REVIEWING THE COLD WA

CASS SERIES: COLD WAR HISTORY
Series Editor: Odd Arne Westad
ISSN: 1471-3829

In the new history of the Cold War that has been forming since 1989, many of the established truths about the international conflict that shaped the latter half of the twentieth century have come up for revision. The present series is an attempt to make available interpretations and materials that will help further the development of this new history, and it will concentrate in particular on publishing expositions of key historical issues and critical surveys of newly available sources.

1. *Reviewing the Cold War: Approaches, Interpretations, Theory*, Odd Arne Westad (ed.)

2. *Rethinking Theory and History in the Cold War*, Richard Saull

NOBEL SYMPOSIUM 107

REVIEWING THE COLD WAR
Approaches, Interpretations, Theory

Edited by
ODD ARNE WESTAD
London School of Economics and Political Science

FRANK CASS
LONDON • PORTLAND, OR

First published in 2000 in Great Britain by
FRANK CASS PUBLISHERS
2 Park Square, Milton Park,
Abingdon, Oxon, OX14 4RN

and in the United States of America by
FRANK CASS PUBLISHERS
270 Madison Ave,
New York NY 10016

Transferred to Digital Printing 2006

Website: www.frankcass.com

British Library Cataloguing in Publication Data

Reviewing the Cold War: approaches, interpretations,
theory
1. Cold War
I. Westad, Odd Arne
327.4'7'073

ISBN 0-7146-5072-2 (cloth)
ISBN 0-7146-8120-2 (paper)
ISSN 1471-3829

Library of Congress Cataloging-in-Publication Data

Nobel symposium (107th: 1998: Lysebu, Norway)
Reviewing the Cold War: approaches, interpretations, theory / Nobel
Symposium; edited by Odd Arne Westad.
p. cm.
Revised papers of a symposium organized by the Norwegian Nobel Institute
at Lysebu in 1998.
Includes bibliographical references and index.
ISBN 0-7146-5072-2 (cloth) – ISBN 0-7146-8120-2 (paper)
1. Cold War. 2. World politics–1945– 3. United States–Foreign relations–
Soviet Union. 4. Soviet Union–Foreign relations–United States.
I. Westad, Odd Arne. II. Title.

D840.N62 1998
327.73047'09'045–dc21   00-031449

Typeset by Vitaset, Paddock Wood, Kent

Cover illustration: reproduced by permission of Corbis Images.

Publisher's Note
The publisher has gone to great lengths to ensure the quality of this reprint
but points out that some imperfections in the original may be apparent

For
the staff and fellows of the Norwegian Nobel Institute –
past, present, and future

Contents

CONTENTS

Notes on Contributors

Yale Ferguson is Professor of Political Science at Rutgers University, Newark.

Aaron L. Friedberg is Professor in the Woodrow Wilson School of Public and International Affairs at Princeton University.

John Lewis Gaddis is Robert A. Lovett Professor of History at Yale University.

Jussi M. Hanhimäki is Lecturer in International History at the London School of Economics and Political Science.

James G. Hershberg is Assistant Professor of History and International Affairs at George Washington University.

Rey Koslowski is Assistant Professor of Political Science at Rutgers University, Newark.

Richard Ned Lebow is Director of the Mershon Center and Professor of Political Science, History, and Psychology at the Ohio State University.

Melvyn P. Leffler is Edward R. Stettinius Professor of History at the University of Virginia, Charlottesville.

Geir Lundestad is Director of the Norwegian Nobel Institute and Adjunct Professor of History at the University of Oslo.

Wilfried Loth is Professor of History at the University of Essen.

Douglas J. Macdonald is Associate Professor of International Relations at Colgate University.

Constantine Pleshakov is an independent scholar and writer who lives in Moscow.

Anders Stephanson is Associate Professor of History at Columbia University.

Antonio Varsori is Professor of International History at the University of Florence.

Odd Arne Westad is Reader in International History at the London School of Economics and Political Science.

William C. Wohlforth is Assistant Professor of Political Science at Georgetown University.

Shu Guang Zhang is Professor of History at the University of Maryland, College Park.

Vladislav M. Zubok is Senior Researcher at the National Security Archive in Washington, DC.

Introduction:
Reviewing the Cold War

Odd Arne Westad

Few, if any, major epochs in international history have faded from view as quickly as the Cold War. In class, I often meet students who wish – but rarely dare – to ask what the Cold War was all about. Not many people going to college in London would, I believe, have wondered in the same way in 1900 about the 'meaning' of the American civil war or the 'significance' of the European colonies in Africa and Asia. For the Cold War, it is not so much a lack of historical memory as it is a lack of relevance – the students see few of the conflict's main points of contention as being of much consequence today.

The most important reason for this lack of relevance is, of course, the collapse of the Soviet Union. With that collapse, one of the main modes of thinking of the twentieth century – Marxism-Leninism – seems to have become inapposite and almost incomprehensible as a world view. I have seen gray-haired former officials of the Central Committee of the Communist Party of the Soviet Union (CPSU) positively blush when explaining the purposes of Soviet involvement in crises and coups around the world. From the vantage point of twenty-first-century Russia, its economic problems and its world role (or lack thereof), it all seems unreal.

The sense of distance, or of a rupture, created by the ideological shift probably explains why both in Russia and, at least in popular terms, in the West the Cold War has come to be seen simply as a conflict of national interests – two giant countries faced each other and battled it out for world supremacy by most means short of all-out war, until one of them was too exhausted to fight any longer. It is interesting to note that this commonly held view – often called 'Realist', for lack of a better term – differs from the views held by an increasing number of historians and international relations experts in the West, who believe that their materials tell them that the Cold War was more about ideas and beliefs than about anything else.[1]

This volume has two main purposes. One is to take up the discrepancy between the two views, and to explore how the Cold War looks in the eyes of leading scholars of international affairs a decade after it ended. The other is to provide some guidance for students who want to understand how the study of the Cold War – both as an historical era and as an international system – has developed, and where the division lines, in terms of approaches to that study, are today. To achieve these purposes, all contributions to the volume are multidisciplinary in scope – the historians and social scientists who contribute address issues across traditional boundaries set by disciplines and fields of inquiry.

The chapters all grew out of a symposium organized by the Norwegian Nobel Institute at Lysebu in the summer of 1998.[2] The institute invited a number of the world's foremost scholars in the field to participate in a debate on what we have learned about the Cold War since the collapse of the Soviet Union. The contributors – all given individual topics – were asked to address their essays to students of the Cold War who want to review the period as a distinct epoch in modern history. After the symposium the essays were revised – in some cases substantially – to form chapters in the present volume.[3]

The authors collected here have – as will be seen – very different answers to many of the key theoretical or interpretative questions posed. Together, however, they do form a fairly representative selection of recent trends in scholarship on the Cold War in Europe, North America, Russia, and East Asia. Many of those represented – although by no means all – have quarrels with the Realist or post-revisionist paradigms in International Relations (IR) and Cold War history. In terms of how the Cold War is generally taught they are therefore perhaps *not* representative as a group; they do, however, seem to cover many of the perspectives which have been at the core of the debate since 1991.

As editor, I need to raise three main caveats in terms of other aspects of the selection of scholars writing for the volume. One is geography and the cultural backgrounds of the contributors. While outside the North Atlantic area Russia and China are well represented, other countries and regions are not. To some extent this is a reflection of the state of scholarship in the field. But it would have been very valuable to have had, for instance, a scholar from or dealing with the Middle East to write one of the chapters.

Another caveat is with regard to gender. It is very unfortunate that there is no scholar presenting issues of gender in the volume, especially since much useful research has recently been undertaken on such issues in relation to the Cold War. Not completely unrelated, perhaps, is the deplorable fact that all the contributors to the volume are men.[4]

Third, all the essays in the volume are interwoven in ways that are not immediately obvious to the reader. They are all products of fairly intense debate at the symposium (and in some cases before and after the meeting) and parts of the chapters are written in direct response to someone else's contribution. Because of this, the chapters tend to have an immediacy and a level of engagement which helps the reader understand the main lines of contention well. On the other hand, each of the essays tends to deal with many different issues in addition to the ones the author is centering on, and it may therefore be necessary to read several chapters to get an impression of the direction the debates are taking.

All chapters are interdisciplinary in approach. The historians and IR specialists who contribute know each other's disciplines and are capable of responding to issues brought up from angles outside the general framework of reference for their own field. Although only one of the main parts of the book concentrates directly on the relationship between history and IR in understanding the Cold War, the rewards and tensions of interdisciplinary debate should be visible throughout.

Approaches

The first four chapters deal with overall reinterpretations of the Cold War and suggestions on how we should study that conflict in the future. The authors bring out at least *four* major themes:

- Is there *a new Cold War history*, and, if so, how does it differ from earlier approaches?

- The necessity for and the opportunities of making new approaches to the study of the period more *comprehensive and versatile* than those that preceded them.

- The need to explain *change* (since we now know that the Cold War had both a beginning *and* an end).

- The apparent centrality of the role of *ideas and beliefs* in the recent work of many Cold War scholars.

Later, I will add some critical comments to the way these four historians try to come to grips with their themes. But, before doing that, it is necessary to briefly resurrect the three major 'schools' in the debates among Cold War historians during the Cold War. These debates – which centered on Cold War *origins* – began with the writings of senior American historians in the 1940s and 1950s, all of whom were influenced by the failure of détente with Nazi Germany in the 1930s, and most of whom viewed Stalin and the Soviet Union as another aggressive antithesis to American freedoms. The common view was that Soviet behavior in Eastern Europe after the war had shown that its policies could not be reconciled with American aims, for reasons ranging from Russian expansionism to Stalin's personality to communist beliefs.[5]

During the 1960s and early 1970s, there was a profound intellectual reaction against this Cold War *orthodoxy*, as there was against other attempts at anti-communist regimentalization of American public life. A number of scholars began to look at the Cold War primarily as an American effort to force its will (and its economic system) upon a reluctant world. Although their enthusiasm for radical thinking was sometimes greater than their research skills, these *revisionists* contributed immensely to the debate on the Cold War – one could almost say that they, through their opposition to orthodox views, created the debate. They also stimulated American authorities to open up official archives, in part to counter revisionist claims.[6]

After the radicalization of the 1960s, and the heated claims and counterclaims in the clashes between orthodox and revisionist Cold War historians, many younger scholars wanted to get rid of the political hyperbole and return to *facts* – as was said by the most prominent of them, John Lewis Gaddis, in 1983; the writing he championed was the 'sober stuff', lacking the 'pungency' of earlier accounts.[7] Assisted by the relative openness of US archives, post-revisionist scholars rewrote Cold War history in the 1970s and 1980s, venturing beyond the European core to the Balkans, Scandinavia, the Middle East, Iran, China, and elsewhere.[8] Their efforts undoubtedly brought Cold War history forward, but the unfortunate thesis/antithesis/synthesis framework in relation to earlier approaches (with post-revisionism, of course, as the synthesis) led to much trouble. In order to clear the middle ground for themselves, many self-proclaimed post-revisionists insisted not only on taking politics (as they knew it) out of the field of history, but also on taking ideas and beliefs out of history as they practiced it. What remained for many post-revisionists, much as for their Realist IR colleagues, were *national interests*; states in conflict with each other along axes of mainly predetermined definitions of themselves as international actors.[9]

For the authors of the first four chapters of the present volume, this background is important. John L. Gaddis, as has been mentioned, was in many ways the founder of the post-revisionist approach. Melvyn Leffler was initially one of Gaddis's revisionist critics, but came increasingly to underline *national security* as a paradigm for explaining Cold War origins (which again, on some issues, brought him into line with IR Realists, by whom Gaddis had also been influenced). Geir Lundestad was one of Gaddis's closest allies in Europe, known for his 'empire by invitation' thesis – that West European elites had 'invited' and, at least to some extent, instigated a strong American role in post-war Europe. Anders Stephanson was (and remains) a radical critic of mainstream Cold War history, emphasizing the conflict as being mainly an American ideological construct.[10]

With the end of the Cold War and the availability of communist source materials in the early 1990s, positions changed. In his latest book, Gaddis challenges some of his own previous views and those of his post-revisionist colleagues. He now insists that a main discovery is the role played by ideas and images on the Eastern side: 'the "new" history is bringing us back to an old answer: that as long as Stalin was running the Soviet Union a Cold War was inevitable ... The more we learn, the less sense it makes to distinguish Stalin's foreign policies from his domestic practices or even his personal behavior.'[11] Lundestad, on the other hand, believes that Gaddis is being far too critical of his own earlier views and that his new views represent a dangerous return to the orthodox school of interpretation. Melvyn Leffler sees ideological postures being adjusted to security needs in both East and West, and that the West, as often as not, was the aggressive side. Stephanson criticizes Gaddis, Leffler, and Lundestad for their lack of understanding of *American* ideology – if it had not been for a particular American view of the world, there would not have been a Cold War. The Cold War, Stephanson argues, was 'the American way'.[12]

As witnessed by the debate between the four in this volume, it is clearly too early to deem the new Cold War history a singular approach, not to mention a 'school'. Rather, as Geir Lundestad suggests, new Cold War history is Cold War history written after the conflict ended and with access to Warsaw Pact documents. It means the culmination, in a historiographical sense, of trends which matured during the 1980s toward making the study of the Cold War *international history*, rather than an outgrowth of the history of American foreign relations. New Cold War history is in its essence multiarchival in research and multipolar in analysis, and, in the cases of some of its best practitioners, multicultural in its ability to understand different and sometimes opposing mindsets.

It is on which tools will be most useful in furthering these processes that the four disagree. Leffler, Lundestad, and Stephanson accuse Gaddis of *overemphasizing* the Soviet contribution to the Cold War, and neglecting the American (and West European) side. Gaddis responds that he is telling the story of what is *new*, of what we have *not* known in the past, and which, according to him, changes our perception of the motives and actions of the Eastern Bloc. To Leffler, especially, this new approach is a continuation of Gaddis's earlier insistence that at the core of the Cold War conflict is the Soviet system and its peculiarities. Leffler believes that Gaddis continues to ignore US actions that led to confrontation, for instance over the occupation of Japan in 1945–46.

The issue of the occupation of Japan is interesting, because the new sources tell us that Leffler in his chapter certainly does not exaggerate Soviet irritation about the way they were excluded from the occupation of Japan. Stalin was furious about being treated 'like a child' by the Western allies, and kept returning to the issue as a major manifestation of US intentions to dominate international capitalism and to isolate the Soviet Union. But, on the other hand, the sources also show that Stalin in 1945 had not *expected* to be in on the occupation of Japan (except in the unlikely case that his forces in the last weeks of war could have landed successfully on Hokkaido), and that he would have considered the Americans naïve if they had volunteered a stake for Moscow. In other words, although Stalin resented the way he was treated on the issue, US behavior fitted in with his preconceived notions of how an imperialist power was supposed to behave, and American offers of a Soviet role in Japan would not necessarily have improved relations.[13]

The example of Soviet post-war policy on Japan shows the need for a new Cold War history to be more *comprehensive* in its approach than earlier generations of scholarship. It also shows, I think, how one can widen the canvas to frame both general mindsets and particular judgments in what was always an interactive relationship. It is the (partial) opening of Eastern archives that gives us the possibility of putting more balance into the design, while the retraining of our skills to use *both* ideational and materialist tools helps us fill in the gaps in our depiction.

Both historians and (especially) political scientist are traditionally poor at explaining *change* – historians because their macro-analytical devices are sometimes rather blunted, and political scientists because their analyses are geared toward a model-building understanding of *what is*. Since we now know that the Cold War had both a beginning *and* an end, many of the earlier approaches to understanding the conflict have to be reworked to take this new form of narrative into account. As several of the contributors to this volume point out, we have not been doing well in this respect so far. Many of the 'new' general accounts of the Cold War are plainly the old static, with an ending tagged on almost as an afterthought. It is primarily in order to overcome this problem that attention to the communist side of the Cold War is important. Without understanding the surprising economic weakness of the Soviet Union, its inherent handicaps in innovation and technology, and its inability to create lasting alliances, we cannot understand why the Cold War ended the way it did. The view of the end of the Cold War as the collapse of the main alternative to capitalism is indeed an incomplete view – at least in my opinion – but it does furnish us with important knowledge to help understand change.

The new Cold War history means the (slow) emergence of new lines of division in the scholarly debate. In the decade to come, it is likely that we will be peeking at what only a few years ago would have been considered strange bedfellows, as debates over modes of interpretation replace the key political discourse of synchronous historiography. Already in this volume, it is striking that John Gaddis and Anders Stephanson have more in common on some issues of interpretative approach than either have with Gaddis's more centrist critics. Future division lines, I think, will be established not on issues of who was to blame for the Cold War, but on how best to understand motives on both sides, and especially on how best to use the new archival sources to get to these motives. In this process, we will probably also see a larger number of similarities between historians and social scientists in terms of difficulties encountered and a growing awareness within the two communities of the need to transmit their findings across the professional divide.

Theory

Unlike international historians, for whom the end of the Cold War initially meant more research opportunities (and therefore often more resources), IR specialists did not at first benefit from the Soviet collapse. On the contrary, many of them were taken to task for not having foreseen these events – for the general public and for quite a number of its own practitioners, IR seems to derive much of its value from accurate predictions. With regard to the Cold War, this is of course a ridiculous debate. The truth is that *nobody* foresaw these rapid changes, except perhaps a few Russian and East European dissidents whom few scholars or politicians cared to listen to at the time. But the soul-searching that went on among IR specialists in the wake of this debate does point to a more general problem: that some IR theories, which have been much used for over a generation, seem to have little *explicatory value* with regard to understanding the Cold War as an international system.[14]

This crisis of theory is particularly acute for various forms of Realism, the concepts and vocabulary of which were often used to explain the *stability* and the *endurance* of a bipolar system. By emphasizing rationalist and materialist lines of inquiry, both classical Realism and the Neo-Realism of the Kenneth Waltz school seem to be of little help in understanding the speedy changes which ended the Cold War in the late 1980s. By their very character, it is argued, contemporary forms of Realism fitted the Cold War system and were perfected in order to analyze it, and therefore missed the boat when the system suddenly started to metamorphose into something different.[15]

These charges against Realism, which gained strength as a result of the end of the Cold War, seem to signify a substantial shift in the focus of discussion within IR theory. But just as with the embattled post-revisionism in international history, it is still premature to say that the new trends are uniformly pointing away from Realist thinking. Some theorists have been arguing that the way the Cold War ended is neither a crucial nor an appropriate case for Realist theory, and that, as Stephen Walt notes, 'criticizing Realism for failing to anticipate the collapse of the Soviet Union is a bit like chiding it for failing to explain the Great Depression, the behavior of subatomic particles, or the causes of cancer'.[16] The post-Cold War system, some scholars would argue, is a much better subject for Realist inquiry. Other writers influenced by Realism are attempting to give ideas and beliefs more of a place in their theoretical toolbox, at the risk of watering down the explicatory value of their overall approach.[17]

The direction in IR which has benefited most from the newfound doubts about Realism is often referred to as Constructivism, an approach which emphasizes the social and cultural context within which a state acts. Most Constructivists see this context as being both domestic and international. At the domestic level, the study of culture and systems of belief can tell us much about a state's aims and about how it acts – more, perhaps, than can be gained from a rational choice approach. With regard to the Cold War, this is essential, it could be claimed, to understand not only the origins but also the intensity of the conflict. At the international level, the study of the spread of norms and the diffusion of ideas can inform our under-standing of change, above the level of any game-theoretical approach. This, it could be argued, is a *sine qua non* for explaining how and why the Cold War ended.[18]

It is interesting to see how the IR debate mirrors, in its own way, the controversies over the new Cold War history. There is, however, one area in which *both* Realism and Constructivism run into trouble, and in which international history probably has more to give. That is the problem of *agency:* In explaining the Cold War, each of these two directions in IR theory are preoccupied with *systems*, and spend much time explaining how their objects' (or their?) system produce testable results. Even Constructivists, who in terms of theory, it seems to me, could easily devolve their system into a looser structure, mostly refrain from doing so – held back, perhaps, by the norms so dominant within their field. This failure to explain agency, both at the individual and collective levels, does project a threshold that both traditions need to overcome in order to explain com-plex phenomena like the life and death of the Cold War.

Both of the authors of the two chapters dealing explicitly with IR traditions in this volume are aware of this problem, and both believe that increasing the empirical understanding of IR theorists can in part rectify it. However, they disagree on which direction such an understanding would take. Ned Lebow is critical of Realism, and believes that it will not be of much use to social scientists or historians who want to take the new evidence seriously. He frames his inquiry primarily in terms of what historians will find of interest in new IR approaches, and believes that those working in new Cold War history so far often have lacked methodological sophis-tication, in part because they have not taken the debates going on in other areas of international relations seriously. William Wohlforth, on the other hand, who seems interested in rescuing Realism, at least in its classical form, believes that the flow of ideas, at least initially, ought to move in the other direction, and that much of the problem can be linked to 'the fact that the field of international relations is not set up to assimilate new historical evidence rationally'.

Culture/Ideology

Both for historians and for IR theorists a major part of the controversies over understanding the Cold War has had to do with what is important and what is less important in terms of research. For a Cold War history revisionist, the *economic* relations between the United States and the rest of the world would be of major importance. For an IR Realist, *power capability* would be a crucial category. Unfortunately, very few scholars are preoccupied with studying the categories which *others* deem to be important, and, as Ned Lebow points out, this is one of the major methodological weaknesses of the field as such.

Part III of the present volume deals critically with two of the vital categories in the present debates, namely *culture* and *ideology*. Both in history and in IR these two concepts take up an increasing part of the scholarly vocabulary; often, it is clear, without much thought being given to how they are used and which implications their use is having for our studies in general. Historians are particularly guilty of such practices, as was shown in some of the debate following the publication of John Gaddis's recent book, *We Now Know*. Instead of trying to work with a category, in Gaddis's case ideology, its usefulness (or lack thereof) was obscured by the imprecision of both supporters and critics.

The two chapters in this part of the book are written by political scientists who attempt to trace both the use of the concepts and the debates which have surrounded them, and show, based on their own research, how the concepts may prove useful in looking at the Cold War. Yale Ferguson and Rey Koslowski look critically at the categories of culture and identity, and call for their measured use in interpretative terms, both by historians and political scientists. While much of the new evidence seems to show that specific cultural traditions *and* developments in the Soviet Union and the United States should figure more prominently in our understanding of the Cold War, there is a danger in the broad use of these terms that some Constructivist scholars are employing. That danger is reductionism, particularly if the use of culture is connected up to a specific understanding of 'national' histories. Instead, scholars ought to review specific elements of cultural practices and see how they might be useful in explaining phenomena that other categories cannot explain.

If, for instance, one believes that the Gorbachev reforms were essential in ending the Cold War, then it seems difficult to avoid discussing both generational changes in perceptions within the Soviet elite and the effects of 'new' forms of social consciousness across borders, for example, environmentalism. Both phenomena have to be seen in a cultural context and can perhaps only be explained in cultural terms. But if one tries to explain Gorbachev's political emergence itself in terms of broader cultural concepts, then one would have to contend with a long tradition of writings on Russian and CPSU (Communist Party of the Soviet Union) political culture, which seem to explain why Gorbachev was *not* possible. Only by limiting the subject of one's inquiry, it seems, will cultural explanations *by themselves* be an important part of the study of the Cold War.

Douglas Macdonald's treatment of *ideology* also seems to point in the direction of theoretical prudence, although Macdonald himself is willing to consider a fairly wide use of the concept for explanations related to the Cold War. The point he is making is that ideology had a particular relevance for the Cold War, both on the revolutionary (Soviet) and the status quo (United States) side. Echoing Gaddis and others, Macdonald believes that 'ideological behavior', particularly among Marxist-Leninist states, is a constituent element of the Cold War. He believes that American ideology does have its own significance, although he does not imply such a far-reaching conclusion as for instance Anders Stephanson. The main value of Macdonald's approach is that in searching for particular problems related to the Cold War where ideology mattered, he avoids making the emphasis on ideas a monocausal or determinist approach.

There are two main categories of analysis not included in this part of the book to which I believe it is necessary to draw special attention for the sake of debate. One is *economic relations* – especially the form economic interaction between countries took during the Cold War, and the effects this had on the political and strategic conflict. There are two important observations that have been made on this category recently. Some scholars have found that Soviet *intentions*, at least during the Stalin era, were to make massive use of strategic raw materials and production capacity in Eastern Europe and China in order to strengthen socialist production in the Soviet Union itself. Economic motives, therefore, should not be ruled out in explaining early Soviet moves in the Cold War.[19]

Another and perhaps more important observation is that American policymakers seem to have understood much more readily than most of us have believed that there was an intrinsic connection between the spread of capitalism as a system and the victory of American political values. The research which has been undertaken on US–West European relations during the Cold War recently seems to underline this, as does research on the US–Japanese alliance – the two winning combinations, it could be argued, during the Cold War. The point here is not so much that the relationship was *exploitative* – the old argument of the historical revisionists – but that American leaders *consciously* took on the role of leader of global capitalism, and were willing to bear at least short-term burdens in order to ensure that the system worked.[20]

Another category which seems promising in order to understand aspects of the Cold War world is *gender*. The research undertaken by scholars such as Frank Costigliola in history and Jean Bethke Elshtain in IR indicates that gender relations were closer to the core of the conflict both in terms of representation and in language than we have previously thought.[21] This view has implications for our understanding of the particular intensity of the Cold War political language – an intensity which, it could be argued, had direct implications for the way the conflict was fought. The terms and style used in speech by leaders in East and West were frequently bound up in gender metaphors; when Stalin spoke in the inner circle of the leadership, for instance, his allusions to the way his Western enemies were treating him sound like a textbook case in the sexualization of language. It is reasonable to think that there are links between Cold War enemy imagery and perceived threats to masculinity – East and West – during the late twentieth century.[22] On the other hand, the character of the conflict seems to have delayed more complete advances toward gender equality on both sides of the ideological divide. The negative repercussions of the Cold War for women were particularly strong in countries under foreign control – South Korea or East Germany under Soviet occupation are cases in point.[23]

Strategies

If those who want to broaden the interpretative or theoretical framework for Cold War studies are correct, then it would be crucial to look more in depth at how these new approaches influence our study of the Cold War strategies of individual states. We therefore asked four scholars, working, respectively, on and originating from the United States, Russia, Germany, and China, to look at the development over time of 'their' countries' positions in the Cold War. The point here is not as much to illustrate national differences in scholarly approach as to indicate how the new information available feeds into our present understanding of the central decisions of the Cold War. All four authors have concentrated on singling out what was important (and what was less important) in the minds of decisionmakers in their individual countries, and on how vital decisions were made.

What emerges is a not too well-defined set of differences in priorities and perceptions. If these authors are to be believed, ideas and beliefs were indeed central to *all* decisions during the early Cold War, and the self-definition of one leadership group was in some cases deliberately constructed to be the negation of that of its defined opponents. For the United States, the Soviet Union, and Germany this situation started to change in the early 1960s, in the sense that conscious ideals of *realpolitik* emerged, while the Chinese leadership remained wedded to a consciously ideological approach to world politics (which, arguably, even premeditated the opening to the United States – as a form of Leninist united front against the more aggressively imperialist Soviet Union). However, even Moscow and

Washington could not free themselves from ideologically based perceptions, except, perhaps, when survival was at stake, as in the case of the Cuban Missile Crisis.

The case of Germany is particularly interesting, as Wilfried Loth explains. His account of Germany's role in the early Cold War emphasizes how American and Soviet policies were formed around their respective perceptions of Germany's future. While Washington was pessimistic about the long-term survivability of capitalism and liberal democracy in a united Germany, Moscow, at least up to the mid-1950s, was more ebullient on the issue, and on several occasions toyed with the idea of making considerable political concessions to open the way to reunification. No plan that we know to have been discussed in Moscow took Western views into consideration to such an extent that it could have formed a possible basis for a compromise. But neither Stalin nor Khrushchev (at least in the early phase) had given up on the perspective of Soviet influence in *all* of Germany, or, for that matter, the belief in the need for an all-German socialist revolution.[24]

The German case also shows that in terms of strategies and decisions it was not just Washington and Moscow that mattered, even in the early Cold War. German leaders – East and West – played a crucial role in furthering Cold War tensions, and thereby ensuring a lasting division of their country. The Cold War, as it relates to Germany, therefore becomes much more than just rivalry for post-war control. It is – importantly in a historical context – the story of the conflict between a conservative and a Marxist direction in German politics, both of which attempted to get superpower support to set up separate states.[25]

In the 1960s – parallel with American and Soviet attempts to change their bilateral relationship – Germany saw the political rise of Social Democrats and CDU liberals who favored activism with regard to the East, and thereby started recovering some of Germany's foreign policy autonomy. The so-called *Ostpolitik* was one of the most important manifestations of a gradual change in the ideological climate in the West and in the East, but also of the relative diffusion of power, particularly in economic terms, from the United States to Western Europe and East Asia, and especially to Germany and Japan. In many ways, this creation of a multipolar international economic system was the most profound change that took place during the Cold War. It helped prepare for the globalization of the capitalist market, it created economic growth, and substantially reduced the room for maneuver both for the Soviet Union and for anti-capitalist regimes in the Third World.

The emergence of China as an independent political actor was another important aspect of the diffusion of global power that took place in the 1960s. Although the significance of the Sino-Soviet split for world politics was reduced by the dramatic turn inward which the Maoist leadership conducted during the Cultural Revolution, long-term implications loomed large in the minds of policymakers East and West. For the Soviet Union the breakdown of the alliance with China meant increased isolation in security terms *and* in economic terms, and a comprehensive ideological challenge to its version of socialism. In Washington, shifting administrations saw an independent China first as a threat to the American intervention in Vietnam, and then as a possible ally in the confrontation with Moscow. The shift in American perceptions were, at least in part, preconditioned by Richard Nixon's belief that the Chinese Communist Party leaders conducted an interest-based, *realpolitik*-oriented foreign policy – the kind of approach he thought he would set up for the United States if it had not been for the bothersome meddling of American public opinion.[26]

Nixon's belief in the transcendence of Mao's foreign policy was almost certainly as misplaced as the president's faith in his own ability to transcend American law. As Shu Guang Zhang explains, Mao and his successor Deng Xiaoping shared a set of ideas about China's place in the world and the need to protect the communist dictatorship which were based squarely on their personal experiences and their visions of China's future. Although the economic and social counter-revolution which Deng and the marshals spearheaded in the late 1970s and early 1980s marked a break with the Marxist past, there is a substantial degree of continuity in China's immediate aims, a continuity which Zhang argues is culturally determined. The 'images, beliefs, ideas, attitudes, aspirations, [and] anxieties' which Zhang catalog have not so far made for a very successful Chinese foreign policy. Instead, post-revolutionary China faces – in part because of its history of bellicosity – a host of regional conflicts and challenges which will pester any Chinese regime well into the coming century.

The two chapters that deal with US and Soviet strategies and decision-making both conclude that the more we know, the less similarity we find between the two states. While the Realist trends of the 1970s and 1980s tended to underline how much the strategic behavior of the two powers had in common, Aaron Friedberg and Constantine Pleshakov argue that in most aspects it was the differences which stood out, and that it definitely was the differences which mattered in the end. Looking primarily at the arms race, Friedberg concludes that it was its political ideology and the role of its political institutions that gave the United States its technological edge. While in ideological terms, there was enough cohesion within the American political elite to secure a continuos dedication of resources to military purposes, there was also enough balance within the political system to make sure that the state did not spend so much that its existence became threatened.

As Pleshakov points out, the Soviet Union was never a 'normal' state in the tradition of European state-building. It was a state which had been deliberately constructed as the *negation* of bourgeois traditions in a much more radical sense than the fascist regimes of the 1930s or the post-colonial African and Asian states of the 1960s and 1970s. It had almost abolished private property and the use of money in any traditional sense, it had created methods for the allocation of resources and the making of political decisions which all depended on the functions of a strongly centralized party bureaucracy, and it had constructed a view of the world and of the future which was as universalistic in approach as it was parochial in content. The only way to understand Soviet foreign policy actions is to interpret them within this framework, and not to attempt generalizations which implicitly assume that the same forces were involved in the making of Stalin's, Khrushchev's, or Brezhnev's priorities as in those of West European or American state leaders.[27]

Pleshakov shares John Gaddis's belief that global hegemony remained the aim of the Soviet Union throughout the Cold War (while putting significantly more emphasis than Gaddis does on immediate strategic – or 'geopolitical', in Pleshakov's terminology – considerations which Soviet leaders had to deal with in the short term). But if this is true, and therefore it was only the fall of the Soviet state which could end the Cold War, how can one then explain what happened in the mid-1980s, when Mikhail Gorbachev instituted a deliberate policy of accommodation with the United States which, arguably, changed the patterns of East–West interaction well before the red flag was lowered over the Kremlin? Were there other periods during the Cold War in which the conflict could have ended or at least changed its character? In the last part of the book, we look more closely at some of these potential turning points.

Turning points?

When first putting this volume together, there was a great deal of discussion as to which periods qualified for this section. Should we concentrate on 'lost opportunities' or on the most dangerous moments of the conflict? Should we primarily discuss changing priorities among different leaders, or longer-term, 'systemic' changes? We decided to concentrate on four periods which are fundamental to our understanding of the conflict – its beginning and end, and the two periods in between in which there seemed to be some chance of accommodation between the principal antagonists – the late 1950s and early 1960s, and the brief period of détente in the 1970s.

A discussion of such turning points may be important not only to avoid the sense of imperturbability to the Cold War conflict which some of the new research may be taken to point toward, but also in order to look more closely at *stages* of the conflict in terms of concrete circumstances. Obviously there was a great deal of change within the superpowers themselves and in the world at large during the 50 years the conflict lasted. What

changed, and what remained relatively stable? And, because of the processes of change, was there any time other than the late 1980s during which
the Cold War could have been called off?

In his essay on the European origins of the Cold War, Antonio Varsori
sees little chance of there *not* being a conflict between the United States
and West European elites on the one hand and Stalin's regime on the other,
because of past ideological hostility and the way World War II ended. The
European 'frontline' of the Cold War, which emerged with the collapse of
Germany and its allies, brought old ideological adversaries face to face.
Both East and West from 1944 to 1947/48 read into each other's actions
what beliefs and prejudices stretching back to before the Russian Revolution told them – that the other side was aggressive and that continued
cooperation could be dangerous. In ways which need to be explored further
by scholars, both sides seems to have been strengthened in their beliefs by
analogies drawn from their experiences with Nazi Germany – while Western
leaders feared the consequences of 'appeasement', Stalin prepared for a
sudden attack on the Soviet Union. As a result, the options for avoiding a
conflict became narrower and narrower in the late 1940s.

Very many New Cold War historians would agree with Varsori. But even
saying that conflict was likely (or almost unavoidable) is not the same as
saying that the *Cold War* was predetermined in its post-1948 form. Post-
war conflict, yes, but 50 years of continuous arms race, global interventions, and division of Europe into two halves seems to depend on more
than what is immediately relevant for an explanation of the breakdown of
the Grand Alliance. One long-term explanation is the profoundly ideological character of the conflict, as Varsori points out. Another explanation suggested by Vojtech Mastny, is the determination of both sides to
avoid war in Europe. Stalin and US President Harry Truman seem to have
shared the view that the institutionalization of conflict into the patterns
that became the Cold War was a necessary price to pay to avoid another
European war, a war which neither of them thought they could win at the
time.[28]

But Cold War *and* peace in Europe could almost be said to be a recipe
for intense conflict in other parts of the world. Stalin showed that by giving
the go-ahead for Kim Il-Sung's attempts at reunifying Korea by force
under a communist regime. US President Dwight D. Eisenhower showed
it by his willingness to have the United States take over France's role as a
counter-weight to revolution in Indochina. And Stalin's successors showed
it by taking the risk of installing nuclear weapons in Cuba, in what became
perhaps the most dangerous moment of the Cold War.

James Hershberg's essay on what is often seen as the first big opportunity at reducing Cold War tensions – Nikita Khrushchev's years in
control of the Kremlin – explains how the Cuban Missile Crisis could arise
out of a period in which both sides had made limited attempts at reaching

some form of accommodation. According to Hershberg, Khrushchev's attempts at reducing Soviet–American tension were directly connected to his fear of war in, or rather over, Europe. Khrushchev believed that socialism needed time to develop ('mature' was the term he often used) in the Soviet Union and Eastern Europe, while 'new' states on the periphery of the capitalist system went through their own socialist revolutions. Increasingly frustrated by the absence of markets and raw materials, capitalism in the West would collapse under pressure from workers' movements and 'progressive' parties, and socialism would triumph *without* war in Europe. But such a strategy supposed that the Soviet Union would be willing to support socialist revolutions on the periphery when they, inevitably, came under pressure from imperialism. The missiles in Cuba were Khrushchev's way of forcing the United States not to destroy Fidel Castro's revolution.[29]

Some scholars have argued that it was only after President John F. Kennedy had shown himself willing to risk nuclear war to prevent Soviet missiles from reaching Cuba – and Khrushchev, as a consequence, had backed down – that a real chance for accommodation between the super-powers emerged. Both sides, it is argued, realized how close to nuclear war they had come, and implicitly agreed to take steps to 'regularize' their competition in the future. Based on what we are getting to know about the later 1960s, this seems to be a dubious preposition. Instead, what seems to have happened is that both sides, and especially the Soviet Union, increased their emphasis on military preparedness and on the need not to lose out in the rivalry for influence in the Third World. Détente, in its classical form, could therefore only come about if the United States, as the strongest power, became willing to limit the arms race on the basis of equality, and to give the Soviet Union a legitimate role in the Third World.

This is exactly what happened under Richard Nixon's presidency, and, as Jussi Hanhimäki shows, exactly the reason why Nixon's détente was unlikely to become a lasting phase in the Cold War, even if its European version was a turning point in East–West interaction. While Nixon and his National Security Adviser Henry Kissinger may have been willing to deal with Moscow as equals, at least in formal terms – to better manage the ascendance of Soviet power, as Kissinger liked to put it – the majority of American policymakers were not willing to grant the Soviet Union such a status. On the contrary, as the Brezhnev leadership in the 1970s started behaving as if they really headed the *other* superpower – investing massively in a blue-water navy and intervening in African civil wars – the American domestic political backlash was acute. As Soviet Third World activism increased, even the core pieces of détente – the arms limitation agreements – were in danger. It is doubtful, however, that Zbigniew Brzezinski's phrase about the Strategic Arms Limitation Treaty laying buried in the deserts of the Horn of Africa is the whole story. A fair part of it, presumably, lies buried under the debris of the Illinois and New York primaries.[30]

Vladislav Zubok is therefore almost certainly right in viewing the 1980s, the last phase of the Cold War, as a continuation of trends that had lasted throughout the conflict. But something obviously had changed. Much of the new literature seems to find the main sources of change in three broad developments, two of which were at the core of the conflict, and one that was tangential to it. In terms of US political ideology, there was during the 1980s a substantial radicalization of American universalism – in part as a reaction against the attacks of self-doubt brought on by Vietnam and Watergate. During Ronald Reagan's presidency, with the economy doing well and the failures of the 1970s forgotten or rewritten, American foreign policy again became imbued with missions: defeating revolutions, opening markets, and instituting democracies.[31]

At the same time the 'other' superpower stumbled. Chronic military overspending during the 1970s ate away at all other forms of state investments – housing, food production, transport. In the mid-1980s the Soviet socialist economy – the surpluses of which were meager under the best of circumstances – was also hit by a sudden and unprecedented drop in prices for many of the raw materials on which its exports depended. The war in Afghanistan was going badly. And in Soviet society – at all levels except the very top – there was a growing ideological disenchantment which probably only radical reform could stem.[32]

Outside the two superpowers other developments seemed to limit the relevance of the Cold War. Islamism became an attractive ideology for Third World radicals opposed to all forms of Western (i.e. US or Soviet) modernization. East Asia's phenomenal economic surge further diffused the world's financial markets. And new initiatives toward a more complete political and economic union in Western Europe made integration within the continent an increasingly attractive option to East Europeans and neutrals. In a world in which other issues became increasingly important, the divides – including the ideological divides – put up by the Cold War seemed to be of less relevance than before.

All of these three broad developments have to be taken into account to explain the Gorbachev phenomenon, the massive and ultimately unsuccessful attempt at saving Soviet socialism through reform. But, while Gorbachev undoubtedly wound down the tensions of previous decades and while the collapse of the Soviet Union in 1991 necessarily meant the end of the Cold War, it is still too early to say that it was the decline and fall of Soviet communism which caused the Cold War to grind to a halt. Such a conclusion is much too dependent on viewing the Cold War conflict as a closed system for which other global developments had little relevance. Perhaps some of the most useful research which could be undertaken on contemporary international history deals exactly with this: the relationship between the Cold War and other determining factors of global developments in the latter part of the twentieth century.

Revisions?

Increasingly important in our understanding of history is its <u>visual repre</u>-sentations. A very successful television series on the Cold War, shown in the United States and Britain in the 1998–99 season, opens each episode with the camera panning along a dark corridor, the walls of which are covered with Cold War images – great dictators, barbed wire, jungle warfare, and bombs. Finally, the camera (and the viewer) emerge into broad daylight. Or is it a little too bright to be just daylight, too luminescent, too incendiary?

For people everywhere the Cold War was very much about survival, and it is the fact that most people in most places did survive that becomes the fundamental truth now that the conflict is over. With the opening of archives, we now know that the conflict was at times even more dangerous than we previously thought, and that the world did move perilously close to the nuclear abyss. It is no surprise, then, that former leaders in East and West have been called upon to justify their roles and their behavior in talks, interviews, and conferences. Attending some of these events, I have been struck by the ability of some of these former policymakers to reflect in a conscious way on the motives they acted on back then, and how they view these actions based on the knowledge they have now. Having ended, the Cold War – as any conflict – seems to call for self-conscious reflection.

This call ought to reach those who make a living from analyzing the Cold War as well. With the increasing willingness to take ideas and beliefs seriously as causal factors, as witnessed both by the new Cold War history and the Constructivist turn in IR, one should have expected more in terms of conscious reflection on the role of the historian or political scientist herself. If this is really a turning point in our understanding of the dominant conflict of the late twentieth century, we ought to be able to tell our readers and students more about the general values and judgments that we put into our analyses. How one views the outcome of the Cold War influences how one tells the story of the conflict – my own background as a <u>Scandinavian socialist</u> predisposes me to a different form of analysis than would that of a Chinese communist or an American liberal, and will also influence my conclusions.

Whatever starting point the scholars represented in this collection may have, it is useful to note that <u>no one argues for monocausality</u> – there is no single factor, be it ideological, economic, or strategic, which can explain the Cold War. Undoubtedly, there has been a turn away from materialist explanations, but only, I think, in so far as they were seen to restrict the general discourse in terms of approach. The most important new research which will be undertaken will probably attempt to create new links between different approaches – for instance between interpretations that underline political and social ideas and those that underline economic relationships.

Another aspect of future Cold War studies is bound to be that less attention will be paid to the bilateral Soviet–American relationship, while other developments that were intertwined with the rivalry between Washington and Moscow will gain in prominence. There are several reasons for this. One is the realization that the Soviet Union was never *the other* superpower, that the gap which separated the communist regime USSR ↔ US from the United States in economic achievement, technological innovation, and overall military capability was so great that it is impossible to place the two in the same category. Then there is the importance of other dimensions of late twentieth-century change – the economic revolutions in East Asia and the rise of political Islam foremost among them – which were connected with, although probably not dependent on, the Cold War. Also, if one looks upon the Cold War as at least in part an ideological project which brought American, West European, and Japanese elites together in opposing revolutionary threats at home and abroad, then it would be natural that scholars show more interest in how these alliances were formed and how American influence helped transform political, economic, and cultural practices within and between its alliance partners. These, in historical terms, rapid changes may constitute the most important revolution of the past fifty years, and perhaps of the whole century.

In redefining the Cold War, we also need to define its central concepts. In this process it is particularly important to find a strong and significant definition of *ideology* – something this volume, in spite of Douglas Macdonald's efforts, proves that we still do not have. In doing so, I think we should heed Macdonald's advice about widening the concept below the level of formal ideologies, while making sure that we do not expand it to such a degree that we make it analytically unhelpful. This means that we ought to consider learning processes, collective experiences, and even psychological patterns as part of the ideological framework on the American and Soviet side, while reserving enough room for formal ideologies for them to form the core of the concept.

A main purpose for such efforts ought to be to demonstrate that there is, in global terms, no *common* sense – groups and individuals tend to think and behave differently depending on their upbringing, their schooling, and the values they have acquired through interacting within social groups. Sometimes their rationalities vary considerably, as was the situation between leaders with a background in the American middle class and leaders who came to power through revolutionary action. We can safely assume that their views of the world had few points of orientation in common. We can also assume that the Cold War meant different things in different parts of the world and among different groups – opportunities and provocations, benefits and immense disasters.

The purpose of this volume is to take stock of the discussion on the Cold War since it ended, and to provoke further explorations. It should be considered an early attempt at showing the value of an interdisciplinary discourse about the character and development of the conflict. We want to show students and scholars alike that such cooperation is possible, and that in the study of the Cold War, as in all other fields of research, the main division is not between an empirical and a theoretical approach, but between restrictive and open forms of scholarship.

NOTES

1 For examples of contemporary Russian views, see the debates in the liberal Moscow newspapers *Segodnia* and *Nezavisimaia Gazeta* during late summer 1997.

2 The editor is grateful to the Symposium Committee of the Nobel Foundation, to the Director-General of the Foundation, Michael Sohlman, and to the staff of the Norwegian Nobel Institute for support which, in different ways, was essential to the holding of this symposium. I am particularly grateful to the Director of the Norwegian Nobel Institute, Geir Lundestad, for his help with this event and all the other projects he stimulated during my time in Oslo.

3 The editor and the authors of the individual chapters are grateful to the commentators at the Nobel Symposium who all did a first-rate job of challenging, pushing, or provoking the key ideas in this volume. These commentators were Mark Bradley, Chen Jian, Alexander Chubarian, Anne Deighton, Kristian Gerner, Jonathan Haslam, Torbjørn Knutsen, Vojtech Mastny, Olav Njølstad, and Stein Tønnesson.

4 All of the three presenters originally invited, who for different good reasons had to withdraw from the symposium, were women.

5 The best summary I know of the orthodox position among Cold War historians is Arthur M. Schlesinger, Jr, 'Origins of the Cold War', *Foreign Affairs*, 46 (1967): 22–52. See also Jerald Combs, *American Diplomatic History: Two Centuries of Changing Interpretations* (Berkeley, CA: University of California Press, 1983), pp. 220–34.

6 The core, so to say, of Cold War revisionism was William Appleman Williams and his students Thomas McCormick, Walter LaFeber, and Lloyd Gardner. In terms of scope the most impressive revisionist contribution is Gabriel Kolko and Joyce Kolko, *The Limits of Power: The World and United States Foreign Policy, 1945–1954* (New York: Harper & Row, 1972)

7 John Lewis Gaddis, 'The Emerging Post-Revisionist Synthesis on the Origins of the Cold War', *Diplomatic History*, 7, 3 (1983): 172. In his programmatic article Gaddis also underlined that the new synthesis presented 'Soviet expansionism as the primary cause of the Cold War', while stressing 'the absence of any ideological blue-print for world revolution in Stalin's mind' (p. 180).

8 See Michael M. Boll, *Cold War in the Balkans: American Foreign Policy and the Emergence of Communist Bulgaria, 1943–1947* (Lexington, KY: University Press of Kentucky, 1984); Geir Lundestad, *America, Scandinavia, and the Cold War* (Oslo: Universitetsforlaget, 1980); Bruce R. Kuniholm, *The Origins of the Cold War in the Near East: Great Power Conflict and Diplomacy in Iran, Turkey, and Greece* (Princeton, NJ: Princeton University Press, 1980); and William W. Stueck, *The Road to Confrontation: American Policy toward China and Korea, 1947–1950* (Chapel Hill, NC: University of North Carolina Press, 1981).

9 Lundestad, whose first book was entitled *The American Non-Policy towards Eastern*

Europe, 1943–1947: Universalism in an Area not of Essential Interest to the United States (Tromsø: Universitetsforlaget, 1975), saw US policymakers in the early Cold War as adopting some 'general guidelines just because they would serve to strengthen the United States at the expense of the Soviet Union' (p. 34). 'After the Second World War was over', Lundestad argues, Soviets and Americans 'reverted to what had basically been their old state of relations' before the war (p. 431).

10 John Lewis Gaddis, *The United States and the Origins of the Cold War, 1941–1947* (New York: Columbia University Press, 1972) – in many ways the founding text of post-revisionism; Melvyn Leffler, 'From the Truman Doctrine to the Carter Doctrine: Lessons and Dilemmas of the Cold War', *Diplomatic History*, 7 (1983): 245–66; Lundestad, 'Empire by Invitation? The United States and Western Europe, 1945–1952', *Journal of Peace Research*, 23 (1986): 263–77; Anders Stephanson, *Kennan and the Art of Foreign Policy* (Cambridge, MA: Harvard University Press, 1989), and 'Fourteen Notes on the Very Concept of the Cold War', http://h-net2.msu.edu/~diplo/stephanson.html.

11 John Lewis Gaddis, *We Now Know: Rethinking Cold War History* (New York: Oxford University Press, 1997), pp. 292, 293.

12 For Leffler's, Lundestad's, and Stephanson's criticism of the 'new' Gaddis, see their respective chapters in this volume.

13 There is much we still do not know about Soviet–Japan policy in 1945–46. My information is drawn from recent memoirs, especially those of Mikhail Kapitsa, *Na raznykh paralleliakh: zapiski diplomata* (Moscow: Kniga i biznez, 1996) and from Sergei Tikhvinskii's recent overview of Russian–Japanese relations, *Rossiia-Iaponia: obrecheny na dobrososedstvo. Vospominaniia diplomata i zametki istorika* (Moscow: Pamiatniki istoricheskoi mysli, 1996). For Stalin's expectations, see Boris Slavinskii, *Pakt o neitralitete mezhdu SSSR i Iaponii: diplomaticheskaia istoriia, 1941–45 gg.* (Moscow: Novina, 1995) and V. M. Barynkin, 'Manchzhurskaia nastypatelnaia operatsiia', *Voenno-istoricheskii zhurnal*, 5 (1995): 14–23.

14 For critical views, see Richard Ned Lebow and Thomas Risse-Kappen, eds, *International Relations Theory and the End of the Cold War* (New York: Columbia University Press, 1995).

15 For the criticism of Realism, see Jeffrey T. Checkel, 'The Constructivist Turn in International Relations', *World Politics*, 50 (1998): 324–48; and, from a more sympathetic viewpoint, William C. Wohlforth, 'Reality Check: Revising Theories of International Politics in Response to the End of the Cold War', ibid., 650–80.

16 Stephen M. Walt, 'The Gorbachev Interlude and International Relations Theory', *Diplomatic History*, 21 (1997): 476.

17 Two summings up of the post-Cold War verdict on Realism are Yosef Lapid and Friedrich Kratochwil, *The Return of Culture and Identity in IR Theory* (Boulder, CO: Lynne Rienner, 1996) and Francis A. Beer and Robert Hariman, eds, *Post-Realism: The Rhetorical Turn in International Relations* (East Lansing, MI: Michigan State University Press, 1996). For the defense, see Benjamin Frankel, ed., *Realism: Restatements and Renewal* (London: Frank Cass, 1996).

18 For a programmatic article on Constructivism, see Alexander Wendt, 'Constructing International Politics', *International Politics*, 20 (1995); for a sympathetic but more critical approach, see Checkel, 'The Constructivist Turn'.

19 See, for instance, Laszlo Borhi's forthcoming work on Hungary, summarized in his 'Hungary Between the Superpowers, 1945–1953', paper presented at the Nobel Institute research seminar, March 1998; or, on China, Shu Guang Zhang, 'Sino-Soviet Economic Cooperation', in Odd Arne Westad, ed., *Brothers in Arms: The Rise and Fall of the Sino-Soviet Alliance, 1945–1963* (Stanford, CA: Stanford

University Press, 1998).

20 For Western Europe, see Geir Lundestad, *'Empire' by Integration: The United States and European Integration, 1945–1997* (Oxford: Oxford University Press, 1998); for Japan, see William R. Nester, *Power across the Pacific: A Diplomatic History of American Relations with Japan* (Basingstoke: Macmillan, 1996); Walter LaFeber, *The Clash: A History of US–Japan Relations* (New York: Norton, 1997); and Michael Schaller, *Altered States: The United States and Japan since the Occupation* (Oxford: Oxford University Press, 1998).

21 Frank Costigliola, '"Unceasing Pressure for Penetration": Gender, Pathology, and Emotion in George Kennan's Formulation of the Cold War', *Journal of American History*, 83 (1997): 1309–39; and his 'The Nuclear Family: Tropes of Gender and Pathology in the Western Alliance', *Diplomatic History*, 21 (1997): 163–83; Jean Bethke Elshtain, 'Feminist Inquiry and International Relations', in Michael W. Doyle and G. John Ikenberry, eds, *New Thinking in International Relations Theory* (Boulder, CO: Westview, 1997).

22 See, for instance, Jennifer L. Milliken, 'Metaphors of Prestige and Reputation in American Foreign Policy and American Realism', in Beer and Hariman, eds, *Post-Realism*.

23 For South Korea, see Katharine H. S. Moon, *Sex among Allies: Military Prostitution in US–Korea Relations* (New York: Columbia University Press, 1997); for the Soviet occupation of Germany, see Norman M. Naimark, *The Russians in Germany: A History of the Soviet Zone of Occupation, 1945–1949* (Cambridge, MA: Harvard University Press, 1995).

24 For perspectives on American policies on Germany which support Loth's view, see Carolyn Eisenberg, *Drawing the Line: The American Decision to Divide Germany, 1944–1949* (New York: Cambridge University Press, 1996); for critical views, see Gerhard Wettig, *Bereitschaft zu Einheit in Freiheit: Die sowjetische Deutschland-Politik 1945–1955* (Munich: Olzog, 1999).

25 For this view, see Hans Peter Schwartz's Adenauer biography, *Adenauer: der Aufstieg, 1876–52* and *Adenauer: der Staatsmann, 1952–67* (Stuttgart: Deutsche Verlags-Anstalt, 1986–91).

26 On the breakdown of Moscow's alliance with China, see Westad, ed., *Brothers in Arms*; for American perceptions, see Allen Whiting, 'The Sino-Soviet Split', in Roderick MacFarquhar and John K. Fairbank, eds, *The Cambridge History of China*, vol. XIV (Cambridge: Cambridge University Press, 1987), pp. 478–538.

27 There is still only a very limited literature on Soviet social history during the 1950s and 1960s; for an overview, see James R. Millar and Sharon L. Wolchik, *The Social Legacy of Communism* (Cambridge: Cambridge University Press, 1994); or, in a pathbreaking Russian work, Petr Vail and Aleksandr Genis, *60-e: mir sovetskogo cheloveka* [The '60s: The World of Soviet Man] (Moscow: Novoe literaturnoe obozvenie, 1996).

28 Mastny's comments at his summing up of the Nobel Symposium; other recent European work underlining the same issues are in Francesca Gori and Silvio Pons, eds, *The Soviet Union and Europe in the Cold War, 1943–1953* (Basingstoke: Macmillan, 1996); and David Reynolds, ed., *The Origins of the Cold War in Europe: International Perspectives* (New Haven, CT: Yale University Press, 1994).

29 The recent literature on the Cuban Missile Crisis is very large – see Hershberg's chapter for references; I have learnt most from Aleksandr Fursenko and Timothy Naftali, *'One Hell of a Gamble': Khrushchev, Castro & Kennedy, 1958–1964* (New York: Norton, 1997), and Michael R. Beschloss, *The Crisis Years: Kennedy and Khrushchev, 1960–1963* (New York: HarperCollins, 1991).

30 On the European dimension, see John van Oudenaren, *Détente in Europe: The*

Soviet Union and the West since 1953 (Durham, NC: 1991); and Richard Davy, *European Détente: A Reappraisal* (London: Sage, 1992). See also Odd Arne Westad, ed., *The Fall of Détente: Soviet–American Relations during the Carter Years* (Oslo: Scandinavian University Press, 1997). According to Zbigniew Brzezinski, 'Détente lies buried in the sands of Ogaden' (*Power and Principle: Memoirs of the National Security Adviser, 1977–81* (New York: Farrar, Strauss & Giroux, 1983), p. 89).

31 For some important issues, see Beth A. Fischer, *The Reagan Reversal: Foreign Policy and the End of the Cold War* (Columbia, MO: University of Missouri Press, 1997).

32 An excellent snap-shot of Soviet society in the 1980s is Stephen Kotkin, *Steeltown, USSR: Soviet Society in the Gorbachev Era* (London: Weidenfeld & Nicolson, 1991).

PART I:
STUDYING THE COLD WAR

1

On Starting All Over Again:
A Naïve Approach to the Study of the Cold War

John Lewis Gaddis

'Outside of a dog, a book is a man's best friend. Inside of a
dog, it's too dark to read.' (Groucho Marx)

I like this quotation from the 'other' Marx because it suggests how limited
our view of the Cold War, until quite recently, has actually been. In
contrast to the way most history is written, Cold War historians through
the end of the 1980s were working within, rather than after, the event they
were trying to describe. We had no way of knowing the final outcome, and
we could determine the motivations of only some – but by no means all –
of the major actors. We were in something like the position of those
puzzled poseurs, Rosencrantz and Guildenstern, in Shakespeare's *Hamlet*,
wondering what in the world was going on and how it was all going to
come out.[1]

We now know, to coin a phrase. Or, at least, we know a good deal more
than we once did. We will never have the full story: we do not have that for
any historical event, no matter how far back in the past. Historians can no
more reconstruct what really happened than maps can replicate what is
really there.[2] We are all in the business of *representation,* and because
representations invariably reflect the nature and purposes of those doing
the representing, there can never be *definitive* histories of anything.[3]
Historians, hence, are by their nature revisionists. Their task is as much to
subvert as to confirm prevailing views – even if these result from earlier
revisions, and even if the effect of challenging them is to revive still earlier
orthodoxies.[4]

Whether we can revise without reconsidering the *labels* we have attached
to one another's work is an interesting question. It is all too easy, in a
controversial field like Cold War history, to let category shape content. We
tend to cram each other into tight historiographical boxes like 'orthodoxy',
'revisionism', 'post-revisionism', 'corporatism', or 'post-modernism', with
the result that we fail to read one another as carefully as we might. If the

substance of what we are doing is new – and much of it surely is – then should not the categories be also? Especially since most of our old ones were themselves artifacts of the Cold War, which is to say, they reflected the view from inside Groucho's dog?

It is, I think, no accident that the parable most often associated with the end of the Cold War was that of the emperor's new clothes. The premise was that a naïve rather than a sophisticated view best detected reality and this chapter tests that hypothesis. I've framed it around a set of impressions a person from Mars might have – someone with no prior memory or knowledge or understanding of the Cold War – if exposed to that subject for the first time. I hope thereby to suggest some new approaches and start some new arguments; in short, to make a fresh start.

Doing so by way of the Martians is not as odd as it might seem, for many of us encounter their equivalents every day. They are not aliens; they are undergraduates.[5]

Naïve Impression no. 1: The Cold War went on for a very long time, and then all of the sudden it went away

That seems obvious enough now, but I cannot recall anyone during the Cold War who thought it obvious at the time. Wars, hot or cold, do not normally end with the abrupt but peaceful collapse of a major antagonist. Such an event had to have deep roots, and yet neither our histories nor our theories came anywhere close to detecting these. Like Rosencrantz and Guildenstern, we were missing a lot.

Nor have we done much better since. We now have several narratives of the Cold War from beginning to end,[6] but none that seeks to place that event within an interpretive perspective that could *explain* such an outcome. Historians are still at the stage of saying, in effect: 'here's what happened, don't push us on why'. The theorists' performance is even less impressive: I have the uneasy sense that international relations theory is still being taught pretty much as if the Cold War had never ended.[7] What would it take, then, to achieve an interpretive breakthrough that would account for why the Cold War lasted so long but ended so abruptly – and so peacefully?

It is worth recalling that two of the most striking revolutions in the history of science – Darwin's and Einstein's – came with the recognition that time and space cannot be separated, that objects and organisms evolve, that structures and processes are *related* to one another. And yet historians and theorists of international relations rarely recognize this: historians prefer tracing processes while remaining vague about structures; theorists describe structures but often fail to place them within the stream of time.[8]

Most historians missed, therefore, a significant structural insight from neo-Realist theory: that, contrary to what geometry might suggest, bipolar systems tend to be more stable than multipolar systems.[9] Neo-Realists, though, found it difficult to explain where bipolarity had come from in the first place, and even greater difficulty anticipating what might happen to it.[10] One group told the story of the Cold War in all of its complexity, but when asked how the Cold War functioned as an international system it had no answer. The other group concentrated on answering that question, but in doing so it treated the Cold War as a static and not an evolving phenomenon, with the result that a focus on stability obscured the instabilities that were rapidly accumulating within the system.

So why can we not have it both ways? Why can we not devise an approach that incorporates both structure and process – that relates space and time – in ways that would respect the historians' concern for complexity on the one hand while permitting theoretical generalization on the other?

I think we can, but only if each discipline adjusts. The historians have got to back off from their preoccupation with particular trees to look at the forest as a whole. If anything, the availability of new documents has caused a regression in this regard: we are probably *less* inclined toward large-scale analysis than we were a decade ago. But the theorists will also need to reconfigure: they will have to abandon a definition of power that accords primacy to military capabilities; they will have to give up their insistence on distinguishing sharply between systems-level and unit-level phenomena; they will have to jettison the curious belief that there can ever be, in this complex and interrelated world, such a thing as an independent variable. Apart from God, of course, who does not figure prominently within international relations theory.

It all sounds rather daunting – until one asks how a child might go about solving the problem. 'What's it like', he or she would probably ask, 'that I already know something about?' Naïve investigators think in terms of metaphors: recognizing that something is *like* something else is how learning takes place. So too, interestingly, do far from naïve scientists. 'To the imaginative theoretical physicist', John Ziman writes,

> axiomization seems a formal and sterile activity. But there is much to be learnt from the mathematical metaphors that are sometimes uncovered in this process – that the behavior of an electron in an atom is 'like' the vibration of air in a spherical container, or that the random configuration of the long chain of atoms in a polymer molecule is 'like' the motion of a drunkard across a village green.[11]

Gaddis, history is a science!

'[T]he scientist learns to talk and think scientifically', Ziman insists, 'in the same way as the infant learns to talk and think about the world of everyday reality.'[12]

These comments struck me with particular force as I was writing the conclusion to *We Now Know*. I was grasping for a way to link the Cold War's chronology to its structure. I did not want to claim – because I do

thus troubles him not to have predicted the end

not believe – that the Soviet Union's collapse was predetermined; but it seemed equally foolish to suggest that so decisive an event could simply have been an accident. As I was pondering this problem, I suddenly found myself thinking about a declining dinosaur: From the outside, as rivals contemplated its sheer size, tough skin, bristling armament, and aggressive posturing, the beast looked sufficiently formidable that none dared tangle with it. Appearances deceived, though, for within its digestive, circulatory, and respiratory systems were slowly clogging up, and then shutting down. There were few external signs of this until the day the creature was found with all four feet in the air, still awesome but now bloated, stiff, and quite dead. The moral of the fable is that armaments make impressive exo-skeletons, but that a shell alone ensures the survival of no animal and no state.[13] The image appealed to me because it was neither static nor reduc-tionist. It implied that the power a state can project externally depends upon multiple systems working together internally, and that to define power – or polarity – in terms of any single capability is to miss most of what is actually happening.

This in turn made me wonder about our old familiar distinction between domestic and foreign policy. Do we not need to look at both, recognizing that each is connected to the other? Medical treatment, however special-ized it may be, cannot succeed without taking into account the entire organism and its surrounding ecosystem. Could it be, then, that physicians have as much to teach us as physicists in seeking to understand inter-national systems and the states that function within them?

We need to find ways, within our histories, to *integrate* structure and process. One way we might do this is to think of great powers as living organisms who have to stay healthy while adapting themselves to shifting environments. Some manage it, others do not, and it should be quite feas-ible within this framework to devise explanations that would satisfy histor-ians and theorists alike. For the historian, such an *ecological* approach would show interconnecting structures evolving through time, a pattern they should certainly find familiar.[14] For the theorists – well, the ones I know speak often enough of billiard balls, dominos, bandwagons, rolling logs, prisoner's dilemmas, stag hunts, and chickens. I fail to see why my metaphorically defunct dinosaur cannot be added to the list.

Naïve Impression no. 2: That the 'superpowers', during the Cold War, were not all that 'super'

The term 'superpower', when it came into common usage at the end of World War II,[15] reflected what was then seen as a unique circumstance: that, at least by traditional standards of measurement, the disparity between the power the United States and the Soviet Union could bring to bear, on the one hand, and the power anyone else could wield, on the other, was greater than it had ever been in the history of the world. It was taken for granted, therefore, that in such a system influence could flow only in one direction: from the big powers to smaller ones, from centers to peripheries. On this point such radically different theories as Neo-Realism, dependency, and world systems could agree[16] – and most early histories of the Cold War were written from that perspective as well.

Long before the Cold War ended, though, there were reasons for questioning this assumption. Historians began suggesting that the US and Soviet spheres of influence were really latter-day empires; but the history of earlier empires had frequently revealed a pattern of peripheries manipulating centers rather than the other way around.[17] Simultaneously, studies on inequality – especially with respect to master–slave relationships and the position of women in society – were showing that subordinate groups were not always powerless: they could and often did carve out zones of autonomy, sometimes even resistance, against those who, to outward appearances, controlled their lives.[18] The 'new' Cold War history, I think, is going to reinforce such arguments, for it is showing that zones of at least relative autonomy existed on both sides during that conflict, and that smaller powers were often in a position to influence the actions of their larger counterparts.

One way to see this is to consider geography, a neglected dimension of Cold War history. We tend to think of the Soviet–US rivalry as a global phenomenon,[19] and in a way it was, since the competition took place within a much wider space than had earlier epic struggles between, say, Germany and France, or England and Spain, or Athens and Sparta. There were always regions, however, that the Cold War bypassed. East and Southeast Asia did not really get caught up in it until the after Mao Zedong's victory in China and the outbreak of the Korean War. The superpower competition had little effect on the Middle East and Latin America until the early 1950s, and Africa got dragged in only a decade or so after that. Other parts of the world always remained more or less apart: India and Indonesia, for example. So a simple analysis that asks *where* the Cold War was taking place at particular times suggests that geography itself made zones of relative autonomy possible. The superpowers were never super enough to operate at full strength everywhere.

What is more interesting is a growing body of evidence showing that even within those countries that were on the 'front lines' the writ of the superpowers did not run as large as we had once thought. Geir Lundestad showed some time ago that the American sphere of influence in Western Europe was not solely the product of Washington's push for it, but rather reflected an invitation extended by the Europeans themselves as a counterbalance to the Russians.[20] More recent studies of the structure of the US empire in Europe show that European preferences often shaped it – that the United States, having been invited in, was not in all respects certain of what to do, and often followed the Europeans' lead.[21]

Even more surprisingly, Norman Naimark has now provided powerful evidence of disarray within the Soviet occupation zone in Eastern Germany, and there are indications of a similar pattern elsewhere in Eastern Europe.[22] Totalitarian rule, it seems, was not always total: there was less autonomy than in the American sphere, but there was enough to allow local actors at least some control over what happened, even under Stalin. By the time Khrushchev came to power, such satellite leaders as Walter Ulbricht and Wladyslaw Gomulka were often in a position to determine the pace if not always the outcome of events.[23] And it now appears that Brezhnev's suppression of the 'Prague spring' in 1968 – once taken as the high point of Moscow's self-confidence about its ability to dominate Eastern Europe – in fact provoked doubts within the Kremlin as to whether it could ever manage this sort of thing again: doubts confirmed when the Politburo decided, prior to the imposition of martial law in Poland in 1981, that the Soviet Union could no longer use its own forces to maintain its authority in that part of the world.[24]

The history of China during the Cold War is one of a secondary power maintaining its autonomy throughout that conflict by alternatively aligning with and defecting from Soviet and US spheres of influence. And both the United States and the Soviet Union found themselves reluctantly committed to military adventures in the Third World through the actions of clients – whether Chiang Kai-shek, Ho Chi Minh, Ngo Dinh Diem, Fidel Castro, or Hafizullah Amin – whom they could not always control.

What many of these episodes have in common is a phenomenon known as the 'tyranny of the weak' – the extent to which a big power rivalry can enhance rather than diminish the influence of small powers, through their ability to threaten defection or collapse.[25] Our understanding of such episodes is underdeveloped, though; and not the least of the opportunities the 'new' Cold War history provides is that of identifying such zones of autonomy, explaining how they evolved, and debating what they meant.

Naïve Impression no. 3: Not everyone during the Cold War thought about things in the same way

The fact that the Cold War never became a hot war would suggest, at first glance, the applicability of a 'rational choice' model for the study of post-1945 international relations.[26] Certainly I implied that in a short-sighted article published in 1986,[27] and not just with respect to the superpowers' handling of nuclear weapons, the aspect of the piece that got the most attention. The 'long peace' thesis presumed a gradual but broad convergence in the thinking of Soviet and American leaders over time: if the Cold War had not begun with a common rationality, then at least this had evolved over several decades. The struggle would probably end, I predicted, on the day when the abnormalities inherent in the Cold War had come to be seen, on both sides, as perfectly normal.

Obviously it would be difficult to reconcile this argument with my dead dinosaur metaphor, and I would not want to try. Part of taking responsibility for what one has said is acknowledging that some of it may have been wrong. I am interested, though, in where a rational-choice approach to Cold War history might still make sense – and even more interested in where it might not.

The case for shared rationality rests chiefly on what the great powers did with the nuclear weapons they produced and deployed in such vast quantities. The fact that nobody used even one against anybody else after 1945 is remarkable enough, given the number of crises during the Cold War that in previous eras might well have produced all-out war. Still more impressive is the fact that this tradition of non-use extended over so wide an array of political, social, and cultural systems. If the United States, the Soviet Union, Great Britain, France, China, India, and Israel could all wind up treating nuclear weapons with respect and restraint, then that would appear to confirm a robust rationality, capable of overriding striking differences in the ways nations organized themselves.

This, at least, is how things looked from inside the Cold War, and the view from outside has not significantly changed it, at least as far as the behavior of national leaders is concerned.[28] Below that level, however, what we are finding is less reassuring. Presumably rational choice models, when applied to the actions of states, assume tight command and control: that decisions are made at the top by policymakers who have a clear vision of expected utility and how to maximize it, and that their subordinates carry out those orders. But do they?

David Rosenberg demonstrated long ago that a considerable gap existed between nuclear strategy as articulated and as implemented in the United States. To understand what really happened, one had to look at what was done with nuclear weapons from the bottom up as well as from the top down.[29] Scott Sagan's more recent work on the Cuban Missile Crisis reinforces that argument: he shows that at several points American alert procedures could have triggered inadvertent nuclear use without official authorization.[30] Nor does what we have learned about Soviet nuclear weapons in Cuba suggest that command and control procedures were any tighter on that side.[31] We know less with respect to the other nuclear powers, declared and undeclared – but enough has surfaced in just the American and Soviet cases to raise real concerns about how far assumptions of nuclear 'rational choice' ought to go.[32]

What about decisionmaking beyond the realm of nuclear weapons? Here the new evidence suggests even stronger grounds for doubting the existence of shared rationality. For example, Stalin appears to have gone through the entire post-World War II period convinced that the capitalists would soon fall out and fight with one another. As a consequence, he neglected clear evidence that the Western Europeans and the Americans were in fact cooperating to balance against the Soviet Union.[33] If a major state *cannot detect* balancing when it is taking place, then that would appear to raise serious questions about the extent to which a realist model of international relations – which presumes at least a common awareness of power balances – can accurately reflect what happened.

The United States assumed, prior to Chinese intervention in the Korean War, that the prospect of heavy casualties would deter Mao from entering that conflict. But, although others in his government did worry about this, the Chairman himself, it seems, welcomed the prospect of huge casualties as a way of legitimizing his revolution.[34] Because standards of rationality differed, what Washington intended as a deterrent Beijing took as an inducement.[35]

Khrushchev appears to have thought that he could threaten repeatedly to use nuclear weapons – ultimately even placing them in Cuba – without eliciting any comparable American response. Far from operating within a 'GRIT' or a 'tit-for-tat' negotiating framework,[36] he favored a strategy of 'bullying' which he none the less expected would alleviate rather than exacerbate Cold War tensions.[37] It was a peculiar logic, unique to its origi-nator, which has yet to fit within the standard repertory of conflict-resolution mechanisms.

The Soviet Union in the post-Khrushchev era repeatedly allowed its policy of seeking détente with the United States to be undermined by the actions of its clients – the North Vietnamese, the Cubans, the Afghans – because it chose not to disavow revolutionary causes in the Third World, even if it had had no hand in proclaiming them.[38] A distant and problem-atic benefit took precedence over immediate and very real costs.

And it now appears to be the case that the Soviet leadership during the early 1980s believed the United States to be on the verge of launching a nuclear first strike against it. Whether because of age or fear or panic, top Kremlin officials took steps to counter a set of dangers that did not exist outside of their own imaginations. The result may have been the second most perilous crisis of the Cold War – all the more so for the fact that Western leaders did not know, until well into it, that it was even taking place.[39]

What each of these situations have in common is a pattern in which a single leader or a small group of advisers decide issues, largely on the basis of emotion and without consulting experts. Although democracies are hardly immune from such practices (witness the recent NATO expansion decision),[40] they do appear to occur more frequently under authoritarianism, and for a reason so simple it is easily overlooked. Autocracy involves the imposition of a single individual's personality upon an entire state – whether Stalin, Mao, Khrushchev, Ceaucescu, or Pol Pot. Such states thus become, in effect, absolute monarchies,[41] a form of government most of the rest of the world gave up long ago precisely because calculations of expected utility by rulers so rarely corresponded with those of the nation as a whole.

If authoritarian structures can produce such 'rationality gaps' within states, what do they imply about shared rationality *among* states? Short-term cooperation is of course possible: collaborating with Stalin to defeat Hitler, for example, or Nixon's rapprochement with Mao. But what are the prospects for long-term compatibility of the kind that builds stable international relationships? Ought we now to extend the 'democratic peace' principle – that democracies do not fight one another[42] – to the broader proposition that democracies and autocracies view the world so differently that only temporary alignments can exist among them?

Probably that is going too far: it is an occupational hazard in trying to construct theory. But the record of the Cold War does, I think, raise questions about the relationship between political *structure* and policy *rationality*. The domestic configuration of states significantly shapes their diplomacy; and, because those configurations differed as dramatically as they did during the Cold War, we probably ought to be more cautious than we have been in assuming that all of that great game's competitors understood its rules in just the same way.[43]

Naïve Impression no. 4: The Cold War had something to do with good and evil

When, in 1983, Ronald Reagan denounced the Soviet Union as the 'focus of evil in the modern world', his speech appalled most academic experts on the Cold War. It was a striking departure from an official rhetoric, extending at least as far back as John F. Kennedy's American university address two decades earlier, that had portrayed the USSR as operating within the same moral universe as the Western democracies.[44] There was, in this view, a potentially deadly conflict; but it was being conducted within certain tacitly understood rules of the game, one of which was not to raise questions of legitimacy.[45] Whatever one thought, one did not say.

It is clear now, though, that citizens of the Soviet Union and its East European satellites saw the 'evil empire' speech rather differently. By the end of the decade, many of them had come to agree with Reagan that the regime under which they lived was, if not evil, then certainly illegitimate.[46] Little in the historical or theoretical literature on the Cold War, even that produced during the 1980s, would have alerted one to such an outcome. For all his superficiality, Reagan managed to anticipate the course of events better than most of us who had spent our lives studying the Soviet–American confrontation. It is worth trying to figure out why this happened.

The principal reason, I think, is that Cold War scholars so strongly resist making moral distinctions. Eyebrows arch, brows furrow, and bodies squirm when anyone raises the issue of good versus evil. It isn't 'scientific', we tell ourselves; it risks introducing bias into our work; it might lead to smugness, complacency, even triumphalist self-congratulation.[47]

But have historians not always known how difficult it is to be objective about anything?[48] Have our post-modernist colleagues not shown *all* generalizations to be socially constructed, save only the one that validates their methodology?[49] These difficulties do not deter historians from commending good or condemning evil when the subject is *not* the Cold War: indeed scholars of race, class, and gender, or slavery, imperialism, and genocide, could hardly function without these categories. Nor are they absent from the work of historians who seek out the voices of everyday life; for among such voices, whether in the modern age or in any other, distinctions between good and evil are ubiquitous.

What is it, then, that makes the Cold War different? Are we to conclude that ordinary people during that conflict did not perceive it in moral terms?[50] Are we to acknowledge that they did, but that this ought not to make any difference in how we retrospectively understand them? There is here, I think, confusion about the proper scope and content of international history. If, on the one hand, we confine it to what leaders said and did to one another, then it is hard to see how it differs from the old diplomatic history most of us have long since rejected. If, on the other hand, it expands to take into account masses as well as elites, then it will have to grapple with what was in *their* minds and what determined *their* actions, whether we as historians approve of these or not.

So what *did* ordinary people during the Cold War really think? Perhaps we should ask them. If we can reconstruct the world of a heretical sixteenth-century Italian miller, or of eighteenth-century Parisian cat torturers,[51] then surely it is not beyond our capabilities to determine how the Cold War shaped the fears and hopes of ordinary Poles, Germans, Czechs, Chinese, Vietnamese, or Guatemalans. I don't know what the outcome of such an investigation would be, but I doubt very much that perceptions of good and evil would be missing from it. Structures of government and the construction of equity have had a lot to do with one another during the Cold War, as they have throughout most of history.[52] We ought not to have to rely on Ronald Reagan to remind us of this.

Naïve Impression no. 5: The Cold War was perhaps not the most important
thing that happened during the last half of the twentieth century

I would not want to end without at least a brief speculation about how the
Cold War may look from the distant future. There is often a gap between
how contemporaries and subsequent chroniclers see particular ages.
Standards of significance change, and it would be quite arrogant to assume
that what *we* think was important about the Cold War all others will also.

One possibility, counter-intuitive now but less so with each passing year,
is that the Cold War will be remembered, not so much as a clash among
superpowers, but as the point at which the long ascendancy of the state reached
its peak and began to wane. States have been growing in power since they
were invented some five centuries ago, and certainly during the first half of
the twentieth century they were stronger than at any point in their history.
George Orwell's horrific vision in his book *1984* assumed that this trend
would continue: his imaginary world was supposed to become our actual world.

But obviously it did not. Does anyone today see states as anything like
that powerful? Have not the processes of economic integration and
political fragmentation – themselves largely set in motion by the Cold War
– halted and perhaps reversed this steady expansion of state authority?[53]
If that is the case, then what was really important about the Cold War may
not be what we are currently focusing on. A *tectonic* analysis of underlying
long-term trends could reveal a very different picture.

To see this point, please put up with one more metaphor, this one based
upon an actual event. The date was 17 October 1989, the Cold War was
well on the way to ending, and at 5.04 Pacific Daylight Time the Oakland
Athletics and the San Francisco Giants were about to take the field in
Candlestick Park to begin the third game of the World Series. Suddenly a
distant rumbling became a frightening shaking, and the great Loma Prieta
earthquake preempted everything planned for that afternoon, as well as
for some time to come. Television cameras, before being knocked off the
air, caught the astonishment on the faces of players, fans, and anchor-
persons alike as they abruptly acquired yet another Shakespearean insight:
that there were more things in heaven and earth than had been dreamt of
– or at least adequately taken into account – in their philosophy.[54]

Something equally surprising may have been happening during the Cold
War – and we have hardly begun to notice.

Conclusion: mapping history

I suggested at the outset an analogy between the writing of history and the
making of maps. Both historians and cartographers represent realities we
cannot replicate. Both vary scale and content according to need: a world

map has a different purpose from one intended to identify garbage dumps in the US state of Connecticut, just as an introductory history textbook differs from an excruciatingly detailed historical monograph. Neither maps nor histories are free from ideology: there is often a political reason for what is shown, and not shown. We evaluate both according to whether they make sense to us: is the representaïion credible? Is the logic plausible? Does the map or the history successfully extend our perceptions beyond what we alone can manage, whether across space or time?

The opening of new archives is like the discovery of a new continent: quick impressions yield to more careful revisions, blank spaces get filled in, and it takes a while to get an accurate or sophisticated representation of what is really there. Throughout this process, we impose a kind of interpretive 'grid' upon the new terrain. Rather like surveyors, our purposes are both orientation and mastery.[55] It makes quite a difference, though, what the units of measurement are.

Cold War historians are of course free to project, onto the 'new' Cold War documentary terrain, old and familiar historiographical categories. We know them well, we have long since decided who fits into which ones, and they are not apt to rattle our graduate students during their oral examinations. They are also likely, however, to reinforce the view many outsiders have of our field as one that is stale, boring, and thoroughly predictable.

But what if we should seize the opportunity that lies before us to map the new archival continent from some different perspectives? What if we recalibrated our surveying instruments so that they could see the Cold War in terms of ecology, or autonomy, or rationality, or morality, or tectonics? Doing so would not be difficult. All it would take would be an open mind, together with a willingness to ask naïve questions. For, as some of our colleagues in livelier fields of history have long since discovered, it is from these that sophisticated answers most often appear.

NOTES

1 Cold War historians might well regard Tom Stoppard's play, *Rosencrantz and Guilderstern Are Dead*, with a certain shock of recognition.
2 For the relationship between maps and landscapes, see John Ziman, *Reliable Knowledge: An Exploration of the Grounds for Belief in Science* (New York: Cambridge University Press, 1978), pp. 77–87.
3 As Ian Lustick has warned his fellow political scientists in 'History, Historiography, and Political Science: Multiple Historical Records and the Problem of Selection Bias', *American Political Science Review*, 90 (September, 1996): 605–18.
4 Anders Stephanson notes, with respect to *We Now Know*, that 'diplomatic historians will find disagreeable Gaddis's return to the perspective of the 1950s'. ('Rethinking Cold War History', *Review of International Studies* (January 1998):

120.) But does this mean that viewpoints are invalid for having originated in particular decades?

5 The earliest memory most of my Yale undergraduates have of the Cold War are the events surrounding its end: the collapse of the Berlin Wall, and later of the Soviet Union itself. Most of them would have been from 9 to 14 years old at the time.

6 Examples include: Richard Crockatt, *The Fifty Years War: The United States and the Soviet Union in World Politics, 1941–1991* (New York: Routledge, 1995); J. P. D. Dunbabin, *The Cold War: The Great Powers and Their Allies* (New York: Longman, 1994); Ralph B. Levering, *The Cold War: A Post-Cold War History* (Arlington Heights, IL: Harlan Davidson, 1994); Ronald E. Powaski, *The Cold War: The United States and the Soviet Union, 1917–1991* (New York: Oxford University Press, 1998); Martin Walker, *The Cold War: A History* (New York: Henry Holt, 1993).

7 William C. Wohlforth writes in his chapter in this volume that 'there is no documented instance of any noted scholar of international relations changing his or her view of any theory in response to fresh historical evidence'.

8 For an excellent if somewhat daunting discussion, see Clayton Roberts, *The Logic of Historical Explanation* (University Park, PA: Pennsylvania State University Press, 1996).

9 Kenneth N. Waltz, *Theory of International Politics* (New York: Random House, 1979), pp. 161–93.

10 For Waltz's flawed predictions, see ibid., pp. 162, 176–83, 204–10. On the origins of bipolarity, see John Gerard Ruggie, 'Continuity and Transformation in the World Polity: Toward a Neorealist Synthesis', in Robert O. Keohane, ed., *Neo-Realism and its Critics* (New York: Columbia University Press, 1986), pp. 131–57.

11 Ziman, *Reliable Knowledge*, p. 21. See also the economist Brian Arthur's short history of modern science as metaphor, quoted in M. Mitchell Waldrop, *Complexity: The Emerging Science at the Edge of Order and Chaos* (New York: Simon and Schuster, 1992), pp. 327–30.

12 Ziman, *Reliable Knowledge*, p. 128. 'Science uses the same mechanisms as in the growing child – sensorimotor coordination of observation and experiment, pattern recognition and the mental transformation of images, communication with a world of "others" and tests to select consensual conceptual schemes – not merely to implant this sense of reality into its practitioners but also as a means of acquiring uniquely faithful knowledge of the material domain', ibid., p. 137.

13 *We Now Know: Rethinking Cold War History* (New York: Oxford University Press, 1997), p. 284.

14 For a clear description of an ecological approach to history, see Paul W. Schroeder, *The Transformation of European Politics, 1763–1848* (New York: Oxford University Press, 1994), p. viii.

15 The first use of the term, I believe, occurs in William T. R. Fox's book, *The Super-Powers* (New York: Harcourt, 1944), although Fox anticipated a tripolar international system with Great Britain a superpower alongside the United States and the Soviet Union.

16 For a convenient overview, see the essays by Ole R. Holsti, Thomas J. McCormick, and Louis A. Perez, Jr, in Michael J. Hogan and Thomas G. Paterson, eds, *Explaining the History of American Foreign Relations* (New York: Cambridge University Press, 1991).

17 See, for example, Ronald Robinson and John Gallagher, with Alice Denny, *Africa and the Victorians: The Climax of Imperialism* (New York: St Martin's Press, 1961); Michael W. Doyle, *Empires* (Ithaca, NY: Cornell University Press, 1986).

18 Examples from American history include: Kenneth M. Stampp, *The Peculiar*

Institution: Slavery in the Ante-Bellum South (New York: Vintage, 1956); Laurel Thatcher Ulrich, *A Midwife's Tale: The Life of Martha Ballard, Based on Her Diary, 1875–1815* (New York: Vintage, 1990); Glenda Elizabeth Gilmore, *Gender and Jim Crow: Women and the Politics of White Supremacy in North Carolina, 1896–1920* (Chapel Hill, NC: University of North Carolina Press, 1996).

19 For example, see Gaddis, *We Now Know*, p. 27.

20 Geir Lundestad, 'Empire by Invitation? The United States and Western Europe, 1945–1952', *Journal of Peace Research*, 23 (September 1986): 263–77. See also Lundestad, *The American 'Empire' and Other Studies of US Foreign Policy in Contemporary Perspective* (New York: Oxford University Press, 1990), pp. 31–115.

21 Such is the argument of William I. Hitchcock, *France Restored: Cold War Diplomacy and the Quest for Leadership in Europe, 1944–1954* (Chapel Hill, NC: University of North Carolina Press, 1998). I am also drawing here upon the forthcoming dissertation of one of my Ohio University graduate students, Alessandro Brogi, which deals with the recovery of self-confidence in France and Italy after World War II.

22 Norman M. Naimark, *The Russians in Germany: A History of the Soviet Zone of Occupation, 1945–1949* (Cambridge, MA: Harvard University Press, 1995). See also Vladislav Zubok and Constantine Pleshakov, *Inside the Kremlin's Cold War: From Stalin to Khrushchev* (Cambridge, MA: Harvard University Press, 1996), especially pp. 48–9; and Vojtech Mastny, *The Cold War and Soviet Insecurity: The Stalin Years* (New York: Oxford University Press, 1996), pp. 19–22.

23 Gaddis, *We Now Know*, pp. 129–31, 143–9, 209–10.

24 Matthew J. Ouimet, 'All That Custom Has Divided: National Interest and the Secret Demise of the Brezhnev Doctrine, 1968–1981', PhD Dissertation, University of Washington, 1997; also, for a summary of more recent information, Raymond L. Garthoff, 'The Conference on Poland, 1980–1982: Internal Crisis, International Dimensions', *Cold War International History Project Bulletin*, 10 (March, 1998): 229–32.

25 The classic work here is Robert O. Keohane, 'The Big Influence of Small Allies', *Foreign Policy*, 2 (Spring, 1971): 161–82.

26 By 'rational choice', I mean the tendency on the part of nations to maximize the expected utility of the actions they take according to shared, not divergent, standards.

27 Gaddis, 'The Long Peace: Elements of Stability in the Postwar International System', *International Security*, 10 (Spring, 1986): 99–142, later reprinted as the final chapter in John Lewis Gaddis, *The Long Peace: Inquiries into the History of the Cold War* (New York: Oxford University Press, 1987).

28 John Lewis Gaddis, Philip Gordon, Ernest R. May, and Jonathan Rosenberg, *Cold War Statesmen Confront the Bomb: Nuclear Diplomacy since 1945* (New York: Oxford University Press, 1999) documents this point in detail.

29 David Alan Rosenberg, 'The Origins of Overkill: Nuclear Weapons and American Strategy', in Norman A. Graebner, ed., *The National Security: Its Theory and Practice, 1945–1960* (New York: Oxford University Press, 1986), pp. 123–95.

30 Scott D. Sagan, *The Limits of Safety: Organizations, Accidents, and Nuclear Weapons* (Princeton, NJ: Princeton University Press, 1993).

31 Anatoli I. Gribkov and William Y. Smith, *Operation ANADYR: US and Soviet Generals Recount the Cuban Missile Crisis* (Chicago, IL: edition q, 1994), discuss these arrangements. See also Gaddis, *We Now Know*, pp. 274–8.

32 A point that carries significant implications for those few theorists who continue to favor the proliferation of nuclear weapons. The pros and cons are conveniently summarized in Scott D. Sagan and Kenneth N. Waltz, *The Spread of Nuclear*

Weapons: A Debate (New York: Norton, 1995).

33 Gaddis, *We Now Know*, pp. 195–8. See also William Curti Wohlforth, *The Elusive Balance: Power and Perceptions during the Cold War* (Ithaca, NY: Cornell University Press, 1993), pp. 76–7; and Mastny, *The Cold War and Soviet Insecurity*, p. 149.

34 Chen Jian, *China's Road to the Korean War: The Making of the Sino-American Confrontation* (New York: Columbia University Press, 1994), p. 193; Shu Guang Zhang, *Mao's Military Romanticism: China and the Korean War, 1950–1953* (Lawrence, KS: University Press of Kansas, 1995), p. 85.

35 Shu Guang Zhang, *Deterrence and Strategic Culture: Chinese–American Confrontations, 1949–1958* (Ithaca, NY: Cornell University Press, 1991), discusses differences in Chinese and American conceptions of deterrence.

36 GRIT is 'Graduated Reciprocation in Tension-Reduction', an idea put forward by the psychologist Charles Osgood in 1959. For 'tit-for-tat', see Robert Axelrod, *The Evolution of Cooperation* (New York: Basic Books, 1984).

37 I have discussed Khrushchev's strategy more fully in *We Now Know*, pp. 234–44. See also Zubok and Pleshakov, *Inside the Kremlin's Cold War*, pp. 174–209.

38 The point is made in Ilya V. Gaiduk, *The Soviet Union and the Vietnam War* (Chicago, IL: Ivan R. Dee, 1996); also in Zhai Qiang, *Comrades and Adversaries: China and the Vietnam Wars, 1950–1975* (forthcoming).

39 Raymond L. Garthoff, *The Great Transformation: American–Soviet Relations and the End of the Cold War* (Washington, DC: Brookings Institution, 1994), pp. 60–2, 135–41. See also Beth A. Fischer, *The Reagan Reversal: Foreign Policy and the End of the Cold War* (Columbia, MO: University of Missouri Press, 1997), pp. 122–40.

40 James N. Goldgeier, 'NATO Expansion: The Anatomy of a Decision', *Washington Quarterly*, 21 (Winter, 1998): 85–102.

41 Absolute in the sense of monopolizing the policymaking process. As suggested above, such states were never absolute in their control over what was happening within their boundaries.

42 See Bruce Russett, *Grasping the Democratic Peace: Principles for a Post-Cold War World* (Princeton, NJ: Princeton University Press, 1993).

43 The tendency to assume shared rationality at the international level is deeply rooted. Melvyn Leffler, for example, distinguishes sharply between the Soviet Union's domestic and foreign policies. The new documents 'reveal a Soviet system as revolting as its worst critics charged long ago'. Nevertheless, '*realpolitik* held sway in the Kremlin. Ideology played an important role in shaping their perceptions, but Soviet leaders were not focused on promoting world revolution. They were concerned mostly with configurations of power, with protecting their country's immediate periphery, ensuring its security, and preserving their rule.' In short, with respect to the outside world, they were normal statesmen. 'Inside Enemy Archives', *Foreign Affairs*, 75 (July/August 1996): 120–35. Similarly, Deborah Welch Larson's recently published *Anatomy of Mistrust: US–Soviet Relations During the Cold War* (Ithaca, NY: Cornell University Press, 1997), documents *perceptions* of divergent rationality in Moscow and Washington, but it does not take up the question of whether at least some of these may have been real.

44 The Kennedy and Reagan speeches, delivered on 10 June 1963 and 8 March 1983, are most easily located in the series *Public Papers of the Presidents*, at the appropriate years.

45 See, on this point, my own 'long peace' article, which listed as one of those rules an acknowledgement of the legitimacy of leadership on both sides Gaddis, *The Long Peace*, p. 243.

46 David Remnick's *Lenin's Tomb: The Last Days of the Soviet Empire* (New York:

Random House, 1993), chronicles this process eloquently.

47 Leffler, in particular, seems to worry about this. See 'Inside Enemy Archives', p. 135; also 'New Approaches, Old Interpretations, and Prospective Recon-figurations', in Michael J. Hogan, ed., *America in the World: The Historiography of American Foreign Relations since 1941* (New York: Cambridge University Press, 1995), pp. 81–4.

48 See Peter Novick, *That Noble Dream: The 'Objectivity Question' and the American Historical Profession* (New York: Cambridge University Press, 1988).

49 Keith Windschuttle, *The Killing of History: How Literary Critics and Social Theorists Are Murdering Our Past* (New York: Free Press, 1996), especially pp. 76, 131, 174.

50 Leffler says as much: 'To frame international politics in the initial post-war years as a struggle between Soviet tyranny and American freedom is to simplify reality and distort the way most peoples around the world understood events.' 'New Approaches, Old Interpretations, and Prospective Reconfigurations', p. 84.

51 Carlo Ginzburg, *The Cheese and the Worms: The Cosmos of a Sixteenth-Century Miller*, trans. John and Anne Tedeschi (New York: Penguin, 1982); Robert Darnton, *The Great Cat Massacre and Other Episodes in French Cultural History* (New York: Basic Books, 1984).

52 R. J. Rummel estimates that some 38,500,000 people died in actual combat during the international and civil wars of the twentieth century. But another 169,202,000 died from what he calls 'democide', a general term he uses to include genocide, political murder, or other forms of indiscriminate killing committed by governments. Of these, Marxist-Leninist regimes accounted for 61 percent of the total, non-Marxist authoritarian governments for another 38.5 percent. Democracies produced only about 0.5 percent, suggesting that 'democide' was 200 times more likely to afflict the citizens of an authoritarian than a democratic state. (This information comes from Rummel's website, http://www2.hawaii.edu/~rummel; but see also his *Death By Government* (New Brunswick, NJ: Transaction Publishers, 1994).) Such figures are always problematic, but even if Rummel should be off by a factor of ten, the pattern would be striking enough.

53 These tendencies are succinctly summarized in Ian Clark, *Globalization and Fragmentation: International Relations in the Twentieth Century* (New York: Oxford University Press, 1997).

54 For the visual evidence, check http://www.kron.com/specials/89quake/nc4.html.

55 James C. Scott, *Seeing Like a State: How Certain Schemes to Improve the Human Condition Have Failed* (New Haven, CT: Yale University Press, 1998), provides a wonderful explanation of this process.

2

Bringing it Together:
The Parts and the Whole

Melvyn P. Leffler

The end of the Cold War and the opening of some archival materials from the former communist bloc has led to an outpouring of interesting papers, insightful volumes of essays, provocative monographs, and one new comprehensive overview of the early Cold War. Collectively, this scholarship represents an important turning point in the evolution of the historiography of post-war international relations. For the first time, the focus of scholarly activity has shifted from the United States and the Western bloc to the Soviet Union and its former allies. At the same time, there has been a noteworthy shift from an emphasis on geopolitics to a stress on ideology, from a concern with interests to a preoccupation with culture, from analyses of the international system and the threats emanating therefrom to a concern with regime-types and with personalities. The result, I think, is a cumulative increase in our knowledge of events and episodes, but not a satisfactory synthesis.[1]

If we are to capture the Cold War in all its complexity, we must become more subtle and textured. We must find a way to see the interconnectedness of many factors. The conflicting interpretive approaches lead us in interesting but sometimes misguided directions because they tend to focus on a specific set of variables and hypotheses rather than allow us to see the interrelatedness of the whole. By necessity, most of us will have to concentrate on particular issues and variables because of the sheer scope of the sources. But, in doing so, I hope we can nevertheless capture the larger context, the thick description, the seamless whole.

By capturing the seamless whole, I would like to think that we could examine both American and Soviet policies and analyze their interaction. I would like to think that we could capture the appropriate elements of geopolitics and ideology and illuminate their interdependence. By the seamless whole, I think we need to reinsert an examination of interests into our narratives as well as a concern with culture, indeed perhaps to illustrate how interests and culture are inextricably intertwined. A concern with regime-types should not distract us from looking at how the international system appears to leaders within those regimes. And we should realize that leaders can feel both very vulnerable and very opportunistic at almost the same moment in time. Precisely because of this fact, we shall lose our grasp of the dynamics of the Cold War if we do not examine events in Western Europe and Eastern Europe, as well as developments on the periphery of Eurasia. Nor will we understand the Cold War if we divorce military strategy from diplomacy, or the domestic polity from the policymakers who make foreign policy. Of course, it is easier to prescribe all of this than to do it oneself. But failure to do it can lead to important errors or distortions, as will be described below.

Revisions

There is no better place to begin than with my own work. In *Preponderance of Power*, I tried to bring together many disparate aspects of the US policy-making process, but I would do parts of it differently if I could begin again with what I now know. I would assign more importance to the role of ideology both in the making of American foreign policy, and, especially, in the making of Soviet foreign policy. In my introduction to the book I stressed that national security was not simply about space and territory; it was about the protection of America's core values, its organizing ideology, its system of liberal capitalism. 'If communism is allowed to absorb the free nations', said Harry S. Truman, 'then we would be isolated from our sources of supply and detached from our friends. Then we would have to take defense measures which might really bankrupt our economy, and change our way of life so that we couldn't recognize it as American any longer.'[2] As was the case with President Woodrow Wilson and President Franklin D. Roosevelt, there was a sense among Truman's advisers that geopolitical balances in the world and the control over economic resources that accompanied those balances had real meaning for the preservation of America's own systems of free markets and democratic capitalism.[3] There was also a knowledge that overcommitments, as a response to geopolitical and geostrategic threats, could undermine that very system of liberal capitalism. Finding the correct mix of domestic and foreign policies to stymie adversaries abroad and preserve an acceptable distribution of power in the international system without imposing a garrison state at home was a formidable and never-ending challenge which President Harry S. Truman and President Dwight D. Eisenhower took very seriously.[4] Yet in my own work, aside from my analysis of the Marshall Plan, I had trouble weaving this story into my examination of US foreign and strategic policies. In other words, I would try even harder to underscore the fact that US officials held very strong beliefs, linking the foundations of democratic capitalism inside the United States to acceptable configurations of power in the international system.

Perhaps I would have illuminated the ideological variable more successfully if I had grappled more systematically with the domestic polity and partisan politics. I do not think that corporatist interpretations and functional interest groups explain the basic motives behind the United States' Cold War posture, but I do think the resonance of anti-communist rhetoric becomes more understandable when you place it in the context of the post-war business offensive against unions, the stiff Southern resistance to civil rights activists and integrationist efforts, and the fierce determination of Republican partisans like Richard Nixon to recapture their dominance in American politics.[5] Amidst the vast panorama of American politics, interest groups and business constituencies could help shape and sometimes even determine specific choices, including the preference for air power, the grudging support for the Chinese Nationalists, and the decisions to reverse course in Japan and intervene militarily in Korea.[6]

If I understated the role of ideology in American Cold War policies, I did so even more noticeably in my brief depictions of Soviet policies. I did so because in thinking about ideology, I kept looking for instances in which Stalin and his advisers and successors fomented revolution abroad or aided and abetted foreign communists. I still think that Stalin after World War II was lackluster and intermittent in his support of communist insurrectionary activity. The disillusionment of some French, Italian, and Spanish leftists was well founded as was the intermittent disappointment of Greek and Chinese communists who looked for Soviet support and did not get it nearly as much as they thought they should. While they did get more of it than was apparent (to me) a decade ago, the new evidence still illuminates the fact that Stalin assigned little importance to the promotion of revolutionary activity. Nowhere beyond its own borders, writes Vojtech Mastny, perhaps with some exaggeration, did the Kremlin 'foresee the establishment of Communist regimes'. 'Despite Stalin's ideological dedication, revolution was for him a means to power rather than a goal in itself.'[7]

But, although other recent writers assign primacy to power politics over ideology, I still think I understated the role of ideology. I did so because I thought about ideology too narrowly. I did not explore how it shaped perceptions of threat, the selection of friends, the assessment of opportunities, and the understanding of what was happening within the international system itself. The analyses of John Gaddis, Vojtech Mastny, William Wohlforth, and Vladislav Zubok and Constantine Pleshakov do convey important insights illuminating how presuppositions about the hostility of the capitalist world, expectations about an economic crisis in the West, and assumptions about intra-capitalist rivalries shaped the contours of Soviet policy and provided comfort that in the long run the Kremlin would triumph. The leaders of the Kremlin were interested primarily in the power of their state and the survival of their regime, but any account that trivializes their faith in the superiority of their system or that obfuscates their conviction that they were engaged in a long-term systemic struggle misses an important part of their belief system. I do not think that these factors dictated the Cold War or determined the goals of the Kremlin, as it came to be waged, but I certainly think that such ideological factors are important in understanding Soviet perceptions, motivations, and behavior. Ideology should help us grasp perceptions of threat and assessments of power balances.[8]

By underestimating the influence of ideology in my own writing, I think I also understated the links between the Chinese, Korean, and Russian communist regimes. The recent literature demonstrates rather persuasively the close coordination of policy between the regimes in Moscow, Beijing, and Pyongyang, at least in the late 1940s and early 1950s. Their interests may not always have converged and Stalin may have possessed some contempt for the Koreans and considerable distrust of the Chinese, but he none the less played a critical role in the decisions leading up to and during the Korean War. In other words, the very good scholarship on Korean and Chinese nationalism that dominated the 1980s does not suffice to explain the dynamics of the Korean War. The ideological affinities of Stalin, Mao, and Kim are critically important to understanding the evolution of the Cold War in East Asia. Moreover, these affinities make some of the perceptions of Washington policymakers somewhat wiser and more credible than some of us thought five or ten years ago.[9]

I also think that the new emphasis on ideology and culture enhances our grasp of the reasons for the success of US policymaking. In his new book, John Gaddis does a superb job of outlining how habits of discourse, political pluralism, and competitive markets enabled the United States to respond thoughtfully and constructively to the needs and pressures of its diverse allies in Western Europe. This new emphasis on democratic discourse adds an important twist and enhances the appeal of the empire by invitation thesis articulated by Geir Lundestad and other post-revisionists. I still believe that this interpretation is misleading in important ways, but Gaddis's focus on democratic culture improves it considerably.[10]

At the same time, the stress on consumer culture and its appeal to Eastern Europeans as well as Western Europeans has helped us to understand the outcome of the Cold War. Not long ago, few of us would have focused on Coke™ and Reeboks, on jazz and rock, on Sesame Street and Donald Duck, but we now know that their appeal perhaps counted for more than the Pershing missiles and the neutron bombs that seemed to dominate the diplomacy of the 1970s. Although we do not know the extent to which US officials grasped these truths, we will need to do a more nuanced job in the future in analyzing the extent to which an understanding of the appeal of consumer culture and individual rights played an important role in configuring Cold War diplomacy. Occasionally, US diplomats and officials did note that the success of Western capitalism would act as a magnet on the East, but they also worried that poverty, unemployment, injustice, and racism would erode the appeal of American democratic capitalism and make our system appear less attractive than its rival.[11]

While the pull of America's consumer culture seems unquestionable, the repugnance of Soviet political culture seems equally so. One of the great advances in our knowledge over the last few years has been the explicit portrayal of the workings of the Soviet system in foreign lands. Nobody reading Jan Gross's account of Soviet troops in Poland in 1939 and 1940, or Norman Naimark's analysis of Soviet occupation policies in Eastern Germany can fail to understand the power of Soviet culture. I say Soviet culture, rather than policy, because one of the signal contributions of this scholarship has been to illustrate that there was no coherent policy, no well-conceived intent. Soviet culture simply replicated itself abroad with all its brutality, its insensitivity to human aspirations, even its indifference to the political needs of communist comrades in foreign lands who were appalled and embarrassed by the rapacity of Soviet troops.[12]

The lack of synthesis

The new scholarship, then, has added immeasurably to our knowledge, but not to an overall synthesis that seems satisfactory to me. There are numerous reasons for this. The tendency to focus on Soviet policy (or on Soviet–Chinese–Korean communist relations) rather than the interactions of Western and Eastern Bloc initiatives has been a noteworthy weakness in the new scholarship. So, too, has been the loss of focus on traditional questions of security, power, and interest. The emphases on ideology and regime-type lack nuance when they are decoupled from an examination of geopolitics and the configuration of the international system. These configurations engendered perceptions of threat and opportunity, and the role of ideological presuppositions cannot be grasped without portraying the systemic backdrop. In other words, the temptation to explain the Cold War in terms of the paranoia of Stalin, the brutality of communism, and the attractions of democratic pluralism and consumer capitalism simplifies the complexity of the historical process and distorts what we now do know about the Cold War.

What is striking in some of the new literature is the failure to look carefully at Soviet security needs. What I would say is especially puzzling is the failure to analyze the suffering and travail of World War II as background for examining Soviet policies. In John Gaddis's recent book, for example, the fact that the Soviet Union lost 27 million people during World War II is mentioned in one sentence. Fear of Germany is not stressed as an important ingredient bearing on Soviet motivations; indeed Stalin is

criticized for not possessing a multilateral approach to security at the end
of the war. In Gaddis's version, Stalin was not reacting to any external
threats, existing or anticipated; he was 'responding predictably to his own
authoritarian, paranoid, and narcissistic predispositions'.[13]

Stalin was, of course, paranoid and brutal, but does this account for the
initial Cold War policies of the Kremlin? Much of the new literature is
loaded with evidence that Stalin and his comrades were greatly pre-
occupied with the revival of German and Japanese power. Kathryn
Weathersby, who has done more research on the Soviet occupation of
Korea than any other person, writes that 'for the rest of his life Stalin
continued to base his policy toward Northeast Asia on the assumption that
Japan would rearm and again threaten the security of the USSR'.[14] Japan,
Stalin was certain, would recover and remilitarize within 20 or 30 years.
'The whole plan of our relations with China', Stalin told Chinese Foreign
Minister T. V. Soong in July 1945, 'is based on this.'[15]

Stalin's concern with Germany, however, greatly exceeded his fear of
Japan. He talked often about the prospect of renewed conflict with
Germany. 'She will recover and very quickly. Give them 12 to 15 years and
they will be on their feet again.'[16] Nor did the specter of German revanchism recede quickly after his death. According to Zubok and Pleshakov,
'the support of the GDR for Khrushchev was first and foremost a
strategic imperative'.[17] Khrushchev wrote to President John F. Kennedy in
December 1961:

> I believe that deep in your heart you will agree with me that the Soviet
> Union after all it has suffered cannot be indifferent to what is
> happening in West Germany. Behind every demand of ours to secure
> lasting peace in Europe and prevent new German aggression … are
> millions of lives of perished Soviet people.[18]

Nobody knowing the history of Soviet–German relations or Russian–
Japanese relations in the twentieth century could doubt the sincerity of
such comments. But, notwithstanding the evident bearing of German and
Japanese reconstruction on Soviet security requirements, this subject
receives rather little attention in the new literature. Instead, Soviet policies
are defined in terms of Stalin's paranoia and the Kremlin's ideology.
Commonplace now is the statement that Stalin sought security at the
expense of all other nations. Stalin sought a Cold War, writes Gaddis, like
a fish seeks water.[19]

But did Stalin seek a Cold War with the United States? Did he define
security in ways that jeopardized the security of the United States, his
principle future adversary? The evidence here is mixed and confusing.
Zubok and Pleshakov, for example, state baldly that Stalin did not want a
Cold War.

Notwithstanding his reputation as a ruthless tyrant, Stalin was not prepared to take a course of unbridled unilateral expansionism after World War II. He wanted to avoid confrontation with the West. He was even ready to see cooperation with the Western powers as a preferable way of building his influence and solving contentious international issues. Thus the Cold War was not his choice or his brainchild.[20]

If it was not his choice or his brainchild, then why did it come about? Arguably, it was because his view of security endangered everybody else. But what were his views? Few look carefully at this subject, but I doubt that many of us would quarrel with the succinct description put forward by David Holloway. He writes that Stalin wanted 'to consolidate Soviet territorial gains, establish a Soviet sphere of influence in Eastern Europe, and have a voice in the political fate of Germany and – if possible – Japan'.[21] The question, then, is why this view of security threatened everyone else. Certainly, it made life unbearable (literally) for many people living on Stalin's borders and circumscribed the sovereignty of Poland, Romania, Bulgaria, Hungary, and Czechoslovakia. But why did this view of security engender such fears in the West?

In the new literature this question is not addressed in any systematic manner. Instead, most writers slip into the ideological/personal argument. Everybody was threatened because Stalin was in control and he was paranoid. Hence Vojtech Mastny writes, 'The forthcoming Cold War was both unintended and unexpected; it was predetermined all the same.' It was predetermined because Stalin had to have enemies in order to justify his hold on power. It was predetermined, say Zubok and Pleshakov, because the imperial/revolutionary paradigm had to resurface. It was predetermined, says Gaddis, because nobody could trust Stalin.[22]

But such arguments do not seem to be supported by the documentation we now have. To blame the Cold War on Stalin, we need to have the evidence to demonstrate that US officials saw something distinctively evil in Stalin during the formative stages of the Cold War, let's say between 1945 and 1948. To blame the Cold War on Stalin, one would have to demonstrate that his view of security was particularly distinctive from that of other Russian/Soviet officials after World War II.

The record is pretty clear on the first of these points. At the end of World War II there is scant evidence that US officials were particularly upset with Stalin the man. Rather, the opposite could be argued. Truman did not mind dealing with Stalin, and some of his closest advisers, for example, Averell Harriman, were favorably disposed toward him. Truman quickly grew agitated by Soviet actions, but neither he nor his leading advisers found dealing with Stalin particularly distasteful. Stalin, Truman noted, was not difficult to do business with. 'I like Stalin', he wrote to his wife. 'He is straightforward. Knows what he wants and will compromise when he can't get it.' If anything, one might be inclined to assail Truman's and his advisers's moral complacency about Stalin and his deeds.[23]

The record is cloudier on the second issue, but there is little reason to believe that, overall, Soviet behavior at the end of World War II would have been different if Stalin were not in power. Would other Kremlin officials have been willing to concede control over Poland? Would they have imposed significantly softer terms on Germany's wartime allies, for example, Romania and Hungary? Would they have quickly withdrawn their troops from Eastern Europe and permitted free elections? Would they have stopped seizing reparations in Germany or withdrawn from northern Korea or refrained from asking to participate in the occupation of Japan? Stalin probably probed a bit more in Turkey and perhaps in Iran, but the record suggests that he had no master plan, that he was not intent on imposing communist regimes, that he supported coalition governments in Western Europe, and that he was not unwilling, at least initially, to collaborate with Chiang in China and the Americans in Korea.[24] One might ask whether other Kremlin leaders might have acted more opportunistically to support communist partisans in northern Italy or France or eschewed relations with Chiang Kai-shek? My point is simply to suggest that if the Cold War is to be blamed on Stalin, a more systematic effort needs to be made to show that Stalin's alleged goals – territorial consolidation, a sphere of influence in Eastern Europe, and some control over German and Japanese power – would have been eschewed by other officials in the Kremlin.

I am struck that the label that Zubok and Pleshakov attach to Stalin's foreign policies is 'cautious expansionism'.[25] The behavior of Soviet troops in Germany was horrible and Soviet repression in Eastern Europe was extensive and Soviet probes and overtures in Iran and Turkey were worrisome, but in and of themselves they hardly support claims that Soviet actions endangered the security of everybody. Some others, however, did feel terribly threatened. The interpretive question, then, is why a policy of cautious expansionism engendered such exaggerated fears of Soviet power.

Analyses that depend primarily on Soviet sources or that focus on Stalin's personality or that dwell on ideology or that emphasize regime-types cannot answer this question satisfactorily. Zubok and Pleshakov concede this point in their conclusion. They start their book stating that the Cold War can be explained by looking at an imperial-revolutionary paradigm and the personalities of the leaders in the Kremlin. By the end of their book, the weight of the evidence and the logic of the facts impel them to inject another variable: the policies of the West, primarily of the United States. The shift from Roosevelt to Truman, the use of the atomic bomb, and the declaration of the Marshall Plan, according to Zubok and Pleshakov, conjured up old threats and ambient anxieties.[26] The Cold War, in other words, was an interactive process.

But the more important point is that the nature of the interaction cannot be understood unless one looks carefully at the configuration of the international system at the end of World War II and the threats and opportunities it engendered. There were vacuums of power in Germany and Japan; there was economic hardship, social turmoil, and political strife in France, Italy, Belgium, Czechoslovakia, Hungary, Poland, and Ukraine; there was impending financial bankruptcy in Britain; there was civil war in China; there were revolutionary nationalist movements contending for power in French Indochina and the Dutch East Indies; there was imperial decay throughout Africa, the Middle East, and Asia. Was this not a world of anarchic states worried about their security? Was this not a world filled with countries experiencing internecine strife, with class factions, if not whole classes, looking for assistance or redemption from states which represented contrasting ways of life?

Histories of the Cold War must take account of the international system and the threats and opportunities it engendered. When Assistant Secretary of War John J. McCloy went to Europe in April 1945, he was horrified by the conditions he observed. 'There is complete economic, social, and political collapse going on in Central Europe, the extent of which is unparalleled in history', he wrote to his boss, Secretary of War Henry L. Stimson.[27] When Stimson met with Truman a few days later, he told the President that there will be 'pestilence and famine in Central Europe next winter. This would be followed by political revolution and Communistic infiltration.'[28] Europe today, Truman was informed, constitutes a breeding ground for 'spontaneous class hatred to be channeled by a skillful agitator'.[29]

Although it is too little emphasized in recent books, indeed almost completely overlooked, the solution to the problems of European reconstruction and stabilization were linked from the outset of the post-war era to the situation in Germany. Truman wrote to Churchill in May 1945, 'From all the reports which reach me I believe that without immediate concentration on the production of German coal we will have turmoil and unrest in the very areas of Western Europe on which the whole stability of the continent depends.'[30]

In most of the new accounts of the Cold War, the perception of chaos in Western Europe is not focused on until we get to the narrative about the Marshall Plan; the story of Germany gets short shrift until we get to the Berlin blockade; and the lost opportunity debate over China gets hardly a word until the Chinese communists are on the threshold of power in 1948. Yet all these issues engulfed Washington in 1945 at the time World War II ended and at the same time that the Soviets were pursuing their own goals in Eastern Europe and eastern Germany. No account will do justice to the origins of the Cold War that does not take cognizance of these developments, events which might accrue to Stalin's benefit even if they were not the result of his actions. Nobody can really understand why Stalin's quest for security in Eastern Europe generated intense fears everywhere unless one grasps that those actions on his immediate periphery coincided with developments elsewhere, which endangered the interests, power, and even survival of the democratic imperial democracies of Western Europe upon which America's own security was perceived to depend.[31]

Although democratic capitalism eventually proved to be more appealing than its ideological rival, this did not seem inevitable in 1945. Throughout Europe and Asia, people associated the two world wars and the great depression with an existing political economy that had to be changed. They wanted more than democratic political reforms; they wanted a more just economic and social order. The leading Catholic newspaper in Czecho-slovakia put it bluntly in May 1945: 'As we renew our economic and social life it is impossible to return to the capitalist system which prevailed here during the first twenty years of our republic. This war put a period at the end of the capitalist era. We stand on the threshold of a new economic and social era.'[32] US officials grasped these sentiments. 'They have suffered so much', said Assistant Secretary of State Dean Acheson, 'and they believe so deeply that governments can take some action which will alleviate their sufferings, that they will demand that the whole business of state control and state interference shall be pushed further and further'.[33]

American threat perception cannot be understood without examining the evolution of the international system and the socio-economic trans-formations caused by depression and war; emphasizing the actions of adversaries or the overtures of friends will not suffice. Nobody forced or invited the Americans to make the decisions they made in 1945, but US officials determined that the production of German coal had to be the number one goal of occupation policy aside from the protection of US troops. Nobody forced or invited US troops into China and Korea, but they went none the less, with several goals in mind, not the least important of which was the containment of Soviet communism. Nobody in the summer of 1945 forced or invited the Americans to contain Soviet probes in the eastern Mediterranean, but by the time of the Potsdam Conference US officials had determined to thwart any Kremlin attempts to control the Dardanelles. Nobody forced or invited the Americans to monopolize the occupation of Japan, but they decided on their own that such a monopoly served US interests and promoted US security.[34]

The Cold War as a complex system

By focusing on the Kremlin and on Sino–Soviet relations, the new literature tends to obfuscate the complex interactions that led to the Cold War. The Cold War meant the division of Europe. The Soviets started it with their policies in Eastern Europe. The Americans intensified it with the initiatives that did so much to split Germany, including the Potsdam provisions on reparations, the creation of Bizonia, the unilateral (or bilateral, but not quadrilateral) increments in Germany's level of industrial production, and, most of all, the consummation of the London agreements of 1948. In her new book on Germany, Carolyn Eisenberg argues that American officials showed little inclination to work out an agreement on Germany, although one might have been possible.[35] For reasons that I have discussed elsewhere, I do not really agree with many of her judgments about the possibility of an accord with the Soviet Union. None the less, I do think that she persuasively illustrates how American interests and ideology powerfully shaped American behavior in western Germany.[36] The new literature focusing on Eastern Bloc sources tends to lose sight of these US (and British) actions in Germany, even while some of them properly highlight the impact of the Marshall Plan on Stalin's decisions in September 1947 to create the Cominform, foment unrest in Western Europe, and clamp down on the countries of Eastern Europe.[37]

The Cold War in Europe was the result of an interactive process in which leaders in many capitals were responding to multiple threats and opportunities to their interests, power, and security (meaning not just territorial security but also regime-type). The threats and opportunities that policymakers perceived emanated from a unique set of geopolitical configurations in the international system interacting with equally unique sets of indigenous variables within their own countries. Ideological predilections, cultural dictates, and historical experience helped shape these officials' assessments of these threats and opportunities. Parsimonious theory and single-minded interpretations cannot do justice to the complexity of the historical process.

This is particularly apparent if we look at another key characteristic of the Cold War, the struggle on the periphery. In the new literature the tendency is to conclude that Stalin's efforts to capitalize on conditions in Western Europe were thwarted by the Marshall Plan; thereafter, he looked to Asia for new successes. His attention turned to China where Mao was beginning to gain the upper hand in the Chinese civil war. Whereas Stalin previously had wavered in his support of the Chinese communists, he now decided to assist the CCP (Chinese Communist Party). 'He had never abandoned his commitment to world revolution', John Gaddis baldly asserts. In this manner, the Cold War came to Asia, and, indirectly to the Third World writ large.[38] Once Mao triumphed, he, too, driven by ideological fervor and revolutionary romanticism, sought to expand the revolutionary process to Korea and Indochina. Indeed, some of the new literature portrays Mao as eager to enter the Korean war. 'There is reason to argue', writes Shu Guang Zhang, that 'rather than merely responding to what was perceived as a compelling threat to their security, Beijing authorities chose to act aggressively, regardless of the calculated high risk and cost.' 'History reveals', says Zhang, that 'the classic romanticism of war is especially attractive to militarily weak, economically underdeveloped nations that passionately hope to expand their power.'[39]

Japan

In some of these new works, albeit not all of them, almost no attention is paid to developments in Japan. In 1947–48, the United States decided to shift attention from the reform of Japan's political and economic institutions to an emphasis on reconstructing the Japanese economy, stabilizing the political center, and aligning its former enemy with the non-communist world. There is a large and excellent literature on the reasoning that impelled this reverse-course strategy, as it came to be called. Almost all of it demonstrates that US officials believed that Japan could not be revived economically without coopting markets and raw materials elsewhere in Northeast and Southeast Asia. The origins of America's embroilment in Indochina, its decisions to loan military assistance to the French, and its concern with Korea, Indonesia, and the Philippines were all heightened by the imperative need to reconstruct and coopt Japan in the struggle against the Soviet-led communist world.[40]

Almost none of this Cold War history receives any emphasis in the new history of the Cold War, and its absence is puzzling and disturbing.[41] It does not appear because the new history focuses on Moscow and Beijing rather than Washington, London, Paris, and The Hague. It does not appear because the new history is inclined to focus on Soviet ideology and Chinese communist culture rather than the perceived interests of policy-makers in Washington who were seeking to rebuild the structures of a world capitalist system and who also felt that their strategic interests would be imperilled if the Kremlin slowly co-opted Japan into a communist sphere.[42]

My argument is not that the latter version is more accurate than the former; my argument is that the new literature errs by largely ignoring American initiatives in Japan and the dangers such initiatives posed to leaders in Moscow and Beijing. If ideological assumptions postulated that capitalist powers would seek to encircle communist regimes, if historical experience taught that Japan would revive and pose a renewed threat, US actions neatly reinforced Marxist-Leninist axioms and the lessons of the past.

More importantly, US thinking about the requirements of Japanese reconstruction beautifully illuminates one strand of analysis explaining why the Cold War did come to the Third World. The imperatives of Japanese reconstruction and the requirements of Western European recovery impelled US officials to be concerned about the periphery, even to intervene on the periphery against their own predilections. Primary and secondary interests blurred when the periphery came to be seen as vital to the core, even if only for symbolic interests, as was the case when the US government intervened in Korea in order to demonstrate that it was a credible hegemon to its Japanese, German, and West European friends as well as to its own people.[43]

The perception of both threat and opportunity in the Third World cannot be grasped without taking cognizance of developments in the international system that were occurring independent of Moscow's and Washington's power. Nationalist movements emerged on their own, challenging British, French, Dutch, and Portuguese power. Many of these nationalists were attracted to Marxist-Leninist principles because they explained away their countries' backwardness; many of them were attracted to command models of economic development because in the 1950s and 1960s they seemed to offer attractive approaches to rapid modernization. Washington perceived threats; Moscow and Beijing saw opportunities. But whether threats or opportunities, they must be explained by analyses that take cognizance of the evolution of the international system.[44]

Of course, Washington and Moscow and Beijing wanted to exploit these developments to further their own interests or thwart those of their adversaries. To do so involved risk-taking, and risk-taking could not occur without the reality, or at least the perception, of military strength. The military arms race had its own momentum and trajectory once it got underway, but it was always linked to policymakers' perceptions of the requirements necessary to deter the adversary. But deterrence was not a static concept; it always had coercive overtones.[45] If you could deter your adversary from military escalation in a crisis, you could gain more freedom to maneuver to achieve your objectives through other means, whether it be shrewd diplomacy, military aid, economic assistance, or covert operations. 'Many people', said Secretary of State Acheson, 'thought that we were trying to hold a ring around Soviet Russia. In fact, we were endeavoring to see to it that freedom of choice rested with us, not the Russians.'[46] This American superiority rankled Stalin and infuriated Khrushchev. Stalin committed huge resources to building his own bomb, while refusing to be intimidated by the American atomic monopoly.[47] Khrushchev sought to gain the same freedom that the Americans possessed by conjuring up the appearance of military strength and then by stealthily and dangerously inserting missiles into Cuba.[48]

Soviet and Chinese communist behavior will be grasped more accurately if ideology is not separated from concrete issues of security and interest and from real and imagined perceptions of threat and opportunity. The Russians and Chinese had reason to suspect that the atomic monopoly and subsequent strategic superiority would infuse American diplomacy with a more offensive spirit; it did. Without its atomic monopoly and subsequent strategic superiority, the United States would not have negotiated the London agreements regarding Germany in the spring of 1948, or airlifted supplies to Berlin, or intervened in Korea, or crossed the 38th parallel, or consummated the Japanese–American security treaty, or rearmed Germany, or repeatedly rebuffed the Kremlin's overtures to sign a separate peace agreement with East Germany. Believing in its own superiority and convinced that the Soviets and Chinese would prefer to avoid war, the United States chose options that otherwise would have appeared far too risky.[49]

In so doing, it engendered real and imagined anxieties in Moscow and Beijing. These anxieties were magnified by the ideological maxims of Marxism-Leninism, but they were not the product of ideology. A revived Germany on Russia's frontiers; a powerful West in the heart of East Germany agitated Khrushchev. 'Do you need Berlin', Khrushchev shouted at Stewart Udall, President John F. Kennedy's Secretary of the Interior. 'Like hell you need it.' In Khrushchev's view, explain Aleksandr Fursenko and Timothy Naftali, Soviet 'interests deserved recognition, and where its interests were stronger than those of the United States ... Moscow should be able to dictate the resolution.'[50] Likewise, Mao could not imagine living with the United States ensconced on China's borders. 'Above all', writes Michael Hunt, Mao's intervention in the Korean War, was 'to prevent the enemy from dominating the Yalu River and thus posing a constant threat to the northeast.'[51] Communist ideology, Hunt concludes, did little 'to transform in any fundamental sense China's inherited strategic calculations and concerns'. Marxist-Leninist ideology, he emphasizes, 'is but one source for policy and ... as a source, it can sustain not one policy but a wide variety of them'.[52]

The Cold War was a complex phenomenon characterized by a rivalry between two powerful states with universalizing ideologies and conflicting systems of political economy. The rivalry led to the division of Germany and Europe, competition on the periphery, and a strategic arms race. Although the belligerents refrained from engaging in direct hostilities with one another, they displayed little incentive to negotiate disputes except on their own terms.

As we learn more about each of the component parts of the Cold War, we will need to adopt more complex interpretations. The new documents from the East tempt us to focus on ideology and personality, but such explanations hardly explain the multidimensional aspects of the Cold War. After all, both Stalin and communism existed in Russia in the 1930s, but few observers would characterize that era as part of the Cold War system. The Cold War occurred in the aftermath of World War II, when an anarchic international system conjured up unprecedented threats and opportunities for leaders in many nations, but most notably for those in the United States and the USSR. Interpreting those threats and opportunities through ideological lenses, cultural traditions, and cognitive habits of mind, American and Russian officials had the incentive and the power to pursue their strategic and economic goals in ways that accorded with their understanding of national interest and their ideological predilections. Their actions triggered reactions in a spiraling model of distrust and recrimination. Meanwhile, other governments (and parties and groups within those nations) sought to exploit the rivalry to enhance their own interests. But one belligerent was far more powerful and rich at the outset of the conflict and possessed a system of political economy that was far more tolerant and ultimately far more appealing and far more productive. The wonder is that the other side imploded without precipitating a major conflict.

Or is it such a wonder? Perhaps the end of the Cold War is more explicable than we usually assume. The Cold War, after all, was the product of a particular time and set of circumstances. In the aftermath of World War II, Soviet power merged with the redemptive appeal of communism. Democratic capitalism had failed during the first part of the century to meet many people's needs. Whether it would do better in the second half was entirely problematic. Would democratic capitalism be able to preserve the peace, avoid depression, provide for the well-being of common men and women? Would it be able to integrate vanquished enemies? Would it be able to accommodate the demands of Third World peoples for national autonomy and modernization? Communists said they could do all these things better than Western governments. The Kremlin's triumph over Nazism, its development of the atomic bomb, and its exploits in space injected credibility to its claims (and threats).

The Cold War ended sequentially and understandably when the United States and its democratic capitalist allies met the challenges of the post-war era; challenges, I would suggest, that inhered not so much from the power of the Soviet Union as from the legacy of the Great Depression and two world wars as well as from the structure of the international system. Democratic capitalist governments demonstrated that they could tame market forces, avoid another great depression, and sustain economic growth, even in the wake of the terrible oil shocks of the 1970s. They demonstrated that they could forgive their enemies, rebuild them, and integrate them into a viable international economy. They demonstrated that, however grudgingly, they could relinquish their imperial heritage, grant independence to the peoples of Asia and Africa, and endure the cycles of revolutionary nationalism that swept many Third World countries during the first generation of their independence.

Notwithstanding occasional and reprehensible lapses of judgment and policy, as in Indochina, the West met the challenges of the post-war world far better than did its ideological rival. The men in the Kremlin claimed the superiority of their system, but failed to produce evidence to support their claim. They failed to provide for their people; they failed to generate continuous economic growth; they failed to sustain the peace within their own borders and empire; and they failed to demonstrate respect for the autonomy of other peoples.

But none of this could have been foreseen in 1945; hence the complex patterns of fear and opportunity that engulfed leaders throughout the globe. Perhaps these leaders grasped that their peoples were more rational than scholars often assume. Perhaps they recognized that when democratic capitalism foundered during the first part of the century, peoples everywhere questioned its viability and relevance; perhaps they intuited that should it succeed in the second half, peoples everywhere would come to see its virtues. But this outcome was not inscribed in the fabric of the universe or the inherent virtues of market capitalism. It was the result of complex interactions between a dynamic international system and its constituent units; between governments operating within that system; between peoples and their governments; between factions, parties, and interest groups.

Our new interpretations of the Cold War will have to take cognizance of all these interactions. It will not suffice to assimilate the new documents from the former communist world. The full story will need to encompass personalities, ideologies, and interests; culture and geopolitics; national traditions and world systems; perceptions of threat and lures of opportunity. The full story will require us to transcend the parts and concentrate on the whole; this will require unprecedented linguistic ability, insight, and imagination. It is a formidable challenge.

NOTES

1 John Gaddis's recent book is the best example of this trend in the evolution of the scholarship on the Cold War. See John L. Gaddis, *We Now Know: Rethinking Cold War History* (Oxford: Oxford University Press, 1997); see also Vladislav Zubok and Constantine Pleshakov, *Inside the Kremlin's Cold War: From Stalin to Khrushchev* (Cambridge, MA: Harvard University Press, 1996); Vojtech Mastny, *The Cold War and Soviet Insecurity* (New York: Oxford University Press, 1996); Shu Guang Zhang, *Mao's Military Romanticism: China and the Korean War, 1950–1953* (Lawrence, KS: University Press of Kansas, 1995); for illuminating volumes of essays, see, for example, Norman Naimark and Leonid Gibianskii, *The Establishment of Communist Regimes in Eastern Europe, 1944–1949* (Boulder, CO: Westview Press, 1997); Francesca Gori and Silvio Pons, eds, *The Soviet Union and Europe in the Cold War, 1943–1953* (London: Macmillan, 1996); Odd Arne Westad, Sven Holtsmark, and Iver B. Neumann, eds, *The Soviet Union in Eastern Europe, 1945–1989* (New York: St Martin's, 1994); contributions by Jonathan Haslam, William C. Wohlforth, Raymond L. Garthoff, Odd Arne Westad, Robert C. Tucker, Robert D. English, and Vladislav Zubok, in 'Symposium: Soviet Archives: Recent Revelations and Cold War Historiography', *Diplomatic History*, 21 (Spring 1997): 217–305.

2 Melvyn P. Leffler, *A Preponderance of Power: National Security, the Truman*

Administration, and the Cold War (Stanford, CA: Stanford University Press, 1992), pp. 13–14.

3 Frank Ninkovich, *Modernity and Power: A History of the Domino Theory in the Twentieth Century* (Chicago, IL: University of Chicago Press, 1994); John L. Harper, *American Visions of Europe: Franklin D. Roosevelt, George F. Kennan, and Dean G. Acheson* (Cambridge: Cambridge University Press, 1994), pp. 34–5, 64–5, 78–9.

4 Aaron L. Friedberg, 'Why Didn't the United States Become a Garrison State?', *International Security*, 16 (1992): 109–42.

5 For the best exposition of the corporatist interpretation, see Michael J. Hogan, *The Marshall Plan: America, Britain, and the Reconstruction of Western Europe, 1947–1952* (New York: Cambridge University Press, 1987); see also Thomas Ferguson, 'From Normalcy to New Deal: Industrial Structure, Party Competition, and American Public Policy in the Great Depression', *International Organization*, 38 (Winter 1984): 41–95; for my own effort to focus appropriate attention on domestic politics, see *The Specter of Communism* (New York: Hill & Wang, 1994).

6 Lynn Eden, 'Capitalist Conflict and the State: The Making of United States Military Policy in 1948', in Charles Bright and Susan Harding, eds, *Statemaking and Social Movements: Essays in History and Theory* (Ann Arbor, MI: University of Michigan Press, 1984); Howard Schonberger, 'The Japan Lobby in American Diplomacy, 1947–1952', *Pacific Historical Review*, 46 (August 1977): 327–59; Bruce Cumings, *The Origins of the Korean War*, vol. II: *The Roaring of the Cataract, 1947–1950* (Princeton, NJ: Princeton University Press, 1990), especially pp. 79–121; for analyses of the relationship of domestic politics to US grand strategy, see Jack Snyder, *Myths of Empire: Domestic Politics and International Ambition* (Ithaca, NY: Cornell University Press, 1991); Thomas J. Christensen, *Useful Adversaries: Grand Strategy, Domestic Mobilization, and Sino-American Conflict, 1947–1958* (Princeton, NJ: Princeton University Press, 1996).

7 Fernando Claudin, *The Communist Movement: From Comintern to Cominform* (Harmondsworth: Penguin, 1975); Paolo Spriano, *Stalin and the European Communists* (London: Verso, 1985); for relations with the Greek communists, see Peter J. Stavrakis, *Moscow and Greek Communism, 1944–1949* (Ithaca, NY: Cornell University Press, 1989); Artiom A. Ulunian, 'The Soviet Union and "the Greek Question", 1946–53: Problems and Appraisals', in Gori and Pons, *Soviet Union and Europe*, pp. 144–60; for even more complex relations with the Chinese communists, see, for example, Chen Jian, *China's Road to the Cold War: The Making of the Sino-American Confrontation* (New York: Columbia University Press, 1994); Segei Goncharov, John W. Lewis, and Xue Litai, *Uncertain Partners: Stalin, Mao, and the Korean War* (Stanford, CA: Stanford University Press, 1993); Odd Arne Westad, *Cold War and Revolution: Soviet–American Rivalry and the Origins of the Chinese Civil War* (New York: Columbia University Press, 1993); Michael M. Sheng, *Battling Western Imperialism: Mao, Stalin, and the United States* (Princeton, NJ: Princeton University Press, 1997); for Mastny's views, see Mastny, *Cold War and Soviet Insecurity*, pp. 21 and 12. Although Gaddis clearly disagrees with this conclusion, Zubok and Pleshakov seem to concur with Mastny. Stalin, they write, 'Used the common ideology of Communist parties to organize Eastern Europe into a "security buffer" for his state.' Zubok and Pleshakov, *Inside the Kremlin's Cold War*, pp. 131, 46–77. David Holloway also places an emphasis on *realpolitik* over ideology. See Holloway, *Stalin and The Bomb* (New Haven, CT: Yale University Press, 1994), p. 168.

8 Gaddis, *We Now Know*; Mastny, *Cold War and Soviet Insecurity*; Zubok and Pleshakov, *Inside the Kremlin's Cold War*; William C. Wohlforth, *The Elusive*

Balance: Power and Perceptions During the Cold War (Ithaca, NY: Cornell University Press, 1993); Douglas J. Macdonald, 'Communist Bloc Expansion in the Early Cold War: Challenging Realism, Refuting Revisionism', *International Security*, 20 (Winter 1995–96): 152–88. My views have been influenced by the publication of Stalin's letters to Molotov and by Molotov's reminiscences. See Lars Lih, Oleg V. Naumov, and Oleg V. Khlevniuk, eds, *Stalin's Letters to Molotov, 1925–1936* (New Haven, CT: Yale University Press, 1995); Albert Resis, ed., *Molotov Remembers: Inside Kremlin Politics: Conversations with Felix Chuev* (Chicago, IL: Ivan R. Dee, 1993).

 9 Jian, *China's Road to the Cold War*; Sheng, *Battling Western Imperialism*; Michael Sheng, 'The United States, the Chinese Communist Party, and the Soviet Union, 1948–1950', *The Pacific Historical Review*, 63 (November 1994): 521–36; Michael Sheng, 'The Triumph of Internationalism: CCP–Moscow Relations Before 1949', *Diplomatic History*, 21 (Winter 1997): 95–104; Odd Arne Westad, 'Losses, Chances, and Myths: The United States and the Creation of the Sino-Soviet Alliance, 1945–1950', ibid., 105–15; John W. Garver, 'Little Chance: Revolutions and Ideologies', ibid., 87–94; Yang Kuisong, 'The Soviet Factor and the CCP's Policy Toward the United States in the 1940s', *Chinese Historians*, 5 (Spring 1992): 17–34; Alexandre Y. Mansourov, 'Stalin, Mao, Kim and China's Decision to Enter the Korean War, September 16–October 15, 1950: New Evidence from Russian Archives', *Cold War International History Project Bulletin*, 6–7 (Winter 1995–96): 94–107.

10 Gaddis, *We Now Know*, pp. 26–53, 198–203, 284–9; Geir Lundestad, '"Empire by Invitation" The United States and Western Europe, 1945–1952', *Journal of Peace Research*, 23 (September 1986): 263–77. My skepticism about the validity of the interpretation rests on the question of whether it was the pull of the Europeans or the perceived interests of Americans that prompted the post-World War II commitments and involvement of the United States in Europe. After World War I, the British and French also 'invited' the Americans, but Washington had a different view of the saliency of perceived threats as well as a lower estimation of the degree of interest that inhered in the stabilization of the Old World.

11 Reinhold Wagnleitner, *Coco-Colonization: The Cultural Mission of the United States in Austria After the Second World War* (Chapel Hill, NC: University of North Carolina Press, 1994); Walter Hixson, *Parting the Curtain: Propaganda, Culture, and the Cold War, 1945–1961* (London: Macmillan, 1997); Timothy W. Ryback, *Rock around the Bloc: A History of Rock Music in Eastern Europe and the Soviet Union* (New York: Oxford University Press, 1990); for a nuanced assessment, see Richard Pells, *Not Like Us: How Europeans Have Loved, Hated, and Transformed American Culture Since World War II* (New York: Basic Books, 1997); for an illuminating discussion of how culture and domestic politics shaped the ideological messages that the United States sent abroad, see Laura Belmonte, 'Defining a Way of Life: American Propaganda and the Cold War, 1945–1959' (Charlottesville, VA: University of Virginia doctoral dissertation, 1996).

12 Norman Naimark, *The Russians in Germany: A History of the Soviet Zone of Occupation, 1945–1949* (Cambridge, MA: Harvard University Press, 1995); Jan T. Gross, *Revolution from Abroad: The Soviet Conquest of Poland's Western Ukraine and Western Belorussia* (Princeton, NJ: Princeton University Press, 1988).

13 Gaddis, *We Now Know*, p. 25; also see Mastny, *Cold War and Soviet Insecurity*, pp. 24–5.

14 Kathryn Weathersby, 'Making Foreign Policy Under Stalin: The Case of Korea', paper delivered at the Norwegian Nobel Institute (Spring 1998), p. 7; see also Kathryn Weathersby, 'Soviet Aims in Korea and the Outbreak of the Korean War,

1945–1950: New Evidence from the Russian Archives', Working Paper of the Cold War International History Project (Washington, DC: Woodrow Wilson International Center, 1993).

15 Goncharov, Lewis, and Xue, *Uncertain Partners*, p. 3.

16 Milovan Djilas, *Conversations with Stalin* (New York: Harcourt, Brace & World, 1962), p. 114.

17 Zubok and Pleshakov, *Inside the Kremlin's Cold War*, pp. 158–61, 197.

18 Department of State, *Foreign Relations of the United States, 1961–1963*, 6 (Washington, DC: Government Printing Office, 1996), 77 (hereafter cited as *FRUS*).

19 Mastny, *Cold War and Soviet Insecurity*, p. 27; Gaddis, *We Now Know*, p. 25.

20 Zubok and Pleshakov, *Inside the Kremlin's Cold War*, p. 276.

21 Holloway, *Stalin and the Bomb*, p. 168.

22 Mastny, *Cold War and Soviet Insecurity*, p. 23; Zubok and Pleshakov, *Inside the Kremlin's Cold War*, pp. 72–7; Gaddis, *We Now Know*, pp. 25, 292–4.

23 Robert H. Ferrell, ed., *Off the Record: The Private Papers of Harry S. Truman* (New York: Harper & Row, 1980), pp. 44–5, 53, 56–7; Robert H. Ferrell, *Dear Bess: Letters from Harry to Bess Truman* (New York: Norton, 1983), pp. 520–2; W. Averell Harriman and Elie Abel, *Special Envoy to Churchill and Stalin, 1941–1946* (New York: Random House, 1975), pp. 533–6; Harriman to Truman, 8 June 1945, in Department of State, *FRUS, Potsdam*, 1: 61; William Leahy, *I Was There* (New York: Whittlesey House, 1950), p. 322; Louis Galambos and Alfred D. Chandler, *The Papers of Dwight David Eisenhower*, vol. VI: 284–7; for the view of James F. Byrnes, see Robert L. Messer, *The End of an Alliance: James, F. Byrnes, Roosevelt, Truman, and the Origins of the Cold War* (Chapel Hill, NC: University of North Carolina Press, 1982), pp. 133–6.

24 These generalizations emerge from Naimark, *Russians in Germany*; Goncharov, Lewis, and Litai, *Uncertain Partners*; Westad, *Cold War and Revolution*; Zubok and Pleshakov, *Inside the Kremlin's Cold War*; Mastny, *Cold War and Soviet Insecurity*; Brian Murray, 'Stalin, the Cold War, and the Division of China: A Multi-Archival Mystery', Cold War International History Project Working Paper No. 12 (Washington, DC: Woodrow Wilson International Center, 1995).

25 Zubok and Pleshakov, *Inside the Kremlin's Cold War*, p. 74; see also Vladislav Zubok, 'Soviet Activities in Europe After World War II', *Problems of Post-Communism* (September–October, 1995): 7.

26 Zubok and Pleshakov, *Inside the Kremlin's Cold War*, pp. 36–51, 275–82.

27 Memorandum for the President, by John J. McCloy, 26 April 1945, Box 178, President's Secretary's File, Harry S. Truman Papers (Harry S. Truman Library, Independence, Missouri).

28 Stimson to Truman, 16 May 1945, Box 157, ibid.

29 Joseph C. Grew to Truman, 27 June 1945, *FRUS, Potsdam*, 1: 267–80; Joseph Grew, *Turbulent Era: A Diplomatic Record of Forty Years, 1904–1945* (Boston, MA: Houghton Mifflin, 1952), vol. II, pp. 1445–50.

30 Truman to Churchill, 24 June 1945, *FRUS, Potsdam*, 1: 612.

31 Leffler, *Preponderance of Power*, pp. 25–141; see also Gabriel Kolko and Joyce Kolko, *The Limits of Power: The World and United States Foreign Policy, 1945–1954* (New York: Harper & Row, 1972); Dale Copeland, *The Origins of Major War: Hegemonic Rivalry and the Fear of Decline* (Ithaca, NY: Cornell University Press, forthcoming), Chapters 6 and 7.

32 Quoted in Igor Lukes, 'The Czech Road to Communism', in Naimark and Gibianskii, *The Establishment of Communist Regimes in Eastern Europe*, pp. 249–50.

33 Testimony, by Dean G. Acheson, 8 March 1945, US Senate, Committee on Banking and Currency, *Bretton Woods Agreements Act*, 79th Cong., 1st sess. (Washington, DC: Government Printing Office, 1945), 1: 35.

34 Leffler, *Preponderance of Power*, 55–99; for an analysis of overall American policy toward East Asia at the end of World War II, see also Marc S. Gallichio, *The Cold War Begins in Asia: American East Asian Policy and the Fall of the Japanese Empire* (New York: Columbia University Press, 1988).

35 Carolyn Eisenberg, *Drawing the Line: The American Decision to Divide Germany, 1944–1949* (New York: Cambridge University Press, 1996).

36 Melvyn P. Leffler, 'The Struggle for Germany and the Origins of the Cold War' (Washington, DC: German Historical Institute, Occasional Paper No. 16, 1997).

37 For the critical role of the Marshall Plan in the division of Europe, see Scott D. Parrish, 'The Turn Toward Confrontation: The Soviet Reaction to the Marshall Plan, 1948', Cold War International History Project Working Paper No. 9 (Washington, DC: Woodrow Wilson International Center, 1994); Mikhail M. Narinsky, 'The Soviet Response: The Turn to Confrontation', ibid.; Geoffrey Roberts, 'Moscow and the Marshall Plan: Politics, Ideology, and the Onset of the Cold War, 1947', *Europe–Asia Studies*, 46 (1994): 1371–86; Zubok and Pleshakov, *Inside the Kremlin's Cold War*, pp. 50–1.

38 Gaddis, *We Now Know*, 67; see also Zubok and Pleshakov, *Inside the Kremlin's Cold War*, pp. 54ff.

39 Shu Guang Zhang, *Mao's Military Romanticism*, pp. 9–10.

40 See, for example, Michael Schaller, *The American Occupation of Japan: The Origins of the Cold War in Asia* (New York: Oxford University Press, 1985); Andrew Rotter, *The Path to Vietnam: Origins of the American Commitment to Southeast Asia* (Ithaca, NY: Cornell University Press, 1987); Howard B. Schonberger, *Aftermath of War: Americans and the Remaking of Japan, 1945–1952* (Kent, OH: Kent State University Press, 1989); Ronald McGlothlen, *Controlling the Waves: Dean Acheson and US Foreign Policy in Asia* (New York: Norton, 1993).

41 Mastny, *Cold War and Soviet Insecurity*; Zubok and Pleshakov, *Inside the Kremlin's Cold War*; Gaddis, *We Now Know*.

42 Note, for example, how belatedly and indirectly Gaddis comes to talk about American interest in rebuilding the structures of world capitalism in chapter 7. Gaddis, *We Now Know*, 189–94. Mastny writes, 'For Stalin, the prize now was Japan', almost totally disregarding the motives, concerns, ramifications, and implications of US initiatives in Japan from late 1947 to 1950. See Mastny, *Cold War and Soviet Insecurity*, pp. 88–9.

43 Thomas D. Lairson, 'Revising Postrevisionism: Credibility and Hegemony in the Early Cold War', in *Re-Thinking the Cold War*, ed. Allen Hunter (Philadelphia, PA: Temple University Press, 1998), pp. 63–90; Robert McMahon, 'Credibility and World Power: Exploring the Psychological Dimension in Postwar American Diplomacy', *Diplomatic History*, 15 (Fall 1991): 455–71.

44 For a provocative new account underscoring these views, an account that combines theoretical discussion and empirical evidence, see Copeland, *Realism and the Origins of Major War*; also Cary Fraser, 'A Requiem for the Cold War: Reviewing the History of International Relations Since 1945', in Hunter, *Re-Thinking the Cold War*, pp. 93–115.

45 Raymond L. Garthoff, *Deterrence and the Revolution in Soviet Military Doctrine* (Washington, DC: Brookings Institution, 1990), pp. 6–9.

46 US Minutes, 4 August 1952, *FRUS, 1952–1954*, 12: 182–3.

47 Holloway, *Stalin and the Bomb*.

48 Aleksandr Fursenko and Timothy Naftali, *'One Hell of a Gamble': Khrushchev,*

Castro & Kennedy, 1958–1964 (New York: Norton, 1997), pp. 178, 180, 182–3, 209.

49 In all these instances, the United States expected the Russians and/or Chinese to react negatively. But because of American strategic superiority, US officials did not expect the adversary to escalate to a level of war. When US and UN troops marched to the Yalu River, policymakers in Washington clearly miscalculated what the Chinese would do. I develop these themes in *Preponderance of Power*, Chapters, 5, 8–11.

50 Fursenko and Naftali, *'One Hell of a Gamble'*, p. 209.

51 Michael H. Hunt, *The Genesis of Chinese Communist Foreign Policy* (New York: Columbia University Press, 1996), p. 189.

52 Ibid., pp. 4, 28.

3

How (Not) to Study the Origins of the Cold War

Geir Lundestad

In this essay I will do three things. First, quite briefly, I shall sketch what could be called the old debate about the origins of the Cold War; then, slightly more fully, I shall outline what is often termed the new debate about the origins of the Cold War; finally, I shall spell out, at somewhat greater length, my own recommendations as to how we should be studying this topic. My argument is that the decades of debate about the origins of the Cold War have delivered less than one could have hoped for, even less than one could have reasonably expected. The reason for this shortcoming is that to a disappointing extent we have focused on the wrong questions. The sooner we correct this focus, the better our analyses will be.

Old Cold War history

In the present context the criteria used in establishing the various schools of interpretation in the debate on the origins of the Cold War are really as important as the schools themselves. It seems to me that the three most useful criteria in categorizing the early scholarly debate were the following: did the scholar in question see the United States (or the West) or the Soviet Union (or the East) as the guilty party behind the Cold War? Largely flowing from the first point, who was seen as the most active party in the transition from World War II to the Cold War? What were regarded as the motive forces behind the foreign policies of the Soviet Union and, particularly, the United States?[1]

Based on these three criteria, three main schools were established: traditionalism, revisionism, and post-revisionism.[2] In capsule, and therefore greatly simplified form, traditionalists tended to see the Soviet Union as largely responsible for the Cold War; they generally regarded the Soviet Union as the active party and described the United States as playing a passive role until the Truman Doctrine and the Marshall Plan; and they saw the defense of democracy in the United States and, even more, in

Western Europe as the main motive force on the American side and the communist-ideological desire for expansion as the main force on the Soviet side.

Revisionists were basically the mirror image of traditionalists. They tended to see the United States as largely responsible for the Cold War; the United States as the active party exploiting a wide selection of instruments ranging from the atomic bomb to many different economic levers, while the Soviet Union only gradually expanded into Eastern Europe; and anti-communism and the promotion of capitalism, the latter in the form of investing surplus capital abroad and exporting surplus goods while importing particularly strategic items, as the main motive forces on the American side, while to a large extent the Soviet Union promoted its security interests.

Post-revisionism was a much vaguer school of interpretation than the other two, representing the middle ground between traditionalism and revisionism. Post-revisionists could therefore blame either the United States or, as most of them did and John Lewis Gaddis among them – Gaddis *was* in many ways post-revisionism – the Soviet Union and Stalin, although post-revisionists generally saw the Cold War as a somewhat more interactive affair than did the other two schools.[3] Post-revisionists tended to describe the United States as more active at an earlier stage than did traditionalists, but as less active than did revisionists. Thus, post-revisionists borrowed from revisionists in their analysis of the various US levers, although they rejected the revisionist view of seeing these levers almost exclusively in a Cold War perspective. On the question of motive forces, post-revisionists tended to answer 'all of the above' in the sense that different motive forces influenced both Soviet and, particularly, American foreign policy, the exact blend of these forces varying from place to place and over time.[4]

One could of course add to these three simple categories. Realism is often seen as an additional school, but political science Realism was mostly of such a general nature that it had little to contribute in the way of detailed analysis of the origins of the Cold War.[5] Realists among historians, such as George Kennan and Louis Halle, are sometimes put in this category, but in fact combine Realism with moralism and could be seen as a sub-category of traditionalism.[6] Corporatism has similarly been mentioned, but corporatism as practiced by Michael Hogan and Charles Maier had less to say about the origins of the Cold War *per se* than about the organization of the Western side. To the extent that they should be placed within the Cold War debate, corporatists had certain basic elements in common with revisionists.[7] Similarly, world systems theory was really more relevant for an analysis of the international structure in general than of the origins of the Cold War, but again even this theory could be seen as a possible subcategory of revisionism.[8]

In a way the old Cold War debate petered out in the 1980s. Apparently, there was not that much to add. Although traditionalists and revisionists continued to write in their old frameworks, there was an impression that the post-revisionists had really 'won' the debate. This was perhaps most clearly seen in the movement toward the broad post-revisionist center by prominent revisionists such as Thomas Paterson, Melvyn Leffler, and Barton Bernstein.[9]

The most interesting new development in the 1980s was the emergence of non-American interpretations of the origins of the Cold War. With the opening of archives in Britain, British historians did, as could be expected, bring back the early perspective of *three* superpowers, a perspective which had been self-evident in 1944–45 when the Cold War arose, but was then rather downplayed by most American historians.[10] It was argued that the Western Europeans 'invited' the Americans to play a larger role in Europe, for economic and soon also for political and military reasons related to the containment of the Soviet Union.[11] Historians from the various countries almost took a nationalist pride in introducing their country as an actor in the origins of the Cold War. Personally, I was happy to bring Norway on stage, particularly in the origins of NATO.[12]

There were, however, many reasons to be skeptical about the early phase of the Cold War debate, one being the extent to which the swings in the debate seemed to follow over-all political trends. While total objectivity is an impossible goal and all historians are part of a wider political context, it could still be argued that the Cold War debate was disappointingly subjective and 'presentist'.[13] Traditionalism dominated until the mid-1960s and was very much a product of the early Cold War climate as this was reflected particularly in the United States. Revisionism was an even more American-dominated product and quite directly mirrored the doubts springing from the Vietnam War. Since the United States was 'wrong' about the Vietnam War, perhaps it had also been wrong about the Cold War? Post-revisionism arose in the early 1970s and, it could be argued, reflected the détente policies of those years. With détente, blame had to be distributed a little more evenly than had been done by the earlier two schools.

New Cold War history

The new Cold War history arose with the end of the Cold War, the collapse of the Soviet Union, and the opening up of new sources, particularly in Russia, but also in other formerly communist countries and in China. (In addition, new sources were opened in Britain and other Western European countries and also in the United States, although most American sources had been made available earlier.)

There were many important new elements in the new Cold War history. The perspective on the Cold War inevitably changed with the end of the

Cold War itself. It is much easier to explain war and conflict when they are over than right in the middle of the process. The geographical broadening of the sources and, less so, of the participating historians – less so because this debate was still dominated by American historians – was very important indeed. During the Cold War the discussion of Soviet foreign policy was based almost exclusively on public sources; now some, but far from all, Russian archives were partly opened, and a new period in the analysis of Soviet foreign policy started.

With the new sources not only in Russia, but also in many other countries, the emphasis from the 1980s in the direction of stressing other actors than simply the two superpowers continued. China certainly became an actor more in its own right, whether one emphasized ideological or more realist considerations behind its foreign policy.[14] All kinds of minor actors appeared on stage, often in disproportionately large roles. North Korea under Kim Il-Sung may have been under strong Soviet influence, but it still had its own views on the unification issue and these views were important in the origins of the Korean War in 1950.[15] Cuba had its own interests to advance, whether during the Cuban Missile Crisis in 1962 or in the events in Angola and Ethiopia in the mid to late 1970s.[16]

There can be no doubt that the new Cold War history represents very significant progress compared to the old one. With the new sources in particular, the study of the origins of the Cold War has been brought to a new level altogether. Again, however, one cannot but help notice the close connection between the interpretations of the historians on the one hand and important political events on the other. The collapse of the Soviet Union and the victory of the West brought the Cold War to an end. This easily led to the conclusion that the Soviet Union must have caused the Cold War. American democratic and free-market ideals were riding high. Despite the warnings against 'triumphalism',[17] there was nevertheless an element of this in the new interpretations of the Cold War. At the same time, it could be no big surprise that also inside Russia itself the new sources and the new freedoms created a mood, particularly among the younger generations, which stimulated renewed emphasis on the horrors of the Soviet past, certainly including Stalin's foreign policy.

New, but still Old

In fact, while much progress has been made in our understanding of the Cold War, the new Cold War history is not quite as new as its representatives generally claim. Despite their pleas to leave the old, stale schools of interpretation behind, some remarkable continuities – rather unfortunate continuities I am going to argue – exist between the old and the new Cold War history. The most remarkable is the ease with which even the new Cold War history can be fitted into the three criteria used for categorizing the old Cold War history debate.

Three books reflect the new Cold War history best: Vladislav Zubok and Constantine Pleshakov's *Inside the Kremlin's Cold War: From Stalin to Khrushchev*,[18] Vojtech Mastny's *The Cold War and Soviet Insecurity: The Stalin Years*,[19] and John Lewis Gaddis's *We Now Know: Rethinking Cold War History*. These three are generally regarded as the leading new over-all interpretations of the Cold War. They are all, more or less, traditionalist in tone.

Attempts have been made to place the new material in a post-revisionist, even slightly revisionist perspective. Melvyn Leffler's 1996 article in *Foreign Affairs* is the most striking example of this.[20] Yet, the momentum in the debate has undoubtedly shifted in a traditionalist direction.

Going back to the three criteria, first, all three books are rather emphatic in blaming Stalin for the Cold War. Zubok and Pleshakov write that 'In the categories of "good guys and bad guys", Stalin was indisputably a bad guy in the Cold War', and that 'It is tempting to lay total blame for the Cold War on the delusions of Stalin and his lieutenants.' Still, they are relatively restrained when they go on to state that Stalin and his lieutenants 'were not the only culprits in the conflict'.[21]

Compared with his book on the early Cold War years, *Russia's Road to the Cold War*,[22] in his new book Mastny sees the Soviet threat as having been greatly exaggerated by the West. Still, Stalin clearly was responsible for the Cold War: 'If the methods Stalin employed to assert his control in the eastern part of the Continent had made the Cold War inevitable, his unfulfilled expectations in the western part made it irreversible.'[23]

In his work more or less founding post-revisionism, *The United States and the Origins of the Cold War, 1941–1947*, Gaddis held out against distributing blame to the final two pages in the book and warned against seeing the Cold War as inevitable.[24] In *We Now Know* he puts moral responsibility right at the heart of his argument when he stresses that '*as long as Stalin was running the Soviet Union a Cold War was unavoidable*' (original emphasis). The West may have had its share of responsibility, but only 'If one could have eliminated Stalin, alternative paths become quite conceivable.'[25] He supports Mastny's early argument that if the West 'bears partial responsibility for the coming of the Cold War', then this is only because of its failure to try containment earlier than it actually did.[26]

On the second criterion, all three books definitely see the Soviet Union as the active part while the West, or rather the United States, since little interest is displayed in Great Britain and other Western countries, are holding back. Again, Zubok and Pleshakov are the most restrained when they argue that 'Stalin's foreign and domestic priorities were limited in nature, and yet they led to tension with the West.' They even see Soviet doubts about post-war cooperation as influenced by Western actions such as the dropping of the atomic bombs, the Marshall Plan, and, after Stalin's death, by later examples of 'America's hard line'.[27] However, these Western elements are introduced only in the final pages of the book and thus there is little actual analysis of how the two sides interacted.

Mastny describes Soviet fears of the West as having been real and the West as stimulating these fears through various subversive activities. Still, Stalin's 'insatiable craving' for security 'was the root cause of the growing East–West tension, regardless of his and his Western partners' desire for manageable, if not necessarily cordial, relations. The forthcoming Cold War was both unintended and unexpected; it was predetermined all the same.'[28]

Gaddis, who analyzed US's policies so brilliantly in *The United States and the Origins of the Cold War*, now asks the question 'Did the Americans attempt to impose their vision of the post-war world upon the USSR?' and even answers that 'No doubt it looked that way from Moscow.' Still, the focus in *We Now Know* is almost exclusively on Soviet actions and Stalin's ambitions: 'What all of this suggests ... is not that Stalin had limited ambitions, only that he had no timetable for achieving them.' One difference between Hitler and Stalin was that 'Where Stalin was patient, prepared to take as long as necessary to achieve his ambitions, Hitler was frenetic, determined to meet deadlines he himself had imposed.'[29]

Finally, on the criterion of the motive powers of Soviet foreign policy, the emphasis on communist ideology is very striking. True, Zubok and Pleshakov see Marxist ideology as being combined with 'traditional Russian messianism' producing 'the revolutionary–imperial paradigm' which is really their basic concept in analyzing Soviet foreign policy under Stalin and even later.[30] For Mastny, the greatest surprise

> so far to have come out of the Russian archives is that there was no surprise; the thinking of the insiders conformed substantially to what Moscow was publicly saying. Some of the most secret documents could have been published in *Pravda* without anybody's noticing.[31]

In *We Now Know* Gaddis goes to great lengths in emphasizing ideas and ideologies: 'The "new" Cold War history will take ideas seriously.' And Gaddis certainly takes ideas seriously, particularly Marxism-Leninism as the fountain of Soviet actions. He even blames the historians for not following the people: '*many people then saw the Cold War as a contest of good versus evil, even if historians since have rarely done so*' (emphasis by Gaddis).[32]

Attacks on Gaddis

What should be done?

What is so negative about this way of studying the Cold War? What should be done to improve this situation? Again, I shall relate my comments to the three criteria which figure so prominently in both the old and the new Cold War history.

First, I have long argued that the focus on blame or responsibility for the Cold War is an unfortunate one. None of us can be entirely objective; most of us pronounce on this question whether we want to or not. The fact that a book focuses on this aspect does not in itself necessarily mean that it is unsatisfactory. Still, I do tend to think that the question of blame is a moral-political one more than it is an historical one. I must admit that after having read hundreds of books and articles on the origins of the Cold War, I am left with a sense of at least partial frustration. We have learnt simply too much about blame-throwing and about the ideological climate from which these various accounts sprang and too little about what exactly happened and why it happened. The admiration for the few who have been able to take a longer historical view increases correspondingly. In an earlier context I have pointed to William McNeill's *America, Britain and Russia*, published in 1953 at the height of the Cold War, as an example of what could be achieved on the basis of a minimum of written sources.[33]

In many of the writings on the Cold War there is the implication that the status quo was more or less sacred, that trying to change the status quo was 'aggressive' while the side upholding the status quo was 'defensive'. Yet, as E. H. Carr argued in *The Twenty Years' Crisis 1919–1939*, published in 1939, 'The moral criterion must be not the "aggressive" or "defensive" character of the war, but the nature of the change which is being sought.' Thus, the American colonists who attacked the status quo by force in 1776 or the Irish who did the same between 1916 and 1920 were not 'necessarily less moral than ... the British who defended it [the status quo] by force'.[34]

This is not meant to imply that the Soviet Union should be compared with either colonial America or Ireland struggling for independence. It does mean, however, that there are always at least two sides to a conflict, that one side is normally trying to change the status quo while the other is upholding it. The conflict arises because neither side is willing to yield. This process is what we should study; then the awarding of points for good or bad behavior simply becomes less interesting. Thus, I think more would have been achieved if we historians had concentrated more on our standard questions of *what* happened and *why* this happened instead of on our explicit or implicit political agendas of distributing blame for the Cold War.[35]

Does this imply a position of moral equidistance between East and West? And what about Gaddis's accusation that the people saw the contest as one of good versus evil while the historians have not seen it in this way? Many historians have indeed seen the Cold War as a contest between good and evil. As I have tried to indicate, this moralism is an important part of the problem with these interpretations. In addition, any historian who writes about the Cold War will have to say something about the attitudes, perceptions, and political structures of the two sides, that they *both* saw this as a struggle between good and evil. The Cold War was a conflict between two basic systems of government; these two systems should indeed be presented and explained. Referring to what others thought is, however, different from the historian himself choosing to analyze the Cold War in terms of good and evil. The essence should be the conflict between the two sides, not the celebration of one of them, although it will of course have to be explained why in the end the Soviet Union collapsed and the West prevailed in the Cold War.

Second, on the question of what was the more active side in the origins of the Cold War, it is time to emphasize *the interaction* between East and West, between the actions of the strongest power the world had ever seen and a country ruled by one of the most suspicious rulers in history. (A most difficult combination under any circumstances.) In the old Cold War debate the emphasis was very much on the actions of the United States, which were analyzed in great detail; Soviet actions were seen as more or less important for US actions, depending on one's over-all interpretation, but too little was really known about the Soviet side to make any study of interaction truly meaningful. In the new Cold War history much more is known about Soviet actions, but once again the new studies are presented in relative isolation, this time without any strong effort to relate Soviet actions to the Western actions which were analyzed in such detail in the first round. This one-sidedness is easily explained by the need to digest the new Russian sources, but it is still an unsatisfactory way of dealing with the origins of the Cold War, as is after all the purpose of the new books.

I would also refer to our experiences in studying World War II. The debate on the origins of this conflict has moved in three rough waves. First came the overwhelming emphasis on Hitler as the guilty person and Nazism as the guilty system, with Hitler having presented rather clear plans as to what he wanted to achieve and then basically carrying out what he had proclaimed he would do; then came the revisionism, especially of A. J. P. Taylor in his *The Origins of the Second World War* from 1961; this revisionism certainly did not stick but it did strengthen a move away from master plans and blueprints and toward the opportunist elements in Hitler's foreign policy. This did not necessarily mean that Nazi Germany and its antagonists acted with equal force and determination, but it certainly meant an added emphasis on the interaction between the two sides. Even if Hitler had his objectives, he was at the same time influenced by what the other major powers did. As Alan Bullock, among others, came to believe, Hitler was both a planner and an opportunist; he had certain preconceived ideas and he was influenced by the actions of others.[36]

If this should be our perspective in studying Hitler, it certainly should be in analyzing Stalin because virtually everybody agrees that Stalin was much more amenable to outside influence than was Hitler. As Mastny describes Stalin, 'Opportunistic rather than reckless, he was not impervious to pressure – his main difference from Hitler.'[37] Or in Gaddis's words:

'Where Stalin sought desperately to stay out of war, Hitler set out quite deliberately to provoke it.'[38]

While as yet we have made little progress on the over-all level in putting the actions of East and West together and studying the interaction between them, at the more detailed level some impressive studies have been presented. The most impressive of them all is probably David Holloway's *Stalin and the Bomb*.[39] Then we always have to remember that there were other powers in addition to the United States and the Soviet Union and that, even in regions where one power had over-all control, circumstances varied from country to country and local actors influenced the pace, and sometimes even the basic outcome, of events. In Eastern Europe, Krystyna Kersten and Norman Naimark have written fine studies about the relationship between the Soviets and the local communists, although there is considerably less in these books about the interaction with the West;[40] an even richer literature is appearing on Sino-Soviet and North Korean–Soviet relations.[41]

Third, while there is much to be said for the upgrading of ideology as a motive force in foreign policy, particularly in Soviet foreign policy since the Soviet Union was a society where matters were frequently both perceived and explained in ideological terms, we should not succumb to the temptation of the one-factor explanation. Revisionists made economic-capitalist considerations into such an explanation on the American side. This was clearly a misrepresentation of US foreign policy. To make ideology into a one-factor explanation for Soviet foreign policy is more understandable, but it would still seem to represent a vast simplification. The reality of American and Soviet foreign policy is much too complex to be captured by such one-factor explanations.

In *We Now Know*, John Gaddis argues that the old Cold War debate, in which he was such a prominent participant, 'emphasized *interests*, which it mostly defined in material terms – what people possessed, or wanted to possess. It tended to overlook *ideas* – what people believed, or wanted to believe.' The new Cold War history – in which Gaddis is equally prominent – 'will take ideas seriously'.[42] It is certainly true that ideas and ideology figure prominently in the new Cold War history, although primarily in the discussion of Soviet foreign policy. Yet, his description of the old debate really refers to more or less Marxist revisionist interpretations, not post-revisionist, and certainly not traditionalist ones.[43]

Thus, while the emphasis on ideology provides a good counter against the assumption of political science realism that ideology is largely irrelevant, in the historical debate on the origins of the Cold War it is definitely nothing new to see ideology as an important motive force in Soviet foreign policy. In fact, one is tempted to argue that this was the very essence of traditionalist interpretations of the Cold War. What Mastny and Gaddis write has been written almost word for word by a steady stream of traditionalists from Herbert Feis to Arthur Schlesinger, Jr. In Feis's words, during World War II the Russian people under Stalin 'were trying not only to extend their boundaries and their control over neighboring states but also beginning to revert to their revolutionary effort throughout the world. Within the next few years *this* was to break the coalition ...' (my emphasis). Or, in Schlesinger's even more striking words, the Cold War 'could have been avoided only if the Soviet Union had not been possessed by convictions both of the infallibility of the Communist word and the inevitability of the Communist world'.[44]

Ideology, even Soviet ideology, is not an all-explanatory factor. Neither is ideology constant; most ideologies, and certainly Marxism-Leninism, contain many different strands, and the emphasis within the ideology may shift over time. Thus, ideologically, Stalin and the Soviet leaders went back and forth between emphasizing the 'contradictions between the capitalist powers' or the conflict between 'the imperialist and the anti-democratic camp and the anti-imperialist and the democratic camp' as the basic antagonism in international relations.[45]

Most of the time, ideology is tempered both by various situational and short-term factors and by deeper considerations, such as security needs, historical legacy, and geographic position.[46] In line with realist interpretations, the greater the security threat, the greater the modifications of ideology seem to be. Soviet history immediately before and also during World War II would seem to provide ample evidence of this. One day Stalin was opposing Nazi Germany; the next he signed a non-aggression pact with it. And, during the Cold War, one day Khrushchev combated capitalism; the next he emphasized 'peaceful co-existence' with it. These approaches may not be entirely antagonistic, but at least they represented a change of emphasis. Changes like these are frequently explained by important events abroad. But this is the very point: situations develop, often, but not always, abroad which influence the way in which ideology is interpreted. (One may of course choose to call even this end product 'ideological', but then ideology becomes a catch-all which simply begs the question of its development over time and the relationship between the many different elements within it.)

This was indeed the way even Lenin himself saw the role of ideology. He referred to the idea that Bolsheviks should always act in an ideologically deterministic way as 'childishness' or an 'infantile disorder'.[47] And, as John Gaddis stressed in his early work, 'Stalin was the master of Communist doctrine, not the prisoner of it, and could modify or suspend Marxism-Leninism whenever it suited him to do so.'[48]

No 'master plan' for Soviet expansion has so far been found in the partly opened archives; neither has a plan for an attack on Western Europe. The few war plans that have surfaced seem to indicate that an advance into Western Europe would take place after the West had initiated hostilities.[49]

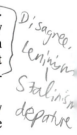

Disagree, Leninism / Stalinism departure

Stalin's foreign policy may in fact be so complicated that it cannot be fully understood at all. As Odd Arne Westad has written, 'To the historian – as to his contemporaries, Soviet and foreign – Stalin's foreign policy is not as much inexplicable in its parts as incoherent in its whole.'[50]

Zubok and Pleshakov's 'revolutionary-imperial paradigm', which introduces the imperial element, would seem to represent a useful starting point for the discussion of motive forces in Soviet foreign policy, but it really dodges the question of what was what in this amalgam.[51]

Mastny underscores the point that the Soviet leaders really believed there was a security threat: 'Whether this was true or not, their constant perception of a threat prevented Soviet leaders from ever feeling sufficiently secure.'[52] Gaddis points out that 'Stalin sought desperately to stay out of war ...'[53] If this is indeed a reasonable interpretation of Stalin's attitude, and I think it is, then realist security concerns would once again seem to be an important modifier of ideology pure and simple.

As Melvyn Leffler points out, other contributors in the new Cold War debate have been much less insistent on the priority and purity of communist ideology.[54] David Holloway writes:

> the policy Stalin pursued was one of *realpolitik*. Left-wing critics would later characterize it, correctly, as statist, because it treated states, rather than classes, as the primary actors in international relations, and because it put the interests of the Soviet state above those of the international revolution.[55]

Or, in the words Goncharov, Lewis, and Xue Litai, with reference to Stalin and Mao, 'the ultimate concern on both sides was not class struggle, but state interests (though the arguments were sometimes couched in revolutionary terms). In the final analysis, *realpolitik* governed [Mao's and Stalin's] thinking and strained their relations.'[56]

The new Cold War interpretations underline the close connection between domestic and foreign policy. In Gaddis's words, 'For the more we learn, the less sense it makes to distinguish Stalin's foreign policies from his domestic practices or even his personal behavior.'[57] Such a connection frequently exists, but at the same time rulers will almost always have more control over domestic than over foreign policy. For that reason too, there will frequently be discrepancies between domestic and foreign policy. Thus, while Stalin was undertaking his purges in the Soviet Union in the mid-1930s, abroad he emphasized the 'popular front' with democratic and socialist parties and cooperation with the Western powers.

Three final points should also be made in this context. First, even a crucially important person such as Stalin can be given too much importance. As Naimark has shown in his fine study of the Soviet zone in Germany, locally in the hundreds of decisions which in sum constituted a policy, Stalin could be rather distant.[58] In a vast empire like that of the Soviet Union even Stalin could only do so much.

Second, the Cold War did not in any way end with Stalin; it continued after his death in 1953. Khrushchev may have reinterpreted ideology and at first this brought the temperature in the conflict down somewhat, only for it to rise to new heights over Berlin and Cuba. This as well would seem to indicate that too much can be made of Stalin's role in the Cold War. The more we get to know, the less likely the theories about 'missed opportunities' appear, during or after Stalin's years in power.[59]

Third, if ideology is so important, then one would think that it was important also on the Western side. True, the United States was a far less rigidly ideological society than the Soviet Union, but its democratic-capitalist ideology certainly influenced the perceptions and explanations of America's leaders.[60] Here too interaction would seem to be the key concept.

Rewriting the Cold War

Thus, while new Cold War history is in many ways an obvious improvement on the old, in the three important ways mentioned it is really a reversal to a rather crude form of traditionalism.

In the third round of Cold War history that will inevitably follow I recommend that we do the following. First, pay less attention to who is to blame for the Cold War and instead focus on the basic questions, what happened and why this happened. Second, move away from analyzing one side or the other and instead emphasize the interaction between the two sides, or, even better, between the many different actors in the Cold War. We may still not have enough sources on the Soviet-Communist side to get into the details of East–West interaction, but there can be little doubt about the direction in which we should attempt to move. Third, stop believing in one-factor explanations for the behavior of the Soviet Union or, for that matter, the United States, and instead analyze how many different factors blended together. When most of us more or less intuitively understand the complexity of the process, why then do we keep coming back to simplistic one-factor explanations for the origins of the Cold War?

NOTES

1 I have dealt at greater length with the historiography in general and the criteria in particular in *The American Non-Policy Towards Eastern Europe 1943–1947: Universalism in an Area Not of Essential Interest to the United States* (Oslo: Scandinavian University Press, 1975), pp. 17–29; *America, Scandinavia, and the Cold War 1945–1949* (New York: Columbia University Press, 1980), pp. 7–35, and

East, West, North, South: Major Developments in International Politics 1945–1996
(Oslo: Scandinavian University Press, 1997), pp. 7–42, especially 7–9.

2 For excellent surveys of the Cold War debate, see Melvyn P. Leffler, 'The
Interpretive Wars over the Cold War, 1945–60', in Gordon Martel, *American
Foreign Relations Reconsidered, 1890–1993* (London: Routledge, 1994), pp. 106–24;
David Reynolds, ed., *The Origins of the Cold War in Europe: International
Perspectives* (New Haven, CT: Yale University Press, 1994), particularly the essays
by Anders Stephanson (pp. 23–52) and Vladislav Zubok and Constantine
Pleshakov (pp. 53–76). See also the references under note 1.

3 John Lewis Gaddis, *The United States and the Origins of the Cold War, 1941–1947*
(New York: Columbia University Press, 1972). For a left-of-center post-revisionist
account, see Daniel Yergin, *Shattered Peace: The Origins of the Cold War and the
National Security State* (Boston, MA: Houghton Mifflin Company, 1977). I have
long considered myself a self-declared post-revisionist. The present essay may well
be regarded as a defense of post-revisionism against certain features of new Cold
War history. Post-revisionism is, however, so vague that it may be seen as much as
a basic attitude as representing a specific interpretation of the origins of the Cold
War. The essence of post-revisionism, as I see it, is reflected in my recommendations
at the end of this chapter.

4 See especially Gaddis, *The United States and the Origins of the Cold War*, chs 6, 8,
and 11.

5 A. J. P. Taylor writes that 'Wars are much like road accidents. They have a general
cause and particular causes at the same time. Every road accident is caused, in the
last resort, by the invention of the internal combustion engine and by men's desire
to get from one place to another.' The 'international anarchy', which is the starting
point of political science realism, might be compared to the internal combustion
engine. It provides a general theory for conflict. Yet, as Taylor also remarks,
'"International anarchy" makes war possible; it does not make war certain.' See
A. J. P. Taylor, *The Origins of the Second World War* (Harmondsworth: Penguin
Books, 1964), pp. 135–6. For an excellent recent article on Realism and other major
political-science interpretations of international relations in general, see Stephen
M. Walt, 'International Relations: One World, Many Theories', *Foreign Policy*
(Spring 1998): 29–46.

6 Lundestad, *America, Scandinavia, and the Cold War*, pp. 4–11; Louis J. Halle, *The
Cold War as History* (New York: Harper & Row, 1967); George F. Kennan,
American Diplomacy, 1900–1950 (Chicago, IL: University of Chicago Press, 1951).

7 Michael J. Hogan, *The Marshall Plan: America, Britain, and the Reconstruction of
Western Europe, 1947–1952* (Cambridge: Cambridge University Press, 1987);
Charles S. Maier, 'The Two Postwar Eras and the Conditions for Stability in
Twentieth-Century Western Europe', *American Historical Review*, 86 (April 1982):
327–52.

8 Thomas J. McCormick, *America's Half Century: United States Foreign Policy in
the Cold War* (Baltimore, MD: Johns Hopkins University Press, 1989); Bruce
Cumings, *The Origins of the Korean War*, vol. II: *The Roaring of the Cataract
1947–1950* (Princeton, NJ: Princeton University Press, 1992).

9 Compare, for instance, Thomas Paterson's revisionist *Soviet–American Confrontation* (Baltimore, MD: Johns Hopkins University Press, 1973) with his post-
revisionist *On Every Front: The Making of the Cold War* (New York: Norton, 1979).
In Melvyn Leffler's case compare his early articles on the Cold War with his more
centrist *A Preponderance of Power: National Security, the Truman Administration,
and the Cold War* (Stanford, CA: Stanford University Press, 1992). With Barton
Bernstein the swing is obvious if you compare his early Alperovitz-inspired writings

(Bernstein, ed., *Politics and Policies of the Truman Administration* (Chicago, IL: Quadrangle, 1972), pp. 15–60) with his many later Sherwin-inspired articles on the atomic bomb.

10 For a review of this trend, see David Reynolds, 'Great Britain', in Reynolds, ed., *The Origins of the Cold War in Europe*, pp. 77–95.

11 See my article 'Empire by Invitation? The United States and Western Europe, 1945–1952', *Journal of Peace Research*, 23:3 (1986): 263–77.

12 Lundestad, *America, Scandinavia, and the Cold War*, especially pp. 167–97.

13 Geir Lundestad, 'Moralism, Presentism, Exceptionalism, Provincialism, and Other Extravagances in American Writings on the Early Cold War Years', in Lundestad, *The American 'Empire' and Other Studies of US Foreign Policy in a Comparative Perspective* (Oxford: Oxford University Press, 1990), especially pp. 14–17.

14 Jian Chen, *China's Road to the Korean War: The Making of the Sino-American Confrontation* (New York: Columbia University Press, 1994); Shu Guang Zhang, *Deterrence and Strategic Culture: Chinese–American Confrontations, 1949–1958* (Ithaca, NY: Cornell University Press, 1992).

15 See the references under note 14; Kathryn Weathersby, 'Korea, 1945–1950: To Attack or Not to Attack? Stalin, Kim Il Sung, and the Prelude to War', *Cold War International History Project Bulletin*, 5 (Spring 1995): 1–9; Weathersby, 'The Soviet Role in the Early Phase of the Korean War: New Documentary Evidence', *The Journal of American–East Asian Relations*, 2 (Winter 1993): 425–58; Sergei Goncharov, John Lewis, and Xue Litai, *Uncertain Partners: Stalin, Mao and the Korean War* (Stanford, CA: Stanford University Press, 1993).

16 The starting point on the Cuban side in the 1970s, as well as on so many other matters relating to the fall of détente, is Raymond L. Garthoff, *Détente and Confrontation: American–Soviet Relations from Nixon to Reagan* (Washington, DC: Brookings Institute, rev edn, 1994). See also Odd Arne Westad, *The Fall of Détente: Soviet–American Relations during the Carter Years* (Oslo: Scandinavian University Press, 1997).

17 John Lewis Gaddis, *We Now Know: Rethinking Cold War History* (Oxford: Clarendon Press, 1997), p. 295.

18 Vladislav Zubok and Constantine Pleshakov, *Inside the Kremlin's Cold War: From Stalin to Khrushchev* (Cambridge, MA: Harvard University Press, 1996).

19 Vojtech Mastny, *The Cold War and Soviet Insecurity: The Stalin Years* (Oxford: Oxford University Press, 1996).

20 Melvyn P. Leffler, 'Inside Enemy Archives: The Cold War Reopened', *Foreign Affairs* (July–August 1996): 120–35.

21 Zubok and Pleshakov, *Inside the Kremlin's Cold War*, pp. 53, 276–7.

22 Vojtech Mastny, *Russia's Road to the Cold War: Diplomacy, Warfare, and the Politics of Communism, 1941–1945* (New York: Columbia University Press, 1979); Mastny, *The Cold War and Soviet Insecurity*, pp. 4–6.

23 Mastny, *The Cold War and Soviet Insecurity*, p. 27, also pp. 23–4.

24 Gaddis, *The United States and the Origins of the Cold War*, pp. 360–1.

25 Gaddis, *We Now Know*, pp. 292, 294. See also pp. 25, 31.

26 Ibid., p. 31. But compare this with his statement that 'This argument by no means absolves the United States and its allies of a considerable responsibility for how the Cold War was fought ... Nor is it to deny the feckless stupidity with which the Americans fell into peripheral conflicts like Vietnam, or their exorbitant expenditures on unusable weaponry ... Nor is it to claim moral superiority for Western statesmen. None was as bad as Stalin – or Mao – but the Cold War left no leader uncorrupted; the wielding of great power, even in the best of times, rarely does' (ibid., pp. 293–4).

27 Zubok and Pleshakov, *Inside the Kremlin's Cold War*, pp. 277–9.
28 Mastny, *The Cold War and Soviet Insecurity*, p. 23. See also pp. 11, 195.
29 Gaddis, *We Now Know*. In order the quotations are from pp. 36, 31, 10.
30 Zubok and Pleshakov, *Inside the Kremlin's Cold War*, pp. 1–8. Their analysis is remarkably close to George Kennan's famous one in the Long Telegram of 22 February 1946. Thus, Kennan wrote that basically Soviet policy 'is only the steady advance of uneasy Russian nationalism, a centuries old movement in which conceptions of offense and defense are inextricably confused. But in the new guise of international Marxism, with its honeyed promises to a desperate and war torn outside world, it is more dangerous and insidious than ever before.' Here quoted from Thomas Etzold and John Lewis Gaddis, eds, *Containment: Documents on American Foreign Policy and Strategy, 1945–1950* (New York: Columbia University Press, 1978), p. 54.
31 Mastny, *The Cold War and Soviet Insecurity*, p. 9. Yet, Mastny also refers to the attempts to advance Soviet power and influence, 'motivated by ideological preconceptions to a much greater degree than suspected ...' (p. 197). So, there must have been some surprises after all, although even they were in an ideological direction.
32 Gaddis, *We Now Know*, pp. 282–3, 286–7.
33 In my opinion William H. McNeill's *America, Britain and Russia: Their Co-operation and Conflict, 1941–1946* (London: Oxford University Press, 1953) was the best analysis of the origins of the Cold War until Gaddis's *The United States and the Origins of the Cold War 1941–1947* was published in 1972. So, with good historical judgment excellent history may indeed be written on the basis of rather limited source materials. The even better combination is of course good historical judgment and a wide array of sources.
34 Edward Hallett Carr, *The Twenty Years' Crisis 1919–1939* (London: Macmillan, 1939), p. 265.
35 Lundestad, *The American 'Empire'*, pp. 11–29, particularly 26–9.
36 For what is still a good collection of articles about the debate on the origins of World War II see Esmonde M. Robertson, ed., *The Origins of the Second World War* (London: Macmillan, 1971). For Bullock's reinterpretation, in part influenced by Taylor, see Alan Bullock, 'Hitler and the Origins of the Second World War', ibid., pp. 189–224. In a telling statement about *Anschluss* Bullock writes that it 'seems to me to provide, almost in caricature, a striking example of that extra-ordinary combination of consistency in aim, calculation and patience in preparation with opportunism, impulse and improvisation in execution which I regard as characteristic of Hitler's policy' (p. 204). For a good recent account, see Donald Cameron Watt, *How War Came: The Immediate Origins of the Second World War* (New York: Pantheon Books, 1989), particularly pp. 30–45. On the one hand, Watt writes that 'Such programmatic elements as can be found in Hitler's foreign policy between 1933 and 1938 were imposed upon him by external fact, not internal vision' (p. 32). On the other hand, Watt also states that Hitler's 'speeches and orders were clearly intended to set forth his aims and how he planned to achieve them. To that extent they represent a programme, or rather a series of directives. They are not, however, consistent enough in direction to be taken for more than this, and yet are too specific to be dismissed as less' (p. 33). See also P. M. H. Bell, *The Origins of the Second World War in Europe* (London: Longman, 2nd edn, 1997), particularly pp. 44–54.
37 Mastny, *The Cold War and Soviet Insecurity*, p. 20.
38 Gaddis, *We Now Know*, p. 10.
39 David Holloway, *Stalin and the Bomb: The Soviet Union and Atomic Energy*

1939–1956 (New Haven, CT: Yale University Press, 1994).

40 Krystyna Kersten, *The Establishment of Communist Rule in Poland, 1943–1948* (Berkeley, CA: University of California Press, 1991); Norman M. Naimark, *The Russians in Germany: A History of the Soviet Zone of Occupation, 1945–1949* (Cambridge, MA: Harvard University Press, 1995). See also Norman Naimark and Leonid Gibianski, eds, *The Establishment of Communist Regimes in Eastern Europe, 1944–1949* (Boulder, CO: Westview, 1997).

41 See the references under notes 14 and 15.

42 Gaddis, *We Now Know*, pp. 282–3.

43 On the American side even some revisionists paid attention to ideology, particularly in the form of anti-communism. This was most noticeable with non-Marxist revisionists such as Gar Alperovitz, David Horowitz, and D. F. Fleming.

44 Herbert Feis, *Churchill, Roosevelt and Stalin: The War They Waged and the Peace They Sought* (Princeton, NJ: Princeton University Press, 1967), p. 655; Arthur M. Schlesinger, Jr, 'The Origins of the Cold War'. Originally published in *Foreign Affairs* (October 1967): 22–52. Here quoted from Schlesinger, *The Crisis of Confidence: Ideas, Power and Violence in America Today* (New York: Bantam Books, 1969), p. 110.

Of course the fact that important points in the new Cold War history represent a reversal to views presented as far back as the 1940s and 1950s does not in itself mean that these interpretations are wrong. This fact would, however, seem to provide little reason for celebrating the quality of historical research on the origins of the Cold War.

45 The latter phrase is from Andrei A. Zhdanov's famous speech at the founding of Cominform in September 1947. See also Mastny, *The Cold War and Soviet Insecurity*, pp. 11–35.

46 For a useful discussion of the role of ideology, see Douglas J. Macdonald, 'Formal Ideologies in the Cold War: Toward a Framework for Empirical Analysis', Chapter 8 in the present collection.

47 Martin Seliger, *The Marxist Conception of Ideology: A Critical Essay* (Cambridge: Cambridge University Press, 1977), p. 108, here quoted from Macdonald, 'Formal Ideologies in the Cold War'.

48 Gaddis, *The United States and the Origins of the Cold War*, p. 360.

49 Mastny, *The Cold War and Soviet Insecurity*, pp. 195–7. See also Vojtech Mastny, 'New Evidence on the NATO–Warsaw Pact Relationship 1949–1969', Paper presented at the Norwegian Nobel Institute, 23 April 1998, pp. 3–8; Holloway, *Stalin and the Bomb*, pp. 271–2.

50 Odd Arne Westad, *Cold War and Revolution: Soviet–American Rivalry and the Origins of the Chinese Civil War* (New York: Columbia University Press, 1993), p. 55. The statement would seem to indicate that Westad does not see ideology as an overriding factor in Stalin's foreign policy. Thus, he also writes that 'The ideological elements in the CCP–Soviet relationship, on which so many Western historians have banked for their explanation of CCP behavior, receded in importance to Yan'an at the very moment when Moscow ceased being a distant ideal' (p. 169).

For a more recent, somewhat different emphasis on Westad's part where, on the one hand, he argues 'that we had been wrong and that ideology may have played a fundamental role in determining the framework for foreign policymaking throughout the Soviet experiment' while, on the other hand, he also states that 'using ideas as important elements in constructing our interpretations of Soviet foreign policy history in no way excludes making use of the essential lessons of realism ...', see Westad, 'Secrets of the Second World: The Russian Archives and Reinterpretations of Cold War History', *Diplomatic History*, 21:2 (Spring 1997):

259–71. The quotations are from 264 and 268.

51 In a later article Zubok further explores the relationship between ideology and *realpolitik*. For this, see his 'Stalin's Plans and Russian Archives', in *Diplomatic History*, 21:2 (Spring 1997): 295–305, particularly 302–4.

52 Mastny, *The Cold War and Soviet Insecurity*, p. 11.

53 Gaddis, *We Now Know*, p. 10, also p. 48.

54 Leffler, 'Inside Enemy Archives', pp. 122–8; Leffler seems to admit that he himself probably put too little emphasis on ideology in *A Preponderance of Power*. For the admission, see his 'Ideology and American Foreign Policy', *The SHAFR Newsletter*, 28:3 (September 1997): 31–8, especially 33, where he writes that 'I felt that in *Preponderance of Power* I had not sufficiently clarified the extent to which correlations of power in the international system were linked to the preservation of America's core values, that is, a system of democratic capitalism at home.' This shortcoming was then presumably remedied in Leffler's *The Specter of Communism: The United States and the Origins of the Cold War, 1917–1953* (New York: Hill and Wang, 1994).

55 Holloway, *Stalin and the Bomb*, p. 168. He also writes that 'Stalin wanted to consolidate Soviet territorial gains, establish a Soviet sphere of influence in Eastern Europe, and have a voice in the political fate of Germany and – if possible – of Japan' (p. 168). This line of reasoning would, however, seem to be slightly at odds with his conclusion, where Holloway states, first, that 'I have been skeptical in this book about the possibility that changes in American policy would have elicited significant shifts in Soviet policy' and, then, that 'All attempts to imagine alternative courses of postwar international relations run up against Stalin himself ... His malevolent and suspicious personality pervades the history of these years. If ever personality mattered in politics, it surely did so in the Soviet Union under Stalin' (p. 370).

56 Goncharov, Lewis, and Litai, *Uncertain Partners*, p. 220.

57 Gaddis, *We Now Know*, p. 293.

58 Naimark, *The Russians in Germany*, pp. 9–11, 58–60, 465–71. It should be pointed out, however, that Naimark primarily studies Soviet policies on the local level in Germany; he is less concerned with Stalin's personal views and role.

59 The only great believer in 'missed opportunities' seems to be Deborah Larson, *The Anatomy of Mistrust* (Ithaca, NY: Cornell University Press, 1997). Gaddis does not really believe in missed opportunities (*We Now Know*, pp. 127–9). Mastny believes that there might have been an opportunity immediately before Stalin's death, but he clearly sees it as rather small (*The Cold War and Soviet Insecurity*, pp. 164–6). For a fine study by a young Norwegian scholar, skeptical to the alleged missed opportunities for German unification in 1952–3, see Stein Bjørnstad, *The Soviet Union and German Unification During Stalin's Last Years* (Oslo: Institutt for forsvarsstudier, 1998).

60 For an excellent recent study of American ideology, but primarily within the Western sphere, see Tony Smith, *America's Mission: The United States and the Worldwide Struggle for Democracy in the Twentieth Century* (Princeton, NJ: Princeton University Press, 1994).

4

Liberty or Death: The Cold War as US Ideology

Anders Stephanson

NSC-68

rhetoric - freedom,
slavery,
totalitarianism

A few weeks after Harry Truman announced his 'Doctrine' in March 1947, Dean Acheson went to Mississippi to give an address about the need for economic assistance to Europe. Joseph M. Jones, who had drafted much of the speech on Acheson's instructions, would later call the event 'history-making', a crucial part of that heroic moment in the spring of 1947 when US policy changed emphatically for the better and grand deeds were accomplished. The point of Acheson's speech was that without restored prosperity in important but now devastated economies abroad there would be no stability in the world and ultimately no security for the United States. It was an argument about political economy combined with a predictable exhortation to action. Attached to it was also a set of allusions, already obligatory, to the new Cold War frame of the Truman Doctrine. Thus Acheson spoke of the imperative to aid 'free peoples' who were struggling to maintain their independence, democracy and freedom 'against totalitarian pressures'.[1]

Acheson was addressing the Delta Council, which is described in *Fifteen Weeks*, Jones's well-known book of the mid-1950s, as 'a remarkable organization of farmers and small businessmen'. The Council, in Jones's view, had been a driving force behind much of the economic diversification that had turned the Delta into 'one of the most progressive and prosperous regions in the South'. Acheson himself writes in his memoirs of 'picturesque but ramshackle shanties giving way to neat, well-fenced farms and painted houses' and remembers the occasion as 'an easy-going, good-natured, shirt-sleeved, thoroughly American one'.[2]

An American occasion it may well have been but perhaps not in the sense Acheson had in mind. The Delta Council was in fact, as the most recent historian of the region puts it, 'an advocacy organization for the large-scale planting and business interests'. One is not surprised to learn that it was lily white in composition and segregationist in spirit. A leading member typically called it 'a striking example of democracy at work', it being open to 'any white person'. In the elections a year later, 95 percent

of this progressive region voted for 'Dixiecrats', extreme white suprema-
cists within a US culture mired in white supremacy.[3]

Several things interest me about this episode. There is, as already implied,
the obvious hypocrisy of Acheson's language, the appeal to global principles of democracy and freedom amidst a Southern regime dedicated to
apartheid and racial oppression. More intriguing is the question of whether
he failed to see the contradiction in 1947 or chose to ignore it. When he
composed his memoirs in the late 1960s, a decade of bitter, sometimes
lethal struggles over civil rights, he must surely have seen the problem; but
he may just have found it impolitic to bring it up. For his memoirs were
meant to counteract the 'mood of depression, disillusion and withdrawal'
among youth in the 1960s, so Acheson wanted to tell a contrasting 'tale of
large conceptions, great achievements, and some failures'.[4]

Such an intentional silence would have been quite in character, for
Acheson did not much care about his rhetorical means as long as his
strategic ends were accomplished. His most immediate object in Mississippi was to generate support for what would eventually become the
Marshall Plan. There was also the long-term aim of putting the United
States systematically into the world in a properly leading position once and
for all. Such circumstances demanded hyperbole. One might thus read
his binary language in an entirely 'tactical' way, as necessary ideological
ornamentation or the kind of 'complexity reduction' required by any
new system in need of distinguishing itself. Even the more ardent Harry S.
Truman, in casting the Cold War as a struggle of freedom against totalitarianism, had acknowledged in an underhanded way that his grand
abstraction had asterisks, hinting that the democratic credentials of Greece
were not perhaps altogether in order and contenting himself with referring
to Turkey, the other designated target of military aid, merely as an 'independent and economically sound state' in need of 'modernization'. It did
not take a cynical observer, moreover, to see that, beyond Truman's
division of the world into two antagonistic forms of life, what was 'really'
at stake at that moment was the strategic importance of the Eastern
Mediterranean: geopolitics in other words.[5]

A strategic analysis, however reductionist, seems to have a certain 'local'
validity here then. The central difficulty, after all, for US policymakers who
think of themselves as 'internationalist' has always been that the outside
matters a great deal less to the United States than the other way around.
Thus the unending quest to justify actions abroad in a way that makes sense
to the public, or more precisely, to sufficiently large segments of the
dispersed ruling class as represented in the dispersed political system. It so
happened here, as Acheson was keenly aware, that the local ruling class of
the cotton kingdom was atypically connected to the world and hence
receptive in principle to his economic logic. Yet he felt compelled ultimately
to put the matter in Truman's dichotomous terms. A purely instrumental

view of ideology as rhetorical means to strategic ends misses the question, then, of why 'internationalists' deployed the particular political language they did and how they came to 'inhabit' it.

✗ *From slavery to totalitarianism* vs. freedom

The historical peculiarities involved were brought home to me forcefully when I reread NSC (National Security Council directive) 68 recently. Three years after Truman's original binary, 'slavery' had replaced 'totalitarianism', a modern neologism, as the central antithesis of 'freedom'. NSC 68, shortly to be given foundational status by the Korean War, revolves indeed almost obsessively around the epic struggle between 'freedom and slavery' – a charged thematic in US history. Would it perhaps have affected Acheson's address to the Delta Council? To speak sternly of the need for a universal struggle against 'slavery' in Mississippi would (one imagines) have triggered mixed feelings among the audience. Yet I was also reminded that numerous propagandists of the revolutionary era, in attacking the putatively despotic attempts of George III to enslave the colonies, did not stop to consider very long, if at all, the central, indeed decisive, role of actually existing slavery in colonial economy and society. Not everyone, it turned out, was born free in the land of the free or was invested with any inalienable rights; but this did not prevent the most uninhibited appeals to such universal principles or induce much sense of contradiction, paradox, and irony.[6]

These initial observations and questions occasioned second thoughts on an earlier attempt that addressed, in part and from another angle, freedom and slavery in the context of the Cold War. That analysis had been prompted by the odd absence within Cold War historiography of any extensive thought on what precisely it was that made the Cold War a Cold War. The focus, however, was on the polarity between war and peace: it seemed that one might begin to disentangle the concept by asking what sort of surrender it presupposed. Following the acute Walter Lippmann, who made the term a concept, I took the US refusal after mid-1947 to engage in normal diplomacy as the defining element in the Cold War; and I saw this in turn as a development of the concept of 'unconditional surrender', taken directly from the Civil War, that Franklin D. Roosevelt had set forth on the eve of the American entry into World War II. He proposed, simply put, that because peace for dictators was really just a covert war, one could never achieve peace with them through negotiation, only by liquidation. This is the thinking that, when translated to the post-1947 period, made it possible for the authors of NSC 68 to intimate that the Soviet Union had initiated the Cold War just by being the Soviet Union and to argue that any negotiations would have to be postponed until the moment (endlessly deferred) when the West had achieved such a position of strength that it could dictate terms. I then argued that the Cold War ended in 1963, when the Kennedy regime 'recognized' the Soviet Union as a legitimate great power and thus laid the foundation for détente (the preconditions being the Sino-Soviet split, the apparently final division of Germany, and, above all, the experience of the Cuban Missile Crisis).[7]

Taking that analysis as a given, then, I want to push the matter further by asking not so much what made the Cold War a Cold War but what made it into a specifically 'American' one. My wager is that just as Roosevelt's reference to the Civil War was not merely one of his typical whims, the related appearance of 'freedom and slavery' in NSC 68 signifies something more than empty rhetoric. The latter trope has a long genealogy in the United States, going back beyond the Civil War through the Revolution into the seventeenth century. It represents, in fact, a deep and extended tradition. Far more intricate than any simple Manichaeanism, that tradition fuses (in the main) radical Protestantism with classical republican and liberal thought, generating a specifically 'American' language of politics, unthinkable anywhere else. It is a language of evil plots, sins and sinners, demons and saviors, corruption and redemption, dramatic choices in the name of humanity by anointed leaders on the edge of the abyss. And it is, also, a language about freedom and slavery and unconditional surrender. Since this peculiar vocabulary is also what, in my view, came to define the Cold War, it seems worthwhile to attempt to chart it, as part perhaps of a more general quest for the sources of the US conduct. Is there, I ask, more than a superficial connection between Patrick Henry's 'Give me liberty or give me death' and 'Better dead than red'.[8]

My central reference point for this necessarily sketchy essay will remain NSC 68, the always useful Kennan intermittently providing auxiliary materials for contrast. It should be underlined that I do not intend to give a 'full' analysis of NSC 68 and its many tensions and contradictions. Rather, I read it exclusively in terms of how its organizing thematic of 'freedom and slavery' relates to a wider historical tradition that perhaps can best be described as 'freedom under siege'. Such an exploration, it should be added, goes against the grain of much recent speculation on the Cold War which tends to focus on the Eastern side of the equation – as though the only controversial aspect regarding the Western side is the adequacy of its response.

Freedom and slavery in the American image

Freedom and slavery form a conceptual field in which the agents of the negative pole take on more than one guise: tyranny, despotism, and totalitarianism, to name the most prominent that are used interchangeably in the 1940s and 1950s. Yet the first principle, the overdetermining *a priori* so to speak, is not the negation, or the specific threat emanating from it or even 'freedom' as such – a master signifier that has taken on quite different concrete meanings and forms in US history.[9] The first principle, rather, is the dynamic notion that freedom is always already under threat, internally as well as externally, and that it must be defended by those so called upon. Freedom (or 'liberty') is understood as independence, as not being dependent on the will of any outside power. This state is natural, something innately given. Any loss of freedom, any movement in the direction of dependence, is defined as 'slavery'. Such dependence/slavery does not have to be actual: the very threat of arbitrary imposition on the still independent self is a form of slavery because it is a constriction, a diminution, of autonomy.[10] The NSC 68 version of this posits that slavery cannot tolerate the very existence of freedom as an idea and must systemically attempt its liquidation. Freedom and its vanguard defender are thus 'mortally challenged by the Soviet system' precisely because diversity and openness are inherently unacceptable to that system in turn.[11]

There are at least four partly overlapping sources for this notion, in one way or another traceable to England in the seventeenth century. First and foremost, there is the Judeo-Christian component which takes two forms. 'Man' is free and has rights to liberty because he is made in the image of God, who is the very definition of independence. This is then coupled with the powerful narrative, much intensified by the radical Reformation, about the persecuted remnant struggling to represent God's righteousness on earth until redemption and the final judgment take place. The outside is evil and evil is by definition hostile and expansive. To confront and struggle against it, however, is not to mix but to suppress and extinguish. As Calvin declared: 'It is the godly man's duty to abstain from all familiarity with the wicked, and not to enmesh himself with them in any voluntary relationship.' Crucially, however, the evil outside is potentially also present on the inside, if nothing else because we are sinners.

The history of the given community can then be written in terms of a series of apostasies, regenerations, and subsequent returns to first principles. To lead a Christian life, meanwhile, is always to resist the ever-present threat of the Devil or Antichrist. The latter 'impostor' becomes an archetype in Protestant thought. The Pope is his first incarnation. For the English, more particularly, it is the Pope's successive agents, the great powers Spain and France, that come to fill the role. For the wayward descendants of this view in New England, however, Antichrist would eventually appear in the guise of London itself; but by then 'anti-popery' had already blended with the general attack on 'tyranny' and 'superstition'. Various anti-Catholic movements, however, will recur in the United States until the Cold War finally makes Catholicism truly 'American' (and thus makes possible, if only barely, the election of the one and only Catholic president).[12]

The classical republican tradition, a strong and surviving one in the political language of the United States, is cyclical and more 'internalist' in that freedom, indissolubly linked to community virtue, is always under threat from the inherent tendency to corruption and degeneration. It is a story about decline and fall, the central analytical reference being the fate of Rome. In the best of cases the story continues with regeneration and a return to virtue. Americans of the eighteenth and nineteenth century often imagined that they had escaped from this infernal historical trap, the continental expanse offering the stage for the final victory of liberty: instead of being a source of corruption, expansion becomes a safeguard against it.[13]

Such self-confident visions became more rare or at least more ambivalent in the twentieth century. As NSC 68 laments, a free society is vulnerable

> in that it is easy for people to lapse into excesses – the excesses of a permanently open mind wishfully waiting for evidence that evil design may become noble purpose, the excess of faith becoming prejudice, the excess of tolerance degenerating into indulgence of conspiracy and the excess of resorting to suppression when more moderate measures are not only more appropriate but more effective.

However, with a huge military buildup in mind, Paul Nitze and his co-authors are in this regard far more optimistic than George Kennan, Nitze's predecessor, for whom domestic ignorance, the corruptions of mass consumption and evils of laxity offered the materials for a veritable Jeremiad on domestic decline, a threat ultimately far more important to him than the actual Soviet one.[14]

The 'modern' liberal discourse on individual freedom, emerging in the American Revolution and becoming fully articulated in the nineteenth century, is significant here chiefly because of its view of government and the role this view plays in the proliferating talk about 'freedom' in the 1930s and onwards. Liberty is individual liberty unconstrained by government except under the rule of (minimal) law. Power is assumed intrinsically to expand, encroach, and corrupt, none more so than centralized state power. Government as a phenomenon is therefore not only to be rigorously restricted in scope, it is by definition always too big, whence it follows that it is also always suspect. Interventionist 'liberals' from the Progressive Era on contest this view in the name of sound management, republican community, countervailing forces to new and gigantic forms of private power, and so forth.

The massive expansion of state authority in the New Deal then turns this conflict into a remarkably polemical one: the 'conservative' or, more accurately, classical liberal reaction to Roosevelt centers on endangered individual and entrepreneurial liberty, after which much of the politics of the Depression comes to revolve discursively around that problem. Roosevelt appropriates this language with great skill and turns it against his accusers, expanding the notion of what it is to be free to include the right to minimal social and economic security and, famously, railing against the despotism of economic royalists. This conception is then readily available to him when he wants to explain to the US public in 1939–41 what is taking place abroad. By connecting lawless aggression with the narrative of the Civil War and the eternal struggle everywhere against creeping tyranny, Roosevelt was able to articulate his long-term goals in terms of the 'four freedoms'. Not until these had been everywhere secured would the struggle end (as would indeed history).[15]

A final aspect of 'freedom under siege' is less pronounced in our context but worth mentioning because it lurks somewhere beneath the surface throughout. It is the idea of ancient Anglo-Saxon liberties. The eighteenth-century argument (of which Thomas Jefferson was a strong proponent) locates the origin of the celebrated ancient English liberties, which the American colonists were presumably fatally about to lose, in the tribal origins of the Teutons. History since the early Middle Ages can then be told as a series of 'usurpations' by alien forces such as the Normans, or, alternatively, by domestic, power-hungry tyrants and other corrupting interests, ever-present threats against which the defenders of ancient freedoms must ceaselessly struggle. In the nineteenth century this narrative becomes deeply enmeshed with quasi-scientific racism and eventually it is submerged in a more general, sometimes overtly imperialist, discourse on 'civilization'.[16]

What is common to these four dispositions is the imperative of vigilance for the sake of preserving freedom (in every sense), as well as the concomitant idea that any loss of freedom is slavery. As the United States is defined as the repository of freedom, any threat to it is a threat of enslavement and is against the basic principles of humankind. Any conflict, consequently, tends to become a question of antagonistic 'ways of life' (to paraphrase the Truman Doctrine). Hence, too, the otherwise peculiar presumption of something called 'the American way' and the auxiliary, more sinister, thesis that something or someone can be 'un-American'.

The negative agent

I now want to explore the character of the negative agent, which is more of a structural position than anything 'real'. Not that it is devoid of reality, but its function is largely derived from the assumption that freedom is under perpetual threat. While the structural space of enmity remains a constant, various concrete targets can fill it. Thus the enslaving tyrant has shifted from (to name but a few) King George III, whose 'long train of abuses and usurpations' aimed to subjugate the colonies 'under absolute Despotism', to the scheming slave power in the 1850s, to autocracy in general and Germany in particular during World War I, to Kremlin-directed world communism after 1947.[17]

As NSC 68 would have it, the enslaving agent is bound by his very nature to destroy freedom and to that extent he is defined by the latter rather than in his own terms. Freedom is always about independence and what drives tyranny to enslave is the functional need to rid the world of any such autonomous sources of potential opposition, inside as well as outside. Consequently, the system is relentlessly searching to destroy what is not identical to itself. Tyranny is, however, also inherently unstable, for it is based in the end on the arbitrary will of the one rather than on the impersonal, constraining rule of law, the precondition of any free system. We recognize much of this analysis from Kennan's early Cold War writings; NSC 68 repeats it in cruder form.

Kennan, incidentally, also articulates an older, Christian theme in this context. One ought not to complain too much about the evil deeds of the Kremlin, he says at the end of the X Article, but be grateful instead

> to a Providence which, by providing the American people with this implacable challenge, has made their entire security as a nation dependent on their pulling themselves together and accepting the responsibilities of moral and political leadership that history plainly intended them to bear.

Evil is a challenge, in short, sent by God to punish his people for their sundry misdeeds and to provide them, ingeniously, with a threat that will serve to regenerate them – if they choose to do the right thing. The same providentialist argument – a standard Christian explanation (against Manichaean heresies) for the existence of evil in a world supposedly governed by an omnipotent God – tends to appear throughout colonial and US history whenever a threat or crisis of difference occurs. Kennan's point, interestingly, follows his critique of the Soviet regime for its structural need of enemies and messianic belief in its own special place in history.[18]

The diagnosis of arbitrariness, lawlessness, and usurpation of liberties is to no little degree derived from classical antiquity and especially the kind of aristocratic critique of individual power-grabbing one finds in Cicero – though it is mediated through neo-Roman thinkers such as Machiavelli. There is, however, a related but more immediate source of particular relevance here, namely Montesquieu. In the mid-seventeenth century he originated the concept of the 'oriental despot', mostly as a coded warning (in the name of moderate aristocracy) that the French monarchy was deviating into a form of 'Asiatic despotism'. Voltaire, more favorably disposed toward both the East and absolute monarchy, said of Montesquieu's concept that he had 'made for himself a hideous phantom in order to fight against it'.[19]

This hideous phantom (for it had very little to do with the actually existing Ottoman Empire, its chief referent) is sharply divided. On the one hand, there is the all-powerful despot, on the other, his totally anonymous subjects, counting for nothing. They prostrate themselves before his every whim, before a despotic will that is wholly arbitrary, lawless, and unpredictable. The result is random executions and torture. The system is devoid of legitimacy and works in the exclusive interest of its secretive ruler. Montesquieu also claims (following Aristotle) that despotic power is irreversible: it can be crushed from outside or collapse under its own internal contradictions but, crucially, it will not evolve into non-despotism. To this image he adds the Oriental lust for goods and sex.[20] That last luridness aside, however, his account could stand as a fairly accurate summary of the US analysis of Stalin's regime.

Montesquieu's contrast between east and west eventually becomes an integral part of the emerging liberal argument about legitimacy, law, and contracts. A legitimate as opposed to arbitrary social order is defined by the degree to which members of civil society are understood to have had a say in its construction, consented to it, and thus sanctioned its laws. Hence the colonial idea in the 1770s that George III was really only a representative, the 'Chief Magistrate' of the empire, and that any monarchical imposition was therefore despotism, usurpation, and slavery, illegitimate acts against which one had the natural right, conceptually speaking, to commit regicide. Members of a properly legitimate order, by contrast, are obliged by their theoretical participation through representation to follow the given rules, which is why, presumably, this is a stable system as opposed to the 'artificial' and essentially fragile structure of despotism. To break the rules is thus criminal to the point of treason, constituting in principle nothing less than an exit from society altogether and the forfeit of all rights to equal status. Extra-legal opposition, consequently, can be treated and punished harshly as criminality. 'No liberty for the enemies of liberty', as the old Jacobin apothegm of Saint-Just would have it.[21]

A similar notion of obligation can then be extended by later liberals to something imagined as the 'international community'. The coalition of World War II, I think, was grasped in the United States as an embryonic form of 'international community' in that contractual sense. When the Soviet Union was then seen lawlessly to break the given agreements – 'not living up to Yalta' – one could reclassify it as just another treacherous gangster regime that had to be liquidated, or, barring that, kept rigidly within its bounds, whilst the United States would reorganize and order the vast part of the now truncated 'one world' that remained 'free' or at least potentially so. The contractual theory of liberal 'society' served in that sense to exacerbate the negative view of the Soviet adversary.

Kennan, in his more historical moods, possibly under Gibbon's influence, sometimes fell into orientalist themes;[22] but the 'despotic' matrix otherwise became part and parcel of a more general image of a particular form of antithetical, non-Western power. A striking contradictory division marks this image, especially in NSC 68. On the one hand, despotism is essentially 'brittle' and unstable because (as already conceived of by Montesquieu) it lacks the organic ties and moderation of legitimate Western society; on the other, unlike the visibly 'regressive' Ottoman Empire, contemporary Soviet despotism is developmentally dynamic, technologically on the advance, and organizationally powerful, capable, in short, of mobilizing immense hostile force. This contrast between weakness and strength is never resolved (or 'combined') into a single analytical frame.

In NSC 68 it thus appears as a constant oscillation. Yet the conceptual problem need not be resolved because the authors are not really interested in analyzing Soviet realities. Their strategic object is the massive mobilization and assertion of US power, but the point is not to launch any fundamental offensive against the bastions of Soviet 'despotism' (the militant rhetorical gestures along these lines are typically short on substance). The aim instead is to create an irrevocable superpower and to order the non-Soviet world, for which purpose it is sometimes useful to posit Soviet strength, sometimes Soviet weakness. The theme of 'irreversibility', the structural inability of the Soviet system to reform and evolve, is assumed; qualitative change, meaning essentially destruction, can only come through the confrontation (as opposed to 'cooperation') with outside power dialectically combined with inside breakdown. On this basis, and the other premise that Soviet despotism is a deadly, expansive threat, one can then proceed to more important things. Hence the curiously formulaic nature of the many passages about Kremlin evils and the absence of any concrete analysis of the Soviet Union. Hence, too, the otherwise astonishing fact that no Soviet experts were consulted during the composition of the policy paper.[23]

Charles Bohlen, one such expert, was thus to complain to Nitze, quite rightly, that there had been no effort to assess 'the great body of Soviet thought in regard to war between states or the even more elementary fact that any war... carries with it major risks to the Soviet system in Russia'; the apparent aim of NSC 68 being, as he added, 'merely to justify the need for military buildup'.[24]

Designs

Bohlen, sensing the abstract form of argument in NSC 68, also criticized its obsession with the 'Kremlin design', the vision, as he put it, of some 'mechanical chess player' with a fully worked out plan for 'world domination'.[25] Here Bohlen had hit upon something with deeper implications than perhaps he realized. The 'Kremlin design' (often referred to as 'funda-mental') is contrasted asymmetrically in NSC 68 with 'the purpose of the United States'. The Soviet regime, then, is a clique in the Kremlin and not comparable to a properly legitimate 'country' such as the United States. That the former has 'designs' while the latter has a 'purpose' is intrinsic to the distinction. For 'design', meaning a secret plot, is a word with a long lineage in the always abundant language of conspiracy in the United States, a language which tends to find such schemes at the center of most alien threats. 'Designs' are the very *modus operandi* of the illicit, enslaving power. Thus Jefferson, for example, writes darkly of 'a deliberate, systematical plan of reducing us to slavery'; and the subsequent Declaration of Independence speaks of the usurping 'design' of the London tyrant. FDR refers to 'the Nazi design to abolish the freedom of the seas' and achieve a 'new world order'. NSC 68 mentions the term no less than 27 times.[26]

The arch-design here is probably to be found in English fears of the Catholic counter-reformation, with its College of Propaganda and sinister, secret vanguard of Jesuits; but there are numerous similar plots in its wake, all aiming to undermine liberty and righteousness. The devious design is typically stealthy in its effectuation, a creeping, slow movement to take over, cunningly orchestrated by secret cabals. Curiously, the advent of secularized rationalism in the eighteenth century reinforces this way of thinking: what appeared on the surface must have some hidden but detect-able cause of an instrumental nature.[27]

Catholics became a favored target in the *antebellum* period, as their religion was not only alien but lethally opposed to true America. 'The systems', as one fervent critic argued, 'are diametrically opposed: one must and will exterminate the other.' Masons and Mormons, on a lesser scale, found themselves denounced in similar ways. But it is in the 1850s and during the Civil War that these political visions reach a crescendo in the attacks on the evil 'Slave Power'.[28]

The American way of conflict

Indeed, abolitionist writings offer a veritable inventory of the kinds of arguments one finds a century later in Cold War thinking. Consider, for example, the bizarre notion of 'Captive Nations', coupling black slaves in the 1850s with Soviet 'satellites' in the 1950s. Thus when William Henry Channing refers to southern politicians as 'a disciplined corps, schooled in the art of managing a small embodied force, so as to subjugate vast multitudes', then one recognizes the formula. Similarly so when Carl Schurz holds that 'the slave power' cannot tolerate free labor, that it 'is impelled by the irresistible power of necessity' to oppress its opponents and that it is systemically forced to seek 'extension by an aggressive foreign policy'. 'The two principles', maintained the powerful preacher Theodore Parker, were 'mutually invasive and destructive' and one must 'overcome the other'. The two could not coexist. The conflict, then, in Seward's famous word, was truly 'irrepressible'.[29]

Against that backdrop, it is intriguing to read Arthur Schlesinger Jr's attack in 1949 on the 'revisionist' historians who had criticized abolitionist 'fanaticism' for its role in bringing about the Civil War. Schlesinger connects abolitionism with anti-Nazism in the 1930s and anti-communism in his own times. Slavery, being a 'betrayal of the basic values of our Christian and democratic tradition', opened up a conflict 'far too profound to be solved by compromise'. Just as one must not fall into any 'sentimental theories about the needlessness of the Civil War', one must not now regard 'our own struggles against evil as equally needless'. For, he concludes, 'the unhappy fact is that man occasionally works himself into a log-jam; and that the log-jam must be burst by violence'.[30]

What manner of suitable 'violence' Schlesinger was prescribing for unsentimental anti-communists of the moment is not clear. The model, however, is clearly Roosevelt's 'internationalist' turn in 1939–40, seen as the reenactment of the activist Civil War period. Roosevelt's own appropriation of Civil War tropes occurred, of course, after the fact so to speak. It was a conscious play on what is today thought of as 'historical memory'. His actions were generated by his immediate experience of the 1930s, which persuaded him that the traditional distinction between war and peace had been blurred by the escalating aggressions of the dictators, by the piecemeal aggression promulgated in the name of 'pacification' as he put it. The only real peace possible with these criminals was thus, in his words, 'the peace that comes from complete surrender'. It was in that context that, later, he invoked Unionist memories of the Civil War and referred to his policy as 'unconditional surrender' – the policy of crushing the Confederacy because it was treason and because it embodied, presumably, the deeply un-American principle of slavery. It was a policy conveniently represented in the person of U. S. Grant, whose initials combined in a single sign the Unionist nation with the total war it implied and required.[31]

In June 1940, along the same lines, Roosevelt's new Secretary of War Henry Stimson declared, on the authority of Lincoln, that the world could no longer survive 'half slave and half free'. Lincoln had used the formulation in his militant 'House-Divided' speech, The Biblical quotation about the House/Nation he had borrowed from Theodore Parker. Stimson then turned the House/Nation into the whole world, wherein one principle or the other would have to emerge victorious. Between two incompatible principles, between self-government and despotism, between the everlasting principles of right and wrong, there could, again, be no compromise. This was very much Roosevelt's stated position as well: there could be no adjudication between 'good and evil', as he said, 'only total victory'.[32]

The no-compromise formula (which Roosevelt had adopted before the United States was actually at war) was a logical stance. If one posits an absolute conflict between eternal principles of moral right and moral wrong, then it makes sense that anything outside the former is by definition wholly unacceptable. An effect of this image of absolute antagonism was that domestic opponents of mobilization tended to be removed from the acceptable political map, classed, as Roosevelt once classed them, as 'appeaser fifth columnists'. Most opponents were crushed politically any-way by Pearl Harbor. Forthwith, they had to accept strong government, though significantly only when the new concept of national security was linked to US freedom, and both to tyrannical aggression. Acheson learn that lesson well. Eisenhower would of course raise some warning flags here; but these were largely gestures. For, as of 1941, it would always be possible in principle to argue the case for enormous military spending on the grounds that 'security' and 'freedom' were in danger. The meaning of 'freedom' was also transformed in the early Cold War: Roosevelt's 'freedom from want' was symbolically replaced by 'free enterprise' and given a much more patriotic and nationalist coloration.[33]

What is established, then, by the manner in which Roosevelt chose to situate the anti-fascist struggle in part as a reenactment of the Civil War (and by extension the American Revolution) is a certain notion of absolute antagonism and enmity.[34] 'Freedom under siege', accordingly, would act to defend itself with all the means at its disposal. The ensuing war did indeed become in every sense a 'total' one, reaching its most unflinching expression on the Western side in vast fire bombings and atomic blasts against civilian populations. The only truly peaceful and secure world would henceforth be one in which outlaws and dictators were extinct and everyone adhered to the fundamental principles of humanity, which, as Wilson had already said, were those embodied in the United States. In essence, this was to argue that everything that is not a true peace is by definition war and that there can be no such peace with certain powers because of qualities in their domestic makeup.[35] Since it turned out that by 1947 the Soviet Union was not only failing to agree to these propositions but actively counteracting them, it had to be an absolute enemy in the manner that Roosevelt had outlined, whether formal conditions of peace obtained or not. In short, there could be no fundamental peace with Moscow and within the world as a whole until the Soviet Union was no longer the Soviet Union.

This, one should add, was not quite what Roosevelt had had in mind when he formulated his position in 1940–41. He was aware, in the end, that not all dictators are alike. The Hitler–Stalin Pact and the Winter War against the Finns could thus be put aside in 1941 and earlier sentiments of geopolitical affinity brought to the fore, narrativized with remarkable success as 'United Nations alliance for eternal peace'. When this story turned out to be 'untrue', it was replaced with equal celerity and power by the idea that totalitarian dictators are, after all, all alike.[36] This view became orthodoxy in the Truman administration.

Yet if NSC 68 thus chooses to define the Soviet Union as a total war against freedom and thinks that only the US counter-threat of 'a global war of annihilation' is preventing more actual aggression, the authors know too that a full-scale war is not about to happen within the immediate future and that it would be a catastrophe. A certain conceptual uncertainty thus pervades the document. For having offered the first fully codified image of the limitlessly evil empire, NSC 68 finds itself a little short on countermoves commensurate with the monstrous nature of the adversary. This particular log-jam, alas, is not resolvable by violence, as morality would dictate, at least not frontal violence. The end result is something very much like the now suspect 'containment' – deemed, symbolically speaking, altogether too passive – coupled with a huge military security state of global reach. Kennan's original formulation was never subject to such conceptual shortcomings, since his 'refusal' of diplomacy was not grounded in any moral notion of an evil empire. For him the Soviet Union was always a historically distinct creation, to be assessed and dealt with as it was, in its particularity. From that angle, Moscow did not constitute a devastating threat, provided the West assembled itself in appropriate ways.[37] Soon indeed, Kennan came to realize that it might be in the Western interest to engage Moscow in a diplomatic manner with realistic proposals. A year after the X Article he had in effect abandoned containment. But by 1948 it was already too late. Containment in the name of moral universals, containment as Cold War if you will, became the order of the day.[38]

It might now be objected that a good deal of what I have said about the United States, historical particularities and religious references aside, would pertain to the Soviet Union as well. After all, a certain Enlightenment heritage marks both. Representing universal interests, the Soviet Union too assumed itself always to be under threat by the (class) enemies of humankind. The difference as regards the Cold War and the reason it is not even in theory a Soviet project can be found in the diverging conception of fascism and alliances. Stalinism came to define the class foundation of fascism in a remarkably narrow manner as the most extreme parts of monopoly capitalism. A rigid stage theory of history combined with the further thesis that capitalism had reached its developmental limits thus made it possible for Stalinist strategy to imagine eventual victory as the mere prevention of future manifestations of fascism and its likes. Consequently, its 'anti-fascist' matrix, unlike that of the United States, was based on a negative rather than positive criterion: a political force that is not explicitly an enemy is, at least potentially, an ally. Anything outside of those 'extremists', even 'good' sections of monopoly capital, could in theory be mobilized within the anti-fascist alliance. Hence the otherwise curious fact that the opposition to the Marshall Plan and communist politics generally after the break in 1947 were situated in a framework of 'national independence' and 'peace' rather than socialism and revolution.

And on that score it is necessary to state the obvious. There was no conceivable reason for Moscow, in its own terms, to act in such a way as to facilitate the emergence of a massively powerful Western anti-Soviet coalition under US leadership. Stalin, contrary to his own interests and with a very limited understanding of how the West operated, may have acted precisely in this manner and thus 'caused' the Cold War. This is certainly arguable. But it remains that the Cold War was not a Soviet project. Amidst the present triumphalism,[39] one might then ask more seriously what it was about the United States and its self-conception that made the Cold War a natural way of being toward the world, why indeed the Cold War turned out to be 'the American way'.

NOTES

Thanks to David Armitage, Ann Douglas, Francois Furstenberg, Eric Foner, Herb Sloan, and Odd Arne Westad.

1 Joseph Mario Jones, *The Fifteen Weeks* (New York: Harcourt, 1964 [1955]), p. 30, ch. 2, *passim*; Dean Acheson, 'The Conduct of Foreign Relations: Requirements of Reconstruction', *Vital Speeches*, 15 May 1947, pp. 485–7. Eric Foner originally alerted me to the Mississippi event. See his *Freedom: An American Story* (New York: Norton, 1998), p. 259.

2 Jones, *Fifteen Weeks*, p. 26; Dean Acheson, *Present at the Creation: My Years in the State Department* (New York: Norton, 1969), p. 228.

3 James C. Cobb, *The Most Southern Place on Earth: The Mississippi Delta and the Roots of Regional Identity* (New York: Oxford University Press, 1992), pp. 207, 226; Nan Elizabeth Woodruff, 'Mississippi Delta Planters and Debates over Mechanization, Labor, and Civil Rights in the 1940s', *Journal of Southern History*, 60:2 (May 1994): 263–84 (quotation, 269). William Wynn, who had invited Acheson (a stand-in for Truman) to the Council, was the 'most prominent lawyer in the Delta' and the owner of a 10,000 acre plantation. See Ann Waldron, *Hodding Carter: The Reconstruction of a Racist* (Chapel Hill, NC: Algonquin, 1993), p. 68. Wynn's name is misspelled in Jones's and Acheson's accounts alike, the latter following the former.

4 Acheson, *Present at the Creation*, preface, n.p. Then again the 'oversight' might also have been sheer Achesonian defiance. Notably, James Chace, Acheson's most recent biographer, retells the Delta story without seeing any irony either: *Acheson: The Secretary of State Who Created the American World* (New York: Simon & Schuster, 1998), p. 171. Chace is an exemplar of a tendency now to turn Acheson into a symbolic representation of the heroic age, sadly passed, when there was a world policy stage for dramatic action to take place in the name of 'American internationalism'.

5 Truman's speech can be found in Jones, *Fifteen Weeks*, pp. 269–74. 'Complexity reduction' is Niklas Luhman's concept. See his *Social Systems* (Stanford, CA: Stanford University Press, 1995).

6 The full text of NSC 68 can be found conveniently in Thomas H. Etzold and John

Lewis Gaddis, *Containment: Documents on American Policy and Strategy, 1945–1950* (New York: Columbia University Press, 1978), pp. 385–442. All page references henceforth are to this edition. On views of slavery in the Revolution, see David Brion Davis, *The Problem of Slavery in the Age of Revolution, 1770–1823* (Ithaca, NY: Cornell University Press, 1975).

7 The original argument was put forth in Anders Stephanson, 'The United States', in D. Reynolds, ed., *The Origins of the Cold War in Europe: International Perspectives* (New Haven, CT: Yale University Press, 1994). The corollary, 'Fourteen Notes on the Very Idea of a Cold War', was first published on *H-DIPLO* and now appears slightly revised in *Rethinking Geopolitics*, eds G. O'Tuathail and S. Dalby (New York: Routledge, 1998). My scope allows no reflection on John F. Kennedy, which is a pity because he thought about foreign relations more systematically than any President since Wilson. Only Richard Nixon compares. Kennedy is also the only one to my knowledge to quote both Patrick Henry's 'liberty and death' and Abraham Lincoln's 'half slave/half free' – neither instance being his finest hour.

8 William Wirt Henry, *Patrick Henry: Life, Correspondence and Speeches*, vol. I (New York: Burt Franklin, 1969 [1891]), p. 266. It is not certain that Henry ever uttered his immortal words for the speech was reconstructed much after the fact. He is alleged to have put it thus: 'Is life so dear, or peace so sweet, as to be purchased at the price of chains and slavery?' No, 'Give me liberty, or give me death.' Whatever the exact wording, it was not an unusual piece of rhetoric. The Second Continental Congress declared itself resolved in 1775 'to die freemen rather than to live slaves'. Henry had perhaps a deeper personal sense for the contradictions involved than his slaveowning colleague Thomas Jefferson. As David Brion Davis says of Jefferson, he had a remarkable 'capacity to sound like an enlightened reformer while upholding the interests of the planter class'. See *The Problem of Slavery*, p. 182; see also Garry Wills, *Inventing America: Jefferson's Declaration of Independence* (New York: Doubleday, 1978), ch. 10.

9 See Foner, *Freedom*.

10 I am following Quentin Skinner, *Liberty Before Liberalism* (Cambridge: Cambridge University Press, 1998), ch. 1. See also Blair Worden's review in the *London Review of Books*, 5 February 1998.

11 NSC 68, 389.

12 I have relied, chiefly, on Christopher Hill, *Antichrist in Seventeenth-Century England* (London: Oxford University Press, 1970); J. G. A. Pocock, *The Machiavellian Moment: Florentine Political Thought and the Atlantic Republican Tradition* (Princeton, NJ: Princeton University Press, 1975), ch. 15; Skinner, *Liberty before Liberalism*; Kathleen Wilson, *The Sense of the People: Politics, Culture and Imperialism in England, 1715–1785* (Cambridge: Cambridge University Press, 1995); Charles Taylor, *Sources of the Self: The Making of Modern Identity* (Cambridge, MA: Harvard University Press, 1989), p. 230; Robert M. Kingdon, 'Calvinism and Resistance Theory, 1550–1580', in *The Cambridge History of Political Thought 1450–1700*, ed. J. H. Burns (Cambridge: Cambridge University Press, 1991), pp. 193–218; Dan Jacobson, *The Story of the Stories: The Chosen People and Its God* (New York: Harper & Row, 1982); Ernest W. Nicholson, *God and His People: Covenant and Theology in the Old Testament* (Oxford: Oxford University Press, 1986); Sacvan Bercovitch, *The Rites of Assent: Transformations in the Symbolic Construction of America* (New York: Routledge, 1993); J. C. D. Clark, *The Language of Liberty 1660–1832: Political Discourse and Social Dynamics in the Anglo-American World* (Cambridge: Cambridge University Press, 1994). Calvin is quoted in Adam Seligman, 'The Eucharist Sacrifice and the Changing Utopian Moment in Post-Reformation Christianity', in *Order and*

Transcendence: The Role of Utopias and the Dynamics of Civilizations, ed. A. Seligman (Leiden: Brill, 1989).

13 See Bernard Bailyn, *The Ideological Origins of the American Revolution* (Cambridge, MA: Harvard University Press, 1967); Pocock, *The Machiavellian Moment*, ch. 15.

14 NSC 68, 403. An outline of Kennan's Jeremiad can be found in my *Kennan and the Art of Foreign Policy* (Cambridge, MA: Harvard University Press, 1989), part III.

15 On 'goverment' and liberalism, see Michel Foucault, *Discipline and Punish* (New York: Vintage, 1979), pp. 89–90; Graham Burchell, C. Gordon, and Peter Miller, *The Foucault Effect: Studies in Governmentality* (Chicago, IL: 1991); and Carl Schmitt, *The Concept of the Political* (New Brunswick, NJ: Rutgers University Press, 1976). On FDR, see Daniel T. Rodgers, *Contested Truths: Keywords in American Politics Since Independence* (New York: Basic Books, 1987), pp. 214–15; Foner, *Freedom*, ch. 9.

16 Reginald Horsman, *Race and Manifest Destiny: The Origins of Racial Anglo-Saxonism* (Cambridge, MA: Harvard University Press, 1981); Garret Ward Sheldon, *The Political Philosophy of Thomas Jefferson* (Baltimore, MD: Johns Hopkins University Press, 1991), pp. 25–7. Jefferson, as Horsman says, *Race and Manifest Destiny* (21), believed in an 'ideal Anglo-Saxon England' featuring 'small political units' and 'an elective king, annual parliaments, a system of trial by jury, and land held in fee simple'. Where this vision eventually terminates can be gauged by the following view on Hawaii, expressed in the House of Representatives in 1898: 'Sir, the fittest will survive. Under the providence of God, Anglo-Celtic civilization is acomplishing the regeneration of the planet. Its progress dispels barbarism and establishes order, dethrones despotism and ushers in liberty. Nothing can stay the onward march of the indomitable race that founded this Republic – the race which sooner or later will place the imprint of its genius and the stamp of its conscience upon civilizations everywhere.' The 'Anglo-Celtic' here was connected explicitly to the overall 'conquest of the world by the Aryan races', 20 January 1898, Appendix to *Congressional Record, 55th Congress, 2nd Sess.* (Washington, DC: US GPO, 1898).

17 The quotations are from the Declaration of Independence.

18 'X' (George F. Kennan), 'The Sources of Soviet Conduct', *Foreign Affairs*, 25:4 (July 1947): 566–82 (quotation 582).

19 On Montesquieu, see Alain Grosrichard, *The Sultan's Court: European Fantasies of the East* (London: Verso, 1998) – Voltaire quoted on 31; and Springborg, *Western Republicanism and the Oriental Prince* (Cambridge: Polity Press, 1992). On the classical aristocratic critique of tyranny, see Hanna Fenichel Pitkin, 'Are Freedom and Liberty Twins?', *Political Theory*, 16:4 (1988): 523–52. Indeed, the aristocratic components (equality before the law, equal right to speak) in subsequent theories of equality are not appreciated enough. The key question in liberalism (as opposed to democracy) is then always who qualifies for such equality, who counts. On Rome, see Chaim Wirszubski, *Libertas as a Political Idea at Rome During the Late Republic and Early Principate* (Cambridge: Cambridge University Press, 1950) and Timothy J. Cornell, 'Rome: The History of an Anachronism', in *City States in Classical Antiquity and Medieval Italy*, eds Anthony Mahlo, Kurt Raaflaub, and Julia Emlen (Ann Arbor, MI: University of Michigan Press, 1991). On Greece, see Kurt A. Raaflaub, 'Democracy, Oligarchy, and the Concept of the "Free Citizen" in Late Fifth-Century Athens', *Political Theory*, 11:4 (1983): 517–44.

20 See Mladen Dolar's introduction to Grosrichard, *The Sultan's Court*. Fear is the central principle of despotism and it envelops even the ruler himself, as Montesquieu argues in *The Spirit of the Laws* (Cambridge: Cambridge University Press, 1989), see esp. Part I. Corruption is not only inescapable but turns in and

feeds on itself.

21 See Foucault, *Discipline and Punish*, pp. 89–90. I owe Saint-Just's apothegm to Michael Christofferson's dissertation 'The Anti-Totalitarian Moment in French Intellectual Politics, 1975–1984', New York: Columbia University, 1997. The peculiar effect of invoking such ethical principles tends to be the exit of ethics: 'Our free society, confronted by a threat to its basic values, naturally will take such action, including the use of military force, as may be required to protect those values. The integrity of our system will not be jeopardized by any measures, covert or overt, violent or non-violent, which serve the purposes of frustrating the Kremlin design, nor does the necessity for conducting ourselves so as to affirm our values in actions as well as words forbid such measures, provided only they are appropriately calculated to that end and are not so excessive or misdirected as to make us enemies of the people instead of the evil men who have enslaved them' (NSC 68, 392). This notorious formulation, ironically, was composed by John Paton Davies, soon to be exiled from the State Department and the country by McCarthyism.

22 William Pietz, 'The "Post-Colonialism" of Cold War Discourse', *Social Text*, 19/20, Fall 1988, 55–75, exaggerates this theme in arguing that the Western concept of totalitarianism in the post-war era essentially amounted to orientalism plus technology. He had more of a point, however, than my acid criticism of it in the same issue would indicate.

23 On the struggles of producing NSC 68, see David Callaghan, *Dangerous Capabilities: Paul Nitze and the Cold War* (New York: HarperCollins, 1990), ch. 4. The 'irreversibility' theme would of course reappear to good effect in Jeane Kirkpatrick's celebrated distinction in the 1970s between authoritarian and totalitarian governments.

24 Bohlen to Secretary of State, 9 October 1951, United States. Department of State. *Foreign Relations of the United States* [FRUS], 1951, vol. I, 181.

25 Bohlen to Nitze, 28 July 1951, ibid., 107. Bohlen lost out here because he accepted (he thought) the basic premises of NSC 68. He was always a better political operator than Kennan, by then departed. However, while aware that something was profoundly wrong, Bohlen did not possess the intellectual depth and stamina to challenge Nitze's onslaught.

26 Jefferson, quoted in Gordon S. Wood, *The Creation of the American Republic, 1776–1787* (Chapel Hill, NC: 1998 [1969]), p. 39; Roosevelt, fireside chat, 11 September 1941, *The Public Papers and Addresses of Franklin D. Roosevelt* (New York: Macmillan, 1942), vol. 10, p. 386. A month later, FDR indicated another Nazi design, referring to a secret map of five future vassal states in the Western hemisphere.

27 On designs and plots, see Wood, *The Creation*, pp. 39–42; David Brion Davis, *The Slave Power Conspiracy and the Paranoid Style* (Baton Rouge, LA: Louisiana State University Press, 1969); Thomas M. Brown, 'The Image of the Beast: Anti-Papal Rhetoric in Colonial America', in *Conspiracy: The Fear of Subversion in American History*, ed. Richard O. Curry and Thomas M. Brown (New York: Holt, 1972); 'David Brion Davis, 'Some Themes of Countersubversion: An Analysis of Anti-Masonic, Anti-Catholic, and Anti-Mormon Literature', in ibid.; Clark, *Language of Liberty*, p. 39; Michael Lienesch, *New Order of the Ages: Time, the Constitution, and the Making of Modern American Political Thought* (Princeton, NJ: Princeton University Press, 1988), p. 208.

28 Davis, *The Slave Power Conspiracy*; quotation Davis, 'Some Themes of Countersubversion', p. 67.

29 Davis, *The Slave Power Conspiracy*, 11, 56, *passim*; Carl Schurz, *The Speeches, Correspondence and Political Papers of Carl Schurz*, ed. Frederic Bancroft (New

York: Putnam's, 1913), vol. 1, pp. 130–3; Theodore Parker, *The Rights of Man in America* (Boston, MA: American Unitarian Association, n.d.), p. 367.

30 Arthur M. Schlesinger, Jr, 'The Causes of the Civil War', *Partisan Review*, 10, October 1949, 969–81, quotations 979, 980.

31 Franklin D. Roosevelt, *The Public Papers and Addresses of Franklin D. Roosevelt. 1940 Volume: War – and Aid to Democracies* (New York: Macmillan, 1941), vol. 9, p. xxx. On the genesis and various aspects of 'unconditional surrender', see Anne Armstrong, *Unconditional Surrender: The Impact of the Casablanca Policy on World War II* (New Brunswick, NJ: Rutgers University Press, 1961); Raymond G. O'Connor, *Diplomacy for Victory: FDR and Unconditional Surrender* (New York: Norton, 1971); Michael Balfour, 'The Origin of the Formula: "Unconditional Surrender" in World War II', *Armed Forces and Society*, 5:2 (1979): 281–301; Charles B. Strozier, 'Unconditional Surrender and the Rhetoric of Total War: From Truman to Lincoln', Occasional paper 2 (New York: Center on Violence and Human Survival, 1987).

32 Stimson quoted in the *New York Times*, 15 June 1940; Franklin D. Roosevelt, State of the Union Address, 6 January 1942, *The Public Papers and Addresses of Franklin D. Roosevelt* (New York: Macmillan, 1943), vol. XI, p. 42. The evidence for Lincoln's borrowing is circumstantial. In 1854, Parker gave a speech which highlighted the metaphor, and Lincoln read his speeches which were passed on by his law partner, one of Parker's correspondents. It was a deeply pessimistic speech: 'See the steady triumph of despotism! Ten years more, like ten years past, and it will be all over with the liberties of America. Everything must go down, and the heel of the tyrant will be on our neck.' Parker, *The Rights of Man in America*, pp. 390–1, 'House Divided' appears on p. 362. The Biblical location is Matthew 12:25: 'Every kingdom divided against itself is brought to desolation; and every city or house divided against itself shall not stand.' A little further on, Jesus says: 'He who is not with me is against me; and he that gathereth not with me scattereth abroad' (King James Bible, the one Lincoln and Parker will have read; see also Luke 11). On Parker, see Perry Miller, 'Theodore Parker: Apostasy Within Liberalism', in Miller, *Nature's Nation* (Cambridge, MA: Harvard University Press, 1967). On Lincoln, see Michael Burlingame, *The Inner World of Abraham Lincoln* (Urbana, IL: University of Illinois Press, 1994), ch. 2.

33 David Green, *Shaping Political Consciousness: The Language of Politics in America from McKinley to Reagan* (Ithaca, NY: Cornell University Press, 1987), ch. 5, Roosevelt quotation on p. 155; Rodgers, *Contested Truths*, p. 214; Foner, *Freedom*, ch. 11. Propagating the United States as the highest condensation of 'the free world' reached formidable expression in the Freedom Train that toured the United States and achieved a massive audience in the Fall of 1947, carrying on display, among other things, the Declaration of Independence and the Gettysburg Address. The proposal to include the Four Freedoms speech was declined.

34 Talking increasingly about fascism in the late 1930s, Roosevelt studiously avoided negative labels such as 'anti-fascist'. But he used the derogatory term with some historical license, dubbing, for instance, the regime of George III 'a fascist yoke'. Green, *Shaping Political Consciousness*, p. 146.

35 Schmitt, *The Concept of the Political*. Here, in part, lies the origin of Wilson's repressive side.

36 A similarly startling shift takes place with regard to 'Red China', a hideous phantom indeed throughout the 1960s but transformed in a few years to a land of idealistic barefoot doctors (and a quasi-ally). Such images have very little anchoring in any real social practices and are thus remarkably changeable.

37 A major difference, it should be said, between the moment of Kennan's erstwhile

attempt to break the Cold War impasse in 1948 and Nitze's call to arms in the spring of 1950 is the alarming advent of Soviet nuclear capability in 1949, the chief reason NSC 68 was generated in the first place.

38 Once the negativity inscribed in the posture (it was never conceived as 'doctrine') of containment was abandoned, so was the concept. Or, alternatively, one might say that it was reduced to a platitude, strategic considerations aside.

39 The identification of 'democracy' with 'free enterprise' and 'the market' is perhaps the most invidious index of this political atmosphere. The emergent debate about 'illiberal democracy' initiated by Fareed Zakaria has, if nothing else, the virtue of again rendering clear that there is no necessary connection between the one and the other. Eventually, perhaps, one will again be able to distinguish 'free enterprise' from 'freedom' and 'democracy'.

PART II:
HISTORY AND THEORY

5

Social Science, History, and the Cold War: Pushing the Conceptual Envelope

Richard Ned Lebow

[handwritten: – Examine questions asked – multiple causation – rank causes – counter-factuals – oral history needed]

East–West accommodation and collapse of the Soviet Union have prompted a reappraisal of the Cold War. This is a natural response to closure; the story line can be interpreted more confidently when the drama has run its course. Reevaluation has also been encouraged by a cornucopia of documents from the archives of former communist countries, and from China, that offer scholars insight into some of the most critical foreign policy decisions of the past 50 years.

The initial products of post-Cold War scholarship are diverse in their ambition and accomplishment. They run the gamut from focused monographs to thematic treatments based on case studies to sweeping efforts to put the entire Cold War into new perspective. Many of these works rely on new evidence, mostly written, but sometimes oral, and have already begun to reshape our thinking. My goal here is not to assess the substantive contribution of these works – they have been widely reviewed. Rather, I want to examine critically the process of historical reevaluation of the Cold War, identify some methodological pitfalls, and urge adoption of some conceptual tools, not commonly employed by Cold War historians, that could facilitate this enterprise.

Good research starts by identifying important questions or puzzles. I contend that Cold War history and international relations theory have been surprisingly unreflective about where their questions come from, and that this has led to some dead ends in both fields. The search for answers has been equally problematic. In Cold War history they most frequently take the form of single-case narratives that attribute key decisions or events to multiple causes. Failure to rank order these causes and explore the relationship between or among them can make such explanations difficult to refute and easy to confirm tautologically. Answers to questions require evidence, and I contend that Cold War history has been too narrowly based on the written record. Documentary evidence is obviously critical, but needs to be augmented – and often corrected – by oral history and interviews.

[handwritten: ✳ use oral history]

There is a widely held view that holds that historians practice narrative-based explanation, and that this is something very different from theory-based explanation.[1] This is a false distinction. Narratives are compatible with and generally rooted in theory, although that theory may not be articulated. Historian Edward Ingram observes: 'The historian's description is a form of analysis (it explains); likewise, narrative (which has nothing to do with chronology) is applied theory, an analytical test of a proposition; each presupposes the other and, without the other, neither can be carried out.'[2] According to political scientist Jack Levy the difference between political science and history 'is not in the use or non-use of theoretical concepts and models, but rather in how they use those concepts and in the importance they attach to being explicit about their analytic assumptions and models'.[3] Historians attempt to explain the particular, but, to do so, they must resort to the general. If even some historical narrative is theory driven, and implicitly employs theory to explain, then the historians who practice this form of narrative could benefit from a more self-conscious approach to method, especially with respect to the construction and evaluation of propositions.

A caveat is in order. Although I use some of the language and concepts of neo-positivism, I am not urging historians to become social scientists. My chapter is not intended – and I hope, is not read – as an exercise in disciplinary imperialism. Elsewhere, I have pleaded with international relations theorists to study the methods and findings of Cold War historians.[4] Learning in our scholarly neighborhood should be a two-way street.

Questions

Graduate education in the social sciences and history privileges explanation. Social science students are taught to build and test theories, and toward this end they study modeling, game theory, statistics, and other forms of data collection and analysis. History students are trained to make and evaluate interpretations. They learn languages and archival skills essential to using documents on which most historical interpretations are based. Graduate education provides students in these disciplines with many of the conceptual and research tools they need to answer research questions. But little, if any, emphasis is devoted to teaching students how to pose the questions that drive their research, or ascertain why they are interesting. The result is a haphazard research agenda where questions come and go in response to political agendas, intellectual fads, and the availability of data. Graduate students and assistant professors choose – or are often encouraged – to write about whatever is 'hot' in their field to increase their chances of getting a job or tenure.

In a highly constrained market, it is understandable that many graduate students and assistant professors follow the path of least resistance. It is more difficult to sympathize with senior colleagues whose research agendas, which have the potential to shape entire fields, are driven by questions whose value rests on unarticulated and unexamined assumptions. My own field of international relations paid a heavy price for this failing.

For international relations scholars in the 1980s, the preeminent problem in the security subfield was 'the long peace' between the super-powers. Specialists considered it remarkable that the superpowers had avoided war, unlike rival hegemons of the past. They were also impressed by the seeming durability of superpower spheres of influence. According to John Gaddis:

> The very fact that the interim arrangements of 1945 have remained largely intact for four decades would have astonished – and quite possibly appalled – the statesmen who cobbled them together in the hectic months that followed the surrender of Germany and Japan.[5]

The burning question in international political economy was the survival of the post-war international economic order despite the seeming decline of the United States, the hegemon that had created this order. Some political economists were surprised that neither Germany nor Japan had attempted to restructure international economic relations to suit their respective interests.[6] Both questions assumed that the robustness of the political and economic status quo was an extraordinary anomaly that required an equally extraordinary explanation.[7]

Attempts to explain the unexpected stability of the post-war political and economic order, and the controversy these explanations provoked, pushed the problem of change out of the pages of the principal journals and into the obscurity where it remained until the Berlin Wall was breached.[8] No major theory of international relations made change its principal focus. Even theories that incorporated some concept of change made no attempt to specify the conditions under which it would occur.[9] In the absence of theoretical interest in change, there was no debate about how or why the post-war order might evolve or be transformed. Scholars became correspondingly insensitive to the prospect that such change could occur.

In a deeper sense, my field's blindness was attributable to the political assumptions that shaped the world view and research agenda of leading scholars. The absence of superpower war seemed extraordinary because of the widely shared belief that the Soviet Union was an aggressive and expansionist adversary; for some, it was the linear descendant of Hitler's Germany. If Soviet leaders from Khrushchev on had been regarded as fundamentally satisfied with the status quo and concerned less with making gains than with avoiding losses – and there is much evidence to support this interpretation – the non-occurrence of World War III would not have required any extraordinary explanation.

Cold War critics were equally myopic. Those who considered the nuclear arms race and its escalatory potential to be the major source of tension in East–West relations directed their scholarly attention to the domestic and international causes of the arms race and the ways it might be halted or stabilized through arms control and security regimes. Once again, there was little recognition or study of the possibility that the underlying conflict might undergo – or indeed, had already undergone – a profound transformation.

The same bias affected the study of political economy. The reigning orthodoxy, imported from classical economics, assumes that states are rational and seek to maximize gain. If scholars had started from the premise that German and Japanese bankers and industrialists, like their counterparts elsewhere in the world's capitalist establishment, were anxious above all else to preserve order and predictability – especially in a system from which they profited so handsomely – they would not have viewed the survival of the post-war international economic framework as anomalous. Japanese and Western European efforts to preserve the system would have been judged simple common sense.

Theory is supposed to free scholars from their political, generational, and cultural biases. In social science, it often does the reverse. Worse still, it confers an aura of scientific legitimacy on subjective political beliefs and prejudices. Logical positivism and other unity of science approaches depict science as independent of the culture, life experiences, and personalities of scientists.[10] But the ideas that propel science to the next stage of inquiry rarely grow out of existing research. Thomas Kuhn and others have shown how revolutions in science are triggered by fundamental shifts in *gestalt* that identify new problems and new kinds of solutions to them.[11] To explain these *gestalt* shifts – in all scholarly enterprises – one must generally look beyond the lab and archive. Research agendas, especially in history and social science, reflect political, institutional, and personal agendas.[12] The 'new international history' is no exception.

The historiographies of World War I and the Cold War illustrate how ideology and current events drive scholarship. The Treaty of Versailles justified reparations by holding Germany responsible for war in 1914. The German government signed the Treaty, but categorically denied its responsibility for the war, and published a selective and carefully edited collection of documents to buttress its claim of innocence. Diplomatic history in the 1920s and 1930s was dominated by the *Kriegschuldfrage*. Predictably, works that upheld the allied position provoked an equal and opposite reaction: revisionist scholarship that shifted the mantle of blame on to the shoulders of Russia, France, and Britain, and attempted to undercut the justification for reparations. Decades later, the Berlin and Cuban Missile Crises revived interest in World War I. Concern that World War III might arise from miscalculation, accidents, loss of control, or runaway escalation led historians and political scientists to mine the crisis of 1914 for contemporary policy lessons. Around the same time, historians began to reexamine the deeper causes and meaning of World War I, its links to World War II, and implications for developments elsewhere in the world.[13] This process has accelerated since the end of the Cold War.[14]

The historiography of the Cold War underwent a parallel evolution. In the 1950s and 1960s, scholarship focused on the question of Cold War 'guilt'. Conservatives and Cold War liberals blamed Stalin, communism, and the Soviet Union. Revisionist scholarship, which began in the 1950s, but really flourished a decade later in response to the Vietnam War, held capitalism and the United States responsible for the Cold War. The collapse of the Soviet Union, and the access this permitted to hitherto unavailable documents, have led some anti-Stalinists in the West to claim victory. By the 1970s, the question of who started the Cold War had become largely *passé*. In response to détente, students of the Cold War shifted their attention to the questions of how a war-threatening conflict was gradually transformed into a more stable rivalry. Now that the Cold War is over, historians will presumably begin to examine the broader meaning of the Cold War, and to do so with an eye on the issues of the moment. A case in point is Paul Schroder's recent work, that uses the concept of the *longue durée* to analyze World Wars I and II and the Cold War as a part of an iterative cycle of the creation, entrenchment, decline, collapse, and reconstitution of legitimate international orders.[15]

Research on World War I and the Cold War shifted in response to contemporary political developments. Scholars looked to the past for guidance about the present. The answers they found reflected their political views and starting assumptions. Neo-positivism and the 'new international history' are naïve in their belief that anything else is possible. Process, not motive, distinguishes good from bad scholarship.

Process begins with identification of an important question or puzzle. These arise when we encounter behavior at odds with our expectations. Expectations are always theory-driven; they are based on underlying beliefs about how the world works. Sometimes these beliefs are well specified, but more often they are unspoken. When we observe a business buy dear and sell cheap, or a state attack a more powerful neighbor, we consider the behavior anomalous because it appears to violate well-established principles of economics and international relations. If we dismiss the actors as ill-informed, incompetent or crazy, the puzzle disappears, although it may give rise to the secondary one of how such people could have achieved positions of authority. To make 'sense' of seemingly anomalous behavior, that is, to square it with accepted principles without relaxing the assumption of rationality, we look for other, situation-specific considerations that may have dictated choice and can ultimately be reconciled with the principles. A business may sell for a loss if there is a glut on the market or its managers expect prices to experience a precipitous decline. A weak state may attack a strong one if its military has a strategy and tactics they expect to negate the adversary's putative advantages.

There is another possible explanation for anomalous behavior: there may be something wrong with the beliefs or principles that make it appear anomalous. These beliefs or principles may rest on inappropriate assumptions, ignore more important determinants of behavior, or have unspecified (or improperly specified) scope conditions. The debate about the end of the Cold War is at its core a controversy about the validity of the principles that shaped Western understanding of the Soviet Union and its foreign policy. Conservatives, including some Realists, insist that the end of the Cold War validated their principles; the Soviet Union's decline compelled Gorbachev to seek accommodation with the West on unfavorable terms. Other Realists contend that their principles are valid, but that the outcome was anomalous because Gorbachev made serious miscalculations. Critics of Realism have used the end of the Cold War to argue that structure is indeterminate, and that the policy choices are significantly shaped by ideas, domestic politics, and the preferences of leaders.[16]

Scholars must always remain open to the possibility that there is something wrong with their premises. They need to make explicit the underlying assumptions that guide their research, and ask themselves what kinds of evidence would lead them to question these assumptions. Self-awareness and self-questioning are the most difficult and most neglected parts of good process, and, as the following section will argue, two of the most essential.

False confirmation

Historical debates are most productive when they focus scholarly attention on underlying assumptions and principles. It often takes strikingly anomalous behavior, as in the case of Gorbachev, to spark such a debate. This is because of the natural cognitive tendency to assimilate information, even when it is disconfirming, to existing beliefs, principles or theories.[17] Motivated bias can reinforce this tendency.[18] Scholars who have built careers on particular interpretations are generally reluctant to recognize problems with those interpretations. When beliefs reflect strong, emotional needs to maintain a particular construction of reality, they can be altogether impervious to discrepant information. The deterrence debate – for many years, a non-debate – gives ample testimony to how cognitive and motivational biases can be reinforcing.

Modern deterrence theory developed in response to the recognition that nuclear wars were too destructive to be rational instruments of war, but their very destructiveness might be exploited to prevent war. The classic formulation of this paradox is found in Bernard Brodie's 1946 study, *The Absolute Weapon*.[19] In the 'golden age' of deterrence theory, the 1950s and 1960s, Bernard Brodie, William Kaufmann, and Thomas Schelling developed formal models of nuclear deterrence. They argued that it could be rational to threaten an irrational act, and explored ways in which deterrent and compellent threats of nuclear annihilation might be made credible.[20]

Deterrence theory gained widespread acceptance in academe and government for intellectual, political, and psychological reasons. Its elegance and simplicity appeared to offer scholars a powerful and widely applicable instrument to analyze and predict strategic behavior. For policymakers, it held out the prospect of exploiting an unusable weapon to achieve political goals. On a deeper level, deterrence was a psychological bulwark against nuclear war. If nuclear war could only come about, as deterrence theory maintained, because an adversary believed that its enemy could not retaliate in kind, war could be prevented by possession of a secure second strike capability.[21]

Deterrence was confirmed tautologically. The United States buttressed its commitments in Berlin (1948–49, 1958–69, 1961), the Taiwan Straits (1954, 1958) and other parts of the world when they appeared threatened by the Soviet Union or China. When no military challenge occurred, politicians and analysts attributed communist restraint to American deterrence. When deterrence failed – the most notable example is the Soviet attempt to deploy strategic missiles in Cuba in 1962 – it was also explained in terms of deterrence theory. Kennedy administration officials and scholars assumed that Khrushchev challenged the United States because of the President's youth; lackluster performance at the Bay of Pigs, Berlin and Vienna Summit had given him good grounds to question American resolve. They attributed Khrushchev's withdrawal of the missiles to Kennedy's credible display of military capability and resolve to use force, if necessary, to take the missiles out.[22] Deterrence was also given credit for the overall absence of nuclear war and the end of the Cold War. The conventional wisdom holds that Gorbachev sought an accommodation because the Soviet Union could no longer compete economically or militarily with the United States.

Recent evidence from Soviet and Chinese archives offers little support for any of these interpretations. In the Taiwan Straits crisis, the Chinese government's goal was to deter Taiwan and the United States from using force against the Chinese mainland.[23] Khrushchev sent missiles to Cuba, not to force a trade-off in Berlin as the Kennedy administration surmised, but to protect Castro from an expected American invasion, offset US strategic superiority, and to get even with the President for deploying Jupiter missiles in Turkey. Kennedy had viewed these measures as prudent, defensive precautions against perceived Soviet threats. His actions had the

unanticipated consequence of convincing Khrushchev of the need to protect the Soviet Union and Cuba from US military and political challenges.
Khrushchev withdrew the missiles to avoid war, but also because of
Kennedy's public promise not to invade Cuba and his secret promise to
withdraw the American missiles in Turkey after a decent interval.[24]

The ultimate irony of nuclear deterrence may be the way in which the
strategy of deterrence undercut much of the political stability the reality
of deterrence should have created. The arms buildups, threatening military
deployments, and the confrontational rhetoric that characterized the
strategy of deterrence effectively obscured deep-seated, mutual fears of
war. Fear of nuclear war made leaders inwardly cautious, but their public
posturing convinced their adversaries that they were aggressive, risk-prone,
and even irrational. In Cuba, we now know, deterrence provoked the kind
of behavior it was designed to prevent.[25]

The intellectual history of deterrence highlights the disturbing ease with
which beliefs can become entrenched, and subsequent information
assimilated to them so the beliefs are confirmed tautologically and increase
their hold over the scholarly and public mind. Even dramatically disconfirming events – this is how I read the Cuban missile deployment and
Gorbachev foreign policy revolution – can be explained away by true
believers. Change, to the extent it occurs, is more likely to be generational;
younger scholars, responding to novel political situations and intellectual
currents, adopt new points of view. This is a slow and inefficient process.
In the twentieth century it has also had disastrous political consequences.
The hardline deterrence strategy that characterized the American
approach to the Soviet Union throughout most of the Cold War was a
response to the failure of appeasement in the 1930s. Appeasement in turn
was a reaction to the more confrontational policies that were believed to
have led to World War I. In each conflict, statesmen and generals prepared
to prevent or fight the previous war.

Overdetermination

The late Sir Isaiah Berlin popularized the Greek poet Archilochus's
distinction between hedgehogs and foxes.[26] Hedgehogs know one big thing,
know it very well, and succeed by invoking it repeatedly. Foxes know many
things, are inventive, and tailor their strategies to circumstances. Social
scientists are more likely to be hedgehogs. Like deterrence theorists, they
look for parsimonious explanations for seemingly complex events and
assume that those explanations, and any strategies based on them, will
be applicable in a wide range of situations. Historians are more likely to
be foxes. They tend to treat every historical situation as unique, and are
likely to propose varied and layered explanations on the assumption that

complex events have complex causes. Reality, in the words of Melvyn Leffler, 'is too complex to be captured by a single theory'.[27] This approach has dangers of its own.

Multiple causation can take two forms. The first, known as over-determination, occurs when several causes are present, any one of which could have produced the observed outcome. The second is when the combined effects of two or more causes are necessary to bring about the outcome. Historians, like their social scientist colleagues, need to specify which use of multiple causation they intend. Historical treatments of the Cold War sometimes fail to do this.

John Gaddis's writings illustrate this problem. In *The Long Peace*, he accepts Kenneth Waltz's contention that bipolarity was the principal structural cause of peace, and, Gaddis adds, for the unexpected stability of the post-war division of Europe.[28] It was an easy structure to maintain, encouraged stable alliances, and reduced the importance of individual defections from either alliance system. But Gaddis also contends that 'what has really made the difference in inducing unaccustomed caution' was nuclear deterrence. He then offers a third cause of peace: the 'rules' the superpowers evolved to regulate their competition. These rules included respect for each other's sphere of influence, a commitment to avoid direct military confrontation and to use nuclear weapons only as an ultimate resort.

Waltz distinguished between 'peace' (the absence of superpower war) and 'stability' (the endurance of the bipolar system). Gaddis elides the two concepts, ruling out the possibility – which came to pass a few years after publication of his book – that a bipolar system could be transformed without a war between its poles. Gaddis fails to tell us whether any or all of his structural and behavioral causes of peace are necessary and sufficient. Could peace have been preserved by any one of them? If not, which was (or were) the most important? And what about the relationship between these several causes? Surely, bipolarity and nuclear weapons were not unrelated; the latter helped to establish the former. Many Realists would probably argue that the rules of the road Gaddis finds so important were a response to bipolarity or nuclear weapons.

Gaddis's most recent book, *We Now Know: Rethinking Cold War History*, has the same problem.[29] He attributes the Cold War to Stalin's personality and ideology. Gaddis has no doubts about it; Stalin sought a Cold War the way 'a fish seeks water'. Stalin also sought to extend Soviet territory and territorial control for security reasons. In Eastern Europe, where this control was ensured through military occupation and the imposition of Soviet-style, puppet governments, Stalin's policy posed a direct challenge to Britain and the United States. But what *really* made the Cold War inevitable, Gaddis argues, was the coercive and crude way in which Stalin pursued his goals. Churchill, Attlee, Roosevelt, and Truman had to defend their policies to voters, and Stalin's failure to conform to the outward forms of democracy (plebiscites, elections, indirect rule through dependent but popularly elected governments) to mask the extension of Soviet power made it unacceptable to British and American leaders.

Following Norman Naimark, Gaddis argues that Stalin's reliance on coercion and brutality was a reflection of the political-economic limitations of the Soviet system.[30] This was most evident in the occupation of Germany, where rape and pillage were unconstrained, and whole factories, rolling stock, equipment, and scientific personnel were forcibly removed to the Soviet Union. The United States was able to exercise influence in more subtle and effective ways, and worked collaboratively with elected governments. Washington also won the support of Western Europeans by providing extensive economic aid and credits for reconstruction. The asymmetry in political, administrative and economic resources between the superpowers accounted 'more than anything else, for the origins, escalation and ultimate outcome of the Cold War'.

Gaddis also maintains that Stalin's foreign policy was a direct extension of his domestic policy, and the overriding goal of both was to intimidate or, better yet, eliminate, potential challengers. Cooperation, other than for purely tactical reasons, was alien to his nature. This leaves the door open to the possibility that another Soviet leader would have pursued a different policy in Eastern Europe and the Far East. But elsewhere Gaddis slams this door shut with his insistence that Stalin, and other officials, like Molotov, were prisoners of Marxist ideology. They believed that sooner or later – perhaps in as little as fifteen years – there would be another crisis of capitalism that would compel the leading capitalist powers to go to war to deflect domestic unrest. The United States would unleash a rearmed Germany against the Soviet Union. For protection, Soviet forces needed to control Germany and extend their defensive *glacis* as far West as possible.

There is an unresolved ambiguity in Gaddis about the Cold War and Stalin's relation to it. The regime, personality, and ideological explanations for the Cold War point to an underlying defensive motivation: the need to expand and assert control to save Stalin and the Soviet Union. But Gaddis also advances a more offensive explanation. Stalin wanted to dominate Europe, and ultimately the world, but, unlike Hitler, he 'was patient, [and] prepared to take as long as necessary to achieve his ambitions'. But in Asia, he threw caution to the wind, succumbed to 'ideological euphoria', and allowed Kim Il-Sung to talk him into an invasion of South Korea. Some of these explanations are contradictory, others are related (but that relationship is left undefined), others may be epiphenomenal (i.e. caused by others), and still others conflate cause and effect. Historians who offer multilayered explanations need to identify what kind of multiple causation they mean (Gaddis uses both interchangeably), distinguish *between* competing causes (offensive vs defensive goals, and personality vs ideology in the case of Gaddis), and rank order those that could be reinforcing (for Gaddis, regime capabilities, ideology, and personality). They also need to describe whatever relationships exist between or among these causes. Failure to do this makes the overall argument impossible to sustain or falsify.

Counterfactual argument

Some prominent historians have dismissed counterfactual thought experiments as idle parlor games.[31] Counterfactual assumptions nevertheless lie at the core of all historical inference.[32] Implicit in every historical interpretation is the counterfactual that the outcome would *not* have occurred in the absence of the stated cause(s). If the Cold War was Stalin's fault, it follows that it would not have happened if a different leader had occupied the Kremlin – unless that leader had wanted that conflict for reasons of his own. Counterfactuals of this kind most often go unexamined. In the Soviet case, one counterfactual has received considerable attention: would communism have evolved differently if Lenin had lived longer, or if he had been succeeded by someone other than Stalin?[33] While this question is unanswerable, attempts to address it have usefully focused attention on the underlying political assumptions that guide and sustain different arguments about the role of Stalin and the nature of the Soviet system, and, in doing so, have encouraged a more sophisticated historical debate.

Counterfactual thought experiments have an important role to play in Cold War scholarship. As noted above, they are a useful device for prodding historians and political scientists to make explicit the assumptions that guide their analysis and interpretations. They are also a useful tool to help formulate and specify. John Gaddis alleges that Stalin was responsible for the Cold War. If Professor Gaddis had asked himself whether there still would have been a Cold War in the absence of Stalin, he would have been forced to decide whether Stalin was a necessary and sufficient condition for that conflict. Removing Stalin from the scene would also have encouraged Gaddis to consider what else about the Soviet Union would have been different. Would foreign policy, for example, still have been subordinate to domestic policy, or subordinate in the same way? Counterfactual thought experiments of this kind could have helped Gaddis to order his explanations and the many links among them.

Counterfactual thought experiments are useful in attacking other explanations. Because every argument has its related counterfactual, critics have two strategies open to them: they can try to offer a different and more compelling account, or try to show that the outcome in question would still have occurred in the absence of the claimed cause(s). John Mueller's account of the Cold War is a nice example of the second strategy. In contrast to the conventional wisdom that attributed the 'long peace' between the superpowers to nuclear deterrence, he argues that Moscow and Washington were restrained by their general satisfaction with the status quo, and secondarily, by memories of World War II and the human, economic, and social costs of large-scale, conventional warfare. The unheralded destructiveness of nuclear weapons was redundant, and possibly counterproductive.[34]

Because historians typically study single cases, history confronts what social scientists call the 'small-n problem'. Single case studies can always be challenged as unrepresentative of the phenomenon in question. Validation is especially difficult when outcomes are attributed to multiple causes. Historians typically attempt to establish causation by process tracing. They try to document the links between a stated cause and an outcome. This works best at the individual level of analysis, but only when there is enough evidence to document the calculations, and the motives behind them, of relevant actors. Even when such evidence is available, it may not permit historians to determine the relative weight of the several causes alleged to be at work, and which, if any, might have produced the outcome in the absence of the others.

Historians who focus on the behavior of actors generally want to understand it in a broader, political, economic, or social context. They often posit underlying explanations for their behavior or for the frames of reference they used to identify problems and appropriate responses to them. Gaddis, as we have noted, believes bipolarity, nuclear deterrence, and the division of Europe were underlying causes of superpower restraint. The evidence for these or any other set of deeper causes is usually circumstantial; documents rarely show the extent to which they were responsible for the behavior in question. When the actor is a group, elite, bureaucracy, or mass movement, the influence of ideas, structures, and institutions are that much harder to track.

To sustain causal inference it is generally necessary to engage in comparative analysis. Within the single-case format – the most common kind of historical scholarship – comparative analysis can take two forms: intra-case comparison and counterfactual analysis. Intra-case comparison breaks down a case into a series of similar interactions that are treated as separate and independent cases for purposes of analysis. Numerous studies of arms control and superpower crises have made use of this technique.[35] Like any form of comparative analysis, intra-case comparisons try to show as much variation as possible on dependent (what is to be explained) and independent (the *expalans*) variables. This is sometimes more difficult to do than in cross-case comparisons. It is also more difficult to establish the independence of cases, as the process and outcome of each case is more likely to influence policy in the next case than it would in cases involving different policymaking elites in different countries. But intra-case comparison confers a singular benefit: it builds variation within a fundamentally similar political and cultural context, controlling better than intercase comparison for many factors that may be important but unrecognized.

Counterfactual analysis introduces variation through thought experiments that add or subtract contextual factors or possible causes, and ask how this would have influenced the outcome.[36] Thought experiments allow researchers to build in the kinds of controls normally achieved only in a laboratory. They suffer from the obvious drawback that it is generally impossible to know with any certainty the consequences of variation introduced by the experimenter. This uncertainty increases dramatically when the experimenter considers second- and third-level consequences of the counterfactual. Suppose we postulate that Archduke Franz Ferdinand was not assassinated in June 1914. This counterfactual involves a minimal rewrite of history; if the carriage carrying the Archduke and his wife had not made a wrong turn, Prinzip would not have had a second opportunity to toss his bomb. Deprived of the pretense provided by the assassination, it seems highly unlikely that Austria-Hungary would have presented Serbia with an ultimatum and have gone to war when it was rejected. World War I would have been averted, at least temporarily. What would have happened next is very hard to say.

The speculative nature of counterfactual thought experiments makes many historians wary of them. But counterfactual analysis does not always have to be as speculative as the possible, longer-term consequences of the survival of Archduke Franz Ferdinand. Deterrence offers a nice counterexample. One of the principal policy 'lessons' of the 1930s is that appeasement whets the appetites of dictators whereas military capability and resolve is likely to restrain them. The failure of appeasement in the 1930s is readily apparent, but the putative efficacy of deterrence rests on the counterfactual that Hitler could have been restrained by France and Britain if they had credibly demonstrated willingness to go to war in defense of the status quo. German documents make this possibility an eminently researchable question, and historians have used these documents to try to determine at what point Hitler was no longer deterrable.[37] Their findings have important implications for any assessment of French and British policy and the broader claims made for deterrence.

The Cuban Missile Crisis is another evidence-rich environment in which to study counterfactuals. Key policy choices, for example, Khrushchev's decision to send and remove missiles from Cuba, and Kennedy's decision to impose a blockade – and subsequent scholarly analyses – were both contingent upon hypothetical antecedents. Kennedy believed, incorrectly, that Khrushchev sent missiles because he doubted his resolve, and would not have sent them if he had taken a stronger stand at the Bay of Pigs and in Berlin. He reasoned that he had to prevent the installation of the missiles to convince Khrushchev of his resolve and deter a subsequent and more serious challenge to Berlin. Such counterfactuals are revealing in and of themselves; they indicate the underlying assumptions about international relations and adversarial goals that policymakers and scholars brought to the crisis. Recent evidence, written and oral, from Soviet and American archives and former officials, makes it possible to explore the validity of many of these counterfactuals.[38]

Even when counterfactuals are speculative, the difference between them and 'normal' history is a matter of degree, not of kind. Documents are rarely 'smoking guns' that allow researchers to establish motives or causes beyond a reasonable doubt. Historical argument is usually built on a chain of inference that uses documents or other empirical evidence as anchor points. Other historians evaluate these arguments on the quality and relevance of the evidence, the logic and propriety of the inferences based on it, and the extent to which that evidence permits or constrains alternative interpretations. Evaluation will also be influenced by the appeal of the underlying, and generally unstated, political and behavioral 'principles' in which the inferences are rooted.

Counterfactual thought experiments are fundamentally similar to historical reconstruction. Suppose we attempted to evaluate the importance of Mikhail Gorbachev for the end of the Cold War by considering the likely consequences for Soviet foreign policy of Andropov's survival or Chernenko's replacement by someone other than Gorbachev.[39] To do this, we would have to study the career and policies of Andropov or an alternative successor to Chernenko (Grishin, Romanov, Ligachev?), and infer their policies on the basis of their past preferences and commitments, the political environment in 1986, and the general domestic and foreign situation of the Soviet Union. There is a lot of documentary evidence relevant to all three questions, evidence that sustains informed arguments about the kind of foreign policies any of these leaders might have pursued. Of course, random events, like Mathias Rust's Cessna flight to Red Square, can have significant influence on policy, and these events, by definition, cannot be predicted. In the final analysis, counterfactual arguments, like any other historical argument, are only as compelling as the logic and 'evidence' offered by the researcher to substantiate the link between the proposed alteration of history and its expected consequence.[40]

Oral evidence

Because many important Chinese and Soviet documents still remain classified, Western students of Soviet foreign policy are often forced to rely on the oral testimony of former officials to reconstruct critical decisions. Some scholars question the value of history constructed on the basis of what they describe as hearsay. Others contend that oral history is a poor

[handwritten: Oral evidence; what's lacking in written sources]

substitute for written sources and contemporary documents.[41] Oral history is rarely intended as a substitute for documents, but rather as a supplement to them. Discussion with former officials can help identify the existence of new documents that may prove critical. It can put existing documents in an appropriate context. Historical accounts based solely on written documents can be as incomplete and misleading as accounts derived entirely from interviews.

In the last decade, thousands of documents pertinent to the Cuban Missile Crisis have been declassified. On the American side, some of these documents, especially the transcripts of the secret Ex Comm tapes, are of enormous importance. These documents do not reveal that behind the back of his Ex Comm, President Kennedy engaged in back channel negotiations with Khrushchev, made a secret concession on the Jupiter missiles in Turkey, and was willing to make a further concession if it was necessary to resolve the crisis. All of this information comes from revelations of former Kennedy administration officials. As they tell it, President Kennedy struggled to find the political room to reconcile the competing demands of foreign and domestic policy. He consequently kept some of his actions and decisions secret not only from the public but from many top government officials. He deliberately misled some of his most trusted officials and advisers like Dean Rusk to protect them and himself from subsequent Congressional inquiries. A history of American policy in the crisis based solely on documents would be very misleading.[42]

The same is true on the Soviet side. The most recent account of Soviet policy in the crisis, by Fursenko and Naftali, makes the most extensive use of Soviet documents. Those documents say nothing directly about Khrushchev's motives for sending missiles to Cuba or his reasons for removing them. Nor do they shed new light on other key Khrushchev crisis initiatives, including the second, Saturday message that so baffled the President and his Ex Comm.[43] Khrushchev's motives, like Kennedy's, need to be inferred from the context, and his off-the-record comments to close advisers and others.

Is the missile crisis unique? I think not. Extraordinary secrecy also surrounded the Bay of Pigs invasion. Within the CIA, the Deputy Director of Intelligence and his directorate were not informed of the operation.[44] Secretary of State Dean Rusk remembers that he was not allowed to consult the Department's Bureau of Intelligence and Research, and that they almost certainly would have provided him with a critical evaluation. He was also prohibited from discussing the operation with senior officials at the State Department. This secrecy, Rusk insists, 'made it very difficult for historians to reconstruct the Bay of Pigs operation, particularly its planning, because very little was put on paper. Dulles, Bissell, and others proposing the operation briefed us orally.' The written records do not include the substance of these conversations.[45]

[handwritten right margin: ex: Cuban Missile Crisis]

American policy during the 1973 Middle East war provides another example. None of the imperatives for secrecy at work in Cuba or the Bay of Pigs was present in this case. Even so, the documents, when released, will be misleading. Henry Kissinger frequently had different versions of documents prepared for different audiences and rarely put anything on record from his extensive back channel discussions. Future scholars, Kissinger noted, will have 'no criteria for determining which documents were produced to provide an alibi and which genuinely guided decisions'.[46] The documentary record is not only misleading but incomplete. As in the missile crisis, the most important decisions grew out of informal conversations among officials that were not recorded.

We must remain wary of interpretations of Cold War decisions and policies based largely, or entirely, on the written record. Archival research must be augmented by oral history. Interviews with former officials can help put documents in context, glean insights into the motives of actors and ferret out secret understandings. In this connection, conferences that bring diverse policymakers together and encourage interaction among them are especially helpful. Experience indicates that these conferences are most likely to be productive when discussion is guided by relevant documents, made available beforehand to all the participants. The documents can be used to refresh the memories of the participants and focus their attention on interpretative controversies or empirical lacunae surrounding critical decisions.

History and social science

My arguments have borrowed heavily from neo-positivist epistemology. I have not spoken of prediction – the holy grail of neo-positivism – because I think predictive theories are impossible in international relations and most other domains of social inquiry. I have assumed that explanation – identification of the causal mechanisms responsible for given outcomes – is a more realistic goal, and one to which many historians aspire. Studies of the Cold War that seek to explain its origins, dynamics, evolution, termination, or relationship to other conflicts, indicate this commitment. Many of these studies reflect a 'soft' positivist epistemology, and can accordingly be evaluated in terms of neo-positivist protocols for hypothesis construction and testing.

Positivism, in its 'hard' and 'soft' formulations, is rooted in an ontology that assumes that reality has an objective existence that is outside and independent of the language and conceptual categories used to describe and analyze it. This assumption, and positivism more generally, has come under increasing attack in the social sciences. The principal alternative in international relations theory, 'Constructivism', is very much in the interpretivist tradition. Like other interpretivist approaches, it assumes that reason and irrationality are constitutive of actors and the societies in which they are embedded. Constructivists emphasize the inter-subjective understandings actors have of themselves, other actors, and their relationships with these actors. Constructivist research suggests that categories of analysis used by international relations scholars often bear little relationship to the categories actors themselves use to frame problems, evaluate their interests, make policy, and draw lessons.[47]

For interpretivists, empathetic understanding from inside (*Verstehen*) not explanation (*Erklären*) is the goal of scholarly inquiry. The purpose of scholarship is to help us understand our lives, individually and collectively. History is a repository of human experience that each generation examines anew from the perspective of its own experience and concerns. There is no one correct way of framing or analyzing a problem, but multiple interpretations that generate different and often equally valuable insights. Interpretivist scholarship also aspires to high professional standards. It can be evaluated by the quality of its narrative. Does it provide a coherent explanation that makes sense of the empirical evidence in terms of the subjective understandings relevant actors have of this evidence, of themselves, and of the social context in which they operate? Other accounts may also 'fit' the evidence, and competing accounts should be evaluated on the basis of their 'generative' properties. Do they highlight and draw attention to hitherto unknown or neglected processes, turning points, and collective understandings that raise interesting questions and prompt research into them? A research agenda may succeed in redefining in fundamental ways our conception of the Cold War.

Neo-positivist and interpretivist epistemologies are both relevant to the study of the Cold War. On the whole, neo-positivism is most appropriate to the 'smaller' questions, by which I mean those internal to the phenomenon under study. In the case of the Cold War, this would include its origins, dynamics, and outcome. Historical analyses of such questions typically aim at 'explanation', and mobilize evidence to document and justify their arguments. At least implicitly, their authors acknowledge that their arguments can be rejected if better and contradictory evidence emerges or if more persuasive interpretations are put forward. Theoretical work in international relations on these questions has been overwhelmingly neo-positivist in orientation, although there is a growing corpus of interpretivist research that examines such questions as the emergence of norms of non-use of chemical, biological, and nuclear weapons, the roots of Gorbachev's foreign-policy revolution, and the transformation of the conflictual Soviet–American relationship into a more cooperative Russo-American one.[48]

The interpretivist perspective is most appropriate to 'bigger' questions that attempt to understand a phenomenon in a broader, external context.

Such interpretations also rely on evidence, but do not rely on it to persuade. It is more often used to illustrate the value of a particular frame of reference for providing insights and understanding. In history, the interpretative research has always been common, and, presumably, more interpretative studies of the Cold War will now appear as that phenomenon has itself become history.

The ongoing epistemological debate in international relations theory has important implications for the relationship between international relations and history. For most of the Cold War, the international relations literature was Realist and neo-positivist, while Cold War history ran the gamut from interpretivist to neo-positivist. These epistemological differences made dialogue difficult; the only real conversations were between realists in both disciplines, and between diplomatic historians and the small community of interpretivist political scientists who used primary historical sources to reconstruct events from the perspectives of the actors involved. Jack Levy argues that the prospect for dialogue is diminishing because of the 'revival of narrative' and the 'linguistic turn' in history, and the further spread of quantitative methods and game theory in international relations.[49] This is an unduly pessimistic view. If interpretivism makes more headway in political science, and if historians become self-conscious and sophisticated in their research strategies, we might move closer together and transcend our disciplinary Cold War.

NOTES

1 See, for example, Edgar Kiser and Michael Hechter, 'The Role of General Theory in Comparative-Historical Sociology', *American Journal of Sociology*, 97 (July 1991): 2; John Lewis Gaddis, 'Expanding the Data Base: Historians, Political Scientists and the Enrichment of Security Studies', *International Security*, 12 (Summer 1987): 3–21.

2 Colin Elman and Miriam Fendius Elman, 'Diplomatic History and International Relations Theory: Respecting Difference and Crossing Boundaries', *International Security*, 22 (Summer 1997): 5–21; Edward Ingram, 'The Wonderland of the Political Scientist', *International Security*, 22 (Summer 1997): 53–63, quote on p. 53.

3 Jack S. Levy, 'Too Important to Leave to the Other: History and Political Science in the Study of International Relations', *International Security*, 22 (Summer 1997): 22–33, quote on p. 25.

4 Richard Ned Lebow, 'The Cold War in Comparative Perspective', forthcoming in Thomas Biersteker, Richard Herrmann, and Richard Ned Lebow, eds, *How the Cold War Ended*.

5 John Lewis Gaddis, *The Long Peace: Inquiries Into the History of the Cold War Era* (New York: Oxford University Press, 1987), p. 218.

6 See Charles Kindleberger, *The World in Depression, 1929–1939* (Berkeley, CA: University of California Press, 1973); Robert Gilpin, *War and Change in World Politics* (Cambridge: Cambridge University Press, 1981). For critical discussions

and alternative explanations, see Robert Keohane, *After Hegemony* (Princeton, NJ: Princeton University Press, 1984), and *International Institutions and State Power* (Boulder, CO: Westview, 1989); Duncan Snidal, 'The Limits of Hegemonic Stability Theory', *International Organization*, 39 (Autumn 1985): 579–614; Volker Rittberger, ed., *The Study of Regimes in International Relations* (New York: Oxford University Press, forthcoming).

7 The focus of Realism is great power relations. In describing the post-war political order as stable, Realists are referring to the stability of Europe, and the *de facto*, and later *de jure* acceptance of its division by East and West. The post-war political 'order' in other regions of the world could hardly be called stable.

8 A literature search reveals that between 1970 and 1990, *International Organization*, *World Politics* and *International Studies Quarterly* published no more than a half-dozen articles whose primary focus was major foreign policy or systemic change.

9 An exception is Gilpin, *War and Change in World Politics*. This point is also made by John Gerard Ruggie, 'Continuity and Transformation in the World Polity: Toward a Neorealist Synthesis', Robert O. Keohane, 'Theory of World Politics: Structural Realism and Beyond', and Robert W. Cox, 'Social Forces, States and World Orders: Beyond International Relations Theory', in Robert O. Keohane, ed., *Neorealism and Its Critics* (New York: Columbia University Press, 1986), pp. 148–9, 179–81, 197–8, 243–5. For a critique of cognitive psychology's failure to deal adequately with change, see Richard Ned Lebow and Janice Gross Stein, 'Afghanistan, Carter and Foreign Policy Change: The Limits of Cognitive Models', in Dan Caldwell and Timothy J. McKeown, *Diplomacy, Force, and Leadership: Essays in Honor of Alexander L. George* (Boulder, CO: Westview, 1993), pp. 95–128.

10 'Unity of science' approaches that see no differences between the goals and proper practices of the social and physical sciences. Logical positivism has for many years been associated with this position, but other approaches, among them positivism, empiricism, subscribe to it as well. There is a lot of confusion in political science, where practitioners routinely use the term logical positivism to refer to all of these approaches. On this subject, see Friedrich Kratochwil, 'Why Sisyphus is Happy: Reflections on the "Third Debate" and on Theorizing as a Vocation', *Sejong Review*, 3 (November 1995): 3–36.

11 Thomas S. Kuhn, *The Structure of Scientific Revolutions* (Chicago, IL: University of Chicago Press, 1962).

12 Michael Oakeshott, *Experience and Its Modes* (New York: Cambridge University Press, 1990); Benedetto Croce quoted in E. H. Carr, *What is History?* (Harmondsworth: Penguin, 1964), pp. 16, 20–1, 29–30; Levy, 'Too Important to Leave to the Other', pp. 26–7; Stephen H. Haber, David M. Kennedy and Stephen D. Krasner, 'Brothers Under the Skin: Diplomatic History and International Relations', *International Security*, 22 (Summer 1997): 34–43, esp. 37–8.

13 See, for example, Hajo Holborn, *The Political Collapse of Europe* (New York: Alfred Knopf, 1963); Arno J. Mayer, *Wilson versus Lenin: Political Origins of the New Diplomacy, 1917–1918* (New Haven, CT: Yale University Press, 1959).

14 The historiography of World War I and the Cold War became intertwined in the Federal Republic of Germany in the 1960s. Anti-capitalist and anti-American feeling ran high among intellectuals, and found expression in the Fischer thesis, which stressed the continuity of German history, from Bismarck through Adenauer, see, for instance, Fritz Fischer, *Bündnis der Eliten: Zur Kontinuität der Machtstrukturen in Deutschland, 1871–1945* (Dusseldorf: Droste, 1979).

15 Paul W. Schroeder, 'The End of the Cold War in the Light of History', unpublished paper, January 1997.

16 See, for example, Kenneth N. Waltz, 'The Emerging Structure of International

Politics', *International Security*, 18 (Fall 1993): 5–43; William C. Wohlforth, 'Realism and the End of the Cold War', *International Security*, 19 (Winter 1994–95): 91–129; Kenneth A. Oye, 'Explaining the End of the Cold War: Morphological and Behavioral Adaptations to the Nuclear Peace?', in Richard Ned Lebow and Thomas Risse-Kappen, *International Relations Theory and the End of the Cold War* (New York: Columbia University Press, 1995), pp. 57–84; Thomas Risse-Kappen, 'Ideas Do Not Float Freely: Transnational Coalitions, Domestic Structures, and the End of the Cold War', in Lebow and Risse-Kappen, *International Relations Theory and the End of the Cold War*, pp. 187–222; Richard Ned Lebow, 'The Long Peace, the End of the Cold War, and the Failure of Realism', in Lebow and Risse-Kappen, *International Relations Theory and the End of the Cold War*, pp. 23–56; Robert G. Herman, 'Identity, Norms and National Security: The Soviet Foreign Policy Revolution and the End of the Cold War', in Peter J. Katzenstein, ed., *The Culture of National Security: Norms and Identity in World Politics* (New York: Columbia University Press, 1996), pp. 271–316; Jeffrey T. Checkel, *Ideas and International Political Change: Soviet/Russian Behavior and the End of the Cold War* (New Haven, CT: Yale University Press, 1997).

17 Human beings use knowledge structures or 'schemas' to cope with the enormous amount of information they receive. Information is assimilated to these schemas. On the limitations of human information processing, see Richard Nisbett and Lee Ross, *Human Inference: Strategies and Shortcomings of Social Judgment* (Englewood Cliffs, NJ: Prentice-Hall, 1980); James Galambos, Robert Abelson, and John Black, eds, *Knowledge Structures* (Hillsdale, NJ: Lawrence Erlbaum, 1986). On biases and heuristics in information processing, see Daniel Kahneman, Paul Slovic, and Amos Tversky, *Judgment Under Uncertainty: Heuristics and Biases* (New York: Cambridge University Press, 1982). For a critique of this model, see Susan T. Fiske and Shelley E. Taylor, *Social Cognition* 2nd edn (New York: McGraw-Hill, 1991), esp. pp. 554–8.

18 Irving L. Janis, *Victims of Groupthink: A Psychological Study of Foreign Policy Decisions and Fiascoes*, 2nd edn (Boston, MA: Houghton-Mifflin, 1972); Irving L. Janis and Leon Mann, *Decision Making: A Psychological Analysis of Conflict, Choice and Commitment* (New York: Free Press, 1977); Richard Ned Lebow, *Between Peace and War: The Nature of International Crisis* (Baltimore, MD: Johns Hopkins University Press, 1981).

19 Bernard Brodie, *The Absolute Weapon* (New York: Harcourt, Brace, 1946).

20 William K. Kaufmann, *The Requirements of Deterrence* (Princeton, NJ: Center of International Studies, 1954); Bernard Brodie, *Strategy in the Missile Age* (Princeton, NJ: Princeton University Press, 1959); Henry A. Kissinger, *The Necessity for Choice* (New York: Harper, 1960); Thomas Schelling, *Controlled Response and Strategic Warfare* (London: International Institute of Strategic Studies, 1965), *Arms and Influence* (New Haven, CT: Yale University Press, 1966).

21 For the psychological roots of deterrence, see Philip Green, *Deadly Logic: The Theory of Nuclear Deterrence* (Columbus, OH: Ohio State University Press, 1966); Robert Jervis, *The Illogic of American Nuclear Strategy* (Ithaca, NY: Cornell University Press, 1984), esp. pp. 22, 36, 37; Steven Kull, *Minds at War: Nuclear Reality and the Inner Conflicts of Defense Policymakers* (New York: Basic Books, 1988).

22 Elie Abel, *The Missile Crisis* (Philadelphia, PA: Lippincott, 1962), pp. 35–6; James Reston, 'What Was Killed Was Not Only the President But the Promise', *New York Times Magazine*, 15 November 1964, p. 126; Arthur M. Schlesinger, Jr, *A Thousand Days: John F. Kennedy in the White House* (Boston, MA: Houghton, Mifflin, 1965), pp. 391, 796; Theodore C. Sorensen, *Kennedy* (New York: Harper & Row, 1965),

pp. 676, 724; Arnold Horelick and Myron Rush, *Strategic Power and Soviet Foreign Policy* (Chicago, IL: University of Chicago Press, 1966), pp. 142–3; Graham T. Allison, *Essence of Decision: Explaining the Cuban Missile Crisis* (Boston, MA: Little, Brown, 1971), pp. 231–5; Alexander L. George and Richard Smoke, *Deterrence in American Foreign Policy: Theory and Practice* (New York: Columbia University Press, 1974), p. 465. For a critique, and a different interpretation of Khrushchev's decision to send missiles to Cuba, see Richard Ned Lebow, 'The Cuban Missile Crisis: Reading the Lessons Correctly', *Political Science Quarterly*, 98 (Fall 1983): 431–58; Raymond L. Garthoff, *Reflections on the Missile Crisis*, rev. edn (Washington, DC: Brookings Institute, 1989); Richard Ned Lebow and Janice Gross Stein, *We All Lost the Cold War* (Princeton, NJ: Princeton University Press, 1994), esp. ch. 4.

23 For an early version of this thesis, Melvin Gurtov and Byong-Moo Hwang, *China Under Threat: The Politics of Strategy and Diplomacy* (Baltimore, MD: Johns Hopkins University Press, 1980), pp. 63–98; Shu Guang Zhang, *Deterrence and Strategic Culture: Chinese–American Confrontations, 1949–1958* (Ithaca, NY: Cornell University Press, 1992), for a more recent study making extensive use of Chinese documents and interviews.

24 Garthoff, *Reflections on the Missile Crisis*, and Lebow and Stein, *We All Lost the Cold War*; James G. Blight, Bruce J. Allyn, and David A. Welch, *Cuba on the Brink: Castro, The Missile Crisis and the Soviet Collapse* (New York: Pantheon, 1993).

25 Lebow and Stein, *We All Lost the Cold War*; Ted Hopf, *Peripheral Visions: Deterrence Theory and American Foreign Policy in the Third World, 1965–1990* (Ann Arbor, MI: University of Michigan Press, 1994).

26 Isaiah Berlin, *The Hedgehog and the Fox: An Essay on Tolstoy's View of History* (New York: Simon & Schuster, 1966).

27 Melvyn P. Leffler, 'New Approaches, Old Interpretations, and Prospective Reconfigurations', *Diplomatic History*, 19 (Spring 1995): 173–96, quote on p. 179; Edward Kiser, 'Revival of the Narrative in Historical Sociology: What Rational Choice Theory Can Contribute', *Politics and Society*, 24 (September 1996): 249–71, offers the view of theory as a 'toolbox', an approach that should be appealing to historical 'foxes'.

28 Kenneth N. Waltz, *Theory of International Politics* (Reading, MA: Addison-Wesley, 1979); Gaddis, *The Long Peace*.

29 John Lewis Gaddis, *We Now Know: Rethinking Cold War History* (New York: Oxford University Press, 1997).

30 Norman N. Naimark, *The Russians in Germany: A History of the Soviet Zone of Occupation, 1945–1949* (Cambridge, MA: Harvard University Press, 1995).

31 According to A. J. P. Taylor, 'a historian should never deal in speculation about what did not happen', *Struggle for the Mastery of Europe, 1848–1918* (London: Oxford University Press, 1954); M. M. Postan writes: 'The might-have beens of history are not a profitable subject of discussion', quoted in J. D. Gould, 'Hypothetical History', *Economic History Review*, 2nd ser., 22 (August 1969): 195–207; See also David Hackett Fischer, *Historian's Fallacies* (New York: Harper Colophon Books, 1970), pp. 15–21; Peter McClelland, *Casual Explanation and Model-Building in History, Economics, and the New Economic History* (Ithaca, NY: Cornell University Press, 1975).

32 James D. Fearon, 'Counterfactuals and Hypothesis Testing in Political Science', *World Politics*, 43 (January 1991): 169–95.

33 George W. Breslauer, 'Counterfactuals Reasoning in Western Studies of Soviet Politics and Foreign Relations', in Philip E. Tetlock and Aaron Belkin, *Counterfactual Thought Experiments in World Politics: Logical, Methodological, and*

Psychological Perspectives (Princeton, NJ: Princeton University Press), pp. 69–94, discusses this literature.

34 John Mueller, *Retreat from Doomsday: The Obsolescence of Major War* (New York: Basic Books, 1989) and the debate on this subject between Mueller, 'The Essential Irrelevance of Nuclear Weapons: Stability in the Postwar World', and Robert Jervis, 'The Political Effects of Nuclear Weapons: A Comment', *International Security*, 13 (Fall 1988): 55–90.

35 See, for example, George and Smoke, *Deterrence in American Foreign Policy*; Alexander L. George and William E. Simmons, eds, *The Limits of Coercive Diplomacy* (Boulder, CO: Westview, 1994); Hopf, *Peripheral Visions*; Robert Jervis and Jack Snyder, eds, *Dominoes and Bandwagons: Strategic Beliefs and Great Power Competition in the Eurasian Rimland* (New York: Oxford University Press, 1991); Thomas Risse-Kappen, *Cooperation Among Democracies: The European Influence on US Foreign Policy* (Princeton, NJ: Princeton University Press, 1995).

36 Tetlock and Belkin, eds, *Counterfactual Thought Experiments in World Politics*.

37 Yuen Foong Khong, 'Confronting Hitler and Its Consequences', in ibid., pp. 95–118.

38 Richard Ned Lebow and Janice Gross Stein, 'Back to the Past: Counterfactuals and the Cuban Missile Crisis', in Tetlock and Belkin, *Counterfactual Thought Experiments in World Politics*, pp. 119–48.

39 George Breslauer and Lebow, 'Leadership and the End of the Cold War', unpublished paper, have conducted such an experiment. We identified other leaders who might have come to power in the Soviet Union, and other responses that the Reagan and Bush administrations might have reasonably had to them – or to Gorbachev – and played out the resulting interaction. We argue that different strategies or tactics by either superpower or their allies might have speeded up, slowed down, altered, or derailed the process of accommodation that led to the Soviet–American entente of 1990–91.

40 In this connection, counterfactual thought experiments should meet seven conditions: possess well-specified antecedents, connecting principles, and consequences; pass the cotenability test (the hypothetical antecedent should not undercut any of the principles or events linking it to the consequent); avoid the conjunction fallacy (the intervening steps in the probabilistic sequence linking antecedent and consequent should be as few as possible); pass the relevance test (preference should be given to hypothesized antecedents that seem most likely to alter the fewest consequences in addition to the hypothesized one); pass the minimal rewrite test (preference should be given to hypothesized antecedents that one can readily defend as feasible without making major alterations in history); be consistent with the understandings and principles of behavior that would be appropriate to normal historical analysis; consider the implications for the consequence of other changes in history the hypothesized antecedent would introduce. Philip Tetlock, 'Distinguishing Frivolous from Serious Counterfactuals', unpublished paper.

41 Mark Kramer, 'Remembering the Cuban Missile Crisis: Should We Swallow Oral History?', *International Security*, 15 (Summer 1990): 212–16.

42 Garthoff, *Reflections on the Cuban Missile*; Lebow and Stein, *We All Lost the Cold War*; Blight, Allyn, and Welch, *Cuba on the Brink*.

43 Aleksandr Fursenko and Timothy Naftali, *'One Hell of a Gamble': Khrushchev, Castro, and Kennedy, 1958–1964* (New York: W. W. Norton, 1997).

44 Raymond L. Garthoff to Malcolm DeBevoise, 22 May 1991.

45 Dean Rusk as told to Richard Rusk, *As I Saw It*, ed. Daniel S. Papp (New York: Norton, 1990), p. 214.

46 Cited by Walter Isaacson, *Kissinger: A Biography* (New York: Simon & Schuster,

1992), p. 827.

47 Robert Jervis, Richard Ned Lebow, and Janice Gross Stein, *Psychology and Deterrence* (Baltimore, MD: Johns Hopkins University Press, 1985), 'Beyond Deterrence', ed. George Levinger, *Journal of Social Issues*, 43 (1987); Paul C. Stern, Robert Axelrod, Robert Jervis, and Roy Radner, eds, *Perspectives on Deterrence* (New York: Oxford University Press, 1989); 'The Rational Deterrence Debate: A Symposium', *World Politics*, 41 (January 1989): 143–266.

48 See, for example, Martha Finnemore, *National Interests in International Society* (Ithaca, NY: Cornell University Press, 1996); Richard Price, 'A Genealogy of the Chemical Weapons Taboo', PhD dissertation, Cornell University, 1994; Herman, 'Identity, Norms and National Security'; Addie Klutz, *Norms in International Relations: The Struggle Against Apartheid* (Ithaca, NY: Cornell University Press, 1995); Karin Fierke, *Changing Games, Changing Strategies: Critical Investigations in Security* (Manchester: University of Manchester Press, 1998).

49 Levy, 'Too Important To Leave to the Other', p. 23.

6

A Certain Idea of Science:
How International Relations Theory
Avoids Reviewing the Cold War

William C. Wohlforth

— IR refuses to care about new developments in history and they should!

The attitude of mainstream scholars of world politics to the relationship between science and history is much like the Bolsheviks' attitude to the relationship between socialism and capitalism. Stalin may have had only the vaguest idea of what the socialism he was supposedly building would look like, but he was absolutely certain of one thing: it would not be capitalism. Today's scholars lack a single vision of what a science of international relations is, but most of them can agree on one thing: it is not history. One consequence of this attitude is that assessing the relationship between international relations theory and the new Cold War history is a vexing task. In this chapter, I explain why my assigned topic is so problematic, show that it need not be so, and make the case for how some of the new information ought to be assimilated.

Good

To get an idea of the barriers to updating theory in response to new historical evidence, consider two related facts. First, there is no documented instance of any noted scholar of international relations changing his or her view of any theory in response to fresh historical evidence. There are, however, instances of scholars abandoning theories whole hog in response to *other* sorts of evidence, such as statistical findings, events, or failed predictions.[1] So the problem is not the relationship between theories and evidence, but the relationship between theories and *historical* evidence.[2] Second, there is in the field today no sense of suspense concerning new revelations about the Cold War. If the top refereed journals, the graduate syllabi of the highest-ranked departments, and the programs of professional meetings are any guide, indifference would best describe the field's official reaction. If scholars thought that historical data about the Cold War might alter the fate of influential theories, surely they would look forward to new releases with some nervous or eager anticipation. This suspense, which is so typical of science, is conspicuous by its absence among scholars of international relations.[3]

The chapter proceeds as follows. In the first section, I show that this reaction to the new evidence is understandable, given the nature of theoretical controversies in international relations, but it is intellectually indefensible in our data-poor field. Moreover, it is probably reversible, since it does not reflect a general problem of relating theories and evidence but instead stems directly from the particular way debates have been organized in recent years. Second, I argue that this lackadaisical approach to historical evidence is particularly costly in the case of the new Cold War history, for the sudden availability of new evidence reflects a unique opportunity to clarify and advance key theoretical debates. The new evidence will influence the theoretical debate; the only question is how. If the process unfolds as it has in the past, new data will be assimilated in a manner that bears scant resemblance to the scientific ideal to which the field aspires. In the final part, I document some intellectual trends that run counter to the field's general reluctance to take historical evidence seriously. Against a backdrop of social scientists eager to get on with the business of predicting and explaining post-Cold War international politics there are some scholarly tendencies that encourage a more disciplined approach to the work of the new Cold War historians.

IR theory and new historical evidence

At first brush, a blasé attitude toward the new evidence seems over-determined. The positivist notion that testing theories is a simple matter of checking the correspondence between theoretical predictions and independent observations has been on the retreat since World War II, while over the past two decades influential new social science theories have undermined faith in the reliability of traditional historical evidence. These intellectual trends and the popular arguments that emerge from them provide the setting – but only the setting – for the more immediate challenge to careful assimilation of the new Cold War materials.

The standard arguments

Compared to their predecessors of twenty or even ten years ago, today's graduate students are wonderfully sophisticated about epistemology. They know that Kuhn and Lakatos came after Popper, and so that the connection between theories and observations is complex. Today's journals are full of references to post-positivism, scientific realism, non-Humean conceptions of causality, Laktosian standards of theory-evaluation, and the like.[4] In short, it is hardly necessary to repeat here the standard list of arguments from philosophers, sociologists, and historians of science that have undermined naïve notions about evidence and falsifiability.

In addition, writings in the field show an increased preoccupation with the special problems presented by the study of world politics. Not only is international politics a 'complex, path dependent system' in Robert Jervis's words, but the phenomena we seek to explain tend to be extremely rare events: wars, crises, alliance change, extended rivalries, and arms races.[5] As long as international politics is construed as relations among states – and mainly great powers at that – we guarantee a focus on small numbers of incomparable complex events. But if international politics is not construed in this way, it becomes indistinguishable from the study of comparative or domestic politics. The statistical sin of underspecification – too many independent variables and too few observations – may be endemic to the subject as we have defined it.

Evaluating theories in these circumstances involves making causal judgments about rare events in a complex system. In other words, it involves doing history – and doing it in a way that many historians find dubious; namely, ranking and rating the causes of major events. And even if it is possible in principle, social psychologists question whether the human mind is up to the task in practice. Experimental research reveals that powerful biases influence even an expert's assessment of the theoretical meaning of new evidence. Since the task of causal explanation is at best extraordinarily difficult, adherents to a theory will almost always have reasonable grounds for rejecting the probative value of disconfirming evidence. Evidence that supports a favored theory, naturally, will be viewed less skeptically.[6]

Moreover, the historical evidence we deal with – the texts produced by decisionmakers and the organizations they head – is likely not only to be incomplete, but ambiguous or systematically biased. Historians, of course, do not need social science theorists to tell them about biased or ambiguous evidence. If any political scientist wants to question the theoretical relevance of new historical findings, his best ally might be a skeptical colleague from the history department. But recent theoretical developments lend a social scientific imprimatur to skepticism about the utility of historical evidence. Game theorists contend that it is precisely the information most necessary for explaining an event that decisionmakers will face the strongest incentives to obscure or misrepresent – to each other and to history. Some game theoretical models undermine the very notion that scholars can ever assess the behavior of decisionmakers, since the statesmen will always know more about the strategic situation they face – how much they know and when they know it, what they really want and how much they want it – than scholars can know.[7]

Organizational theories and cognitive psychology, on the other hand, question the veracity of diplomatic documents for the opposite reason: decisions are rarely, they suggest, made 'rationally' in the sense of game theory, but people face incentives to tell false tales of rationality after the fact.[8] Thus, we have one body of theory telling us that diplomatic documents concerning any strategic interaction will inevitably support multiple, opposed interpretations, and another insisting that if any coherent story of rational calculation none the less emerges, it is most likely fictional.

The final, predictable argument concerns the limits of the new Cold War evidence itself. The outpouring of new data is only dramatic when compared to what we used to know about the Cold War, rather than what we need to know or actually do know about other historical cases. The fact that the former Soviet bloc was composed of unusually secretive regimes that sought unusual degrees of social control makes any release of new information about them particularly exciting. Yet, as Jonathan Haslam has noted, it is misleading to speak of the 'opening' of Soviet archives.[9] The documents which most historians regard as essential to reconstructing high-level decisionmaking lie in archives which remain closed to almost all scholars. What we have is a truly dramatic quantitative increase in the availability of second-level materials – embassy reporting, some Foreign Ministry and Central Committee papers, interviews, and memoirs – and sporadic, semi-regulated access to top-level documentation concerning a few key episodes, including the Korean War, the Cuban Missile Crisis, and the end of the Cold War.

As a result, many new Cold War historians seem understandably reluctant to forward bold new interpretations. The standard approach seems to be to assimilate all the relevant new information, clarify its relation to what we knew, and conclude with tentative suggestions about how the new findings alter previous views. Most historians seem still to be grappling with the new materials themselves. If that is the case, political scientists might ask, why should we rush in? It would be imprudent to alter our confidence in established theories in response to such incomplete evidence. Let's give the historians time to sort things out themselves, and then we'll see whether there is any need to rethink anything.

Three confounding pathologies

The standard arguments add up to skepticism about the implications of the new evidence, but they are insufficient to explain international relations scholars' approach to it. They would come into play only if the relationship between contending theories and the explanation of the Cold War were evident. If the theoretical stake in explaining the Cold War were clear, scholars would have no choice but to treat new evidence about the Cold War explicitly. If they did so, all the arguments about causal inference, biased interpretation, ambiguous evidence, and the limits of the new material would apply – just as similarly challenging methodological arguments apply to other kinds of evidence and other sorts of tests. To understand the field's unstudied indifference, it is necessary to look beyond

the universal challenges of scientific inference, and even the specific difficulties of studying world politics, to three particular pathologies that
conspire to confound the relationship between historical evidence and the
evaluation of IR theories.

First is ambiguity about history. All too often, the relationship between
theories or theoretical debates and the explanation of specific historical
episodes is profoundly ambiguous. True, by the 1980s, many of the central
debates quite clearly had nothing to do with the Cold War. In the long-
running debate between neo-liberal theories and Kenneth Waltz's Neo-
Realism, for example, the former simply conceded the Cold War as a topic
to the latter. Much of the debate in those years centered on explaining cooperation among capitalist states. Scholars argued over the likely effects
of US decline – without explicitly considering the US–Soviet rivalry. In
keeping with this arrangement, the current attack on Neo-Realism focuses
(with a few exceptions) on post-Cold War developments rather than on
retrospective explanations of the Cold War itself.[10]

However, even when theories and theoretical arguments do seem related
to the Cold War, the extent to which they are sensitive to our understanding
of that event is shrouded in ambiguity. The culprit here is the scholarly
aspiration to universalism. International relations theories are written to
explain relations among states in all times and places. As a consequence,
the degree to which their validity hinges on the explanation of any one
episode is always unclear. For this reason, 'critical cases' – that is,
events that must conform to a theory's expectations if that theory is
true – never occur in international relations.[11] Neo-Realism is an extreme
but illustrative case in point. Despite the fact that Kenneth Waltz's
Theory of International Politics was influential in part because it seemed
to explain the stability of the Cold War, one looks in vain in that book or
in any other of Waltz's writings for clear language indicating the extent to
which the theory's veracity hinges on any particular understanding of the
Cold War.[12]

The same problem occurs in less acute form even in the work of case-
study researchers. Jack Snyder's *Myths of Empire*, for example, attracted
the attention of specialists on the Cold War in part because of its ambitious
explanation for Soviet 'overexpansion'.[13] But the Soviet case is only one
of five Snyder considers, and it is by no means the most important. It is
unlikely that any finding about the Cold War which undercuts that one
case would substantially alter the status of Snyder's work. Again, not only
do all the standard arguments about theories and evidence in world politics
potentially undermine the implications of any such finding, but the degree
to which Snyder's theory really hinges on its portrayal of the Cold War is
arguable.

The universalistic aspiration and the related conviction that science
cannot resemble history ensure that scholars do not articulate theories

IR's use of game theory

and theoretical arguments that can be advanced by the accumulation of historical evidence.[14] Finely grained historical explanations of specific episodes simply seem boring and irrelevant in this context, since arguments about theory are not formulated in a manner that allows them to advance in response to such accounts

The second pathology is the tendency toward zero-sum methodology wars. Built in to some methodological approaches is a necessarily all-or-nothing approach to historical explanation. For example, some (though clearly not all) understandings of game theory contribute to a strict belief that historical explanation and social science theory are antithetical to each other. According to Bruce Bueno de Mesquita, 'The use of game theory almost assures that a thick [historical] analysis cannot be undertaken.' The reason, in his view, is that game theory is geared toward the creation of abstract, highly simplified models of general causation. And, 'when the objective is to explain general phenomena, the causality implied by a theory of how variables relate to each other, thick analysis [history] serves to distort and mislead'.[15] William Riker puts it in similarly stark terms: 'the search for and discovery of genetic [historical] explanations precludes scientific generalization'.[16]

Such thinking has two consequences. First, it creates incentives for those scholars who believe that historical research does have theoretical implications to adopt a similarly absolutist stance in reply. Second, as soon as any theoretical debate also becomes such an all-or-nothing methodology dispute, the possibility of advance by empirical inquiry is excluded, since each side dismisses the findings of the other on methodological grounds. In these instances, the field's inherent ambiguity about history revolves itself into a zero-sum impasse concerning the relevance of history to theory. An example of this sort of impasse was the debate on rational deterrence theory. Case-study researchers, many working with cognitive or social psychology, found time and time again that real decisionmakers just do not perform the mental calculations implied by rational deterrence theory, and their preferences simply do not accord with the expectations of influential theoretical models. The response of many rational deterrence theorists was that case study research is irrelevant to science. In addition, they contended, assumptions that can be expressed mathematically are necessary components of theory. Hence the debate was: 'your assumptions are inaccurate; you can't explain these data sets' vs 'you don't have a theory; those data sets don't matter'.[17]

Third is the pathology of zero-sum paradigm wars.[18] The all-or-nothing quality of theoretical controversies in international relations makes them hard to update in response to new historical evidence, which is always tentative and incomplete. Zero-sumism works on both sides of any debate. Those who question a theory face incentives to claim that new evidence falsifies it; in response, defenders of the theory reject the relevance of the evidence. Thus, theories are either completely corroborated or totally falsified. Lost in the competitive atmosphere is any language for discussing how degrees of confidence might be revised in response to new data. Zero-sum paradigm wars simply do not translate well into the multicausal world of historical research. Incentives in the discipline call for claiming 'priority' for some cause or causal mechanism, or touting the fact that some cause 'matters' as a finding of major significance. Evidence is interpreted in terms of zero-sum exchanges between partisans of different causes or levels of analysis. It is international *versus* domestic influences, power *versus* ideas, or institutions *versus* interests. This sort of language is off-putting, naïve, and obviously wrongheaded to historical researchers.

Missed opportunities

These pathologies produce a research practice that is indefensible from the standpoint of the very commitment to science which has marked the academic study of world politics from its origins in the 1930s. After all, the field faces a severe data shortage created by its focus on relations among major states in anarchic systems. Methodologists tell us to expand the observable implications of theories.[19] In practice, however, scholars restrict the empirical implications of their theories by failing to specify how they relate to historical data. It is well known that *events* influence the fate of theories. No student of international relations would deny the fact that the popularity of liberal, Marxist, and Realist theories has altered in response to major events in the international system, from the origins of World War II to the end of the Cold War. If events influence theories, then they are logically connected to the *explanation* of those events. To the extent that popular research practice denies this connection, it is contradictory and profoundly unscientific.

Defenders of the status quo may contend that I am overstating my case. Surely, historical evidence is assimilated in theoretical debates. I agree. The question is, how is it assimilated? It does not take a doctorate in psychology to predict the answer. If debates are not framed with an eye toward their advancement in response to new historical evidence, such evidence will be assimilated opportunistically. That is, at the level of the individual, the theoretical school, and indeed the discipline as a whole, new evidence will enter the discussion in a manner guaranteed not to upset cherished beliefs and practices. An instructive example of this practice is again the rational deterrence debate. While dismissing the scientific status of case-study research, game theorists changed their models to accommodate historical findings that underscored the complexity and uncertainty of real-world decision problems.[20] In this manner, the cumulation of detailed historical evidence influenced how scholars formulated their theories in an *ad hoc*, informal manner, without altering their stated beliefs about the irrelevance of historical research to social science.

If the new evidence on the Cold War is assimilated in this backhanded manner, it will be tragic indeed. For, with due regard to its important limitations, the evidence to hand bears directly on central theoretical arguments in world politics. If crucial information on power, perceptions of power, ideas, and domestic politics during the Cold War is not central to the study of world politics, it is difficult to imagine what is. In the three subsections that follow, I review the evidence on power and ideas, and then predict its fate at the hands of international relations scholars if we do not change the way we do business.

Power

'If there is any distinctively political theory of international politics, balance of power theory is it', writes Kenneth Waltz.[21] He has a point: were it not for balance-of-power theory (and, with only slight exaggeration, without Waltz himself), one wonders what international relations scholars would do with themselves. A large proportion of writing in the field is taken up with defending, critiquing, or elaborating this venerable theory. At root, the theory posits a relationship between the distribution of material capabilities among states and things that matter to scholars and statesmen, such as war, cooperation, alliances, and crises.

The new sources are giving us new information in three key areas of decisive importance for understanding how the material distribution of capabilities influenced world politics for the half-century after 1945. First, we are learning about the actual relationship of military and economic capabilities. Sporadic archival releases, as well as much more plentiful memoirs and interviews, are giving us a new picture of Soviet strength during the Cold War.[22] We now have much more information about the size, composition, disposition, and state of training and discipline of the Soviet armed forces; about the development, deployment, and reliability of Soviet nuclear weapons and ballistic missiles; and about the real state of the Soviet economy, the proportion of resources devoted to defense and imperial control, and the drain imposed by subsidies to allies. On balance, this evidence shows a Soviet Union with a much more tentative grasp on superpowerdom than nearly all observers imagined until recently. In short, *Moscow's Potemkinism worked* in misleading everyone, including scholars, about Soviet power and hence the overall balance of power. Thus, the new evidence renders one of the central puzzles of the Cold War for balance-of-power theory – the *imbalance* of power between the main protagonists – even more puzzling.

Second, the new sources improve our understanding of Soviet perceptions of power. The key to Moscow's Potemkin strategy was to advertise an inflated self-assessment of the Soviet Union's relative capabilities. And one thing the Kremlin could indeed do better than its Western rivals was to control public discourse. In these circumstances, one would expect an unusually large gap between public and private assessments of power. While much more documentation is needed – especially concerning assessments of the military balance – new sources do underscore this large gap between public and private assessments.[23] For much of the early Cold War, Soviet decisionmakers appeared to be quite sober about the existing relationship of power but bullish about trends (as a result of both rational expectations and ideological interpretation of evidence). Expectations of capitalist economic crises or inter-imperialist squabbling buoyed Stalin's hopes, while an expected socialist economic boom raised Khrushchev's. It was only in the period of high Brezhnevism in the early 1970s that we see some evidence of Soviet bullishness about the existing balance of power. But even then the realities of poor relative Soviet economic performance were beginning to penetrate Soviet minds.

The third stream of evidence concerns the effects of asymmetries in the distribution of material capabilities. As John Gaddis has argued, the new evidence underscores the costs of thinking about 'power' as a mono-dimensional structure.[24] What seems to matter most in the Cold War is less how power resources are distributed than how *symmetrically* different elements of power are distributed. The fact that the Soviet Union had some but not all the attributes of superpower status seems to have underlain many of the difficulties the two sides had in cooperating. If one looks simply at the aggregate indicators of national capabilities, one is hard pressed to understand how the West could ever have felt challenged and how the Soviets could ever have made a plausible claim to political parity with the United States. What seems to have produced the dissonance was Moscow's possession of plausibly equal or superior capabilities in particular categories of power: conventional military forces, ideological appeal, nuclear weaponry, and overall military might. Hence the Soviet sense of entitlement to superpower parity coupled with insecurity about its recognition. Hence the West's strong reaction to Moscow's claims coupled with the conviction that the Russians could ultimately be kept in their place. The asymmetrical distribution of power resources made a political equilibrium based on a stable material balance – the basic aim of détente – extraordinarily difficult to achieve in practice.[25]

Ideas

Since the end of the Cold War, a substantial literature has emerged built on the premise that 'ideas matter' in explaining international politics.[26] Scholars contributing to this literature reject the classical social scientists' belief that human behavior can be explained in terms of material structures and the incentives they create. They question the modern game theorists' assumptions that actors' preferences can be derived from the logic of strategic situations, that strategic incentives will induce decision-makers to choose rationally, and that different decisionmakers operating in a similar strategic environment will have similar beliefs about how the world works. For them, actors' preferences and causal beliefs cannot be external to theory and explanation. Even generalizing theorists, they argue, need to know how people come to want the things they want. And that knowledge, they contend, is only obtainable if one studies the ideas that govern how people see and respond to their circumstances.

The new Cold War evidence seems tailor-made for this intellectual trend in political science, for it has supported an increased emphasis on ideology. The simple fact that classified documents do not reveal Soviet decision-makers talking in private like Hans Morgenthau has itself influenced the debate. 'The greatest surprise so far to have come out of the Russian archives', Vojtech Mastny notes, 'is that there was no surprise: the thinking of the insiders conforms substantially to what Moscow was publicly saying. Some of the most secret documents could have been published in *Pravda* without anybody's noticing.'[27] The fact that there was no 'double bookkeeping' lends support to those who contend that Leninist ideas shaped thinking and action.

In addition, the new sources point toward the sporadic emergence behind Kremlin walls of hardheaded, realistic, and cost-conscious *alternative* approaches to Soviet security. For example, Zubok and Pleshakov suggest that, had Beria and Malenkov had their way, the Soviet Union might have charted a more prudent course and possibly avoided over-extension in the rivalry with the United States.[28] Other sources show how clearly the costs of Third World expansionism were perceived in Brezhnev's Moscow. But these security-centered *realpolitik* tendencies repeatedly lost out against a more encompassing, global vision for Soviet policy. And a recurring cause may have been ideology: genuine ideological commitment, ideologically induced optimism about global trends, and the instrumental use of ideology by those interested in a forward policy. By revealing the existence of alternatives and at the same time seeming to show how ideology systematically stacked the deck against them, the new sources dramatically enhance the case for the causal role of ideas.

As a result, the new evidence has clearly nudged Cold War historiography in the direction of ideas. Gaddis, for example, argues that 'the new sources ... seem to suggest that ideology often *determined* the behavior of Marxist-Leninist regimes'.[29] Zubok and Pleshakov, while they highlight the cynicism of Soviet leaders, nevertheless include their 'revolutionary-imperial paradigm' as one of three key factors governing Moscow's conduct of the Cold War.[30] For these scholars, many of the big puzzles of the Cold War – why a relatively weak Soviet Union often seemed so keen to compete with wealthy West, why it took actions that fostered co-operation among adversaries, and why, when the costs of this behavior became apparent, it found it so hard to extricate itself from its over-extended position – can only be explained by placing great importance on ideology.

Scholars who tackle more discrete questions are also lending support to the importance of ideas. For Chen Jian, neither the closeness of the early Sino-Soviet alliance nor the intensity of the later antagonism can be understood without placing considerable weight on the force of ideology.[31] Why did Moscow select the alliance partners it did? Why were these alliances so hard to manage? Ideology, according to Odd Arne Westad, is an important part of the answer.[32] Fursenko and Naftali's account of the Cuban Missile Crisis repeatedly returns to ideology as both a basic moti-vation for behavior and a powerful influence on the interpretation of evidence. 'For Khrushchev', they argue, 'Cuba was the physical embodi-ment of the Communist future.'[33] In Fursenko and Naftali's narrative, the Soviet leader's rough Leninist conceptual lenses repeatedly led him to misperceive the workings of the US democracy in fateful ways.

How the new data will enter the debate

The fate of this new information is predictable. The advent of Construc-tivist theory in international relations has reignited the old debate over materialism versus idealism.[34] Constructivists are thus likely to seize on the new evidence to argue that Soviet material weakness makes it even harder to explain bipolarity as a consequence of an underlying material structure. Citing new Cold War historians, they will argue that Marxist-Leninist ideas and the Soviets' self-identification as revolutionaries really deter-mined the structure of international politics in the Cold War. Not only were the material underpinnings of bipolarity far weaker than was apparent before, but the importance of ideas now appears greater. The basic prediction of structural theory, idealists will argue, was that different kinds of states will 'socialize' to a given material structure. The new evidence may be interpreted as showing not only how resistant the Soviet Union was to such socialization, but that the Cold War was the *result* of Moscow's resistance. Constructivists will argue that when Soviet thinking finally did come to resemble American and West European perceptions, the Cold War ended.[35] Thus, Neo-Realism – or indeed any theory that posits a single material structure to which all states react – is not only irrelevant in explaining the Cold War, it has causality exactly backwards.

In addition, the new evidence bears directly on the fundamental precepts of rational deterrence theory and the applicability of specific game-theoretical models to the Cold War crises and arms competition. Overall, it appears strongly to support the contention that real decisionmakers do not think like deterrence theorists, and it surely will be used to buttress the case of scholars who are skeptical of rational choice approaches. So far as we are able to reconstruct the strategic preferences of Soviet leaders during tense Cold War crises or in key decisions concerning the arms race, they appear to be utterly inexplicable in terms of influential models. Khrushchev's diplomacy is particularly paradoxical. Even if his missile deception had been successful, there is still no rational explanation (that I am aware of) for his conviction that a nuclear stalemate somehow conferred a special bluffing advantage on him. Yet this belief helped lead the superpowers to the brink of thermonuclear war. Thanks to the work of Naftali and Fursenko, we now know that Khrushchev was willing to risk nuclear war (perhaps, but by no means surely, local in character) to defend Cuba despite overwhelming real American local and strategic superiority. The obvious next step for scholars who are skeptical of rational deterrence theory is to compare 'One Hell of a Gamble' to some of the more sophisticated game-theoretical treatments of that event. The result will surely make their basic point.[36]

Unfortunately, the responses of many Realist and rationalist scholars are easy to predict based on their past reactions to similar evidence. Waltz and those who share his understanding of theory will assert that evidence concerning decisionmakers' ideas is irrelevant to testing a general theory that predicts only general patterns of outcomes over the long term.[37] As far as the new data on power are concerned, the response will be that the theory never stated that Moscow had to be as powerful as some might have thought it was in the Cold War. To provide the material underpinnings of bipolarity, the Soviet Union only had to meet two requirements: to be much more powerful than any other state except the United States; and to be capable of threatening the security of the United States. The new evidence undermines neither requirement. It adds historical detail that is useful for explaining the nuances of the Cold War, but has little bearing on general theories of international politics.

Rationalist responses, too, can be predicted from earlier scholarly exchanges concerning similar evidence. They will dismiss or downplay the findings on statistical grounds: selection bias (since most of the action in deterrence theory concerns unobservables -- wars, crises, or challenges that do not occur -- focus on Cold War crises skews the results by selecting only evidence of general deterrence failures); underidentification (too many variables, not enough cases); and unreliable, non-replicable measurement of variables (especially of preferences, since game theory highlights decisionmakers' incentives to lie about what they want).[38] But the real point of disagreement will be the basic contention that explanation of behavior in specific cases is irrelevant or even damaging to the theoretical project. Without the simplifying assumptions of rationality and rational updating of beliefs, theory as these scholars understand it is not possible. Since this understanding of theory excludes historical explanation, detailed historical findings that contradict some model are seen not so much as challenges to that particular model, but as challenges to the very idea of theory.

The key here is that the new Cold War evidence is not qualitatively different from similar historical evidence concerning this and other events. The debate over Neo-Realism already 'knew' before 1991 that the Cold War was inexplicable in terms of the theory. The rational deterrence debate already 'knew' that decisionmakers do not think like game theorists. More evidence that these things are so will not alter these debates.

Breaking the impasse

Thus, the danger is that the new evidence will enter the debate without providing a clarifying reality check for existing theories. Years hence, it may be hard to say exactly how evidence has influenced theories, and whether any claimed advances in understanding resulted from brilliant deduction or backhanded induction. And, the reason will not be the general epistemological conundrums that are so popular with scholars, but the specific pathologies I spelled out above. Ambiguity about history hinders any real confrontation with the new evidence. Because theories are written and theoretical arguments are proposed without clarifying their implications for historical evidence of this kind, the sudden discovery of a treasure trove of new data may end up having little probative value. Zero-sum attitudes to methodological differences promote irreconcilable stances concerning the meaning of new historical evidence. And zero-sum paradigm rivalry ensures that the new evidence must be shoehorned into a debate over ideas vs power as the 'ultimate' cause. Again, the incentives are for extreme claims for the importance of one's favored causal factor and endless defensive moves to protect favored theories from problematic evidence.

How to break the impasse? The answer is simple: recognize that IR is a historical science. That implies stating clearly the relationship between specific theoretical arguments and the historical explanation of specific events like the Cold War; being much more attentive to how the causal mechanisms of different theories work together to produce outcomes; and a problem-oriented focus rather than an exclusive orientation toward competition between paradigms and methods. It is easy to dismiss the possibility of any such change since it would strike so many of the field's gatekeeping personalities as so deeply wrongheaded, and it contradicts the peculiar attitude toward science that is thoroughly enmeshed in the history and culture of the discipline.[39] Nevertheless, there are two intellectual trends and one popular research program that appear to be working in this direction.

The breakdown of Realism into many discrete Realisms has generally been interpreted within the classical paradigm-war framework as a 'weakening' or 'degeneration' of the theory.[40] From the perspective of the (generally untenured) scholars who are largely responsible for proliferating Realisms, however, nothing could be farther from the truth. On the contrary, ending Neo-Realism's hegemony over Realist thinking produces a series of goods: overall, it weakens the hold of the paradigm-war framework over the discipline, facilitating less causal and methodological absolutism and more explanatory cooperation; and it frees Realist scholars to explore new hypotheses about power. Once liberated from Waltz's particular understanding of theoretical parsimony, which allows little variation in structure and equates power with a monodimensional index of military capabilities, Realists can generate models that are much more helpful in tackling specific explanatory problems. Of particular relevance to the new Cold War evidence is newer research on differentiated structures of power; asymmetrical resource endowments, and status competition.[41]

The trend toward greater sophistication of qualitative research is also serving to disarm some of the methodological warriors. Historical case researchers in political science are caught between three lines of intense criticism: game theorists tell them that they are methodologically naïve and that the evidence they use is hopelessly biased; post-modernists say much the same thing, from a rather different point of view; and then historians helpfully come along and castigate them for being too theoretical, too interested in generalization, and sloppy in their use of historical sources. While they will never satisfy these audiences, case researchers are becoming a lot more sophisticated about the philosophical and methodological underpinnings of their work.[42] Whether this will result in better work is uncertain. But it clearly does help researchers present their work in terms that interlocutors in other research traditions can understand. The result will be to bridge some of the communications breakdowns that bedevil IR debates.

Finally, *democratic peace research* is a heartwarming example of a focus on an explanatory problem coupled with resolute methodological pragmatism. Both democracies and wars are so few in number that the data shortage which I contend is endemic to all questions of interest in IR is clear to all but the most obtuse scholars. Since statistics simply know no solution to the inferential problems posed by the democratic peace argument, researchers of all stripes recognize the limits of correlational findings and welcome new data generated by historical research.[43]

And the new evidence on the Cold War does bear on the question of how democracy affects states' strategic behavior. Arguments about how democracies behave imply corollary arguments about non-democracies. The Cold War, in which a democratic and an authoritarian coalition faced off, is a wonderful laboratory for exploring theoretical conjectures from the democratic peace literature. At first glance, much of the new evidence from the former Soviet bloc seems to support many recent theoretical arguments for the superior strategic efficiency of democracies: that democratic leaders, beholden to powerful publics, can make more credible commitments in crises; that democracies select better personnel, allow freer flow of information to decisionmakers, constrain the irrational interests of organizations and interest groups, and are better able to delegate authority for more efficient decisionmaking and warfighting.[44] Though many of these arguments smack of triumphalism, they are worthy of investigation; and one way to evaluate them is to compare democratic and non-democratic decisionmaking in a similar strategic environment.

Though limited, the new evidence on this score is striking. If the first big surprise of the new archival releases was that ideology permeated the system, surely the second one was the dismal intellectual and organizational capabilities of the Soviet system and its leaders. Throughout the Cold War, Westerners were all too aware of the inefficiencies and absurdities in how their own policy sausage was made. Soviet secrecy fed fantasies of a hyper-efficient totalitarian state where Leninist Bismarcks plotted intricate strategies completely free from domestic constraints. The reality was more banal. The private Stalin, Khrushchev, and Brezhnev were even less impressive intellectually than they appeared in public. A system which leaves its foreign policy in the hands of people with the intellectual firepower of Molotov and Gromyko for most of the Cold War has clearly got problems selecting decisionmakers. The quality of the analytical papers that have been released is generally unimpressive. As many Sovietologists long suspected, the tendency of all organizations to stifle dissent once the top leader makes a decision appears to have been especially strong in the Soviet Union. The propensity of executives to make snap decisions without deep analysis or careful weighing of expected costs and benefits appears particularly strong in Soviet leaders. Had a US president acted like Khrushchev – for example, by issuing in the country's name stern ultimata on Berlin with absolutely no endgame in mind, and then permitting them to fizzle out with no discernible result – he would have surely been punished severely at the polls and in his relations with Congress.

Evidence on how the Soviet Union's authoritarian structure affected its strategic behavior, as well as on how Washington's and Moscow's dramatically different political cultures may have contributed to miscommunication and missed signals, could be extremely helpful in evaluating popular conjectures about how democratic norms and institutions affect international relations. Ironically, however, the new Cold War research is weakest on the domestic context of Soviet foreign policy – precisely the area in which IR scholarship might be most capable of assimilating it rationally. The main culprits here are the limited access to archives and the built-in propensity of the Soviet system to mask policy disagreements. But, to an outsider, at least, scholarly trends in the historical profession may bear some of the responsibility. Historians who delve deeply into Soviet domestic affairs seem interested in anything – culture, identity, historical memory – as long as it is not foreign affairs. The new international historians seem transfixed by international, multiarchival research. Lost in the mix, at least for the time being, is research that marries knowledge about the international context of the Cold War with in-depth expertise on Soviet domestic and bureaucratic politics.

The lesson is that the manner in which academics break up their subjects always imposes certain costs. However we choose to organize inquiry, something falls between the cracks. In the case of international relations in the United States, a certain idea of science leads to a discipline biased against the rational assimilation of historical data – a bias which may be particularly costly now. After all, the new Cold War history is a motherlode for international relations theory. With all of its limitations, the new evidence is for international relations theory what a large new fossil discovery is for paleontology. While it does not constitute a controlled experiment, and its extent is limited and far from what is needed to resolve basic explanatory disputes, it is undeniably new, and it bears on contending theories about how world politics works. Suddenly, we are confronted with fresh evidence on the balance of power during the Cold War, how elites perceived this balance, how the ideas they professed shaped those perceptions and subsequent strategic choices, how leaders balanced domestic and international imperatives, and how changing material incentives influenced ideas.

All of this information is central to fundamental theoretical controversies in international relations, and it constitutes a major challenge to the field. The challenge does not derive from the fact that the new findings underscore the inadequacies of standard theories of international relations. The weakness of international relations theory in providing valid explanations is well known – especially to the scholars who deal with it on a daily basis. There is no need for new evidence to make that point – the data to hand before 1991 were more than sufficient to demonstrate it. By its very suddenness and scope, however, the cascade of new information has underscored the fact that the field of international relations is not set up to assimilate new historical evidence rationally.

What is needed to rectify the situation is not utopian, but a simple recognition of IR's status as a historical science. We need to reconcile the aim to generalize with the detailed kinds of historical data we routinely obtain about international events. While this combination of general and particular may not come easily to many minds, it is a standard attitude in science. As A. N. Whitehead observed in 1925:

All the world over and at all times there have been practical men, absorbed in 'irreducible and stubborn facts': all the world over and at all times there have been men of philosophic temperament who have been absorbed in the weaving of general principles. It is this union of passionate interest in the detailed facts with equal devotion to abstract generalizations which forms the novelty in present society.[45]

It is that union which international relations scholarship needs and has never achieved. Paleontologists do it. Biologists do it. Meteorologists do it. Why can't we forge general theories that can be checked against the stubborn facts of history?

NOTES

1 In one of the best examples, a founder of regional integration theory abandoned it in part because it failed to anticipate one perturbing variable: Charles De Gaulle. See Haas, 'The Obsolescence of Regional Integration Theory', Research Series No. 25, Institute of International Studies, University of California, Berkeley, 1975.

2 Throughout, I restrict my comments to international relations as practiced in the United States. For a contrasting, more optimistic view, see Colin Elman and Miriam Fendium Elman, 'Diplomatic History and International Relations Theory: Respecting Differences and Crossing Boundaries', *International Security*, 22: 1 (Summer, 1997).

3 As Murray Gell-Mann put it, 'When suspense seems to be lacking in a particular field, controversy may erupt about whether it is truly scientific' (*The Quark and the Jaguar: Adventures in the Simple and the Complex* (New York: W. H. Freeman, 1994), p. 78).

4 For a review, see Martin Hollis and Steve Smith, *Explaining and Understanding International Relations* (Oxford: Clarendon, 1990)

5 Robert Jervis, *System Effects: Complexity in Social and Political Life* (Princeton, NJ: Princeton University Press, 1997). For a succinct statement of the data shortage that is endemic to the field, see Philip E. Tetlock and Aaron Belkin, *Counterfactual Thought Experiments in World Politics: Logical, Methodological and Psychological Perspectives* (Princeton, NJ: Princeton University Press, 1996), ch. 1.

6 A brilliant discussion of this issue, which reports experimental results, is Phillip E. Tetlock, 'Theory-Driven Reasoning about Possible Pasts and Probable Futures in World Politics: Are We Prisoners of Our Preconceptions?', Ohio State University, unpub. MS, n.d.

7 James D. Fearon notes this implication of rationality assumptions in 'Threats To Use Force: Costly Signals and Bargaining in International Crises', PhD diss., University of California, Berkelely, 1992, ch. 3. This is a logical conclusion of common game theory assumptions: that efficient choosers are promoted to decisionmaking roles; and that decisionmakers choose rationally among available options, given their preferences and the information available to them. In other words, history is efficient. The implication is that scholarly criticism of decisionmakers is the result of one of two things: either the scholar has different preferences than the decisionmakers; or the scholar's critique is based on hindsight.

8 I deal with these issues at greater length in 'New Evidence on Moscow's Cold War:

Ambiguity in Search of Theory', *Diplomatic History*, 21:2 (Spring 1997).

9 See Jonathan Haslam, 'Russian Revelations and Understanding the Cold War', in ibid.

10 This point is exemplified by two major post-1991 'paradigm-debate' volumes: Sean M. Lynn-Jones and Stephen Miller, eds, *The Cold War and After: Prospects for Peace* (Cambridge, MA: MIT Press, 1993); and David A. Baldwin, ed., *Neorealism and Neoliberalism: The Contemporary Debate* (New York: Columbia University Press, 1993).

11 Harry Eckstein, 'Case Study and Theory in Political Science', in Fred I. Greenstein and Nelson Polsby, eds, *Handbook of Political Science*, vol. 7, *Strategies of Inquiry* (Reading, MA: Addison-Wesley, 1975), pp. 79–137.

12 Waltz, *Theory of International Politics* (Reading, MA: Addison-Wesley, 1979). For two seemingly devastating critiques of Neo-Realism's ability to account for the Cold War, see R. N. Lebow, 'The Long Peace, the End of the Cold War, and the Failure of Realism', in Lebow and Risse-Kappen, eds, *International Relations Theory and the End of the Cold War* (New York: Columbia University Press, 1995); and R. Harrison Wagner, 'What was Bipolarity?', *International Organization*, 47:1 (Winter 1993).

13 *Myths of Empire: Domestic Politics and International Ambition* (Ithaca, NY: Cornell University Press, 1991).

14 I pursue this argument in relation to the debate on the end of the Cold War in 'Reality Check: Revising Theories of International Politics in Response to the End of the Cold War', *World Politics*, 50 (July 1998).

15 Bruce Bueno de Measquita, 'The Benefits of a Social-Scientific Approach', in Ngaire Woods, ed., *Explaining International Relations Since 1945* (Oxford: Oxford University Press, 1996), pp. 64, 71.

16 Riker, 'Comments on Case Studies and Theories of Organization Decision-Making', in *Advances in Information Processing in Organizations*, vol. II (Greenwich, CT: JAI Press, 1985), p. 63.

17 For a succinct summary of this impasse, see James DeNardo, *The Amateur Strategist: Intuitive Deterrence Theories and the Politics of the Arms Race* (Cambridge: Cambridge University Press, 1995), ch. 1.

18 My thinking on this issue owes an intellectual debt to Stephen Brooks, who connects the prevalent 'zero-sumism' in international relations research to assumptions built into Neo-Realist theory. See Brooks, 'Dueling Realisms', *International Organization*, 51:2 (Spring 1997).

19 Gary King, Robert O. Keohane, and Sidney Verba, *Designing Social Inquiry: Scientific Inference in Qualitative Research* (Princeton, NJ: Princeton University Press, 1994).

20 George Downs, 'The Rational Deterrence Debate', *World Politics*, 41:2 (January 1989).

21 Waltz, *Theory*, p. 117.

22 David Holloway, *Stalin and the Bomb: The Soviet Union and Atomic Energy* (New Haven, CT: Yale University Press, 1994) and Matthew Evangelista, *Unarmed Forces: The Transnational Movement to End the Cold War* (Ithaca, NY: Cornell University Press, 1999), for example, clarify our understanding of the state of Soviet military programs in key periods of the Cold War. Among memoirs, Sergei N. Khrushchev's *Nikita Krushchev: Creation of a Superpower* (University Park, PA: Pennsylvania State University Press, 1999) is revealing on Khrushchev-era Soviet missile programs. In addition, the outpouring of memoirs by Soviet-era figures includes many by military-industrial managers – exploited by Holloway and Evangelista – that provide new insights into the state and functioning of the Soviet economy.

23 This theme is especially strong in Vojtech Mastny, *The Cold War and Soviet Insecurity: The Stalin Years* (Oxford: Oxford University Press, 1996); and Alexander Fursenko and Timothy Naftali, *'One Hell of a Gamble': The Secret History of the Cuban Missile Crisis* (London: John Murray, 1997). New evidence reported in these volumes and many other sources causes me to revise somewhat my earlier estimates of Soviet power and self-assessments of power reported in *The Elusive Balance: Power and Perceptions During the Cold War* (Ithaca, NY: Cornell University Press, 1993).

24 Gaddis, *We Now Know: Rethinking Cold War History* (Oxford: Clarendon, 1997), ch. 10.

25 This argument – which was advanced well before the new sources became available – finds confirmation in documents and oral history conferences of the Carter–Brezhnev project. See Odd Arne Westad, ed., *The Fall of Détente: Soviet– American Relations during the Carter Years* (Oslo: Scandinavian University Press, 1997).

26 See Peter J. Katzenstein, ed., *The Culture of National Security: Norms and Identity in World Politics* (New York: Columbia University Press, 1996) and Judith Goldstein and Robert O. Keohane, eds, *Ideas and Foreign Policy: Beliefs, Institutions and Political Change* (Ithaca, NY: Cornell University Press, 1993).

27 Mastny, *The Cold War and Soviet Insecurity*, p. 9.

28 Vladislav Zubok and Constantine Pleshakov, *Inside the Kremlin's Cold War: From Stalin to Khrushchev* (Cambridge, MA: Harvard University Press, 1996), ch. 5.

29 Gaddis, *We Now Know*, p. 290.

30 Zubok and Pleshakov, *Inside the Kremlin's Cold War*, pp. 275 ff.

31 *China's Road to the Korean War: The Making of Sino-American Confrontation* (New York: Columbia University Press, 1994); and 'A Crucial Step Toward the Sino-Soviet Schism', *Cold War International History Project Bulletin*, 8–9 (Winter 1996–97).

32 Westad, 'The Road to Kabul: Soviet Policy on Afghanistan', in Westad, ed., *The Fall of Détente*; 'Moscow and the Angolan Crisis, 1974–76: A New Pattern of Intervention', *Cold War International History Bulletin*, 8–9 (Winter 1996–97).

33 Fursenko and Naftali, *'One Hell of a Gamble'*, p. 355.

34 A good introduction to the debate is Katzenstein, ed., *Culture*, chs 1–2.

35 In fact, they already have. See Rey Koslowski and Friedrich Kratochwil, 'Understanding Change in International Relations: The Soviet Empire's Demise and the International System', in Lebow and Risse-Kappen, eds, *International Relations Theory*.

36 Fursenko and Naftali, *'One Hell of a Gamble'*, ch. 11; and 'The Pitsunda Decision: Khrushchev and Nuclear Weapons', *Cold War International History Bulletin*, 10 (March 1988).

37 See, for a particularly vivid example, Waltz's response to Paul Shroeder's historical critique of Neo-Realism in Waltz, 'Evaluating Theories', *American Political Science Review*, 91:4 (December 1997).

38 A good example of this kind of historical challenge and rationalists' response is the following exchange: R. Ned Lebow and Janice Gross Stein, 'Deterrence: The Elusive Dependent Variable', *World Politics*, 42:3 (April 1990) and Paul Huth and Bruce Russett, 'Testing Deterrence Theory: Rigor Makes a Difference', ibid. (July 1990).

39 In three different papers, John Lewis Gaddis has developed the argument that IR's understanding of science is indeed peculiar: 'International Relations Theory and the End of the Cold War', *International Security*, 17 (Winter 1992–93); 'History, Science and the Study of International Relations', in Woods, *Explaining*; and

'History, Theory and Common Ground', *International Security*, 22:1 (Summer 1998). For a historical explanation of the origins of IR's attitude to science, see Dorothy Ross, *The Origins of American Social Science* (New York: Cambridge University Press, 1991).

40 On the breakdown of Realism, see Brooks 'Dualing Realisms', and sources cited therein. For the 'paradigm war' interpretation of the breakdown, see John Vasquez, 'The Realist Paradigm and Degenerative versus Progressive Research Programs: An Appraisal of Neotraditional Research on Waltz's Balancing Proposition', *American Political Science Review*, 91:4 (December 1997).

41 Examples include Randall Schweller, *Tripolarity and the Second World War* (New York: Columbia University Press, 1998); Edward Mansfield, 'Concentration, Polarity and the Distribution of Power', *International Studies Quarterly*, 37:1 (March 1993).

42 An exemplar is Andrew Bennett and Alexander George, *Case Studies and Theory Development* (Cambridge, MA: MIT Press, forthcoming). On greater sophistication in the use of secondary historical materals, see Ian S. Lustick, 'History, Historiography, and Political Science: Multiple Historical Records and the Problem of Selection Bias', *American Political Science Review*, 90:3 (December 1996).

43 See the discussion in Miriam Elman, *Paths to Peace: Is Democracy the Answer?* (Cambridge, MA: MIT Press, 1997) and James Lee Ray, *Democracy and International Conflict: An Evaluation of the Democratic Peace Proposition* (Columbia, SC: University of South Carolina Press, 1995), ch. 4.

44 For examples, see James D. Fearon, 'Domestic Political Audiences and the Escalation of International Disputes', *American Political Science Review*, 88:3 (September 1994); Dan Reiter and Alan C. Stam III, 'Democracy and Battlefield Military Effectiveness', *Journal of Conflict Resolution*, 42:3 (June 1998); and Stephen Van Evera, *Causes of War: Power and the Roots of Conflict* (Ithaca, NY: Cornell University Press, 1999).

45 Alfred North Whitehead, *Science and the Modern World: Lowell Lectures, 1925* (New York: New American Library, 1948), p. 10.

PART III:
CULTURES AND IDEOLOGIES

7

Culture, International Relations Theory, and Cold War History

Yale Ferguson and Rey Koslowski

Analysts for years have been debating how and why the Cold War began and evolved the way it did, and the debate is heating up again as more information becomes available from archives and personal recollections. We also now have yet another debate over how and why the Cold War ended – and why virtually no one predicted its demise. Richard Ned Lebow and Thomas Risse-Kappen observe: 'Neither realists, liberals, institutionalists, nor peace researchers recognized beforehand the possibility of such momentous change, and they have all been struggling to find explanations consistent with their theories.'[1] Historians and social scientists alike are all now looking back, trying to establish what exactly happened and why.

Our assignment in the Nobel Symposium that fostered this volume was to assess the impact of 'culture' and 'national roles' on the Cold War, and it is essential to put such emphases in the context of other theoretical perspectives. Ours is by no means an easy task, as we shall explain, partly because of the ambiguity inherent in the concept of 'culture' itself and partly because of the ambiguities involved in other approaches as well. Different approaches often overlap. Moreover, there remains the challenge of establishing a clear link between the matters a particular theoretical lens highlights and the apparent course of the Cold War.

We have divided this chapter into two sections. The first puts the culture approach in context by examining several other theoretical perspectives. The second explores 'culture' as a concept and its influence on various stages and aspects of the Cold War.

Explaining the Cold War: a cornucopia of theories

Several 'schools' of theory have been applied to the task of explaining the Cold War, some only implicitly, especially in works by historians. Many historians are still uncomfortable with 'theory', although what they write unavoidably reflects one theoretical perspective or another. The fact that

there are a number of approaches which sometimes overlap is not necessarily lamentable. Each approach spotlights a somewhat different aspect
of 'reality'. Some may be more useful in explaining one stage or dimension
of the Cold War than another. That said, let us examine each of several
approaches briefly, in turn.

The individual actor, role, and the bureaucratic state

All collectivities are ultimately reducible to individuals. But the personality
and impact of individual actors is not easy to discern. How do we 'read'
personality? From personal diaries and papers, or must we infer personality from actions? How to generalize about the patterns we observe?
Personality categories used by psychologists rarely proceed beyond the
stereotypes advanced in popular psychology, such as classifications of US
presidents as active/positive. Individuals who fit the classic model of a
paranoid sometimes act in that deviant mode and yet may function relatively 'normally' on given days. How do we distinguish personality from
role? That problem is illustrated by the dolls that appeared in Russia during
the early 1990s, with Yeltsin nested on the outside, followed by Gorbachev,
Brezhnev, Khrushchev, Lenin, and so on back to the tsars. How do we
know when leaders' actions are mere reflections of their 'national interest',
history, or 'culture' or when they are simply responding as most individuals
would to a particular chain of events?

Personality might be particularly useful to explain Soviet actions in the
Cold War, given that country's tradition of authoritarian leadership. Few
doubt that Stalin himself had much to do with the Soviet side of the Cold
War equation in the formative years. However, consider the recent debate
between John Lewis Gaddis and Anders Stephanson that raises questions
as to what Stalin was actually 'like' and what influences explain his behavior.

Gaddis puts most of the blame for Soviet authoritarianism and the Cold
War on Stalin himself. Gaddis writes: 'Stalin had conflated the requirements of national with personal security in a completely unprecedented
way.' The historical figure he most sought to emulate was Ivan the Terrible.
'Stalin's choices, as much as Lenin's legacy or the requirements of Marxist
ideology, transformed the government he ran and even the country he
ruled, during the 1930s, into a gargantuan extension of his own patho-
logically suspicious personality.'[2] 'World politics was an extension of Soviet
politics, which was in turn an extension of Stalin's preferred personal
environment: a zero-sum game, in which achieving security for one meant
depriving everyone else of it.'[3] Gaddis states unequivocally that 'as long
as Stalin was running the Soviet Union a Cold War was unavoidable'.

The Cold War could hardly have happened if there had not been a
United States and a Soviet Union, if both had not emerged victorious

from World War II, if they had not had conflicting visions of how to organize the post-war world. But these long-term trends did not in themselves *ensure* such a contest ... Individuals ... personify contingency.

Also, 'Stalin built a system durable enough to survive not only his own demise but his successors' fitful and half-hearted efforts at "de-Stalinization" ... Not until Gorbachev was a Soviet leader fully prepared to dismantle Stalin's structural legacy.'[4] Will Gaddis's next book attribute, perhaps properly, the end of the Stalinist system and the Cold War largely to Gorbachev alone?

So far, so clear in Gaddis's analysis, but there is more. He takes issue with Henry Kissinger's characterization of Stalin as 'brutally realistic, prepared to take as long as necessary to achieve his goals, willing to adapt ideology as needed to justify them'. In Gaddis's view, 'ideology often *determined* the behavior of Marxist-Leninist regimes', including that of Stalin. Why, except for ideology, asks Gaddis, would Soviet leaders persist with collective agriculture when it had plainly failed. Stalin additionally believed, despite strong indications to the contrary, that the next war would take place within the capitalist world. 'Ideology also helps to explain Stalin's uncharacteristic aggressiveness in the months preceding the Korean War. He interpreted Mao's victory as evidence that the revolutionary tide, contained in Europe, had shifted to Asia. He fell, as a consequence, into a kind of geriatric romanticism ...'[5] Stalin in this regard resembled Mao and Hitler. Both Hitler and Stalin 'dedicated themselves to implementing internationalist ideologies' and 'subordinated geopolitical logic to authoritarian romanticism'.[6]

That might seem to describe a different sort of dictator. Gaddis points out, moreover, that 'there seems to have been something about authoritarians that caused them to lose touch with reality'. So would any authoritarian, especially Marxist, have done as much as Stalin did? In sum, do we blame the system, the tsarist legacy, Marxist ideology, and/or Stalin's dementia for all or most of the troubles? Stephanson is disturbed by Gaddis's description of Stalin as a 'romantic'. Stephanson rejoins:

It is not an epithet that comes readily to mind when one thinks of Stalin. Nasty, brutish, cunning, lots of horrible things, but *romantic*? I think not. However, Gaddis seems to mean nothing more than that Stalin really was a communist, doctrinely bound and so incapable of seeing reality for what is was ... After him, this romanticism became a perverse sort of sentimentality within the Soviet leadership, geriatric over-exertion, a futile attempt to find revolutionary roots long since lost. Hence, for example, Khrushchev's attachment to Cuba.[7]

That is persuasive, but personality has somehow gone missing in the process.

The other major figures, at the end of the Cold War, were, of course, Gorbachev and Ronald Reagan. Reagan was a democratic president known for delegating, while Gorbachev inherited the centralized Soviet system. Yet, argues Lebow, there had to be reciprocity from Washington before Gorbachev's initial attempts at conciliation could proceed to genuine accommodation. Lebow observes: 'When Reagan changed his opinion of Gorbachev, he also modified his view of the Soviet Union and quickly became the leading dove of his administration.'[8] While Lebow thus stresses that it took not one individual, but two, to tango, Janice Gross Stein places her emphasis on Gorbachev, albeit in a curiously back-handed way. By contrast with Stalin, in her view, Gorbachev was central precisely because he had few preconceived notions and was therefore unusually receptive to learning. Does she once again shift from the individual: who or what then filled Gorbachev's near-empty vessel? Writes Stein: 'The answer to the question of how Gorbachev learned is that he learned in part from those in the Soviet Union who had been thinking about security for a long time, in part from the meetings he held with senior officials abroad, and in part through ... trial-and-error.'[9] Thomas Risse-Kappen maintains, somewhat differently, that four transnational networks or 'intellectual communities' influenced Gorbachev: a liberal arms control community in the United States, Western European peace researchers, European policy-makers in Social Democratic and Labor parties, and natural scientists in various Russian institutes.[10] If his interpretation is accepted, we have shifted even further away from the individual, to transnational linkages in civil societies, and thereby closer to the liberal perspective discussed below.

In Stein's view, Gorbachev's own learning was only the beginning of a much wider process: 'Although individual learning by doing was a necessary condition of foreign policy change, it is not a sufficient explanation ... Gorbachev's new thinking activated the engine of policy change, but politics determined whether, when, how far, and in what ways change occurred.'[11] 'Politics' in this case involved 'co-optation of intellectual and political entrepreneurs, coalition building and some institutionalization, and further policy change'. The process from the very outset in 1985 was highly tentative and never complete: 'Gorbachev changed the top leadership in the Foreign Ministry and the International Department of the Central Committee, put civilians with defense expertise on the staff of the Central Committee, and named policy intellectuals to his personal staff.' Yet no broad-based consensus in favor of new thinking emerged, and it remained 'politically contested'. The opposition gained strength in 1990-91, and 'Gorbachev was forced to give greater attention to traditional thinkers and to slow somewhat the pace of policy change.'[12] In August 1991, indeed, whatever force Gorbachev as a personality exerted was almost extinguished in a military coup, and that episode brought yet another strong personality, Boris Yeltsin, to the fore. At the same time, Soviet politics moved into a more pluralistic phase.

Vladislav M. Zubok would no doubt agree with Stein that Gorbachev and others went through a learning process at a dizzying pace, but Zubok's assessment of Gorbachev is that the personality vessel he brought to his central role in the Soviet system was not even near empty. Zubok stresses that Gorbachev 'represented the educated, Westernized part of the next generation of Soviet political elites ... the last cohort of reformers that the moribund Soviet elites could muster at this fateful moment'. Some of this generation were literally grandsons of revolutionaries who had been killed by Stalin, and Gorbachev himself had come to a personal belief in the necessity for 'Communism with a human face'. 'He found his soul-brothers among revisionists of the communist creed, Eurocommunists, Social Democrats, and among the apostles of "social Christianity", including, most surprisingly, Pope John Paul II.' Zubok is clear that he believes the fall of the USSR and its empire would never have taken place had not the entire system been in the throes of a 'multi-faceted crisis'. However, given the crisis context and Gorbachev's role at the center of the governing structure, what he decided was crucial. Writes Zubok: 'Gorbachev's choice to remain "a good Tsar", to avoid force, proved to be decisive in a political system where the will of the leader since Stalin's times was the imperative' and was a crucial factor in 'the complete and peaceful nature of the Soviet collapse.'[13]

Liberalism: democracy and capitalism

So-called liberal interpretations of Cold War history suffer, among other things, from a central ambiguity as to what 'liberal' actually means. Michael Doyle, for example, argues that 'liberalism' involves a shared commitment to the civil liberties of citizens, a state with a representative legislature and the consent of an electorate, recognized rights of private property, and free-market economic decisions.[14] Some liberals of that order (though not Doyle) would insist that the Cold War ended, fundamentally, because democracy triumphed over Soviet-style authoritarianism and capitalism vanquished state socialism. The ultimate expression of that sort of triumphalism is Francis Fukuyama's 'end of history' thesis.[15] Other persons who might be classified as political liberals in the United States favor advancing democracy and human rights, but also advocate a higher measure of income redistribution and regulation of market forces. They are the American version of European social democrats and are keen to distance themselves from the nineteenth-century brand of liberalism associated with Adam Smith and twentieth-century US political conservatives.

Few would deny that notions of democracy and free-market capitalism are currently riding high in global affairs. But the extent to which either or both account in some essential way for the various stages of the Cold War is vague in the extreme. To be sure, the Soviet Union's oppressive political structure and its imposition upon Eastern Europe initially offended US democratic sensibilities. However, we might well ask, if US devotion to political liberty was inherently so great, why were US sensibilities not more often troubled than they were by ruthless dictatorships prevailing in Latin America and elsewhere in the non-communist world? Perhaps the key in terms of explaining US behavior was economics rather than democracy? The Soviet Union was not only authoritarian but also socialist. Although a Latin American tyrant like the Dominican Republic's Raphael Trujillo was a 'son of a bitch', he was also (in FDR's characterization) 'our son of a bitch', a firm friend of the United States and the Western Alliance who welcomed private investment from the Colossus of the North. That does not quite work either. If economics is key, how, then, do we explain the Nixon administration's accommodation with Mao's communist China? Mao was, in Stephanson's words, 'a dictator whose revolutionary credentials were much more convincing than Stalin's and whose personality was every bit as excessive'. Mao, after all, had 'unleashed the most astonishing case of revolutionary utopianism in the whole post-war era, namely, the Cultural Revolution'.[16] When Nixon and Chou En-lai exchanged toasts, there was no hint of the market liberalizations in China that were ultimately to follow.

A purer version of the liberal thesis is that democracy and capitalism are fundamental longings of human nature, which in due course were destined to overwhelm any and all competitors. If such longings exist, why did they not manifest themselves in widespread rebellion in the Soviet empire years earlier? Power theorists would insist that Soviet rule was introduced through the barrel of a gun and enforced when required, in Hungary (1956) and Czechoslovakia (1968), by tanks and superior force generally. Of course, coercion had much to do with Soviet control, but the level of force available to Moscow could never have kept subject peoples compliant without substantial complicity at least on the part of many of their elites.

As Alec Nove put it, quoting Tallerand, 'one cannot indefinitely sit on bayonets'. In Czechoslovakia and Romania 'party colleagues obeyed not just because they feared the consequences of not doing so, but because at that time they believed in Moscow and Stalin, in the ultimate triumph of communism, or in the linking of their careers with those who seemed to them most likely to win'.[17] In Russia itself, '[t]here was the traditional Russian fear of disorder, *bezporyadok*, fear of anarchy, the need felt for a strong state, and also some pride in the great-power status of the USSR (in reality of Russia)'.[18] There is no doubt that many in the USSR and subject territories, with no experience of democracy in any form, tolerated or even welcomed and supported Soviet authoritarian rule. For much of its life, the Soviet empire delivered adequate economic welfare and, if not political liberty, at least a degree of order and sense of participation in one of the two superpowers in the contemporary world. Where does stability and collective pride fit into the liberal scale of human needs?

The power tradition: Realism, economic performance, and Neo-Realism

Like liberalism, Realism as an approach to understanding global politics suffers from near-fatal ambiguity, which indeed, its critics have long observed, has also been one of its major strengths. Since it is all things to all analysts, much of Realism is impossible to disprove. Classic Realism in modern times is inevitably associated with the writings of Hans J. Morgenthau, especially his famous dictum: 'All states pursue their national interest defined in terms of power.' His vision of global politics dominated by states is clear enough, but what is 'national interest defined in terms of power'? More to the point, what is *not* related to power? Morgenthau's position on that score, we shall argue, omits a principal factor contributing to the influence of both of the protagonists in the Cold War.

Let us examine each component of the Classic Realist position, in turn, with reference to the Cold War. First, states are the primary actors in world politics. The Cold War contest between West and East, as Geir Lundestad (Gaddis notes) observed years ago, was one between rival empires and not fundamentally between or among 'states' or 'nation-states' in any traditional sense.[19] To be sure, the NATO allies were states, but what made the Cold War a bipolar contest was their agglomeration into an alliance of 'the West' or 'Free World' led by the United States. Likewise, the Soviet Union was always less a state than a successor of the multiethnic empire of the tsars, which was further extended into Eastern Europe 'satellites' after World War II.[20]

What, then, of 'national interest'? Morgenthau asserts that this is an 'objective' concept, that anyone can see that decisionmakers opt for policies that enhance their state's power. There are, of course, grave difficulties with any such assumption. First, few decisionmakers seek 'power' for its own sake: they try to mobilize whatever resources they can in order to advance particular goals. Power for what? is the key question. Second, foreign-policy decisionmakers regularly disagree about the specific goals they should be pursuing and how those translate into policies. Some ends may conflict with other ends, some may be entirely incompatible, and in any event there must be priorities.

Actual outcomes are extremely hard to predict or even to explain in retrospect. Stephanson, for example, remarks:

> Every explanation of the Cold War that centres on blaming Stalin does indeed have to face the simple fact (no one disputes it) that the

Cold War was not in his interest. Enter, therefore, the theory of Stalinist blunders, be it in the form of excessive security demands, faulty ideological lenses, personal paranoia or all the above.[21]

As Stephanson notes, Gaddis solves the problem of interest by insisting that Stalin made the national interest virtually identical with his personal paranoia. But the hubris was perhaps not Stalin's, rather that of outside analysts who assert that they somehow know better than the leader of the Soviet Union what sort of security demands were 'excessive', why ideology was not an appropriate guide for action, or why a dictator whose paranoid instincts had served him well should not be entitled to construe 'national interest' any way he pleased!

Risse-Kappen similarly points to the shortcomings of the Realist assertion that it was Reagan's realist-style arms buildup that drove the Soviets to capitulate. Under comparably gloomy economic circumstances, in 1983, Moscow withdrew from negotiations and proceeded to produce and deploy nuclear weapons. Moreover, 'some new thinkers argue that Reagan's buildup actually made it harder for them to push for changes in the Soviet security outlook'. Risse-Kappen stresses:

> The transformation of Moscow's foreign policy was contested all along: the reaction of conservatives in the military and other institutions to the Reagan buildup was the opposite of the Gorbachev coalition's. That the latter prevailed must be explained by the dynamics of Soviet domestic politics rather than assumed away theoretically.[22]

In addition, Risse-Kappen observes, Realists should have particular difficulties explaining the Germans' early 'Gorbimania'. '[T]he risks involved in a premature and overly accommodative reaction to Gorbachev could just as easily have led the Germans to adopt a cautious policy similar to the United States.'[23]

So much for 'objective' national interests or the plain dictates of power strategies, even if power is what is wanted. Morgenthau himself, it must be said, fulminated about the woeful situation that – despite his repeated pleas for recognition of mutual interests, pragmatism, and prudence – decisionmakers were forever going astray. Rather than heeding the dictates of Realism, they were making decisions based on ethnic prejudices, religion, ideology, jingoistic nationalism, and all sorts of other irrelevances. Woodrow Wilson and idealists of his ilk simply would not go away. In fact, the ultimate irony for our concerns is that, as Lebow and Risse-Kappen note, Morgenthau viewed the Cold War as an 'ideological struggle':

> He argued that the rise of mass politics and democracy had swept away the transnational aristocracy that had provided the common

norms necessary for a balance-of-power system to work. Without those constraints, post-war international politics had become a Manichaean struggle between contending forms of nationalistic universalism.[24]

Remarkably, then: Morgenthau was not only an idealist – in advancing prescriptions that many did not follow – but a flaming liberal as well.

Morgenthau also failed to grasp one critical dimension of power. Analysts can debate forever (and probably will) the degree to which ideology influenced the main protagonists in the Cold War drama. But who can gainsay that ideology was a major weapon in the power arsenals of both the Soviet Union and the United States? Would Soviet influence have ever been as significant on the global scene had the USSR not advanced the utopian Marxist vision of a classless and egalitarian society? Would the United States have kept the Western alliance in line and competed effectively elsewhere without its opposite vision of a 'Free World', civil liberties, private property, representative government, and so on? Even in the later stages of the Cold War, as Joseph S. Nye so accurately predicted, the 'soft power' possessed by the United States more than compensated for some relative decline in its global economic dominance.[25]

Explanations based on assessments of economic performance – distinct from liberal arguments about the inevitable appeal of capitalism as a model – get at the Realist's emphasis on capabilities from a different and more persuasive direction. Power, including military power, ultimately rests mainly upon the size and efficiency of a state's or empire's economy. A related notion popularized by Paul Kennedy is 'imperial overstretch', a situation in which an empire's new external adventures and/or challenges from rivals prove to be an intolerable economic burden.[26] In the case of the Soviet empire, analysts frequently point to the USSR's financial subsidies to client states and other aid programs designed to enhance Soviet influence, the disastrous intervention in Afghanistan (comparable to the US involvement in Vietnam), and the final impossibility of matching the Reagan military buildup.

Were the Soviet empire's economic difficulties an important reason for its eventual decline and fall? Almost certainly, yes, yet the precise relationship remains debatable. Economic strength is difficult enough for domestic elites and masses to measure, let alone foreign adversaries, and the connection between perceptions and behavior is more elusive still. The best intelligence estimates of Western analysts, based on highly suspect Soviet statistics and often shamelessly overinflated to make a case before the US Congress, was that the USSR was the second major economy in the world, threatened in that ranking only by Japan. The view among knowledgeable Soviet elites was far different, as discussed by Nove: 'Not only was the USSR not "catching up and overtaking", as Khrushchev had hoped and forecast, it was falling further behind.' The 'centralized and bureaucratized planning system' simply could not rise to the challenge of the scientific-technical and especially the information revolutions. Early market-oriented reforms in Hungary and Poland came to naught. Soviet agriculture was hopeless. Leningrad economist A. Illarionov (quoted by Nove) put the Soviet Union in the same category with other 'semi-developed' countries like Spain, Ireland, Venezuela, Greece, Uruguay, Argentina, Portugal, Chile, and Brazil. And the Soviets had to face a doubling of US arms spending and a sci-fi threat like 'Star Wars'.[27]

So why did the entire economic house of cards not collapse many years earlier? Gaddis and other analysts suggest that the Soviet Union maintained a very effective facade because it went for the biggest bang (in geopolitical terms) for the ruble – nuclear weapons and quantities of other military weapons and personnel. Stephanson counters:

> Gaddis seems not to see where his logic is carrying him. If the military dimension kept the Soviet Union in business, perhaps it had not actually been in the Western interest to militarize the division of Europe and build countless encircling military alliances around the Communist bloc in the 1940s and '50s.

In Stephanson's view, Reagan's big buildup mattered only, if at all, because the United States had earlier encouraged the USSR to play military games: 'The power of the commodity would have erased the Soviet Empire long before Ronald Reagan's posturings became the political mainstream.'[28] Gaddis's reply, surely, would be that Stalin's warped personality was such that military games and containment of possible Soviet aggression were inevitable.

Doyle suggests that we can make too much of the failure of socialism both as a model and in its actual performance. He proposes that we envisage some sort of socialist ownership of the means of production that none the less relies on capital markets to enhance efficiency. For example, 'pension funds ... would own the economy but would themselves be owned on an egalitarian basis'. Moreover, in his view, communism worked exceedingly well from a performance standpoint during the era of heavy industry between 1930 and 1970.[29] The problems of the system came in shifting gears from heavy industry to services and entering the high-tech information age, except in a few sectors like space science.

Confronted with economic stagnation, why did Gorbachev and his associates not opt for sweeping capitalist-style economic reforms, while still maintaining strict authoritarian political controls? That, of course, is what the communist Chinese did, ultimately vowing not to repeat the USSR's mistake of political before economic reforms? Obviously, we need to consider other factors than lags in economic performance to explain why the Soviet system unraveled so quickly.

Yet another variant of Realism that was perhaps the dominant explanation for the Cold War, during much of its history, is Neo-Realism. According to Kenneth Waltz, a bipolar distribution of capabilities in the international system almost guarantees hostility between the two protagonists. Yet, paradoxically, bipolarity contributes to overall stability in the system because one superpower balances the other and both are capable of keeping lesser powers in line. Waltz thus seemed to offer a useful theoretical explanation for what Gaddis[30] and others came to term 'The Long Peace', the longest period in modern global history with no direct war between or among the great powers. However, Waltz has often been criticized, justly in our opinion, not only for extreme reductionism but also for his limited ability to explain changes in the system. Rey Koslowski and Friedrich V. Kratochwil observe that the end of the Cold War appears incompatible with the Waltzian perspective in two ways:

> First ... the Soviet bloc disintegrated. Second, and even more damaging, change did not follow a path derived from any of neo-realism's theoretical propositions. It was not the result of a hegemonic or systemwide war. It was not due to different alliance patterns or the emergence of another superpower ... It was not the outcome of a sudden gap in military capabilities or of US compellence as envisaged by John Foster Dulles's rollback.[31]

Another strain of Neo-Realist theory, typified by the work of Robert Gilpin, accepts change as a perennial feature of the international system and a relationship between stability, legitimacy, and international institution-building, and admits more attention to the economic dimension of power.[32] (Oddly, though a micro-economic analogy to markets inspired Waltz's equilibrium model, he is as preoccupied with military balances and security issues as any traditional Realist.) Gilpin's own assessment of the Cold War era draws heavily on Paul Kennedy, E. H. Carr, and Samuel Huntington (vintage 1967). He writes:

> The dynamics of international affairs can in fact, be told largely in terms of the rise and fall of successive dominant powers and their empires. Sooner or later, however, an imperial structure fragments from within or is destroyed by rising powers on its periphery ... [S]ubordinate peoples may again enjoy self-determination [although frequently at the price of] political instability and inter-group conflict that ceases only with the emergence of a new imperial rule or an equilibrium among the contending forces.[33]

Gilpin describes the twentieth century as being 'especially strewn with the debris of former great powers' and quotes Huntington's early forecast that, among the three expansionist powers (the Soviet Union, China, and the

United States) only the United States would not find itself frustrated by the year 2000.[34] A new liberal international order will emerge, Gilpin believes (as Carr suggested), only if there is a power distribution favoring liberal states, widespread acceptance of the legitimacy of the status quo, and rules and international institutions underpinning the new order.[35]

Two things are worth emphasizing about Gilpin's analysis. Its Realist roots are evident in Gilpin's reference to 'successive dominant powers and their empires'. The implication seems to be that empires are just add-ons to great-power states, not a different type of political entity altogether. His reliance upon Kennedy suggests that he accepts the importance of economics and the notion of imperial overstretch. However, like all Neo-Realists, Gilpin remains most comfortable with a parsimonious description of international structure that, in turn, derives from the relative capabilities and interaction of 'billiard-ball' states.[36]

Polities, post-internationalism, and non-state-centric Constructivism

The penultimate cluster of theoretical approaches in our overview are those which share a vision of global politics that involves a wide range of political actors; the importance of ideology, identity, and rules; and continual dynamism as well as significant continuity at, and across, many levels of the system as a whole.

'Constructivism' as an approach has two distinct branches. One popularized in the United States by Alexander Wendt is unabashedly state-centric. However, Wendt does make an additional important observation that decisionmakers respond mainly to their *perceptions* (rather than 'objective' nature) of the external environment and may alter that environment by their actions.[37] A second, far more sophisticated branch of Constructivism, pioneered separately by Friedrich V. Kratochwil and Nicholas Onuf,[38] also accepts the 'subjective' aspect of decisionmaking and the impact of actors' behavior upon system-wide structures and trends (and vice versa) – but there is much more. The actors that make up the global system are themselves changing as they evolve 'new conceptions of identity and political community'. For example, the rise of modern nationalism in Europe significantly transformed the character of 'states'. Similarly, different rules and structures evolve at the 'international level'.[39] Koslowski's and Kratochwil's Constructivist analysis of the demise of the Soviet empire emphasizes shifts in official thinking and doctrines, and in civil societies, both in the USSR and in Eastern Europe, as well as the influences that rapid changes in the USSR, Eastern Europe, and the broader international system had upon one another.[40]

The polities approach to understanding global politics developed by Yale H. Ferguson and Richard W. Mansbach intersects in interesting ways with the post-international perspective of James N. Rosenau.[41] Both approaches argue that present-day states have been increasingly challenged by the forces of transnationalism and also subgroupism, to such an extent that there has been a significant shift of authority and influence to other types of actors. 'Governance' thus involves many different types of actors within their respective domains, not just states. Ferguson/Mansbach and Rosenau also see a dynamic pattern of simultaneous integration and fragmentation of actors occurring at every level of the global system (Rosenau's term is 'fragmegration'). New actors are born; some existing ones prosper and expand in territory, function, or influence; some stagnate; and still others contract or die.

The Ferguson/Mansbach model – drawn in part from an analysis of six pre-Westphalian historical systems – is a world of many different types of 'polities' (families, cities, firms, empires, and so on) that coexist, cooperate, and conflict and also often overlap, layer, and nest. A significant portion of the capacity to mobilize personnel and resources stems from the construction of an effective ideology that sharpens identity and legitimizes rules, institutions, and leadership. Although, within limits, individuals and groups can be coerced into submission to authority, loyalty goes only to those polities that deliver the requisite psychological and material rewards.

Applied to the Cold War, the polities approach easily accommodates the different sorts of empire created by the two main protagonists and the variety of political forms within the Soviet empire and the USSR itself. This approach does not explain policies advanced by either side to the conflict by Realist power-seeking or Neo-Realist system-level determinism. Rather, policies are choices made by individual and group decision-makers, with all their personality and institutional biases, responding, in part, to perceptions of demands emanating from both their own societies and the bipolar contest. The polities model also leads us to focus on the extent to which, particularly, the Soviet empire's persistence rested upon coercion and/or upon the capacity to meet its subjects' needs for group identity and material welfare. Lastly, the model highlights the living museum of old polities, identities and loyalties that nested in Eastern Europe and the USSR, waiting for an appropriate moment to reassert themselves.

Culture and the Cold War

'Culture' has long been a lens through which historians and social scientists viewed the politics of the Soviet Union and the United States, as well as diplomacy in general. Of late, 'culture' has been returning to IR theory, as Lapid and Kratochwil observe in a recent volume.[42]

However, Lapid suggests (quoting Jepperson and Swindler), the 'cargo' carried on 'culture's ship' is in serious need of an 'inventory'.[43] At one end of the analytical spectrum, the concept of culture is almost impossible to distinguish from the kinds of 'civilizations' (e.g., 'Islamic civilization') that Huntington has lately been predicting will 'clash' in the next stage of global politics,[44] which category he seems to distinguish from a narrower 'national identity'.[45] By contrast, Peter J. Katzenstein's definition of 'culture' is clearly tied to the nation-state, that is:

> a broad label that denotes collective models of nation-state authority or identity carried by custom or law ... both a set of evaluative standards (such as norms or values) and a set of cognitive standards (such as rules and models) that define what social actors exist in a system, how they operate, and how they relate to one another.

His 'emphasis' is 'on what is collective rather than subjective'.[46]

Moving towards the more self-consciously subjective end of the spectrum, we have Lapid's statement: 'Embracing the idea that cultures and identities are emergent and constructed (rather than fixed and natural), contested and polymorphic (rather than unitary and singular), and interactive and process-like (rather than static and essence-like), can lead to pathbreaking theoretical advances.'[47] Lastly, there is R. B. J. Walker's judgment that we can have almost anything we want:

> [T]he significance of the concept of culture in the analysis of international relations is not that it offers a convenient category of socio-scientific explanation, or a convincing account of human nature, or a helpful classification of the different kinds of human practices there have been. Rather it hints at all the uncertainties of modernity, and at a multitude of struggles – on the grounds of tradition or postmodernity, of gender, race, religion and ethnicity, or socialism or capitalism, of the Other, of the future, of the local community, or the state and of the planet – to reconstitute the conditions of human existence in the face of tremendous structural transformations.[48]

Since there is a long tradition of understanding politics in terms of 'culture', it should come as no surprise that many historians and political analysts explicitly interpreted the Cold War in terms of cultural differences and national characteristics. Moreover, even those who emphasized other factors and perspectives – national interests and power, ideology, economics – often included an implicit cultural dimension to their analysis or cultural subtexts in their narratives.

Political culture in comparative politics and diplomatic history

The idea of culture, 'spirit', or 'mores' shaping the politics of a people or nation goes back to Aristotle[49] and Thucydides.[50] As Gilpin notes:

[I]n explaining the outbreak of the Peloponnesian War, Thucydides told us that the critical factor was the contrasting characters of the Athenians and the Spartans. The former were energetic, democratic, inventive; they saw and seized opportunities opening up by the development of sea power and long-distance commerce and consequently grew in wealth and power. The Spartans lacked initiative and failed to take advantage of the new opportunities for wealth and power.[51]

Despite the early origins of cultural explanations of politics, their development only begins wholeheartedly with Montesquieu's *Spirit of the Laws*;[52] reactions to the Enlightenment's universalistic notions of human nature on the part of Rousseau, particularly his discussion of particular 'mores' of certain peoples such as the Poles and Corsicans;[53] and Burke's evocation of custom and conventions in his depiction of society as a contract between 'those who are living, those who are dead, and those who are yet to be born'.[54] Herder elaborated the insights of Rousseau into a framework for understanding history[55] arguing that 'we live in a world we ourselves create' and that 'language expresses the collective experience of the group'.[56] He thereby laid the basis for the subsequent development of modern 'scientific history'[57] and produced its first systematic theory of 'political culture'.[58] Herder's concept of the plurality of human histories was often implicitly and explicitly framed against the universalism of his teacher Kant. Nevertheless, later in his life, Kant classified humanity by physical appearance and race in *Anthropology from a Pragmatic Point of View* (1974), particularly in a section subtitled 'On How to Know a Man's Interior from His Exterior'.[59] Although Herder became a progenitor of nationalism by providing a framework for understanding human history as the development of distinct cultures and national characteristics, he insisted that there was no *Favoritvolk* and maintained a cosmopolitan vision of coexisting multiple cultures which was perhaps no less cosmopolitan than that of Kant.

Tocqueville's work was pivotal for both political culture and future interpretations of the Cold War in terms of cultural differences and national characteristics. Echoing Montesquieu's and Rousseau's notion of 'mores', Tocqueville offers an explanation of politics shaped by an acute sense of the differences between Americans and Europeans, particularly the French. He also goes beyond laying out a method for the comparison of democratic societies in terms of cultural characteristics by predicting the rise of the United States and Russia to superpower status and starkly setting out their differing characteristics.

The American fights against natural obstacles; the Russian is at grips with men. The former combats the wilderness and barbarism; the latter, civilization with all its arms. America's conquests are made with the plowshare, Russia's with the sword. To attain their aims, the former relies on personal interest and gives free scope to the unguided strength and common sense of individuals. The latter in a sense concentrates the whole power of society in one man. One has freedom as the principal means of action; the other has servitude.[60]

Tocqueville's prediction became an enduring feature of Cold War historiography, and some historians developed his contrast between Americans and Russians as a framework for explaining the Cold War itself. Perhaps most notably, Louis Halle sets up the narrative of *The Cold War as History* with chapters on 'The behavior of Moscow as a reflection of Russia's historic experience' and 'American behavior as a reflection of experience opposite that of the Russians'. Referring to Tocqueville, Halle writes:

He foresaw that what in fact came to pass would come to pass regardless of the ideological label attached to the authoritarian regime that governed Russia. The implications of this seem essential to an understanding of the Cold War. The behavior of Russia under the Communists has been Russian behavior rather than Communist behavior.[61]

A focus on national characteristics was also pervasive in writings about comparative politics at the end of the nineteenth century. Moreover, these writings often subscribed to the 'social Darwinism' of Walter Bagehot[62] and Herbert Spencer[63] as well as the racial theories of Gobineau,[64] which represented the biological 'reductionist episode in the intellectual history of political culture'.[65] For example, the political scientist Woodrow Wilson writes in the first chapter of what may have been the first comparative politics textbook:

In order to trace the lineage of the European and American governments which have constituted the order of social life for those stronger and nobler races which have made the most notable progress in civilization, it is essential to know the political history of the Greeks, the Latins, the Teutons, and the Celts principally, if not only, and the original political habits and ideas of the Aryan and Semitic races alone. The existing Governments of Europe and America furnish the dominating types of today. To know other systems that are defeated or dead would aid only indirectly towards an understanding of those which are alive and triumphant, as the survival of the fittest.[66]

The rise of the Nazis to power did much to discredit such 'biological reductionism'. At the same time, the puzzle posed by the rise of Nazism among one of the world's most educated and 'civilized' people spurred the development of psycho-cultural theories[67] in the 1940s. These theories interpreted 'aberrant' German political behavior in terms of family structure and childhood socialization notions borrowed from Freudian psychology.[68] Russian,[69] Japanese,[70] American,[71] and European politics[72] received similar treatment. The pyscho-cultural approach was soon discredited for its emphasis on early childhood instead of on the full cycle of human experience, as well as its impressionistic approach and lack of empirical evidence. To a certain extent the psycho-cultural approach to understanding politics lived on in more empirically based discussions of German 'authoritarian personalities'[73] and psycho-histories that focused not on societies as a whole but on all-powerful individuals, like Hitler, Stalin, and Mao, whose *Führerprinzip*, or 'personality cults', enabled personal characteristics to take on a society-engulfing life of their own.[74]

While the rise of fascism and communism prompted explorations of mass movements and revolutionary change, comparative political analysis remained dominated by typologies of formal institutions with extensive descriptions of legal structures well into the 1950s. Finding inspiration in Max Weber's studies of social action, sociologists Talcott Parsons and Edward Shils developed a systematic approach to studying the subjective orientations of behavior[75] and then political scientist, Gabriel Almond, applied this behavioral approach to the analysis of the belief and feelings of individuals toward formal political institutions.[76] Almond and Sidney Verba (as well their many associates and students) adapted new techniques of survey research and the increasing availability of computing power to test Tocqueville's assertions about the cultural basis of stable democracy and expanded the analysis beyond the United States to a wider universe of democratic successes and failures.[77] In contrast to the behavioralists who endeavored to make the study of political culture into a rigorous social science through systematic collection of data and quantitative analysis, the anthropologist Clifford Geertz drew from Weber's notion of *Verstehen* ('understanding') in his definition of sociology as 'the interpretive understanding of social action'[78] to develop an interpretive approach to culture itself.

> Believing, with Max Weber, that man is an animal suspended in webs of significance he himself has spun, I take culture to be those webs, and the analysis of it to be therefore not an experimental science in search of law but an interpretive one in search of meaning.[79]

Geertz provided an alternative method of 'thick description', in which the description of behavior is nested within description of the meaning of that behavior.

The heyday of political culture in comparative politics during the early 1960s did not last long. Students' questioning of authority during the

Vietnam War led many future scholars to neo-Marxist dependency theory which held that political values and attitudes were just part of the 'superstructure' of an international political economy characterized by neo-colonialism. For those who eschewed Marxism, the American civil rights movement reinvigorated more traditional liberal universalism, which bridled at the notion of national characteristics. In a somewhat contradictory vein, liberal toleration encouraged a celebration of differing cultures, which, for many, led to cultural relativism. Nevertheless, liberal cultural relativism remained positive in tone toward all cultures. For example, suggestions that, owing to their political cultures, some states were capable of practicing democracy while others were not seemed at first old-fashioned and then 'politically incorrect'.

While some of those who looked to economics for answers to political questions turned to Marxism, others embraced neo-classical micro-economics. Rational-choice theory uses analogies from micro-economics to explain politics in terms of cost-minimizing, benefit-maximizing, rational individuals. Values, attitudes, culture all become epiphenomenal. As adherents to cultural explanations of politics were assaulted from either side by economics, their own methodological differences set the stage for vicious battles within political science departments, often fought over the subject matter of political culture, between 'behavioralists' and 'interpretivists'. In the wake of these methodological battles, rational-choice theory had little difficulty gaining ground rapidly during the 1980s. It then assumed a commanding position in the early 1990s, with the demise of Marxism in the academy after the collapse of communism in Eastern Europe.

Although psycho-cultural explanations of Soviet behavior in terms of Russian child-rearing practices did not survive very long after the war, explaining Soviet behavior in terms of national characteristics did. In his long telegram, George Kennan set the tone with his focus on the 'traditional and instinctive Russian sense of insecurity'.[80] Historians such as Richard Pipes, as well as political scientists like Zbigniew Brzezinski, have explained the course of the Russian Revolution in terms of a social revolution that reverted to Russian traditions of autarchy.[81] Political scientists who adopted the behavioral method attempted to include the Soviet Union in comparative analysis of political culture, but it was difficult, if not impossible, to gather appropriate survey data. None the less, scholars employing a cultural approach to the study of Soviet politics simply supplemented what survey data were available with a much more historically grounded analysis.[82] They also developed an interpretive approach beholden more to anthropology than to the behavioralist movement in political science.[83] Moreover, rather than simply interpreting Soviet behavior in terms of traditional Russian characteristics, these scholars argued that the particular implementation of communist ideology in the

Soviet Union under Stalin produced a distinctive 'Soviet political culture'.[84] This model, in turn, was reproduced outside of Russia itself by 'Stalinists' like Boleslaw Bierut in Poland, Walter Ulbricht in East Germany, Matyas Rakosi in Hungary, Gheorghe Gheorghiu-Dej in Romania, and Klement Gottwald in Czechoslovakia.[85]

Successive generations of political scientists and historians reiterated the idea, pioneered by Tocqueville, of a distinct American political culture that shaped American foreign policy.[86] Whether it was Americans' Puritan self-conception as an exemplary 'city upon the hill' propelling self-righteous missionary zeal, their propensity to form civil associations promoting self-government (Tocqueville), or their lack of a feudal tradition and class-consciousness prompting a liberal world view,[87] American politics came to be seen as 'exceptional' – neither conforming to established patterns of European political regimes and parties nor accepting of the practices of classical balance of power diplomacy. While behavioralists used survey methods to ascertain the distinctive features of American politics,[88] political culture became perhaps an even more enduring framework of American historiography.[89] For example, Richard Hofstadter elaborated these themes in his *American Political Tradition*,[90] and in his Pulitzer Prize-winning study of the Progressive era wrote:

> The center of attention in these pages is neither the political campaigns, the enactments of legislatures, the decisions of the courts, nor the work of regulatory commissions, but the ideas of participants – their conceptions of what was wrong, the changes they sought and the techniques they thought desirable ... While my book is ... primarily a study of political thinking and of political moods, it is not a study of our high culture, but of the kind of thinking that impinged most directly upon the ordinary politically conscious citizen.[91]

Cultural interpretation of the Cold War was also grounded in a cultural approach to general diplomatic history. For example, although historians such as Harold Nicholson explained the development of diplomacy as the evolution of a shared set of symbols and rules, he argued that there were 'marked differences in the theory and practice of the several great powers ... caused by variations in national character, traditions and requirements'.[92] Adda Bozeman took a similar tack in her far-ranging examination of the history of 'international relations' of premodern civilizations as well as the early modern period, and subsequently concluded that

> political systems are grounded in cultures, that present day inter*national* relations are therefore by definition also intercultural relations; and that scholarly analysts in the West would be more

successful in their respective callings if they would examine the cultural infrastructures of the nations and political systems they are dealing with.[93]

Framed by cultural explanations of foreign policy practices in general diplomatic history as well as cultural themes of American historiography, it should come as no surprise that American diplomatic histories of the Cold War have often rested on the notion of an exceptional American political culture.[94] American exceptionalism acquired a positive sheen in the moralism of traditional approaches that blamed the Soviet Union for the Cold War[95] and a negative cast in revisionist accounts that portrayed America's espousal of a universalistic liberalism as a belief in cultural superiority and a rationalization for expansionism.[96] Although the 'Realists' like Kennan and Halle may have deplored basing US foreign policy on value-laden depictions of American exceptionalism, as our previous quotations of Halle make clear, they had no such reservations about explaining Soviet behavior in cultural terms. It was only the rise of the post-revisionist approach that sanitized Cold War historiography by clearing out much of the overtly cultural dimensions of explanation.[97]

The influence of culture in the Cold War and its aftermath

According to historians working with documents from the newly opened Soviet archives, it appears that 'ideas' had a much greater impact on the Cold War and its end than the Realist emphasis on power would have one believe.[98] This has opened the doors of historical interpretation to ideology and culture as explanatory factors. Culture, broadly defined, does play an important role in politics and it is a useful, if limited, prism for understanding certain aspects of the Cold War and its end.

It is not, however, always that easy to distinguish between 'ideology' and 'culture'. And when the difference is clear, the question arises as to which kind of ideas – 'ideological' or 'cultural' – are more important. Practically speaking, if ideas were important to the course of the Cold War, what kind of ideas? Marxist or Russian? Liberal (capitalist) or American? And which were more important – when and where?

If one begins with a very expansive conception of culture as how people think (Hofstadter), or the provision of meaning (Geertz), or in terms of 'ideas, norms and values', as Mark Bradley suggested,[99] then culture encompasses ideology, or can be considered synonymous with a broad definition of ideology as 'world view'. In this case, the importance of culture to understanding the Cold War goes without saying and the emerging archival evidence may be used to demonstrate it. The challenge for the historian or political analyst then becomes one of identifying such cultural world views and demonstrating exactly how they influenced the course of the Cold War. If one begins with a narrow traditional conception of culture as national characteristics, it is easier to distinguish culture from ideology and make comparisons between the two; however, the significance of culture may be somewhat more dubious.

Cultural approaches that focus on national characteristics all too easily degenerate into various forms of simplistic stereotyping and cultural determinism. Although there may be some validity to claims that most people in particular countries have certain habits and customs – for example, the French are more likely to drink wine, and the Norwegians aquavit – most such habits and customs have little to do with public policy. More relevant to politics, there have been many 'democracies' and 'authoritarian' regimes, and we have to be prepared to distinguish what is 'special' about American, Soviet, or Chinese varieties and the direct connections of that to what their respective governments actually did. We are back to such questions as to what extent Nicholas II, Stalin and Gorbachev were all in a sense Russian Tsars, or very different personalities operating in different political systems with different world views. The long tradition of understanding the Cold War in terms of national characteristics discounts individual agency for that of the group, people, or nation. Moreover, a cultural approach to explanation may become cultural determinism, if one views the Cold War as the inevitable outcome of national characteristics.

Occasionally, however, national characteristics seem to be significant in explaining the political course of events. China is a case in point, perhaps not surprisingly, in view of the exceptionally long history of Chinese civilization. John Gaddis has commented that, in certain practical cases, culture is more important than ideology noting that Chinese culture, particularly its Sino-centric universalistic conceptualization of the 'Middle Kingdom', has overwhelmed Marxist ideology and taken precedence. The Chinese communist leadership may have suppressed this particularly Chinese world view, initially in deference to Stalin, but this suppression has proved temporary.[100] The rapid expansion of a distinctively Chinese family-based 'Confucian' capitalism[101] within a communist country supports Gaddis's point and reminds us of the commonly expressed notion that 'Chinese communists are more Chinese than communist'. However appealing this argument may be, interpreting the international behavior of China utilizing such a concept of a uniquely Chinese world view is really no different than Halle's argument (above) that 'The behavior of Russia under the Communists has been Russian behavior rather than Communist behavior.'

Still, purging culture completely from explanations because of fears of replacing analysis with explanation via cultural stereotype may be going too far. Moreover, while many scholars find explanations based on national characteristics difficult to apply and even 'politically incorrect', that does not mean that the objects of their inquiry, be they specific leaders or the people at large, are equally reticent about making sweeping generalizations about 'the other'. As Westad notes, archival material that was never meant to be made public contains plenty of stereotypes to describe enemies as well as allies.[102] As Mark Bradley pointed out, interviews with policymakers may reveal personal world views governed by cultural chauvinism and even racism.[103] In such cases, researchers need to be open to the influence of culture, national characteristics, and race on the course of events, if only as a factor in the perceptions of actors and the decisions they took as a result of those perceptions.

While cultural perceptions of leaders and their followers would be one promising line of inquiry, the use of culture as a leader's tool is another related way in which culture was important to the course of the Cold War. Culture became a political tool in Stalin's hands not only in the nationalist recasting of Marxist theories of economic determinism that identified the proletariat as the new 'Soviet man' and socialism with the Soviet Union,[104] but also within the communist movement itself. Stalin insisted on the supremacy of a distinctly Soviet model of communism among the world's communist parties, even if it had to be imposed by force. Following Stalinist logic, indigenous communist parties of Eastern Europe, such as the Polish Communist Party co-founded by Rosa Luxembourg, could not be truly socialist because they were not of Soviet origin and therefore must be fronts for counterrevolution. After the Red Army occupied Eastern Europe, those communists, such as Wladyslaw Gomulka, who led the resistance against the Nazis, were replaced with cadres who had spent the war in the Soviet Union.

Culture also became a tool of US foreign policy. In the 'public diplomacy' of the airwaves, simplification was the rule and, all too often, explanations of East European misery slipped from blaming the communist leadership of the Soviet Union to blaming 'the Russians'.[105] By contrast, the Voice of America news service projected a positive spin on the development of the United States' increasingly prosperous society, while music programing appealed to the young people on the other side of the Iron Curtain through Western 'youth culture'.

Jazz, rock and roll, jeans, Hollywood and Coca-Cola became weapons in a the contest over living standards that Khrushchev and Nixon spotlighted in their famous 'kitchen debate'. This debate marked a certain transformation of the Cold War itself – a move, or expansion, of the arenas of competition from the military and political to the economic and cultural.[106] Not only did the Cold War influence the production of culture,[107] but, in a sense, popular culture itself became political. Indeed, the image of East Germans abandoning their Trabants and crossing into West Germany to purchase Western consumer goods has been a metaphor for the popular explanation of the Cold War's end as just one more step toward a global consumer culture. In retrospect, several historians have commented that this popular culture as 'soft power'[108] perhaps played a much greater role in the end of the Cold War than previously acknowledged.[109]

It was also suggested that the new Cold War historiography needs to take a page from cultural studies and social history, analyze the conflict from the 'bottom up' and ask 'the ordinary people', what they thought about the Cold War and whether or not it was a matter of good and evil.[110] One interesting approach to such research would be to compare the cultural perceptions and the cultural stereotypes of the political leadership to that of 'the ordinary people' they targeted with their political use of culture. If Soviet and American policymakers explicitly used culture as a tool, to what extent did their cultural perceptions, and even stereotypes, resonate with their target audiences, whether at home or abroad?

If one follows Hofstadter and regards culture in broad terms as how people think about political behavior and also following Geertz's definition of culture as concerning the provision of meaning, then the Cold War itself increasingly became more than a phenomenon and a name for a phenomenon. It was also a symbolic framework that provided meaning for the political behavior of governments and of societies in general.[111] As Lundestad points out, Cold War history was not immune from 'presentism' or 'a history reflecting present political purposes'. While Lundestad refers to the confrontation of traditional moralism by New Left revisionism in the 1960s and 1970s, he maintains that 'the 1980s broke with earlier periods in that historical writings did not reflect the changing political climate in the same way that scholarship from earlier periods had done'.[112]

Indeed, Gaddis's attempt to overcome the intellectual conflict between traditionalists and revisionists over who started the Cold War did ameliorate the left–right politics of Cold War history. Nevertheless, his concept of 'The Long Peace' can also be interpreted in cultural terms. That is, 'The Long Peace' and its increasing popularity among historians was perhaps indicative of an institutionalization of the practices of Cold War bipolarity and thereby itself became part of the edifice of Cold War culture. The growing acceptance of the characterization of the Cold War as a period of stability is only a step away from viewing the Cold War as 'normal'.[113] While the Cold War was a set of practices governed by a particular set of norms that facilitated the reproduction of those practices, a danger arises when expectations develop that these practices would continue indefinitely. Once the stability of the Cold War was not viewed as historically contingent, but as an inevitable product of the structure of the international system, historical description slipped into more dangerous political science predictions, themselves supported by a cross-disciplinary intellectual milieu nested with the larger popular culture of the Cold War. As the Cold War passed into history, the notion of Cold War comfort found fulsome expression in John Mearsheimer's paean to its stability.[114] The romanticization of a Cold War culture, however, is proving to be less effective than the earlier Romantics' reversal of the Enlightenment's dark characterization of the Middle Ages.

As mentioned at the outset, historians and international relations scholars found themselves flat-footed when the Cold War abruptly came to an end. A focus on certain cultural dimensions that may have been overlooked at the time provide useful insights into the development of political movements driven by a reawakening of national political identities and a shift in political culture toward the values of environmentalism.

Even though the Soviet Union was a multiethnic empire that was reconstituted as a federation of republics, international relations theorists usually treated the Soviet Union as if it were a unitary nation-state. For instance, up until very recently it has been a common practice to use the terms 'Russia' and 'Soviet Union' interchangeably.[115] The practice reflected an unwarranted faith in the resilience of the totalitarian system as well as a belief that nationalism was a component of Soviet cohesion and power because the population identified with the Soviet state rather than with the Russian Federation or the other republics.[116] When nationalist social movements prompted the communist leaders of the Ukrainian Republic to declare its 'sovereignty' in July 1990 and Lithuanian communists to declare Lithuanian independence shortly thereafter, it became abundantly clear that nationalism was a factor of disintegration rather than cohesion. While the mistake of discounting nationalism is understandable, this mistake dramatically demonstrates the perils of underestimating the importance of culture and political identity in the conceptualization of international relations theory.

In addition to increased interest in nationalism, the political culture approach is experiencing a revival within comparative politics, which is in large measure due to the work of Ronald Inglehart. Through decades of survey research of advanced industrial societies, Inglehart has chronicled the values and attitudes of changing generations[117] and he has identified the emergence of 'post-materialist values', particularly among young middle-class people.[118] Post-materialist values such as environmentalism and participatory democracy provide another issue dimension of party competition beyond traditional left–right competition on socioeconomic policy such as private versus public property, influence of government in economic planning, redistribution of wealth, and the expansion/contraction of social welfare programs.[119] Although the societies of Eastern Europe and the Soviet Union were by no means as rich as those of Western Europe, some exhibited aspects of a similar 'culture shift' toward the post-materialist value of environmentalism.[120] This shift politically manifested itself with the emergence of environmental movements including: the successful effort to encourage Gorbachev to cancel plans to reverse the flow of Siberian rivers for the sake of irrigating Soviet Central Asia;[121] the unprecedented and wide-ranging protests that arose after the Chernobyl disaster;[122] and group Ecoglasnost's leadership of the protest that triggered the toppling of Bulgarian Communist Party leader Todor Zhivkov, and its subsequent emergence as a popular political party.[123]

Kristian Gerner commented that these environmental movements do not support the argument that there is a larger cultural shift because they are epiphenomenal to nationalist movements that simply have used environmentalism for nationalist ends.[124] The confluence of nationalism and environmentalism has a long history (in the United States, going back at least to Theodore Roosevelt) and this synergy has magnified the effects of both movements over time.[125] Moreover, the fact that nationalists have used environmentalism (or environmentalists have used nationalism) does not undermine the basic point that intergenerational culture shifts to these 'post-materialist values'[126] were more important to the collapse of communism than the dominant Realist theories and diplomatic histories anticipated.

If it was the end of the Cold War that led to wholesale reevaluation of IR theory, it has been the aftermath of the Cold War, particularly the rise of nationalist movements in Eastern Europe and in the former Soviet Union, that has brought the salience of political identity and culture to the fore. Nascent civil societies find themselves challenged by anti-democratic renditions of national political identity. Despite the collapse of communism and the Soviet Union, some fear that authoritarianism is so ingrained in the Russian character that renewed hostilities with the West may be just a matter of time, as the Russian character reasserts itself and overwhelms Russian democracy and economic reform.[127] On this point, we can only hope that the proponents of that particular cultural interpretation are wrong.

NOTES

1 Richard Ned Lebow and Thomas Risse-Kappen, 'Introduction: International Relations Theory and the End of the Cold War', in Richard Ned Lebow and Thomas Risse-Kappen, eds, *International Relations Theory and the End of the Cold War* (New York: Columbia University Press, 1995), p. 1.

2 John Lewis Gaddis, *We Now Know: Rethinking Cold War History* (New York: Oxford University Press, 1997), pp. 8–9.

3 Ibid., p. 15.

4 Ibid., pp. 292–3.

5 Ibid., p. 290.

6 Ibid., p. 10.

7 Anders Stephanson, 'Rethinking Cold War History', *Review of International Studies*, vol. 24, no. 1 (January 1998): 121–2.

8 Richard Ned Lebow, 'The Search for Accommodation: Gorbachev in Comparative Perspective', in Lebow and Risse-Kappen, *International Relations Theory and the End of the Cold War*, p. 179.

9 Janice Gross Stein, 'Political Learning by Doing: Gorbachev as Uncommitted Thinker and Motivated Learner', in Lebow and Risse-Kappen, *International Relations Theory and the End of the Cold War*, p. 243.

10 Thomas Risse-Kappen, 'Ideas Do Not Float Freely: Transnational Coalitions, Domestic Structures, and the End of the Cold War', in Lebow and Risse-Kappen, *International Relations Theory and the End of the Cold War*, pp. 195–7.

11 Stein, 'Political Learning by Doing', p. 245.

12 Ibid., pp. 244–5.

13 Vladislav M. Zubok, 'The Collapse of the Soviet Union: Leadership, Elites, and Legitimacy', in Geir Lundestad, ed., *The Fall of Great Powers: Peace, Stability, and Legitimacy* (Oslo: Scandinavian University Press/Oxford University Press, 1994), pp. 166–70.

14 Michael W. Doyle, 'Liberalism and the End of the Cold War', in Lebow and Risse-Kappen, *International Relations Theory and the End of the Cold War*, p. 88.

15 Francis Fukuyama, *The End of History and the Last Man* (New York: Free Press, 1992).

16 Stephanson, 'Rethinking Cold War History', 123.

17 Alec Nove, 'The Fall of Empires – Russia and the Soviet Union', in Lundestad, *The Fall of Great Powers*, p. 135. However, Nove does not go so far as to argue that the mass of citizenry in 'the satellites' regarded Soviet rule as legitimate. He says that 'there was acceptance, there being no alternative' (p. 143).

18 Ibid.

19 Geir Lundestad, 'Empire By Invitation? The United States and Western Europe, 1945–1952', *Journal of Peace Research*, vol. 23 (Sept. 1986): 263–77.

20 See, for example, Geoffrey Hosking, *Russia: People and Empire* (Cambridge, MA: Harvard University Press, 1997).

21 Stephanson, 'Rethinking Cold War History', 123.

22 Risse-Kappen, 'Ideas Do Not Float Freely', p. 191.

23 Ibid.

24 Lebow and Risse-Kappen, 'Introduction', p. 16.

25 Joseph S. Nye, *Bound To Lead: The Changing Nature of American Power* (New York: Basic Books, 1990).

26 Paul Kennedy, *The Rise and Fall of Great Powers: Economic Change and Military Conflict from 1500 to 2000* (New York: Random House, 1987).

27 Nove, 'The Fall of Empires – Russia and the Soviet Union', pp. 137, 139.

28 Stephanson, 'Rethinking Cold War History', 123–4.

29 Doyle, 'Liberalism and the End of the Cold War', pp. 92–3.

30 John Lewis Gaddis, *The Long Peace: Inquiries into the History of the Cold War* (New York: Oxford University Press, 1987).

31 Rey Koslowski and Friedrich V. Kratochwil, 'Understanding Change in International Politics: The Soviet Empire's Demise and the International System', in Lebow and Risse-Kappen, *International Relations Theory and the End of the Cold War*, p. 129.

32 See by Robert Gilpin, *War and Change in World Politics* (Cambridge: Cambridge University Press, 1981); and 'The Richness of the Tradition of Political Realism', in Robert Keohane, ed., *Neorealism and Its Critics* (New York: Columbia University Press, 1986), pp. 301–21.

33 Robert Gilpin, 'The Cycle of Great Powers: Has It Finally Been Broken?', in Lundestad, *The Fall of Great Powers*, p. 313.

34 Ibid., pp. 313, 320.

35 Ibid., pp. 317, 328–9.

36 We do not discuss the Institutionalist school of IR theory associated with the work of Robert Keohane in this chapter, since it focuses on the evolution of international institutions (most of which did not involve the USSR) and has little to tell us about the Cold War.

37 See, for example, by Alexander Wendt, 'Anarchy Is What States Make of It: The Social Construction of Power Politics', *International Organization*, vol. 46, no. 2 (Spring 1992): 391–426; and 'Identity and Structural Change in International Politics', in Yosef Lapid and Friedrich Kratochwil, *The Return of Culture and Identity in IR Theory* (Boulder, CO: Lynne Rienner, 1996), pp. 47–64.

38 See especially Friedrich V. Kratochwil, *Rules, Norms, and Decisions: On the Conditions of Practical and Legal Reasoning in International Relations and Domestic Affairs* (Cambridge: Cambridge University Press, 1989); Nicholas Onuf, *World of Our Making: Rules and Rule in Social Theory and International Relations* (Columbia, SC: University of South Carolina Press, 1989); and Vendulka Kubálková, Nicholas Onuf, and Paul Kowert, eds, *International Relations in a Constructed World* (Armonk, NY: M. E. Sharpe, 1998).

39 Koslowski and Kratochwil, 'Understanding Change in International Politics', p. 136.

40 Ibid., pp. 144–59.

41 See Yale H. Ferguson and Richard W. Mansbach, *Polities: Authority, Identities, and Change* (Columbia, SC: University of South Carolina Press, 1996), 'The Past as Prelude to the Future: Identities and Loyalties in Global Politics', in Lapid and Kratochwil, *The Return of Culture and Identity in International Relations Theory*, pp. 21–44; 'Beyond Inside/Outside: Political Space and Westphalian States in a World of "Polities"', *Global Governance*, vol. 2, no. 2 (May–Aug. 1996): 261–87; 'History's Revenge and Future Shock', in Martin Hewson and Timothy Sinclair, eds, *Approaches to Global Governance Theory* (Albany, NY: State University of New York Press, 1999); and James N. Rosenau, especially, *Along the Domestic–Foreign Frontier* (Cambridge: Cambridge University Press, 1997); *Turbulence in World Politics* (Princeton, NJ: Princeton University Press, 1990); and 'Governance in the Twenty-first Century', *Global Governance*, vol. 1, no. 1 (Winter 1995): 13–43.

42 Lapid and Kratochwil, *The Return of Culture and Identity in IR Theory*.

43 Yosef Lapid, 'Culture's Ship: Returns and Departures in International Relations Theory', in Lapid and Kratochwil, *The Return of Culture and Identity in IR Theory*, p. 3.

44 Samuel P. Huntington, *The Clash of Civilizations and the Remaking of World Order* (New York: Simon & Schuster, 1996).

45 Samuel P. Huntington, 'The Erosion of American National Interests', *Foreign Affairs*, vol. 76, no. 5 (Sept.–Oct. 1997): 28–49.

46 Peter J. Katzenstein, 'Introduction: Alternative Perspectives on National Security', in Peter J. Katzenstein, ed., *The Culture of National Security: Norms and Identity in World Politics* (New York: Columbia University Press, 1996), pp. 6–7.

47 Lapid, 'Culture's Ship', p. 8.

48 R. B. J. Walker, 'The Concept of Culture in the Theory of International Relations', in Jongsuk Chay, ed., *Culture and International Relations* (New York: Praeger, 1990), pp. 12–13.

49 For example, Aristotle referred to a 'state of mind which creates revolutions', in *Politics*, book V, chapter 2, in Richard McKeon, ed., *The Basic Works of Aristotle* (New York: Random House, 1941), pp. 1234–5.

50 Thucydides, *History of the Peloponnesian War*, trans. Rex Warner (London: Penguin, 1972), pp. 39–46.

51 Gilpin, *War and Change*, p. 96.

52 Especially Book 19, 'On the laws in their relation with the principles forming the general spirit, the mores, and the manners of a nation', Montesquieu, *Spirit of the Laws* (1748), trans. and ed. Anne M. Cohler, Basia Carolyn Miller, and Harold Samuel Stone (Cambridge: Cambridge University Press, 1989).

53 Jean-Jacques Rousseau, *The Government of Poland*, trans. Willmoore Kendall (Indianapolis, IN: Hackett, 1985); and Jean-Jacques Rousseau, *The Constitutional Project for Corsica*, in Frederick Watkins, trans. and ed., *Political Writings* (Edinburgh: Nelson, 1953).

54 Edmund Burke, *Reflections on the Revolution in France* (1790) in Walter J. Bate, ed., *Selected Writings of Edmund Burke* (New York: The Modern Library, 1960), p. 407.

55 Johann Gottfried Herder, *Ideen zur Philosophie der Menschengeschichte* (4 vols 1784–1791).

56 F. M. Barnard, ed. and trans., *Herder on Social and Political Culture* (Cambridge: Cambridge University Press, 1969).

57 R. G. Collingwood, *The Idea of History* (Oxford: Oxford University Press, 1946), pp. 86–93.

58 F. M. Barnard, 'Culture and Political Development: Herder's Suggestive Insights', *American Political Science Review*, vol. 63 (1969): 379–97, at 392.

59 *Anthropology from a Pragmatic Point of View* (The Hague: Nijhoff, 1974), trans. Mary S. Gregor; Immanuel Kant, *Anthropologie in Pragmatischer Hinsicht*, in *Immanuel Kants Werke*, ed. Ernst Cassier (Hildesheim: Gerstenberg, 1973), Vol. 8, pp. 214–15. For a discussion of 'Kant's Anthropological Odyssey', see Michael Brint, *A Genealogy of Political Culture* (Boulder, CO: Westview Press, 1991), pp. 58–65.

60 Alexis de Tocqueville, *Democracy in America*, ed. J. P. Mayer, trans. George Lawrence (Garden City, NY: Doubleday, 1969).

61 Louis Halle, *The Cold War as History* (New York: Harper & Row, 1967), p. 11.

62 Bagehot, *Physics and Politics*.

63 Herbert Spencer, *The Man versus the State* (1884), ed. E. Mack (Indianapolis, IN: Liberty Classics, 1981)

64 Arthur de Gobineau, *Selected Political Writings*, ed. M. D. Bliss (London: Cape, 1970).

65 Gabriel A. Almond, 'Foreword' to Richard J. Ellis and Michael Thompson, *Culture Matters: Essays in Honor of Aaron Wildavsky* (Boulder, CO: Westview Press, 1997), pp. vii–viii.

66 Woodrow Wilson, *The State: Elements of Historical and Practical Politics* (Boston, MA: D. C. Heath & Co., 1889), p. 2.

67 Norman Leites, 'Psycho-Cultural Hypotheses About Political Acts', *World Politics*, vol. 1, no. 1 (1948): 102–19.

68 See Rudolph M. Lowenstein, 'The Historical and Cultural Roots of Anti-Semitism', in Geza Roheim, ed., *Psychoanalysis and the Social Sciences* (New York: International Universities Press, 1947), pp. 313–56.

69 Geoffrey Gorer and John Rickman, *The People of Great Russia: A Psychological Study* (London: Cresset Press, 1949).

70 Ruth Benedict, *The Chrysanthemum and the Sword: Patterns of Japanese Culture* (Boston, MA: Houghton Mifflin, 1946).

71 Geoffrey Gorer, *The American People: A Study in National Character* (New York: Norton, 1948).

72 Ruth Benedict, 'The Study of Cultural Patterns in European Nations', *Transactions of the New York Academy of Sciences*, series II (1946), no. 8, 274–9.

73 Theodore Adorno *et al.*, *The Authoritarian Personality* (New York: Wiley, 1964).

74 Philip Pomper, *The Structure of Mind in History: Five Major Figures in Psychohistory* (New York: Columbia University Press, 1985); Philip Pomper, *Lenin, Trotsky, and Stalin: The Intelligentsia and Power* (New York: Columbia University Press, 1990); Richard H. Solomon, *Mao's Revolution and the Chinese Political Culture* (Berkeley, CA: University of California Press, 1971).

75 Talcott Parsons and Edward Shils, *Toward a General Theory of Action* (Cambridge, MA: Harvard University Press, 1951).

76 Gabriel A. Almond, 'Comparative Political Systems', *Journal of Politics*, vol. 18 (1956): 127–38.

77 Gabriel A. Almond and Sidney Verba, *The Civic Culture* (Princeton, NJ: Princeton University Press, 1963).

78 Max Weber, *The Theory of Social and Economic Organization*, ed. Talcott Parsons (New York: The Free Press, 1947), p. 88.

79 Clifford Geertz, *The Interpretation of Cultures* (New York: Basic Books, 1973), p. 5.

80 George Kennan, 'The Long Telegram of 22 February 1946', in Martin McCauley, *The Origins of the Cold War* (London: Longman, 1983), p. 113.

81 See Richard Pipes, *Russia Observed: Collected Essays on Russian and Soviet History* (Boulder, CO: Westview, 1989); and Zbigniew Brzezinski, 'Soviet Politics: From Future to the Past?', in Paul Cocks *et al.*, *The Dynamics of Soviet Politics* (Cambridge, MA: Harvard University Press, 1976).

82 See, for example, Frederick C. Barghoorn and Thomas F. Remington, *Politics in the USSR*, 3rd edn (Boston, MA: Little Brown, 1986).

83 See Robert C. Tucker, 'Culture, Political Culture, and Communist Society', *Political Science Quarterly*, vol. 88 (1973): 173–90; and Stephen White, *Political Culture and Soviet Politics* (London: Macmillan, 1979).

84 Robert C. Tucker, *Political Culture and Leadership in Soviet Russia: From Lenin to Gorbachev* (New York: Norton, 1987).

85 See Robert Tucker, ed., *Stalinism* (New York: Norton, 1987).

86 For an overview, see Gabriel Almond, *The American People and Foreign Policy* (New York: Harcourt, Brace, 1950), especially chapter 3, 'American Character and Foreign Policy'.

87 Louis Hartz, *The Liberal Tradition in America* (New York: Harcourt, Brace, 1955).

88 See Almond and Verba, *The Civic Culture*; Sidney Verba and Norman Nie, *Participation in America: Political Democracy and Social Inequality* (New York: Harper & Row, 1972).

89 See Stephen Welch, *The Concept of Political Culture* (New York: St Martin's Press, 1993), pp. 147–58.

90 Richard Hofstadter, *The American Political Tradition* (New York: Alfred Knopf, 1948).

91 Richard Hofstadter, *The Age of Reform* (New York: Vintage, 1955), p. 6.

92 Harold Nicholson, *Diplomacy*, 5th edn (Oxford: Oxford University Press, 1950), p. 127.

93 Adda Bozeman, *Politics and Culture in International History*, 2nd edn (New Brunswick, NJ: Transaction Publishers, 1960), pp. 5–6.

94 Geir Lundestad, *The American 'Empire'* (Oxford: Oxford University Press, 1990), pp. 17–20.

95 See, e.g., Arthur M. Schlesinger Jr, 'The Origins of the Cold War', *Foreign Affairs*,

vol. 46 (Oct. 1967): 22–52.

96 See, e.g., William Appleman Williams, *The Tragedy of American Diplomacy*, rev. edn (New York: Delta Books, 1962).

97 See John Lewis Gaddis, *The United States and the Origins of the Cold War 1941–1947* (New York: Columbia University Press, 1972).

98 See Odd Arne Westad, 'Secrets of the Second World: The Russian Archives and the Reinterpretation of Cold War History', *Diplomatic History*, vol. 21, no. 2 (Spring 1997): 259–71; and Robert D. English, 'Sources, Methods, and Competing Perspectives on the End of the Cold War', *Diplomatic History*, vol. 21, no. 2 (Spring 1997): 283–94.

99 From Mark Bradley's comments on this chapter at the Nobel Symposium.

100 John Gaddis's comments on this chapter at the Nobel Symposium.

101 See 'Culture is Destiny: A Conversation with Lee Kwan Yew', *Foreign Affairs*, vol. 73, no. 2 (March/April 1994): 109–26.

102 Westad, 'Secrets of the Second World', p. 266.

103 Mark Bradley's comments on this chapter at the Nobel Symposium.

104 See Klaus Mehnert, *Stalin versus Marx* (Port Washington, NY: Kennikat Press, 1953).

105 For examples, see Walter L. Hixson, *Parting the Curtain: Propaganda, Culture and the Cold War, 1945–1961* (New York: St Martin's Press, 1997), ch. 2.

106 From James Hershberg's comments on this chapter at the Nobel Symposium.

107 See Stephen J. Whitfield, *The Culture of the Cold War* (Baltimore, MD: Johns Hopkins University Press, 1994).

108 See Nye, *Bound to Lead*.

109 John Gaddis, James Hershberg and several other participants in the Nobel Symposium made this point.

110 See John Gaddis's contribution to this volume.

111 See Whitfield, *The Culture of the Cold War*.

112 Lundestad, *The American 'Empire'*, pp. 16–17.

113 This is not a matter of whether one thinks that such stablity was 'good' or 'bad', at issue is the degree scholars could take it for granted in their analysis.

114 John Mearsheimer, 'Why We Will Soon Miss the Cold War', *The Atlantic Monthly*, vol. 266, no. 2 (August 1990): 35–50.

115 For instance, see Waltz, *Theory of International Politics*, pp. 191–3 and the index entry for 'Russia (USSR)' on p. 248.

116 As Morgenthau put it, 'The average Russian worker and peasant has nobody to look down upon, and his insecurity is intensified by the practices of the police state as well as by a low standard of living. Here, too, a totalitarian regime projects these frustrations, insecurities, and fears onto the international scene where the individual Russian finds in the identification with "the most progressive country in the world", "the fatherland of socialism" vicarious satisfaction for his aspirations for power. The conviction, seemingly supported by historic experience, that the nation with which he identifies himself is constantly menaced by capitalist enemies serves to elevate his personal fears and insecurities onto the collective plane. His personal fears are thus transformed into anxiety for the nation. Identification with the nation thus serves the dual function of satisfying individual power drives and alleviating individual fears by projecting both onto the international scene' (Hans Morgenthau, *Politics Among Nations*, pp. 114–15).

117 See Ronald Inglehart, *The Silent Revolution: Changing Values and Political Styles among Western Publics* (Princeton, NJ: Princeton University Press, 1977).

118 See Ronald Inglehart, 'Post-Materialism in an Environment of Insecurity', *American Political Science Review*, vol. 81 (1981): 1289–303; Ronald Inglehardt,

Culture Shift in Advanced Industrial Society (Princeton, NJ: Princeton University Press).

119 See Arend Lijphart, *Democracies* (New Haven, CT: Yale University Press, 1984), pp. 139–41.

120 Such environmentalism may seem at odds with the trend toward consumerism mentioned above, however, as the explosion of marketing products as 'green' to the baby boom amply demonstrates, consumers are often able to find psychic satisfaction by subsuming mutually contradictory values in their purchases.

121 See Robert G. Darst, Jr, 'Environmentalism in the USSR: The Opposition to River Diversion Projects' *Soviet Economy*, vol. 4, no. 3 (1988).

122 Ann Sheehy and Sergei Voronitsyn, 'Ecological Protest in the USSR, 1986–1988', Radio Liberty Research Report, 11 May 1988.

123 Jiri Pehe, 'The Green Movements in Eastern Europe', Report on Eastern Europe, Radio Free Europe, 16 March 1990.

124 Comments on this chapter at the Nobel Symposium.

125 See Daniel Deudney, 'Ground Identity: Nature, Place, and Space in Nationalism', in Lapid and Kratochwil, *The Return of Culture and Identity in IR Theory*.

126 Ingelhardt identifies right-wing nationalist and xenophobic movements as aspects of the intergenerational culture shift.

127 Richard Pipes, 'Is Russia Still an Enemy?', *Foreign Affairs*, vol. 76 (Sept.–Oct. 1997): 65–78.

8

Formal Ideologies in the Cold War: Toward a Framework for Empirical Analysis

Douglas J. Macdonald

Empirical analysis of political life entails the comprehension of the interrelationship between material reality and the ideational constructs that humans create to understand that reality. As the great French political scientist Raymond Aron noted: 'The purpose of the empirical study of international relations consists precisely in determining the historical perceptions that control the behavior of collective actors and the decisions of the rulers of the actors.'[1] In this context, ideological behavior is that part of political life where the ideational abstractions of human values and the definitions of interests they engender, which are what bring people to politics in the first place, are foisted upon and tested against material reality. Karl Marx captured this dualistic, interactive mode of causation succinctly with his famous maxim that humans attempt to decide history through their own efforts (agency), but do not do so within situations of their own choosing, that is, they are constrained by material circumstances beyond their control (structures) that emerge from the social and political systems in which they operate.[2]

International politics reflects this same dilemma. Yet structures do not always restrict behavior, but can also present occasions for action. State interaction within the international system places important constraints on human agency under certain environmental conditions associated with threats (potential costs), but also offers opportunities (potential benefits) for purposeful political behavior through human volition under other conditions. An important facet of determining how these conditions shape international politics is that of values and beliefs, that is, the role that purposes play in political life. Political actors not only react to the exigencies presented by their material environment, but also behave proactively, that is, they try to shape those material forces in ways that will affect the future. In political life, this pursuit of values is most commonly reflected in ideological behavior.

The usual way of attempting the goal of shaping material reality for a great power is the establishment of the 'practices, principles, and institutions' that will lead to the acceptance and perpetuation of norms and rules, what James Rosenau has called 'routinized arrangements', thus creating particular political orders.[3] These can be limited to particular regions, such as the 'American System' set up with the Monroe Doctrine, or can be more universal in scope and aims. Ideologies represent ideational blueprints for the purposeful creation and maintenance of such political orders, which are more typically universal in their pretensions.[4] In the aftermath of the Cold War, during which a bipolar material structure appeared to explain so much of international politics, scholars are becoming more interested in ideational causation. This entails explaining the mutual causality of agency and structure – ideational and material factors respectively – and their roles in shaping contention over international orders.[5]

Thus I return to a paraphrase of Marx's formulation: political actors rationally pursue ideological goals, but not under structural conditions of their own choosing. This intermittent pursuit of particular orders can be thought of as ideological *behavior* because it includes the concept of a dialectical, rather than dichotomous, relationship between beliefs (political thought) and the actions (political deeds) they inspire that is more representative of real world activity in political life.

Ideologies in the Cold War

Despite its importance as an analytical concept for understanding political behavior, and rich literatures on ideology and its effects on domestic politics in various nations, scholarly attention has been selective to the study of ideology in the analysis of international politics.[6] Many observers simply use the concept as an instrument of disparagement for behavior of which they do not approve. In scholarly debates over the Cold War in the United States, for example, many early traditionalists portrayed the USSR and its allies as fanatical, ideological states bent on immediate world domination, with the United States often treated as a pragmatic, reactive entity. In contrast, many revisionists of the 1960s portrayed the United States as a rapacious, ideological state bent on world domination through spreading democratic capitalism, with the USSR reacting in a relatively non-ideological and defensive manner to these provocations. Partly in reaction to these approaches, many post-revisionists and realists downplayed the importance of ideology in decisionmaking in both superpowers, although often the United States was criticized more in this regard.[7] In each instance, the assumption was made that ideological thinking is in direct contradiction to, and in fact often precluded, pragmatic decisionmaking and blinded leaders to political realities.

Ideological behavior was far more common on both sides of the Cold War than these analytical approaches suggest. Indeed, since Leninist or liberal ideologies were well entrenched among the relevant American, Russian, and Chinese elites long before the onset of the Cold War, they can be seen as preexisting systems of belief that had major causal effects on the development of the political contention. This may be more obvious for Leninists than for liberals, but it is true for both. These systems of belief were aimed at the final goal of creating particular international orders, the liberal states favoring reformist change and the Leninist states favoring revolutionary change.

While both the United States and the USSR had historically been critical of the European balance of power system, they had also attempted to remain aloof from European politics in the 1930s. The destruction of the traditional European system during World War II, including the beginning of its demise in the colonies of Africa, the Middle East, and Asia, led to a global power vacuum that set the structural stage for the intersubjective ideological contention over what would replace it. The irony was that neither Leninism nor American-style liberalism accepted traditional balance of power politics philosophically, but structural realities meant that this was the most to be hoped for in the short run given deep ideational conflicts over the determination of the post-war order.

For the Americans, it was the possibility of adapting the traditional system to create a new world order that convinced them to become involved in the way that they did after the war. There is a good deal of historical evidence that suggests many Americans have found it very difficult from their beginnings as a people to fight a war if it is not in support of the creation of a new political order rather than more narrowly defined economic or security goals.[8] In the twentieth century, prominent American liberals such as John Dewey would not support the United States' entry into World War I until they were convinced that the United States would be fighting against the ideological dominance of autocracy in Europe and replacing the European system with a new world order.[9] Disappointment over the failures of Versailles in this regard added to isolationist sentiment following the war. For example, John Foster Dulles, a member of the American contingent at Versailles, and later to return to internationalism in spades, promoted isolationism prior to Pearl Harbor because he saw the Allies, as Ole Holsti notes, 'fighting merely to destroy the Nazi regime, not to build an international order'.[10] Yet many Americans continued to press for the support of liberal international institutions throughout the 1930s to create a new world order to avoid war.[11] President George Bush returned to this quest when he called for the construction of a New World Order after the Gulf War of 1991. Without this type of appeal, American ideological principles often produce skepticism over, and domestic resistance to, military action that is not in reaction to direct attack.[12] This approach to world politics is the result of a combination of liberal ideology and the structural good fortune the United States has enjoyed throughout much of its history.

Once ideological behavior is conceptualized analytically as a set of beliefs in service to the construction of a particular world order, it can be seen that both the First and Second Worlds were consistently driven in their policies by their respective ideologies during the Cold War, albeit within the context of a rational recognition of the material constraints created by international interactions with opposing forces. The new evidence flowing from the East in the aftermath of the end of the Cold War largely supports such a view. Recent works on Soviet and Chinese international behavior during the Cold War, based on post-Cold War evidence, show a strong tendency on the communists' part to act according to ideological principles more often than was believed among Western academics at the time. Recent treatments of American foreign policy also suggest that ideological thinking was influential in shaping decisions.[13]

The Cold War was far more than a struggle for a desirable balance of power writ in interest-based material terms, as orthodox Marxists, Realists, or post-revisionists might argue, although it was that. It was also a struggle between competing and in many ways mutually exclusive ideational blueprints for constructing international political orders. As the American Sovietologist Alex Inkeles noted near the beginning of the Cold War:

> Certainly a knowledge of [decisionmakers'] fundamental beliefs is hardly sufficient for the explanation of men's actions in the real world. But insofar as these actions reflect a mutual adjustment between ideology and social realities, an understanding of ideology becomes a necessary condition for an understanding of the action.[14]

More than 40 years later, a post-Cold War Russian historian, working with access to Soviet documents that Inkeles could only have dreamed of, made a similar point: 'There could be tension between *realpolitik* and ideological goals. But usually both considerations had to be reconciled before decisive action could be approved.'[15] Harold Hinton characterized Chinese foreign policy for much of the Cold War in the same way: ideological and national interests intersected 'usually in combination rather than separately'.[16]

Thus the widely perceived contradiction between ideological beliefs and national interests is a somewhat misleading dichotomy, at least in terms of the political actor having *permanently* to choose one or the other. Rather, ideological political actors (ideologists) oscillate between relatively principled (that is, behavior more directly aimed at achieving the long-term goals of a particular order) and relatively pragmatic (that is, behavior more directly concerned with the short-term survival of a polity) conduct based

on their rational calculation at any given historical moment of the opportunities and constraints presented by material reality during the pursuit of
ideologically defined final goals.[17] The national interest is decided within
the context of both types of considerations. In attempting to bring the
goals of preserving, reforming, or destroying the existing political order to
fruition, adherents of ideologies are forced to participate in the short-term
ends–means analysis and cost–benefit trade-offs inherent in all political
life. Ideologies must include technical prescriptions for their realization,
and ideologists in power know this, or quickly learn it. Ideology therefore
does not necessarily exclude the use of reason to determine policies, as
many analysts insist.[18]

Such an approach attempts to explain the ideological behavior of
groups of political elites, not that of philosophers and theorists, and
certainly not the masses, although all of these subjects typically have been
of central concern to students of ideology. It emphasizes what Steven
Levine has termed the 'formal ideology' of structured belief systems, in
contrast to what he terms 'informal ideology', the latter being more
susceptible to cultural and personality influences.[19] Both have their importance analytically, but they can also be usefully analyzed separately. The
elite approach focuses attention on the behavior of the people who make
and shape decisions in governments – the final interpreters and decisionmakers of a political system – not with an ideology's 'consumers' or
innumerable abstract theorists. Collective ideological consensus, rather
than doctrinal disputes, is also emphasized.[20] Political elites utilize ideological thinking instrumentally to orientate themselves to ('defining the
situation') and predict (planning action) reality far more than is recognized
in many scholarly treatments.[21] It may be, as Alfred G. Mayer has noted,
that ideological pronouncements by elites take on some of the characteristics of 'Sunday sermons' or 'Independence Day proclamations' for
many people in any society (that is, nice sounding, but essentially empty,
phrases), although in my opinion this is too cynical and general a statement
of the importance of morality to ethics or ideology to politics. But, as
Mayer also notes, it is usually those who give the sermons who believe them
the most fervently.[22]

How not to think about ideology

Despite playing such a crucial role in domestic politics, ideology has long
been disparaged by many as a useful concept for analysis of international
politics. This reflects what George Lichtheim has called 'some deeper
uncertainty about the status of ideas in the genesis of historical movements' among many historians and social scientists.[23] A summary of the
reasons underlying such disparagement will allow the identification of

some of the basic issues involved in the analysis of ideological behavior more generally.

The 'invisibility' of ideology in international relations theory is largely a product of the dominance of the Realist paradigm in the discipline. There are strong prescriptive overtones to many Realist critiques of ideological behavior. The critics often appear to be saying that ideologists *should* not act for these reasons, which subtly translates into the idea that they *could* not 'really' be doing so. As Sasson Sofer has noted: 'Man's commitment to ideology as a possible origin of his action has always bewildered the realist.'[24] The empirical evidence for making these judgments is based on abundant observed gaps between beliefs and behavior in political life. The apparent disparities between the beliefs proclaimed and the behavior produced in political actors are seen by many social scientists and historians as indications and evidence of tortured rationalizations at best, and rank and cynical hypocrisy at worst. This moral skepticism is nothing new. As Rousseau noted of the Europe of his day: 'So much humanity, in principle, so much cruelty in deed.'[25]

Such skepticism sets in motion a scramble for alternative materialist explanations that might be quite at odds with the actual mindset and decisionmaking frame of reference of the ideologist under study. Despite this manifest disparity between general beliefs and particular actions, only the most cynical observers would say that therefore such beliefs are meaningless or do not affect behavior in important ways, especially in looking to create a future political order. All people contradict themselves. A lack of congruity between beliefs and actions is not necessarily evidence for a lack of relevance unless it can be shown to be wholesale and permanent.

Academic specialization more generally has also taken its toll, and has led to various pronounced parochialisms, even among those scholars who do take the study of ideological behavior seriously. Frederic Fleron and Rita Kelly pointed to these tendencies in Soviet studies in 1970, emphasizing that those most concerned with the analysis of international politics are those most resistant to the notion that ideological thinking has an important effect on decisionmaking.[26] The basic idea is that the dominant modes of causal explanation in history and social science – material interests, international structures, and historically determined cultural patterns – are pervasive and powerful enough to negate, generally if not completely, any potential effects that formal ideological thinking might have. Since the analyst allegedly thinks like a disinterested rationalist, especially among materialists it is assumed that the politician can and should also.[27] Such explanations typically consist of hypothesized ulterior motives and hidden meanings that relate back to a rationalist causal relationship to structural factors such as economic or political power. Although at times clearly justified, the materialist approach, if taken to extremes, can also lead to a sterile structuralism devoid of the vagaries of human agency.

Two additional areas of disparagement that follow from the standard critiques lie in assumptions of ideological determinism and symmetrical implementation of policies. Some analysts posit that, since ideologists supposedly adhere to ideological prescriptions in a monocausal and deterministic way, ideology must therefore dictate every action. Since there is abundant evidence to demonstrate that this is not the case, ideology is therefore not a credible way to view beliefs and their effects on actions. These analysts do not claim that ideology is deterministic – quite the opposite. But they do insist that any theory about it must make this claim, thereby setting up a straw man argument. As Donald Treadgold concludes in his survey of Western views of the Sino-Soviet split:

> A tendency among modern social scientists ... is to assume a rigoristic, quasi-moralistic stance in regard to ideology, and Communist ideology in particular; if ideology can be shown to be affected by secular and especially power forces, there is a readiness to explain it away and reduce it to something quite different, on the grounds that those professing it must be hypocrites only masking their contemptible self-serving motives by high-flown rhetoric.[28]

Such ideological determinism implies that ideologists must always take the strategic and tactical political offensive for ideology to be shown to influence behavior. Such a constancy of political posture is not possible in the real world. This approach also analyzes ideology primarily by the lack of influence it has on behavior, a necessary but excessively narrow standard of judgment when used alone. In other words, ideology sometimes drives behavior directly and sometimes indirectly. But pointing to those instances in which it is temporarily put aside in no way 'disproves' the fact that in other circumstances ideology is crucial to understanding behavior.

Similarly, some analysts argue that if an ideologist does not display ideological constancy in each theater of operations, in each situation, and with symmetrical intensity, ideology cannot be said to be shaping behavior in any area. Yet, as we shall see, neither of these critiques captures the complexities of the policy world in which ideational and material factors intersect. Both give beliefs a 'false autonomy' in the complex processes of decisionmaking in the real world.[29] Even powerful revolutionary movements with strong ideological motivations are sensitive to and constrained by the potential effects of material forces that oppose them.[30] Moreover, although ideologies set parameters for the political strategies and tactics that may be credibly employed, within any belief system there remain a wide variety of means that can be justified in pursuit of final goals. If this were not so, ideologists would rarely disagree on the manner of implementation in their political actions.

Thus, much of the literature on the subject of ideology in international politics holds that political elites generally do not 'really' believe in ideological principles, are avoiding 'reality' if and when they do, and therefore that ideology is not particularly useful as an analytical device. Behavior that appears to contradict fundamental principles is taken as evidence that they do not matter. These tendencies create misconceptions concerning the functions of ideological thinking in political decision-making. What is needed is a more practical and empirically based understanding of the complicated relationships among values, beliefs, and the relative possibilities for action in particular historical circumstances. Such an understanding should incorporate the dialectical relationship between structurally induced reactive behavior and ideologically induced proactive behavior.

Toward a more useful concept of ideology

Critiques of the use of ideological behavior as an analytical construct in international politics, whether from an historical, political theory, or social-science perspective, share a common theme: they often posit that there is a inherent dichotomy between ideological thinking and national interests in political behavior. This is especially true among international relations analysts. These criticisms, including those from academic international relations theories such as Realism (which underestimates the importance of agency), Constructivism[31] (which underestimates the importance of structural constraints), or liberalism (which underestimates the importance of both agency and structural constraints), entail the classic dichotomous analytical formulation of structures *versus* agency.

An ideological approach suggests that a dialectical analytical attention to structures *and* agency offers more insight into the decisionmaking process because this is how decisionmakers typically see the world. Many dichotomous critics assume that the national interest can be either objectively determined (for example, Realism) or is inherently subjectively determined (for example, Constructivism). But the national interest is a combination of objective (structural) and subjective (ideational) factors that cannot be isolated from one another so easily. As Hannes Adomeit notes in his examination of Soviet risk-taking, 'the problems with the dichotomy of Soviet ideology and the Soviet national interest can be alleviated provided the two elements are seen not as contradictory, but as *complementary* aspects of Soviet policy'.[32] The same can be said of the United States and the People's Republic of China, or perhaps any Great Power with ideological ambitions.[33]

Most modern ideologies, especially if their ideologists are elites in power, are no less concerned with comprehending reality than are other forms of political thought. Ideologies are based on a desire for purposeful political behavior, that is, to move material reality in a particular direction. Ideologies serve multiple purposes for ideologists, which is why they are so important to them and why they sometimes hold on to such beliefs in the face of incredible challenges to their viability. They are used simultaneously as guides for action, analytical tools for the interpretation of reality, a means of planning, and as a basis for political legitimation. Ideologies therefore give decisionmakers a means to *orient* themselves to their environment, normatively *evaluate* their own behavior and that of others, and *predict* the future, at least for the long term.[34]

But ideological behavior also cannot be separated from practical compromises, from the inherent trade-offs between long-term and short-term political goals, and ideologists in power, as opposed to some on the sidelines, know this. As Martin Seliger notes, 'All action-oriented thought, from political philosophy down to party politics, from the outset contains pragmatic considerations.'[35] Lenin, for example, a leader whose ideological comprehension of the world cannot be seriously questioned, often made reference to the necessary distinctions between 'general fundamental aims' and 'the aims of direct and immediate action' in Bolshevik policy. Indeed, he referred to the idea that Bolshevism should act unfailingly in an ideologically deterministic way as 'childishness' and an 'infantile disorder'.[36] Such tactical flexibility suggests a need to reformulate the concept of ideological behavior and give it a more inclusive definition that synthesizes agency and structural considerations under a single analytical framework in order to capture these concerns that are so widespread in political life.

Strategic orientation: status quo versus revisionist states

I will begin with some assumptions from Realist analysts about the basic strategic orientations of the Great Powers in the Cold War. The Realist school holds that states act primarily according to the dictates of the covering law of the balance of power, that is, structural factors (which they generally define as the relative distribution of economic and military capabilities) largely determine the actions of states in the anarchical 'state of nature' that is the international system. That is not to say that there is no agency, but it is an agency severely constrained by structures. Realists make three major assumptions concerning international politics: (1) the system is anarchic, that is, states obey no common authority higher than themselves, and the state, therefore, is the primary actor in international politics; (2) although short-term cooperation is possible, the nature of the relations among states is fundamentally competitive or conflictual; and (3), states pursue material goals over time, with a great deal of emphasis placed on economic and, especially, military security.[37] While there is a good deal of variation among Realist analysts, these common assumptions are generally held.

In classical Realism, strategic orientations of Great Powers can be divided into two categories. As Arnold Wolfers influentially noted, *status quo states* are those that may desire change but 'have renounced the use of force as a method for bringing it about', although, I would add, they are likely to use force to preserve the existing order if necessary. *Revisionist states* are those that are 'bent on changing the *status quo*', including in some circumstances by military force, and will accept the existing political order 'only with utter resignation'.[38] Although they used different terminology, classical Rrealists such as Hans Morgenthau, Frederick Schuman, Henry Kissinger, Johannes Mattern, and the historian E. H. Carr utilized similar classifications of states and their strategic orientations.[39] In general, notwithstanding some notable exceptions, the intentions of the liberal powers in the Cold War were oriented to maintaining the existing international political order, while those of Leninist states were oriented to undermining and eventually destroying it.

Much of the conflict of the Cold War can be usefully analyzed according to these basic categories, and they are largely compatible with an ideological approach. The difference between the Realist and ideological analyses is the former's claim, especially among structural realists, that material factors largely determine strategic orientation. Constructivists, on the other hand, might argue that only ideational factors determine strategic goals. In contrast, an ideological approach suggests that the strategic orientation of a state is only partially determined by its current power position. Final goals matter in state behavior, even in the short term. While not clean and neat predictors of behavior, Realist theories lead us to expect that revisionist states will tend toward expansionist behavior, while status quo states will tend toward containing behavior. But Realist analysis has been inadequate in explaining how and why such orientations are chosen, and here Constructivist approaches can offer a useful analytical complement by reminding us that strategic orientations flow from, rather than are merely rationalized by, beliefs and values. Stated simply, states that intend to destroy the existing international political order will presumably have a consistently different frame of reference regarding what constitutes legitimate behavior than those bent on preserving it, whatever their relative power position. As the psychologist Philip Tetlock notes: 'what counts as a rewarding or punishing consequence in the international environment critically depends on the ideological assumptions of the beholder …'.[40] Therefore, both ideational and material factors should be included in the analysis of state behavior.[41]

Variation in strategic orientation leads to variation in behavior. Status quo states, being relatively satisfied with the existing order, fear the uncertainty caused by systemic instability and act to prevent it. This expands the goals of foreign policy considerably, as the status quo power, especially a superpower, such as the United States, views all states not aligned with revisionist states as potential losses to its security.[42] A loss of any country to what was seen as a monolithic communist bloc created a good deal of strategic anxiety in the United States throughout the Cold War, as with China in the 1940s, Cuba in the 1950s, and Indochina, southern African countries, and Nicaragua in the 1970s (Iran was lost to hostile forces in 1979, but not to communists aligned with the Soviets). All three periods were followed by ones of greater ideological and material commitments to containing communism.[43] On the basis of American behavior in the Cold War, we can expect status quo states in a bipolar system to behave proactively (ambitiously) to preserve the existing order when threatened and reactively (cautiously) when facing potential opportunities for advancement. Given their general satisfaction with existing structures, status quo states are less likely to take risks to make strategic gains.[44] Put simply, there is enough for them to do in holding on.

Revisionist states tend to behave differently in the face of threats and opportunities. Short of war, revisionist states opportunistically promote instability to loosen the constraints of existing structures and open the potential for furthering their long-term final goal of undermining and replacing the entire existing international political order. Not all instability is valued by revisionist states, certainly not those developments that could threaten their own security or sphere of influence. But their general strategic orientation is to value, and even promote, instability in the spheres of influence of others in order to undermine the existing order. Communist behavior in the Cold War suggests that revisionist states tend to behave proactively (ambitiously) when presented with opportunities, and reactively (cautiously) when facing threats.[45] The Cold War, at least at the sub-nuclear level of contention, represented the political results of the thrust and parry of these varying strategic orientations in the Great Powers.

Ideology and political order: Martin Seliger's synthetic framework

The definition of ideology is a conceptual minefield, since there is no universally, or even generally, accepted understanding of the term and its role in politics. I do not intend to sweep this minefield, only tiptoe through it, borrowing as I go, in order to create an operational research framework for an ideological perspective and a more useful and accurate way of understanding the Cold War. In doing so, I rely heavily on the inclusive concept of ideology of the political theorist Martin Seliger, based originally on his study of Israeli political parties and their domestic ideological behavior. Seliger argues that most definitions of ideology are excessively narrow and need to be extended conceptually to offer an empirically meaningful definition of the concept.

Eschewing the dominant restrictive definitions in the literature that portray ideological thinking as applying to particular sets of beliefs that are extremist or unrealistic, or the analytically problematic definition of ideology as any set of dominant ideas, Seliger offers the following inclusive definition:

> sets of factual or moral propositions which serve to posit, explain and justify ends and means of organized social action, especially political action, irrespective of whether such action aims to preserve, amend, destroy or rebuild any given order. According to this conception, ideology is as inseparable from politics as politics from ideology.[46]

In this sense, ideologies are concerned with existing or potential social and political orders, that is, with the structure of the system. Note also that in Seliger's definition either support for (preserve/amend) or opposition to (destroy/rebuild) the existing political order is ideological. This is an important inclusion because of ideological thinking's central concern with the moral determination of legitimate authority. As Edward Shils argues: 'The evaluation of authority is the center of the ideological outlook, and around it are integrated all other objects and their evaluations.'[47] Ideologies are necessarily concerned with the normative distribution of the means of power in particular political systems, domestic or international. Viewed in this way, international competition in the Cold War was a political struggle (with economic and military components) over the perpetuation or destruction of competing normative visions of the international order.

Since ideological thinking is action-oriented thought concerning the legitimacy of political authority, it is subject to inevitable tensions between long-term final goals (moral prescriptions) and the short-term expediencies of survival in the material world (technical prescriptions) that are perhaps greater than other types of more abstract political thought. This inherent tension between ideological belief systems and the material world leads to ideological change over time.[48] Indeed, those changes are what bridge the gap between beliefs and actions. As Seliger notes further:

> when ideology is made to function in the here and now it becomes subject to strains and stresses that endanger its, in any case, relative consistency. In fulfilling its function of guiding political action, each political belief system is faced with the challenge of change. All such systems must deal with change, attempting either to perpetrate or to prevent it. In the process they are confronted with the challenge of changing themselves.[49]

The doctrinal changes in ideologies that some critics offer as evidence that the ideologies were meaningless in the first place are the result of an inevitable process of agency and structure intersecting.

Some brief examples will illustrate the point. The disappointment that emerged from the failed predictions of Lenin's theory of imperialism changed it over the years from a description of capitalist behavior in the 1920s to a description of the inherent characteristics of capitalists by the 1960s; that is, it went from being a theory of what capitalists *do* to a theory of what capitalists *are*. Although scholars may complain that these shifts represent the analytical abandonment of the original concept, it continued to shape Soviet and Chinese policies well into the 1960s and beyond.[50] Similarly, 'peaceful coexistence' went from a temporary 'breathing space' for a beleagured regime, to a doctrinal shift that attempted to use the capitalists, to a basic principle of Soviet foreign policy. Yet in the 1920s this 'did not imply that the Soviet Union had become reconciled to capitalism. On the contrary, it was another, more favorable form of the struggle against capitalism.'[51] This was also true when Nikita Khrushchev announced it as a principle of Soviet foreign policy in 1956. Peaceful coexistence, it was argued, would sharpen the contradictions among capitalists by removing the threat from the existence of the USSR as a unifying factor in inter-capitalist relations.[52] Such doctrinal shifts are necessary to maintain a focus on final goals and tactical flexibility in the face of a material reality that often fails to respond to ideologically derived predictions. Thus we should not be surprised if, as Shils notes, '[e]ven the most systematically elaborated ideology, like all systems of belief, scientific and nonscientific, contains inconsistencies, ambiguities, and gaps'.[53]

In addition to the tensions between long-term and short-term goals, the demands for change lead to a second set of tensions among adherents. This is also an inevitable aspect of action-oriented political thought: 'Out of the interdependence between thought and action, action-oriented thought arises; and out of the permanence of the interaction a tension evolves within action-oriented thought itself.'[54] It is in these grey areas that ideologists carry out their sometimes brutal internecine conflict. This process of adapting philosophical thought for political action leads to the well-known propensity of ideologists to split into factions over the relative consistency of the ideological behavior of the polity (faction, party, nation-state, alliance). Seliger describes this process: 'Compromises cause ideology to bifurcate into the purer, and hence more dogmatic, fundamental dimension of argumentation and the more diluted, and hence more pragmatic, operative dimension.'[55] While the longer-term goals of ideological thinking may remain the same, and largely must remain the same for it to maintain coherence as a system of beliefs, much ideological argumentation centers on the tension between short-term tactics connected to the reactive expediencies of survival and the longer-term, proactive desire to promulgate the ideology and create a particular order. This is why 'true believers' so often become disenchanted with ideologist elites as the 'official' ideological thinking changes over time, and break off from the ruling group in some sort of purification ritual, create factions to challenge the leadership's interpretation of events, give up on major portions of the belief system more generally, or all three. Both Titoism and the Sino-Soviet split during the Cold War in large part can be better explained by this process than by power or interest-based material explanations alone, and these examples illustrate the *prima facie* importance of ideological behavior in international politics.[56] For status quo states, strategic losses or compromises with the forces of revisionism cause similar internal ideological anxieties among hard-liners and shift policy debates in their direction.

Two main analytical innovations follow from Seliger's reconfiguration of the concept of ideology: (1) an acceptance that ideologies and the thinking of their adherents must change over time to survive, that is, ideological thinking is not static but dynamic, and therefore ideologists in power must *adapt*;[57] and (2) ideological behavior is characterized by two *necessary* dimensions: *fundamental* (normative, ends-oriented moral prescriptions)[58] and *operative* (empirical, means-oriented technical prescriptions).[59] Both of Seliger's innovations challenge the notions of ideological determinism and symmetrical implementation as viable modes of analysis for ideological behavior.

Both fundamental and operative dimensions represent ideological behavior as long as final goals, whether revisionist or status quo, continue to inspire actions over time. They should be understood as varying means of pursuing the same ends along a continuum, not either–or states of being. Viewed this way, the typical dichotomy posited between 'progressive internationalist' (that is, strongly emphasizing moral prescriptions) and 'conservative internationalist' (that is, strongly emphasizing technical prescriptions) approaches to international politics among American political elites, for example, are not separate and dichotomous orientations, but rather different dimensions of the same phenomenon of ideological behavior in service to final goals.[60] Similarly, in the Soviet case, following Lenin's death the Communist Party of the USSR split into factions representing similar dimensions of political behavior that continued until its demise: one desiring the proactive pursuit of international revolution, the other a more reactive group that counselled caution in spreading the revolution based on the expedients of survival in a hostile, capitalist world.[61] Chinese elites went through similar factionalization in the 1950s and 1960s.[62] In this sense, the ideological framework portrays the ideologist in cognitive terms as both a short-term 'problem solver', trying to survive in a very uncertain environment, and a long-term 'consistency seeker', who tries to bring his values and beliefs to bear on his actions.[63] Moral prescriptions represent the *direct* attempt to pursue final goals, while technical prescriptions represent *indirect* attempts to do so, including by biding one's time or tactically retreating. Thus consistency of purpose does not translate into constancy of behavior, nor should we expect it to do so.

It is this area of the respective roles of fundamental and operative dimensions that leads structural and ideological determinists to their most consistent and serious error. Such analysts assume that temporary switches to technical prescriptions translate into, and provide conclusive proof for, a permanent abandonment of moral prescriptions. Structural Realists, for example, argue that the exigencies of the anarchy of the international system 'socialize' regimes, regardless of ideological intensity of belief, into abandoning moral prescriptions over time.[64] Every seeming contradiction between long-term principles and short-term pursuit of narrowly defined goals supposedly provides evidence that 'ideology doesn't matter, only power (or material interests, or expedience) does'. Consistent subsequent attempts to interject moral prescriptions into the policy choices of states are explained away by such critics as stupidity, hypocrisy, or window-dressing for domestic or other propaganda purposes. In other cases, analysts simply express consistent surprise and confusion over the recurrence of the patterns of fundamentalist behavior in political actors who are supposedly driven only by power politics.[65]

The ideological perspective suggests that an exclusive reliance on power politics and technical prescriptions to explain international politics is based on fallacious and misleading assumptions. If a group of ideologists shifted permanently into the operative dimension, it would become 'socialized' into expediency alone, as structural Realist theory predicts it will, and would no longer be acting fundamentally. It is an assumption in the ideological perspective that ideologists do not do this, but instead become *semi-socialized:* states act as realists predict under certain conditions, but will seek longer-term goals under other, less threatening conditions.[66] Thus states act along a continuum of behavior depending on perceptions of threats and opportunities, ranging from the need for survival, to avoiding relative losses, to achieving relative gains, to pursuing primacy or hegemony. These actions are often taken, however, in pursuit of ideological values and beliefs and the creation or preservation of a particular global order. It is this consistent return to first principles over time that material approaches to understanding international politics alone cannot explain adequately. Ideational approaches, on the other hand, have difficulty in explaining why sometimes ideological beliefs appear to matter and at other times they do not. Both ideational and structural analyses are necessary to explain how and why states act, and the study of formal ideology intersecting with structural considerations offers an efficient and relatively parsimonious means to do so.

Toward a useful concept of ideology

Agency and structure offer partial causal explanations for political behavior, although their relative salience varies according to particular historical circumstances. Neither is monocausally deterministic, and such implicit standards of judgment are not helpful in understanding political behavior. Structural constraints (largely represented as actual and potential threats created by state interactions), since they are often perceived by the decisionmaker as directly connected to survival and therefore are a precondition to the pursuit of other ideological goals, have a greater short-term salience than the purist pursuit of final goals. Ideologically derived final goals, since they are perceived by the decisionmaker as indirectly connected to survival, but also shape perceptions of a preferred and secure structural environment, have a greater long-term salience to political action. A proactive pursuit of such goals for revisionist states is likely when structures appear to offer opportunities for advancing toward a new political order with relatively low levels of threats. Status quo states, on the other hand, aim their policies at maintaining structural constraints to prevent and discourage such behavior. The trade-offs inherent in such short-term and long-term political calculations constitute the essence of rational decisionmaking in ideological states.

Traditionalist and revisionist treatments of the Cold War failed to include such ideational factors systematically because each school of thought assumed that only one side of the conflict was acting ideologically. Each claimed a qualified form of ideological determinism for the side it was criticizing most (the East for the traditionalists; the West for the revisionists). They were not necessarily wrong, although both schools sometimes displayed a weakness for the ideological stereotype, but rather half right. Post-revisionists and Realists downplayed ideational factors beyond rational psychological reactions to threats, and at times came close to structural determinism in their concentration on material factors and relative lack of interest in ideational factors. All were unable to explain adequately why the protagonists in the Cold War, particularly the revisionist Leninist states, consistently returned to ideological behavior over time.

This analysis suggests that formal ideologies should be given greater prominence in explaining behavior on both sides of the Cold War. Theories about situational variables such as structural constraints and opportunities, or ideational variables such as the cultural or cognitive 'construction' of reality, can only take an analyst so far if used in isolation. A more complicated reality needs to be incorporated into our thinking about interactive behavior during the Cold War.

NOTES

1 Aron quoted in John A. Hall, 'Ideas and the Social Sciences', in Judith Goldstein and Robert O. Keohane, eds, *Ideas and Foreign Policy: Beliefs, Institutions, and Political Change* (Ithaca, NY: Cornell University Press, 1993), p. 41.

2 Marx was, in my view, a structural determinist who saw morality and ideas as epiphenomenal. For a discussion of the agency of individual leaders by a historian, see Philip Pomper, 'Historians and Individual Agency', *History and Theory*, 35 (1996): 281–308. For a more narrow definition of structures, see Kenneth Waltz, *Theory of International Politics* (Reading, MA: Addison-Wesley, 1979), pp. 80–1.

3 This 'determinability of determinism' has deep roots in Western political thought that run from Plato's ideal Republic to Montesquieu to Rousseau to Locke to Marx, with many adherents in between and after. Thus Montesquieu's maxim that 'at the birth of states it is the leaders of states who make the institution[s] and afterwards it is the institution[s] which shape the leaders of states' is fundamental to the desire for the construction of political orders, domestic or international. The institutionalization of an order perpetuates the preferred values. For a discussion of the determinability of determinism, see Martin Seliger, *The Marxist Conception of Ideology: A Critical Essay* (Cambridge: Cambridge University Press, 1977), p. 17. For a discussion of liberal orders, see Robert Latham, *The Liberal Moment: Modernity, Security, and the Making of Postwar International Order* (New York: Columbia University Press, 1997), ch. 2, Rosenau quoted on p. 35.

4 Both Leninist and liberal ideologies aim at the construction of universal political orders as the final goals of their belief systems, but based on obviously quite different, and in important respects mutually exclusive, ideas of legitimate practices, principles, and institutions. I am *not* arguing for moral equivalence here, but functional equivalence in the sense that these very different concepts of what constitutes legitimate order drove policy. More is known about Leninist ideology in this regard, since communists were quite self-conscious about public theorizing about international politics. See, for example, Margot Light, *The Soviet Theory of International Relations* (New York: St Martin's, 1988). Although less self-reflective, the Americans also seek a particular political order as a final goal of their ideology. For recent treatments see Latham, *The Liberal Moment*; John M. Owen, *Liberal Peace, Liberal War: American Politics and International Security* (Ithaca, NY: Cornell University Press, 1997), esp. ch. 2; George W. Egerton, 'Collective Security as Political Myth: Liberal Internationalism and the League of Nations in Politics and History', *The International History Review*, 4 (November 1983): 475–627. Others have also drawn strong connections between ideologies and institutional creation and maintenance domestically. See Karl Loewenstein, 'Political Systems, Ideologies and Institutions: The Problem of Their Circulation', *The Western Political Quarterly*, 6 (March 1953): 689. Similarly, Martin Seliger argues that the laws and political institutions of any society 'reflect the specific value-judgments of political belief systems, or compromises over them' (*Ideology and Politics* (New York: The Free Press, 1976), p. 103).

5 For examples of post-Cold War critiques of the existing Neo-Realist research agenda of international politics, especially its materialist biases, see Peter J. Katzenstein, ed., *The Culture of National Security: Norms and Identity in World Politics* (New York: Columbia University Press, 1996); Michael W. Doyle and G. John Ikenberry, eds, *New Thinking in International Relations Theory* (Boulder, CO: Westview Press, 1997); Douglas J. Macdonald, 'Communist Bloc Expansion in the Early Cold War: Challenging Realism, Refuting Revisionism', *International Security*, 20 (Winter 1995/96): 152–88. The leading proponent of 'Constructivism',

which emphasizes agency in international relations theories, in political science in the United States is Alexander Wendt. See Wendt, 'The Agent–Structure Problem in International Relations Theory', *International Organization*, 41 (Summer 1987): 335–70; Wendt, 'Constructing International Politics', *International Security*, 20 (Summer 1995): 71–81. For an examination of the analytical problem from the perspective of the philosophy of science, see David Dessler, 'What's at Stake in the Agent-Structure Debate?', *International Organization*, 43 (Summer 1989): 441–73. For the renewed interest of historians in question of ideology in the Cold War, see 'Symposium: Soviet Archives: Recent Revelations and Cold War Historiography', *Diplomatic History* (Spring 1997): 217–305, esp. Odd Arne Westad, 'Secrets of the Second World: The Russian Archives and the Reinterpretation of Cold War History', 263–8.

6 For some useful works from the rather voluminous literature on ideology in domestic politics, see first the invaluable guide to treatments of the concept in the 1940s and 1950s, Norman Birnbaum, 'The Sociological Study of Ideology (1940–1960): A Trend Report and Bibliography', *Current Sociology*, 9 (1960): 91–172. See also, Joseph S. Roucek and Charles Hodges, 'Ideology as the Implement of Purposive Thinking in Social Sciences', *Social Science*, 11 (January 1936): 25–34; Joseph S. Roucek, 'A History of the Concept of Ideology', *Journal of the History of Ideas*, 5 (October 1944): 479–88; Edward Shils, 'The Concept and Function of Ideology', in David L. Sills, ed., *International Encyclopedia of the Social Sciences, Volume 7* (New York: The Free Press, 1968), pp. 66–76; George Lichtheim, 'The Concept of Ideology', *History and Theory*, 4 (1965): 164–95; Giovanni Sartori, 'Politics, Ideology, and Belief Systems', *American Political Science Review*, 63 (June 1969): 398–411. For recent works that do look at ideology and foreign affairs, see Alexander L. George, 'Ideology and International Relations: A Conceptual Analysis', *Jerusalem Journal of International Relations*, 9 (1987): 1–21; Sasson Sofer, 'International Relations and the Invisibility of Ideology', *Millennium: Journal of International Studies*, 16 (1987): 480–521; Walter Carlsnaes, *Ideology and Foreign Policy: Problems of Comparative Conceptualization* (Oxford: Basil Blackwell, 1987).

7 Macdonald, 'Communist Bloc Expansion in the Early Cold War', pp. 154–8.

8 David M. Fitzsimons, 'Tom Paine's New World Order: Idealistic Internationalism in the Ideology of Early American Foreign Relations', *Diplomatic History*, 19 (Fall 1995): 569–82.

9 John C. Farrell, 'John Dewey and World War I: Armageddon Tests a Liberal's Faith', *Perspectives in American History*, 9 (1975): 299–340. For a broader analysis of the period, see Thomas J. Knock, *To End All Wars: Woodrow Wilson and the Quest for a New World Order* (New York: Oxford University Press, 1992). Knock points out that there was a good deal of variation between 'progressive' and 'conservative' internationalisms in the period, the former emphasizing change and the latter emphasizing stability. But there were enough similarities between the positions to distinguish a distinctive liberal view of world order. After the overthrow of the Russian Tsar in March 1917, Wilson was able to portray the stuggle as one between autocracy and democracy and support for entering the war increased precipitously. Ibid., p. 138.

10 Ole R. Holsti, 'Cognitive Dynamics and Images of the Enemy: Dulles and Russia', in David J. Finlay, Ole R. Holsti, and Richard R. Fagen, *Enemies in Politics* (Chicago, IL: Rand McNally, 1967), p. 37 fn. 30. See also, Robert R. Bowie and Richard H. Immerman, *Waging Peace: How Eisenhower Shaped An Enduring Cold War Strategy* (New York: Oxford University Press, 1998), p. 56. Although Bowie and Immerman reject the term 'isolationist', they do confirm the anti-

interventionism in Dulles's thought in the 1930s in similar terms.

11 Warren F. Kuehl and Lynne K. Dunne, *Keeping the Covenant: American Inter-nationalists and the League of Nations, 1920–1939* (Kent, OH: Kent State University Press, 1997).

12 On the Lockean ideological roots of the self-defense principle in American foreign policy more generally, see Edward Weisband, *The Ideology of American Foreign Policy: A Paradigm of Lockian [sic] Liberalism* (Beverly Hills, CA: Sage Publications, 1973), pp. 11–16; Roger D. Masters, 'The Lockean Traditions in American Foreign Policy', *Journal of International Affairs*, 21 (1967): 253–77.

13 For recent works based on new evidence from the East that, in my view, support the ideological perspective empirically, although not necessarily analytically, see John Lewis Gaddis, *We Now Know: Rethinking Cold War History* (New York: Oxford University Press, 1997); Michael Sheng, *Battling Western Imperialism: Mao, Stalin, and the United States* (Princeton, NJ: Princeton University Press, 1998); Vladislav Zubok and Constantine Pleshakov, *Inside the Kremlin's Cold War: From Stalin to Khrushchev* (Cambridge, MA: Harvard University Press, 1996); Vojtech Mastny, *The Cold War and Soviet Insecurity: The Stalin Years* (New York: Oxford University Press, 1996); David Holloway, *Stalin and the Bomb: The Soviet Union and Atomic Energy* (New Haven, CT: Yale University Press, 1994); Sergei N. Goncharov, John W. Lewis, and Xue Litai, *Uncertain Partners: Stalin, Mao, and the Korean War* (Stanford, CA: Stanford University Press, 1993); Chen Jian, *China's Road to the Korean War: The Making of the Sino-American Confrontation* (New York: Columbia University Press, 1994). For recent treatments of the role of ideology in American foreign policy, see Tony Smith, *America's Mission: The United States and the Worldwide Struggle for Democracy in the Twentieth Century* (Princeton, NJ: Princeton University Press, 1994); Douglas J. Macdonald, *Adventures in Chaos: American Intervention for Reform in the Third World* (Cambridge, MA: Harvard University Press, 1992).

14 Inkeles quoted in David Apter, 'Ideology and Discontent', in David Apter, ed., *Ideology and Discontent* (New York: The Free Press, 1964), p. 17. Inkeles is discussing Soviet ideology, but his insight has an application to other forms of ideological thought also.

15 Vladislav Zubok, 'Stalin's Plans and Russian Archives', *Diplomatic History*, 21 (Spring 1997): 303.

16 Quoted in, Donald W. Treadgold, 'Alternative Western Views of the Sino-Soviet Conflict', in Herbert J. Ellison, ed., *The Sino-Soviet Conflict: A Global Perspective* (Seattle, WA: University of Washington Press, 1982), p. 336.

17 I have argued that this oscillation between principles and pragmatism was reflected in the behavior of the United States in the Third World during the Cold War, in Macdonald, *Adventures in Chaos*, esp. chs 1–2. See also Inis L. Claude, Jr, 'The Tension Between Principle and Pragmatism in International Relations', *Review of International Studies*, 19 (July 1993): 215–27, and the classic Robert E. Osgood, *Ideals and Self-Interest in America's Foreign Relations* (Chicago, IL: University of Chicago Press, 1953).

18 For examples of this dismissiveness toward ideology as 'irrational', see Alan Cassels, *Ideology and International Relations in the Modern World* (London: Routledge, 1996), pp. 3–4.

19 Steven I. Levine, 'Perception and Ideology in Chinese Foreign Policy', in Thomas W. Robinson and David Shambaugh, eds, *Chinese Foreign Policy: Theory and Practice* (New York: Oxford University Press, 1994), pp. 30–46.

20 For the consensus view of American ideology, see Louis Hartz, *The Liberal Tradition in America* (New York: Harcourt, Brace, and World, 1955); Weisband,

The Ideology of American Foreign Policy; William J. Dixon and Stephen M. Gaarder, 'Presidential Succession and the Cold War: An Analysis of Soviet–American Relations, 1948–1988', *Journal of Politics*, 54 (February 1992): 156–75; Scott L. Feld and Bernard Grofman, 'Ideological Consistency as a Collective Phenomenon', *American Political Science Review*, 82 (September 1988): 773–88. For consensus treatments of Soviet ideology, see John Lenczowski, *Soviet Perceptions of US Foreign Policy: A Study of Ideology, Power, and Consensus* (Ithaca, NY: Cornell University Press, 1982); Peter Rutland, 'The Search for Stability: Ideology, Discipline, and the Cohesion of the Soviet Elite', *Studies in Comparative Communism*, 24 (March 1991): 25–57.

21 On 'definitions of a situation' as an orientation to one's environment based on one's belief system, see Katarina Brodin, 'Belief Systems, Doctrines, and Foreign Policy', *Cooperation and Conflict*, 8 (1972): 98.

22 Alfred G. Mayer, 'The Functions of Ideology in the Soviet Political System', *Soviet Studies*, 17 (January 1966): 284. Mayer is discussing the Soviet system, but I believe that the point is valid more generally. For the concept of studying elite ideology more generally, see Robert D. Putnam, 'Studying Elite Political Culture: The Case of "Ideology"', *American Political Science Review*, 65 (1971): 651–81; Putnam, *The Beliefs of Politicians: Ideology, Conflict, and Democracy in Britain and Italy* (New Haven, CT: Yale University Press, 1973), esp. chs 1–2. Lucian Pye notes further: 'Work on the elite political culture involves skill in interpreting ideologies, in characterizing operational codes, and in defining the spirit and calculations that lie behind high-risk political behavior.' Quoted in Putnam, 'Studying Elite Political Culture', p. 652.

23 Lichtheim, 'The Concept of Ideology', p. 164.

24 Sofer, 'International Relations and the Invisibility of Ideology', p. 514. The 'invisibility' of ideology noted above is taken from Sofer's title.

25 Quoted in Anders Stephanson, 'Fourteen Notes on the Very Concept of the Cold War', on the internet at http://h-net2.msu.edu/~diplo/ stephanson.html, p. 7.

26 Frederic J. Fleron and Rita Mae Kelly, 'Personality, Behavior and Communist Ideology', *Soviet Studies*, 21 (January 1970): 297–8. For an earlier dissection of Sovietologists along generally similar lines, see Daniel Bell, 'Ten Theories in Search of Reality: The Prediction of Soviet Behavior in the Social Sciences', *World Politics*, 10 (April 1958): 327–48.

27 For criticisms of this tendency, especially among social scientists, see Herbert A. Simon, 'Rationality as Process and as Product of Thought', *American Economic Review*, 68 (May 1978): 1–16; Simon, 'Human Nature in Politics: The Dialogue of Psychology with Political Science', *American Political Science Review*, 79 (June 1985): 293–304.

28 Treadgold, 'Alternative Western Views of the Sino-Soviet Conflict', p. 339.

29 The phrase is Daniel Bell's, see 'Ten Theories in Search of Reality', pp. 347–8. For a critique of analysts who portray ideology in a 'dogmatic, even doctrinaire sense ... as a static entity', see Carl J. Friedrich, 'Ideology in Politics: A Theoretical Comment', *Slavic Review*, 24 (December 1965): 614.

30 Odd Arne Westad, 'The Foreign Policies of Revolutionary Parties: The CCP in a Comparative Perspective', in Michael H. Hunt and Niu Jun, eds, *Toward A History of Chinese Communist Foreign Relations, 1920s–1960s* (Washington, DC: Woodrow Wilson International Center for Scholars, 1994), p. 117.

31 I am using the common term 'Constructivist' as an umbrella category for various scholars utilizing cultural, identity, and other ideational concepts as their primary analytical focus. For a recent debate over the relative utility of material and ideational approaches among international relations scholars, see Michael C.

Desch, 'Culture Clash: Assessing the Importance of Ideas in Security Studies', *International Security*, 23, 1 (Summer 1998): 141–70, and Ted Hopf, 'The Promise of Constructivism in International Relations Theory', in ibid., 171–200.

32 *Soviet Risk-Taking and Crisis Behavior: A Theoretical and Empirical Analysis* (London: George Allen and Unwin, 1982), p. 58.

33 N. Gordon Levin, Jr argues that 'Woodrow Wilson's vision of a liberal world order of free trade and international harmony did not oppose but rather complemented his conception of the national interests …', *Woodrow Wilson and World Politics: America's Response to War and Revolution* (New York: Oxford University Press, 1968), pp. 13–14. For arguments that the national interest is constructed from objective and subjective criteria, see William T. R. Fox, 'E. H. Carr and Political Realism: Vision and Revision', *Review of International Studies*, 11 (1985): 1–16; Arnold Wolfers, *Discord and Collaboration: Essays on International Politics* (Baltimore, MD: Johns Hopkins University Press, 1962), pp. 147–65; Robert G. Kaufman, 'A Two Level Interaction: Structure, Stable Liberal Democracy, and US Grand Strategy', *Security Studies*, 3, 4 (Summer 1994): 678–717. Constructivist theory strongly emphasizes the subjective determination of the national interest, excessively so in my view. See Wendt, 'Constructing International Politics', pp. 71–81.

34 John B. Thompson, *Studies in the Theory of Ideology* (Berkeley, CA: University of California Press, 1984), p. 151; Sofer, 'International Relations and the Invisibility of Ideology', p. 491. Ideologies may, of course, vary widely in the extent to which these particular functions are important to them. In the early stages of the Cold War, American Secretary of State Dean Acheson differentiated communism from democracy, in part, on the issue of prediction of the future. Since no one can predict the future, said Acheson, liberals fundamentally disagreed with Leninists who claimed 'a monopoly of the knowledge of what was right and what was wrong for human beings' from which all their other actions sprang. Dean Acheson, 'Tensions Between the United States and the Soviet Union', *Department of State Bulletin* (27 March 1950), pp. 473–8 quote from p. 473. The point is not whether Acheson is accurate or not (I believe he is), but that different ideologies place varying emphases on particular aspects of their belief systems.

35 Martin Seliger, 'Fundamental and Operative Ideology: The Two Principal Dimensions of Political Argumentation', *Policy Sciences*, 1 (1970): 326.

36 Lenin's distinctions between fundamental and immediate aims are quoted from Seliger, *The Marxist Conception of Ideology*, p. 6. Lenin's 'childishness' quote is in Seliger, *Ideology and Politics*, p. 108. Lenin also famously called such ideological rigidity an 'infantile disorder.' On Lenin as ideologist, see also Adam B. Ulam, *The Bolsheviks: The Intellectual, Personal, and Political History of the Triumph of Communism in Russia* (New York: Macmillan-Collier, 1968); George Brinkley, 'Leninism: What It Was and What It Was Not', *The Review of Politics*, 60 (Winter 1998): 151–64; Apter, 'Ideology and Discontent', p. 19; J. D. Armstrong, *Revolutionary Diplomacy: Chinese Foreign Policy and the United Front Doctrine* (Berkeley, CA: University of California Press, 1977), pp. 1–46; Robert C. Tucker, *Stalin in Power: The Revolution From Above, 1928–1941* (New York: Norton, 1990), pp. 25–43.

37 This is a common formulation of realist theory. See Michael Mastanduno, David A. Lake, and G. John Ikenberry, 'Toward a Realist Theory of State Action', *International Studies Quarterly*, 33 (December 1989): 459.

38 Wolfers, *Discord and Collaboration*, pp. 125–6. See also, Randall L. Schweller, 'Bandwagoning for Profit: Bringing the Revisionist State Back In', *International Security*, 19 (Summer 1994): 72–107.

39 Randall L. Schweller, 'Neorealism's Status-Quo Bias: What Security Dilemma?', *Security Studies*, 5 (Spring 1996): 99–101.

40 Philip E. Tetlock, 'Learning in US and Soviet Foreign Policy: In Search of An Elusive Concept', in George W. Breslauer and Philip E. Tetlock, eds, *Learning in US and Soviet Foreign Policy* (Boulder, CO: Westview Press, 1991), p. 27.

41 For an interesting discussion of the interactive effects of various strategic orientations, see Noel Kaplowitz, 'Psychopolitical Dimensions of International Relations: The Reciprocal Effects of Conflict Structure', *International Studies Quarterly*, 28, 4 (December 1984): 373–406.

42 Thus Erich Weede argues that the status quo nature of US policy during the Cold War led to the inclusion of virtually all non-Communist states within its sphere of influence. Erich Weede, 'US Support for Foreign Governments, or Domestic Disorder and Imperial Intervention, 1958–1965', *Comparative Political Studies*, 10 (January 1978): 502. Typically, this was a matter of much debate in the United States government. For the internal debates over symmetrical and asymmetrical containment policies, see John Lewis Gaddis, *Strategies of Containment* (New York: Oxford University Press, 1982).

43 The debate over foreign policy in the Third World centered on varying means of meeting the communist threat, not over whether to meet it. For the role of strategic losses in causing shifts in policy orientation, see Macdonald, *Adventures in Chaos*, ch. 2.

44 The behavior of status quo states closely resembles that predicted by prospect theory, in which 'the theory argues that people tend to be risk-averse for gains (this was generally known before) but simultaneously to be risk-acceptant for losses (this was the surprise).' Robert Jervis, 'Political Implications of Loss Aversion', *Political Psychology*, 13, 2 (1992): 187. See also, Jack S. Levy, 'An Introduction to Prospect Theory', *Political Psychology*, 13, 2 (1992): 283–310; Daniel Kahneman and Amos Tversky, 'Prospect Theory: An Analysis of Decision Under Risk', *Econometrica*, 47, 2 (March 1979): 263–91; William A. Boettcher III, 'Context, Methods, Numbers, and Words', *Journal of Conflict Resolution*, 39, 3 (September 1995): 561–83. In contrast to prospect theory, which suggests that this is universally true, I believe that the theory describes the tendencies of status quo powers but not revisionist ones.

45 I have argued this in Macdonald, 'Communist Bloc Expansion in the Early Cold War.'

46 Seliger, *The Marxist Conception of Ideology*, p. 1; see a far more detailed definition in Seliger, *Ideology and Politics*, pp. 119–20. Seliger's theory of ideology deals almost exclusively with domestic political orders. I have adapted it for application to the international political order.

47 As Shils notes further: 'Ideologies are always concerned with authority, transcendent and earthly, and they cannot, therefore, avoid being political except by the extreme reaction-formation of complete withdrawal from society.' Both quotes from Shils, 'The Concept and Function of Ideology', p. 68. Rokeach's influential work on belief systems, and a good deal of the psychology of ideology literature, concentrates on little else but attitudes toward authority. See Milton Rokeach, *The Open and Closed Mind: Investigations into the Nature of Belief Systems and Personality Systems* (New York: Basic Books, 1960).

48 Steve Levine, following the analysis of the China historian Benjamin I. Schwartz, argues that such changes represent ideological 'disintegration' and 'decay'. Levine, 'Perception and Ideology in Chinese Foreign Policy', pp. 31–2. But altering belief systems represents decay only if they are expected never to adapt to changing circumstances. Seliger's insight is that ideologies must adapt as they interact with

material reality. Proponents of such adaptation not only do not see such change as decay, but usually present it as ideological renewal.

49 Seliger, 'Fundamental and Operative Ideology', p. 326.

50 For example, James Roberts complains that these changes emptied the theory of all meaning. See James W. Roberts, 'Lenin's Theory of Imperialism in Soviet Usage', *Soviet Studies*, 29 (July 1977): 353–72. For another example of doctrinal adaptation, see Richard Nordahl, 'Stalinist Ideology: The Case of the Stalinist Interpretation of Monopoly Capitalist Politics', *Soviet Studies*, 26 (April 1974): 239–59.

51 Light, *The Soviet Theory of International Relations*, p. 33.

52 Ibid., p. 51. For discussions among the post-Stalin leadership of the Soviet Union, even prior to Khrushchev's switch to 'peaceful coexistence' in 1956, of the unifying effects on the non-communist world of the Stalin–Molotov hard line, see the Plenum discussions on the question in *Cold War International History Project Bulletin*, 10, 'Leadership Transition in a Fractured Bloc' (March 1998), pp. 34–60. Ironically, Khrushchev went on after 1957 to nullify any such potential effects by his bellicose behavior that alarmed the West in the late 1950s and early 1960s. He might have done so unintentionally, in part, while trying to calm fears among fundamentalists at home and abroad that the USSR had become a status quo power, as the Chinese were then charging. For example, in October 1958 the Chinese Ambassador to the USSR noted with some satisfaction that Khrushchev, in apparent response to Chinese complaints, had begun to emphasize 'the correctness of our position that war must not be feared and peace cannot be begged [for]'. Quoted in Shu Guang Zhang, 'Sino-Soviet Economic Cooperation', in Odd Arne Westad, ed., *Brothers in Arms: The Rise and Fall of the Sino-Soviet Alliance, 1945–1963* (Stanford, CA: Stanford University Press, 1998), p. 211.

53 Shils, 'The Concept and Function of Ideology', p. 70. See also, Seliger, *Ideology and Politics*, p. 98.

54 Seliger, 'Fundamental and Operative Ideology', pp. 326–7. For treatments of ideology that include similar thought-action aspects of ideological thinking, see Apter, 'Ideology and Discontent', p. 17; Sartori, 'Politics, Ideology, and Belief Systems', pp. 402–3. The difference is that Seliger's framework synthesizes the elements into a single concept, whereas the others maintain a relatively strict separation between the two.

55 Seliger, *Ideology and Politics*, p. 120.

56 This is not to say that the splits were merely over differences in doctrine and excluded material interests, but those interests were often ideologically defined. For an early examination of doctrinal splits in the Yugoslav case, see T. Peter Svennevig, 'The Ideology of the Yugoslav Heretics', *Social Research*, 27 (Spring 1960): 39–48. The dominant view of the Yugoslav–Soviet split since the 1950s, largely derived from the Yugoslavs themselves, is now being revised with the opening of Russian archives and demonstrates the interplay between ideational and material factors. See Leonid Gibianski, 'The 1948 Soviet–Yugoslav Conflict and the Formation of the "Socialist Camp" Model', in Odd Arne Westad, Sven Holtsmark, and Iver B. Neumann, eds, *The Soviet Union in Eastern Europe, 1945–89* (New York: St Martin's, 1994), pp. 26–46; Gibianski, 'The Soviet–Yugoslav Conflict and the Soviet Bloc', in Francesca Gori and Silvio Pons, eds, *The Soviet Union and Europe in the Cold War, 1943–53* (London: Macmillan, 1996), pp. 222–45. For a series of excellent articles on the mix of material and ideological factors in the Sino-Soviet relationship, see Westad, ed., *Brothers in Arms*, especially Odd Arne Westad, 'Brothers: Visions of an Alliance'; Niu Jun, 'The Origins of the Sino-Soviet Alliance'; Constantine Pleshakov, 'Nikita Khrushchev and Sino-Soviet Relations';

and, Chen Jian and Yang Kuisong, 'Chinese Politics and the Collapse of the Alliance'.

57 Policy adaptation can be distinguished from policy learning in that adaptation does not question underlying theories and values in a belief system, does not challenge final goals (what Ernst Haas calls 'ultimate purposes'), and emphasizes altering the means of action but not the ends. For this distinction, see Ernst B. Haas, 'Collective Learning: Some Theoretical Speculations', in Breslauer and Tetlock, eds, *Learning in US and Soviet Foreign Policy*, pp. 72–3. See also, Michael Waller, 'The Soviet Union's Adaptation to Change in the Communist Movement: A Framework for Analysis', *Journal of Communist Studies*, 2 (September 1986): 235–50.

58 Moral prescriptions differ from technical prescriptions in that, although they also depend on the description and analysis of facts, they apply value judgments to the factual world and are intended to 'contribute towards its ordering, serving to stigmatize, repress, recommend and protect given forms of behaviour, i.e., social facts'. Seliger, *Ideology and Politics*, p. 104.

59 Technical prescriptions are those dealing with 'expedience, prudence and efficiency' and are 'more or less directly derived from facts, i.e., from their descriptive and classificatory as well as from their analytical and causal perception and presentation.' Ibid., p. 104.

60 For the emergence of 'progressive' and 'conservative' internationalisms in the Wilsonian period, see Knock, *To End All Wars*, pp. 48–69. Christopher Hill has argued that such idealism and realism became inexorably interconnected in liberal thought in 1939 in reaction to the failures of 'progressive' assumptions of a fundamental harmony of interests among states. See Christopher Hill, '1939: The Origins of Liberal Realism', *Review of International Studies*, 15 (1989): 319–28. For the continuation of the ideological contention in attenuated form during the Cold War, see Macdonald, *Adventures in Chaos*, chs 1–2. For the strategic consequences of such domestic political contention, see Gaddis, *Strategies of Containment*.

61 Tucker, *Stalin in Power*, p. 39. This problem also existed, of course, while Lenin was alive. George Brinkley notes that Lenin, virtually alone among the leading Bolsheviks, argued in 1918 that Russia had to make peace with all capitalist states in the short run to protect the Soviet state from the dangers to its survival from capitalist encirclement in order to overthrow capitalism in the long run. See his 'Leninism', p. 161. As would be predicted by bureaucratic and organization models for understanding state behavior, these policy splits became institutionalized and typically led to an incremental and opportunistic approach to the promotion of revolution, not its abandonment. For this policy outcome, see Jan S. Adams, 'Incremental Activism in Soviet Third World Policy: The Role of the International Department of the CPSU Central Committee', *Slavic Review*, 48 (Winter 1989): 614–30.

62 For Chinese factionalism see Andrew Hall Wedeman, *The East Wind Subsides: Chinese Foreign Policy and the Origins of the Cultural Revolution* (Washington, DC: The Washington Institute Press, 1987); Kuo-kang Shao, *Zhou Enlai and the Foundations of Chinese Foreign Policy* (New York: St Martin's Press, 1996); Steven M. Goldstein, 'Nationalism and Internationalism: Sino-Soviet Relations', in Robinson and Shambaugh, eds, *Chinese Foreign Policy*, pp. 224–265; and the essays in Westad, ed., *Brothers in Arms*.

63 For a discussion of 'problem solving' and 'consistency seeking' models of cognitive behavior, see Alexander L. George, 'The Causal Nexus Between Cognitive Beliefs and Decision-Making Behavior: The "Operational Code" Belief System', in Lawrence S. Falkowski, ed., *Psychological Models in International Politics* (Boulder, CO: Westview Press, 1979), pp. 98–9. See also, Carlsnaes, *Ideology and Foreign*

Policy, pp. 101–2. As Tetlock notes, there are 'powerful cognitive psychological and political accountability pressures to demonstrate consistency in policies over time …' (Tetlock, 'Learning in US and Soviet Foreign Policy', p. 28).

64 Waltz, *Theory of International Politics*, pp. 74–7. Armstrong agrees on the socialization of revolutionary regimes, see D. Armstrong, *Revolution and World Order* (New York: Oxford University Press, 1993), p. 307. Although not a structuralist, the Realist Stephen Walt also argues that ideology may matter in the short run, but quickly loses its influence on policies, even among revolutionary regimes. Stephen M. Walt, *Revolution and War* (Ithaca, NY: Cornell University Press, 1996). Thus realist theorists argue that ideology may matter in the short term, but does not in the long term for an established great power, that is, states become 'socialized' into realist behavior by the constraints placed on them by material reality. Neither Waltz nor Walt defines ideology beyond the most general terms. I am arguing the opposite: ideology may be temporarily abandoned in the short term, but it continues to matter in the long term. My emphasis on the relationship between ideologies and seeking particular political orders makes the long-term focus more relevant in understanding how ideas affect policies, an area in which realists are notoriously deficient.

65 Zubok and Pleshakov, *Inside the Kremlin's Cold War*, pp. 1–173.

66 For differing views of the pursuit of long- and short-term state goals among realists, see Stephen G. Brooks, 'Dueling Realisms', *International Organization*, 51 (Summer 1997): 445–77.

PART IV:
STRATEGIES AND DECISIONMAKING

9

The United States and the Cold War Arms Race

Aaron L. Friedberg

Over the course of the Cold War, the United States devoted enormous resources to achieving and maintaining an advantage over the Soviet Union in most areas of military technology. Indeed, for the better part of half a century, reliance on qualitative superiority was at the heart of US military strategy, and its pursuit was the central, defining feature of the entire American defense effort.

What were the origins of this desire for technological supremacy and of the institutional mechanisms put in place to attain it? What may have been the connections between the structure of the R&D system set up during the 1940s and 1950s and the manner in which it functioned over time? And what impact did the continuing American pursuit of technological advantage have on the course and ultimate conclusion of the Cold War?

My progressively more speculative answers to these increasingly complex and difficult questions may be summarized as follows.

First, both the sheer size and strategic centrality of the American technological effort, and the key attributes of the US government's Cold War research and development system (its general administrative decentralization, heavily military focus, and extensive reliance on private institutions for the performance of research) were shaped by the essential characteristics of the American domestic regime that gave it birth (in particular, its liberal ideology, and its open, fragmented political institutions).

Second, the US research system was large and diverse enough to be highly productive of innovations but it was also, at the same time, sufficiently structured to be subject at key moments to 'top-down' strategic direction and control.

Finally, especially in its later stages, the ongoing American pursuit of technological advantage had a significant impact on the course of the Cold War. The increasingly desperate efforts of the Soviet leadership to keep pace with the United States in military technology appear to have imposed serious long-term burdens on their economy. In the 1980s, fear of falling ever further behind played a part in persuading the Soviet military to tolerate Mikhail Gorbachev's wide-ranging and ill-fated attempts at reform.

Structure[1]

Scale

The vigor with which the United States pursued military-technical advance and qualitative superiority during the Cold War reflected the intensity of a set of complementary beliefs about the respective strengths and weaknesses of the US and Soviet (or, more generally, the 'free world' and 'totalitarian') systems, and about the specific character of the strategic competition between them.

From the beginning of the Cold War it was generally accepted that the superior extractive capacities of the communist states gave them certain inherent military advantages. Thanks both to the sheer size of the populations and economies under their control and to their ability to tax and conscript virtually without constraint, the Soviets and their allies could generate enormous forces in peacetime and even bigger ones, on short notice, in the event of war. Free from democratic constraints, to say nothing of considerations of human decency, the leaders of what were described as the 'slave states' could also afford to use their forces with a reckless disregard for casualties. Unless they were willing to adopt similar domestic powers and battlefield tactics, the nations of the free world would have to offset the advantages of their rivals by substituting firepower for manpower, capital for labor, quality for quantity.

This line of argument first began to emerge at the close of World War II and, by the beginning of the 1950s, it had congealed into strategic dogma. As early as November 1945 James Forrestal recorded in his diary the observation that, in any future war involving 'a combination of Russia and the Asiatic powers the manpower available to such a combination would be so tremendous and the indifference to the loss of life so striking that it would present a very serious problem to this country'.[2] Even before the Chinese entry into the Korean War, allusions to what Chairman of the Joint Chiefs of Staff General Omar Bradley in a 1949 article termed 'the hordes of the East' had begun to appear in Western strategic debate.[3] After December 1950 such references became commonplace. In Europe, as in Asia, communism had at its disposal a 'horde of expendable manpower'.[4] But, if war came, the United States could not 'meet hordes with hordes'.[5] Instead, superior numbers would have to be offset by superior weaponry.

In the late 1940s and early 1950s this reasoning underlay an increasing American reliance on atomic and thermonuclear weapons.[6] However, as the Soviets demonstrated their capacity, not only to put large numbers of men in uniform, but to supply them with advanced and steadily improving equipment, the logic of countering quantity with quality began to be more generally applied. Maintaining a US advantage would require, not the acquisition of a single 'winning weapon', but the development and deployment of a steady stream of new military systems. 'Achievement and maintenance of technological superiority, both in the short run and for an indefinite period of years ...' and in conventional as well as nuclear weapons, had become, in the words of one government report, 'indispensible'.[7] 'The Cold War', wrote the Executive Secretary of the President's Science Advisory Committee in 1955, 'has become, in large measure, a technological race for military advantage.'[8]

Fortunately for the United States, the same imbalance in internal characteristics that made such a strategy necessary was widely believed also to make it feasible. The very domestic strength that permitted the totalitarian states to extract human and material resources in such quantities from their own societies also tended, in the long run, to supress their capacity for innovation. Totalitarian regimes, claimed wartime science tsar Vannevar Bush, were rigid, arbitrary, heirarchical, and regimented; they were, by their nature, intolerant of heresy, individual genius, the free movement of peoples and ideas, and the 'winnowing of chaff by competition and criticism' on which true scientific progress inevitably rested. While the Soviets' superior extractive powers gave them certain advantages, in the long run the 'democratic system ... is not only the best system ... it is the strongest system in a harsh contest'.[9]

As MIT President Karl Compton explained in 1949, reliance on advanced technology was:

> in line with the American achievement to which we owe our economic strength and standard of living. I refer to our per capita productive power ... [O]ur American workman or farmer produces more goods, and usually with less effort, than the workers of any other country. It is in our tradition, therefore, to follow this policy by providing our soldiers, sailors, and airmen with equipment which will multiply as much as possible their power as fighting men ... [W]e must ... substitute the maximum of mechanical power and technical skill for brute human force if we should again have to fight ... We must rely on continual technological progress to keep us secure against any possible competitor.[10]

Organization

The importance that American leaders attached to maintaining a qualitative edge over the Soviet Union may have made a large-scale research and development effort inevitable. But the intense desire for advantage did not, in itself, dictate the manner in which that effort would be organized within the federal government. Indeed, given the perceived urgency of stimulating rapid and sustained technological advances, the administrative structure that had emerged by the end of the 1950s must appear somewhat puzzling.

Despite repeated calls for unity of effort and concentration of authority, the system that took shape during the first full decade of the Cold War was characterized above all by its pluralism and decentralization. Far from being the product of a unified national master plan, the federal investment in science and technology represented instead the sum total of the independent activities of an assortment of parallel agencies, each intent on pursuing its own goals.[11]

The absence of a strong controlling mechanism at the core of the entire post-war government research system was not due to any lack of interest in building one. As World War II drew to a close, former New Deal Democrats in Congress and the executive branch put forward plans for the creation of a new, powerful, permanent federal agency authorized to conduct its own research, direct the research activities of all other government departments, and support work on problems of potential medical, military, and commercial importance carried out in non-governmental institutions.[12]

But proposals for the creation of a strong central science agency aroused intense opposition. Conservative Congressional Republicans, eager to block and if possible to roll back any further expansion in the powers of the federal government, warned that such an entity would bring a 'large sector of our national economy ... under the centralization, control, and supervision of Washington' and that it would become 'a link in the chain to bind us into the totalitarian society of the planned state'.[13] Businessmen and industrial researchers worried about possible federal interference (or competition) with their own expanding R&D programs.[14] The nation's top scientists feared that a powerful new agency would bureaucratize and politicize the research process and interfere with the conduct of 'free science ... carried on by free men whose guide is truth'.[15] The combined force of these objections defeated administration plans and 'assured the pluralistic, loosely coordinated nature of the nation's science effort'.[16]

Powerful centrifugal forces were also at work in the narrower realm of military research. Here, as at the overall national level, bureaucratic resistance to centralization was reinforced by Congressional reluctance to permit ever greater concentrations of executive power. While President Truman and President Eisenhower sought repeatedly to promote unity of effort among the armed services by enhancing the powers of the top civilian and military leaders of the new national military establishment, Congress tended to act in ways that slowed or moderated their efforts at reform.[17] Until the late 1950s, Congressional resistance was sufficiently powerful to defeat repeated attempts to impose even a modest measure of central control over defense research.

Without the Sputnik crisis (which was widely interpreted as revealing flaws in the American research system) Congressional approval for reforms designed to increase the ability of the Secretary of Defense to control military R&D would simply not have been forthcoming.[18] President

Eisenhower, long convinced of the inadequacies of the existing system and, in particular, of the harmful strategic and fiscal consequences of inter-service rivalry, did not need to be persuaded of the need for change. What was required, he argued, was the creation of a 'real boss over research and engineering' with the authority to 'minimize duplication and rivalry among the three services'.[19] Even Eisenhower could not get all that he wanted, but his personal authority in matters military and the prevailing crisis atmosphere finally permitted a modest measure of centralized con-trol over defense research. As one of its key provisions, the Defense Reorganization Act of 1958 created the position of a civilian Director of Defense Research and Engineering (DDR&E) authorized 'to approve, modify, or disapprove programs and projects of [the military] departments and other Defense agencies ... and ... to initiate or support promising programs and projects for research and development'.[20]

Scope

Despite its size, the scope of the American Cold War research program was actually quite narrow. The great bulk of all federal research expendi-tures (generally on the order of 80–90 percent of each year's budget) went to support the development of defense, space, or energy-related technolo-gies.[21] As would-be reformers have often pointed out with regret and some puzzlement, in marked contrast to many of its allies and economic com-petitors, over the course of the Cold War the US government spent virtually nothing on supporting civilian, industrial research for its own sake, nor did it create powerful new agencies for that purpose.[22]

A non-interventionist approach to commercial innovation was consis-tent, both with the dominant American position in most technological fields at the end of World War II, and with the resurgent post-war faith in 'free markets' and 'free enterprise'. Proposals for direct federal funding of industrial research (some of it to be carried out in government labora-tories), and changes in the patent laws to ensure public ownership of all discoveries paid for, even in part, with tax dollars, were attacked as un-necessary, disruptive, and even 'socialistic'.[23] By the early 1950s it was generally agreed that, as Vannevar Bush put it, the government's role in promoting commercial innovation should be confined to sustaining 'the flow of new scientific knowledge through support of basic research' and aiding education to ensure 'the development of scientific talent'.[24]

Means

A final distinguishing feature of the Cold War research system was the way in which it mobilized 'private energies on a large scale for public purposes'.[25] From the end of World War II to the end of the Cold War, roughly three-quarters of the annual government defense research budget was expended in corporate and university laboratories or in facilities owned by the government but operated by private organizations; only the remaining 25 percent went to pay for work done by federal employees in federal laboratories.[26]

The Cold War contract system was a product of both pragmatic and ideological considerations. As during World War II, when the practice was first used on a large scale, contracting out for research permitted the government rapidly to draw on the talents of a wide range of industrial and academic researchers. Private research institutions were generally believed to be more flexible, innovative, and cost-effective than their public sector counterparts, especially those operating under direct military control. At a moment of great national danger, and in the midst of a confrontation with a supremely statist rival, the contract system also maintained a reassuring degree of separation between the public and private spheres. Arrangements under which the government paid private entities to do research for it 'resonated symbolically to the culture of the marketplace'; they were compatible with American economic ideology in a way that no other means of mobilizing the nation's scientific resources could possibly have been.[27] Whatever its practical merits, the contract system was also America's symbolic answer to what Winston Churchill had called the 'perverted science' of totalitarianism.[28]

In the late 1940s and early 1950s, the executive branch, with an occasional nudge from Congress, moved quickly to consolidate and expand its reliance on private research institutions. Any inclination on the part of the military services to go back to their traditional dependence on 'in-house' research was discouraged by new peacetime procurement regulations, which mandated a continuation of wartime practices for buying research from the private sector, and by edicts from the newly formed Office of the Secretary of Defense, which declared that government-owned laboratories would receive 'only those projects that cannot be contracted for with academic or industrial facilities'.[29] Even in entirely new and especially sensitive areas, such as the development of atomic energy, strong preference was to be given to the use of research contracts with private institutions.[30]

Function

By the end of the 1950s (and, in most respects, by the end of the calendar year 1950) the United States had in place the institutions with which it would conduct its half of the Cold War technological competition. The American Cold War research system was large, substantially decentralized, narrowly focused, and heavily reliant on the private sector. How did that system actually work? And how did the system's structure influence the manner in which it functioned?

There are two closely related issues here. First is the question of the connection between structure and innovation. The standard view, among critics and celebrants alike, is that the American R&D system was highly productive of technological advances, and that its performance was directly related to its organizational form. This interpretation is essentially correct, but also incomplete.

More controversial is the question of the relationship between structure and control. Certainly, among academic observers (as well as some knowledgeable, if disgruntled, former practitioners), the conventional wisdom has been that the American research system was essentially impervious to strategic direction. In this account, the same features that made the system so productive of new ideas also tended to make it extremely difficult to control. The United States had what political scientist Matthew Evangelista has called a 'bottom-up' system, one in which there was 'vigorous activity at the base and weak control at the top'.[31] In such a system new ideas tended to bubble freely to the surface, emerging as an endless stream of ever more sophisticated weapons, regardless of the larger implications for American (to say nothing of global) security.[32] This assessment is inaccurate. To a far greater degree than is generally acknowledged, the Cold War research system was subject at critical junctures to a substantial measure of central strategic control. In contrast to the Soviet Union, where rigid, hierarchical command structures tended to stifle innovation, the United States was able to enjoy the benefits of 'bottom-up' innovation without sacrificing entirely the capacity for 'top-down' control.

Innovation

The overall decentralization of the federal R&D system frustrated those with a preference for planning and bureaucratic rationality, but it meant that there were multiple sources of support for a wide range of research ventures. Although the reforms of the 1950s did lead to a significant strengthening of the institutions of central control, the defense research system also retained a considerable measure of disorderly diversity. In this, as two RAND analysts pointed out in 1960, it continued to have a good deal in common with the civilian sector, where 'duplication, rivalry, and ... apparent waste' led nevertheless to 'the most progressive and advanced [economy] in the world'.[33]

The fact that the great bulk of defense research was performed by private industry also had powerful stimulative effects. While the Cold War was under way, advocates praised 'the flexibility, innovative nature, technical competence' and competitive spirit of industry, and applauded the way in which the pursuit of contracts (and profits) encouraged private defense firms to take risks and to push forward the technological frontier.[34] Critics, describing the same phenomena, deplored the fact that the use of 'large private corporation[s], dependent on government orders, created an "industrial imperative" for rapid product improvement'.[35] While the language differed, the fundamental conclusion was the same: whether for good or ill, heavy reliance on private, profit-making enterprises (as compared with state-owned arsenals) tended to promote rapid military-technical advance.

In the long run, however, it was not only the structure of the defense research establishment as such, but its placement in the American economy that gave it a decisive advantage. In ways that the founding fathers of Cold War science and technology policy could not fully have anticipated, the *restrictions* on the institutions they established seem to have contributed to their eventual strategic success.

The constraints on the organizational structure and functional scope of the federal research system meant that the government could influence, but could not control, the larger course of national technological development. The defense research establishment (and the closely related space and energy R&D efforts) were lodged within, and, through the contract mechanism, connected to a civilian commercial and academic research system which tended to grow in relative size and independence as time wore on. If the federal science apparatus had been organized differently, if it had been more highly centralized and broader in scope, the evolution of post-war science and technology would have been much different, and even more heavily shaped by the demands of the state, than was in fact the case. Instead, the federal government's influence as the driving force of technological progress tended to diminish as time passed. In terms of their impact on the arms competition, the results were unintended, unanticipated, and, for the United States, highly beneficial.

During the first half of the Cold War, the federal government dominated the national scientific and technological enterprise, contributing between one half and two thirds of the total dollars spent each year on research. The end of the space program's explosive growth phase, and the continued, steady expansion in privately funded research combined, after the mid-1960s, to produce a steady decline in the government's share of national R&D spending. By the second half of the 1970s, and for the first time since the onset of the Cold War, industry and academia had replaced government as the leading supplier of research dollars.[36]

The relationship between the government-funded, largely defense-oriented research system, and its increasingly vigorous, privately funded, mostly commercially oriented counterpart changed over time. From the 1940s to the 1960s most of the technologies being developed for defense purposes were either unrelated to, or significantly more advanced than, those being pursued primarily for commercial reasons. Intercontinental ballistic missiles and thermonuclear weapons had no obvious civilian applications, and government sponsors led the way in developing such things as jet engines and nuclear power plants. Non-defense, high-technology industries were, if anything, competitors with the military and space programs for scarce scientists and engineers. As the term 'spin-off' suggests, to the extent that there was a flow of ideas between the two, the balance of exchange appeared heavily to favor the civilian sector over its defense-driven counterpart.

Gradually at first, and then with increasing rapidity, this balance began to shift. In the 1960s and 1970s the semiconductor and electronic computer industries, which had been nurtured initially by government agencies and whose early evolution had been shaped primarily by their needs, entered a phase of accelerated, autonomous, commercially driven development. As their possible civilian applications became more obvious, innovations that had been launched by the defense and space programs were picked up and exploited by a private sector responding to commercial incentives and acting largely beyond the reach of governmental direction or control. The stimulus of unconstrained commercial competition (involving first American, and then West European and Asian-based firms as well) forced technological development further and faster than it would otherwise have gone. By the mid-1970s the pace of advance in electronics, telecommunications, and computers was clearly being set by the civilian sector.[37]

In the closing two decades of the Cold War the presence of a large, vibrant, and independent civilian high-technology sector emerged as a decisive strategic advantage for the West. In contrast to the 1950s and 1960s, commercial research was now clearly producing substantial, tangible benefits for defense. Lacking a similar amplifier and accelerator for their own military research efforts, and able to gain access to Western technology only sporadically, stealthily, and at great expense, the Soviets began, in a number of crucial respects, to fall further and further behind.

By the mid-1970s American defense officials had begun to note that, if taken together, the perfection of 'precision guided ordnance, stand-off control of battlefield weapons, powerful new forms of surveillance, command and control, night vision and remotely piloted vehicles' might have revolutionary effects.[38] Fortunately, it was precisely in the electronic technologies that underlay all of these systems that the United States appeared to be gaining ground on the Soviets. The driving force behind this advance, in turn, was the vitality of the commercial sector. As Malcolm Currie, Director of Defense Research and Engineering, observed in 1975: 'Wherever we have leads of several years to a decade, and where our leads seem to be increasing, it is important to note that large civilian markets exist in the US.'[39] In contrast to the United States, the inability of 'Soviet civilian R&D to contribute substantive benefits ... to military programs' was 'one of the great failures of the Soviet system'. The task facing the US research establishment, Currie concluded, was how best to exploit its inherent advantages and, in particular, its proximity to a dynamic private sector.[40]

As the pace of the commercially driven electronic revolution continued to accelerate, the extent of the American advantage became even more evident. By the mid-1980s US intelligence analysts were reporting that much of the overall Soviet disadvantage in advanced military technologies could be traced to failings in a handful of 'underlying technologies', in particular, computers (where 'the Soviets lag the United States by 5 to 15 years ... and appear to be falling further behind'), microelectronics production techniques (where 'the Soviets have been unable to achieve high-quality mass production both of electronics grade silicon and the micro-electronic devices themselves sufficient to their needs'), and precision instrumentation to monitor experiments and control production.[41] These, of course, were the areas in which Western civilian industry had been most active and innovative.

Control

Whether they place the final blame on the 'military technical community', capitalist arms makers, or ambitious scientists, 'bottom-up' theorists share a common understanding of the American innovation process.[42] Top decisionmakers do little more than ratify choices that have already been made for them. In this view, it was because its upper echelons were so weak in comparison to its lower layers that the American research system was endlessly productive of innovations, and largely responsible for driving the arms race.

In its description of the dynamic character of American defense research, this account has much to commend it. Looking at the entire course of the Cold War competition, however, the 'bottom-up' version of events is clearly inadequate. Decisions taken at the top of the system in the early 1950s, and again in the mid-1970s and early 1980s, were critically important in initiating and accelerating movement along several key avenues of technological advance. More damaging to the 'bottom-up' theorists is the fact that in the late 1950s and early 1960s, high-level decisionmakers were also able to *stop* several species of new weapons for which there appeared to be overwhelming support at the lower reaches of the system.

The superpower arms race can usefully be divided into two distinct cycles, or what Soviet theorists identified as two successive 'revolutions in military affairs'.[43] The first cycle involved the playing out of technological possibilities that had become evident during the course of World War II, most notably the perfection of nuclear weapons and incontinental range ballistic missiles. This process was essentially complete by the beginning of the 1960s. In the mid-1970s a second cycle of rapid change began, this one driven by advances in electronics, and characterized by the development of conventional weapons of extraordinary accuracy and lethality.

Top US decisionmakers played key roles at each of the major turning points in the Cold War technological competition.

Neither the hydrogen bomb nor the ICBM, the premier products of the first cycle, can be understood adequately as the result of a 'bottom-up' innovation process. While both weapons had their supporters among the ranks of scientists and military men, each also had powerful detractors. It was precisely the *absence* of a lower-level consensus on how best to proceed that seemed to demand a decision from above. Given the comparative weakness of the institutions of central control in the early stages of the Cold War, these interventions were carried out by *ad hoc* committees, formed at the request of top civilian decisionmakers. It was the recommendations of such committees that led to the acceleration of the hydrogen bomb and the ballistic missile programs.

In 1950, an intense dispute among the nation's leading scientists over whether to attempt to build a thermonuclear weapon was resolved by a presidentially appointed special committee of the National Security Council. Three years later, as part of a general reexamination of strategy following the 1952 presidential election, the new Secretary of Defense ordered the Air Force to review all guided missile programs. This request was followed by the formation of an *ad hoc* group of scientists and engineers which, in February 1954, recommended a dramatic acceleration in ICBM development. Although many high-ranking air force officers continued to prefer manned bombers, the report of the so-called 'Teapot Committee' was decisive in forcing the development and eventual deployment of long-range ballistic missiles.[44]

If the lower levels of the defense research establishment had had their way, the late 1950s and early 1960s would have been marked by redoubled efforts to exploit the technological breakthroughs of the preceding decade. Nuclear reactors would have been used to power manned aircraft and unmanned cruise missiles of virtually unlimited range. The perfection of the hydrogen bomb would likely have been followed by the development of nuclear explosives with higher yields, specially tailored effects, and novel applications (including detonation in space to propel rockets or disrupt enemy communication systems). The same techniques used to put unmanned satellites in earth orbit, or to loft nuclear warheads from one corner of the planet to another could also have been employed to create an entire panoply of new space weapons – space planes to fight duels high above the earth's atmosphere and attack targets on its surface; manned space stations from which all points on the globe could be observed (and bombarded); unmanned nuclear weapons in permanent orbit, ready to smash down on enemy territory with little or no warning; bases on the moon from which retaliation could be unleashed, even after the home country had been destroyed in a surprise attack.[45]

All of these ideas (and others like them) were in wide circulation at the close of the 1950s. Spurred on by Sputnik, scientists, aerospace industrialists, the armed services (especially the air force), and their allies in Congress were poised to take what seemed to most to be the next logical steps forward in the military-technical competition with the Soviet Union. And yet, with very few exceptions, these steps were never taken. By the mid-1960s virtually all of the more ambitious (or far-fetched) schemes for radically new weapons had been effectively derailed, or killed outright. The delay or cancellation of the Aircraft Nuclear Propulsion program, Project Pluto (a planned supersonic cruise missile powered by a 500 megawatt nuclear reactor), Project Dyna-Soar (a manned space bomber prototype), and a military Manned Orbiting Laboratory, and the quiet shelving of plans for bombs in orbit and bases on the moon, led critics to complain that top civilian decisionmakers were orchestrating a 'slow-down in the Pentagon'.[46]

This assessment was basically correct. The centralizing institutions put into place after Sputnik had been intended to focus the disparate programs of the military services and, by so doing, to *accelerate* the pace of the nation's overall defense research effort. But these same institutions could be, and soon were, used to achieve the opposite objective. Poised atop the military R&D establishment, the Director of Defense Research and Engineering had the authority to overrule the armed services and to slow or cancel even their most prefered programs. When he had the support of the Secretary of Defense (and when the two of them enjoyed the sympathetic ear of the head of the President's Science Advisory Council), the DDR&E could make his decisions stick, even in the face of fierce resistance from the military.[47] Beginning in the late 1950s, and with increasing frequency in the 1960s, this is precisely what happened: pressure from above was decisive in blocking or redirecting a stream of innovations that appeared to be bubbling up vigorously from below. If the US defense research system had operated solely and simply according to a 'bottom-up' principle, the arms race would have run a far different, and possibly more dangerous, course.[48]

In addition to cancelling programs, the DDR&E also had the authority to influence the composition of the overall defense research budget, to encourage the military services to pursue what he regarded as particularly promising technologies, and, where necessary, to initiate research on his own, using the Advanced Research Project Agency to set up contracts with industry and university laboratories.[49] In the mid-1970s the DDR&E began once again to play the role of stimulator, rather than dampener, of innovation. The primary impetus for exploiting the military potential of ongoing advances in electronics came, initially, from the top of the defense research system. Within the armed forces, the idea that a new generation of highly capable, comparatively inexpensive weapons might transform the character of warfare (and render existing aircraft, ships, and armored vehicles obsolete into the bargain) was met at first with a measure of skepticism, if not outright hostility. Nevertheless, successive DDR&E preached the gospel of the coming revolution to the military and to Congress, pushed the services to pursue emerging technologies, and, most important, provided funding for the development of prototypes to demonstrate the feasibility and utility of new weapons systems. By the early 1980s, some of these had started to enter into large-scale production and the military had begun to debate the best ways of exploiting their potential. In 1991 new weapons and modified concepts of operation were employed, with dramatic results, by the United States against Iraq.[50]

Not all high-level initiatives were equally productive of tangible results. The 1980s also saw the launching of the Strategic Defense Initiative, perhaps the single most spectacular example of the 'top-down' direction of American technology policy during the Cold War. In the early 1980s, the notion that the United States should initiate a crash program to build defenses against ballistic missile attack (and that it should place heavy reliance on doing this with space-based, directed energy weapons) had virtually no support. With the exception of a handful of civilian researchers at one of the nation's two nuclear weapons laboratories, this idea had few backers in the military or in the relevant sectors of the defense industry. While supportive of continuing research, DARPA (Defense Advanced Research Projects Agency) and the office of the Undersecretary of Defense for Research and Engineering apparently concluded in 1981–82 that revolutionary breakthroughs in missile defense technology were not imminent, and that space-based systems would be especially costly and vulnerable to countermeasures. Far from reflecting a carefully constructed, 'bottom-up' consensus, therefore, President Ronald Reagan's decision to launch an accelerated missile defense program was based on minimal consultation with his political advisers and a handful of outside enthusiasts. By all accounts, the 1983 speech in which this decision was announced provoked shock and some dismay at every level of the government. Whether they applaud it as a bold end-run around a stodgy bureaucracy, or abhor it as an ill-considered, ill-conceived leap in the dark, most subsequent analysts agree that the launching of the Strategic Defense Initiative was 'very much a presidential decision ... it was a "top-down" decision rather than one reached ... after prolonged gestation in the defense establishment'.[51]

Impact

What impact did the manner in which the United States conducted its half of the military technical competition have on the course and eventual conclusion of the Cold War?

Among academics (and former practitioners turned academics) the dominant view during at least the last two decades of the Cold War was that the continuing American pursuit of technological advantage was wasteful, at best, and, at worst, dangerous. With the onset of nuclear parity, the possibility of either superpower obtaining a meaningful military edge appeared to have evaporated. Under these conditions, it was assumed, the endless development and deployment of new weapons would most likely leave both countries poorer, but no more secure. An on-going qualitative arms race would probably produce a stalemate at ever higher levels of technological achievement and expense. In addition, there was always the danger, however remote, that a breakthrough would give one side a temporary advantage (or at least its *appearance*), thereby increasing the risk of war. For these reasons, it was widely believed, an end to the qualitative competition was not only desireable, but imperative.[52]

That the Cold War ended when and how it did suggests a very different interpretation of the impact of the high technology arms race. In retrospect, the balance of military capabilities between the superpowers appears to have been much more stable than was commonly assumed at the time. For most of the duration of the Cold War (and especially after the mid-1960s, by which time both the United States and the Soviet Union had acquired secure second strike nuclear forces) successive advances in weaponry led primarily to efforts by each superpower to match or counter the capabilities of its rival, rather than to radical shifts in strategic behavior.

Despite the language in which it is sometimes discussed, the qualitative arms race was not all of a piece. The superpowers were not (in Paul Warnke's memorable phrase) 'apes on a treadmill', running harder and harder just to stay in place.[53] Over time the nature of the technological competition changed, and so too did the capacity of the two superpowers to conduct it. Instead of a treadmill, the more apt metaphor may be a marathon or, better still, a biathalon. In retrospect, as I have suggested, the 50-year arms race can be divided into two 'events' or phases. If, in the first phase (the nuclear missile revolution of the 1940s and 1950s), the capabilities of the two competitors were roughly equally matched, in the second (the electronics revolution of the 1970s, 1980s, and 1990s) the United States enjoyed some decisive advantages. Both the cumulative effects of a 50-year arms race, and the more immediate stresses and anxieties induced by falling further behind in its latter phase, appear to have contributed to the demise of the Soviet Union and the end of the Cold War.

Keeping pace with the United States required the Soviet leadership to divert a large percentage of their country's technological resources from civilian to military uses. This made it extremely difficult for the USSR to negotiate the transition from an era of extensive growth (driven by the addition of ever larger quantities of land, labor, and capital), to an age of intensive growth (in which technological advances produced more output for every unit of input).[54] Statistical analyses and anecdotal evidence suggest that, from the mid-1960s onwards, at the same time as they were struggling to increase overall national economic productivity, the Soviets were also shifting money and manpower from civilian to military R&D.[55] Instead of speeding up, in the 1960s and 1970s 'technological progress slowed down, generating less economic growth exactly when it was needed most'.[56] Over a period of decades, the pursuit of military technological parity (if not superiority) contributed to a deterioration in Soviet economic performance. In this way, the qualitative arms race helped set the stage for the fatal reform experiments of the 1980s.[57]

Soviet political leaders and economic planners had always been concerned, not only with their country's absolute level of technological performance, but with their position in relation to the advanced industrial economies of the West. During the 1960s and 1970s, anxiety on this issue came to focus especially on the rapid advances in electronics and computing that were together largely responsible for what Soviet theorists identified as a new 'scientific-technological revolution'. As Western progress in these areas accelerated, and as their own efforts faltered, Soviet fears of being left behind grew deeper.[58]

Whatever the consequences for Soviet economic performance of failing to keep up with the West, the potential military implications were at least equally troubling. By the early 1980s, top Soviet defense officials (most notably Chief of the General Staff, Marshal N. V. Ogarkov) had begun to speak of a new 'military-technical revolution' in which 'the latest achievements of electronics and other technical sciences' would permit 'rapid changes in the development of conventional means of destruction'. In the very near future, these developments would include 'the emergence ... of automated reconnaissance-and-strike complexes, long-range, highly accurate, terminally guided combat systems, unmanned flying machines, and qualitatively new electronic control systems'.[59] In Central Europe in particular, Soviet strategists warned that the exploitation by the United States of its evident advantage in emerging technologies might tip the balance of military capabilities away from the Warsaw Pact and toward NATO.[60]

From the Soviet point of view, the timing of these developments could hardly have been worse. In the late 1970s and early 1980s, the deteriorating performance of the Soviet economy had forced a reduction in the rate of growth in defense spending. Now the West was accelerating its own expenditures and pushing the military-technical competition in troubling new directions. In the late 1970s, many top Soviet political and military leaders had also finally concluded that, for the foreseeable future, there was no possibility of being able to fight and win a nuclear war. Far from ending the military competition, however, the mutual cancellation of the superpowers' strategic nuclear forces simply increased the importance of their conventional capabilities. In this arena, especially in Europe, the Soviets seemed at first to have significant advantages in terms of the size and geographical positioning of their ground and air forces. But it was precisely these advantages that Western technological dynamism was threatening to erase.[61]

For Ogarkov, at least, the problem was clear: the Soviet Union's military power, its international stature, and, perhaps ultimately its survival depended on its ability to keep up with the West in the development and deployment of new, high-technology weapons. But how was this desirable goal to be achieved? Following his elevation to Chief of the General Staff in 1977, and with increasing urgency and openness until his removal from power seven years later, Marshal Ogarkov campaigned for higher rates of growth in defense expenditures, shifts in military investment away from old weapons (especially strategic nuclear weapons) and toward new ones (especially high-technology conventional systems), and increased 'integration' of the civilian and military economies, in other words, for an even greater extension of military control over the remaining industrial and scientific resources of the civilian sector.[62]

Ogarkov's prescription, and the outspoken manner in which it was proffered, were unacceptable to his political superiors, and his dissent from their decisions contributed directly to his dismissal in September 1984. Ogarkov's *diagnosis*, on the other hand, appears to have won increasing acceptance among his military colleagues, and, after March 1985, it clearly resonated with the views of the new political leadership.[63] Although he was as much concerned with promoting national welfare as with protecting national security, Gorbachev, like Ogarkov, stressed the importance of accelerating the rate of technological advance. In direct contrast to Ogarkov, however, Gorbachev proposed to achieve this end by cutting defense spending and shifting resources from the military to the civilian sectors.[64]

For the military leadership, acceptance of Gorbachev's initial program represented a considerable gamble but one which, in the end, they were willing to take.[65] After several years of open and bitter disputes, the fall of Ogarkov and the rise of Gorbachev were followed by a marked improvement in civil–military relations. Military writers offered cautious praise for reform and placed considerable emphasis on the strategic benefits to be derived from a general acceleration of 'scientific-technical progress'. 'After all', reasoned one analyst, 'the leading directions of scientific-technical progress ... are simultaneously the basic catalysts of military-technical progress.' Gorbachev's program of 'accelerated development ... offers new potential for military building, too'.[66] Anxious to avoid being left behind in a military-technical revolution, the Soviet military were acquiescing in a process of economic and political reform that would soon lead to revolution of a very different kind.

In his 1949 book, *Modern Arms and Free Men*, Vannevar Bush asserted the existence of a connection between the fundamental character of a nation's domestic political regime and its capacity for technological innovation. Whatever the apparent strengths of the totalitarian states, Bush maintained, over time the democracies would prove themselves better able to generate knowledge, wealth, and military power. He wrote:

> The philosophy that men live by determines the form in which their governments will be molded. Upon the form of their government depends their progress in utilizing the applications of science to raise their standards of living and in building their strength for possible war.[67]

Bush was here expressing a fond hope, rather than making a confident prediction. Nevertheless, with the benefit of hindsight, we can see that he was right. In the race to develop 'modern arms', 'free men' do seem indeed to have a decided, and, in the long run, a decisive advantage.

NOTES

1 This section draws on a chapter of my book, *In the Shadow of the Garrison State: American Anti-Statism and its Cold War Strategy* (Princeton, NJ: Princeton University Press, 2000).

2 Walter Millis, ed., *The Forrestal Diaries* (New York: Viking, 1951), p. 108.

3 General Omar Bradley, 'This Way Lies Peace', *Saturday Evening Post* (15 October 1949), p. 168.

4 Anonymous, 'The Case for Tactical Atomic Weapons', *Army*, vol. 6, no. 8 (March 1956): 24.

5 Vannevar Bush, 'Organization for Strength', Remarks at Tufts College Centennial Celebration, Medford, MA, 11 October 1952 (typescript, National War College Library, Washington, DC), p. 3.

6 Thus, in the words of one Congressional enthusiast, 'Atomic weapons used tactically are the natural armaments of numerically inferior but technologically superior nations. They are the natural answer to the armed hordes of the Soviet Union and its allies.' J. K. Mansfield, Chief of Special Projects, 'Some Comments on Tactical Atomic Weapons', Memorandum for the Chairman of the Joint Committee on Atomic Energy, 15 August 1951. In Harry S. Truman Library, PSF, Subject File: National Security Council, Atomic, Folder: Atomic Energy – Expansion of the Atomic Energy Program.

7 Report by the ODM-Defense Working Group, 'Achieving and Maintaining US and Free-World Technological Superiority Over the USSR', 20 December 1955. *Foreign Relations of the United States, 1955–1957, Volume XIX* (Washington, DC: US Government Printing Office [GPO], 1990), pp. 173–7.

8 David Z. Becker, Executive Secretary of the Science Advisory Committee. Quoted in Daniel J. Kevles, 'Cold War and Hot Physics: Science, Security, and the American State, 1945–56', *Historical Studies in the Physical and Biological Sciences*, vol. 20, no. 2 (1990): 239.

9 Vannevar Bush, *Modern Arms and Free Men: A Discussion of the Role of Science in Preserving Democracy* (New York: Simon & Schuster, 1949), pp. 207, 204, 8. On the issue of democratic versus totalitarian science see also John R. Baker, *Science and the Planned State* (London: Allen & Unwin, 1945).

10 Karl T. Compton, 'Science and National Strength: Some Lessons from World War
Two', Address at the dedication of the Aeroballistics Facility, Naval Ordnance
Library, 27 June 1949 (mimeo, National War College Library, Washington, DC).

11 See Kenneth Jones, 'The Government Science Complex', in Robert H. Bremner and
Gary W. Reichard, eds, *Reshaping America: Society and Institutions, 1945–1960*
(Columbus, OH: Ohio State University Press, 1982), p. 320.

12 See the discussion of Senator Harley Kilgore's proposal for a permanent 'Office of
Scientific and Technical Mobilization', in Hearing before a Subcommittee of the
Senate Committee on Military Affairs, *Scientific and Technical Mobilization*, 78th
Congress, 1st sess. (Washington, DC: US GPO, 1943), pp. 1–8.

13 From a statement issued during the 1946 debate over the National Science
Foundation. Quoted in J. Merton England, *A Patron for Pure Science: The National
Science Foundation's Formative Years, 1945–57* (Washington, DC: National Science
Foundation, 1983), pp. 47–8.

14 On business hostility to Kilgore's proposals see Daniel J. Kevles, *The Physicists:
The History of a Scientific Community in Modern America* (New York: Knopf,
1977), pp. 344–5.

15 Bush, *Modern Arms and Free Men*, pp. 248–9.

16 Report Prepared for the Task Force on Science Policy, House Committee on Science
and Technology, *A History of Science Policy in the United States, 1940–1985*, 99th
Congress, 2nd sess. (Washington, DC: US GPO, 1986), p. 19. For more on this
struggle see also John Walsh, 'Truman Era: Formative Years for Federal Science',
Science, vol. 179 (19 January 1973): 263; England, *A Patron for Pure Science*,
pp. 61–82.

17 As Robert Art explains, whatever their other motives, 'Congressmen have
traditionally seen their ability to influence defense policy enhanced under a
decentralized structure and have feared loss of influence under a more centralized
one ... Therefore, not surprisingly, American's defense establishment has reflected
the pluralistic and decentralized nature of America's national governmental
system.' Robert J. Art, 'Introduction: Pentagon Reform in Comparative and
Historical Perspective', in Robert J. Art, Vincent Davis, and Samuel P. Huntington,
eds, *Reorganizing America's Defense: Leadership in War and Peace* (New York:
Pergamon-Brassey's, 1985), p. xvi. For useful overviews see also Vincent Davis, 'The
Evolution of US Central Defense Management', and William J. Lynn, 'The Wars
Within: The Joint Military Structure and Its Critics', in ibid., pp. 149–67, 168–204.

18 According to the Gaither Commission Report, issued shortly after the launch of
the first Soviet satellite: 'We are faced with an enemy who is able, not only ruthlessly
to concentrate his resources, but rapidly to switch from one direction or degree of
emphasis to another.' The United States, on the other hand, had 'lost ability to
concentrate resources ... and to change direction or emphasis with the speed that
a rapidly developing international situation and rapidly developing science and
technology make necessary'. Security Resources Panel of the Science Advisory
Committee, *Deterrence and Survival in the Nuclear Age* (Washington, DC: Office
of Defense Mobilization, 1957), pp. 8–9.

19 Eisenhower to Ann Whitman and 3 April 1958 message to Congress, quoted in
Robert A. Divine, *The Sputnik Challenge: Eisenhower's Response to the Soviet
Satellite* (New York: Oxford University Press, 1993), pp. 129, 131.

20 Michael H. Armacost, *The Politics of Weapons Innovation: The Thor-Jupiter
Controversy* (New York: Columbia University Press, 1969), pp. 235–6. In addition
to the research programs and facilities of the three services, the DDR&E also had
within his control the resources of the newly created Advanced Research Projects
Agency (ARPA). Established initially as a 'special projects agency', ARPA became,

in effect, the research arm of the DDR&E. On the battle over the 1958 reforms see Divine, *The Sputnik Challenge*, pp. 128–43; Lynn, 'The Wars Within', pp. 174–81.

21 For an overview of post-war federal investments in research and development, see David Mowrey and Nathan Rosenberg, *Technology and the Pursuit of Economic Growth* (New York: Cambridge University Press, 1989), pp. 123–68. For the breakdown of federal research by function, see the figures in Linda R. Cohen and Roger G. Noll, *The Technology Pork Barrel* (Washington, DC: Brookings Institution, 1991), pp. 32–3.

22 For comparisons of public spending on industrial research in the US, France, Germany, Japan, and the UK, see Alexander H. Flax, 'Interdiffusion of Military and Civil Technologies in the United States of America', in Philip Gummett and Judith Reppy, eds, *The Relations Between Defence and Civil Technologies* (Boston, MA: Kluwer Academic Publishers, 1987), p. 127.

23 As the president of one industrial research association put it: 'Those who are spending millions of their hard-earned money in the development of processes and in the study of further application of scientific knowledge to the ... problems of production, are completely floored with the thought that ... the results of their research can be taken away from them and made available to the public at large.' This would 'do incalculable harm to the very thing that made America supreme under a system of free enterprise'. A. R. Ellis, President of the American Council of Commercial Laboratories, quoted in *Scientific and Technical Mobilization*, pp. 240–1.

24 Bush's views on the government's role in commercial innovation are laid out in *Science: The Endless Frontier* (Washington, DC: US GPO, 1945), pp. 2–3, 5–7, 13–17.

25 Bruce L. R. Smith, 'Accountability and Independence in the Contract State', in Smith and D. C. Hague, eds, *The Dilemma of Accountability in Modern Government: Independence versus Control* (New York: Macmillan, 1971), p. 14.

26 The FY 1984 Defense Department research budget breakdown was: 23 percent in-house, 71 percent industry, 4 percent universities, and 2 percent federal contract research centers. Franklin A. Long and Judith Reppy, 'The Decision Process for US Military R&D', in Kosta Tsipis and Penny Janeway, eds, *Review of US Military Research and Development* (1984) (New York: Pergamon-Brassey's, 1984), p. 7. In 1989, the figures were 26 percent intramural, 65 percent industry, 3 percent universities, and 5 percent FFRDC. John A. Alic, Lewis M. Branscomb, *et al.*, *Beyond Spinoff: Military and Commercial Technologies in a Changing World* (Boston, MA: Harvard Business School Press, 1992), p. 102.

27 Larry Owens, 'The Struggle to Manage Science in the Second World War: Vannevar Bush and the Office of Scientific Research and Development' (mimeo, University of Massachusetts, Amherst, 12 October 1993), p. 5.

28 On the origins of the wartime contract system see A. Hunter Dupree, 'The Great Instauration of 1940: The Organization of Scientific Research for War', in Gerald Holton, ed., *The Twentieth Century Sciences* (New York: Norton, 1972), pp. 457, 459. For more on the origins of the research contract, see Irvin Stewart, *Organizing Scientific Research for War: The Administrative History of the Office of Scientific Research and Development* (Boston, MA: Little, Brown, 1948), pp. 12–13, 191–9. James B. Conant, *My Several Lives: Memoirs of a Social Inventor* (New York: Harper and Row, 1970), p. 236, and Vannevar Bush, *Pieces of the Action* (New York: William Morrow, 1970), pp. 38–9. The best and most comprehensive treatment of the transition to the Cold War is Clarence H. Danhof, *Government Contracting and Technological Change* (Washington, DC: Brookings, 1968), pp. 39–69. Regarding the presumed superiority of private over public research

organizations see, for example, an essay by the President of the California Institute
of Technology, Lee A. Dubridge, 'Science and Government', *Chemical and Engineering News*, vol. 31, no. 14 (6 April 1953): 1384–90. Also Report to Congress by
the Commission on Organization of the Executive Branch of Government (Hoover
Commission), Research and Development in the Government (Washington, DC:
US GPO, May 1955), p. 16.

29 OSD directive, quoted in Danhoff, *Government Contracting*, p. 56.

30 See Harold Orlans, Contracting for Atoms (Washington, DC: Brookings, 1967),
    p. 6. Also Morgan Thomas, *Atomic Energy and Congress* (Ann Arbor, MI:
    University of Michigan Press, 1956); Richard A. Tybout, *Government Contracting
    in Atomic Energy* (Ann Arbor, MI: University of Michigan Press, 1956).

31 Matthew Evangelista, *Innovation and the Arms Race: How the United States and
    the Soviet Union Develop New Military Technologies* (Ithaca, NY: Cornell Uni-
    versity Press, 1988), p. 56. See especially pp. 22–82.

32 For another variant of this view see Herbert York, *Race to Oblivion: A Participant's
    View of the Arms Race* (New York: Simon & Schuster, 1970), pp. 238–9. York was
    the first Director of Defense Research and Engineering in the Department of
    Defense.

33 Charles J. Hitch and Roland N. McKean, *The Economics of Defense in the Nuclear
    Age* (Cambridge, MA: Harvard University Press, 1960), pp. 256–8.

34 See the comparison of the US and Soviet systems in Statement by William J. Perry,
    Undersecretary of Defense, Research, and Engineering to the Congress of the
    United States, *The FY 1979 Department of Defense Program for Research,
    Development, and Acquisition*, 95th Congress, 2nd sess. (Washington, DC: Depart-
    ment of Defense, 1 February 1978), pp. II-4 to II-6. Quote from p. II-6.

35 Mary Kaldor, 'The Weapons Succession Process', *World Politics*, vol. 38, no. 4 (July
    1986): 595. Kaldor attributes the superior technological dynamism of the West to
    the behavior of the 'supply institutions' (i.e., industry) rather than the preferences
    of the 'demand institutions' (i.e., the military), which she regards as inherently
    conservative. She conludes that, 'in the East, the supply institutions are funda-
    mentally bureaucratic organizations with the same inertial tendencies that are
    characteristic of the demand institutions; therefore there is not the same pressure
    for technological change' ibid. See also Mary Kaldor, 'Military R&D: Cause or
    Consequence of the Arms Race?', *International Social Science Journal*, vol. 35, no.
    1 (1983): 25–43, and Mary Kaldor, *The Baroque Arsenal* (New York: Hill & Wang,
    1981). Kaldor draws inspiration from an earlier article by James Kurth, 'Why We
    Buy the Weapons We Do', *Foreign Policy*, no. 11 (Summer 1973): 33–56.

36 See tables in Mowery and Rosenberg, *Technology and the Pursuit of Economic
    Growth*, pp. 126–7.

37 For useful overviews of developments in two closely related and extremely
    important industries see Richard C. Levin, 'The Semiconductor Industry', and
    Barbara Goody Katz and Almarin Phillips, 'The Computer Industry', in Richard
    R. Nelson, *Government and Technical Progress: A Cross-Industry Analysis* (New
    York: Pergamon Press, 1982), pp. 9–100, 162–232.

38 Statement by Dr Malcolm R. Currie, Director of Defense Research and Engi-
    neering, before the House Armed Services Committee, The Department of Defense
    Program of Research, Development, Test and Evaluation, FY 1976, 94th Congress,
    1st sess. (Washington, DC: Department of Defense, 21 February 1975), p. I-23.

39 Ibid., p. II-10.

40 Ibid., p. II-16.

41 Statement by Rear Admiral Robert Schmitt, Deputy Director, Defense Intelligence
    Agency in Hearing Before the Subcommittee on Economic Resources, Com-

petitiveness, and Security Economics of the Joint Economic Committee, *Allocation of Resources in the Soviet Union and China – 1985*, 99th Congress, 2nd sess. (Washington, DC: US GPO, 1986), p. 115.

42   Examples of the first view include Evangelista, *Innovation and the Arms Race*, and Harvey Brooks, 'The Military Innovation System and the Qualitative Arms Race', in *Deadalus*, vol. 104, no. 3 (Summer 1975): 75–97. The second view is expressed in the works of Mary Kaldor cited above. The third interpretation appears in the work of authors such as Solly Zuckerman, Nuclear Illusion and Reality (New York: Viking Press, 1982), p. 103 and Hugh E. DeWitt, 'Labs Drive the Arms Race', *Bulletin of the Atomic Scientists* (November 1984): 40–2. Herbert York, in *Race to Oblivion*, tends toward the view that scientific progress itself (and, in particular, the superior progress of American science) drives the arms race.

43   For the Soviets, successive military revolutions were one part of a larger process of scientific and technological change. In Soviet parlance, the *first* revolution of the twentieth century involved the widespread introduction of tanks, trucks, and aircraft in the 1920s and 1930s. The events of the forties and fifties and the seventies and eighties were therefore the second and third revolutions in military affairs. See William E. Odom, 'Soviet Force Posture: Dilemmas and Directions', *Problems of Communism*, vol. 34 (July–August 1985): 1–14.

44   The story of the H-bomb decision has been told many times and from a variety of angles. See especially Richard G. Hewlett and Francis Duncan, *Atomic Shield: A History of the United States Atomic Energy Commission (Volume II, 1947/1952)* (Washington, DC: US Atomic Energy Commission, 1972), pp. 362–409; Gregg Herken, *Cardinal Choices: Presidential Science Advising from the Atomic Bomb to SDI* (New York: Oxford University Press, 1992), pp. 34–65; Herbert York, *The Advisors: Oppenheimer, Teller, and the Superbomb* (San Francisco, CA: W. H. Freeman, 1976); Robert G. Gilpin, *American Scientists and Nuclear Weapons Policy* (Princeton, NJ: Princeton University Press, 1962); and Jonathan B. Stein, *From H-Bomb to Star Wars* (Lexington, MA: Lexington Books, 1984), pp. 15–49. Regarding the ICBM see Jacob Neufeld, *The Development of Ballistic Missiles in the United States Air Force, 1945–1960* (Washington, DC: Office of Air Force History, 1990), especially pp. 93–118, 239–44; Edmund Beard, *Developing the ICBM* (New York: Columbia University Press, 1976), especially pp. 129–246; Michael R. Terry, 'Formulation of Aerospace Doctrine From 1955 to 1959', *Air Power History*, vol. 38, no. 1 (Spring 1991): 47–54; Stephen P. Rosen, *Winning the Next War: Innovation and the Modern Military* (Ithaca, NY: Cornell University Press, 1991), pp. 245–9.

45   Most of these possibilities are discussed in Paul B. Stares, *The Militarization of Space: US Policy, 1945–1984* (Ithaca, NY: Cornell University Press, 1985), pp. 38–91; and Jack Manno, *Arming the Heavens: The Hidden Military Agenda for Space, 1945–1995* (New York: Dodd, Mead & Co., 1984), pp. 15–119. For a humorous but informative overview of some of the 'wacky wonder weapons' of the 1950s see Stephen Budiansky, 'The Wrong Stuff: The Cold War's Legacy of Weird Weapons Lives On', *US News and World Report* (16 July 1990): 49–51. For examples of contemporary commentary and a sense of the substantial support enjoyed by proposals for the expanded military exploitation of space see Donald Cox and Michael Stoiko, *Space Power: What It Means To You* (Philadelphia, PA: J. C. Winston Co., 1958); M. N. Golovine, *Conflict in Space: A Pattern of War in a New Dimension* (New York: St Martin's Press, 1962); J. S. Butz, Jr, 'Hypersonic Glider Studied As 'Manned Missile' Hope', *Aviation Week*, vol. 66, no. 11, (18 March 1957): 72–3, 75, 77; 'Military May Accelerate Lunar Base Plan', *Aviation Week*, vol. 69, no. 13 (29 September 1958): 18; Ford Eastman, 'Argus Potential as Weapon Described', *Aviation Week*, vol. 70, no. 14 (6 April 1959): 31; 'USAF Considering

Moon Base by 1968', *Aviation Week*, vol. 70, no. 17 (27 April 1959): 26–7; 'Military Use Seen For Base on Moon', *Aviation Week*, vol. 71, no. 7 (26 October 1959): 61; Walter R. Dornberger, 'Dornberger Sees Space as Military Area', *Aviation Week and Space Technology*, vol. 75, no. 12 (18 September 1961): 57–9, 61; 'Military Space Technology Needs Are Urgent', *Aviation Week and Space Technology*, vol. 75, no. 13 (25 September 1961): 93; George Alexander, 'USAF Aims as Military Space Supremacy', *Aviation Week and Space Technology*, vol. 75, no. 14 (2 October 1961): 28–9; Don Schanche, 'General of Outer Space', *The Saturday Evening Post*, vol. 234, no. 40 (7 October 1961): 78, 80, 82, 84; Russell Hawkes, 'High-Priority Military Space Pace Urged', *Aviation Week and Space Technology*, vol. 75, no. 15 (9 Octoer 1961): 30.

46 Hanson W. Baldwin, 'Slow-Down in the Pentagon', *Foreign Affairs*, vol. 43, no. 2 (January 1965): 262–80. For another critical assessment of Defense Department policy in this period see Klaus Knorr and Oskar Morgenstern, *Science and Defense: Some Crticial Thoughts on Military Research and Development* (Princeton, NJ: Center of International Studies, Policy Memorandum no. 32, 18 February 1965). On the demise of the Dyna-Soar see 'Dyna-Soar's History Full of Re-Examinations', *Aviation Week and Space Technology*, vol. 79, no. 4 (22 July 1963): 233, and York, *Race to Oblivion*, pp. 129–30. York also deals at length with the cancellation of the atomic airplane, ibid., pp. 60–74. See also, W. Henry Lambright, *Shooting Down the Nuclear Plane*, Inter-University Case Program no. 104 (Indianapolis, IN: Bobbs-Merrill, 1967).

47 Thomas McNaugher notes that, although the initial changes were made during the Eisenhower Administration, it was Secretary of Defense Robert McNamara who began fully to 'exploit ... the new powers and the new agencies', in particular, by giving the DDR&E 'far more power than he had had in the 1950s'. Thomas L. McNaugher, *New Weapons Old Politics: America's Military Procurement Muddle* (Washington, DC: Brookings Institute, 1989), pp. 41, 53. The central role of the DDR&E (in alliance with the director of PSAC) in killing the nuclear airplane is described in Lambright, *Shooting Down the Nuclear Plane*, pp. 30–1.

48 As Paul Stares points out: 'In hindsight ... the level of the US effort in this area seems remarkably restrained when set against the public anxieties of the late 1950s [and] the interests of the services and industry in space weapons ... Contrary to what was expected at the dawn of the space age an arms race in the true meaning of the term has been surprisingly absent from space.' Stares, *The Militarization of Space*, pp. 19–20. In explaining this outcome Stares stresses the role of arms control agreements in heading off an intensified military space competition in the early 1960s. But, as his careful account makes plain, it was American self-restraint, imposed on an unwilling military, that made these agreements possible, rather than the other way around.

49 On the ability of the DDR&E to act either as a 'stimulator or a dampener of technological innovation', see Ted Greenwood, *Making the MIRV: A Study of Defense Decision Making* (Cambridge, MA: Ballinger, 1975), p. 147.

50 The complete story of the making of this revolution in military affairs has yet to be told. See articles by (or based on interviews with) the Carter Administration's Director of Defense research: William J. Perry and Cynthia A. Roberts, 'Winning Through Sophistication: How to Meet the Soviet Military Challenge', *Technology Review*, vol. 88 (July 1982): 27–35; William J. Perry, 'Desert Storm and Deterrence', *Foreign Affairs*, vol. 70, no. 4 (Fall 1991): 64–82; also Eliot Marshall, 'William Perry and the Weapons Gamble', *Science*, vol. 211, no. 13 (February 1981): 681–3; Michael Getler, 'Cruise Missiles: US Reliant on New Technology', *Washington Post* (30 June 1980), p. 1. The role of the office of the Director (later Undersecretary)

of Defense Research and Engineering in nurturing the new technologies is made plain in its annual reports to Congress. The annual reports of the Secretary of Defense for this period also identify DARPA as the principal source of initial funding for the development of long-range cruise missiles, 'fire-and-forget' precision guided munitions, greatly improved space surveillance and target acquisition systems, new techniques for information processing to assist in command, control, and communications, and 'unconventional technologies' such as the 'Assault Breaker' program, 'an integrated anti-armor surveillance and engagement concept for NATO'. See Secretary of Defense Donald H. Rumsfeld, *Annual Defense Department Report FY 1978* (Washington, DC: US GPO, 1977), pp. 263–71. Secretary of Defense Harold Brown, *Department of Defense Annual Report FY 1979* (Washington, DC: US GPO, 1978), pp. 287–9. Secretary of Defense Harold Brown, *Department of Defense Annual Report FY 1980* (Washington, DC: US GPO, 1979), pp. 257–8. Although the public statements do not reveal it, the DDR&E and DARPA were also heavily engaged at this time in funding the development of low-observable or 'Stealth' technologies. See Ben R. Rich and Leo Janos, *Skunk Works* (Boston, MA: Little, Brown, 1994); Bill Sweetman, *Stealth Aircraft* (Osceola, WI: Motorbooks, 1986), pp. 59–82.

51 For a highly critical account, see Sanford Lakoff and Herbert F. York, *A Shield in Space? Technology, Politics, and the Strategic Defense Initiative* (Berkeley, CA: University of California Press, 1989), pp. 1–47, 252–90. Quote from p. 6. Regarding the lukewarm attitudes of DARPA and Richard DeLauer, the Undersecretary of Defense for Research and Engineering, see ibid., pp. 10–11, 15. For a far more sympathetic account of the 1983 decision see Donald R. Baucom, *The Origins of SDI, 1944–1983* (Lawrence, KS: University of Kansas Press, 1992). Baucom, the official historian of the Defense Department's Strategic Defense Initiative Organization, places Reagan at center stage, but he also emphasizes the role of a handful of non-governmental space defense boosters, including former head of Air Force intelligence Daniel Graham. See especially pp. 139–200. For other accounts see Herken, *Cardinal Choices*, pp. 208–16. According to Herken, top Defense Department officials learned of the contents of Reagan's speech only hours before it was given. Also emphasizing the 'top-down' nature of the decision are Stares, *The Militarization of Space*, pp. 225–9; and Stein, *From H-Bomb to Star Wars*, pp. 51–91. Evangelista notes that 'at first glance ... the Strategic Defense Initiative ... appears to contradict the bottom-up generalization about US weapons innovation'. But he goes on to claim, that, because space-based beam weapons were first advocated by Edward Teller and some members of the staff of the Lawrence Livermore Laboratory, SDI 'is not such a notable departure from the norm of US weapons innovation as it first appears'. See Evangelista, *Innovation and the Arms Race*, pp. 257–61. This argument is unconvincing. Given the skepticism expressed by other top administration officials, it is clear that, without Reagan's intervention, Teller's ideas would have gone nowhere. What would later come to be referred to as 'the President's vision' may not have sprung fully formed from his brow (or from some half-forgotten movie script), but the SDI program was still very much the product of his own imagination. On Teller and Livermore see William J. Broad, *Star Warriors* (New York: Simon & Schuster, 1985).

52 For sophisticated expressions of these views see Evangelista, *Innovation and the Arms Race*, pp. 1–5. York, *Race to Oblivion*, pp. 228–39. For another example (among many), see Ralph E. Lapp, *Arms Beyond Doubt: The Tyranny of Weapons Technology* (New York: Cowles, 1970). Lapp, a physicist, was involved in the atomic bomb project and later worked for the Defense Department.

53 Paul C. Warnke, 'Apes on a Treadmill', *Foreign Policy*, no. 18 (Spring 1975): 12–29.

54 On the transition from extensive to intensive growth, see Stanley H. Cohn, 'Soviet Intensive Economic Development Strategy in Perspective', in Joint Economic Committee, *Gorbachev's Economic Plans (Volume I)*, 100th Congress, 1st sess. (Washington, DC: US Government Printing Office, 1987), pp. 10–26. Early (1969–75) Soviet debates on how to increase the pace of technological change and productivity growth are reviewed in Bruce Parrott, *Politics and Technology in the Soviet Union* (Cambridge, MA: MIT Press, 1983), pp. 231–305.

55 For statistical analysis, see Vladimir Kontorovich, 'The Long-Run Decline in Soviet R&D Productivity', in Henry S. Rowen and Charles Wolf, Jr, eds, *The Impoverished Superpower: Perestroika and the Soviet Military Burden* (San Francisco, CA: Institute for Contemporary Studies, 1990), pp. 255–70. Kontorovich concludes that, 'resources were shifted from civilian to military R&D in 1965–1985', ibid., p. 267. Soviet *émigrés* reported an increasing use of civilian scientists in military research beginning in the late 1960s. See Arthur J. Alexander, *Soviet Science and Weapons Acquisition*, R-2942-NAS (Santa Monica, CA: RAND, August 1982), pp. 28–30.

56 Vladimir Kontorovich, 'Technological Progress and Research and Development', in Ellman and Kontorovich, eds, *The Disintegration of the Soviet Economic System* (London: Routledge, 1992), pp. 217–38. Quote from p. 217. Further evidence is presented in the essays by Stanislaw Gomulka, Padma Desai, and Vladimir Kontorovich included in 'The Soviet Growth Slowdown: Three Views', *AEA Papers and Proceedings*, vol. 76, no. 2 (May 1986): 170–85

57 On the deteriorating performance of the Soviet economy and its role in stimulating reform, see, among many others, Jerry F. Hough, *Opening Up the Soviet Economy* (Washington, DC: Brookings, 1985); Ed A. Hewitt, *Reforming the Soviet Economy* (Washington, DC: Brookings, 1988); Henry Rowen, 'Central Intelligence Agency Briefing on the Soviet Economy', in Erik P. Hoffmann and Robbin F. Laird, eds, *The Soviet Polity in the Modern Era* (New York: Aldine Publishing, 1984), pp. 417–46. On collapse as the unintended consequence of reform see, for example, Coit D. Blacker, *Hostage to Revolution: Gorbachev and Soviet Security Policy, 1985–1991* (New York: Council on Foreign Relations, 1993); Michael Ellman and Vladimir Kontorovich, 'Overview', in Ellman and Kontorovich, eds, *The Disintegration of the Soviet Economic System*, pp. 1–39; John Gooding, 'Perestroika as Revolution from Within: An Interpretation', *Russian Review*, vol. 51, no. 1 (January 1992), pp. 36–57.

58 On the discussion of a a new 'scientific-technological revolution' in the late 1960s and early 1970s see Parrott, *Politics and Technology in the Soviet Union*. On faltering Soviet efforts to keep pace in computers see Martin Cave, 'Computer Technology', in Amann, Cooper, and Davies, eds, *The Technological Level of Soviet Industry*, pp. 377–406. The failure of indigenous development programs led quickly to intensified efforts to buy or steal Western technology. See S. E. Goodman, 'Technology Transfer and the Development of the Soviet Computer Industry', in Bruce Parrott, ed., *Trade, Technology, and Soviet–American Relations* (Bloomington, IN: Indiana University Press, 1985), pp. 117–40. Unfortunately for the Soviets, computers and the increasingly miniaturized components of which they were constructed proved extremely difficult to 'reverse engineer' and copy. According to one account it took Soviet engineers longer to copy the IBM 360 computer 'than IBM took to develop it in the first place'. Shelley Deutch, 'The Soviet Weapons Industry: An Overview', in Joint Economic Committee, *Gorbachev's Economic Plans* (Volume 1), pp. 424–5. For an assessment of where the two superpower's stood in this crucial area by the mid-1980s see Richard W. Judy, 'The Soviet Information Revolution: Some Prospects and Comparisons', in Joint Economic

Committee, *Gorbachev's Economic Plans* (Volume 2), 100th Congress, 1st sess. (Washington, DC: US GPO, 1987), pp. 161–75.

59 The quotes are from two articles by Ogarkov, one published in May 1983 and the other in May 1984. See Dale R. Herspring, *The Soviet High Command: 1967–1989* (Princeton, NJ: Princeton University Press, 1990), pp. 174–5. For an overview of Ogarkov's thinking see Mary C. Fitzgerald, 'Marshal Ogarkov and the New Revolution in Soviet Military Affairs', *Defense Analysis*, vol. 3, no. 1 (1987): 3–19.

60 See Michael J. Sterling, Soviet Reactions to NATO's Emerging Technologies For Deep Attack N-2294-AF (Santa Monica, CA: RAND, August 1985); Phillip A. Petersen and Notra Trulock III, 'A "New" Soviet Military Doctrine: Origins and Implications', *Strategic Review* (Summer 1988): 9–33.

61 The best treatment of the evolving Soviet analysis of these developments is Herspring, *Soviet High Command*, pp. 119–214. In the second half of the 1970s and the early 1980s the rate of growth in Soviet defense spending appears to have fallen from 4–5 to 2 percent per year. Jeremy R. Azrael, *The Soviet Civilian Leadership and the Military High Command, 1976–1986*, R-3521-AF (Santa Monica, CA: RAND, June 1987), p. 7.

62 On Ogarkov's program see Brian A. Davenport, 'The Ogarkov Ouster: The Development of Soviet Military Doctrine and Civil/Military Relations in the 1980s', *Journal of Strategic Studies*, vol. 14, no. 2 (June 1991): 129–47. Also Herspring, *Soviet High Command*, pp. 192–202.

63 Regarding the reasons for Ogarkov's ouster, see Herspring, *Soviet High Command*, pp. 218–24. Herspring notes that, despite his removal, 'One of the most interesting aspects of the early 1980s was the degree to which Ogarkov's ideas in the military-technical area seem to mirror those later espoused by Gorbachev.' He also points out that: 'Ogarkov's constant harping on the need for the Soviet military to do a better job in reacting to the demands of modern technology helped lay the groundwork for the implementation of Gorbachev's policy of perestroika in the armed forces', ibid., pp. 169, 192. For more background see also Michael Checinski, 'The Legacy of the Soviet War-Economy and Implications for Gorbachev's Perestroika', *Journal of Soviet Military Studies*, vol. 2, no. 2 (July 1989): 206–40.

64 On the mobilization of defense resources to promote economic development, see Julian Cooper, 'Technology Transfer Between Military and Civilian Ministries', in *Gorbachev's Economic Plans (Volume 1)*, pp. 372–87.

65 For similar conclusions see Abraham S. Becker, 'Gorbachev's Defense–Economic Dilemma', in *Gorbachev's Economic Plans (Volume 1)*, pp. 372–87; Russell Bova, 'The Soviet Military and Economic Reform', *Soviet Studies*, vol. 40, no. 3 (July 1988): 385–405.

66 Quotes from two articles by Major-General M. Yasyukov, one published in October 1985, the other in December 1986. See Abraham S. Becker, *Ogarkov's Complaint and Gorbachev's Dilemma: The Soviet Defense Budget and Party–Military Conflict*, R-3541-AF (Santa Monica, CA: RAND, December 1987), p. 34. For more on early Soviet military responses to the reform process see George G. Weickhardt, 'The Soviet Military-Industrial Complex and Economic Reform', *Soviet Economy*, vol. II, no. 3 (1986): 193–220.

67 Bush, *Modern Arms and Free Men*, p. 9.

10

Studying Soviet Strategies and Decisionmaking in the Cold War Years

Constantine Pleshakov

The subjectivity of professional writing of history is generally amazing. Of course, there is such a thing as an absolute truth or historical fact – when a Cold War historian writes that Joseph Stalin died in 1953, indisputably, this is a hard-and-fast fact. But when he amplifies, saying that Stalin died on 5 March some imaginative colleagues of his would already disagree, insisting that the dictator had died several days earlier and that his death was concealed by his entourage for some self-serving purpose.[1] If we do choose to stick with the absolute majority of available sources, we would still insist that on the fifth day of March, 1953, the ruler of the Soviet Union gave up the ghost. However, if, for the purposes of accuracy, we would like to be more precise and make inquiries about the details of that happy event, we will face a wide range of evidence, and our conclusion, based on the evaluation of the evidence, will almost certainly still be inconclusive.

For instance, if we ask about the medical causes of Stalin's death, we will now meet a spectrum of hypotheses so wide – from poison to stroke – that any further firm judgment would be impossible, and each of us would be tempted to use the version which appeals most to our general understanding of what went on in Soviet politics in early 1953. Even if Stalin's mummy is dug up from beneath Red Square and thoroughly examined by an independent group of experts, I am sure that historians (and others) would still dispute their findings. We always attempt – consciously or subconsciously – to put any 'fact' within our own frameworks of historical or analytical understanding.

The last ten years or so have released tens of thousands of pages from Soviet, Chinese, and East European archives, many of them sensational. No doubt, the picture of the Cold War we have now is much fuller and richer than was ever the case before the conflict ended. Most scholars, in Russia and elsewhere, agree that Cold War studies have been transformed. In terms of knowledge, we do have much more than we had before, on almost all aspects of the field, be it in history or political science. But do we *understand* more about the core strategies and decisions on both sides than we did before the avalanche of new materials started rolling?

If we cannot now understand the circumstances of Stalin's death, our chances of knowing his strategies or understanding his decisions do not look good. With the end of the Cold War, we have seen little change in the interpretive wrappings in which these issues come to us, and we still learn at least as much about an author's political viewpoint or general view of history and/or the Soviet Union than we do about Stalin's decisions. It would be silly for a historian not to acknowledge that he has other concerns beside accuracy and certainty. Besides traditionalism, revisionism, post-revisionism, and post-modernism, there is such a thing as historians' ego. An eternity ago, back in the 1980s, the best Cold War historians of the United States would spend hours of their precious time persuading us, their Soviet counterparts, that it was North Korea which had started the Korean War. They were right, of course, and we (or at least most of us) knew that they were right, but that discussion, as many today, are not just conducted for the purpose of historical accuracy.

Strategies

Great power strategies pertain to the murky kingdom of wishes, intentions, perceptions, ideas, and dreams. There is hardly much *a priori* meaning in expressions like 'strategic priorities of a nation' or 'strategic necessity', or 'general strategy'. For Stalin it was a strategic necessity to reclaim Port Arthur (Lüshun) from China, for Khrushchev it was a strategic necessity to give it back to Mao Zedong.[2] In April 1950, for Stalin it was a strategic necessity to support Kim Il-Sung in unleashing the Korean War, for Molotov and Beria in March 1953 the urgent necessity was to bring the war to an end.[3] Each person, or each political leader, for that matter, is operating within his or her own unique strategic framework. Two leaders, very close to each other in time and even in office space, may have two absolutely different strategies, even if the goals they pursue are similar.

Within a Soviet context, the 'tyrannical' Joseph Stalin and the 'democratic' Nikita Khrushchev shared many foreign policy goals. However we view Khrushchev – whether he was the last revolutionary or the first reformer in the Kremlin – his objectives were more or less similar to those of his awesome predecessor, be it on the global or regional level (with the obvious exception of regions, easily accessed by Khrushchev, but hardly accessible to Stalin at all, like the Caribbean or Indochina). Both Stalin and Khrushchev wanted to see the worldwide victory of communism and its embodiment – the Soviet empire. Nothing could be more erroneous than to suggest that the Kremlin after Stalin was satisfied with the status quo in international affairs. If it had been so, why would Khrushchev have actively interfered in Cuba, Egypt, and Congo and Brezhnev in Indochina, Ethiopia, and, finally, Afghanistan?

However, if there was little or no difference in the foreign policy *goals* of Stalin and his immediate successor Khrushchev, their *strategies* were rather dissimilar. In terms of perceptions between the two, it was the difference between the stick and the carrot – although one may with good reason argue that Nikita Khrushchev in a few cases used the carrot as a baton. In hindsight, the contrast between the strategies applied looks astonishing indeed: only a year and a half after the death of Stalin – the leader who had done his best to humiliate Mao Zedong back in 1949 – Khrushchev went to China to suggest to Mao Zedong what looked like a fair – if not equal – partnership.

In economic terms, Stalin's strategy in China was basically colonial in the traditional European sense. He wanted to get physical control over Chinese natural resources and communications, to create a Soviet protectorate in Manchuria and, if possible, in Xinjiang. Khrushchev, on the other hand, had launched, what almost amounted to a process of decolonization with regard to China, emphasizing Beijing's sovereignty and attempting to make China work with Moscow in more subtle ways – through the bonds created by Soviet economic, military, and technological assistance.[4]

Stalin would hardly have agreed with Khrushchev's strategies in China or, for that matter, in the West. Most probably, these methods would have struck the Boss as too straightforward and soft, lacking subtlety and determination. But were the two leaders pursuing different goals in China? Was Khrushchev yielding Moscow's supremacy among socialist countries in East Asia and in the communist camp in general? Not at all.

Decisionmaking

What then about the way Soviet leaders *arrived* at their strategies, the processes of making decisions and creating policy? If strategies belong to the terrain of perceptions, could decisionmaking be called the terra firma of politics?

During the Cold War years, decisionmaking in the USSR underwent tremendous change – from the Bolshevik Party to the fist of a dictator to the hands of an oligarchy. In this sense the decisionmaking processes in the Soviet Union were extremely fluid – there was, in general, much less change in how decisions were arrived at in the United States during the Cold War, for instance between 1947, 1957, and 1967. What did, in a way, protect the decisionmaking process from collapse was its ideological content, which, particularly in its latter phase, made sure that the way issues were approached was conservative and backward-looking, connected to ideals rather than to immediate solutions. The state machine itself evolved only slowly, but the machine could be used in different modes. Stalin used it for great terror, Khrushchev for a modest thaw; the people who were opening the doors of the Gulag in 1957 were the same people who had been locking them in 1947. Likewise, a decade of almost continuous changes in the decisionmaking process, on both domestic and foreign policy, did not influence the Soviet state machine's ability and its determination to crush the 1962 Novocherkassk workers' uprising.

Twelve years and a dramatic change of leadership (in 1964) separate the two Soviet interventions in Europe – in Budapest (1956) and in Prague (1968). But the *content* of the two decisions of the Kremlin do not much differ from each other. The Politburo of 1968 had little cadre continuity with the Presidium of 1956 (with the evident exception of people like Leonid Brezhnev and Mikhail Suslov), but the form of the ideas presented was rather similar in spite of the mechanisms of decisionmaking: alarm signals from the Foreign Ministry and secret services; heated discussions in the narrow circle of oligarchs in the Kremlin; talks with native East European 'revisionists'; consultations with socialist allies; and finally discussion at the Politburo and the taking of a vote.[5]

Of course, there is a huge difference between a personal dictatorship (Stalin's) and the rule of an oligarchy (under Khrushchev and Brezhnev), and in terms of the decisionmaking process the contrast is striking indeed. But in the core *ideas* that went into decisionmaking as a system, there was a very considerable continuity between 1945 and 1975, and perhaps even later.

Stalin had created a pyramid of foreign policymaking with its ministries, secret services, Central Committee departments, academic experts, mass media mouthpieces, and the rest. The edifice was complicated and elaborate, but Stalin did not use it in full and probably never intended to. Normally, under Stalin, only part of the pyramid was working actively in each particular case – the rest of the edifice was, for different reasons, often shut down. For his successors, this pyramid became fully operational. They changed the office hours and clearance procedures, but they did not have to invent anything structurally new. The innovation they made was to make place for an oligarchy on top; instead of a dictator's study, they built a meeting-hall.

There was even room for a form of 'dissent'. Foreign policy experts like Georgy Arbatov, Georgy Bovin, Fedor Burlatsky, or Oleg Troyanovsky were allowed to speak up on some issues. But Stalin also kept his 'closet liberals', men like Maxim Litvinov and Yakov Suritz, as foreign-policy consultants for emergencies which demanded special expertise. The main difference between the 1940s and 1960s was that Litvinov for ten years slept with a revolver on his bedside table – to shoot himself in case of arrest, while Arbatov's main worry for his personal safety was connected to yoga exercises in his rooms in the Central Committee building. A difference in situation, no doubt, but in basic ideals of the system – not much. Both Litvinov and Arbatov were kept by the system as exotic birds with silver tongues, in cages: Litvinov in an iron cage, Arbatov perhaps in a golden cage.[6]

Sources of Soviet conduct

One of the most politically charged statements a contemporary historian may make, is that democracies have triumphed over dictatorships in the Cold War. In other words, reason and experience tell us that dictatorships will *inevitably* lose in the international arena to democracies, that popular vote and pluralism are more durable political tools than repression and persecution.

It is hard to dispute the point that throughout the Cold War years the Soviet Union was a dictatorship, be it the authority of one person or the collective authority of the oligarchy. The Soviet dictatorship suppressed popular dissent and did not ask its people for guidance.[7] But, I will argue, it is not true to say that the Kremlin always ignored what the Soviet grass-roots had to say about its foreign policy. If the Soviet leaders had ignored all forms of public opinion, they would have lost their jobs 60 years ago, and not only a decade ago.

No police state – even in Orwell's *1984* – could survive without taking into account the views of its citizens. Of course, in a democracy leaders monitor public opinion, asking the people what sort of foreign policy the majority wants to have and using this knowledge to build up a reasonably popular foreign policy course. In a dictatorship, the leadership probes the public mood in order to know what sort of foreign policy the potential *opposition* wants to have and uses this knowledge to avoid foreign-policy behavior which might be good for the enemies of the regime. In a democracy, foreign policy interaction between people and the government is more or less positive; in a totalitarian state, it is negative.

Throughout the years, the Kremlin did stay in touch with the domestic reality of the country. One of the major tasks of the Soviet secret police was to report on the moods of the rank-and-file, foreign-policy concepts included. Of course, the easiest solution to any dissent was to arrest and perhaps to execute. But the attitude of the authorities was much more complex, for even Stalin could not arrest all potential adversaries and doubters. The regime could not be sure that the outside world would not influence the domestic situation and attempt to assist a real or potential opposition. The Kremlin was carefully following what the Soviet peoples were saying about events abroad, and the main departments of the Central Committee had as one of their special tasks to devise ways in which Soviet foreign policy could be presented domestically in a way which would suit these ideas.

One of the motivations for Stalin to launch his full-scale confrontation with the West, the Cold War, was his fear that Western ways might become too popular in the USSR after World War II. Stalin's armies had seen Europe, and the impact of that was immense. For the next 40 years the war veterans remembered their shock at the material splendor of European cities like Budapest and Prague, the agricultural abundance of Slovakia and Pomerania, the magnificent German roads, Czech shoes, and Viennese bakeries. These matters counted more than formal ideologies. They raised doubts about the very basis of the communist regime. Stalin was afraid of 'new Decembrists' – people influenced by the West in the same way as the mutinous Russian veterans of the Napoleonic wars in 1825. For once, his fears were not unreasonable: in January 1946, the NKVD was reporting that war veterans were already distributing anti-Soviet leaflets.[8] Even Stalin could not have all the suspects arrested or killed; his whole army became his number one suspect. What he could do and what he did, was to make an Iron Curtain and pull it down tight, to seal the country from alien winds.

Democracy and dictatorship are important categories in international relations, but I fear that theorists often prefer the general thesis that dictatorship inevitably loses in the long run because it is convenient. In some cases, and the Soviet Union may be one of them, we may be mixing up two different categories – political totalitarianism and economic inefficiency. Perhaps these two aspects are not connected. Perhaps it is possible to guard the Gulag camps not with Alsatians, but with imported hi-tech?

The problem here, of course, is China. If all the countries that 'won' the Cold War had been democracies there would not be an issue at all. The authoritarian regime headed by the Chinese Communist Party (CCP) is a big problem for a Cold War theorist who will insist that when dictatorship faces foreign policy challenges, it is not as successful in dealing with them as a free nation. The universal Hegelian pattern – from obtuse dictatorship through ordeals and collapse to wise democracy – is challenged by China's case. We may have to see how Beijing handles the challenges of the future – and not least the issues of information and technology – before we can tell how the CCP regime influences our thinking about the Cold War.[9]

Ideology

How important was ideology in Soviet foreign policymaking? It is perhaps here we find the great divide between different groups of Cold War historians. In my book with Vladislav Zubok, we argue that great power expansionism and communist ideology had to some extent merged in the Soviet case.[10] Our critics told us that it was too easy a solution for such an intricate dilemma. However, I still believe that it is almost always better to explain something as a combination of several elements than as a Manichaean choice of 'either–or'. Pure phenomena, be it the ultimate red color, or an absolute imperial power, or a government of ideologues, belong to the domain of pure theory, not history.

It is hard to say when Soviet ideology finally expired. Ideas hardly have an exact expiry date. But, at least in the Soviet case, they had a 'best before' date. Soviet ideology was 'best before' 1939, when Stalin concluded his alliance with Hitler, thus dropping for a while the banner of communist internationalism. But ideology still had a role to play in Soviet foreign policymaking for the next forty years or so. One may argue that the Soviet invasion in Afghanistan in 1979 had used ideology mainly as a smoke screen. But the invasion in Czechoslovakia in 1968 was the product of ideological as well as of geopolitical thinking.

It is important that the last generation of Soviet leaders – which also became the first generation of leaders of the independent post-Soviet states, be it Russia or Azerbaijan – finds it extremely difficult to live in the world of harsh *realpolitik* without the cushion of ideology. Brought up in the 1940–50s with its communist Russianness as an ideological pivot of state, current leaders feel uneasy when surrounded only by barrels of oil, kilograms of gold and tons of their national currency. Hence their desire to make a new state ideology. Boris Yeltsin used different versions of Russian nationalism, Geidar Aliev is maneuvering between the Turkic idea and Islam, and Alexandr Lukashenko, between fascism and communism. When the communist dragon was defeated, many modern leaders discovered that they were actually missing the verbal flame and smoke coming from its throat.

Culture?

Culture ought to be an extremely useful methodological category or analytical framework for all historians or international relations experts. But its usefulness often becomes buried under imprecision and vague formulations. When a historian cannot explain something, he is far too often tempted to term it an effect of 'cultural factors' or, even worse, 'well-known cultural archetypes'. But it would be silly to imply that throughout this century, even before the Great War and the social revolutions it caused, leaders of different European countries were not in conflict over basic cultural differences.

It may be useful here to think in terms of the effects of cultural stereo-types. When the French Ambassador to St Petersburg, Maurice Paleo-logue, reported in 1916 that 'Russians can grasp the reality of the present and future only through day-dreaming', he did not hesitate to explain it by the geographical misfortune of the Russian nation: 'How possibly could you, travelling through the steppes in a blizzard, not zigzag all the time, when you cannot see anything ahead of you?' About this time, W. Somerset Maugham also compared the Russian national character to 'the boundless steppes of Russia'. Paleologue continued to believe that Russians were more easily influenced by oral presentations than by the written word. Maugham noticed that Russians loved to talk 'far into the night'.[11]

Yet, the problem comes when one starts taking these stereotypes as objectively meaningful archetypes. Used in this way, national culture is as difficult to capture as the hue of the sky. Artists refer to an 'Italian' or 'Parisian' sky; Shelley says that the sky of northern Italy 'hangs heavily', Yves Montand praises the '*ciel de Paris*', but, if shown photographic images of the two, both would almost certainly have failed to identify 'their' sky – provided that the Italian sky was not pierced by the dome of Santa Maria del Fiore and the French by the Tour d'Eiffel.[12] Of course, anthropologists tell us that it is possible to suggest a scholarly classification of national archetypes, such as perceptions of space (distance) and time (pace), borders (natural, historical, ethnic, and mythological), state (community, ruler, or God), and self. The problem we have is to use these general values to explain conflict or cooperation as a result of the actions of individuals.

Talking about 'Russian' (or American, or Chinese, or Norwegian) culture in general is similar to talking about the average body temperature in a hospital. Will we get a Russian national cultural type if we summarize Joseph Stalin, Vyacheslav Molotov, Lazar Kaganovich, and a peasant from the Archangel region and then divide the sum of 'culture' by four? Is it safe to suggest more complex symbols of culture than the samovar, caviar, vodka, babushka, and matreshka for Russia, chopsticks, the bicycle, bamboo, and shark's fins' soup for China, and cheeseburger, Coca-Cola, skyscrapers, dollars, and cowboys for the United States? Stalin, if my reading is correct, preferred Georgian wine to Russian vodka and did not care much about samovars; to the best of my knowledge, he was never interested in matreshkas; and as for babushkas, his closest relations with any of them were with those old communist ladies whom he had shot toward the end of his career.

Causes

The one concept with which historians always have trouble is causality. This is, I believe, in part because causality as used by historians is in its origins a religious concept, particularly linked to the great monotheistic religions. To Jews, Christians, and Moslems the search for a purpose is directly linked to understanding God's will and His laws.

Causality in historical writings takes this preoccupaton with purpose as its starting point. Discussing the Emperor Augustus, Suetonius (*c.* 70–*c.* 140 AD) informs us about his habits and deeds in detail; we learn that Augustus was subject to 'certain seasonal disorders', that he wore 'no fewer than four tunics' in wintertime, and that he restored 'ruined or burned temples' – but the Roman historian is mostly avoiding the subject of causality.[13] The British classical author Edward Gibbon (1737–94), on the contrary, is more than willing to be 'causal' (and judgmental) while discussing the same emperor: 'A cool head, an unfeeling heart, and a cowardly disposition, prompted him, at the age of nineteen, to assume the mask of hypocrisy, which he never afterwards laid aside.'[14] As we can see, Gibbon is up to writing what we would term psychological biography, explaining Augustus' rule through his personal neuroses. Arnold Toynbee discusses Augustus already in strictly systemic terms and puts him into a 'historical' chain of causality, claiming, for example, that Augustus was unconsciously paving the way for Saint Paul.

Our role, after the disasters of the twentieth century, is to reflect on our own position as writers of history in a more conscious fashion, knowing that every explanation is potentially loaded with misperception. Since our intellectual pedigree is so dominated by nineteenth-century positivism, we know that the origins of our use of causality links up to Charles Darwin, or, for that matter, Henri Stendhal. We therefore have to be careful not to become just followers of a great tradition.

If we take this responsibility seriously, we are bound to have an exceptionally hard time explaining Soviet diplomatic history. Since we are dealing with a tyrannical regime, built upon ideas, but also upon arbitrariness and the rulers' tantrums, how can we distinguish between the influence of geopolitical challenges or cultural archetypes and the impact of the dictator's flu? What, for example, about some crucial leadership changes in the 1940s? Why did Stalin, out of nowhere, pick the young and inexperienced Andrei Gromyko for the position of Soviet Ambassador to the United States? Because he wanted to have the diplomatic service radically renewed? Because Stalin liked Gromyko's NKVD (secret police) file or because he liked Gromyko's necktie?

With luck and a lot of labor, we may hope to get a clearer vision of how things were done in the Kremlin. As to ever fully explaining events, I am somewhat more skeptical.[15] With the flow of new archival documents from the Russian archives becoming thinner and thinner with every year, historians will be tempted to fall back on dubious tools of interpretation. Our main mission may, however, be the age-old responsibility of storytelling. As Joseph Brodsky's Emperor says, 'What one conquers is up to the scholars' quills.'[16]

NOTES

1 For example, see Robert Conquest, *Stalin: Breaker of Nations* (New York: Viking, 1991), p. 313. Various reference books take this date for granted (e.g., *The 1988 Almanac* (Boston, MA: Houghton Mifflin, 1987), p. 127, though, symbolically enough, this particular volume also gives Stalin's date of death as 6 March (p. 259) – so much for accuracy). See also Abdurakhman Avtorkhanov, *Zagadka smerti Stalina* [The Mystery of Stalin's Death] (Frankfurt: Posev, 1976).

2 Nikita Khrushchev, *Khrushchev Remembers* (Boston, MA: Little, Brown, 1970), p. 466; and Cold War International History Project Bulletin (*Cold War International History Bulletin*), no. 4 (1994): 60–1.

3 Kathryn Weathersby, 'New Findings on the Korean War', *Cold War International History Bulletin*, no. 3 (Fall 1993): 15; Sergei N. Goncharov, John W. Lewis, and Xue Litai, *Uncertain Partners: Stalin, Mao and the Korean War* (Stanford, CA: Stanford University Press, 1993), pp. 121–7.

4 Khrushchev, *Khrushchev Remembers*, p. 464.

5 Roi Medvedev and Dmitry Ermakov, *Seryi kardinal. M. A. Suslov: politicheskii portret* [Grey Cardinal: M. A. Suslov: A Political Portrait] (Moscow: Respublika, 1992), pp. 131–3, 174–5; Fedor Burlatsky, *Vozhdi i sovetniki* [Chiefs and Advisers] (Moscow: Politizdat, 1990), pp. 113–25.

6 Ilya Erenburg, *Liudi, gody, zhizn* [People, Years, Life] (Moscow: Sovetskii pisatel,1990), p. 210; Burlatsky, *Vozhdi i sovetniki*, p. 40.

7 Yet, some analysts, for instance Stephen Cohen, tend to take a very different view, thus fully demonstrating the role of the analyst's political partisanship in interpreting seemingly simple facts.

8 Quoted in Conquest, *Stalin*, p. 271. Vladislav Zubok and Constantine Pleshakov, *Inside the Kremlin's Cold War: From Stalin to Khrushchev* (Cambridge, MA: Harvard University Press, 1996), p. 37.

9 The prevailing optimistic view is eloquently advocated by Francis Fukuyama, *The End of History and the Last Man* (New York: Free Press, 1992).

10 Zubok and Pleshakov, *Inside the Kremlin's Cold War*, pp. 12–15.

11 Maurice Paleologue, *Tsarskaia Rossiia nakanune revoliutsii* [Tsarist Russia on the Eve of Revolution] (Moscow: Mezhdunarodnie otnosheniia, 1991), p. 18. W. Somerset Maugham, *Collected Short Stories* (London: Mandarin, 1994), vol. 3, p. 226.

12 Shelley quoted in *Library of World Poetry*, ed. William Cullen Bryant (New York: Avenel Books, 1970), p. 335.

13 Suetonius, *The Twelve Caesars* (New York: Penguin Books, 1979), pp. 99, 71.

14 Edward Gibbon, *The Decline and Fall of the Roman Empire* (New York: The Modern Library, n.d.), vol. I, pp. 30, 63, vol. II, p. 22.

15 Let me suggest a quiz: How do you explain White House motivations in the August 1998 attacks on Sudan and Afghanistan? Now, how many chose Monica Lewinsky and how many Islamic terrorism? Then compare notes.

16 Joseph Brodsky, *So Forth* (New York: Farrar, Straus & Giroux, 1996), p. 112.

11

Germany in the Cold War: Strategies and Decisions

Wilfried Loth

Germany was both a cause of and a battleground for the Cold War. If the Allies succeeded in working out a joint peace settlement for the defeated Germany, chances might have been that they would be able to limit conflicts in other areas as well and to further expand Allied cooperation. If, however, cooperation failed, this would inevitably lead to the division of Germany and the formation of the NATO bloc in the West and the Warsaw Pact in the East. This, in turn, over and over again forced the security dilemma of the East and the West.

Between cooperation and division

The initial willingness of both the East and the West to cooperate in general affairs and with regard to Germany in particular refutes the thesis of the Cold War's inevitability. Skeptical voices certainly made themselves heard from the beginning. As early as the summer of 1945, George F. Kennan considered the intention to 'govern Germany in cooperation with the Russians' a 'delusion'.[1] In a conversation with the leaders of the German Communist Party, Stalin at the same time conjured up the danger that 'there will be two Germanies'.[2] The speed with which the Soviet occupation forces took to looting in 1945 and 1946 also shows that they lacked confidence that the alliance of the victors would prevail.

Yet, with regard to the German question, the American as well as the Soviet government aimed at preventing such a break. James F. Byrnes believed his offer of a Four Power Agreement to be concurring with Roosevelt's principles. Until the spring of 1947, Lucius D. Clay worked hard to carry out the Potsdam Agreement for the constitution of a central administration for occupied Germany. Stalin also wanted to secure German unity and to put the Potsdam Agreement into effect, although at times he acted undiplomatically in dealing with the Western powers. From the Moscow Conference of Foreign Ministers in the spring of 1947 on,

Molotov's conduct left no doubt that he really wanted to cooperate with the West in working out an agreement on a peace treaty for Germany. At the London conference in the winter of 1947, he 'almost desperately' tried to bring about an accord on the early establishment of a German central government.[3]

The motives for the American and Soviet all-German strategies are obvious: the Americans pursued the general philosophy of the open door policy and hoped to create liberal conditions in Germany, which would reduce the danger of renewed German aggression. They also feared the costs of the division of Germany, which would result in a permanent American military commitment in Europe. Policymakers did not think that such a commitment could be justified domestically and financially. The Soviets, on the other hand, feared a Western European military bloc dominated by the United States. In this case, they expected the American imperialist 'reactionary circles' to prevent the elimination of fascism's social basis in the Western zones, thereby increasing the threat of another war. Also, the Soviet Union desperately needed reparations from industrial West Germany and from the Ruhr area in particular.

Neither American nor Soviet policymakers expected the Germans to accept the long-term division of their nation. As the new primary sources clearly show,[4] Stalin hoped to make use of the Germans' opposition to division – a division which the West obviously pursued ever since the Moscow Council of Foreign Ministers. On the other hand, the Americans, and especially the French, feared that the West Germans might turn to the Soviet Union to rescue German unity. In their ideological images, Moscow feared an alliance of American and (West) German imperialism, while the West was frightened by the thought of an alliance of Soviet and German totalitarianism.

This fear of a German–Soviet alliance explains why the West decided to form blocs but still made several attempts to come to terms with the Soviet Union with regard to the German question. The key concept, neutralization, aimed at excluding Germany from the East–West conflict, and was supposed to be a first step towards détente in general. Under the influence of the Berlin Blockade, the British military governor Brian Robertson was the first to favor this concept. Shortly afterwards – and without knowledge of the British suggestion – Kennan, of all people, also came to fear the consequences of his own recommendations. In the spring of 1952 the Policy Planning Staff of the State Department, now under the leadership of Paul M. Nitze, again advocated the neutralization of Germany and increasingly emphasized that such an agreement might initiate the retreat of communism from Eastern Europe. After Stalin's death, even Winston Churchill thought the time had come to discuss the neutralization of Germany with the Soviet leadership – in the interest of détente and in order to forestall dangerous German aspirations to unify.[5]

Meanwhile, Soviet interest in a joint agreement on Germany continued undiminished. As can be gathered from the new sources, Stalin did not sway indecisively between the consolidation of the GDR (German Democratic Republic – East Germany) on the one hand and new offers for negotiations on the other. Instead, he gave absolute priority to unity and a peace treaty, especially in view of the alternative, that is the formation of a powerful Western military bloc with US and German troops in the center of Europe. After a meeting with Stalin in May 1951, the SED Politburo had to admit 'self-critically' that '[t]he main task lies in the development of a policy for all of Germany'.[6] In the second half of 1951, a commission of the Soviet Foreign Ministry worked out a draft for a peace treaty, which the East wanted to submit to the West for negotiation. The Stalin Note of 10 March 1952, was worded very carefully in order not to provide the opponents of a peace settlement with a pretext to decline the offer.[7]

Since the concessions offered in the Stalin Note did not bring the West back to the negotiation table, Stalin for the most part gave up, ordering the SED leadership to 'organize your own State now'.[8] He allowed Ulbricht to proclaim the construction of socialism in the GDR. After Stalin's death, however, his successors approached the West again. The documents of the Moscow foreign ministry confirm that Beria was not the only one who pursued new initiatives, as his opponents later claimed, and that he was not in a minority. For the session of the Council of Ministers' Presidium on 27 May 1953, Foreign Minister Molotov submitted a draft resolution recommending 'the early realization of free all-German elections after withdrawal of the occupation forces of all Powers from Germany'. The draft also recommended 'not to oppose the question of restoration of German unity to the proposal of the three [Western] Powers concerning the realization of free all-German elections'.[9]

There is no reason to doubt the various claims that the Soviet Union favored German unity based not on socialism but on the 'completion of the bourgeois-democratic revolution'. The internal orders never indicated anything different, and, if one takes a sober look at it, it could not have been in the Soviet interest to do otherwise. Stalin's repeated claims that socialism could be realized in a parliamentary democratic way[10] in this context seem to have been an attempt to reconcile ideological principles and Soviet interests and to soothe the disappointed Germans' comrades.

The West German option

The Soviet leadership's persistent attempts to win German support in concluding a peace settlement show that the consolidation of the division of East and West could not be achieved without the consent of the West Germans. If they were willing to pay the price of neutrality for reunification, then the Western occupying powers would not be able to deny it to them, no matter what the consequences of a neutral Germany for the design of the Western alliance. In the West, the Germans, therefore, played a specific part in the Cold War.

This part certainly turned out differently from what Stalin had hoped for and what Churchill had feared. As early as the summer of 1945, Konrad Adenauer, who later became the first Chancellor of the Federal Republic, concluded that 'the Soviet occupied part' of the German Reich 'is lost to Germany for an incalculable period of time'.[11] 'He elaborated on 31 October 1945, in a letter to the Mayor of Duisburg, Heinrich Weitz:

> Russia more and more withdraws from cooperation with the other great powers and acts at its own discretion in the territory it governs. In the territory it governs there already rule different economic and political principles than in the other part of Europe. Thus, the division of Eastern Europe, the Soviet area, and Western Europe is a fact.

Therefore, Adenauer concerned himself mostly with the new organization of the state of the Germans in that 'part of Germany not occupied by Russia'. In his view, Western Germany constituted 'an integral part of Western Europe', and he intended to keep it that way.[12]

Shortly after he wrote off the Eastern Zone he also came to fear the expansion of communism: in March 1946, he alerted an old acquaintance he had known in the Weimar Republic and who had emigrated to the United States, the Social Democrat Wilhelm Sollmann, that 'the danger is great'. 'Asia moved up to the Elbe', and: 'only an economically and mentally healthy Western Europe under the leadership of England [sic] and France, a Western Europe of which a fundamental part is the part of Germany not occupied by Russia, can stop the further mental and massive advance of Asia'.[13] For the future of the Germans, Adenauer from now on envisioned an economically and politically consolidated West Germany as an equal partner of the West in the struggle against Soviet expansion.[14]

In essence, Kurt Schumacher, the leader of the West German Social Democrats, concurred. Although he and Adenauer later quarreled passionately over tactical questions of Western integration, Schumacher, too, considered the Eastern occupation zone 'lost' as early as the fall of 1945. He did not think that in the presence of Soviet occupation forces Social Democratic policies could be pursued in the East. Accordingly, he concentrated on building up a strong Social Democratic Party in the Western zones only. He hoped that the party's strong anti-communism would help the Social Democrats to become influential with the Western occupation powers. Schumacher categorically opposed the creation of an all-German Social Democratic Party, which in his view would only advance Soviet influence on the development of the Western zones. He continued to reject this possibility, even when Otto Grotewohl's Social Democratic Berlin Central Committee urged a Reich-wide organization of social democracy. This organization aimed at parrying communist pressure to unite the two workers' parties as soon as possible, but the only advice Schumacher offered his discouraged East German comrades in the Winter of 1945 and 1946 was to dissolve the party in the Eastern zone.[15]

However, in the immediate post-war years neither Adenauer nor Schumacher could publicly state that a new German state could only be created in the West. The German public favored the politically correct demand that the four occupation powers build a bridge between the East and the West that would serve as an element of communication between the four powers, secure German unity, and decisively aid the establishment of a new peace order. In his first programmatic speech to the executive of the Eastern zone's Christian Democratic Union on 13 February 1946, the party's chairman Jakob Kaiser, stated what many thought:

> I think the meaning of these events, which are so hurtful to us, lies in the mutual stimulation of the nations, in the mutual coordination towards a European union, which will allow all of Europe to advance to social forms that will make possible a new and lasting understanding.[16]

These ideas dominated the discussions in magazines and political circles,[17] and made Kaiser believe that he would become the leader of an all-German Christian Democratic Union and the man in charge in the new Germany.

Yet, the influence of the skeptics and the particularists sufficed to prevent an articulation of the all-German interest. In a discussion with the party leadership in Wennigsen in the beginning of October 1945, Grotewohl argued in favor of expanding the Social Democratic Central Committee and including representatives of the Western zones and the old party executive that had been in exile in London. His suggestion aimed at the constitution of a provisional party executive, but failed. Instead, Schumacher was authorized to act as the party's representative for the Western zones. This deprived the Eastern Central Committee of its strongest argument against an immediate union of the workers' parties. After that, Schumacher's (justified) attacks on this forced union stood in the way of any serious reflection on the situation in occupied Germany. Accordingly, the West German advocates of an understanding between the East and the West lost ground within the SPD.

Meanwhile in the Christian Democratic Union (CDU), Jakob Kaiser also lost ground due to the attacks of the Social Democrats (SPD). When Adenauer managed to win the support of the middle class and the anti-Prussian forces, Kaiser also failed to follow through his claim to a leadership position. In February 1947, he barely managed to organize a nation-wide working group of the Christian Democratic Union and the Christian Social Union, which, however, was never really active. An all-German party organization was missing in the Christian Democratic Union as much as it was missing in the Social Democratic Party.

Neither did Kaiser succeed in organizing the 'national representation' of all parties in the run-up to the Moscow Conference of Foreign Ministers in early 1947. Schumacher rejected discussions with the SED, thereby allowing Adenauer to point to the SPD's negative attitude in order to weaken any CDU commitment. Thus, the British and the Americans no longer saw any need to overcome French resistance to this project. The French occupation authority and the politicians in favor of separation 'cooperated' in a similar fashion in letting the Munich Conference of Ministers fail in June 1947: when the chief ministers of East Germany were prevented from giving a statement on the constitution of a central administration, they saw themselves forced to leave the Conference even before it officially started. The head of Saxony-Anhalt, Erhard Hübener, failed to organize another meeting of the chief ministers. When twelve leading politicians met privately in Berlin Wannsee on 9 November 1947, Schumacher punished the most prominent Social Democratic participant, Paul Löbe, by excluding him from the committee for foreign affairs of the party.

Adenauer and Schumacher succeeded in their strategy of separation, because two factors severely handicapped German nationalism. After the break-down of the Third Reich, the identification with National Socialism, which had brought an incredible catastrophe on the world, had discredited nationalism itself. In living under occupation many found it appropriate to hold back on national questions. Also, many were insecure or honestly looked for a new start beyond the idolization of the nation-state. Second, the fear of Soviet communism overshadowed any feelings of national unity. Age-old fears of threats to civilization and the latent fear of a social revolution led to a highly selective perception of the realities in the Soviet occupied zone and of Soviet policies towards Germany. Former *Wehrmacht* members, who knew of the realities of the German war of extermination in the East, often feared an Eastern pay back.

The break-down of nationalism and the fear of communism led pragmatic West Germans to concentrate on the obvious: the reconstruction of political life in their region and their zones of occupation. Thus, they neglected the fate of the Germans in the East. When Grotewohl advocated a joint organization of the SPD in all four zones of occupation, the chair of the SPD district Westliches Westfalen wrote to Schumacher that he considered the constitution of an all-German SPD a problem of the future but not of the present: 'now, our shirt is nearer than our jacket'.[18] In view of such attitudes, an all-German approach that actively opposed the tendency toward the East–West division could not possibly push through.[19]

On the other side, the break of solidarity hidden in the concentration on the West made many Germans hesitate to actively participate in intensifying the East–West conflict. This could be seen in June of 1948, when the Western Allies put the foundation of a West German state on their agenda. In view of the public's wait-and-see mood, the chief ministers of the Western zones of occupation only agreed to a 'basic law for the uniform administration of the Western zone of occupation', which the military governors enforced and which left responsibility for the consolidation of the split with them. Two years later, the discussion on German rearmament and the integration of Germany in the Western alliance increased resistance even more. Even after the outbreak of the Korean War a majority of the people opposed rearmament: only 40 percent of the West Germans agreed to a 'European Army with German participation', while 45 percent opposed the German defense contribution.[20]

These indecisive and contradictory attitudes of the West German population enabled determined and resourceful politicians to assume a major role in Germany's political arena. In reacting to the Berlin Blockade, the Berlin Mayor Ernst Reuter, for example, pushed the West German chief ministers to proceed with the organization of a West German state. His appeal to defend the freedom of West Berlin helped to weaken any reservations that this might hasten the division of Germany. Of all the tactical mistakes that Stalin made in the Cold War, the Berlin Blockade turned out to be the biggest one.

For the most part, it was Konrad Adenauer who pushed rearmament and Western integration. He not only made use of the Korean War to provoke negotiations with the West on a West German defense contribution, but also became active in the discussion of the most extensive concessions the Soviet leadership had made as yet: he implored the Western governments not to accept the Stalin Notes of 10 March and 9 April 1952. He put off the critics of Western integration within his own ranks and within the opposition by promising that if the West stood firm now, the Soviet Union would soon – in 'not many years' – extend its offers even more: it would accept freedom in the 'whole European East'.[21]

It is remarkable that Adenauer's judgment of the Soviet initiative of early 1952 corresponds exactly to the analyses of our newest research: he viewed it as a consistent continuation of a political approach pursued since 1945. 'If one really looks at it', he told the constituting assembly of the Protestant Christian Democratic working group in Siegen on 16 March 1952, 'it is hardly anything new. Next to a strong nationalist touch, it aims at the neutralization of Germany and wants to prevent the progress of the creation of the European defense union and European integration.'[22] As opposed to historians who later analyzed the notes, Adenauer definitely took Stalin's offer seriously.

He just did not think it was an attractive offer. From his point of view, neutralization would not only lead to the withdrawal of Soviet troops from the Eastern occupation zone (a topic he hardly ever discussed), but also to the withdrawal of the United States from Europe. In Adenauer's opinion, this would then lead to a situation in which Western Europe would be under permanent pressure from the only great military power left and in which naïve or opportunist nationalists would help the communists to seize power in Germany. 'Bismarck talked about his nightmare', he told a journalist in June 1953.

> I also have a nightmare: its name is Potsdam. The threat of a joint policy of the great powers that would be to Germany's disadvantage has existed since 1945, and continued to exist even after the founding of the Federal Republic. The foreign policy of the Federal Republic always aimed at moving out of this danger zone. Germany must not fall between the millstones, otherwise it is lost.[23]

Considering a joint policy of the Great Powers as a threat? Adenauer could not have articulated his preference for the Western bloc more clearly.

In trying to move out of this dangerous zone Adenauer made use of a variety of factors that were to his advantage. First, in being a privileged partner in his talks with the West he had acquired strategic advantages. Second, his opponent's inconsistency and lack of decisiveness turned out to be in Adenauer's favor as well. The success of the economic reconstruction and the ability to overcome the crisis of reconstruction against the background of the 'Korea Boom' of 1951, resulting in the first signs of the economic miracle, also was to his advantage. These factors expanded Adenauer's domestic basis and increased the West Germans' perception of the sacrifices they would have to make for a new all-German beginning. Additionally, the Stalin Note came too late to really impress the West Germans. Stalin too readily agreed to the GDR's proclamation of the construction of socialism, and the upheaval of 17 June 1953 also helped Adenauer's position.

Ulbricht's revolution

At the same time, in the Eastern zone of occupied Germany, Walter Ulbricht and his social revolution also moved out of a danger zone. The parallelism of the interests of the first Federal Chancellor and those of the SED General Secretary has often been debated. The new primary sources indicate more clearly that there also existed a certain parallelism in their actions. One can hardly imagine the Federal Republic's integration in the West without Adenauer or a politician comparable to him, as much as one cannot imagine the GDR without an Ulbricht.

This does not mean that Ulbricht's intentions differed from Stalin's from the start. Both inner conviction and concern for his political survival guided his acceptance of the directives of the Soviet Union's great leader. Not only did he accept Stalin's dictum that revolution in Germany was not on the agenda and that one had to pursue cooperation with the Western Allies instead, Ulbricht also worked hard to carry through Stalin's intentions with his confused and oftentimes disappointed comrades. 'In the period of opposition to Fascism', he declared in the planning commission of the Moscow exiles in April 1944,

> of Hitler's war, and in the period of setting up a new democracy, the party defers efforts to realize its final goal. In the struggle in Hitler's war and participation in setting up a new democracy, the extermination of the German reaction, the party sees the creation of the prerequisites for the propagation of its final goal.[24]

However, while in the West the initial dictatorship of education gradually evolved into the granting of more and more freedoms, the communist perception of the world in terms of class struggle led to the dictatorship of the SED Secretary. If one suspected the class enemy's manifestation in each and every deviating opinion, then there was no choice but to control everything oneself. The newest research shows that Ulbricht and Sergeii Tulpanov, the party official of the Soviet Military Administration (SMA), supported each other in this process. Colonel Tulpanov considered Ulbricht the most reliable organizer among the Germans and promoted him accordingly. Ulbricht's successes increased Tulpanov's influence in the occupation administration and he also gained some influence in Moscow.[25]

Initially, Ulbricht and Tulpanov did not notice that the consolidation of the party dictatorship in the Eastern zone objectively contradicted Stalin's agenda for policies for Germany. The failure of the London Council of Foreign Ministers in December 1947 showed that Germany was divided. Moscow, nevertheless, kept insisting on its determination to continue the struggle against 'the imperialist and anti-democratic camp'.[26] Thus, it seemed obvious to conclude that the situation in the Eastern zone was revolutionary and that this revolution had to be carried through in all of Germany, if the country were to be unified. Tulpanov believed to concur with Stalin when he told the SED leadership, in May 1948, that 'in fact, the party is in power and leads the struggle of the conquest of all of Germany'.[27]

The political adviser of the SMA Vladimir Semyonov soon told Tulpanov in plain terms that he was mistaken: 'I clearly told Tulpanov what I thought and especially emphasized that statements of this sort may not be made without previous sanctioning of the Central Committee of the CPSU (B).'[28] On his next visit to Moscow in December of 1948,

Ulbricht heard that his proclamation of the transition to socialism had gone too far. Wilhelm Pieck jotted down the results of the conversation with Stalin: 'No transition to people's democracy yet', 'situation not the same as in the people's democracies', 'no unified state yet – not yet in a position to take power'.[29]

Of course, Tulpanov and Ulbricht immediately promised to do better. However, this could not protect Tulpanov from being discharged, albeit with some hesitation, probably because his excellent knowledge of the language, the country, and the party made him indispensable. In the winter of 1948–49, he first had to contend with a limitation of his authority and then was dismissed for good.[30] Ulbricht, on the other hand, held his own, because, as a result of the break with Tito, Stalin gave absolute priority to the strict control of the foreign party organizations. In the Soviet zone of occupation no one but Ulbricht was better suited for this task. Therefore, Stalin continued to accept Ulbricht's conversion of the SED to a 'party of a new type'. Apparently he did not realize that this further damaged his political project for Germany.

Ulbricht, of course, did not content himself with transforming the SED into a Stalinist cadre party. He also intended to secure its monopoly in the GDR and to advance the 'socialist transformation' wherever this was possible. German unity, in his view, required the application of the GDR's order to all of Germany, and was to be brought about by the 'struggle' of the 'democratic forces' against the Western monopolies and the Adenauer regime they had created. In his draft for his speech at the second Party Conference of the SED, which he submitted to the Moscow leadership for approval in March 1952, he characterized the SED's task as providing 'leadership in the fight to accomplish a peace treaty and fulfill the great national task – establishment throughout Germany of a democratic and peaceful order modelled on the German Democratic Republic'.[31]

It is characteristic that Ulbricht's speech did not meet with approval in this form. Mikhail Gribanov, the leader of the German desk in the Foreign Ministry, complained about a lack of consideration for the struggle for unity: the SED leadership behaved 'as if the existing division of Germany will continue for ever'.[32] It is hard to say to what extent Ulbricht now recognized the contradiction. The objective 'democratic order' left room for interpretation and the struggle for this order could be pursued in various ways. Therefore, Ulbricht may well have misunderstood Stalin's criticism as tactical correction. However, it is also conceivable that he evaluated the Moscow stipulations critically and consciously utilized the linguistic ambivalence to pursue his own objectives. At any rate, the fascination of power and belief in the revolution led him to push the Soviet dictatorship as far as possible in the direction he considered appropriate.

With uncanny certainty, Ulbricht made use of any fluctuations and insecurities in Stalin's policy. When the boss of the Kremlin ordered the

SED in April 1952 to organize its own state, the East German leader asked directly for permission to proclaim a 'People's Democracy' and to make it the party's purpose 'to lead the working class forward along the path of constructing socialism'.[33] After the Moscow Politburo approved the 'course of forcing the construction of socialism in the GDR *as had been begun by the SED*',[34] Ulbricht went a step further: he announced 'that constructing socialism has become the *fundamental* task in the German Democratic Republic'.[35] In the following months he pursued this construction with his inherent radicalism and mercilessness, and extensively used the scope the Moscow declaration left him.

Ulbricht also utilized the confusion created by Beria's fall at the end of June 1953. As opposed to what has been suggested earlier, the suppression of the 17 June 1953 insurgency did not complete Ulbricht's fall from power.[36] The preparations for a new initiative to negotiate with the Western powers continued, as did the criticism of the 'course of forcing the construction of socialism in the GDR'. On 26 June the Commission for the Organization of the SED Politburo decided to cancel the function of the Central Committee's General Secretary. Practically, this completed Ulbricht's loss of power. It was only his conduct after Beria's arrest that saved him. On 3 July he managed to convince a representative of the Soviet High Commission to support the retention of the office of the First Secretary; and until 18 July he convinced the majority of the Politburo as well as the High Commissioner Semyonov that he enjoyed the trust of the new Moscow leadership.[37]

In fact, an order from Moscow to keep Ulbricht in any case has yet to be found. In view of the confused balance of power after Beria's fall, which complicated communication on the strategic track, such an order could not have been given. There were more important things to tend to in Moscow than to interfere with the domestic debate of the East German party leadership. Meanwhile, however, Semyonov feared that such an order might be given, and Herrnstadt and Zaisser, the spokesmen of the faction that opposed Ulbricht, thought that one existed. Accordingly, they stopped talking, thereby allowing Ulbricht to triumph.

In view of this decisionmaking process Ulbricht appears to have been a revolutionary in his own right – in developing his own course he is comparable to a Tito, Gomulka, or Mao, and in his technique of influencing Stalin to Kim Il-Sung. His 'socialist revolution' certainly depended on Soviet military presence, but his political measures saw to the continuation of this prerequisite – even though the Soviet occupation authority had initially hoped to withdraw after the conclusion of a peace treaty. The socialist transition in the Soviet zone of occupation compares to the transformation in the other countries that later formed the Warsaw Pact: Moscow did not intend the changes to take this form, but national communist forces advanced them in the shadow of the Red Army. They were then sanctioned by the Cold War, which they themselves had helped to provoke.

The turning point and its aftermath

The rescue of Ulbricht on 18 July 1953, marks precisely the point at which the structure of the Eastern and Western blocs ceased to be at risk. Until then, Soviet initiatives again and again had interfered with the Western plans of an integrated NATO including the Federal Republic. At the same time, the West doubted whether this form of Western integration was really necessary, reasonable, or even inevitable. Ulbricht's return to power stabilized the strongest obstacle to an agreement on a joint settlement of the German question. Stalin's successors did not manage to remove this obstacle: After 17 June 1953, they had to be careful not to expose the SED regime to further shocks. Furthermore, the instrumentalization of obvious disagreements on *Deutschlandpolitik* (the extent of which still is not known) in the power struggle against Beria limited their freedom of action.

Accordingly, the Soviet leadership continued the campaign to organize all-German elections, but they did not any longer care about its credibility. At an informal meeting at the Geneva summit in July 1955, Nikolai Bulganin told Anthony Eden that he could not possibly return from this conference and 'here in Geneva ... have agreed upon the immediate reunification', as this would not be understood in Moscow. When Nikita Khrushchev joined the conversation, however, Bulganin continued to say that he and Khrushchev were prepared to give their foreign minister corresponding directives; the ministers should deliberate the theme of 'reunification', and discuss corresponding services they expected in return.[38]

It was only after this signal of a willingness to negotiate did not show any concrete results that Khrushchev dismissed his plans for neutralization for good. In official negotiations Bulganin pointed out that meanwhile there had developed considerable difficulties, which complicated such an arrangement:

> In the meantime, two Germanies have formed – the GDR and the Federal Republic of Germany – each with its economic and societal structure. It is clear that under such circumstances, the question of a mechanistic melding of the two parts of Germany cannot be touched upon, since that would be an unrealistic question.[39]

And Khrushchev openly provided the GDR with a guarantee of continuance, which it had still not obtained. When the Soviet delegation stopped in Berlin on their return to Moscow, Khrushchev declared that

there was 'no whole Germany at present; two German states exist ...
nothing else is realistic'. And then, amidst 'long, continuos applause': 'The
German question cannot be solved at the expense of the interests of the
German Democratic Republic'; 'eliminating all its political and social
achievements' would not be possible.[40]

Thus, the summer of 1955 saw the end of a process that until then had
been the central theme of the Cold War: the formation of blocs in the East
and the West as a means of establishing a new international order after
the European state system had collapsed following National Socialist
expansion. What followed in the history of the Cold War – the antagonism
of the two blocs and the efforts to contain the conflict – differed in its
structure from the process of the formation of blocs, making it advisable
to make a chronological distinction in the study of the conflict.[41] The Cold
War was not over yet, but the German question had been settled in a way
that fundamentally changed the conflict's character. The new problems
evolving from the blocs' antagonism soon led to the question of whether
the term 'Cold War' still adequately characterized the events.[42]

The two German states at first opposed the efforts to contain the Cold
War. Adenauer only wanted to agree to an understanding on armaments
limitation if the German question were first settled in his favor: a complete
Soviet renunciation of the GDR and the reunification of Germany within
the Western alliance. When he realized that the Western partners were no
longer prepared to tolerate this precondition, he tried to at least prevent
any arrangements that would have included recognition of the GDR under
international law and which would thus have established the division of
Germany for an indefinite period of time.[43] Ulbricht, on his side, pressed
Khrushchev to cancel the Four Power status of Berlin and to hand control
of the transition routes to West Berlin over to the GDR – thereby disregarding the danger of an armed conflict with the Western powers that this
might have provoked.[44]

Only gradually, in a long and painful learning process after the construction of the Berlin Wall in August 1971, did the West Germans come
to understand that détente also constituted a means to ease the consequences of division. In July 1963, Egon Bahr declared that a recognition
of communist security needs would result in the 'loosening up of the
borders and of the Wall'.[45] Maybe, it would even offer a means to restore
German unity. Although this might not necessarily be a result of détente,
it was the only path left after the failure of the neutralization plans. When
the successes of the administration of Willy Brandt and Walter Scheel from
1969 to 1972 officially implemented this train of thought, the Federal
Republic came to be one of the main driving forces of détente. The GDR,
on the other hand, was now on the defensive. Much to the chagrin of the
Moscow leadership, Erich Honecker had to pay for economic support by
granting humanitarian concessions, thereby allowing himself to get caught

on a 'golden hook' (a term coined by Julii A. Kvitsinskii), unable to escape.[46]

The absence of pre-determination

The primary sources of Western and Eastern archives make the process of the bloc formation appear much more open than contemporaries thought at the time. Research, thus, questions the interpretation of history which the winners of the debates in the post-war period made until the mid-1950s. There seems to have been more flexibility and common ground between the victorious powers than contemporaries impressed by the myths of the Cold War cared to believe; the part Germans in the East and the West played in the decisionmaking process, which led to the foundation of two German states, proved to be more substantial. In this respect, the disclosure of the new primary sources contributes to the depolarization of our understanding of the Cold War: the impression that the Cold War was mostly determined by decisionmakers in Moscow or Washington cannot be maintained.

NOTES

1 Quoted from George F. Kennan, *Memoirs 1925–1950* (Boston, MA: Little, Brown and Company, 1967), p. 264.
2 Conversation on 4 June 1945, in Rolf Badstübner and Wilfried Loth (eds), *Wilhelm Pieck – Aufzeichnungen zur Deutschlandpolitik 1945–1953* (Berlin: Akademie-Verlag, 1994), pp. 50–2.
3 As described by Marshall in a message to his Assistant Secretary Lovett, 12 December 1947, *FRUS 1947*, II, pp. 764f.; also see Martina Kessel, *Westeuropa und die deutsche Teilung: Englische und französische Deutschlandpolitik auf den Außenministerkonferenzen von 1945 bis 1947* (Munich: Oldenbourg, 1989); Wilfried Loth, *Stalins ungeliebtes Kind: Warum Moskau die DDR nicht wollte* (Berlin: Rowohlt, 1994), pp. 83–8, and 98f.; Carolyn Eisenberg, *Drawing the Line: The American Decision to Divide Germany, 1944–1949* (New York: Cambridge University Press, 1996), pp. 289–308.
4 See esp. Loth, *Stalins ungeliebtes Kind*, which is now also available in Italian and English translation: *Figliastri di Stalin: Mosca, Berlino et la formazione della RDT* (Urbino: Quattroventi, 1997); *Stalins Unwanted Child: The Soviet Union, the German Question and the Founding of the GDR* (London/New York: Macmillan, 1998). A Polish translation will be published by Philip Wilson, Warsaw.
5 See Rolf Steininger, 'Wie die deutsche Teilung verhindert werden sollte. Der Robertson-Plan aus dem Jahre 1948', in *Militärgeschichtliche Mitteilungen* 33 (1983): 49–89; Wilfried Loth, *The Division of the World, 1941–1955* (London/New York: Routledge, 1988), pp. 204f.; Reinhard Neebe, 'Wahlen als Test. Eine gescheiterte Initiative des Politischen Planungsstabs im State Department zur Stalin-Note vom 10. März 1952', *Militärgeschichtliche Mitteilungen* 45 (1989): 139–62; Josef Foschepoth, 'Churchill, Adenauer und die Neutralisierung

Deutschlands', *Deutschland-Archiv* 17 (1984): 1286–301; Klaus Larres, *Politik der Illusionen: Churchill, Eisenhower und die deutsche Frage 1945–1955* (Göttingen: Vandenhoeck & Ruprecht, 1995).

6 Internal resolution of the SED Politburo, 2 June 1950, quoted in Loth, *Stalins ungeliebtes Kind*, p. 169.

7 See for the new details of the bureaucratic process, Stein Bjørnstad, *The Soviet Union and German Unification During Stalin's Last Years* (Oslo: Institutt for Forsvarsstudier, 1998), pp. 64–73, 78–91.

8 Conversation on 7 April 1952, Soviet Protocoll in *Cold War International History Project Bulletin* 4 (Fall 1994), p. 48.

9 Published by Elke Scherstjanoi, 'Die sowjetische Deutschlandpolitik nach Stalins Tod 1953. Neue Dokumente aus dem Archiv des Moskauer Außenministeriums', in *Vierteljahrshefte für Zeitgeschichte* 46 (1998): 497–549, here 539–43.

10 See Loth, *Stalins ungeliebtes Kind*, pp. 32f., and also p. 146.

11 Adenauer's note of 9 October 1945, on a conversation with representatives of the *New Chronicle* and the Associated Press in *Adenauer, Briefe 1945–1947*, ed. Hans-Peter Mensing (Berlin: Siedler, 1983), p. 124.

12 Ibid., pp. 130f.

13 Ibid., p. 191.

14 More details on Adenauer's politics are given by Hans-Peter Schwarz, *Adenauer. Vol. I: From the German Empire to the Federal Republic, 1876–1952* (Oxford/Providence: Berghahn, 1995). See also Josef Foschepoth (ed.), *Adenauer und die Deutsche Frage* (Göttingen: Vandenhoeck & Ruprecht, 1988).

15 See Klaus Sühl, 'Schumacher und die Westzonen-SPD im Vereinigungsprozeß', in Dietrich Straritz and Hermann Weber (eds), *Einheitsfront – Einheitspartei. Kommunisten und Sozialdemokraten in Ost- und Westeuropa 1944–1948* (Cologne: Verlag Wissenschaft und Politik, 1989), pp. 108–28.

16 Quoted in Werner Conze, *Jakob Kaiser. Politiker zwischen Ost und West 1945–1949* (Stuttgart: Deutsche Verlags-Anstalt, 1969), p. 68.

17 See Wilfried Loth, 'German Conceptions of Europe during the Escalation of the East–West Conflict, 1945–1949', in Josef Becker and Franz Knipping (eds), *Power in Europe? Great Britain, France, Italy and Germany in a Postwar World, 1945–1950* (Berlin/New York: de Gruyter 1986), pp. 517–36.

18 Letter of 21 September 1945, quoted in Sühl, *Kurt Schumacher*, p. 118.

19 See other examples in Wilfried Loth, 'Die Deutschen und die deutsche Frage. Überlegungen zur Dekomposition der deutschen Nation', in Loth (ed.), *Die deutsche Frage in der Nachkriegszeit* (Berlin: Akademie-Verlag, 1994), pp. 186–200.

20 Polls taken in November 1950, quoted in Wilfried Loth, 'The Korean War and the Reorganization of the European Security System 1948–1955', in Rolf Ahmann, Adolf M. Birke, and Michael Howard (eds), *The Quest for Stability: Problems of West European Security 1918–1957* (Oxford: Oxford University Press, 1993), pp. 465–86, here p. 480.

21 Executive meeting of the *Bundestag* faction of the CDU on 25 March 1952, recorded in: Hermann Pünder, *Von Preußen nach Europa: Lebenserinnerungen* (Stuttgart: Deutsche Verlags-Anstalt, 1968), p. 488.

22 *Siegener Zeitung*, 17 March 1952.

23 Interview with Ernst Friedländer, in *Bulletin des Presse- und Informationsamtes der Bundesregierung*, Bonn 1953, Nr. 109, p. 926 (13 June 1953).

24 Session of 24 April 1944, quoted in Peter Erler, Horst Laude, and Manfred Wilke (eds), *'Nach Hitler kommen wir.' Dokumente zur Programmatik der Moskauer KPD-Führung 1944/45 für Nachkriegsdeutschland* (Berlin: Akademie-Verlag, 1994), p. 169.

25 Next to Loth, *Stalins ungeliebtes Kind*, see Norman M. Naimark, *The Russians in Germany: A History of the Soviet Zone of Occupation, 1945–1949* (Cambridge, MA, and London: Harvard University Press, 1995), as well as the memories of Semyonov, published posthumously: Vladimir S. Semyonov, *Von Stalin bis Gorbatschow. Ein halbes Jahrhundert in diplomatischer Mission 1939–1991* (Berlin: Nicolaische Verlagsbuchhandlung, 1995), esp. pp. 261ff.

26 Zhadonov at the constituting conference of the Cominform, *The Cominform: Minutes of the Three Conferences 1947/1948/1949* (Milan: Feltrinelli, 1994), pp. 224f. Apparently, the SMA or the SED leadership did not receive more detailed directives in the winter of 1947/48.

27 Draft of presentation of 8 May 1948, published in Badstübner and Loth, *Wilhelm Pieck*, pp. 216–27, here p. 217.

28 Semyonov, *Von Stalin bis Gorbatschow*, p. 262.

29 Conversation of 18 December 1948, quoted in Badstübner and Loth, *Wilhelm Pieck*, pp. 259–63.

30 Naimark, *Russians in Germany*, pp. 341–5.

31 Quoted in Bjørnstad, *Soviet Union*, p. 75.

32 Gribanov to Vyshinsky, ibid.

33 Ulbricht to Stalin, 1 July 1952, published in Dietrich Staritz, 'Die SED, Stalin und der "Aufbau des Sozialismus"', *Deutschland-Archiv* 24 (1991): 686–700, here 698f.

34 Formulated in a resolution of the Committee of the Council of Ministers of the USSR on 27 May 1953, published in *Beiträge zur Geschichte der Arbeiterbewegung* 32 (1990): 651–4.

35 Draft of a resolution of 8 July 1952, quoted in Loth, *Stalins ungeliebtes Kind*, p. 189.

36 Ibid., p. 208.

37 Ibid., pp. 211–14.

38 Public Record Office (PRO) Cabinet Papers (55)99. 27 July 1955, CAB 129/76, reported in Rolf Steininger, Deutsche Frage und Berliner Konferenz 1954, in Wolfgang Venohr (ed.), *Ein Deutschland wird es sein* (Erlangen: Straube, 1990), pp. 37–88, here p. 87.

39 *Europa-Archiv* 10 (1955): 8061.

40 Ibid., 8121.

41 Cf. my proposal in *The Division of the World*, pp. 304–6.

42 For an assessment on the basis of the new evidence, see Wilfried Loth, *Helsinki, 1. August 1975. Entspannung und Abrüstung* (Munich: Deutscher Taschenbuch-Verlag, 1998).

43 For this see Hans-Peter Schwarz, *Konrad Adenauer. Vol. II: The Statesman: 1952–1967* (Oxford/Providence, RI: Berghahn, 1997).

44 Documented in Hope M. Harrison, 'Ulbricht and the Concret "Rose". New Archival Evidence on the Dynamics of Soviet–East German Relations and the Berlin Crisis, 1958–1961', *Cold War International History Project Working Paper* 5, May 1993; and Michael Lemke, *Die Berlin-Krise 1958–1963. Interessen und Handlungsspielräume der SED im Ost–West-Konflikt* (Berlin: Akademie-Verlag, 1995).

45 *Dokumente zur Deutschlandpolitik. IV. Reihe, Bd. 9* (Frankfurt am Main: A. Metzner, 1978), pp. 572ff.

46 Julii A. Kvitsinskii, *Vor dem Sturm. Erinnerungen eines Diplomaten* (Berlin: Siedler, 1993), p. 261. On the Moscow's helpless concern see ibid., pp. 255–66.

12

China's Strategic Culture and the Cold War Confrontations

Shu Guang Zhang

The opening of archives – especially from Russia and China – has fostered a 'new' Cold War history. While many are busy digging new materials, however, few have taken on the task of making theoretic sense of the new historical evidence. Whether or not strategic culture, for example, would be a viable conceptual framework remains unexplored. States have armed forces and armed forces have strategies; but the way those armed forces are organized and used show variations. Do these variations matter in international conflict resolution? Or, did they matter in the Cold War confrontations? To address these large questions, it is useful to look at a particular case such as China. As the threat and use of force are central to China's history,[1] any discussion of China's strategic behavior might need to begin with its cultural underpinnings. This chapter, therefore, takes strategic culture as an analytical framework to assess the PRC's (People's Republic of China's) strategic behavior, and to identify China's traditions, values, beliefs, attitudes, symbols, and culturally based ways of 'adapting to the environment and solving problems' with respect to the threat or use of force.[2] This chapter will concentrate on the Cold War period with a particular emphasis on Mao Zedong's strategic outlook.

Chinese strategic culture and its symbols

Strategic culture as a system of symbols embodies assumptions about what constitutes national security. One such assumption is that security problems and military power may ebb and flow, but historical consciousness will linger, thus perpetuating an ideological system and political culture.

To identify the nation's cultural roots, students of contemporary China would have to examine the late Zhou Dynasty, known as the spring–autumn (770–476 BC) and the Warring States (475–221 BC) periods. Celebrated as the Golden Age of Chinese philosophy, those years produced many great thinkers, whose influence was sustained for well over 2,000 years. While Confucianism stands out as the most important source of Chinese political culture, Legalism is one of the keys to an understanding of China's strategic traditions.

Legalism was mainly represented by Shang Yang (390–338 BC) and Han Fei Zi (280–233 BC). Almost a hundred years apart, Shang and Han shared many common beliefs. In contrast to Confucianism, they took a pessimistic view of human nature: human nature is fundamentally evil and humans are thus inclined to vicious behaviour. Severe laws and harsh punishments are the only means of bringing about order and security, no matter how hateful to the people they are. As the ruler's objective is to create a prosperous and powerful state, people are to be made mutually responsible for one another's actions. Extending such a 'realist' attitude into foreign policy, they accepted the basic characteristics of the multistate system of their time: a number of equal and sovereign states fighting for survival and supremacy in a world of anarchy. To them, a state's security invariably relies on the ruthless exercise of power.[3]

A significant figure among the Legalists was Sun Zi. A native of the state of Qi, born in the sixth century BC, Sun Zi and his *Arts of War* are remembered by the Chinese as the paramount articulation of military strategy and tactics in the recorded history of China.[4] Regarding warfare as the most important of all state affairs, Sun Zi writes extensively on how to wage war effectively. Along with other traditional strategists, including Wu Zi and Wei Liao Zi, Sun Zi has perpetuated such concepts as 'not fighting but subduing the enemy', 'the best policy is to attack the enemy's strategy', 'know your enemy and know yourself, in a hundred battles, win a hundred victories'. His systematic discussions of statecraft, strategy, tactics, organization, mobilization, and diplomacy became the core of Chinese strategic traditions through centuries-long teaching and practice.

Despite the condemnation of later ages, Legalism left a lasting mark on Chinese civilization. Through the triumph of the Qin state over Zhou in 246 BC and the imperial system that the Qin dynasty (246–206 BC) organized, it accounts partially for the highly centralized government of later times and its harsh and often arbitrary rules, and, more importantly, for the constant mass rebellions and tenacious government suppressions in Chinese history. Often in the name of the 'Mandate of Heaven', which manifests itself only through the acceptance of a ruler by his people, use of force has been justified by both rebels – sometimes invaders – and oppressors. There are numerous instances of China resorting to violence in resolving political, territorial, economic, and ethnic conflicts. Rebellion and invasion constantly bring about wars, and often result in changes of political rule, known in Chinese history as the dynastic cycles. As much as totalitarianism, rebellion constitutes a major component of Chinese political culture.

Contemporary Chinese attitudes toward the threat and use of force are rooted in the nation's experiences with foreigners in recent times. The Opium War of 1839–42 marked the beginning of Western imperialism in China. From then on, the search for a way to survive in the new and challenging world dominated Chinese thought. This search entailed a hard struggle against hurt pride, and pervasive feelings of 'national humiliation' accompanied by a disdain for things foreign. The images of 'foreign devils', Western gunboats, unequal treaties, international settlements with signs of 'No Chinese and Dogs Allowed' planted deep seeds of distrust and hatred toward foreigners.

The deepening crises at the turn of the century led to the emergence of patriotic movements. The 'May 4th' movement (1919) became the banner of Chinese patriotism. The Japanese invasions (1931–45) deepened the fear of becoming a *'wangguolu* [slave without a nation]'. 'September 18th' – the date of Japanese invasion of China's Northeast in 1931 – and the 'Nanjing Massacre' (1937), are inscribed in Chinese history as monumental reminders of the sufferings and humiliations inflicted on the nation by foreigners. But the search for a way to survive also constituted new visions – advocated in particular by a good number of Chinese reformers – such as 'self-strengthening', 'learning the superior barbarian technique with which to repel the barbarians', 'using the barbarians against the barbarians', and 'forming a united front against foreign invasions'. The call for 'national liberation', recreation of an independent and sovereign China and restoration of the nation's prestige in the world appealed to the Chinese people.

It was in the midst of this popular anxiety and aspiration for 'a new China' that Mao Zedong (1893–1976) and his fellow revolutionaries emerged. Throughout his political career, Mao took as his primary goal the complete liberation of the nation from 'imperialist' domination. He and his comrades were determined that 'a new China' should resume 'her rightful place' among the nations.[5] In formulating a revolutionary line, Chinese communist leaders undoubtedly learned from the contributions and writings of Marxist revolutionary leaders and other thinkers from various ages. But it was from the rich Chinese experience of warfare, along with the long history of peasant uprisings and Chinese communist revolutionary wars, that they obtained and formulated the essence of their military thought. Under Mao, the Chinese Communist Party (CCP) leadership's revolutionary line and military thought had invariably dictated the attitude and behavior of the PRC in regard to the threat and use of force.

The CCP leaders regarded the use of force as 'the highest form' of revolution.[6] As a communist, Mao inherited a distinctively Marxist-Leninist war philosophy. He accepted class struggle as a framework in which to conceive and develop the origins and nature of a modern war.[7] Mao, in his readings of Marx and Engels, came to regard war as 'the highest form of struggle for resolving contradictions ... between classes, nations, states, or political groups'.[8] Accepting the inevitability of war as long as there was a class struggle, Mao found war and politics closely related. Quoting Clausewitz that 'war is the continuation of politics', he asserted that 'war is politics and war itself is a political action'.[9] In his view, only by examining war from a political point of view could one fully understand the essence of warfare.[10]

The relationship between war and politics led Mao to believe that 'victory is inseparable from the political aim of the war'.[11] In his view, the common masses would only support a just war. Popular support would create 'a vast sea in which to drown the enemy, create the conditions that will make up for [one's] inferiority in arms and other things, and create the prerequisites for overcoming every difficulty in the war'.[12] Therefore, the setting up of political aims has remained a top priority for the CCP leadership whenever force is used.

The CCP leaders saw political mobilization and indoctrination as an integral part of revolutionary war. Mao defined political mobilization as a means of 'telling the army and the people about the political aim of the war'. It is absolutely necessary for every soldier and civilian to understand why the war must be fought and how it concerns his or her interests. Mao advocated popular and extensive war propaganda to this end.[13] Given political mobilization's 'immense importance', Mao and his fellow leaders had devoted enormous efforts to winning popular support in the civil war with the Nationalists. There has existed a consensus among the leaders that the CCP's final victory owed a great deal to political and mass mobilization.[14]

The CCP maintained a long tradition of politicizing its armed forces. Mao himself had vehemently advocated the party's absolute control of its army. To him, such control must hinge upon 'the system of Party Representatives' in the army which was 'particularly important at company level'. With party branches organized on a company basis, the party representatives would be able to 'guide' both political training and indoctrination.[15] Mao found it imperative that all military affairs be discussed and decided upon by the party before being carried out.[16] Mao's teachings on political control and indoctrination have fostered a persistent institutional culture that has shaped the force and command structure of the People's Liberation Army (PLA). As a result, the political commissar system and CCP party committees exist in the military to this date.[17]

The CCP leaders regarded human power, not weapons, as the decisive factor in war. Mao maintained that military capability was where one's military-strategic thinking should begin. Without downplaying the 'objective conditions', such as weaponry, equipment, and other war materials, he placed greater emphasis on 'subjective conditions' of war-waging capability, by which he meant the spirit, attitudes, beliefs, political quality, and morale of the armed forces. Mao regarded war as the highest manifestation of a human's 'conscious dynamic role' and the supreme test of the human spirit in transforming the objective world. 'War is a contest of strength', he wrote in 1938, 'but the original pattern of strength changes in the course of war. Here the decisive factor is subjective effort – winning more victories and committing fewer errors.' Although the objective factors would make such a change possible, Mao thought, 'in order to turn the possibility into actuality both correct policy and subjective effort are essential. It is then that the subjective plays the decisive role.'[18]

A belief in human superiority has persistently gripped the Chinese leadership, the military, and the nation. The slogans of *Ren de yinsu di yi* [The human factor is the first and most important thing] and *Ren ding sheng tian* [Man will triumph over nature] dominated the psychology and mindset of the leadership. Despite its recent emphasis on *junshi xiandai hua* [military modernization], the Chinese communist leadership's reliance on the dynamic role of human consciousness in the forms of political and moral strength remains unaltered.

Mao found in the history of war that wars were usually fought under only two circumstances: an absolutely strong power fought against an absolutely weak power, or a relatively strong power battled with a relatively weak power.[19] He then maintained that a transformation between the weak and the strong might occur in a dialectical manner. This law of the unity of opposites, Mao believed, governed the change 'from inferiority to parity and then to superiority'.[20]

How would 'inferiority' transform into 'superiority'? Mao thought the answer lay in 'each side's subjective ability in directing the war'. Acknowledging that 'in his endeavor to win a war a military man cannot overstep the limitations imposed by the material conditions', he argued that 'within these limitations, however, he can and must drive for a final victory'. Here, Mao believed it was 'man's dynamic role' that determined the fate of war. Because, 'whatever is done has to be done by human beings ... [and therefore] war and final victory will not come about without human action'.[21]

Mao discovered many instances in Chinese war history which supported his thesis. In the Battle of Chengpu (203 BC), the Battle of Kunyang (23 BC), the Battle of Guandu (AD 200), the Battle of Chibi (AD 208), the Battle of Yiling (AD 222), and the Battle of Feishui (AD 383), he believed that the weaker states' conscious activity changed their military inferiority into military superiority. Therefore, Mao had predicted that China would eventually defeat a more powerful Japan. He was confident that the PLA would prevail over the better equipped and outnumbered Nationalist army. He also optimistically calculated that the conventional Chinese forces could beat the 'armed-to-the-teeth' US military in Korea. Not surprisingly, Mao's teachings on how a weak army could defeat a stronger enemy have spread all over the world, inadvertently stimulating numerous revolutionaries – Ho Chi Minh, Fidel Castro, and perhaps even Saddam Hussein.

Founding 'established norms'

Mao's revolutionary line and military thought guided the CCP's struggle through different stages with many twists and turns. The majority of the Chinese communists appeared to have attributed the founding of 'a New China' in 1949 to Mao Zedong's thought. More importantly, Mao's teachings on revolution and armed struggle remained the 'established norms'. It is hardly surprising that these norms played a pivotal role in shaping the PRC's attitude and policy toward security issues throughout the Cold War period.

The CCP's oversensitivity to foreign interference and domination have dictated Beijing's perception of external threat. For most of the PRC's history, 'anti-interventionism' and 'anti-hegemonism', as defined by the CCP leadership, governed the way Beijing perceived threats to the state. The regime was primarily concerned with threats from 'American imperialism' in the 1950s. That concern soon developed into strong opposition to both 'Soviet social-imperialism' and 'American imperialism' in the 1960s and early 1970s. Whilst it dropped its strong anti-American stance after the normalization of Sino-American relations, China continued to denounce Soviet expansionism through the early 1980s.

Geopolitics, ideology, and the historical consciousness of foreign domination all played a crucial role in Beijing's threat perception. This role was best reflected in the ways the CCP leaders had conceived of the danger of US military intervention in the 1950s. Geopolitically, Mao's 'intermediate zone' concept reasoned that, since the US and the USSR were separated by 'a vast zone which includes many capitalist, colonial, and semi-colonial countries in Europe, Asia, and Africa, before the US reactionaries have subjugated these countries, an attack on the Soviet Union is out of the question'. Naturally, China must be one of these countries and probably among the first the US intended to subjugate.[22]

In ideological terms, Mao saw US China policy within the context of imperialism. Believing that the shrinking of domestic and foreign markets caused irreconcilable contradictions in capitalism, Mao saw the United States 'sitting on a volcano'. This situation, he predicted, would drive Washington to 'draw up a plan for enslaving the world, to run Europe, Asia, and other parts of the world like wild beasts'.[23] Mao and other CCP leaders also believed that the US government was counter-revolutionary by nature: the US intervened often on behalf of reactionaries. Important instances included Frederick Ward's 'Ever-Victorious Army' in China that assisted the Qing regime against the Taiping uprising in 1860–63, US participation in the international intervention against the Chinese Boxer rebellion in 1900–01, and intervention against the Bolshevik revolution in Russia in 1918–19.[24]

The CCP leaders for a long time distrusted US policy toward China.

Their few dealings with the US in the 1940s had made them feel cheated and humiliated. The Marshall mission of 1946, they at first believed, had been intended to mediate China's civil war impartially, but its outcome had not been in line with CCP expectations. Mao explained

> The policy of the US Government is to use the so-called mediation as a smoke screen for strengthening Chiang in every way and suppressing the democratic forces in China through Chiang Kai-shek's policy of slaughter so as to reduce China virtually to a US colony.[25]

The CCP leaders thus quickly jumped to the regretful conclusion: '[since] it was the first time for us to deal with the US imperialists, we did not have much experience. Consequently, we were taken in. Now with experience we won't be cheated again.'[26]

Throughout the 1950s and 1960s Beijing consistently worried about 'three dangerous spots': the Korean peninsula, the Taiwan Strait, and Indochina where the CCP leaders saw the most likely US armed actions against China. Early in 1949, Mao had warned the party that 'the US might send armed forces to occupy some of China's coastal cities and directly engage us [there]'.[27] To him, the United States might execute its hostility toward China in three ways: first, 'they will smuggle their agents into China to sow dissension and make trouble'; second, 'they will incite the Chinese reactionaries, and even throw in their own forces, to blockade China's ports'; and, third, 'if they still hanker after adventures, they will send some of their troops to invade and harass China's frontiers'. All of these were 'not impossible'.[28]

To counter the perceived US threat, Beijing chose to rely on Soviet protection. However, the CCP's alertness to Soviet domination led to the Sino-Soviet split in the late 1950s, eventually causing Beijing to treat the USSR as the major potential aggressor. From the outset, relations between Mao and Stalin were full of mutual distrust. While Stalin suspected Mao of being another Tito, Mao feared that the USSR would always want to dominate China.[29] To obtain Soviet protection and assistance, however, Mao had to accept a Soviet presence in China's Northeast and Xinjiang through a secret agreement in 1950 that China would 'not allow the citizens of a third country to settle or to carry out any industrial, financial, trade, or other related activities [there]'.[30]

Mao, like other leaders, was haunted ever after by this secret agreement. It reminded the Chinese of the unequal treaties that the West had forced the Qing Emperors to sign. At a meeting with Mikoyan in April 1956, Mao referred to the secret deals on the Northeast and Xinjiang as 'two bitter pills' that Stalin had forced him to swallow. The following year he complained to Gromyko that 'only imperialists' would think of forcing China to accept such a treaty. In his contempt for the agreement, Mao was determined to terminate the deal, when in 1958 he spoke of 'two "colonies", the Northeast and Xinjiang, where the people of third countries were not permitted to settle down'.[31]

Meanwhile, Mao distrusted Moscow's intention to incorporate China's coast into its Far Eastern defence system. In 1958, Soviet Minister of Defence Radion I. Malinovskii suggested 'jointly' building a powerful long-wave radio station linking the Chinese Navy with the Soviet Navy in the Far East. The USSR would provide the technology and most of the money needed.[32] Soviet Ambassador to Beijing Pavel F. Iudin also proposed to Mao that the Soviet Union and China establish a joint fleet 'for a common defence in the Far East'.[33] The CCP leaders immediately worried that the Kremlin might aim to control China militarily. Beijing responded that China would only accept technological assistance from the Soviet Union; there would be no joint ownership.[34] Mao also told Iudin: 'we will build [the station and the fleet] by ourselves and will accept your assistance only'. He lectured Iudin that 'if you want to talk about political conditions [of assisting us in building the fleet], we will never accept [your request]. … You may accuse me of being nationalist, but I then can accuse you of bringing Russia's nationalism over to China's coast.'[35]

The Taiwan Strait crisis of 1958 witnessed a turning point in the Sino-Soviet relationship. Counting on Soviet nuclear deterrence in the event of war with the United States, however, the CCP leadership deeply suspected Moscow of having intentions to control China, and deliberately kept the Soviets uninformed of its plans for shelling the Jinmen and Mazu offshore islands, and declined Khrushchev's offer of nuclear protection.[36] After visiting the United States in September 1959, Khrushchev came to Beijing and criticized Beijing's 'reckless' policy toward the US. He pointed out that China's bombardment of the offshore islands had 'created a big problem' for the USSR. He then requested Beijing to renounce the use of force against Taiwan, and implicitly pressured Mao to accept Taiwan's independence. Mao and other Chinese leaders were convinced that Moscow would accommodate Washington at the expense of China's interests, and that Beijing could no longer rely on the USSR unless it was prepared to sacrifice its own sovereignty.[37]

Concerned about the possible threat from the two superpowers, the CCP leadership were prepared to fight in an 'imminent, large-scale, and nuclear war' [zaoda, dada, dahezhanzheng] from 1949 through the late 1970s. Consequently, the PRC's defence and foreign policy was, for the most part, directed to finding ways of surviving, delaying, and ultimately preventing such a war.

In view of its place in the world, the PRC aspired to act as a leading revolutionary state in world politics. The Chinese had for centuries maintained an idealized vision of China as the center of the earth, and of world politics as evolving around it in a hierarchical way. The reality, though, was far more cruel than the perception, especially since the early 1800s. From the moment that Mao proclaimed 'the Chinese people have thus stood up', he was determined to restore China to its rightful place. Not surprisingly, the CCP aspired to redress the balance in the international system.

Anxious to rid China completely of its humiliating image in the times of Western pressure, the CCP leaders decided that the new regime would 'refuse to recognize the legal status of any foreign diplomatic establishment and personnel of the Kuomintang period, abolish all imperialist propaganda agencies in China, take immediate control of foreign trade and reform the customs system'.[38] During the period 1949–50, the CCP established two principles on foreign affairs: 'make a fresh start', and 'clean the house first and then entertain [foreign] quests'.[39] According to Zhou Enlai, these two principles were crucial in order 'to clean up the vestiges of the influences of imperialism in order not to leave them space for their further activities'.[40] As 'the old China has been dependent on the imperialists not only in the economic sphere but also in the sphere of culture and education', Zhou asserted, the Chinese people had been 'exploited economically and polluted politically'. In order to 'expose and eradicate the evil influence of imperialism, we should neither rely on the imperialists nor be afraid of them'.[41]

Aware that only the two superpowers in the post-war world had the potential to inflict serious damage on China, Beijing came around to playing the great-power triangle game. Given the hostile US policy toward the PRC, Mao 'leaned' to the Soviet side. Although ideological links and China's need for economic aid were important factors, national security was the key concern. 'The basic spirit of the alliance treaty', Mao had stated in January 1950, 'should be to prevent the possibility of Japan and its ally [the United States] invading China', and 'with the treaty, we will be able to use it as a big political asset to deal with imperialist countries in the world'.[42] Ideology and economic leverage, however, did not forestall the collapse of the Sino-Soviet alliance in the late 1950s when Beijing increasingly feared the 'danger from the north'. As Sino-Soviet friction expanded into mutual military buildup along the border and then in armed clashes in the late 1960s, Beijing immediately played the 'American card'. The PRC's 'Ping-pong diplomacy' in the spring of 1971 resulted in the normalization of US–China relations two years later and openly declared opposition to Soviet 'hegemony' in the Asia-Pacific region.[43]

While its ability to play in the superpowers' league was limited, Beijing had wanted to be recognized as an important member of the society of states. This intention was evident in the PRC's tenacious efforts to replace the Nationalist regime in the United Nations and in other international organizations. More importantly, from the mid-1950s through the end of the 1970s, Beijing devoted most of its attention to relations with Third World countries. It was China's 'international duty', Mao declared in 1956, 'to actively support all the national independent and liberation movements not only in Asia but also in Africa and Latin America'.[44] Beijing worked hard at portraying itself as a 'true and reliable friend' of all the developing countries. During the Suez crisis of 1956, Mao told the Egyptian Ambassador to Beijing that China would 'do everything possible to support the Egyptian people's struggle to protect their sovereign rights over the Suez Canal'. Whatever Egypt needed from China, he stressed, 'we will provide if we have, and our assistance has no [political] conditions attached'. To support Iraq against possible Western intervention under the 'Eisenhower Doctrine' in 1958, Mao decided to shell the offshore islands to divert US military strength from the Middle East. Soon after Castro's revolution succeeded in Cuba, Beijing extended diplomatic recognition. To counter the growing threat of American intervention in 1960, Zhou Enlai cabled Castro that 'if ever needed, the Chinese people and government will offer all the necessary assistance that Cuban people request for their struggle for independence and freedom'. Despite its economic weakness, Beijing had provided a good number of countries with extensive economic aid and dispatched a large number of *yuan wai* [aiding foreign countries] teams, including military advisers, medical doctors, engineers, and agricultural experts.[45]

Beijing seemed to want to represent the interests of the weak, the poor, and the oppressed. In the leaders' view, new China's foreign policy would be appealing to all the countries worldwide which suffered from 'imperialist exploitation', and the China factor would have to be counted. The CCP kept fighting vigorously to augment its influence and prestige in world politics.

In conflict resolution, Beijing consistently emphasized the demonstration of resolve and strength. Whenever under threat, the CCP leaders tended to act on the basis of *yiyan huan yan, yiya huan ya* [an eye for an eye and a tooth for a tooth]. According to them, China should never hesitate to use force as long as it obtained *dao* [justice or moral support]. This belief was rooted in the old Chinese teaching *dedao duozhu shidao guazhu* [a just cause enjoys abundant support while an unjust cause finds little support]. Therefore, the CCP always made the setting up of political objectives for the use of force one of their priorities. *Kangmei yuanzha* [To resist the US and aid Korea] became the political slogan for mobilizing domestic support and soliciting international sympathy during China's intervention in Korea. *Fan di* [anti-imperialism], and later *fan ba quan zhuyi* [anti-hegemonism], dictated the nationwide political campaigns throughout the 1950s and the 1960s. *Renwu heren* [We are driven beyond the limits of tolerance] and *beipo fanji* [We are compelled to strike back] served as explanations of Chinese use of force in the border wars with India (1962), the Soviet Union (1969), and Vietnam (1979). Almost every time that China prepared to resort to violence in pursuit of foreign-policy goals,

Beijing would organize a series of public rallies and 'mass demonstrations' in Beijing or other major cities to show popular support.

Beijing was inclined to treat international crises as not necessarily bad. The Chinese traditionally view crises in dialectical terms. The term 'crisis' in Chinese stands for *shi* [a situation] embodying both *wei* [danger] and *ji* [opportunity]. Mao genuinely believed that all crises were dialectical in terms of their strong and weak points, their advantages and disadvantages, their dangers and opportunities. Thus, he considered any crisis to be both negative and positive, believing that a dangerous situation could be turned to his advantage. In many ways Mao adopted the Legalist principle *bupo buli busai buliu buzhi buxing* [there is no construction without destruction, no flowing without damming and no motion without rest]. This preference in part explains why China initiated intervention in Korea in 1950 and the Taiwan Strait crises in 1954–55 and 1958. By initiating limited and well-controlled crises, Beijing expected to clearly demonstrate China's resolve to counter international pressure. Before deciding to shell Jinmen and Mazu in 1958, Mao asserted that the reason why 'Dulles looks down upon us [is] that we have not yet completely shown and proven our strength'. So the best way to deal with the fearsome US imperialists was to 'demonstrate our boldness'.[46] As Mao later explained, the decision to shell the offshore islands was based upon the thesis of 'the fear of ghosts', which he had derived from *Liaozhai Zhiyi*, a traditional Chinese collection of ghost stories. Mao stated:

> All the stories tell us only one truth, that is, do not be afraid of ghosts. The more you are afraid of them, the less likely you are to survive, and the more likely [it is that] you will be eaten up by the ghosts. We were not afraid of ghosts; and we bombed Jinmen and Mazu.[47]

The CCP also regarded the use – not merely the demonstration – of force as a final resort in international conflict. Although Sun Zi teaches that the best strategy is 'to subdue the enemy without fighting', he clearly advocates taking short-term military action [*fabin*] to prevent the enemy from launching general war [*famou*]. Mao and other CCP leaders perfectly understood Sun Zi's doctrine. Beijing's intervention in Korea, 'tension diplomacy' regarding the Taiwan Strait, and Mao's 'rope around the neck' strategy all reflected the Chinese calculation that short-term belligerency would enhance long-term security.[48] Mao insisted on armed intervention in Korea because he could not tolerate waiting 'year after year unsure of when the enemy will attack us'. Beijing bombarded the offshore islands not as a prelude to an invasion of Taiwan but to demonstrate that China would never concede US dominance of the Taiwan Strait. Chinese troops actively engaged the Soviet force at Zhenbaodao in 1969 to send out a message that Beijing would not be bullied by Soviet threats of a nuclear 'preemptive attack'. More recently the Chinese 'counteroffensive' against the Vietnamese was aimed at 'teaching the little hegemonist a lesson'.[49]

During the Cold War, the CCP persistently adhered to the doctrine of 'People's War' as the basis of its defence policy. The Chinese have traditionally stressed the importance of human power in war. Inheriting this tradition, Mao and his comrades formulated the People's War doctrine through their armed struggle. The doctrine incorporated the central elements of guerrilla warfare, the use of protraction, and the political control and indoctrination of the armed forces. Attributing its revolutionary victory to the slogan of 'People's War', the CCP had little doubt that China would eventually defeat any foreign invaders no matter how powerful they were.[50]

Having tasted modern warfare in Korea, however, from mid-1950s to the early 1960s the military tended to want more modern technology without abandoning the doctrine of People's War. This new orientation bore the personal imprint of Defence Minister Peng Dehuai and Chief of General Staff Luo Ruiqing. But shortly afterward, they were accused of being 'purely militarists', and had to step down. In 1965, the new Defence Minister Lin Biao published the essay 'Long Live the Victory of the People's War'. Lin described the People's War as 'a doctrine for the defence of China against various types of war ranging from a surprise long-range nuclear strike combined with a massive ground invasion to a conventional ground attack with limited objectives'. The doctrine was 'premised on participation of the whole populace and mobilization of all the country's resources for as long as it takes to defeat any invader'. The main objective of fighting a People's War against invaders was 'to deter potential enemies by making it clear that any invasion of China would be a very expensive proposition and one with no chance of a satisfactory resolution'.[51] *Quanmin jiebing* [Turning the entire population into a military force] had become a central element in China's defence policy throughout the 1970s.

As China's foreign policy changed significantly in the 1970s, so did its defence priorities. Beijing adapted its strategic doctrine to the changing world, consequently constituting the doctrine of 'People's War under modern conditions'. Still stressing the human factor, technology began to be accorded much more weight. The leaders felt it imperative that China modernize its armed forces so as to improve both conventional and nuclear capabilities. Since the late 1970s this new strategy has slowly but surely reoriented Beijing toward military upgrading. However, Beijing has continued to emphasize the need to rely on active defense on the home territory, with greater attention given to an in-depth and three-dimensional defence system.[52] This change, however, entails no fundamental alternation in China's strategic preferences, while allowing for changes at operational levels.

Beijing has invariably reoriented its active defense strategy. To the

strategists, there should be an effective combination of tactical and guerrilla offensives. Mao's principle of 'luring the enemy in deep', an integral
part of active defense, is still relevant. Nevertheless, modern conditions
have made Chinese strategists downplay excessive 'hit-and-run' tactics.
Now attaching more importance to the defense of cities and industrial
centers, China in the 1980s left the strategy of using its cities as bait for
invaders.[53]

Undoubtedly, Beijing still stresses strategic defense in the initial stage of
the war, because active defense consisting of positional, mobile, and
guerrilla warfare will enable the PLA to seize the initiative and reverse the
fate of war. No matter how badly Beijing aspires to build a 'blue-water
navy', the core of China's defense is the nation's inner land with the 'Great
Southwest [da xinan]' as the last line of defence.

Beijing maintained a revolutionary attitude toward nuclear weapons.
When the CCP took power in 1949, its armed forces consisted of a large
number of light infantry troops. Embarking upon its own nuclear program
in 1955, the PRC has since become a major nuclear power. Interestingly,
Beijing's discovery of and attitude toward nuclear weapons has followed a
tortuous path.

Mao at first did not believe that nuclear weapons fundamentally
changed military and political realities. Proclaiming his famous thesis,
'All reactionaries are paper tigers' in 1946, he specifically regarded the
atomic bomb as 'a paper tiger which the US reactionaries use to scare
people'. Although admitting that the atomic bomb was 'a weapon of mass
slaughter', he maintained that 'the outcome of a war is decided by people,
not by one or two new types of weapon'.[54]

Mao's contempt for the atomic bomb played an important role in
China's intervention in Korea. Considering whether Chinese intervention
might provoke US atomic attack, Mao asserted in September 1950: 'We
will not allow you [the US] to use the atomic bomb [against us]. But if you
won't give it up, you could as well use it.' Even if Washington were to
launch a nuclear attack on China, Mao insisted that 'we will respond with
our hand grenades. We then will use your weakness to tie you up and finally
defeat you.'[55] Mao obviously saw the atomic bomb as having little military
utility. The purpose of imperialist policy, he later explained, was exploitation and 'the object of exploitation is man. ... If man is killed, what's the
use of occupying soil? I don't see the reason for the atomic bomb.
Conventional weapons are still the thing.'[56]

However, by the mid-1950s Beijing took a serious look at the danger of
nuclear war. Mao now felt that nuclear weapons were becoming 'real
tigers'. In 1958 he called for preparations for the worst outcome of a
nuclear attack. 'We have no experience in atomic war', Mao explained. 'So,
how many [people] will be killed cannot be known. The best outcome may
be that only half of the population is left, and the second best may be only

one-third.' The party therefore should adopt a 'scientific' attitude toward nuclear threat: 'We are afraid of atomic weapons and at the same time we are not afraid of them ... We do not fear them because they cannot fundamentally decide the outcome of a war; we fear them because they really are mass-destruction weapons.'[57]

To counter the US nuclear threat, Beijing decided to build China's own nuclear weapons. Mao declared in January 1955 that 'sooner or later, we would have to pay attention to the matter [of nuclear weapons]. Now, it is time for us to pay attention to it.'[58] Mao stressed in 1956 that 'in today's world, if we don't want to be bullied by others, we should have atomic weapons by all means'. To him, 'this is an issue of strategic policy'.[59] Naturally, Mao reassessed the value of nuclear weapons. 'In essence, from a long-term point of view, from a strategic point of view', he believed, '[they] must be seen for what they are – paper tigers. On this we should build our strategic thinking. On the other hand, they are also living tigers, iron tigers, real tigers which can eat people. On this we should build our tactical thinking.'[60]

Afraid that the superpowers' confrontations might drag China into war, Beijing's main concern was how to survive a general and nuclear war. China voluntarily adopted the principle of no-first-use, and decided to rely on retaliatory second-strike capability. Beijing's 'Guidelines for Developing Nuclear Weapons' of 1958 made it clear that China's purpose in developing nuclear weapons was 'to warn our enemies against making war on us, not in order to use nuclear weapons to attack them'; and to this end, 'we have no intention of developing tactical nuclear weapons'.[61]

China's development of the bomb also aimed at breaking the nuclear monopoly of the superpowers. 'If we are not to be bullied in the present-day world', Mao stressed in 1957, 'we cannot do without the bomb.'[62] At a special Politburo meeting of 1961, Foreign Minister Chen Yi insisted that China should develop nuclear weapons at any cost, 'even if the Chinese people have to pawn their trousers for this purpose'. He explained that 'as China's minister of foreign affairs, at present I still do not have an adequate back-up. If we succeed in producing the atomic bomb and guided missiles, then I can straighten my back.'[63]

Mao simply would not accept the two superpowers' nuclear monopoly. In a letter to Khrushchev, dated 6 June 1963, he argued that the Soviet Union aimed at 'maintaining dominance over other socialist states' by providing them with nuclear protection but not nuclear technology. 'That is why you want to develop [nuclear weapons] alone and prohibit other brother states from building [the bomb] ... so that all the [socialist states] would obey you and you control [us] all.' He thus declared: 'The Chinese people will never accept the privileged position of one or two superpowers because of their monopoly of the nuclear weapons in today's world.'[64] Learning of China's first successful atomic explosion on 16 October 1964,

Mao asked Zhou to immediately release the 'good news' to the world that China had eventually broken the 'nuclear monopoly of the nuclear powers'. Beijing claimed that China's success in making nuclear weapons would greatly encourage the revolutionary people of the world.[65]

Indeed, Beijing encouraged other Third World countries to build their own atomic weapons. When asked at a press conference on 29 September 1965, whether China would share nuclear technology with other developing countries, Chen Yi referred to Mao's statement that 'China sincerely wishes that the Asian and African countries would be capable of developing their own atomic bomb, [because] the more countries can build the bomb the better.' What Mao meant, Chen explained, was that

> as soon as the small and weak nations acquire their own atomic weapons, the nuclear monopoly would be broken, the one or two superpowers could no longer wave nuclear weapons to blackmail [us], and the nuclear overlords could not but sob out their grievances in the corner [of the world].[66]

China's acquisition of nuclear weapons was unmistakably for national security. Mao adopted the conviction that nuclear weapons, with their tremendous psychological impact, were an integral part of deterrent strength. He had long held that a balance must exist between maintaining sizeable regular forces to deter or repel conventional attack and building a small nuclear capability to deter nuclear attack. This had become a major theme that Mao stressed again and again through the 1960s. At different points, he stated that China's nuclear weapons 'will not be numerous even if we succeed [in the strategic weapons program]'; that 'the success [of our strategic weapons program] will boost out courage and scare others'; and that 'in any case, we won't build more atomic bombs and missiles than others'. More important was his statement in the mid-1960s that China would adhere to the principle of 'building a few [nuclear weapons] with small quantity but high quality' [you yidian, shao yidian, hao yidian].[67] Mao's instructions were reflected in Beijing's official policies toward nuclear weapons in the 1960s and 1970s, and most of them remain in effect to this day.

Identity, self-reliance, and the use of force

In the final analysis, the CCP leadership maintained a revolutionary attitude and behavior toward threats and the use of force. This 'strategic culture' was deeply rooted in the nation's history of warfare, recent experience of foreign 'humiliation', rebellious and revolutionary ideology, and the CCP's long armed struggle for political power. It definitely bore the personal imprint of Mao Zedong.

The PRC's revolutionary line on warfare has transcended the regime's foreign and defense policy. However, the extent of its impact should be measured not only in terms of Beijing's great-power aspirations but also in the context of China's defense posture. Despite its long-sustained aspiration to challenge and change the existing international system and play in the great-power league, Beijing has been preoccupied with how it can restore international respect for the new China, best defend itself and survive another general war, probably nuclear. Despite the self-serving nature of the People's War doctrine, the CCP leaders have wanted to make the best of China's natural and human resources, which are all they have to rely on. Despite its revolutionary rhetoric, frequent use of force to resolve international conflicts, all-out support to Third World countries' national liberation, and vigorous pursuit of nuclear weapons, Beijing has adhered to a defensive posture and relied on a deterrence by denial of victory to aggressors.

Beijing's oversensitivity to foreign dominance has geared the country toward national security. From 1949 to the late 1990s, the CCP launched numerous political campaigns partly because of its concerns over external threat. The 'Three-Antis, Five-Antis' of 1951–53 aimed at mobilizing the nation's resources for the war in Korea. The Great Leap Forward and the People's Commune Movements in 1958 were intended to further release the productive energy of the society so as to *chaoying ganmei* [overtake Britain and catch up America] in industrial production. The CCP's call to *da ban minbingshi* [organize contingents of the people's militia on a grand scale] and *quanmin jiebing* [to turn every citizen into a soldier] were to prepare the nation for potential nuclear attacks. This was reinforced by the slogan of *Beizhan beihuang weirenmin* [be prepared against war, be prepared against natural disasters, do everything for the people] in the early 1970s. As a result, the bulk of resources – human and natural – were devoted to arms expansion and modernization. Indeed, as political control and indoctrination has extended to every corner of society, the whole society and economy has been virtually militarized. Nevertheless, power changes but historical consciousness persists.

It remains a difficult task to characterize Chinese strategic culture. There are four main analytical problems. First, culture has changed, especially in recent decades. The causes of change are various but the influence of external culture is a key factor. China, which had been fundamentally free from Western influence until the late eighteenth century, has become slowly and often reluctantly adaptive to modern trends for well over a century. Clearly, no country forgoes its ancient heritage entirely, and certainly not if that heritage is as illustrious as that of China. But the rise and fall of Confucianism, the rise and fall of republicanism, and the rise and possible fall of communism that China has undergone have affected the nation's politics, society, and certainly its strategic behavior. It would be a mistake to regard strategic culture as static.

Second, history is a primary source of strategic culture, but the influence of different historical periods varies. The existing literature presents no succinct answer as to whether historical or more recent antecedents are part of Chinese strategic culture. Mary McCauley warns that 'we must know just which period "history" refers to – when it begins and ends – how we can assess the influence of that period with the influence of the more immediate past'.[68] Hence, it is dubious to assume a relatively unbroken chain between historical strategic preferences and contemporary policy.

Third, there is the problem of identifying a strategic cultural identity. There may well be such a 'strategic cultural person' in China who occupies political and military institutions, or manages international crises, or directs wars. However, questions such as what has made this person the representative of China's strategic traditions and whether this person's influence has transmitted across space and through time deserve attention. As Confucius – the most influential philosopher in ancient China who lived around 551–479 BC – was regarded as China's 'political cultural person', numerous Chinese and Western scholars treat Sun Zi – whose writings on the military arts became the late Zhou (400 BC) classic – as China's 'strategic cultural person'. Although some similarities are identifiable between Sun Zi and contemporary Chinese strategists, it would, however, be simplistic to 'assume from the existence of two similar sets of beliefs at different periods of time … that they enjoy an unbroken existence'.[69]

Fourth, political ideology must not be ignored in any discussion of strategic culture. China has produced its own political ideology, Confucianism, which has influenced many of China's neighbors with different ideologies for centuries. Domestically, the Confucian ideology calls for a benevolent bureaucracy under a virtuous ruler. In foreign-policy terms, it emphasizes technocratic expertise and easy international contacts between elites relatively unfettered by pressure groups; it condemns the use of force and regards morality as the organizing principle of human society and thus the international community. Emphasizing the absence of logical absolutes, Confucius stressed 'the judicious balancing of inner virtues and external polish' which set the East Asian pattern of compromise, of always seeking the middle path. It best represents the Chinese '*He* (Union)' approach to conflict resolution.[70] However, Legalist ideology, standing in opposition to Confucianism, has yet to be stressed in the studies of Chinese strategic culture. Placing great emphasis on violence and power, Legalism has served as a primary guideline not only to the ruling elites, but also to the peasant rebels in traditional China and the communists in modern China. Thus, it is inappropriate to cast off the effect of the tradition of rebellion on the Chinese attitude to national security.

NOTES

1 From the Western Zhou (1100 BC) through the end of the Qing dynasty (1911) as many as 3,790 wars, domestic and foreign, and rebellions are identified. Since its foundation in October 1949, the People's Republic of China (PRC) has resorted to force as an instrument of foreign policy *ten* times. The PRC's use of force includes China's intervention in Korea (1950–53), military involvement in the first and second Indochina wars (1950–54, 1965–73); twice shelling Jinmen/Mazu offshore islands (1954–55, 1958); military suppression of rebellion at Tibet (1959); the Sino-Indian border war (1962); the Sino-Soviet border war (1969); military counter-attack on Vietnam (1979); and the Sino-Vietnamese border war (1981–89). For a recent study of Chinese strategic culture, see Alastair Iain Johnson, *Cultural Realism: Strategic Culture and Grand Strategy in Chinese History* (Princeton, NJ: Princeton University Press, 1996); also see Shu Guang Zhang, *Strategic Culture and Deterrence: Chinese–American Confrontation, 1949–1958* (Ithaca, NY: Cornell University Press, 1992).

2 Ken Booth, 'The Concept of Strategic Culture Affirmed', in *Strategic Power: USA/USSR*, ed. Carl G. Jacobsen (New York: St Martin's Press, 1990), p. 121.

3 Legalist ideas are summarized in John K. Fairbank, Edwin O. Reischauer, and Albert M. Craig, *East Asia: Transition and Transformation* (Boston, MA: Houghton Mifflin, 1989), pp. 53–4.

4 See for example, Xie Guoliang, 'On Sun Zi's Thought on Waging an Effective War', in *Sun Zi xintan* [New Exploration on Sun Tzu] (Beijing: n.p., 1990), p. 33.

5 Stuart Schram, *Mao Tse-Tung* (Baltimore, MD: Penguin Books, 1972), p. 16.

6 Mao Zedong, 'Problems of War and Strategy', *Selected Military Writings of Mao Tse-Tung* (Peking: Foreign Languages Press, 1967), p. 269 (hereafter cited as *SMW*).

7 Xia Zhennan, 'On the Relationship between War and Politics', *Mao Zedong sixiang yanjiu* [Studies of Mao Zedong Thought], no. 3, 1987, pp. 48–9. See also Bob Avkian, *Mao Tsetung's Immortal Contributions* (Chicago, IL: RCP Publications, 1979), pp. 39–40.

8 Mao, 'Problems of Strategy in China's Revolutionary War', December 1936, *SMW*, p. 78.

9 Mao, 'One Protracted War', May 1938, ibid., p. 226.

10 Ibid., p. 227.

11 'Problems of Strategy in China's Revolutionary War', ibid., p. 81.

12 'On Protracted War', ibid., p. 228.

13 Ibid., pp. 228–9.

14 For how the CCP leadership stressed the importance of political mobilization, see Jiang Siyi, ed., *Zhongguo Renmin Jiefangjun zhengzhi gongzhuo shi: 1924–1950* [History of the Chinese People's Liberation Army's Political Work, 1924–1950] (Beijing: Jiefangjun, 1984), pp. 1–94.

15 Mao's report to the CCP Central Committee, 'The Struggle in the Chingkang [Jinggang] Mountains', 25 November 1928, *SMW*, pp. 29–30.

16 Mao, 'On Correcting Mistaken Ideas in the Party', December 1929, ibid., pp. 53–6. For a good Western study of the CCP's military and political command structure, see William W. Whitson, *The Chinese High Command: A History of Communist Military Politics, 1927–1971* (New York: Praeger, 1973).

17 Jiang, *Zhongguo Renmin Jiefangjun zhengzhi gongzuo shi*, pp. 90–5.

18 Mao, 'On Protracted War', *SMW*, p. 235.

19 Liu and Shan, *Mao Zedong junshi bianzhengfa yanjiu*, pp. 68–9.

20 'On Protracted War', *SMW*, p. 217. See also Liu and Shan, *Mao Zedong junshi*

bianzhengfa yanjiu, pp. 68–71.

21 'On Protracted War', *SMW*, p. 225.

22 Mao, 'Talks with the American Correspondent Anna Louise Strong', August 1946, *Selected Works of Mao Tse-tung* (Peking: Foreign Languages Press, 1967), vol. IV, p. 99 (hereafter cited as *SW*).

23 Mao, 'The Present Situation and Our Tasks', 25 December 1947, ibid., vol. IV, p. 172.

24 Zhang Shu Guang, *Deterrence and Strategic Culture: Chinese–American Confrontations, 1949–1958* (Ithaca, NY: Cornell University Press, 1992), pp. 16–18.

25 Mao, 'The Truth about US "Mediation" and the Future Civil War in China', 29 September 1946, *SW*, vol. IV, p. 109.

26 Zhang, *Deterrence and Strategic Culture*, pp. 18–19.

27 CCP Central Committee document, 'The Current Situation and Our Tasks in 1949', 8 January 1949, *Wenxian yu yanjiu* [Manuscripts and Studies], October 1984, pp. 1–3.

28 Ibid.

29 Sergei N. Goncharov, John W. Lewis, and Xue Litai, *Uncertain Partners: Stalin, Mao and the Korean War* (Stanford, CA: Stanford University Press, 1993), pp. 26–8.

30 Ibid., p. 121.

31 Ibid., p. 122.

32 Letter, Malinovskii to Peng Dehuai, 19 April 1958, *Dangdai Zhongguo waijiao* [China Today: Diplomacy] (Beijing: Shehui kexueyuan, 1987), p. 112.

33 Ibid., p. 113.

34 Minutes, Mao's conversation with Iudin, 22 July 1958, *Mao Zedong waijiao wenxuan* [Selected Works of Mao Zedong on Diplomacy], ed. the Ministry of Foreign Affairs and Central Division of Archives and Manuscripts (Beijing: Dang'anguan, 1994), pp. 322–33.

35 Ibid., pp. 328–33.

36 Zhang, *Deterrence and Strategic Culture*, pp. 254–6.

37 *Dangdai Zhongguo waijiao*, pp. 115–16.

38 Mao, 'Report to the Second Plenary Session of the Seventh Central Committee of the CCP', *SW*, vol. IV, pp. 435–6.

39 *Zhonggong Zhongyang wenjian xuanji* [Selected Documents of the CCP Central Committee] (Beijing: Zhongyang wenxian, 1985), vol. XV, pp. 302, 308.

40 Zhou Enlai, *Zhou Enlai xuanji* [Selected Works of Zhou Enlai] (Beijing: Renmin,1984), vol. II, pp. 85–7.

41 Ibid., pp. 10–11.

42 Telegram, Mao to the CCP Central Committee, 2 January 1950, *Jianguo yilai Mao Zedong wengao* [Mao's Manuscripts since the Founding of the People's Republic] (Beijing: Zhongyang wenxian, 1987), vol. I, p. 215.

43 *Dangdai Zhongguo waijiao*, pp. 217–24.

44 Ibid., p. 128.

45 Ibid., pp. 128–34.

46 Mao's speech at the Eighth Party Congress, 23 May 1958, *Mao Zedong Sixiang wansui* [Long Live Mao Zedong Thought] (Beijing: n.p., 1967), part 1, p. 217.

47 Mao's speech at the Sixteenth Supreme Conference for State Affairs, 15 April 1959, ibid., p. 290.

48 Zhang, *Deterrence and Strategic Culture*, p. 96.

49 *Dangdai Zhongguo waijiao*, pp. 106, 122, 285.

50 Mao, 'Our Great Victory in the War to Resist US Aggression and Aid Korea and Our Future Tasks', 12 September 1953, *SW*, vol. V, pp. 115–18.

51 Ngok Lee, *China's Defence Modernization and Military Leadership* (Sydney:

Australian National University Press, 1989), p. 140.

52 Ibid., p. 148.

53 Ibid., p. 150.

54 Mao, 'Talk with American Correspondent Anna Louise Strong', August 1946, *SW*, vol. V, pp. 100–1.

55 Mao's speech at the ninth session of the Central Chinese Government Council, 5 September 1950, cited in Division of Military History, the Chinese Academy of Military Science, ed., *Zhongguo Renmin Zhiyuanjun kangMei yuanChao zhanshi* [Combat History of the Chinese People's Volunteers in the War to Resist America and Aid Korea] (Beijing: Jiefangjun, 1988), pp. 6–7.

56 Mao's speech at the meeting of regional officials, 12 December 1958, *Mao Zedong Sixiang wansui*, p. 256.

57 Commentary of *Renmin Ribao*, 'To Watch For US War Preparations', 31 January 1958, *Renmin Ribao*.

58 Li Jie, Lei Rongtian, and Li Yi, eds, *Dangdai Zhongguo hegongyie* [China Today: Nuclear Industry] (Beijing: Shehui kexue,1987), p. 4.

59 Mao, 'On Ten Relationships', 25 April 1956, *Mao Zedong Sixiang wansui*, pp. 45–6.

60 Mao's speech at a meeting of the Politburo of the CCP Central Committee held at Wuchang, 1 December 1958, see *SW*, vol. V, pp. 98–9.

61 John W. Lewis and Xue Litai, *China Builds the Bomb* (Stanford, CA: Stanford University Press,1988), p. 70.

62 Mao Zedong, 'On the Ten Major Relations', *SW*, vol. V, p. 288.

63 Cited in Lewis and Xue, *China Builds the Bomb*, p. 130.

64 The CCP Central Committee to the Soviet government, 6 June 1963, *Dangdai Zhongguo waijiao*, p. 121.

65 Statement of the Government of the People's Republic of China, *Renmin Ribao*, 16 October 1964, p. 1. For the English version, see 'Appendix A', in Lewis and Xue, *China Builds the Bomb*, pp. 241–3.

66 Hu Sisheng, 'One Word to Shock the World: Comrade Chen Yi at a Press Conference', in *Huiyi Chen Yi* [Recollections of Chen Yi] (Beijing: Zhongyang wenxian, 1980), p. 215.

67 Xue Litai, 'Chinese Nuclear Strategy', paper presented at the Workshop on Strategic Culture and China, 13 May 1992, Ohio University, Athens, OH, 2.

68 Mary McCauley, 'Political Culture and Communist Politics: One Step Forward and Two Steps Back', in *Political Culture and Communist Studies*, ed. Archie Brown (New York: M. E. Sharpe, 1984), p. 22.

69 *Political Culture and Communist Politics*, p. 24.

70 Fairbank, Reischauer, and Craig, *East Asia*, pp. 44–6.

PART V:
TURNING POINTS

13

Reflections on the Origins of the Cold War

Antonio Varsori

This chapter deals with issues connected to the scholarly debate about Cold War origins.[1] The 'Cold War', in this context, may be defined as the conflict between two systems which were the standard-bearers of two contrasting world views (or *Weltanschauungen*). Both systems, in different ways, had a need to assert themselves worldwide and could leave no room for the other system's values and models. Such a vague definition, which stresses the ideological, almost 'religious' character of the conflict, may lead to the rejection of the mid-1940s as the outbreak of the Cold War, and support the historiographical approach which singles out 1917 as the origin of the East–West conflict.[2] But there are other factors which would lead us to focus our attention on the last stages of World War II and on the immediate post-war period. There is the proximity in Europe of the two opponents' armies which would magnify any conflicting interests. There is also the growing awareness – or belief – on the part of the 'decisionmakers' in both camps (governments, diplomats, the military, public opinion, influential political, economic, or social groups) that the conflict was *unavoidable*.

During the final stages of World War II the victorious powers had for the first time in their history a sort of common border which runs through Europe 'from Stettin to Trieste'.[3] No line existed (yet) in East Asia, where the United States appeared to exert an almost undisputed influence, undermining the roles of Britain and France,[4] and the result of the Chinese civil war was still uncertain.[5] Europe was therefore the first battlefield, the core of the 'Cold War', at least untill the early 1950s.[6]

The issue of the inevitability of the conflict forces us to pose the question: who were the enemies? If we may assume that Washington and Moscow played the paramount roles in unleashing the 'Cold War', the East–West conflict more broadly speaking was mainly the outcome of a failure to achieve a lasting peace settlement in Europe. To this failure, however, numerous international actors contributed. In fact, the immediate post-war period was only to a limited extent bipolar. If in the communist world the Soviet Union was still the undisputed 'Fatherland of

Socialism', in the Western camp both Britain and France had still, at least in theory, the role of 'great powers'.[7] Neither should one forget the influence exerted by the European context itself – by the German question and by the smaller states – on the chain of events that marked the failure of the wartime 'Grand Alliance'.[8] We therefore have to look more closely at a broad European international context in order to understand the origins of the Cold War.

The new American role in Europe

It is an almost impossible task to sketch out in a few lines US President Franklin D. Roosevelt's wartime policy toward the Soviet Union. At any rate, we may assume that, in spite of some doubts and second thoughts, the President believed in the survival of the 'Grand Alliance', as well as in a continuing cooperation with Stalin, which would favor the creation of a stable and lasting world order.

Roosevelt's 'Grand Design' was built on some definite assumptions. There was to be a new international order mainly shaped by Washington's war goals – the creation of the United Nations, the role played by the 'Four Policemen', and a revival of free trade – which aimed at reconciling Wilsonian idealism and *realpolitik*. The Soviet Union had given up its 'communist' and revolutionary character and was going to transform itself into an ordinary great power, perhaps not too different from the British empire. Future differences of opinion with Moscow were regarded as likely, but compromise solutions would always be feasible, since Stalin seemed to comply with the 'rules' of a traditional diplomatic game.[9]

Not all American diplomats or political leaders unconditionally shared Roosevelt's opinions. The common struggle against Nazi Germany had not wiped off the negative view of both the Soviet Union and the communist ideology fostered by the 'Red Scare', the images of the great Moscow trials, and the Nazi–Soviet alliance.[10] In the minds of numerous US policymakers the 'Great Patriotic War' hardly concealed the reality of a totalitarian nation which was alien, if not fiercely hostile, to American traditions, values, and interests. In January 1943, for example, William Bullit, former US Ambassador to Moscow, wrote that Russia 'moves where opposition is weak. He stops where opposition is strong. He puts out pseudopodia like an amoeba ... If the pseudopodia meet no obstacle, the Soviet Union flows on.'[11]

Roosevelt had, however, a firm control on US foreign policy. Furthermore the powerful American propaganda instruments that had been set up during the war had been able to spread the image of the gallant and grateful 'Russian' – not Soviet – ally, who, under Stalin's leadership, had first stopped and later defeated Hitler's armies.[12] Last but not least, Soviet reality was very far from the average American's everyday experience and although some politicians, diplomats, and military leaders foresaw a post-war world shaped by a growing US international role, few policymakers would be eager to admit that such a development would mean a permanent and direct American involvement in every part of the world or dealing with a new 'neighbor' in Europe, the Soviet Union.

Roosevelt's death did not mean a radical and immediate change in Washington's attitude toward the Soviet Union, although the new President's unsympathetic view of communist ideology is well known. Melvyn Leffler has stressed how both Harry Truman and his advisers:

> felt a deep ambivalence about the emergence of Soviet power. On the one hand they felt that wartime cooperation had to be perpetuated if peace and security had to be achieved. On the other hand, they believed that they had to monitor Soviet behavior lest another totalitarian behemoth seek control of countries, bases, resources, and labor that may some day allow it to endanger American security and jeopardize the peace of the world.[13]

Slowly but surely, analyses of Soviet policies led growing numbers of US diplomats, politicians, and military leaders to believe that the Soviet Union had never changed its 'true' character and that under the surface of Stalin's patriotic aims there were the threatening goals of a revolutionary leader, whose thought was shaped by an aggressive ideology.

It was mainly through their daily dealings with Russian authorities about the European settlement that most US policymakers convinced themselves that Roosevelt had been 'deceived' by Stalin and that Moscow had no intention whatsoever of complying with the 'rules of the game' sketched out during the war.[14] The experience of US representatives in Europe and their reports had a very significant impact on Washington's attitude. The American members of the Allied Control Commissions, which operated in the defeated Eastern European countries, had direct experience of what they perceived as the totalitarian methods through which the Soviets and their local allies imposed communist rule. According to them, Soviet policies left no room for manoeuvre for the Western powers. They were the ones who listened to pleas and warnings by the leaders of local anti-communist opposition parties for whom the Cold War was already a tragic reality.[15] Similar warnings were put forward by moderate anti-fascists in the Western European countries, such as in Italy and France, where communist parties came out of the war as leading political forces sharing power in broad anti-fascist coalition governments.

The point which was so powerful, I think, for American policymakers both in Washington and abroad was to compare the room allowed communist parties in Western Europe and the weak and decreasing influence left to non-communist anti-fascist parties in East Central European nations. As Harry Truman put it later in his life, 'if the Russians'd lived up to their agreements that they made at Yalta, there wouldn't be any trouble at all, but they didn't; they never lived up to an agreement they made ever'.[16] The meaning of such a remark may be further clarified by what Averell Harriman stated in a speech 'off the record' held in March 1946 at the New York Union Club. Harriman told his audience:

> [Russia's] principal object ... was to cover her western borders with a screen of friendly countries. This ... was in conformity with agreement reached in conferences with the British and the Americans; unhappily, there was a wide difference between the American and the Russian interpretation of the term 'friendly'. For America it would connote an attitude something like that of Mexico, but for Russia, intolerant of opposition and used to liquidation as the sole means of dealing with opposition, it meant complete domination of the country before it is ready to regard it as 'friendly'.[17]

Such difficulties and fears were magnified by the German situation. Germany had been the main culprit of the war, but it was also the main symbol of the victory achieved by the 'Grand Alliance', as well as the main context where peace could be won or lost. In Germany the victorious powers had decided to cooperate and US authorities had to deal with the Soviets on an equal footing. Contrasts in the thinking about Germany's post-war settlement surfaced almost immediately.[18]

There is little doubt that the Truman Administration was trying to be faithful to some aspects of Roosevelt's foreign policy. The peace treaties with Germany's minor allies (Italy, Romania, Bulgaria, Hungary, and Finland) signed in early 1947 by the victorious powers owed much to compromises which involved both Washington and Moscow.[19] It is not surprising that in mid-1946 some Western European diplomats still thought that the US authorities were bound to continue cooperation with the Soviet Union and feared a comprehensive agreement with Moscow. This, they thought, could bring the Truman Administration back to the isolationist tradition.[20]

By mid-1946 many of these worries had been put to rest. The events in East Central Europe, the obstacles created by the Soviet Union during the Foreign Ministers' Conferences, the failure of the atomic energy negotiations,[21] the suspicions about Moscow's intentions toward Germany, the apparent Soviet threat to Turkey and Iran had already laid down the basis for a radical change in US policies toward the Soviet Union. As the heading of a *Life* editorial article put it bluntly: 'Why Kid Around? There is No Misunderstanding between Russia and the West. There is a Conflict'.[22]

In the minds of US decisionmakers and in American public opinion the

Soviet Union was replacing Germany and Japan as the main threat to American values and ideals.[23] Historical comparison offered further suggestions: if isolationism had not safeguarded the United States from Nazi and Japanese aggression, isolation would not save the American people from a more dangerous enemy: international communism. The need to confront – to 'contain' – such a threat was pointed out in George Kennan's 'long telegram', which offered a clear-cut analysis and seemingly viable solutions to decisionmakers in Washington who were looking for such a conceptual framework.[24]

In that same period most American decisionmakers reached the conclusion that the United States had to develop some form of worldwide responsibilities. Washington had to safeguard and strengthen the leading international position it had built during World War II, which was not only the consequence of military and economic power, but also of a moral superiority. The United States had to face a new potential enemy, whose first aim was to fill the power vacuum which the war had created in Europe. That meant for the United States to confront the Soviet Union in the 'old continent'.[25] Of course public opinion and especially Congress had to become accustomed to such a new international reality as a part of US political thought to which the tradition of 'Manifest Destiny' seemed to give directions.[26]

By the summer of 1946 most US decisionmakers appeared determined to contain the Soviet Union along the border which had been created by the war and highlighted in Churchill's 'iron curtain' speech.[27] In March 1947 the communist threat to Greece – till then a minor issue in Washington's political agenda – offered Truman the chance 'to sell' to Congress and American public opinion a new policy which was a radical departure from the comfort which the political elite and the American people had felt about external threats in the previous decades.[28] The Truman Doctrine was also a warning to the Soviet Union and an early guarantee to Washington's future allies: the United States was ready to challenge Stalin's aims in every part of the world.

In spite of the fact that the Truman Doctrine was not an open 'declaration of war' against the Soviet Union, most of American public opinion felt that the international context had dramatically changed and communist Russia was now an enemy. But the United States was not ready to wage the Cold War alone; the Administration had found a strategy – 'containment' – and a theater of operations – Europe – but they needed active allies, as well as an effective and coherent Western system. We should not forget that the US attitude was imbued with a sort of missionary zeal: for the third time in its history, after 1917 and 1941, the US was going to save the world – meaning Europe – and this time build a new and peaceful international order.

The Western European nations appeared eager to be saved by the United

States.[29] The Marshall Plan, which aimed at creating a Western system through which the containment of the Soviet Union could be implemented, was a first step in such a strategy.[30] A few weeks after the launching of the Marshall Plan an external observer, a Canadian diplomat, summed up the new American attitude which was emerging from the early conflict with the Soviet Union:

> the United States, as the most powerful and highly developed democratic and capitalist state, is anxious to maintain the existing system of democratic values and free enterprise in the areas under United States political control, and this involves a desire to expand the defence area of that system. This desire, which is shared by the overwhelming majority of the population in the United States, is partly the result of a desire to retain the benefits of a free way of life and partly the result of the dominant belief that the capitalist system is superior to the Soviet system.[31]

By mid-1947 the United States had definitely entered the Cold War through the European door.

Britain: the resumption of traditional conflict?

During World War II both leading decisionmakers in London and British public opinion appeared to share the view that Britain and the Soviet Union had to cooperate in the post-war period.[32] Most Foreign Office officials seemed to believe that Russia had come back to its 'normal' imperial tradition. Of course nobody in Whitehall would forget that Tsarist ambitions and British imperial interests had clashed fiercely during the nineteenth century in the Eastern Mediterranean and in Asia, almost in the same way as Bolshevik Russia and international communism had been regarded as major threats to British interests. The continuing 'great game' along the Indian North-West frontier, the Zinoviev letter, and the 'General Strike' had been the symbols of an early 'Cold War' which had already opposed Britain to the Soviet Union.[33] But in 1907 Russia and Britain had worked out a lasting compromise which had transformed itself into an alliance against Imperial Germany. Now, once again, London and Moscow shared the same enemy and, in a pragmatic way, Britain and Russia would win the war and work out a stable peace, in particular in Europe.

It was mainly the British Foreign Office which in 1943 advocated the Soviet Union's involvement in the Allied administration of the European countries which would be liberated by Anglo-American armies.[34] Of course, such a forthcoming attitude was based on some 'realistic' assumptions, which did not exclude a more negative view of Stalin's foreign policy. A partial recognition of Russia's great-power role in Western Europe would allow Britain to have a say in those Eastern European countries which would be liberated by the Red Army. Most British decisionmakers also realized that in the post-war period a weakened British empire would face a powerful Soviet Union on a European continent where the traditional powers which might face Moscow's growing influence would have disappeared or would be severely weakened. And nobody in London could be certain about Washington's eagerness to be deeply involved in post-war Europe. Britain would be almost helpless in a confrontation with Russia without America's support.[35]

Some compromise with Stalin appeared to be the only feasible solution in order to 'contain' the growing strength of Russia. Such an attitude would explain Churchill's attempts at a 'percentage agreement' with the Soviet leader – it was an almost desperate effort to reconcile London's awareness of its own weakness and Britain's ambitions at maintaining its great power role, British fears that Soviet motives were still influenced by communist ideology, and Whitehall's hope that Stalin's policy was now mainly shaped by traditional imperial aims.[36]

Britain's policy toward the Soviet Union did not appear to change dramatically after the Labour Party's electoral victory in July 1945. On the other hand, the new Attlee Cabinet had to take into careful consideration the sympathetic feelings toward Russia which influenced the Labour rank and file, while the Labour left strongly advocated a close relationship between communist Russia and the new socialist Britain.[37] But the new Foreign Secretary Ernest Bevin had a deeply embedded negative view of communist motives and tactics – and of communist leaders – which he had fought against as a trade union leader in the 1920s and 1930s.[38] It was never difficult for Bevin to apply the conceptual and ideological framework of British trade unionism to the international scene: Moscow's foreign policy was only an adaptation of well-known Leninist strategies, which *inter alia* aimed at conquering power and destroying their adversaries through perfidious tactics.

Much against his instincts, until 1946 Bevin accepted the need of some form of cooperation with Moscow.[39] It is very likely that the Foreign Secretary's attitude was more the consequence of his doubts about Britain's strength, of Washington's uncertainties, and of British public opinion rather than a firm belief in future Soviet compliance with the 'rules of the game' sketched out by the 'Big Three' during the final stages of the war. In the meantime, British diplomats who had to deal with the Soviets on the European continent experienced the same disillusionment, frustration, and anger which their US colleagues were reporting to Washington in the same period.[40] In his memoirs the British *chargé d'affaires* in Moscow, Frank Roberts, has stressed how in early 1946 he had the chance to discuss

Stalin's foreign-policy aims with his US colleague, George Kennan. Kennan showed the text of his 'long telegram' to Roberts, who soon afterwards sent off his own long despatches to London.[41] Roberts's views appeared to be slightly milder than Kennan's, and the British diplomat wrote:

> Unlike George Kennan, I took into account our historical relationship with Russia, always ideologically hostile, often involving conflicts of interest worldwide, but rarely leading to war ... and resulting in cooperation and alliance in major world conflicts against Napoleon, the Kaiser, and Hitler.[42]

Nevertheless the British *chargé* added that 'in London there was a tendency in some circles to rule out any kind of cooperation with the kind of country which they thought we had so accurately described'. In early April 1946, Cristopher Warner, the head of the Foreign Office Northern Department, stated in an important memorandum that 'the Soviet Government, both in their recent pronouncements and in their actions have made it clear that they have decided upon an aggressive policy, based upon militant communism and Russian chauvinism' and he suggested that 'we must at once organise and coordinate our defences ... and we should not stop short of defensive-offensive policy'.[43]

Although such alarming evaluations appeared to be shared by British military leaders,[44] Bevin could not challenge the Soviet/Russian threat without clear-cut US backing, a wide consensus on the part of British public opinion, and a victory over the Labour left.[45] Furthermore, the Foreign Secretary and his close advisers could not forget that Churchill's 'iron curtain' speech had been strongly criticized both in Britain and in the US by the press and the most influential opinion-makers as a harmful provocative move toward the Soviet Union.[46]

Between the second half of 1946 and early 1947, however, the public's attitude toward Moscow radically changed. In August 1946 a Gallup poll showed that 61 percent of those questioned in Britain thought that the wartime friendship among Britain, the US, and the Soviet Union had disappeared, while in September a further poll stated that 41 percent of the people questioned nurtured 'less friendly' feelings toward Russia as opposed to only 8 percent who felt 'more friendly'.[47] In spring 1947 the Labour Party experienced a definite swing to the right.[48] Above all, in late 1946 in Germany, Britain and the United States began to cooperate in order to 'contain' Moscow's goals, as showed by the close cooperation on occupation policies toward Germany.[49] By early 1947 the British Cabinet, the Foreign Office, and the military leaders had already reconciled themselves with the perspective of a 'Cold War'. Such feelings would be shared in a few months by the majority of British public opinion and by most Labour members.

But British leaders remained concerned with Washington's attitude and felt the need to lead the United States to a long-term commitment which would avoid the risk that Britain could be left alone to wage a 'Cold War' against Moscow. It is not surprising that Bevin felt the need to have a *casus belli* in order to mobilize British public opinion and justify a 'declaration of war' which would prove to Moscow that a powerful Western alliance was in the making and entangle the Truman administration in the European 'battlefield'. The *casus belli* was offered in late February 1948 by the Prague coup. As Dennis Healey, at that time a leading member of the Labour Party, wrote in his memoirs about the Czechoslovak events:

> To me, as to million of others, Soviet behaviour after the war came as a bitter disappointment. We had thought, as Bevin told the Labour Party Conference in 1945, that 'Left could speak to Left'. What I saw for myself in Eastern Europe was typical of Stalin's approach to all who did not accept his dictates.[50]

The 'Prague coup' could be exploited in part due to a historical myth: if Tory Britain had failed in 1938 to save Czechoslovakia from Nazi aggression as a consequence of 'appeasement', in 1948 Labour Britain would be ready to face another totalitarian regime through all the means at its disposal.[51] It is not surprising that only a few days after Prague, in March 1948, Britain played a major role in the creation of the Brussels Pact, the main purpose of which from the British perspective was to serve as a 'declaration of Cold War'.[52]

France: the reluctant cold warrior

In December 1944 General Charles de Gaulle visited Moscow and signed an alliance which committed France and the Soviet Union to a common policy against German revanchism.[53] Between 1941 and 1944 the leader of 'France Libre' had increasingly focused his attention on the Soviet Union as a vital asset in France's foreign policy. De Gaulle was an anti-communist by tradition and he had never concealed his suspicions about the French Communist Party's aims. He thought, however, that Stalin's Soviet Union would share Russia's traditional goals and hoped that it was possible to revive the French–Russian alliance which from the 1890s to 1914 had helped France to overcome Sédan and the ensuing international isolation, as well as to face imperial Germany.[54] Obsessed at points with historical analogies, General de Gaulle could not forget how the moderate politicians of the 'Troisième République', as a consequence of their lack of confidence in the Soviet Union, had wasted the vital asset of the Soviet–French alliance which perhaps would have saved Czechoslovakia and the remnants of the French security system in East Central Europe in 1938.[55]

It is possible that de Gaulle in 1945 began to show some doubts about Stalin's motives. The anti-fascist coalition which replaced him in 1946 had initially few such doubts. The three major parties in the coalition – the Catholic Mouvement Républicain Populaire (MRP), the socialists, and the communists – expressed much eagerness to develop friendly relations with Moscow. The French Foreign Minister, Georges Bidault, hoped that France might avoid any involvement in the emerging conflicts between Moscow and the 'Anglo-Saxon' powers. During the negotiations that led to the drafting of the Italian peace treaty, Bidault did his best to work out some viable compromise which would overcome the deadlock between the British and American positions on the one hand, and the Soviet views on the other.[56] Until the eve of the Four Foreign Ministers' conference held in Moscow in March–April 1947 the Quai d'Orsay thought that Paris and Moscow shared common aims and could develop a common policy toward Germany.[57]

But in its domestic politics a cold war was already influencing France: the relations between the moderate parties in government and the Communist Party were becoming more and more strained as the French communists strove for more power and the moderate political forces began to fear the aspirations of the Parti Communiste Français.[58] During the Moscow meeting Bidault's hope in a French–Soviet agreement had also been frustrated by Stalin's policy toward Germany. After Truman had stated his 'Doctrine', the French Foreign Minister realized that wartime cooperation was a past experience and that it would be impossible to work out a lasting European settlement acceptable in Paris on the basis of the 'Grand Alliance' cooperation. A few weeks later the French Prime Minister Ramadier ousted the Communist Party from the coalition government.

In spite of the internal political developments, of Paris joining the Marshall Plan, and of the growing social unrest fostered by the Communist Party, most French decisionmakers had difficulties in reconciling themselves to a Europe-wide Cold War.[59] At least till 1948, the French 'Cold War' was mainly regarded as an *internal* factor – the fierce struggle between the moderate parties and the French communists, which the former considered a dangerous and powerful 'Fifth Column' aiming at overthrowing a democratic regime through revolutionary means.[60] France's attitude towards the Soviet Union was on the contrary far more cautious. Of course the French moderate leaders felt themselves in a weaker position and they did not dare to show a 'provocative' attitude toward the Soviets, for, as de Gaulle put it,[61] between the Red Army and the French border there was only the distance of two *etapes* of the Tour de France cyclists. Stalin, de Gaulle thought, could also rely on an effective internal ally.

Furthermore, there was the still unsettled German problem and the early fear that the Cold War could mean Germany's political and military rebirth.[62] It is of some significance that in early 1948, in spite of the Truman Doctrine, of the Marshall Plan, of Bevin's 'Western Union' speech, the French authorities exerted strong pressure on their British and Benelux partners in order to have in the Brussels Treaty a statement about the German threat, as well as to avoid in the same agreement any reference which might appear provocative to the Soviet Union.[63] As late as July 1948, in an important memorandum 'Conceptions stratégiques d'ensemble', the French Chief of Staff, General Georges Revers, foresaw a 'guerre entre le Bloc Anglo-Saxon et l'URSS';[64] although in Revers's opinion France would be an almost obvious ally of the 'Anglo-Saxon' powers in a war against the Soviet Union, the French commander seemed to imply that France would not completely share Britain's and Washington's interests and goals.

Only in the second half of 1948 did the French authorities begin to accept the reality of Paris's involvement in the international dimension of the Cold War as the consequence of Washington's commitment to Europe's security. But, as France's later foreign policy would demonstrate, most French decisionmakers who concentrated on defeating the internal enemy (i.e., the French Communist Party) entered the Cold War with the undeclared hope that sooner or later France would be able to conclude a sort of 'separate peace' with the Soviet Union.[65]

The Soviet Union: Stalin's options

In spite of new evidence from Soviet archives and much recent work on Stalin's foreign policy,[66] there still seems to be some uncertainty about Moscow's motives in the process which led to the unleashing of the Cold War. Soviet foreign policy was not only the outcome of Stalin's decisions – it is likely that there were different opinions in the Kremlin leadership. But it is difficult to deny that Stalin played a more immediate role in comparison with his Western counterparts in shaping his country's post-war foreign policy.[67] The most recent studies based on Russian archival sources seem to demonstrate that during the final stage of World War II Stalin had no clear-cut strategy which aimed at imposing communist rule over the European continent, although he was definitely interested in creating a sphere of control in East Central Europe which may be regarded as a Soviet counterpart of the *cordon sanitaire* which the Soviet Union had experienced – and deeply resented – in the 1920s.[68]

Stalin appeared to have had a cautious attitude which did not exclude flexibility and the obvious interest to seize any opportunity which might strengthen Moscow's international position. As Vladislav Zubok and Constantine Pleshakov and other scholars seem to infer, Stalin's thought was a synthesis of Marxism-Leninism and Russian nationalist tradition,

which was the consequence of his personal, cultural, and political experience. Such an approach favored the identification of Moscow's goals with
communist aims and vice versa.[69] As a disciple of Marx and Lenin, Stalin
knew very well the role of tactics and strategy. In the Soviet leader's mind
the conflict between communism and capitalism was an unavoidable
feature of world history and in the end communism – that is the Soviet
Union – would triumph over capitalism. But since nobody in 1945 – Stalin
included – could foresee when such an ultimate goal would be achieved, in
the short run tactical agreements could be worked out with capitalist
powers, if such agreements would safeguard Soviet/Russian interests and
would offer Moscow the chance to maintain some foothold in the capitalist
world.[70]

In the earlier stages of the 'Grand Alliance' Stalin appeared mainly
concerned with the recovery of the territories Lenin had been compelled
to cede at Brest-Litovsk and during the Civil War (i.e., parts of Poland,
Bessarabia, the Baltic states).[71] But when during the war Moscow's military
and political role grew and it became obvious that the Red Army would
liberate East Central Europe, it also became clear to Stalin and the Soviet
leadership that these nations were a 'security belt' which could protect the
Soviet Union from capitalist aggression.[72] Of course, such a strategy did
not exclude adaptations to local situations, as well as to Allied policy. Stalin
never refused to negotiate with Washington and London on any relevant
issue: from the creation of the United Nations to Germany's fate, from
Moscow's participation to the war with Japan to Europe's post-war settlement.

Stalin would be ready to work out some comprehensive compromise
with the Allied powers also because he was aware of his own country's
economic and military weakness. The Kremlin was obviously most interested in some form of cooperation over Germany, which could become
once again a capitalist power and could unleash once again aggression
against Russia. But in a long-term perspective, Stalin's pledges of
cooperation with the capitalist powers was only a truce. He was convinced
that sooner or later the Western powers would come back to an aggressive
mood.[73] The toughening of Washington's and London's attitude during the
first half of 1946 on various issues – the political situation in East Central
Europe, the peace treaties, Germany's future, and the sharing of atomic
secrets[74] – were regarded as symptoms of the revival of capitalist hostility.

The Kremlin's attitude toward the 'Big Three' continuing cooperation
changed quite radically in spring 1946 and once again Soviet propaganda
began to magnify the inevitability of the conflict between the communist
and the capitalist worlds.[75] But it was the developments in Allied policies
toward Germany and, above all, the Marshall Plan – which, in the eyes of
Soviet leaders, aimed at reviving a dying capitalist system in Europe –
which provided evidence that the Western powers were going to break the

truce with the Soviet Union. In doing so, they were trying to deny Russia the territorial advantages and the international 'status' it had won through a war which had cost millions of lives.[76]

Conflict and war, although in this case a 'cold' one, were obvious features in the minds of leaders who tried to understand reality, on the one hand, through elementary ideological frameworks which stressed the vital role of dialectics and class struggle, and on the other, through the heritage of a traditional Russian vision of the external world.[77] The Cold War was only a phase in an historical process, the dynamics of which a disciple of Marx and Lenin would know well. When the Cominform was created in 1947, Soviet leaders had already reconciled themselves to such a new phase of world history.[78]

The European context

At the end of World War II the future opponents in the Cold War had a common border which divided Europe. In some areas, such as Germany, this frontier could be changed by internal or international factors, and the uncertainty this created fueled suspicions and misperceptions, and favored the intensification of conflict.[79]

The main actors in the early Cold War years had a particular interest in Europe's future: on the West European side, France was a traditional continental power and obviously focused its attention on the continent, as the new European settlement and in particular the fate of Germany was closely tied to Paris's international role and security.[80] Britain was both a European and a world power, which had always showed a keen concern about Europe's balance because such a balance would have vital consequences for London's imperial role, as well as for Britain's security and economic interests.[81]

Russia had become a vital element in European politics in the late seventeenth century and the Soviet leaders of the Stalin generation had a Eurocentric approach to foreign affairs. This approach was both a consequence of Russia's traditional foreign policy aims and a legacy of an ideology which was born in Germany and which had always stressed the role of the working class in industrialized nations.[82]

The United States, albeit a non-European power, had close cultural and political links with Europe and these links strongly influenced leading US decisionmakers – George Kennan and Dean Acheson are good examples – who played decisive roles in shaping Washington's post-war foreign policy.[83] In addition, of special importance to the United States was the influence post-war European powers still exerted in Africa and in Asia.

The European continent not only became the main battlefield and the main prize in the early Cold War, but its leaders contributed to the conflict and to shaping its main characters. In some European nations the Cold War had emerged already during World War II – by 1944 the open struggle between anti-communist forces and local communist parties was already a definite feature in Poland and Greece,[84] not to speak of the unsuccessful attempts to maintain some room for political manoeuver on the part of anti-communist groups in nations such as Romania and Bulgaria.[85] For most members of European moderate elites communism and the Soviet Union were traditional enemies and many anti-communist politicians resented the close cooperation the Western powers had developed with Moscow during the war, as well as the friendly relations that some Western representatives had with local communist leaders who they regarded as mere stooges of the Soviet Union.

In East Central Europe anti-communist feelings and traditional fears of Russian expansionism sometimes overlapped. In Western Europe the model of anti-fascist cooperation among communist and non-communist forces appeared initially to be more successful, but many French, Italian, or Belgian moderate politicians did not share the enthusiasm widely engendered by the common struggle against the Nazi and fascist enemies and regarded the wartime cooperation with the communists as a temporary solution, which was mainly the outcome of a transient international situation.[86] They waited, sometimes with hope, sometimes with deep worry, for the end of the 'Grand Alliance'.

In Italy, for example, the Christian Democrat leader, Alcide De Gasperi, who in December 1944 had been appointed Foreign Minister and in December 1945 Prime Minister, appeared faithful to the 'anti-fascist' coalition and tried to maintain friendly relations with the Soviet Union, but never concealed his suspicions about communist intentions. De Gasperi used to point out that the moderate political forces needed open support on the part of Washington, London, and Paris.[87] During his visit to Washington in January 1947, De Gasperi realized that American policy towards the Soviet Union and toward Europe was beginning to change radically: Truman was no longer eager to 'appease' the Russians and the United States were ready to engage themselves in Europe. It is not surprising that on his return to Italy De Gasperi took the first opportunity to oust the Communist Party from his government. A few weeks later the US Administration launched the Marshall Plan, which Italy almost immediately joined.

De Gasperi, like Ramadier, like other Western European moderate anti-communist leaders, could feel that they had concurred in showing, especially to the US and British authorities, the risks related to maintaining an 'unnatural' coalition between communists and democratic forces. Such an attitude was shared by both Christian Democrat and Social Democrat German politicians who were trying to build a new democratic Germany and showed a very tough attitude toward the German communists.[88] By mid-1947 the ambiguous political atmosphere engendered by the 'Grand Alliance' had been dispelled: the communists, who had always been perceived as uneasy and unlikely allies, were once again natural enemies.

Understanding the origins of the Cold War

For the Cold War, as for most historical eras, there was no single point of origin. Its roots were in a complex and sometimes contradictory process, which lasted roughly from 1944/45 untill 1947/48.[89] This process was related to the failure to achieve a lasting peace in Europe, which all the victorious powers regarded as the most relevant area to be settled after the end of the war. The European continent had been the center of international affairs and through the colonial system it still exerted its political and economic control, albeit in an increasingly shaky fashion, in most of Asia and Africa. Europe's and especially Germany's fate had been at the core of the victorious powers' post-war planning, for ideological, economic, and strategic reasons.[90] Post-war Britain, France, and Russia originated in traditional European powers, viewing the continent's future as the core of their respective projects. The United States was, it could be argued, becoming a 'European' power, at least to a much greater extent than it had been at any other time in its history. The Cold War was, initially, a European affair.

In this European context, it is not difficult to find stages on the road to conflict: the Sovietization process in East Central Europe; Washington's refusal to share atomic secrets; the early conflicts about the United Nations; peace treaties with Germany's allies, and Germany itself; the 'Truman Doctrine' and the Marshall Plan; and the creation of the Cominform. But also at the end of World War I the 'Big Four' had quarreled on many important issues, had nurtured contrasting world strategies and reciprocal suspicions. In spite of that in the early 1920s a new world war among the victorious powers would have appeared an unlikely event, and they had worked out a peace settlement, albeit an unsatisfactory one, as they shared common political, cultural, and psychological values and attitudes.[91] In the 1920s the only real international 'outsider' was Bolshevik Russia, as even Stresemann's Germany was looking for political rehabilitation through diplomacy.

In order to understand the roots of the 'Cold War', we must therefore stress not only specific decisions, but the influence exerted on most decisionmakers and public opinion by cultural, psychological, and ideological factors.[92] Both in the West and in the East the Cold War did not emerge as a sudden revelation. It appeared to confirm beliefs, convictions, prejudices, which were already well rooted: to some, the Soviet Union was showing its 'true' communist face and its aspiration to world domination; for others, the United States and their Western European allies had quickly come back to their obvious capitalist nature, bent on an aggressive policy toward the 'Champion of Socialism'.[93] Neither the Western powers nor the Soviet Union would accept the opponent as a viable partner in a long-term perspective, although, as John Lewis Gaddis has recently noted, in 1945 numerous US and British decisionmakers were eager to maintain some form of cooperation with the Soviet Union if Stalin would be ready to comply with their 'rules of the game'.[94]

As the 1940s drew near its end, Marxism-Leninism offered both opponents an easy key to understand its enemy's long-term goals and the inevitability of conflict. In Stalin's opinion capitalism was an obvious rival – in the eyes of Western decisionmakers every attempt at compromise on the part of the Soviet Union could be dismissed as a mere tactical move. The Cold War was not only a matter of conflicting economic, strategic, and political interests, although we must not forget these aspects. It involved ideological beliefs, psychological convictions, deep-rooted prejudices. To a certain extent the Cold War was similar to the revolutionary wars of the Napoleonic era and to the religious wars which devastated Europe during the sixteenth and the seventeenth centuries. Only when one of the ideologies that had shaped the twentieth century – communism – appeared to have lost its worldwide attraction, and the political instruments it had created had collapsed even in the country where it had first triumphed, could the Cold War come to an end.

NOTES

1 See for example M. P. Leffler and D. S. Painter (eds), *Origins of the Cold War: An International History* (London/New York: Routledge, 1994). See also G. Lundestad, *East, West, North, South: Major Developments in International Politics 1945–1996* (Oslo: Scandinavian University Press, 1996), pp. 1–42, and his 'How (Not) to Study the Origins of the Cold War', ch. 3 in this volume.

2 In this connection see, for example, the remarks in a very recent contribution on the Cold War: R. E. Powaski, *The Cold War: The United States and the Soviet Union 1917–1991* (New York/Oxford: Oxford University Press, 1998), p. 306.

3 On the role of frontiers in international relations see, for example, the thoughtful remarks in J.-B. Duroselle, *Tout empire périra: Théorie des relations internationales* (Paris: Armand Colin, 1992), pp. 49–62.

4 On the contrasts between the United States and Britain see, for example, C. Thorne, *Allies of a Kind: The United States, Britain and the War Against Japan, 1941–1945* (New York: Oxford University Press, 1978); on the contrasts between the United States and France, especially in Indochina, see, for example, J. de Folin, *Indochine 1940–1955: La fin d'un rêve* (Paris: Perrin, 1993), pp. 61–75; I. Wall, *L'influence américaine sur la politique française 1945–1954* (Paris: Balland, 1989), pp. 328–38; J. Valette, *La guerre d'Indochine 1945–1954* (Paris: Armand Colin, 1994), pp. 29–34.

5 See the evaluations in J. L. Gaddis, *We Now Know: Rethinking Cold War History* (Oxford: Clarendon Press, 1998), pp. 54–5 or O. A. Westad, *Cold War and*

Revolution: Soviet–American Rivalry and the Origins of the Chinese Civil War 1944–1946 (New York: Columbia University Press, 1993).

6 For a broad evaluation on Europe as the main prize in the early Cold War see, for example, A. DePorte, *Europe between the Super-Powers: The Enduring Balance* (New Haven, CT/London: Yale University Press, 1979) and W. Loth, *The Division of the World 1941–1955* (London: Routledge, 1988). Furthermore, see the introduction in C. S. Maier (ed.), *The Cold War in Europe: Era of a Divided Continent* (New York: Markus Wiener, 1991).

7 On Britain's and France's hopes and ambitions see J. Becker and F. Knipping (eds), *Power in Europe? Great Britain, France, Italy and Germany in a Postwar World 1945–1950* (Berlin/New York: W. de Gruyter, 1986).

8 See the interesting remarks in D. Reynolds, 'Introduction', in D. Reynolds (ed.), *The Origins of the Cold War in Europe: International Perspectives* (New Haven, CT/London: Yale University Press, 1994), pp. 1–21. See also the results of the international conference 'The Failure of Peace in Europe: 1943–48', held in Florence in 1996. The proceedings of the Florence conference are due to be published shortly (A. Varsori and E. Calandri (eds), *The Failure of Peace in Europe (1943–48)* (London: Macmillan, 2000)).

9 On Roosevelt's policies see, for example, J. L. Gaddis, *The United States and the Origins of the Cold War 1941–1947* (New York: Columbia University Press, 1972). For an exhaustive analysis of Roosevelt's foreign policy see R. Dallek, *Franklin D. Roosevelt and American Foreign Policy, 1932–1945* (New York/Oxford: Oxford University Press, 1979), in particular the chapters in Part IV.

10 A series of reports drawn up by the British Embassy in Washington between late 1944 and mid-1945 showed how US public opinion had mixed feelings toward the Soviet Union. While well-rooted negative attitudes had not disappeared, most Americans hoped that it would be possible to continue some form of cooperation with Moscow in the post-war period; see Public Record Office (hereafter PRO), Foreign Office 371 (hereafter FO 371), Nos. 44606, 44607, 44608. For a broad assessment see J. L. Gaddis, *Russia, the Soviet Union and the United States: An Interpretive History* (New York: McGraw-Hill, 1990), pp. 87–143, and P. G. Boyle, *American–Soviet Relations From the Russian Revolution to the Fall of Communism* (New York/London: Routledge, 1993), pp. 17–39.

11 Quoted in D. Fromkin, *In the Time of the Americans* (New York: Vintage Books, 1996), p. 595. On Bullit's critical view of the Soviet Union see D. Mayers, *The Ambassadors and America's Soviet Policy* (New York/Oxford: Oxford University Press, 1994), p. 117.

12 See, for example, Henry Luce's attitude, quoted in W. LaFeber, *The American Age: US Foreign Policy at Home and Abroad, 1750 to Present* (New York: W. W. Norton & Co., 1994), p. 437. For Hollywood's attitude see C. R. Koppes and G. D. Black, *Hollywood Goes to War* (New York: The Free Press, 1987).

13 M. P. Leffler, *A Preponderance of Power: National Security, the Truman Administration and the Cold War* (Stanford, CA: Stanford University Press, 1992), p. 30.

14 On the 'Grand Alliance', see, for example, R. Edmonds, *The Big Three: Churchill, Roosevelt and Stalin in Peace and in War* (London: Penguin Books, 1992).

15 See B. Arcidiacono, *Alle origini della guerra fredda: Armistizi e Commissioni di controllo alleate in Europa orientale 1944–1946* (Florence: Ponte alle Grazie, 1993). See also R. Pruessen, '"Unpleasant Facts" and Conflicted Responses: US Interpretations of Soviet Policies in East Central Europe, 1943–1948', in Varsori and Calandri (eds), *The Failure*. For a broad evaluation see G. Lundestad, *The American Non-Policy towards Eastern Europe, 1943–1947* (New York: Columbia University Press, 1978).

16 M. Miller, *Plain Speaking: An Oral Biography of Harry S. Truman* (New York: Berkeley Books, 1974), p. 209.
17 PRO, FO 371, N 4152/971/38, British Consulate (New York) to British Embassy (Washington), 11 March 1946.
18 On Germany's situation see, for example, W. Krieger, 'Germany', in Reynolds (ed.), *The Origins*, pp. 144–66, and W. Loth's contribution to the conference. On US policy toward Germany see W. Krieger, *General Lucius D. Clay and Die Amerikanische Deutschlandpolitik, 1945–1949* (Stuttgart: Klett-Cotta, 1987), and T. A. Schwartz, *America's Germany: John J. McCloy and the Federal Republic of Germany* (Cambridge, MA: Harvard University Press, 1991).
19 See the remarks in I. Poggiolini, 'Some Reflections on Post-World War II Peace-Making Practices (1947–51)', in A. Varsori (ed.), *Europe 1945–1990s: The End of An Era?* (London: Macmillan, 1995), pp. 17–27. For a broad analysis see, for example, J. L. Gormly, *From Potsdam to the Cold War: Big Three Diplomacy 1945–1947* (Wilmington, DE: Scholarly Resources Inc., 1990).
20 See, for example, *I Documenti Diplomatici Italiani*, X series, vol. IV (Rome: Ministero Affari Esteri, 1994), Doc. no. 88, Quaroni (Moscow) to Rome, 31 July 1946.
21 On the nuclear issue see G. Alperovitz, *The Decision to Use the Atomic Bomb and the Architecture of an American Myth* (New York: Knopf, 1995). From the viewpoint of the present chapter the negative reactions on the part of both US public opinion and politicians to the discovery of some espionage cases related to nuclear research appear interesting; see, for example, H. Thomas, *Armed Truce: The Beginning of the Cold War 1945–46* (London: Hamish Hamilton, 1986), pp. 195–6.
22 *Life*, 27 May 1946. In June 1946 *Life* published an interesting article by John Foster Dulles ('Thoughts on Soviet Foreign Policy and What to Do About it', *Life*, 3–10 June 1946) which stressed the increasing difficulties in relations between the United States and the Soviet Union. For a comment on this article see PRO, FO 371, N 8550/971/39, despatch no. 1446, Lord Inverchapel (Washington) to C. A. F. Warner (FO), 26 June 1946, confidential.
23 PRO, FO 371, AN 3041/1002/45, Butler to Harvey, 25 September 1946.
24 On Kennan's 'long telegram' see D. Yergin, *Shattered Peace: The Origins of the Cold War and the National Security State* (London: Penguin Books, 1977), pp. 168–71. See also A. Stephanson, *Kennan and the Art of Foreign Policy* (Cambridge, MA: Harvard University Press, 1989), pp. 45–53, and D. Mayers, *George Kennan and the Dilemmas of US Foreign Policy* (New York/Oxford: Oxford University Press, 1988), pp. 97–101.
25 On Europe's role in America's approach to the Cold War see, for example, Gaddis, *We Now Know*, pp. 26–53.
26 For the origins of the 'Manifest Destiny' see LaFeber, *The American Age*, pp. 94–6.
27 See, for example, the conversation the British Chargé d'Affaires in Washington, Balfour, with two top State Department officials; PRO, FO 371, N 8694/97/38, Balfour to Warner, 24 June 1946.
28 Leffler, *A Preponderance of Power*, pp. 142–7.
29 On this aspect see G. Lundestad, 'Empire by Invitation? The United States and Western Europe 1945–52', *Journal of Peace Research*, September 1986, pp. 263–77 and G. Lundestad, *'Empire' by Integration The United States and European Integration, 1945–1997* (Oxford: Oxford University Press, 1998), pp. 29–39.
30 On the Marshall Plan see J. Gimbel, *The Origins of the Marshall Plan* (Stanford, CA: Stanford University Press, 1977); M. Hogan, *The Marshall Plan: America, Britain and the Reconstruction of Western Europe 1947–1952* (Cambridge/New

York: Cambridge University Press, 1987); D. W. Ellwood, *Rebuilding Europe: Western Europe, America and Postwar Reconstruction* (London/New York: Longman, 1992); R. Girault and M. Levy-Leboyer (eds), *Le Plan Marshall et le relèvement économique de l'Europe* (Paris: Comité pour l'histoire économique et financière de la France, 1993); see also Leffler, *A Preponderance of Power*, pp. 182–219.

31 *Documents on Canadian External Relations*, vol. XIII, *1947* (Ottawa: Queen's Printer, 1993), Document no. 226, Draft memorandum by Head, Second Political Division, 30 August 1947, top secret, pp. 367–82; 368–9.

32 For a broad evaluation of Britain's changing attitude toward the Soviet Union see G. Warner, 'From "Ally" to Enemy: Britain's Relations with the Soviet Union, 1941–48', in F. Gori and S. Pons (eds), *The Soviet Union and Europe in the Cold War, 1943–53* (London: Macmillan, 1996), pp. 293–309.

33 F. S. Northedge and A. Wells, *Britain and Soviet Communism: The Impact of a Revolution* (London: Macmillan, 1982).

34 See B. Arcidiacono, *Le 'précédent italien' et les origines de la guerre froide: Les alliés et l'occupation de l'Italie 1943–1944* (Brussels: Bruylant, 1984).

35 For Britain's policy toward the Soviet Union during World War II see, for example, the remarks in V. Rothwell, *Britain and the Cold War 1941–1947* (London: Jonathan Cape, 1982).

36 B. Arcidiacono, 'Dei rapporti tra diplomazia e aritmetica: lo "strano accordo" Churchill–Stalin sui Balcani (Mosca, ottobre 1944)', *Storia delle relazioni internazionali*, 5, 2 (1989): 245–78. For an example of Britain's attitude see PRO, FO 371, N 678/20/38, memorandum 'Russia's Strategic Interests and Intentions From the Point of View of her security' by the Joint Intelligence Sub-Committee, 18 December 1944, top secret.

37 M. Caedel, 'British Political Parties and the European Crisis of the Late 1940s', in J. Becker and F. Knipping (eds), *Power in Europe? Great Britain, France, Italy and Germany in a Postwar World 1945–50* (Berlin/New York: de Gruyter, 1986), pp. 137–62.

38 Northedge and Wells, *Britain and Soviet Communism*, pp. 198–9. See also G. Warner, 'Ernest Bevin and British Foreign Policy, 1945–1951', in G. A. Craig and F. L. Loewenheim (eds), *The Diplomats 1939–1979* (Princeton, NJ: Princeton University Press, 1994), p. 106.

39 A. Bullock, *Ernest Bevin: Foreign Secretary 1945–1951* (London: Heinemann, 1983), p. 473.

40 See, for example, *Documents on British Policy Overseas*, series I, vol. VI, *Eastern Europe 1945–1946* (London: HMSO, 1991).

41 See PRO, FO 371, N 4156/97/38, despatch no. 189, F. Roberts (Moscow) to E. Bevin, 17 March 1946, confidential and N 4157/97/38, despatch no. 190, F. Roberts (Moscow) to E. Bevin, 18 March 1946, secret. Both despatches are quoted in DBPO, series I, vol. VI, pp. 315–31. Furthermore, see S. Greenwood, 'Frank Roberts and the "Other" Long Telegram: The View from the British Embassy in Moscow', *Journal of Contemporary History*, 25 (1990): 103–22.

42 F. Roberts, *Dealing with Dictators: The Destruction and Revival of Europe 1930–70* (London: Weidenfeld & Nicolson, 1991), p. 109.

43 Quoted in J. Lewis, *Changing Direction: British Military Planning for Post-War Strategic Defence, 1942–1947* (London: The Sherwood Press, 1988), p. 363.

44 D. C. Watt, 'British Military Perceptions of the Soviet Union as a Strategic Threat 1945–50', in Becker and Knipping (eds), *Power in Europe?*, pp. 325–8.

45 In late October 1946, 22 Labour MPs wrote a public statement in which they condemned Bevin's policy toward Russia and advocated close cooperation with

both the United States and the Soviet Union; see PRO, FO 371, N 14755/97.38.
46 On Churchill's speech, see F. J. Harbutt, *The Iron Curtain: Churchill, America and the Origins of the Cold War* (New York/Oxford: Oxford University Press, 1986).
47 G. H. Gallup (ed.), *The Gallup International Opinion Polls: Great Britain 1937–1975*, vol. I, *1937–1964* (New York: Random House), pp. 136–8.
48 Bullock, *Bevin*, p. 398. See also R. O. Morgan, *Labour in Power 1945–1951* (Oxford: Clarendon Press, 1984), pp. 238–9.
49 A. Deighton, *The Impossible Peace: Britain, the Division of Germany and the Origins of the Cold War* (Oxford: Clarendon Press, 1993).
50 D. Healey, *The Time of My Life* (London: Michael Joseph, 1989), p. 100.
51 See D. Chuter, 'Munich, or the Blood of Others', in C. Buffet and B. Heuser (eds), *Haunted by History: Myths in International Relations* (Oxford: Berghahn, 1998), pp. 65–79.
52 See A. Varsori, *Il Patto di Bruxelles (1948): tra alleanza atlantica e integrazione europea* (Rome: Bonacci, 1988).
53 See G. Andreini, '"La belle et bonne alliance": i rapporti franco-sovietici (1941–1945)', *Storia delle relazioni internazionali*, 10–11, 1 (1994/95): 25–62.
54 G. H. Soutou, 'General de Gaulle and the Soviet Union, 1943–5: Ideology or European Equilibrium', in Gori and Pons (eds), *The Soviet Union*, pp. 310–33, and G. H. Soutou, 'De Gaulle's Plans for Post-War Europe', in Varsori and Calandri, *The Failure*.
55 On France's 'Soviet' policy during the 1930s, see J.-B. Duroselle, *Politique étrangère de la France: La décadence 1932–1939* (Paris: Imprimerie Nationale, 1979).
56 On Bidault's foreign policy see, for example, J. Dalloz, *Georges Bidault, biographie politique* (Paris: L'Harmattan, 1992), pp. 123–56.
57 P. Gerbet, *Politique étrangère de la France: Le relèvement 1944–1949* (Paris: Imprimerie Nationale, 1991), pp. 259–68 and in particular, C. Buffet, *Mourir pour Berlin: La France et l'Allemagne 1945–1949* (Paris: Armand Colin, 1991).
58 See, for example, G. Elgey, *Histoire de la IVème République*, vol. I, *La République des illusions 1945–1951* (Paris: Fayard, 1969), pp. 99–293; S. Berstein and P. Milza, *Histoire de la France au XXe siècle*, vol. III, *1945–1958* (Brussels: Complexe, 1991), pp. 44–68.
59 See J. W. Young, *France, the Cold War and the Western Alliance, 1944–1949* (Leicester/London: Leicester University Press, 1990).
60 See the journalistic reconstruction in T. Wolton, *La France sous influence: Paris–Moscou 30 ans de relations secrètes* (Paris: Grasset, 1997), pp. 89–113.
61 J. Charlot, *Le gaullisme d'opposition 1946–1958* (Paris: Fayard, 1983), p. 82.
62 Gerbet, *Le relèvement*, pp. 279–91; Buffet, *Mourir pour Berlin*, pp. 77ff.
63 Varsori, *Il Patto di Bruxelles*.
64 Service Historique de l'Armée de Terre, 1K331, Fonds Revers, box 7, memorandum 'Conceptions stratégiques d'ensemble', 20 July 1948, *très secret*.
65 See G. H. Soutou, 'Pierre Mendès France et l'URSS 1954–1955', in R. Girault (ed.), *Pierre Mendès France et le role de la France dans le monde* (Grenoble: PUG, 1991), pp. 177–206, and A. Varsori, 'Alle origini della prima distensione: la Francia di Pierre Mendès France e la ripresa del dialogo con Mosca (1954–1955)', *Storia delle relazioni internazionali*, 8, 1–2 (1992): 63–98.
66 See, in particular, Gori and Pons (eds), *The Soviet Union*; V. Zubok and C. Pleshakov, *Inside the Kremlin's Cold War: From Stalin to Khrushchev* (Cambridge, MA: Harvard University Press, 1996) and V. Mastny, *The Cold War and Soviet Insecurity: The Stalin Years* (New York/Oxford: Oxford University Press, 1996); also see the publication of both essays and Soviet documents by the 'Cold War International History Project'.

67 See the most interesting remark in E. Aga Rossi and V. Zaslavsky, *Togliatti e Stalin: Il PCI e la politica estera staliniana negli archivi di Mosca* (Bologna: Il Mulino, 1997), pp. 14–15.

68 On Stalin's wartime policy, see V. Mastny, 'Soviet Plans for Postwar Europe', in Varsori and Calandri (eds), *The Failure*; see also V. O. Pechatov, 'The Big Three After World War II: New Documents on Soviet Thinking about Post War Relations with the United States and Great Britain', Cold War International History Project, Working Paper no. 13.

69 Zubok and Pleshakov, *Inside the Kremlin's Cold War*, pp. 16–17; Mastny, *The Cold War*, pp. 12–13. On Stalin see D. Volkogonov, *Stalin: Triumph and Tragedy* (New York: Grove Weidenfeld, 1992).

70 Aga Rossi and Zaslavsky, *Togliatti e Stalin*, pp. 55–74. See also S. Pons, 'L'Italia e il PCI nella politica estera dell'URSS (1943–1945)', in F. Gori and S. Pons (eds), *Dagli archivi di Mosca: L'URSS, il Cominform e il PCI 1943–1951* (Rome: Carocci, 1998), pp. 19–70.

71 See, for example, the claims that Stalin put forward in 1942 during the negotiations for the Anglo-Soviet treaty: S. M. Miner, *Between Churchill and Stalin: The Soviet Union, Great Britain and the Origins of the Grand Alliance* (Los Angeles, CA: University of California Press, 1988) and A. Giglioli, 'La sorte degli stati baltici: un "acid test" nei rapporti anglo-sovietici durante la seconda guerra mondiale', *Storia delle relazioni internazionali*, 9, 2 (1993): 67–97.

72 See, for example, the evaluations in C. Gati, *The Bloc that Failed: Soviet-East European Relations in Transition* (Bloomington/Indianapolis, IN: Indiana University Press, 1990), pp. 3–28. For an extensive analysis see V. Mastny, *Russia's Road to the Cold War: Diplomacy, Warfare and the Politics of Communism, 1941–1945* (New York: Columbia University Press, 1976).

73 For a comprehensive analysis of Stalin's policies, see Zubok and Pleshakov, *Inside the Kremlin*, pp. 36–46 and Mastny, *The Cold War*, pp. 23–9; see also the comments by Dallin and Taubman in Gori and Pons (eds), *The Soviet Union*, pp. 185–94. For a different view see C. Kennedy-Pipe, *Stalin's Cold War: Soviet Strategies in Europe, 1943 to 1956* (Manchester/New York: Manchester University Press, 1995).

74 On the nuclear issue see D. Holloway, *Stalin and the Bomb: The Soviet Union and Atomic Energy 1939–1956* (New Haven, CT/London: Yale University Press, 1994). Holloway argues that Stalin did not believe an international control of atomic energy could be a feasible goal (pp. 161–5).

75 See the interesting remarks in PRO, FO 371, nos 47786 and 47893.

76 S. D. Parrish and M. N. Narinsky, 'New Evidence on the Soviet Rejection of the Marshall Plan, 1947: Two Reports', Cold War International History Project Working Paper no. 9.

77 For some fascinating inlooks, see I. B. Neumann, *Russia and the Idea of Europe* (London/New York: Routledge, 1996).

78 A. Di Biagio, 'The Marshall Plan and the Founding of the Cominform, June–September 1947', in Gori and Pons (eds), *The Soviet Union*, pp. 208–21.

79 See W. Loth's chapter in this volume. See also W. Loth, *Stalins ungeliebtes Kind: Warum Stalin die DDR nicht nollte* (Berlin: Rowohlt–Berlin Verlag, 1994).

80 See, for example, Gerbet, *Le relèvement, passim*.

81 See Rothwell, *Britain and the Cold War*, which stressed the 'European' dimension of Britain's interests.

82 See, for example, Mastny, *The Cold War*, p. 12.

83 On those links see W. Isaacson and I. Thomas, *Wise Men: Six Friends and the World They Made* (New York: Simon & Schuster, 1986) and J. L. Harper, *American Visions of Europe* (Cambridge: Cambridge University Press, 1994).

84 On Poland see, for example, K. Kersten, *The Establishment of Communist Rule in Poland, 1943–1948* (Berkeley, CA: University of California Press, 1991). On Greece see J. O. Iatrides, *Revolt in Athens: The Greek Communists Second Round* (Princeton, NJ: Princeton University Press, 1972).

85 For a broad analysis of Communists' seizure of power in East Central Europe see, for example, H. Carrère d'Encausse, *Le grand frère: L'Union Soviétique et l'Europe sovietisée* (Paris: Flammarion, 1983), pp. 13–134; B. Fowkes, *The Rise and Fall of Communism in Eastern Europe* (London: Macmillan, 1993), pp. 6–51.

86 See the interesting remarks about De Gasperi in Aga Rossi and Zaslavsky, *Togliatti e Stalin*, pp. 116–17.

87 A. Varsori, 'De Gasperi, Nenni, Sforza and Their Role in Post-War Italian Foreign Policy', in Becker and Knipping (eds), *Power in Europe?*, pp. 89–116.

88 As for the Social Democrats see, for example, D. Staritz and A. Sywottek, 'The International Political Situation as Seen by the German *Linksparteien* (SPD, SED and KPD) between 1945 and 1949', in Becker and Knipping (eds), *Power in Europe?*, pp. 213–24. For a broader view see D. L. Bark and D. R. Gress, *A History of Germany*, vol. I, *From Shadow to Substance 1945–1963* (Oxford: Blackwell, 1993), pp. 93–230.

89 For a reconstruction see, for example, R. B. Woods and H. Jones, *Dawning of the Cold War: The United States Quest for Order* (Chicago: Elephant Press, 1994).

90 See, for example, Ellwood, *Building Europe*, pp. 3–60.

91 On the post-Versailles settlement see, for example, S. Marks, *The Illusion of Peace* (London: Macmillan, 1980).

92 These aspects have been pointed out in numerous contributions, see, for example, the chapters in this volume by D. J. Macdonald and by Y. Ferguson and R. Koslowski.

93 See the remarks by P. Grosser, *Les temps de la guerre froide* (Brussels: Complexe, 1995), pp. 19–49. The role of the ideological aspects seems to suit in particular the early phase of the Cold War.

94 Gaddis, *We Now Know*, pp. 24–5.

14

The Crisis Years, 1958–1963

James G. Hershberg

It is in the 'crisis years' 1958–63 that the history of the Cold War perhaps comes closest to fitting Gibbon's famous definition of history itself as, 'indeed, little more than the register of the crimes, follies, and misfortunes of mankind'[1] – and, this chapter contends, the new evidence that has emerged in recent years from both communist (and former communist) and Western archives and sources only reinforces that impression. Encompassing such events as the Taiwan Straits, Berlin, U-2, Laotian, Congo, and Cuban Missile Crises, the Sino-Soviet schism, Sino-Indian border clashes, the collapse of East–West negotiations in Paris in 1960, and of a nuclear-testing moratorium the following fall, and an unmatched concentration of (frequently acrimonious) summitry involving the encounters of the unpredictable, raucous figure of Nikita Sergeevich Khrushchev with a vast cast of communist and capitalist luminaries (Mao, Eisenhower, De Gaulle, Castro, Kennedy, and Marilyn Monroe), this half decade has long been recognized as the period of the most acute and dangerous tensions between 'East' and 'West', as well as of deepening contradictions within the communist realm between Moscow and Beijing.

Periodization, as all historians know, can be a dangerous and tricky business. This chapter, for example, considers the years 1958–63 as some sort of 'turning point' in Cold War history. The selection of such 'turning points' invites immediate deconstruction (or nit-picking): why not 1953–56 – the start of 'post-' and 'de'-Stalinization; or 1975/79–81 – the Soviet empire overstretches abroad and stagnates at home? I raise the issue not to be churlish, but to underline one early conclusion from the early phases of the emergence of communist bloc evidence on the international history of the Cold War: it frequently plays havoc with the traditional narrative constructed on the basis of Western evidence,[2] using a periodization largely based on the comings and goings of US and/or Soviet leaders.

Still, there can be little doubt that the period from 1958 to 1963 did indeed mark a turning point in the Cold War, as the tensions which had been accumulating since the end of World War II sharpened and intensified through a series of crises that repeatedly appeared to bring the globe to the precipice of nuclear war. To paraphrase the terminology employed by Chairman Mao, it was a time when neither the East nor West Wind prevailed over the other, but the synergy of gusts in various directions produced a maelstrom which buffeted international relations. This tempestuous passage of thrusts and counterthrusts, of political, military, and ideological jousting, climaxed, of course, with the frightening brinkmanship of the October 1962 Cuban Missile Crisis, an experience which sobered Washington and Moscow to the point where both superpowers evidently decided that continuing along the same path would be simply too dangerous. Following their near-hit with catastrophe, both sides took steps to moderate the intensity of their rivalry, and to try to ensure that subsequent direct tests of strength, especially in the vital arena of Europe, would be limited to political, economic, and ideological struggle, while military battles could be shunted off to Third World proxies and the nuclear race kept within predictable, negotiable channels.

As many commentators then and since have noted, it was in this period stretching from the Taiwan Straits Crisis of 1958 through the Cuban Missile Crisis, that the West and its enemies finally adopted some 'rules of the game', which pointed toward safer limits of Cold War competition and away from a 35-year-long period in which, as Louis J. Halle put it, 'the populations of the West lived continuously in a terrible fear ... [when] we, in the West, saw almost no possibility of saving ourselves from the intolerable darkness that was overspreading the world from the East'.[3]

Away from bipolarity

If one new challenge facing Cold War historians is, in fact, a 're-periodization' of the era, another is the need for at least a partial 'retro-active de-bipolarization' of much of the Cold War's history. Increasingly, just as the 'post-Cold War' world's multipolar nature has been spotlighted by analysts, the emerging evidence of complex two-way relations between superpowers and their allies during the Cold War hardly conforms to the classic models of blocs marching in lock-step unison presented to the public at the time. There is a need for increased attention to the roles of neutral or semi-neutral states and groupings (not only the formal 'Non-Aligned Movement' but regional, national, and transnational forces, e.g., Islam), who struggled, like the Jeff Daniels character in Woody Allen's film *The Purple Rose of Cairo*, to break out of the Cold War narrative scripted by and in Washington and Moscow. And, to a considerable extent, it appears that, while much of the American public (and at least some of the leadership) only appreciated the genuineness and intensity of the defection of the People's Republic of China from the 'Sino-Soviet bloc' in the late 1960s, in reality the alliance between the two communist giants had never been as smooth or coherent as presented to the outside world even at its heyday in the early to mid-1950s.

To the extent that the international system could ever accurately be described as a confrontation of two *unified* global blocs in the early Cold War, that bipolarity began to dissipate rapidly with the unilateral decision by the Beijing leadership, primarily Mao Zedong, to radicalize the Chinese revolution in 1958, both domestically (by launching the Great Leap Forward) and in foreign policy (by secretly signaling displeasure to Moscow over Sino-Soviet relations and, soon thereafter, by starting the Taiwan Straits Crisis). One major finding from recent Chinese evidence on the Great Leap Forward,[4] is that Mao's turn to the left in the spring of 1958 appears to have been even sharper, broader, and, to return to Gibbon, more criminal and misfortunate than was generally appreciated by Western observers at the time. Indeed, now estimated to have affected at least 30 million people, the famine caused by the Great Leap Forward (comparable in many respects with that induced in Ukraine in the 1930s by Stalin's collectivization schemes) looms in retrospect as perhaps the single greatest human disaster of the Cold War period.[5]

To judge from recent accounts, Mao's radical shift at home beginning in early 1958, and accelerating in the summer or fall of that year, seems also to be growing in importance in its impact on explanations of Chinese foreign policy. Much as the Chinese historian Chen Jian accentuated the role domestic politics may have played in China's entry into and involvement in the Korean War in 1950–53,[6] other scholars have persuasively argued that mobilizing and energizing the Chinese population for the Great Leap Forward's Herculean economic and ideological targets constituted a crucial motive underlying Mao's initiation of the Taiwan Straits Crisis and, more broadly, his exacerbation of tension in Chinese foreign policy.[7] As Michael Hunt puts it, both before and after it seized power in 1949:

> domestic concerns mingled inextricably with international pressures to produce CCP [Chinese Communist Party] foreign policy. Decisions on foreign and domestic policy did not occupy different lobes in the collective mind of the CCP. It could not be otherwise. The party sprang from a domestically defined ideological agenda – a pre-occupation with China's political and social transformation and its economic development, and these basic, long-range concerns fundamentally shaped the CCP's approach to external relations.[8]

The new Cold War history therefore has a far different emphasis with regard to China than the concentration on the idea of a 'strategic probe' which preoccupied Eisenhower administration officials pondering the use of nuclear weapons to defend Mazu and Jinmen (Matsu and Quemoy), and believing that Mao's principal immediate objective was the military conquest of those offshore islands if not Taiwan itself. Several Chinese scholars based in the United States, writing in the early and mid-1990s, have stressed differing (yet complementary or at least not mutually exclusive) motives in explaining Mao's actions in launching the offshore islands crisis.[9] Zhai Qiang endorses the contention, which Mao himself stressed in some contemporaneous internal speeches, that it was primarily designed to offer tangible, albeit indirect, support to Arab forces in Iraq and Lebanon struggling against US and British 'imperialism' (in contrast to Moscow's passivity) and only to a 'lesser extent' related to domestic factors such as the Great Leap Forward.[10] Shu Guang Zhang relates the military attacks to a policy of 'active defense' to 'improve China's strategic position' as well as to ensnare the Americans and Nationalist Chinese in the 'noose' of the offshore islands (which Mao described as a convenient lever for Beijing to use to apply pressure or raise tensions whenever it desired).[11]

As some recent analyses suggest, a new understanding of Mao's initiation of the 1958 crisis is emerging that finds both a temporal and a substantive link to his simultaneous secret ratcheting up of tensions with his putative communist ally in Moscow.[12] In fact, Mao's secret decision in the summer of 1958 to detonate an explosion in Sino-Soviet relations – muffled to the outside (Western) world but loud, clear, and shrapnel-filled to its intended target in the Kremlin – is itself a major finding that has become documentable only in recent years: the Chairman's bitter screed to Soviet envoy Pavel Yudin on 22 July 1958[13] represented a fateful choice to escalate the grumblings and resentment toward the post-Stalin leadership in Moscow into expressions of outright contempt, distrust, and hostility. These sentiments were only slightly and temporarily moderated during Khrushchev's emergency visit to Beijing a week later, and it now seems clear that Mao's decision to approve the shelling of the offshore islands, three weeks after the Kremlin leader departed, represented a deliberate snub to Moscow, as well as the more obvious military challenge to the United States.[14]

Meshing with the view that Mao triggered the crisis as a deliberate defection from the spirit if not the letter of the Sino-Soviet alliance and the bipolar world it signified, Constantine Pleshakov and Vladislav Zubok conclude that

> the [Taiwan Straits] crisis of 1958 was not Khrushchev's war. Not only had the crisis been unleashed by Moscow's main ally at its own risk, but it was also a provocation to the Kremlin to change its new post-Stalin politics (which were regarded in Beijing as a betrayal of the 'common cause') and perhaps even to challenge the leadership of the worldwide Marxist empire. The Quemoy and Matsu crisis was therefore of paramount importance as a manifestation of the disintegration of the absolute bipolarity of the early Cold War.[15]

In explaining the collapse of the Sino-Soviet alliance, several leading Chinese scholars adopt, in Chen Jian and Yang Kuisong's phrase, a 'domestic-oriented approach'. During the 'pivotal' year 1958, as Mao revved up the processes of the Great Leap Forward, Chen and Yang see the CCP Chairman as increasingly perceiving potential tensions in Beijing's relations with the USSR through the lens of his radicalizing crusade in China's domestic political priorities. 'Indeed', they write, in assessing Mao's harsh treatment of Khrushchev and other Soviet representatives that summer, 'when Mao was turning his own revolutionary emotion into the dynamics for the Great Leap Forward, it is not surprising that he had the same offensive-oriented mood in dealing with his Soviet comrades.'[16]

While the new evidence hardly clarifies in any definitive way the precise, evolving complex of motives behind Mao's actions in 1958, it seems clear that US policymakers and military planners could only dimly perceive that Beijing's shelling of the offshore islands was not simply or solely a Chinese communist military foray against Taiwan and the United States, let alone a coordinated Sino-Soviet 'probe' to 'test' American or Western 'resolve', but in fact represented only one visible manifestation of an upheaval in Mao's China that was at least as much directed toward Moscow as toward Washington and, even more, inwardly directed. As Shu Guang Zhang concludes, it appears that both Beijing and Washington mishandled the Taiwan Straits Crisis in important respects and were, indeed, fortunate to escape without stumbling into a wider conflict.

Khrushchev and Berlin

The summer 1958 Straits Crisis – which ebbed after Beijing agreed to the resumption of Sino-American ambassadorial talks in early September – presaged another, even more suspenseful crisis that fall, when Khrushchev on 27 November issued his six-month ultimatum calling for a German peace treaty to be signed by the victors of World War II or else Moscow would sign a bilateral pact with the GDR that threatened to cut off Western access to West Berlin. Although it seems plausible that Beijing's profoundly radical swerve must have exerted a kind of gravitational pull within the communist solar system, a causal link between Mao's foreign policy actions in the summer of 1958 and Khrushchev's launching of the Berlin crisis that fall has only been postulated,[17] but not concretely established,[18] on the basis of the new evidence emerging from Russian and East German archival sources.[19]

Nevertheless, some parallels between the Taiwan Straits and Berlin Crises in their broader Cold War significance seem to emerge from the analyses based on communist-side archives in recent years. Like the Far

Eastern crisis which preceded it, the Kremlin's reopening of the Berlin issue in the menacing terms of the November 1958 ultimatum struck many US observers, both in government and in the public at large, as yet another sign of Soviet (and indeed Sino-Soviet) communist confidence, assertiveness, and aggressiveness in the wake of Sputnik and other spectacular technological achievements in 1957–58. As in the Taiwan Straits, communist military forces appeared to enjoy an overwhelming local conventional superiority, a fact which immediately raised for Western leaders the unpalatable alternatives of surrender or escalation to nuclear weapons should the adversary decide to force the issue. Given the danger, widely recognized at the time, of escalation to general and/or nuclear war over Berlin, the questions naturally arise, as they did in the Taiwan Straits Crisis, of how well or poorly US and Western leaders appear to have understood the goals and motives on the communist side.

While a definitive assessment of Khrushchev's motives in triggering and handling the Berlin Crisis remains elusive, extensive releases from Russian and East German archives strongly indicate that, as with the Taiwan Straits Crisis, they included a more complex mix of offensive and defensive aims, and were more influenced by intra-alliance and domestic political considerations, than Western observers and the public could appreciate at the time. Clearly, as Marc Trachtenberg has argued,[20] and as some previously hidden Soviet–East German and Soviet–Polish exchanges in the period leading up to Khrushchev's ultimatum confirm, one key motive was to undermine the process of West Germany's rearmament and, above all, nuclearization within the NATO alliance.[21] Certainly, also, it seems likely that Khrushchev felt emboldened by what he regarded as his successful nuclear bluster and bluff during the 1956 Suez Crisis,[22] and by the rush of adrenaline provided by Sputnik, to engage in nuclear pressure tactics on Berlin – which he once famously described as the 'testicles of the West' ('Every time I give them a yank they holler').[23]

At the same time, new evidence strengthens the view (held by some Soviet experts in the West at the time) that Khrushchev's bluster over Berlin masked significant weaknesses and constraints that in some ways compelled him to act as much out of desperation as of confidence. Also, his control of the situation on the communist side was not nearly as complete as many in the West imagined or presumed. In particular, Hope M. Harrison's work illuminates the extent to which, as she put it, 'the tail wagged the dog' – that GDR influence on Soviet policy during the crisis of 1958–61 was, in several respects, 'much more important than previously believed'.[24] Making extensive use of both Russian and East German archival records, Harrison shows how Socialist Unity Party (SED) leader Walter Ulbricht was, paradoxically, able to parlay the GDR's economic weakness into political strength in bargaining with the Soviets. Ulbricht knew that the Kremlin was loath to pour needed resources into an ally's stagnant economy whose brightest citizens were fleeing, but even less able to afford risking the collapse and loss of its most crucial military-strategic satellite, the symbol of its victory in World War II, and the putative showpiece of the Soviet empire in Central Europe.

Ulbricht was able to employ the 'tyranny of the weak' to blackmail Moscow into pumping resources into the East German economy and into waging a political campaign to elevate the GDR's prestige and stem its brain drain by plugging the escape hatch of West Berlin. As Harrison points out, 'Ulbricht's influence over Khrushchev actually grew as East Germany moved closer to collapse'. Records of Soviet–East German exchanges cited by Harrison also reveal that on many occasions actions taken during the crisis by East German *Volkspolizei* to harass Western diplomats in East Berlin or at border crossings – steps which Western officials presumed stemmed from a decision by Khrushchev to 'tighten the screws' – were actually taken independently by Ulbricht and the SED leadership without consulting the Soviets, and in some cases eliciting protests and scoldings from Moscow.[25] In Harrison's view, Ulbricht's enhanced leverage helped drag Khrushchev further into the Berlin Crisis than he otherwise may have wanted to go. Again, as in the Taiwan Straits Crisis, a simple bipolar model is insufficient to explain the course of events.[26]

Other recent studies have also pinpointed domestic and personal factors operating on Khrushchev which made him predisposed to act as he did during the crisis. One key finding is the extent to which Khrushchev's actions in the post-Stalin succession struggle, dating to his role in the June 1953 arrest and subsequent execution later that year of Lavrentii Beria, inhibited his options *vis-à-vis* East Germany and Ulbricht. In particular, once he had accused Beria of having been ready to sell out the GDR in exchange for a deal with the West for a demilitarized, unified Germany, and followed that up with similar charges against Malenkov two years later, Khrushchev could hardly do anything but the utmost to prop up the sagging East German state when it appeared on the verge of economic (and thus political) bankruptcy.

It is also correct to highlight the immediate foreign-policy consequences of the Soviet leader's desires to redirect resources away from conventional military forces to the USSR's civilian economy. James Richter writes:

> In domestic policy [Khrushchev] had essentially promised that rapid economic growth would resolve the post-Stalinist tension between preserving the Party's leading role and raising the status of society. Such promises placed his foreign policy in a double bind, however: he had to show progress toward establishing the Soviet Union in the international role he had envisioned during the succession, but at the same time he hoped to restrain – or even reduce – defense spending to preserve investment resources for his ambitious domestic program.[27]

Despite gaining ascendancy in the leadership by mid-1957, in order to convince the Presidium, the party elite, and skeptical military leaders to go along with his proposals, Khrushchev needed foreign-policy successes. To him, a chief foreign-policy goal – a barometer of Soviet (and his own) stature as an equal superpower to Washington – was Western acceptance and recognition of the post-World War II order in Europe, the fruits of the Red Army's victory over Nazism, a triumph embodied in the existence (and persistence) of a communist German state.

Even as the Berlin Crisis sharpened and softened, and even amidst rants about the danger of war with the West if it did not cave in to his demands for a new arrangement regarding Germany, until the spring of 1960 Khrushchev nursed hopes of an arms control breakthrough with the United States that could allow him to score a statesmanlike triumph in international relations. This would fit neatly into his scheme to build up the Soviet Union's domestic economy, both for the good of his country's people and as the most sensible way for socialism to compete with capitalism in the thermonuclear age. In late 1959, after he had permitted his first six-month Berlin ultimatum to expire in exchange for an invitation from Eisenhower for a long-desired summit talk in the United States, the Soviet leader shifted toward improved relations with the West and away from the increasingly tenuous alliance with the radicalizing Chinese.

Khrushchev also tried to bring to fruition his goal of reorienting the militarized Soviet society in the direction of the civilian economy. At the December 1959 CPSU CC Plenum, records of which have recently emerged from Moscow archives, Khrushchev received approval for the dramatic troop cuts he would announce the following month. In a revealing memorandum prepared for the Presidium explaining the decision,[28] clearly dictated by Khrushchev, the Soviet leader lays out his rationale for cutting military forces 'by perhaps a million or a million and a half' (the final figure was 1.2 million) troops.

Khrushchev's reasoning both illuminates a previously hidden story of the nuclear arms race – the rise of a Soviet 'New Look' philosophy that indeed accompanied a Khrushchevian version of Dulles's 'brinkmanship' – and also, in some respects, shows a far-sighted leader seeking to improve the lot of his people, attain international disarmament measures, and presaging the 'preemptive concession' tactics of Mikhail Gorbachev almost three decades later.

The CPSU leader confidently declared that this 'very powerful, fantastic step' would not only not endanger Soviet security, but in fact help socialism gain 'major political, moral, and economic advantages' in the competition with capitalism, and undercut 'aggressive, militarist circles' in the West who doubted Moscow's sincerity in seeking disarmament. Succumbing to the temptations of nuclear weaponry that had already so seduced American leaders, Khrushchev boasted that, since 'we are in an excellent position with [regard to] missile-building' (having perfected the 'serial production of these rockets') and 'now have a broad range of rockets and in such quantity that can virtually shatter the world', the USSR could safely drastically reduce its conventional forces (perhaps even to a 'territorial militia') while maintaining all of its military commitments – 'I think that it would not make sense now to have atomic and hydrogen bombs, and to maintain at the same time a large army.' In a remarkably prescient paragraph, Khrushchev continued,

> We have already said many times that our ideological debates with capitalism will be resolved not through war, but through economic competition ... Some comrades might object that we could cut armaments, while the enemy would not. But it is debatable if the enemy would be doing the right thing ... since they would devour their budgets, reduce the economic development of these countries, thereby contributing to the increasing advantages of our system.[29]

The Cuban Missile Crisis

The Cuban Missile Crisis finally showed most dramatically how dangerous Khrushchev's emphasis on nuclear strategies – and the outcomes of nuclear choices by both Cold War rivals since 1945 – had become. When viewed with additional attention to domestic and intra-alliance factors, Khrushchev's decision to send nuclear missiles to Cuba becomes more understandable, but the series of actions by both Soviet and US leaders (plus, to a lesser extent, Cuban leaders) that created the crisis nevertheless seems worthy of Gibbon's admonition. In leading the world to near-catastrophe, both Khrushchev and Kennedy (and, for that matter, Eisenhower) made choices that in retrospect appear reckless, irresponsible, disproportionate, and lacking thoughtful analysis.

A full review of the impact of recent evidence and scholarship on the Cuban Missile Crisis is obviously beyond the scope of this chapter.[30] But, in general, the evidence makes both Khrushchev and Kennedy look even 'worse' (i.e., more reckless, irresponsible, short-sighted) *before* the crisis, but even 'better' (i.e., more wise, statesmanlike, sensible, rational) *during* the crisis.

Probably the single most important revelation about the crisis since the new sources began to emerge concerns Khrushchev's previously unknown *second* nuclear deployment to Cuba in 1962, that of tactical nuclear weapons to accompany the strategic medium- and intermediate-range ballistic missiles that were later discovered by US U-2 reconnaissance flights in mid-October. Although an account published in the mid-1960s by former State Department official Roger Hillsman contained a little-noticed allusion to US naval aerial intelligence detecting the presence of tactical atomic weapons in Cuba during the crisis,[31] the first concrete indication that Soviet tactical weapons had actually been emplaced in Cuba prior to the crisis emerged at a January 1992 Russian–American–Cuban 'critical oral history' conference of scholars and former officials in Havana. At the conference, General Anatoly I. Gribkov, who in 1962 helped oversee the deployment of Soviet nuclear weapons to Cuba, nonchalantly revealed that the forces on the island included nine atomic warheads for short-range surface-to-surface 'Luna' ('Frog') rockets.[32]

Gribkov's assertion sparked an uproar, including declarations by some scholars and former officials, including former Defense Secretary Robert S. McNamara, that the crisis now appeared to have been even more dangerous in retrospect given the fact that US officials had failed to detect the weapons and would have been under irresistible pressure to launch a nuclear retaliation had a US invasion force against Cuba come under atomic attack. It also engendered skepticism by others about the veracity of Gribkov's story or whether it truly signified that the threat of nuclear war during the crisis had been greater than previously believed. In the year or two after the Havana conference, additional details on the tactical nuclear weapons issue seeped out of Moscow sources, in the form of articles and memoirs by former Soviet military officers. Stunningly, the additional reports stated that in fact the Soviets had deployed as many as 162 warheads to Cuba, including 102 tactical warheads (80 for tactical cruise missiles, 12 for Luna rocket launchers, six bombs for IL-28 bombers, and four mines) rather than the nine originally revealed by Gribkov.[33]

Equally sensational, alarming, and even more controversial, was Gribkov's claim at Havana that Khrushchev had not only deployed tactical battlefield nuclear weapons to Cuba prior to the crisis but predelegated authority to local commanders to use them if the situation required it.[34] Further investigation in Moscow uncovered both Khrushchev's draft instructions prior to the crisis, which indeed provided for the Soviet military commander in Cuba (General Issa Pliyev) to use the tactical nuclear weapons in the event of a US attack and a simultaneous cut-off of communications between the island and Soviet Defense Ministry authorities in Moscow – *and* Khrushchev's revocation of that authority on 22 October, a few hours before Kennedy's speech, an order which was 'categorically' reaffirmed on 27 October as the crisis neared its climax.[35]

Potentially still more disturbing, in terms of Khrushchev's ability to control the decisionmaking process involving the tactical weapons, was Gribkov's additional assertion that 'under cover of darkness' on the night of 26–27 October, as fears of a US invasion of Cuba rose sharply, Pliyev had unilaterally ordered the movement of some of the tactical nuclear warheads from storage facilities closer to delivery vehicles so they could be more quickly available for use – a decision that allegedly prompted

Moscow's reiteration of its earlier order against employing any nuclear weapons without approval.[36]

While since 1992 scholars have continued to dispute vigorously the details of the Soviet tactical weapons disclosures and their significance on the broader issue of nuclear danger during the crisis,[37] additional disclosures from Russian archives have removed serious doubt about the actual presence of tactical weapons in Cuba during the crisis, and shed more light on Khrushchev's decision to send them. In particular, Aleksandr Fursenko and Timothy Naftali's *'One Hell of a Gamble': Khrushchev, Castro, and Kennedy, 1958–1964*, published in 1997 and based on unusual (and, regrettably, in some cases, exclusive) access to materials in Russian military, intelligence, and presidential archives, offers an account of how Khrushchev, in early September 1962, apparently acting *after* he believed Kennedy had signaled his awareness of the secret missile deployment, had upped the ante by ordering an emergency immediate additional deployment of tactical nuclear weapons to Cuba by plane (extra cruise missiles plus warheads for the IL-28s) in order to defend the island in case Washington attacked.[38] This supplementary, expedited delivery of a variety of battlefield nuclear weapons suggests, Fursenko and Naftali argue, that Khrushchev was preparing to use nuclear means to defeat, not merely deter, a US invasion of Cuba. At the same time, the military drew up (but Defense Minister Radion Malinovskii did not sign) an order explicitly pre-delegating authority to Pliyev to use those means for that purpose should contact with Moscow be broken off and the Americans attacked.[39]

Further clarification on Khrushchev's September decisions regarding tactical nuclear weapons emerged in early 1998. Fursenko and Naftali describe the documents which then came to light as 'arguably ... more revelatory about Khrushchev's understanding of nuclear weapons than any other documents currently available from Russian archives' and enshrine September 1962 'in the pantheon of Cold War turning points'.[40] What makes the handwritten memoranda from senior Defense Ministry officials to Khrushchev (with the leader's notations), on the composition and method of delivery of the expedited shipment of tactical nuclear weapons to Cuba, potentially so important? In one sense they establish that Khrushchev did maintain a semblance of caution and a desire to retain 'firm control' over events, for one document contains the clear injunction that the nuclear weapons be used only 'upon signal from Moscow' – a piece of evidence that finally confirms that Pliyev was *not* given pre-delegated authority to use the weapons, remark Fursenko and Naftali. But the documents also imply, in greater detail, Khrushchev's readiness to rely on these tactical weapons for defense, not deterrence, to 'ratchet up the incipient crisis' by rushing tactical weapons into the breach even after he evidently sensed that JFK knew that nuclear missiles were on their way to Cuba, to, in effect, 'embrace a nuclear warfighting strategy' to hold onto the socialist outpost 90 miles off the Florida coast.

Ever since the crisis, and from all directions, Khrushchev has come under sharp criticism for deploying nuclear MRBMs and IRBMs to Cuba – for taking what was widely viewed as a risky, reckless, irresponsible gamble that nearly plunged the world into World War III – but the gradually deepening revelation about the supplementary, massive, and equally secret deployment of tactical nuclear weapons, even after the realization that a military showdown over the island might be imminent, casts his actions into an entirely new level of 'adventurism', to use the term used by those who later ousted Khrushchev, or criminality, in Gibbon's phrase.[41] The suddenness of his September decisions too speaks volumes, for as Fursenko and Naftali write, his 'embrace of a nuclear warfighting strategy ... happened too fast [for military assessment of the implications of placing tactical nuclear weapons in Cuba]. It seems we must come to the conclusion that Moscow placed tactical nuclear weapons on the battle-field without any analysis of the threshold between limited and general nuclear war.'[42]

There is no space here for an in-depth exploration of the reasons behind Khrushchev's *two* nuclear deployment decisions to Cuba of 1962 – no definitive contemporaneous 'smoking gun' documents have emerged to confirm a single motive, or a precise hierarchy of motives – but in light of the above analyses of the Taiwan Straits and Berlin Crises it is worth noting again the apparent increased cogency of domestic and intra-alliance factors. The domestic economic factors which had pushed Khrushchev to propose his January 1960 military troop cuts, an initiative that was put on the back burner after the U-2 crisis and the collapse of the East–West summit in Paris that May and the subsequent resumption of tensions over Berlin in 1961, still plagued the USSR.[43] Like Eisenhower (a leader concerned about excessive military spending who presided over the deployment of US tactical nuclear weapons along with a 'trip-wire' troop contingent to the front line of the Cold War in Germany in an area of Soviet conventional military superiority, and ordered a major policy shift toward 'conventionalizing' nuclear weapons), and two American presidents who had used threats of nuclear retaliation to defend the isolated capitalist oasis of Berlin, Khrushchev could not defend Cuba conventionally and evidently saw atomic arms as the one, best, and only way to safeguard Havana as well as, perhaps, redress the strategic balance on the cheap.[44]

Indeed, even though in some respects the logic of the situation dictated the move if Khrushchev refused to concede Cuba's eventual conquest by its giant capitalist neighbor, it may well be, as John Lewis Gaddis has ventured,[45] that 'inadverten[tly] ... the Americans gave' Khrushchev 'the idea of using *missiles* to defend the Cuban revolution' by responding to Sputnik in fall 1957 by pushing NATO allies to accept medium-range nuclear missiles as stopgap symbols of America's continued extended deterrence commitment despite claims of a 'missile gap' – an offer taken up by only Italy and Turkey, in a story that has now been crisply told by Philip Nash in *The Other Missiles of October*.

It is also clear that Khrushchev faced intense pressures from within the communist world to shore up Moscow's position in Cuba in spring 1962 as well as to assure the survival of Castro's regime. The Western researcher who has received perhaps the most extensive access to Russian archives on the crisis, Timothy Naftali, in a November 1997 talk to the American Association for the Advancement of Slavic Studies, in Seattle, listed two intra-alliance factors that seemed far more important in explaining Khrushchev's deployment than such old standbys as the nuclear balance or possible bargaining over Berlin. One consideration, also described in *One Hell of a Gamble*, stemmed from Castro's purge of hard-line communists in March 1962 (the 'Escalante affair'), which led to the expulsion of the Soviet Ambassador and evidently fanned fears in Moscow of a 'backlash' by Castro against the USSR.[46] With cooperation 'disrupted' and mutual suspicions growing, Khrushchev seems to have felt a pressing need to reaffirm and cement the basic alliance with Havana, 'to demonstrate to Castro personally and dramatically that the Soviet Union would defend his revolution'.[47]

While his book with Fursenko mentions the desire for a 'bold move to remind Washington of Soviet power, to ensure that the Kremlin received the respect it deserved from Washington' as Khrushchev's most likely coequal motive for sending in the missiles, Naftali has since added another likely suspect: Soviet concern over China. But Naftali did not offer the most common variant of the China syndrome – Khrushchev's desire to rebuff Beijing's charges that Moscow was a 'paper tiger' unwilling to stand up to the imperialists – but instead stated that a key reason for deploying the missiles had been a genuine and growing Soviet fear, exacerbated by the Escalante affair, about the extent of Chinese influence in Cuba itself and the risk that the revolution might turn toward their chief, and increasingly bitter, rival for leadership in the world communist movement.

Clearly it is too soon to apportion conclusively the relative importance of the domestic and intra-alliance motives noted above compared to others involved in Khrushchev's perilous step – especially defense of Cuba, the strategic balance, and countering US nuclear deployments on the Soviet periphery (Naftali and Fursenko looked for evidence of a connection to Berlin, but found none) – but the new evidence suggests that explanations and accounts rooted solely in dynamics of East–West relations will ring increasingly hollow.

JFK and Cuba

While the foregoing analysis of the Taiwan Straits and Berlin episodes gives relatively lesser import than in the past to US actions for provoking the crises, in the case of Cuba the evidence that has emerged in the past decade suggests that, while not as foolhardy as Khrushchev's succumbing to nuclear temptation, Kennedy's semi-covert campaign to topple Castro was comparably ill-advised, misguided, irrational, and disproportionate to the stakes involved. Above all, his failure to consider the risk that his military muscle-flexing and covert harassment might provoke Castro and Khrushchev to take desperate countermeasures nearly proved catastrophic. One need hardly dwell on the story of the Kennedy administration's efforts to get rid of the Castro regime between the April 1961 Bay of Pigs debacle and the missile crisis 18 months later – the assassination plots, the Operation Mongoose program of covert operations – which have been known to the general public since the post-Watergate Congressional investigations of the CIA in the mid-1970s.

But the past decade has seen some important shifts in the historiography as well as the emergence of new evidence from both East and West with significant implications for assessing the impact of JFK's policies before and during the crisis. While the Cubans have always viewed the 'October Crisis' as merely the next stage in a running melodrama of *Yanqui* hostility, only in the past decade has this history of US–Cuban bilateral interactions become seriously integrated into the American-centric history of the 'Cuban Missile Crisis', which until then was usually viewed primarily or even exclusively as a US–*Soviet* crisis which happened to take place in Cuba. Since, in this view, Khrushchev's overriding goal had been to alter the nuclear balance rather than to defend Cuba (a claim dismissed by most American officials and analysts as *post factum* propaganda to rationalize his failed gambit), the pre-crisis history of Washington's actions against Havana was generally shunted aside in favor of a recital of an East–West narrative involving the 'missile gap', Vienna, Berlin, etc.

In recent years, additional evidence has disclosed that US military, covert operations, and assassination planning against Castro was more extensive than previously realized, and all but confirmed JFK's personal involvement in them, while Russian evidence has tended to confirm that the 'defense of Cuba' claim had been at least one genuine motive, if not necessarily the decisive one, behind Khrushchev's spring 1962 decision to send the nuclear missiles. In particular, the evidence cited by Naftali and Fursenko suggests that Khrushchev's *personal* commitment to the Cuban revolution came earlier than was previously realized and was clearly deeper than most US officials suspected then or historians believed later.

While not necessarily excluding the likelihood that Khrushchev also desired to improve the USSR's standing in the nuclear balance, the revelation of his genuine commitment to and concern for the survival of the Cuban revolution confirms the need to reassess the consequences of Washington's tough line toward Havana in 1961–62. As Lebow and Stein argue, US as well as Soviet conduct leading up to the missile crisis illustrate the pitfalls of provocative 'threat-based strategies' that encourage mutual escalation rather than moderation.[48] Documents declassified and findings published over the past decade have further illuminated US policies and decisionmaking, especially JFK's personal role, regarding the Bay of Pigs,[49] and the synchronization and intensification of military contingency planning with Operation Mongoose covert operations. The latter indicates serious consideration, if not approval, of some form of military action against Cuba, even prior to the discovery of the nuclear missiles in mid-October or in response to a possible Soviet move against Berlin.[50] We also know more about the level of the Kennedys' knowledge and approval of various assassination plots against Castro.[51]

As important as this stronger evidence of JFK's own willingness to take risks is the lack of any findings (of which this author is aware, at any rate) that any serious studies were undertaken or top-level discussion held to assess the full range of possible Soviet reactions to aggressive US actions, or even hints of actions (such as massive military exercises to practice amphibious landings in the Caribbean), even if they were mere bluffs or contingency plans, that threatened the survival of the Cuban revolution and Castro personally.[52] Washington's apparent insensitivity to the domestic and intra-alliance pressures on Khrushchev may have contributed to this misjudgment, just as the Soviet leader's evident misreading of JFK's domestic political context probably fostered his underestimation of the intensity of the American's likely response to the missiles, regardless of whether they were discovered before or after the Congressional elections in November.

Learning from history? 1962

Given the new evidence on the feckless behavior of both leaders prior to the crisis, the ability of Kennedy and Khrushchev to turn on a dime and pull back from the abyss after the crisis started, and to resist unforeseen developments that could have led to undesired escalation during it, appears even more impressive. As we have learned only since the declassification of Ex Comm tapes and transcripts and other documents since the mid-1980s, JFK seems to have initially leaned toward military action to remove the missiles after learning of their presence on the morning of 16 October, but over the next five days shifted to accepting the option of a blockade ('quarantine') to give diplomacy and political-military pressure short of violence time to work.[53] He also repeatedly rejected pressures for air-strikes or invasion, especially after the fatal downing of Major Anderson's U-2 on 27 October, despite grumbled charges of appeasement from some bellicose military leaders.[54] He coped with, or at least avoided actions that exacerbated the effects of ('managed' is too strong a term), accidents and incidents that could have intensified the crisis;[55] was willing to countenance a deal with Castro that would have left the Cuban revolution in power so long as Havana evicted the Soviets and their missiles;[56] and, finally, became the Excomm's leading 'dove' on 27 October (ready to trade the Jupiters in Turkey for a Soviet withdrawal of the missiles in Cuba covertly and secretly lay the groundwork for a public swap[57] if Khrushchev rejected the private offer).

All of this is in stark contrast to the steely-eyed Cold Warrior who 'went eyeball to eyeball' until the other fellow 'blinked', portrayed by Camelot acolytes and hagiographers in the mid-1960s. Collectively, the evidence now tends to suggest that had Khrushchev not 'blinked' first on the 28th, Kennedy would have done so himself soon thereafter, or perhaps ordered a tightening of the blockade, rather than authorize an invasion of Cuba that risked killing thousands of Soviet personnel and further escalation with all the nuclear implications that entailed (including those involving the tactical nuclear weapons of which Kennedy was unaware). But for JFK to confound Gibbon, he would have had to show a different kind of profile of courage by being willing to back down in the face of severe public pressure.[58]

In light of what we now know about his willingness to risk local nuclear war to defend Cuba, Khrushchev's retreat is even more remarkable, especially since he had to switch gears even more quickly than Kennedy, i.e., in only two days rather than six – between 22 October, when after JFK's speech he defiantly vowed to run the blockade, and 24 October, when he not only resisted suggestions to retaliate by laying a counter-blockade around Berlin (which Kennedy seems to have expected) but also ordered his weapons-carrying ships to stop and turn around rather than dare the Americans to open fire. By the weekend of 26–28 October, even while trying to get the best deal possible, Khrushchev hastily beat a retreat from the confrontation rather than extend it at the increasing risk of a direct military clash with the Americans – especially after receiving a communication from Castro on the night of the 26th (first disclosed in 1990) in which the Cuban urged Khrushchev to be willing to initiate nuclear war in retaliation for a US invasion of Cuba.[59]

The new evidence of the domestic and intra-alliance pressures on Khrushchev make his crisis-resolving decisions even more fortunate than many in the West realized, for he surely sensed that he would have to pay a high price in terms of prestige, in domestic leadership circles, with the Chinese (who sharply criticized him for backing down), and especially, at least in the short term, in his relations with Castro, which were indeed strained both by the outcome of the crisis and by the Soviet leader's failure to consult with Havana both on the inclusion of Turkey in the bargaining and on the 28 October letter to JFK, which essentially accepted US terms, including UN inspection, which Castro angrily rejected.

In his comparative analysis of crises in US foreign policy, Michael Hunt has commented:

> Viewed internationally, a crisis is made up of narratives that seldom overlap, or for that matter even converge, in a way that puts all parties in the same narrative framework. Rather, the distinct narratives intertwine, and as they do, each narrator appropriates narrative fragments from the others, prompting in turn the revision or extension of that party's narrative. Thinking of policymakers as creators of narratives may help us see more clearly the many unpredictable twists a crisis (like a piece of fiction) may take. And thinking of a crisis as the interweaving of narratives spun out by each of the major participants in the crisis underlines not just the complexity but also the subjectivity of the phenomenon we struggle to pin down ...[60]

Perhaps one of the most vital achievements of Kennedy and (especially) Khrushchev at the height of the Cuban Missile Crisis, then, and the most fortunate turn of the 1958–63 'turning points', came when both leaders, facing the national analogue of Johnson's imminent hanging that concentrates the mind, managed to transcend the various competing narratives that had driven them to so many dangerous policy choices over the previous months and years and to link up in a shared narrative that both men, finally, understood – one that stressed mutual survival, avoiding the very real possibility of thermonuclear war, above all others.

The safe resolution of the nuclear crisis in the Caribbean indeed constituted a 'turning point' in the Cold War and, in the words of Zubok and Pleshakov, 'marked the watershed between the first, virulent stage of the Cold War and the second, long period of truce, when the competition between the two superpowers was constrained by a mutual fear of nuclear force'.[61] This chapter does not accept Anders Stephanson's contention that the Cold War essentially did end in 1963,[62] or Gaddis's implicit argument that it could and should have then ended had the United States played its cards correctly (and not become fixated on nuclear weapons as a sensible barometer of political strength as the USSR increasingly become a mono-dimensional, i.e., exclusively militarily competitive, superpower).[63] None the less, it agrees that an essential transformation in the dynamics of the US–Soviet confrontation at the core of the Cold War did occur in these years – a turning point, if one prefers – that constituted a kind of phase change in its history.

Although if Khrushchev's Gorbachevian impulses had extended to accepting a few more on-site inspections it could have ended far more successfully by yielding a comprehensive instead of a limited test ban treaty in the summer of 1963, the aftermath of the missile crisis inaugurated a trend toward greater stability and predictability in US–Soviet bilateral and nuclear arms relations[64] as well as their rivalry in Berlin and Central Europe, although the benefits of the 'Long Peace' did not, alas, extend to certain areas of the Third World in which the superpower rivalry was sublimated. The final break between Moscow and Beijing in the summer of 1963 also helped intensify the trend toward multipolarity which would within a decade lead to the open triangular diplomacy of the early 1970s, and at the same time liberated the Kremlin to pursue a limited détente with Washington and take measures to avoid further crises even if the ideological, political, and even military rivalry hardly abated.

NOTES

1 Edward Gibbon, *The Decline and Fall of the Roman Empire*, abr. edn, ed. and intro. Dero A. Saunders (New York: Penguin Books, 1952, 1985), p. 106.
2 To make the point I'll take three examples, from Sino-Soviet, US–Soviet, and Sino-American relations. In the Sino-Soviet relationship, one finds signs of discord even at the alliance's putative highpoint in 1950 and aspects of cooperation even when it has seemingly dissolved into schism a decade later; and, as for US–Soviet relations, materials in the Lyndon Johnson Library seem to be pushing the origins of 'détente' back to the mid-1960s, even though it did not manifest itself openly until the Nixon–Kissinger eras. Finally, the breakthrough in relations between Washington and Beijing, usually dated to 1971 (the initiation of 'ping-pong diplomacy' and Kissinger's secret trip to the PRC), now must be pulled back at least to the spring of 1969, as Mao's advisers urged a strategic counterweight to Moscow in the wake of the violent clashes along the Sino-Soviet border, and perhaps even to 1968, when Beijing appears to have regarded the Soviet invasion of Czechoslovakia as an ominous indication that the 'Brezhnev Doctrine' enforcing discipline on the socialist commonwealth could also be applied to the Chinese – the real point being that what is usually depicted as Nixon's playing of the 'China card' was no less Mao's playing of an 'American card'.
3 Louis J. Halle, *The Cold War As History*, with a new epilogue (New York: Harper Perennial, 1967; Harper & Row, 1991), p. 138 fn. 2.
4 Jasper Becker, *Hungry Ghosts: Mao's Secret Famine* (New York: Holt, 1996, 1998).
5 For discussions of casualty estimates and Western reactions to the famines caused by the Great Leap, see Becker, *Hungry Ghosts*, chs 18, 20.
6 Chen Jian, *China's Road to the Korean War: The Making of the Sino-American Confrontation* (New York: Columbia University Press, 1994).
7 Thomas J. Christensen, *Useful Adversaries: Grand Strategy, Domestic Mobilization, and Sino-American Conflict, 1947–1958* (Princeton, NJ: Princeton University Press, 1996), esp. pp. 194–241.
8 Michael H. Hunt, *The Genesis of Chinese Communist Foreign Policy* (New York: Columbia University Press, 1996), p. 228.
9 For English translations of some of the new Chinese-language evidence, see 'Mao Zedong's Handling of the Taiwan Straits Crisis of 1958: Chinese Recollections and

Documents', trans. and annot. Li Xiaobing, Chen Jian, and David L. Wilson, *Cold War International History Project Bulletin* [*CWIHPB*], 6–7 (Winter 1995/96): 208–26.

10 Zhai Qiang, *The Dragon, the Lion, and the Eagle: Chinese–British–American Relations, 1949–1958* (Kent, OH: Kent State University Press, 1994), p. 181. Like most other recent analysts, Zhai Qiang sees Mao's initiation of the crisis as stemming from a mixture of factors: 'to stop Chiang's harassment against the mainland, to show Beijing's defiance of the United States, to divert American attention from the Middle East, to contest the Soviet advocacy of détente with the West, as well as to mobilize the domestic population ...'.

11 Shu Guang Zhang, *Deterrence and Strategic Culture: Chinese–American Confrontations, 1949–1958* (Ithaca, NY: Cornell University Press, 1992), pp. 233–5.

12 Li Xiaobing, 'The Second Taiwan Straits Crisis Revisited', paper presented at the Cold War International History Project/University of Hong Kong conference on 'New Evidence on the Cold War in Asia', 9–12 January 1996.

13 See *CWIHPB*, 6–7 (Winter 1995/96): 155–8.

14 For a dissenting view, see Mark Kramer, 'The USSR Foreign Ministry's Appraisal of Sino-Soviet Relations on the Eve of the Split, September 1959', *CWIHPB*, 6–7 (Winter 1995/96): 174. Kramer writes that while not explicitly informed of the imminent shelling of the offshore islands, Khrushchev was told in Beijing 'in general terms' of plans to 'bring Taiwan back under China's jurisdiction' and 'welcomed' the military attacks when they occurred.

15 Vladislav Zubok and Constantine Pleshakov, *Inside the Kremlin's Cold War: From Stalin to Khrushchev* (Cambridge, MA: Harvard University Press, 1996), p. 211.

16 Chen Jian and Yang Kuisong, 'Chinese Politics and the Collapse of the Sino-Soviet Alliance', in Odd Arne Westad, ed., *Brothers in Arms: The Rise and Fall of the Sino-Soviet Alliance, 1945–1963* (Stanford, CA: Woodrow Wilson Center Press/Stanford University Press, 1998).

17 Vladislav M. Zubok, 'Khrushchev and the Berlin Crisis (1958–1962)', CWIHP Working Paper No. 6 (Washington, DC: Wilson Center, May 1993), pp. 6–7; Zubok and Pleshakov, *Inside the Kremlin's Cold War*, pp. 198–9.

18 Hope M. Harrison, in 'Ulbricht and the Concrete "Rose": New Archival Evidence on the Dynamics of Soviet–East German Relations and the Berlin Crisis, 1958–1961', CWIHP Working Paper No. 5 (Washington, DC: Wilson Center, May 1993), p. 9, cites a letter from Soviet Deputy Foreign Minister N. Patolichev to the CPSU CC of 13 August 1958 – ten days before Mao started the shelling of Jinmen – proposing an East German initiative to counter West German unification schemes; the CPSU CC Presidium approved Patolichev's proposal on 15 August and relayed it officially to the East German communist leadership on 23 August, the same day the Taiwan Crisis started. This does not preclude, of course, the possibility that Mao's private rebukes to Khrushchev had prodded him toward more militant action, or that the Far East crisis influenced his subsequent moves, but tends to undermine the theory that the Soviet leader's 27 November ultimatum originated from the desire to match or respond to Beijing's aggressive actions. See also Hope M. Harrison, 'The Bargaining Power of Weaker Allies in Bipolarity and Crisis: The Dynamics of Soviet–East German Relations, 1953–1961' (PhD dissertation, Columbia University, 1993), pp. 162, 212–13.

19 James G. Richter, *Khrushchev's Double Bind: International Pressures and Domestic Coalition Politics* (Baltimore, MD: Johns Hopkins University Press, 1994), p. 115.

20 See Marc Trachtenberg, *History and Strategy* (Princeton, NJ: Princeton University Press, 1991), pp. 169–234 and *A Constructed Peace: The Making of the European*

Settlement, 1945–1963 (Princeton, NJ: Princeton University Press, 1999).

21 See, for example, Douglas Selvage, 'Khrushchev's November 1958 Berlin Ultimatum: New Evidence from the Polish Archives', *CWIHPB*, 11 (Winter 1998): 200–3, on a key conversation between Gomulka and Khrushchev on the eve of the latter's November 1958 ultimatum.

22 See Zubok and Pleshakov, *Inside the Kremlin's Cold War*, pp. 190–2. See Khrushchev's boasting about the impact of his threats during Suez to his colleagues in excerpts from the transcript of the CPSU CC Plenum, 24 and 28 June 1957, *CWIHPB*, 10 (March 1998): 54–5, 60.

23 Quoted in Cyrus Szulzberger, *Last of the Giants* (New York, 1970), p. 860.

24 For Harrison's findings, see 'Ulbricht and the Concrete "Rose"'; and 'The Bargaining Power of Weaker Allies in Bipolarity and Crisis', ch. 4.

25 Bruce Menning, who gained limited access to Soviet general staff archives on the crisis, found comparable cases of military incidents involving GDR harassment of Western officials that occurred without Soviet approval or foreknowledge. See papers presented by Menning at the CWIHP conference on 'New Evidence on Germany and the Cold War, 1945–1962', University of Essen, Germany, June 1994, and at a conference on NATO and Warsaw Pact archives held by the US Army Center for Military History and the US Department of Defense, near Washington, DC, March 1994.

26 Harrison, 'The Bargaining Power of Weaker Allies in Bipolarity and Crisis', p. 248.

27 Richter, *Khrushchev's Double Bind*, pp. 102ff.

28 For the text of the memorandum as well as an introductory essay and annotations, see Vladislav M. Zubok, 'Khrushchev's 1960 Troop Cut: New Russian Evidence', *CWIHPB*, 8–9 (Winter 1996/97): 416–20.

29 Ibid. See also Richter, *Khrushchev's Double Bind*, p. 121.

30 Important English-language works on the Cuban Missile Crisis since the end of the Cold War include Michael R. Beschloss, *The Crisis Years: Kennedy and Khrushchev, 1960–1963* (New York: HarperCollins, 1991); Dino A. Brugioni, *Eyeball to Eyeball: The Inside Story of the Cuban Missile Crisis* (New York: Random House, 1991); James G. Blight, *The Shattered Crystal Ball: Fear and Learning in the Cuban Missile Crisis* (Lanham, MD: Littlefield Adams, 1992); James A. Nathan, ed., *The Cuban Missile Crisis Revisited* (New York: St Martin's Press, 1992); Laurence Chang and Peter Kornbluh, eds, *The Cuban Missile Crisis: A National Security Archive Documents Reader* (New York: New Press, 1992); James G. Blight, Bruce J. Allyn, and David A. Welch, *Cuba on the Brink: Castro, the Missile Crisis, and the Soviet Collapse* (New York: Pantheon, 1993); Scott D. Sagan, *The Limits of Safety: Organizations, Accidents, and Nuclear Weapons* (Princeton, NJ: Princeton University Press, 1994), pp. 53–155; General Anatoli I. Gribkov, *Operation ANADYR: US and Soviet Generals Recount the Cuban Missile Crisis* (Chicago, IL: edition q, 1994); Richard Ned Lebow and Janice Gross Stein, *We All Lost the Cold War* (Princeton, NJ: Princeton University Press, 1994), pp. 19–145; Mark J. White, *The Cuban Missile Crisis* (London: Macmillan, 1996); Mark J. White, *Missiles in Cuba: Kennedy, Khrushchev, Castro and the 1962 Crisis* (Chicago, IL: Ivan R. Dee, 1997); Aleksandr Fursenko and Timothy Naftali, *'One Hell of a Gamble': Khrushchev, Castro, and Kennedy, 1958–1964* (New York: Norton, 1997); Ernest R. May and Philip D. Zelikow, *The Kennedy Tapes: Inside the White House during the Cuban Missile Crisis* (Cambridge, MA: Harvard University Press, 1997); Philip Nash, *The Other Missiles of October: Eisenhower, Kennedy, and the Jupiters, 1957–1963* (Chapel Hill, NC: University of North Carolina Press, 1997); James G. Blight and David A. Welch, eds, *Intelligence and the Cuban Missile Crisis* (London: Frank Cass, 1998); Graham T. Allison and Philip D. Zelikow, *Essence of Decision:*

Explaining the Cuban Missile Crisis, 2nd edn (Chapel Hill, NC: University of North Carolina Press, 1999). Also see the compilations of declassified US documents published by the State Department since 1997: *Foreign Relations of the United States, 1961–1963*, esp. vols X (*Cuba, 1961–Sept. 1962*) and XI (*Cuban Missile Crisis and Aftermath*) and the microfiche compilation to both volumes.

31 See Roger Hilsman, *To Move a Nation: The Politics of Foreign Policy in the Administration of John F. Kennedy* (New York: Dell (paperback edn), 1967), pp. 159, 215, 227. Hilsman decades later acknowledged that the United States did not have evidence that the nuclear-capable tactical weapons had been accompanied by atomic warheads (Hilsman, *The Cuban Missile Crisis: The Struggle Over Policy* (New York: Praeger, 1996), pp. 116–17).

32 See Blight, Allyn, and Welch, *Cuba on the Brink*, pp. 56–63, and Raymond L. Garthoff, 'The Havana Conference on the Cuban Missile Crisis', *CWIHPB*, 1 (Spring 1992): 2–4.

33 The higher figures first appeared in Lieut.-Gen. Anatolii Dokuchaev, '100-dnevnyi yadernyi kruiz', *Krasnaya zvezda*, 6 Nov. 1992, p. 2, and were repeated in Gribkov and Smith, *Operation ANADYR*, p. 4. See Blight, Allyn, and Welch, *Cuba on the Brink*, pp. 356–63, on scholarly reactions to the initial discrepancy. Gribkov elaborated on his disclosures and his reasons for failing to speak openly at a CWIHP oral history workshop at the Wilson Center in Washington, DC on 5 April 1994. There is some confusion as to whether 4 or 6 nuclear mines were sent, and whether they actually arrived, so the number of tactical warheads at issue is between 98 and 104. See Raymond L. Garthoff, 'US Intelligence in the Cuban Missile Crisis', paper presented at the September 1997 CWIHP Wilson Center conference on 'Intelligence and the Cuban Missile Crisis', pp. 32–3, 35–6, fns 24, 46. The Russian Defense Ministry archives and Presidential archives have remained frustratingly out of reach on this issue.

34 See Blight, Allyn, and Welch, *Cuba on the Brink*, pp. 353–6.

35 See Gribkov and Smith, *Operation ANADYR*, pp. 7, 62–3, 181–2.

36 Ibid., p. 63, and Gribkov comments at CWIHP oral history workshop, Wilson Center, Washington, DC, 5 April 1994. Mark Kramer has cited contrary accounts from other Soviet military authorities in Cuba at the time (Kramer, '"Lessons" of the Cuban Missile Crisis for Warsaw Pact Nuclear Operations', *CWIHPB*, 8–9 (Winter 1996/97): 348–54, esp. 349, 353–4, fns 117–8, and 'The Cuban Missile Crisis and Nuclear Proliferation', *Security Studies*, 5:1 (Autumn 1995), pp. 171–9.

37 See Kramer's exchange with Arthur M. Schlesinger, Jr, in *The New York Review of Books*, 28 May 1992, following Schlesinger's account of the Havana conference, 'Four Days with Fidel: A Havana Diary', in the 26 March 1992 issue; Blight, Allyn, and Welch, *Cuba on the Brink*, p. 414 fn. 4; Mark Kramer, 'Tactical Nuclear Weapons, Soviet Command Authority, and the Cuban Missile Crisis', and James G. Blight, Bruce J. Allyn, and David A. Welch, 'Kramer vs. Kramer: Or, How Can You Have Revisionism in the Absence of Orthodoxy?', both in *CWIHPB*, 3 (Fall 1993): 40, 42–6 and 41, 47–50; James G. Blight and David A. Welch, 'Risking "The Destruction of Nations": Lessons of the Cuban Missile Crisis for New and Aspiring Nuclear States', *Security Studies*, 4:4 (Summer 1994), pp. 811–50; Kramer, 'The Cuban Missile Crisis and Nuclear Proliferation'; James G. Blight and David A. Welch, 'On Historical Judgment and Inference: A Reply to Mark Kramer', *Security Studies*, 5:4 (Summer 1996): 172–82; and Mark Kramer, '"Lessons" of the Cuban Missile Crisis for Warsaw Pact Nuclear Operations', *CWIHPB*, 8–9 (Winter 1996/97): 348–54, esp. 349.

38 Fursenko and Naftali, *'One Hell of a Gamble'*, pp. 206–13.

39 Ibid., pp. 212, 243; and Gribkov and Smith, *Operation ANADYR*, pp. 5–6, 183.

40 Aleksandr Fursenko and Timothy Naftali, 'The Pitsunda Decision: Khrushchev and Nuclear Weapons', *CWIHPB*, 10 (March 1998): 223–7. But also see Raymond L. Garthoff, 'New Evidence on the Cuban Missile Crisis: Khrushchev, Nuclear Weapons, and the Cuban Missile Crisis', *CWIHPB*, 11 (Winter 1998): 251–62, which takes a more skeptical view of the idea that the new evidence supports the assertion that Khrushchev's sending of additional tactical nuclear weapons to Cuba in September 1962 constituted an 'embrace of a nuclear warfighting strategy'.

41 Ironically, had Khrushchev deployed *only* tactical nuclear weapons which could not reach the United States, suitable only for defensive use, and publicly announced their existence as a deterrent to an invasion of Cuba, he might well have got away with it – at least, Kennedy would have had a far harder time depicting such a deployment as a grave threat to US security and rousing the public and the Western world behind him for a firm response, including the threat of military force, to compel Moscow to withdraw them.

42 Fursenko and Naftali, 'The Pitsunda Decision', p. 225.

43 As evidenced in late May 1962 by the Novocherkassk workers' uprising. For released Russian documents on the crushing of the protest, see *Russian Social Science Review*, 33:5 (1992).

44 Even after the Bay of Pigs, US officials could not put themselves in Khrushchev's shoes sufficiently to see that he might take action comparable to US policy in Europe and Berlin, and most subsequent analysts (e.g., Graham Allison) dismissed the possibility. See Allison, *Essence of Decision*, pp. 47–50, and the author's previous comment in Hershberg, 'Before "The Missiles of October": Did Kennedy Plan a Military Strike Against Cuba?', in Nathan, ed., *The Cuban Missile Crisis Revisited*, p. 278 fn. 116.

45 John Lewis Gaddis, *We Now Know: Rethinking Cold War History* (Oxford: Oxford University Press, 1996), p. 263.

46 The present author is working on an article on the Kennedy Administration's response to reports of Soviet–Cuban tensions and its consideration of the possibility of trying to establish a secret dialogue with Castro in 1962, possibly through third parties.

47 Fursenko and Naftali, *'One Hell of a Gamble'*, p. 183.

48 Lebow and Stein, *We All Lost the Cold War*, chs 1–6.

49 See, e.g., James G. Blight and Peter Kornbluh, eds, *Politics of Illusion: The Bay of Pigs Invasion Reexamined* (Boulder, CO: Lynne Rienner Publishers, 1998).

50 See Hershberg, 'Before "The Missiles of October": Did Kennedy Plan a Military Strike Against Cuba?' *passim*. But also see the qualification in Hershberg, 'New Evidence on the Cuban Missile Crisis: More Documents from the Russian Archives', *CWIHPB*, 8–9 (Winter 1996/97): 271–2, 276–7 fns 8–11.

51 See, e.g., Seymour M. Hersh, *The Dark Side of Camelot* (Boston, MA: Little, Brown, 1997), ch. 17.

52 Some former senior Kennedy Administration officials, such as McNamara, have conceded that Soviet or Cuban leaders could reasonably have got the impression in 1962 that Washington intended to invade, even while vehemently denying that this was the case.

53 See Excomm records of 15–22 October in May and Zelikow, *The Kennedy Tapes*.

54 See May and Zelikow, *The Kennedy Tapes*, for many examples in which military leaders urged an air strike or invasion and express frustration at his evident reluctance to authorize an attack.

55 As detailed in Sagan, *The Limits of Safety*.

56 The present author is working on an article on this episode.

57 On JFK's views during the Excomm discussions on 27 October, see the minutes and

transcripts of the sessions (originally published in *International Security* in its Summer 1985 and Winter 1987/88 issues) in May and Zelikow, *The Kennedy Tapes*; for documents on the secret arrangement on the Jupiters, see Jim Hershberg, 'Anatomy of a Controversy: Anatoly F. Dobrynin's Meeting with Robert F. Kennedy, 27 October 1962', *CWIHPB*, 5 (Spring 1995): 75, 77–80, and Hershberg, 'More on Bobby and the Cuban Missile Crisis', *CWIHPB*, 8–9 (Winter 1996/97): 274, 344–7; on the 'Cordier Ploy', in which JFK laid the groundwork for a public trade, see James G. Blight and David A. Welch, *On the Brink: Americans and Soviets Reexamine the Cuban Missile Crisis* (2nd edn, New York: Noonday, 1990), pp. 83–4. See also Lawrence Freedman, *Kennedy's Crisis Years: Berlin, Cuba, Laos and Vietnam* (New York: Oxford University Press, 2000).

58 In terms of intra-alliance pressures, Kennedy faced fewer obstacles to a compromise settlement than Khrushchev, for, despite subsequent claims that a trade over the Turkish Jupiters would have threatened NATO, probably most Western European allies, especially the British (who had never been especially upset over Cuba and thought the Americans overwrought on the issue), would have been relieved at a compromise – whereas the Kremlin leader had to deal with hard-line views in Havana and Beijing who, on the surface at least, appeared gung-ho for battle.

59 See Blight, Allyn, and Welch, *Cuba on the Brink*, apps, for English translations of the relevant Castro–Khrushchev correspondence, which was first disclosed in the third volume (*Khrushchev Remembers: The Glasnost Tapes*) of the Soviet leader's tape-recorded memoirs.

60 Michael H. Hunt, *Crises in US Foreign Policy: An International History Reader* (New Haven, CT: Yale University Press, 1996), p. 425.

61 Zubok and Pleshakov, *Inside the Kremlin's Cold War*, pp. 236–7.

62 Professor Stephanson made this argument in the course of a 14-part essay on the electronic discussion group H-DIPLO in, I believe, 1996.

63 Gaddis, *We Now Know*, pp. 291–2.

64 With the possibly crucial exception of the US–Soviet crisis of late 1983, depending on the accuracy of the claim by Oleg Gordievsky that the open political tensions accompanied a largely secret nuclear crisis that marked the most dangerous moment since the Cuban Missile Crisis. For an exploration of the possible implications of this account for the thesis that nuclear weapons exerted an increasingly 'stabilizing' effect on the Cold War after 1962 as both powers reaped the benefits of 'nuclear learning', see James G. Hershberg, 'Reconsidering the Nuclear Arms Race: The Past as Prelude?', in Gordon Martel, ed., *American Foreign Relations Reconsidered, 1890–1993* (London: Routledge, 1993), pp. 187–210.

15

Ironies and Turning Points:
Détente in Perspective

Jussi M. Hanhimäki

It was probably Urho Kekkonen's greatest moment. The early August 1975 meeting at Helsinki's Finlandia Hall was the largest such meeting in post-war history to date. It brought together representatives from 35 countries. Among them were all European countries except for Albania (but including the USSR, the United States, and Canada). The representatives, who included such men as Gerald R. Ford and Leonid I. Brezhnev, had gathered in the Finnish capital to sign the Helsinki Final Act, the concluding document of the Conference for Security and Cooperation in Europe (CSCE), a result of several years of painstaking negotiations. Some observers referred to the gathering in Helsinki as the peace conference that finally ended World War II in Europe. Others would describe the entire process as one in which 'never have so many struggled for so long over so little'.[1] Be that as it may, Kekkonen, the Finnish President who acted as the formal host of the conference, surely deserved some acclaim for the undertaking that was one of the more visible moments of the détente process. Surely, his 'bridge-building' efforts were worthy of international recognition. Perhaps Kekkonen even deserved the Nobel Peace Prize?

This was, undoubtedly, Kekkonen's view and that of his supporters at home and elsewhere (not least in the USSR). In fact, according to a recent biography of Kekkonen, the Finnish President was one of the 'front-runners' in the fall of 1975 when the Norwegian Nobel Committee, at the time headed by Aase Lionaes, made its final decision. Kekkonen lost. To the Committee's mind, a gentleman named Andrei Sakharov was more deserving of the award.[2]

The reason why I decided to open this chapter with this piece of Nobel Peace Prize history is not because I think that Kekkonen suffered some grave injustice in 1975. Nor is it because the first version of this chapter was delivered at a symposium supported by the Norwegian Nobel Institute, or because this chapter will feature a number of other Peace Prize winners (such as Willy Brandt and Henry Kissinger) and runners-up (Richard Nixon). Instead, I raise it because it seems to me that the two men in question illustrate some of the major points that I wish to make about détente as a turning point.

Both candidacies were based largely on the conclusion of the Helsinki Accords in August 1975, one of the highlights of European détente. Yet, I would argue, the two men represented two very different aspects of détente. On the one hand, Kekkonen's candidacy was based on his role as the facilitator of the conference. Aside from bolstering his own considerable ego, Kekkonen had been pushing for the conference since the late 1960s because he thought it was important for Finland's national interest, international image, and stable relations with the Soviet Union.[3] Kekkonen's achievement was in facilitating an agreement that did, as a number of observers have pointed out, end the post-war era in Europe; an agreement that, in the minds of Kekkonen as well as of many others in Finland, the USSR, and elsewhere, stabilized the division of Europe.

Sakharov, on the other hand, was the human rights candidate, whose selection was influenced (but hardly determined) by the part of the treaty (Basket III) that recognized human rights as an aspect of international security. While he was an internationally renowned human rights advocate and the first Soviet citizen to receive the Peace Prize, Sakharov's open criticism of the treatment of dissidents in the USSR had for a long time been a thorn in the Kremlin's flesh. It came as no surprise to most, then, that the Soviet press branded Sakharov an 'enemy of détente' and called him a 'Judas for whom the Nobel Peace Prize was thirty pieces of silver from the West'.[4] Accordingly Sakharov was denied a visa and prevented from attending the ceremonies in Oslo.

The two men thus illustrate the multifaceted role of détente as, for lack of a better term, a turning point. There was the 'Kekkonen side', a non-ideological strand that was meant to formalize a state of affairs and recognize the status quo of the Cold War. And there was the 'Sakharov side', a challenge, based largely on moral and ideological arguments, to the legitimacy of the Cold War order, or at least to the legitimacy of the totalitarian rule that was endemic on one side of that order.

In this chapter I will argue that détente was a turning point in at least three ways. First, it meant an end to the post-war adjustment to the division of Europe (and 'the world'). Second, it meant a beginning of a new phase in the Cold War characterized by ongoing, if not always successful, negotiations (SALT, CSCE, etc). Third, and perhaps most importantly, détente of the early 1970s had a long-term impact: that is, it accelerated the process of exchanges between East and West, a process that, it seems safe to argue, bore fruit in the late 1980s as the communist order in Eastern Europe and the Soviet Union collapsed peacefully. What I would contend then, is simply that in both its European and Soviet–American varieties détente was a significant turning point in the history of the Cold War; in part because of the treaties signed, but even more so due to the processes it either accelerated or set in motion.

A new kind of Soviet–American relationship?

The course of Soviet–American détente is well known. And while its origins may be traced back to various points, even as early as the mid-1960s, there is no question that its best-known phase was the Nixon–Kissinger years, particularly the three years between 1971 and 1974. This was, naturally, the period that included the 1971 'conceptual breakthroughs' in the Backchannel, the Moscow Summit of 1972 where the SALT I agreements were signed, the Summit of 1973 that led to the PNW agreement, and the 1974 tentative SALT II agreements of Vladivostok (agreements that Nixon – having bowed out of office in August 1974 – could only watch from the sidelines).[5] It was also a time when the term 'triangular diplomacy' became a permanent part of our vocabulary, particularly after the announcement of Kissinger's secret trip to China in July 1971 and the Nixon visit in February of the following year. By the 1972 US presidential elections, as Robert Schulzinger notes, even the critics, both at home and abroad, 'could only mutter and look embarrassed as Nixon and Kissinger rewrote the script of post-World War II foreign policy'.[6]

All in all, it was a remarkable set of deals and summits that constituted a significant break with the atmosphere of the late 1960s, when America's growing involvement in Vietnam and the Warsaw Pact's invasion of Czecho-slovakia had marred the tentative efforts at détente made during that decade. The early 1970s also stood in extremely sharp contrast to the crisis years of the late 1950s and early 1960s that Jim Hershberg discusses in chapter 14. Whereas the Soviets and the Americans had been, in October 1962, on the brink of nuclear confrontation, they signed, less than ten years later, the first strategic arms limitation agreement. From the American perspective, more-over, there were the deliciously promising prospects that the normalization of Sino-American relations in the early 1970s and the apparently permanent split in Sino-Soviet relations, had opened up. Suddenly, at the end of Nixon's first term, the United States was back in the driver's seat of international relations. It would appear even more firmly in that seat with the January 1973 Paris settlement that enabled the United States to bring back its last remaining troops from Vietnam. As Henry Kissinger reminisces, in early 1973 'we were confident that in the second term we would travel the road of our hopes and that we would walk a path leading to a better future'.[7]

One should bear in mind that the principal actors on the American side (Kissinger and Nixon) had relatively modest goals in their quest for détente. It was not aimed at ending the Cold War but rather at changing the methods and framework used to fight it. After all, the SALT agreements notwith-standing, surely one must acknowledge that Nixon was right when he promised in his inaugural address that we were entering 'an era of negotiations'.[8] Indeed, even if the Nixon–Kissinger détente doctrine failed to deliver a new 'global equilibrium' or a true 'structure of peace', it did introduce some vital – and given the Vietnam War crucial – restraints for American foreign policy.

As David C. Hendrickson puts it in his review of William Bundy's *A Tangled Web* (a highly critical account of foreign policymaking in the Nixon years), Nixon and Kissinger managed 'to de-emphasise the ideological warfare of the preceding generation [and thus] gave American diplomacy considerable flexibility and resilience, constituting valuable warnings against the over-reaching of the previous epoch and important insurance against the prospect of the unilateral abdication that then beckoned'.[9] In short, from the perspective of American foreign policy, of Soviet–American relations, of international relations at large, the characterisation of the early 1970s as a turning point is not only justified, it is an unalterable fact.

And yet, one might wonder if all this was in vain. While the early 1970s can be seen as having launched a new American approach *vis-à-vis* the Soviet Union, things began to go wrong very soon after 1972. Indeed, it is obvious that the hopes and promises of the early 1970s for a permanent shift in the Soviet–American relationship were not to be realized. Soviet–American détente began to fall apart as domestic troubles plagued the second – and only half-completed – Nixon administration, and as the Americans and Soviets engaged in a proxy contest for influence in the Middle East. After Nixon's ignoble exit in August 1974 this decline of détente only accelerated as the term itself became so unpopular in the United States that Gerald Ford banned its use in his 1976 presidential campaign. And while a SALT II treaty was eventually signed during the Carter Administration in 1979, that agreement was, even at the time of its signing, doomed to failure – a failure confirmed by American domestic opposition to such a deal. In the early 1980s a new Cold War (or a second Cold War) was under way, spurred on by Ronald Reagan's confrontational rhetoric and a renewed arms race.[10] By that time the new kind of Soviet–American relationship that Nixon and Kissinger had envisioned was surely a thing of the past.

Out of control: Détente and Soviet globalism

In fact, it had become clear already by the time Nixon left office in 1974 that the ideas of concreteness, restraint, and linkage that Kissinger in his memoirs identified as the keys to the new Soviet–American relationship did not work. In particular, these notions did not allow the United States any significant amount of 'control over Soviet behavior'. Sticks and carrots simply did not work the way they were supposed to when it came down to Soviet–American relations in the Third World. If anything, the Soviets got out of control in the mid and late 1970s as they intervened more boldly and at increasing frequency in Africa and, in an ultimate show of misjudgment, sent their troops to Afghanistan.

Why did the Soviets intervene in the 1970s more boldly and more globally than before? There are two possible reasons. The first was, of course, the fact that while Kissinger and Nixon may have preached restraint and talked about not seeking unilateral advantages, they did not themselves always practice what they preached. An example of this might be the 1973 Middle East war and the peace process that followed. Kissinger may have acted in a more even-handed manner *vis-à-vis* the principal adversaries in the regional crisis than his predecessors did in the 1960s but the prize that was awarded after extensive shuttle diplomacy was a clearly enhanced American role in the region.[11] For the Soviets, however, this coincided with their own diminished influence. While blaming the lack of concerted cooperation on America's NATO allies 'jealousy' over joint Soviet–American efforts, Kissinger privately acknowledged to Anatoly Dobrynin the basic fact that 'détente had its limits' when it came down to regional conflicts. Thus, to the Soviets the Americans' successful quest for increased influence in the Middle East surely translated to a 'unilateral advantage' and an indication that Washington was more than happy to maximize its power in a particular region (witness also the increased aid given to the Shah of Iran immediately after the 1972 Soviet–American summit in Moscow).[12]

So why should the Soviet Union not do the same? After all, viewed through the lenses of Soviet leaders, détente had been possible because the Americans had finally been convinced that the USSR was their approximate equal. That much had, after all, been recognized in the SALT agreements that were based on the assumption of nuclear parity. The legitimacy of the Soviet hold in Eastern Europe was, moreover, in the process of being recognized as well (see below) only a few years after the USSR had aroused moral outrage by the Warsaw Pact invasion of Prague. If anything, détente appeared to acknowledge Moscow's stature as the other legitimate superpower at the time when America's power was waning. And, if the Soviet Union was now a superpower, it surely had the right to act in that manner; it had gained the right to be more than a mere regional power in Eastern Europe. In short, instead of allowing the US more control over Soviet behavior, détente may actually have encouraged the new interventionism that was evident in the USSR's support to communist revolutionaries in Angola, Ethiopia, Somalia, and elsewhere.[13] If the American goal in implementing détente had been to create a new kind of geopolitical equilibrium – or 'a structure of peace' as Nixon liked to call it – then the Soviets refused to play ball.

The American inability to control Soviet behavior via a selective use of carrots and sticks was particularly evident in the different ways in which Americans and Soviets interpreted the end of the Vietnam War. According to his memoirs, Kissinger, for one, assumed that the January 1973 Paris Peace Accords somehow enhanced the 'prestige' of the Nixon Administration and freed his hands to, among other things, 'turn confidently to the Third World'.[14]

Ironically, the reaction in Moscow was quite similar if based on a diametrically opposite view of the significance of Washington's exit from Indochina. To the Soviets, as to much of the rest of the world, the end of the Vietnam

War in no way enhanced American prestige. Rather, it did the opposite. As Iliya Gaiduk argues, the Soviets, already in a triumphant mood because of the American acknowledgment of nuclear parity, were encouraged to turn even more 'confidently' to the Third World by the American withdrawal from Vietnam and the anti-interventionist domestic scene in the United States. As Gaiduk puts it: 'inspired by its gains and by the decline of US prestige resulting from Vietnam and domestic upheaval, the Soviet leadership adopted a more aggressive and rigid foreign policy, particularly in the Third World'.[15] It seemed that – notwithstanding the debacle with the People's Republic of China – history was, indeed, on the side of the Soviet Union.

Ideology, moralism, and realpolitik

Another reason why a lasting détente proved impossible was in the inability to minimize the role of ideology and moralism in the context of Soviet–American relations. This was, Kissinger would remind us, not for the lack of effort from the American side. Indeed, as he argues in *Diplomacy*, Kissinger thought that Nixon 'was the first president since Theodore Roosevelt to conduct American foreign policy largely in the name of the national interest'.[16] In the context of Kissinger's own thinking in the early 1970s this meant that during the Nixon Administration the United States moved away from the ideological excesses of the previous decade. And, to be sure, given both the disillusionment at home and the nature of the post-Khrushchev Soviet leadership, time appeared ripe for the purging of ideological excesses from the conduct of Soviet–American relations.

But even Kissinger, no matter how many *realpolitik* rabbits he pulled out of his hat, could not achieve the impossible. He could not stop Americans from moralizing, from criticizing the European-style *realpolitik* that was never far from Kissinger's approach. Indeed, because of his immense success in terms of the 'rabbits' (SALT, opening to China, ending the Vietnam War, etc.), when things went wrong the only logical reaction at home was a shift toward overmoralizing and overideologizing, be it in the form of Carter's human rights agenda or Reagan's return to the rhetorical style of John Foster Dulles. While part of such moralizing was undoubtedly due to the unfolding of Watergate that cast a shadow over the often secret machinations of the Nixon–Kissinger team, the fundamental problem was that when one stripped away the drama surrounding, say, the opening to China, there was little domestic consensus – and even less enthusiastic support – for a foreign policy that, to most observers, appeared devoid of moral principles.[17]

When it came down to the Soviets, one could argue that while détente did not necessarily increase the role of ideology in the conduct of Soviet foreign policy, the encouraging signs of American decline in the early 1970s surely strengthened the conviction inside the Kremlin that the Soviet system was ripe for expansion. Indeed, there had always been an uneasy coexistence between communist ideology, the Russian imperial past, and the penchant for *real-politik* in the conduct of Soviet foreign policy. In fact, the two were part of the same package that Vladislav Zubok and Constantine Pleshakov, in their account of foreign policymaking inside the Kremlin during the Stalin and Khrushchev years, like to refer to as the revolutionary-imperial paradigm.[18]

I would therefore maintain that while ideology alone hardly explains Soviet imperial posturing in, say, Angola or the Horn of Africa during the 1970s, the appearance that the capitalist world was in retreat certainly convinced many that the socialist alternative was on the rise. As one Politburo member put it in December 1977: '*Détente* is creating favorable conditions for the struggle for national liberation and social progress.'[19] Whether one reads this as a genuine ideological statement or as a statement made to justify Soviet imperial involvement in Africa, it indicates that the Soviet leadership saw no difficulty in reconciling the new interventionism in the Third World with Soviet–American détente.

Unexpected outcomes

Viewed with the benefit of post-Cold War hindsight, therefore, Soviet–American détente of the early 1970s had two significant but mostly unexpected outcomes. The most glaring one was that the Nixon–Kissinger détente doctrine and the Soviet–American rapprochement of the early 1970s seem to have encouraged the opposite type of Soviet behaviour than that for which Nixon and Kissinger had hoped. To be sure, as Odd Arne Westad has pointed out, the Soviet role in, say, the Angolan civil war of 1974–76 was perhaps justified by both strategic and ideological convictions. Nevertheless, the new Soviet interventionism was ultimately the result of inflated expectations. These expectations were in turn encouraged by the (to the Soviets) accumulating evidence of American weakness – retreat from Vietnam, anti-interventionist domestic opinion, the acceptance of nuclear parity with the Soviet Union – and not tempered by the confrontation with China. It was their view of the future that convinced the Kremlin to make moves that would confirm its place in the sun as the other, truly global, superpower.[20]

On the other hand, this Soviet behavior worked in the long term to weaken rather than to strengthen the Soviet Union. That is, as the USSR embarked on its adventures in Africa and elsewhere, it engaged in the type of exercise that fits so well into Paul Kennedy's notion about the decline of great powers.[21] The Soviets were about to discover, as had the Americans in Vietnam, that acquiring allies in the Third World was a complicated affair, one in which the superpower could rarely meet the expectations it fed by its initial instalments of aid, and one in which the return for your investment was rarely, if at all, measurable. Indeed, 'going global' with far less impressive resources than the United States proved not only costly to the USSR but, possibly, detrimental.

With the great benefit of hindsight one can argue that the ultimate irony of the Soviet–American détente of the early 1970s is that by encouraging the sort of behaviour it was meant to discourage, the Nixon–Kissinger détente doctrine actually promoted the eventual collapse of the USSR, the ultimate goal of post-war American foreign policy. It did not, however, come about the way the designers of containment or, for that matter, the practitioners of détente had thought it would. The Soviet Union did not, after all, collapse because the United States and its Western allies had effectively contained its expansion. Rather, it was the belief that the tide of history was on the Kremlin's side that contributed to the demise of the Soviet state as the aging Brezhnev Politburo embarked on those adventures that Kissinger's principles of restraint and linkage were meant to prevent.[22] A similar irony was experienced within the context of European détente.

European détente: end of the post-war era

While its origins and process were closely linked to those of Soviet–American détente, European détente did have a life of its own. On the one hand, the issues involved in the East–West détente process in Europe were different from those discussed between Soviet and American leaders; instead of nuclear arms the Europeans focused on a wider range of issues from economic and cultural exchanges between East and West to the formalization of Europe's post-war borders. On the other hand, European détente was, far more than its Soviet–American sibling, a dynamic process that stretched from the mid-1960s well into the 1980s when superpower détente was already dead on its tracks.[23]

While the origins of European détente can be traced to the fragmentation of the European alliance systems (e.g., France's exit from NATO's integrated military structure in 1966) and the independent initiatives of Charles De Gaulle in the mid-1960s, the signing of the main treaties associated with the process coincided with Soviet–American détente.[24] The first set of these agreements included the 1970 Soviet–West German and Polish–West German Treaties, the September 1971 four power agreement on Berlin, and the December 1972 Basic Treaty between East and West Germany. All of these were, either directly or indirectly, results of the changes that had taken place in West German foreign policy during the 1960s as Bonn's foreign policy shifted from the Adenauer-era Hallstein Doctrine to the *Ostpolitik* advocated by Willy Brandt's Social Democratic Party.[25]

European détente thus appeared to signal an end to the ongoing squabbles about the division of Germany, the main prize in post-war Europe. With the 1970–72 treaties and the signing of the CSCE in 1975 it appeared, at least to the Soviet and East German leaders, as though there would now be permanently two Germanies.[26] That the 1968 Warsaw Pact invasion of Czechoslovakia had passed without much more than a series of moral condemnations from the United States and its NATO allies gave credibility to the belief that the West had, in fact, approved – or at least accepted as unalterable fact – Soviet hegemony in Eastern Europe. As Anatoly Dobrynin reminisces, 'the relatively weak Western reaction to the invasion of Czechoslovakia proved to Moscow that Western governments were not prepared to commit themselves militarily on the territory of the Warsaw Treaty powers'. (Significantly, he adds that 'this weighed in the balance in the Kremlin when it decided on a new invasion, in Afghanistan, slightly more than a decade later'.[27])

If this was the lesson learned in the Kremlin in 1968 there can be little doubt that the Soviet leaders assumed, and many in the West disapprovingly feared, that the 1975 Helsinki Accords' Basket I that spelled out the 'inviolability of borders' was equal to a multilateral acknowledgment of the legitimacy of Soviet control in Eastern Europe. Indeed, on one level, the CSCE appeared to be the peace conference that finally formalized the status quo of Cold War Europe. With some justification James Mayall and Cornelia Navari could, therefore, title their 1980 selection of documents on détente *The End of the Post-War Era*.[28] Yet, much as in the case of superpower détente there were unexpected outcomes associated with both the CSCE process and détente in general.

Engagement and erosion

If détente ended Europe's post-war era it also meant the acceleration of a new dynamic process of economic and cultural exchanges that was going to climax in 1989. One should note, though, that this was hardly evident to observers until after the end of the Cold War. In 1980, for example, Mayall and Navari maintained that

> although *détente* had finally ended the post-war period, it had not given rise to a new international order. Rather, it had created an entirely new and uncomfortable context of relations for all the great powers, a context which was to require an entirely new set of rules; and *détente* itself could not provide those rules.[29]

It was, perhaps, a valid observation at the time, although the emphasis put on 'great power relations' itself betrays a certain narrowness of perspective. Indeed, six years later Vojtech Mastny applauded the same facets of détente in general and the Helsinki process in particular that Mayall and Navari had found so disappointing in 1980. According to Mastny, the 'open-endedness of the Helsinki process' was its greatest strength, because it 'served to expand the substance of security by inducing its participants to redefine their concepts of security and relate them to human rights'.[30] If one compares Mastny's 1986 statement with two other observations, written with the benefit of post-Cold War hindsight, the growing stock of the CSCE process becomes even clearer.

First, take Henry Kissinger, who in the 1970s was rather skeptical about the value of the CSCE, particularly its human rights agenda.[31] In his 1994 book *Diplomacy* however, Kissinger writes that: '[the CSCE] came to play an important dual role: in its planning stages, it moderated Soviet conduct in Europe and, afterward, it accelerated the collapse of the Soviet Empire'.[32] Second, take Raymond Garthoff – rarely to be found in agreement with Kissinger – who writes in *Détente and Confrontation*

> *Détente* in Europe developed naturally, involving countries and peoples more than political acts and institutions. It emerged on a much more solid basis than the later, more dramatic rise of US–Soviet *détente* precisely because it involved the interests of peoples rather than just the sometimes fickle interests of leaders.[33]

What both Kissinger and Garthoff appear to be saying is that European détente was far more than a process of negotiations (although even this, as Kissinger acknowledges, was rather significant). While the CSCE may not have created a new set of rules of behavior between states, European détente prompted and accelerated a set of challenges 'from below' that transformed the East–West relationship. If the operative word that characterized this relationship had previously been 'division', the relationship during détente was best described by the term 'engagement'. If pre-détente European international relations had been about erecting walls between East and West, détente era European international relations focused on building bridges.

This was evident in two ways. First, the Human Rights Basket (Basket III) of the CSCE had, as is now widely acknowledged, a far-reaching impact. Indeed, to paraphrase Mastny, one of the reasons why European détente was a major turning point, was the introduction of the notion that human rights mattered in the general framework of European international relations. Andrei Sakharov's selection as the recipient of the 1975 Nobel Peace Prize foreshadowed a decade-and-a-half long process during which men like Vaclav Havel, Lech Walesa, and Sakharov challenged, eventually successfully, totalitarian rule in Eastern Europe and the USSR.[34]

One of the ironies of this process was that very few of the signatories of the Helsinki Accords foresaw the challenge that such a 'soft' issue as human rights would eventually present to the Cold War order. It was certainly not envisioned by Leonid Brezhnev when he traveled to Helsinki in 1975, triumphant that he was about to achieve what had eluded his predecessors: a multilateral acknowledgment of the legitimacy of the Soviet bloc. Indeed, as Anatoly Dobrynin puts it, the Third Basket of the Helsinki Accords 'gradually became the manifesto of the dissident and liberal movement, a development totally beyond the imagination of the Soviet leadership'.[35]

Similarly, one needs to add, the ultimately successful challenge of the human rights advocates was, in 1975, beyond the imagination of most Western leaders. While Henry Kissinger, for example, may hail the CSCE as a key achievement in retrospect, he had, in the early 1970s, little interest in the Helsinki process. Indeed, for Kissinger, the CSCE was a sideshow that remained, perhaps understandably, secondary to the more pressing needs of Soviet–American relations, triangular diplomacy, or the 1973–74 crisis in the Middle East. What made things worse for him was that the spin given to the CSCE during the 1976 presidential elections in the United States was almost wholly negative.[36]

If Basket III had its unexpected long-term consequences, perhaps even more important in the long term was the role of economic relations, underlined in Basket II of the Helsinki Accords. While the détente era in Europe saw no birth of a stable pan-European economic structure, it did, in the long run, provoke a deepening crisis of expectations in the Soviet bloc that was to undermine the future of what Harriet Friedmann calls 'Warsaw Pact Socialism'. As Friedmann argues, however, the real 'culprit' for this crisis was not détente or the CSCE process but another development, largely unrelated to détente that may, in the 1970s, have added to the Soviet leaders apparent sense of their nation's growing power *vis-à-vis* the West.[37]

This was the oil crisis in 1973 that enhanced the Soviets' position as a global oil exporter. Ironically, the increased exports to the West and the growing hard currency earnings of the USSR also meant that the price of Soviet oil went up for East Europeans who, while looking Westwards for increased trade, were heavily dependent on Soviet energy resources. Although the USSR continued to subsidize its oil sales to Eastern Europe, the latter region was, as Friedmann puts it, increasingly 'caught in the scissors of deteriorating terms of trade with both the USSR and the West'.[38] That is, not only did Soviet oil prices go up in the 1970s but East European exports to Western Europe were not competitive enough in Western markets, and the Soviets, instead of using their oil earnings to restructure their internal economy or to increase purchases from Eastern Europe, used their hard currency to purchase consumer goods from the West. Because most of the superior Western goods were available only in elite specialist stores, the benefits of the Soviet 'oil boom' were, at best, meager for the average Soviet citizen.

Thus, the energy crisis in the West had an abundantly ironic impact on the Soviet bloc. While initially it may have increased the confidence of some Soviet leaders in their economic ability to embark on costly external adventures (see above), the mismanagement of the proceeds did little to promote the integration of Warsaw Pact economies. In fact, it drove the East Europeans to borrow increasingly from the West and further eroded the legitimacy of socialism by creating internal barriers between the privileged and the underprivileged. Moreover, even the limited access to Western goods heightened internal pressures within a number of Soviet bloc countries and highlighted the inferiority of the socialist system in providing consumer goods to its citizens.

The limited economic opening to the West that took place during détente thus served to strengthen what one could call the 'magnet effect'. This is perhaps best summarized by Vladislav Zubok, who has pointed out that while the Kremlin's effort to partially integrate the East with the West may have had some positive economic benefits for the Soviet bloc,

> its strategic consequence was very negative for the integrity of the Soviet regime. The new emphasis on foreign imports was undermining the autarkic ethos in East European and Soviet economies, and at the same time was preparing a revolution of expectations in Eastern European countries and inside Soviet elites who began to dream of Western goods and living standards.[39]

If the human rights provisions of the CSCE had given a certain legitimacy to Soviet dissidents, Soviet economic mismanagement and the inherent problems of Warsaw Pact Socialism were to provide the socioeconomic background against which the dissidents' voices would resonate loudly in the 1980s.

The ironies of détente

There is no question that détente did not change the era of Cold War confrontation to one of East–West cooperation. And yet, one can hardly argue in retrospect that Nixon was wrong when he proclaimed in his inaugural address in early 1969 that we were entering 'an era of negotiations'. Ironically, those negotiations remained within certain parameters and were restricted by the boundaries that were a legacy of previous decades' uncompromising positions. While there were numerous and sometimes crucial agreements, there was to be no end to confrontation and competition. Indeed, the qualitative change that détente brought to the Soviet–American, and broader East–West, relationship is aptly described by John L. Gaddis, who maintains that détente 'institutionalized negotiations as a form of Cold War competition'.[40]

While this may be the case détente also left far-reaching and crucially important legacies that became evident only in the 1980s. In fact, while détente did not end the Cold War, it may have accelerated the ending of it. The misreading of an American willingness to negotiate with the USSR and Washington's ignoble exit from Vietnam as signs of weakness, along with the inflated notion of one's power that may have been translated into the heads of a number of Soviet leaders during détente, surely helped these leaders to assume that in the second half of the 1970s the time was ripe for a global grab, or if not a grab at least a probe. These probes were costly and led to the overextension of the Soviet empire, which had, to begin with, far less impressive resources at its disposal than the United States. Indeed, one might argue that the greatest mistake of the Brezhnev Politburo was to assume that the Cold War was a zero-sum game and that the side-effects of the American disaster in Vietnam necessarily translated to a Soviet opportunity to assert its power on a global scale.

Lastly, and possibly most importantly, the era known as détente brought with it the realization of what could best be characterized as a strategy of engagement. With the success of *Ostpolitik*, the signing of the CSCE, and even with the opening to China, were unleashed processes that, with the aid of new information technology, culminated in 1989. In the 1970s and 1980s the notions of human rights increasingly undermined the legitimacy of totalitarian control in the Soviet bloc. At the same time, the gradually increasing East–West trade led to rising (and unmet) expectations inside the Soviet bloc. A decade and a half after the signing of the Helsinki Accords, the lure of the West, the promise of democracy, and the appeal of free markets then coincided with disillusionment in communist rule and the inefficiencies of socialism to produce a true revolution in what soon became known as 'the former Soviet bloc'.

A word of caution is in order. While one can, with the benefit of hindsight, make the above connections between détente and the end of the Cold War, the historian must always hold back when building such causal links. In the case of the issues discussed in this chapter such caution is doubly important. After all, it was hardly predetermined that the Soviets would choose the path of imperial overextension in the mid-1970s; should different leaders have been in power at the time the Soviet Union might have, just as well, used its enhanced prestige and increased oil revenues to restructure both the Soviet economy and the USSR's relationship to the rest of the world. What détente presented to the Brezhnev Politburo was a new set of choices and circumstances, not a clear-cut roadmap. The choices they made were perhaps disastrous, but they were not necessarily illogical at the time. Most importantly, however, the consequences of such choices – as well as the consequences of the choices and decisions made on the Western side – were far from clear to the principal actors in the 1970s.

It is time to return to Kekkonen and Sakharov and leap forward to 1986. It was perhaps fitting that Kekkonen died in the fall of that year, for it was then becoming clear that his type of static view of a permanently divided Europe was beginning to crumble. Soon after the Finnish President died Andrei Sakharov received a phone call from one Mikhail Gorbachev. The Soviet leader asked the 1975 Nobel Peace Prize winner to return to Moscow from his internal exile in Gorky.

It was a phone call that in itself symbolized the next significant 'turn' in the Cold War. Again, one might add, this 'turn' was to lead to some unexpected outcomes, including a Nobel Peace Prize for Gorbachev himself.

NOTES

1 *New York Times*, 21 July 1975, cited in Henry Kissinger, *Diplomacy* (New York: Simon & Schuster, 1994), p. 760.

2 Juhani Suomi recounts Kekkonen's Peace Prize 'campaign' in his recent biography. Suomi, *Liunnytyksen akanvirrassa. Urho Kekkonen, 1972–1978* (Helsinki: Otava, 1998).

3 On Kekkonen's efforts and goals regarding the CSCE see ibid. and Suomi, *Taistelu puolueettomuudesta: Urho Kekkonen 1968–1972* (Helsinki: Otava, 1996); Jussi M. Hanhimäki, *Scandinavia and the United States: An Insecure Friendship* (New York: Twayne's, 1997), pp. 143–6; and *Jukka Tarkka, Suomen kylmä sota: Miten viattomuudesta tuli voima* (Helsinki: Otava, 1992), pp. 139–48.

4 Cited in Irwin Abrams, *The Nobel Peace Prize and the Laureates* (Boston, MA: G. K. Hall, 1988), p. 213.

5 The most exhaustive study dealing with Soviet–American détente is Raymond Garthoff, *Détente and Confrontation: American-Soviet Relations from Nixon to Reagan* (Washington, DC: Brookings Institute, 1994). Some of the other works that deal with these issues include Coral Bell, *The Diplomacy of Détente: The Kissinger Era* (New York: Cambridge University Press, 1977); William P. Bundy, *A Tangled Web: The Making of Foreign Policy in the Nixon Presidency* (New York: Hill & Wang, 1998); Robin Edmonds, *Soviet Foreign Policy: The Brezhnev Years* (Oxford: Oxford University Press, 1983); Michael B. Froman, *The Development of the Idea of Détente: Coming to Terms* (London: Macmillan, 1991); John L. Gaddis, *Strategies of Containment: A Critical Appraisal of Postwar American National Security Policy* (New York: Oxford University Press, 1982); Robert S. Litwak, *Détente and the Nixon Doctrine: American Foreign Policy and the Pursuit of Stability, 1969–1976* (Cambridge: Cambridge University Press, 1984); Keith Nelson, *The Making of Détente: Soviet–American Relations in the Shadow of Vietnam* (Baltimore, MA: Johns Hopkins University Press, 1995); Robert Schulzinger, *Henry Kissinger: Doctor of Diplomacy* (New York: Columbia University Press, 1989); Richard Thornton, *The Nixon–Kissinger Years: The Reshaping of American Foreign Policy* (New York: Paragon House, 1989); Adam B. Ulam, *Dangerous Relations: The Soviet Union in World Politics* (Oxford: Oxford University Press, 1983). One should also consult the documents in William Burr, ed., *The Kissinger Transcripts* (New York: The Free Press, 1998).

6 Schulzinger, *Doctor of Diplomacy*, p. 101.

7 Henry Kissinger, *Years of Upheaval* (Boston, MA: Little, Brown, 1982), p. 8.

8 Nixon's inaugural address can be found in *Public Papers of the President: Richard Nixon, 1969* (Washington, DC: US GPO,1970), pp. 1–4. On Nixon and Kissinger's foreign policy thinking see (in addition to books cited in fn. 5 above), for example, John L. Gaddis, 'Rescuing Choice from Circumstance', in *The Diplomats, 1939–1979*, ed. Gordon A. Craig and Francis Lowenheim (Princeton, NJ: Princeton University Press, 1994), pp. 564–92; Joan Hoff, *Nixon Reconsidered* (New York: Basic Books, 1994); Richard Weitz, 'Henry Kissinger's Philosophy of International Relations', *Diplomacy and Statecraft*, 2, 1 (1991): 103–29. Both of them have, of course, also written a number of books on foreign policy, both before and after they were in office.

9 David C. Hendrickson, 'All the President's Acumen', *Foreign Affairs*, 77, 3 (May–June 1998), 117. On the renewed debate about Kissinger's role see Robert Kagan, 'The Revisionist: How Henry Kissinger Won the Cold War, or so He Thinks', *The New Republic* (21 June 1999): 38–48; John Lewis Gaddis, 'The Old World Order', *The New York Times Review of Books* (21 March 1999): 6–7; Philip Zelikow, 'The

Statesman in Winter', *Foreign Affairs*, 78, 3 (May–June 1999); Kissinger, 'No Tapes, No Secrets', *Foreign Affairs*, 78, 4 (July–August 1999).

10 On the decline of détente see the essays in Odd Arne Westad, *The Fall of Détente: Soviet–American Relations during the Carter Years* (Oslo: Scandinavian University Press, 1997). For an earlier appraisal see Fred Halliday, *The Making of the Second Cold War* (London: Verso, 1986).

11 For basic overviews of US policy during and immediately after the 1973 October (Yom Kippur) War see William B. Quandt, *Peace Process: American Diplomacy and the Arab–Israeli Conflict since 1967* (Washington, DC: Brookings Institute, 1993); Schulzinger, *Doctor of Diplomacy*, pp. 142–62; and Bundy, *A Tangled Web*, pp. 428–73. For an analysis of Soviet policy, see Galia Golan, *Soviet Policies in the Middle East from World War II to Gorbachev* (Cambridge: Cambridge University Press, 1990). See also Garthoff, *Détente and Confrontation*, pp. 404–57; Victor Israelyan, *Inside the Kremlin during the Yom Kippur War* (University Park, PA: Pennsylvania University Press, 1995); and Carol R. Saivetz, 'Superpower Competition in the Middle East and the Collapse of *Détente*', in Westad, *The Fall of Détente*, pp. 72–94.

12 Anatoly Dobrynin, *In Confidence: Moscow's Ambassador to America's Six Cold War Presidents* (New York: Basic Books, 1995), p. 325. On American policy toward Iran in the early 1970s see James A. Bill, *The Eagle and the Lion: the Tragedy of American–Iranian Relations* (New Haven, CT: Yale University Press, 1988), pp. 183–215.

13 For details see the *Cold War International History Project Bulletin* (hereafter *CWIHP*), 8–9 (Winter 1996–97), especially the articles by Westad on Angola and the documents from Russian and East German archives on the Horn of Africa. For general accounts of Soviet policy in the Third World see also Andrzej Korbonski and Francis Fukuyama, eds, *The Soviet Union and the Third World: The Last Three Decades* (Ithaca, NY: Cornell University Press, 1987); Edward A. Kolodziej and Roger E. Kanet, eds, *The Limits of Soviet Power in the Developing World: Thermidor in the Revolutionary Struggle* (Basingstoke, UK: Macmillan, 1988); Margot Light, ed., *Troubled Friendships: Moscow's Third World Ventures* (London: Macmillan, 1993); Alvin Z. Rubinstein, *Moscow's Third World Strategy* (Princeton, NJ: Princeton University Press, 1989); William E. Odom, *On Internal War: American and Soviet Approaches to Third World Clients and Insurgents* (Durham, NC: Duke University Press, 1992).

14 Kissinger, *Years of Upheaval*, 6. Thus, when détente faltered the explanation Kissinger offered was captured in one word that had little to do with his foreign policy: Watergate. This view is captured also in Kissinger's much-awaited third volume of his memoirs. Henry Kissinger, *Years of Renewal* (New York: Simon & Schuster, 1999).

15 Ilya Gaiduk, *The Soviet Union and the Vietnam War* (Chicago, IL: Ivan Dee, 1996), p. 250.

16 Kissinger, *Diplomacy*, p. 731.

17 This view comes across, among others, in the most recent critical account of Nixon–Kissinger foreign policy, Bundy, *A Tangled Web*.

18 Vladislav Zubok and Constantine Pleshakov, *Inside the Kremlin's Cold War* (Cambridge, MA: Harvard University Press, 1996). In fact, as much is implied in Adam B. Ulam's classic (but by now much outdated) history of Soviet foreign policy, *Expansion and Coexistence: The History of Soviet Foreign Policy* (New York: Praeger, 1968).

19 Quoted in Garthoff, *Détente and Confrontation*, p. 588.

20 Westad, 'Moscow and the Angolan Crisis, 1974–1976', *Cold War International*

History Project Bulletin, 8–9 (1996–97): 21–31.

21 Paul Kennedy, *The Rise and Fall of Great Powers: Economic Change and Military Conflict from 1500 to 2000* (New York: Vintage, 1987).

22 For a largely similar argument see Westad, 'The Fall of *Détente*'.

23 On European détente see, in addition to sources cited in fn. 5: Richard Davy, ed., *European Détente: A Reappraisal* (London: Sage, 1992) and John van Oudenaren, *Détente in Europe: The Soviet Union and the West since 1953* (Durham, NC: Duke University Press, 1991).

24 On De Gaulle's policies see, for example, Hugh Gough and John Horne, eds, *De Gaulle and Twentieth Century France* (London: Edward Arnold, 1994) Michael Harrison, *France: A Reluctant Ally* (Baltimore, MD: Johns Hopkins University Press, 1981); Robert O. Paxton and Nicholas Wahl, eds, *De Gaulle and the United States: A Centennial Appraisal* (Oxford: Oxford University Press, 1994).

25 On these changes see, among others, Hans W. Gatzke, *Germany and the United States: A 'Special Relationship?'* (Cambridge, MA: Harvard University Press, 1980); Wolfram F. Hanrieder, *Germany, America, Europe: Forty Years of German Foreign policy* (New Haven, CT: Yale University Press, 1989); Barbara Marshall, *Willy Brandt, A Political Biography* (London: Macmillan, 1997), pp. 48–96; Gottfried Niedhart, 'The Federal Republic's *Ostpolitik* and the United States: Initiatives and Constraints' (paper presented at the 1996 Commonwealth Fund Conference, University College, London); Michael J. Sodaro, *Moscow, Germany, and the West from Khrushchev to Gorbachev* (Ithaca, NY: Cornell University Press, 1990), pp. 72–225; Angela Stent, *From Embargo to Ostpolitik* (Cambridge: Cambridge University Press, 1981).

26 On the East German quest for legitimacy see A. James McAdams, *East Germany and Détente: Building Authority after the Wall* (Cambridge: Cambridge University Press, 1985) and Sodaro, *Moscow, Germany, and the West*, pp. 108–264.

27 Dobrynin, *In Confidence*, p. 184.

28 James Mayall and Cornelia Navari, eds, *The End of the Post-War Era: Documents on Great-Power Relations 1968–1975* (Cambridge: Cambridge University Press, 1980).

29 Ibid., p. 25.

30 Vojtech Mastny, *Helsinki, Human Rights, and European Security* (Durham, NC: Duke University Press, 1986), p. 33.

31 See John J. Maresca, *To Helsinki: The Conference on Security and Cooperation in Europe 1973–1975* (Durham, NC: Duke University Press, 1985), esp. ch. 10. This is also evident from a number of memos by various British diplomats involved in the CSCE. At the time when the negotiations got seriously under way in 1972, for example, a slightly frustrated Counsellor at the British Embassy in Washington, M. D. Butler, reported to London that 'Kissinger does not regard the CSCE as being a "serious" affair, partly because he is busy with other things and partly because he probably does not yet know what kind of tone he will wish to give to US/Soviet relations after the [May 1972] Moscow visit'. *Documents on British Foreign Policy Overseas: The Conference on Security and Cooperation in Europe*, series III, vol. II (London: Stationery Office, 1997); ibid., p. 34, fn. 2.

32 Kissinger, *Diplomacy*, pp. 759–60.

33 Garthoff, *Détente and Confrontation*, p. 140.

34 While the significance of human rights in the collapse of totalitarianism in Eastern Europe and the Soviet Union is generally acknowledged, specialized literature on the subject is limited and much of it outdated. See, however Mastny, *Helsinki*; A. Bloed and P. van Dijk, eds, *Essays on Human Rights in the Helsinki Process* (Boston, MA: M. Nijhoff, 1985); and Bennett Kovrig, *Of Walls and Bridges* (New York: New

York University, 1991), pp. 166–227.

35 Dobrynin, *In Confidence*, p. 346.

36 See Schulzinger, *Doctor of Diplomacy*, pp. 210–36; Walter Isaacson, *Kissinger* (New York: Simon & Schuster, 1992), pp. 653–72, 693–704.

37 Harriet Friedmann, 'Warsaw Pact Socialism: *Détente* and the Disintegration of the Soviet Bloc', in *Re-Thinking the Cold War*, ed. Allen Hunter (Philadelphia, PA: Temple University Press, 1998), pp. 213–31. The following paragraphs are based largely on this article.

38 Ibid., p. 214.

39 Vladislav Zubok, 'The Soviet Union and European Integration from Stalin to Gorbachev', *Journal of European Integration History*, 2, 1 (1996): 92.

40 Gaddis, 'Why Did the Cold War Last as Long as it Did?', in Westad, *The Fall of Détente*, p. 155.

16

Why Did the Cold War End in 1989?
Explanations of 'The Turn'

Vladislav M. Zubok

Why did the confrontation between the superpowers in the second half of the 1980s transform itself into the collapse of communism and the end of the Soviet empire? The answer may seem obvious: the Soviet empire imploded under internal and external pressure. Yet nobody could foresee this happening in 1985, when Mikhail Gorbachev, a young and confident leader of the Soviet Union, met with US President Ronald Reagan in Geneva. In fact, even when some world leaders proclaimed the end of the Cold War in 1988, most still remained skeptical. It took the peaceful revolutions in Eastern Europe the very next year to prove that the Cold War was dead.

Explaining the end of the Cold War may be as tricky as explaining its origins: as in any transition from one international order to another, there was much dynamism and uncertainty and many choices. All previous 'turning points' of Cold War history (the years after Stalin's death, the aftermath of the Berlin and Cuban Missile Crises, the détente of the early 1970s and its fall) were phases in the Soviet–American confrontation cycle. After almost four decades, this rivalry began to look like the immutable status quo of international affairs, seen by some analysts as the lesser of evils. A 'Realist' perspective on foreign affairs, predominant in the West, had ready explanations for the durability of the confrontation, but saw it ending most likely in a 'hegemonic war'. Indeed, a peace, based on something other than mutual assured destruction, seemed to be a vision as fantastic as the sleeping Brünnhilde in the Wagnerian epic. Both could be reached only through the wall of fire, but in our case the fire was nuclear apocalypse. For this reason, prudent observers preferred to treat the Cold War as 'peace' for lack of better alternatives.[1]

The sudden peaceful transformation of the international landscape and disappearance of the Soviet Union perplexed most observers and thinkers. Many books and articles are written about the 'enigma' of the end of the Cold War (although even more attention is devoted to the end of the Soviet Union). As many discover, it is impossible to explain the end of the Cold

War within the framework of international relations or the history of Russian/Soviet foreign policy alone. A more comprehensive study of Cold War history leads researchers into areas far beyond the traditional scope of methods and issues of diplomatic history.[2] In the United States the basic issues have already been discussed for years: the nature of American 'empire' and its ideology, US Cold War strategies, and their relevance to a relative decline of US power.[3] The first post-communist publications in Russia also began to assess similar broad questions: the costs of Soviet empire, Stalin's legacy and the failure of reforms, and the importance of internal and external factors in the collapse of the Soviet Union.[4]

This chapter will summarize the main lines of argument in the first wave of literature on the end of the Cold War. It will also look at the most recent evidence resulting from my own research and several concurrent international projects. It will also briefly reflect on the relevance of this new field of study for the historiography of the Cold War.

The debates

With the events so fresh and so dramatic, it is not surprising that political and ideological passions are still smoldering in the literature on Soviet–US relations in the 1980s. The collapse of the Soviet Union left the United States as the winner in the Cold War by default. This created a strong temptation to regard the decades of confrontation through 'triumphalist' lenses – winners are above criticism – and to claim that US foreign policy, strategies, and policies from Truman to Reagan were vindicated and justified. The former intelligence chief Robert Gates in his memoirs proclaims the triumph of the strategy of containment, formulated in 1946 by George F. Kennan – the vindication of 'the belief that, denied new conquests, the inherent weaknesses of Soviet communism ultimately would bring it down'.[5]

The 'triumphalist' agenda reaches even further among some hard-line members of the Reagan Administration (Caspar Weinberger, Robert McFarlane, Richard Pipes, Richard Pearle, and Edward Rowney). Peter Schweitzer, who interviewed many of them for his tendentious book *Victory*, concludes that the Reagan administration turned the tide of the Cold War, that had developed in the 1970s in favor of the Soviet Union, against Moscow. The hard-line 'triumphalists' stress discontinuity; the abandonment of approaches of previous administrations, primarily of the Carter administration, who had acknowledged the bipolar status quo and sought to cultivate the Soviet Union's responsible role in it; instead, the Reagan administration in its early years used all the means, short of actual warfare, to bring the Soviet empire down. Schweitzer disclosed for the first time a number of secret policies between 1981 and 1987 – military, economic, political, and psychological – that, in his view, were responsible for the collapse of the Soviet empire and 'victory' of the West.[6]

Critics of 'triumphalism', among them former Secretary of State George Shultz, former US Ambassador to Moscow Jack Matlock, and some CIA analysts, admit that the direct impact of US pressure on the Soviet Union could hardly have won the Cold War.[7] However, the United States did play a considerable role, largely due to the sustained course of 'realism, strength, and dialogue' with Gorbachev. Matlock argues that this course was born by the bitter lessons of the fall of détente. Since 1984 the State Department and the President linked progress in reduction of armaments to military non-intervention in 'Third World' conflicts, greater respect for human rights, and a free exchange of information and ideas. Reagan adopted this policy in his speech of 16 January 1984, well before Gorbachev came to power. Matlock is strongly convinced that this 'agenda' was later accepted by the Gorbachev leadership and provided a mutual basis for gradually reducing the tensions of the Cold War.[8]

The argument between the 'triumphalists' and their political opponents is not only about the consequences of US foreign policy, but about Soviet intentions and the interpretation of Moscow's 'new thinking'. The 'triumphalists' always mistrusted the gradual change in Gorbachev's reformist intentions and do so even today.[9] Robert Gates, for instance, concluded that Gorbachev's goal was 'to restore the Soviet Union to good health politically and economically and thereby allow it to retain its place as a superpower with global interests and ambitions, a communist superpower in more dimensions than military strength'.[10]

The 'non-triumphalists' claim that precisely the change in Moscow's intentions ended the cycle of fear and tension. Matlock praises Gorbachev and his followers for abandoning the Marxist–Leninist concept of 'class struggle' and old policies that were as much against the interests of Soviet society as they were against Western interests. Matlock even claims that if the Soviet Union had succeeded in reforming itself and remained a great power, it would have become 'a friend and a potential partner' of the United States.[11] For him (in retrospect) the Cold War effectively was over at the end of 1988.

Among Western political scientists and historians, many – critical of American Cold War policies – fear that 'triumphalist' interpretations of the end of the Cold War may fortify that US foreign policy ideology that had once led the US into the Vietnam War. Intellectually, they sympathize with Soviet reformers and explore the role of 'new thinking' and the personality of Mikhail Gorbachev in the transformation of late 1980s. Raymond Garthoff in his meticulous study concluded that the dismantling of the confrontation happened exclusively because of Soviet concessions and 'new thinking', while the Reagan administration largely pocketed them and continued its Cold War tactics on other fronts, particularly in Third World conflicts.[12]

The British scholar Archie Brown does not conceal his Gorbyphilia. He contends that the end of the Cold War had little or nothing to do with US strategies, pressures, or engagements, but rather with a potential for reform and revolution inside the Soviet system. In his opinion, the Reagan administration slowed down changes by its obtuse policies and blind anti-communism. Without Gorbachev's reforms, the Cold War may have still continued. Brown writes:

> The conservative American opponents of the foreign policy of Shultz and Reagan – and of the arch-enemy, Gorbachev – would later have the gall to claim some credit for winning the Cold War ... It is, however, clear that, if Reagan and Shultz had been unwise enough to listen to them, the opportunity to change the character of East–West relations presented by Gorbachev's leadership would have been missed.[13]

Even some IR Realists deal to some extent with the changes in Soviet ideas when interpreting the end of the Cold War: William Wohlforth analyzes the Soviet leadership's perceptions during the Cold War and concludes that only under Gorbachev could the Soviet Union have changed from a challenger in the international system to a status quo power. He registers a quantum leap in Soviet perceptions of the world after 1985. Ironically, this happened in 'the most unstable period since World War II'. Wohlforth writes:

> When Mikhail Gorbachev took the helm of the Communist Party in March of that year, his country was seen from within and without as a formidable but troubled superpower that under energetic leadership was likely to emerge as a more capable competitor of the United States (itself to be thought in decline). Five years later the same observers saw the Soviet Union as a pitiful, disintegrating, anachronistic giant that could pose no threat to the great powers save the aftershock of its own collapse.[14]

For a moderate Realist such as Wohlforth, Soviet perceptions just followed, albeit belatedly, the real balance of power.

Not so for the Canadian scholar Jacques Levesque. He concludes that 'new thinking' and Gorbachev's personality played an outstanding, unique role in transforming the realities of power and in ending the Cold War. Gorbachev replaced the faded Stalinist imperial consensus with a new neo-Leninist utopia, based not on force and party monopoly, but on consensus

and pluralism. This, more than anything else, led to the quick disappearance of the Soviet empire in 1989 as a major factor of the Cold War.
He writes:

> Rarely in history have we witnessed the policy of a great power
> continue, throughout so many difficulties and reversals, to be guided
> by a such an idealistic view of the world, based on universal recon-
> ciliation, and in which the image of the enemy was constantly
> blurring, to the point of making it practically disappear as the
> enemy.[15]

On the Russian side, the divergences essentially parallel those in the
West; there is strong tendency toward 'cross-breeding' between American
and Soviet schools of thought on the end of the Cold War. A large and
increasingly vocal group, including most veterans of the Gorbachev
Administration, the military, and the former KGB, claim that the United
States 'won' because it developed external insidious and subversive policies
(usually associated with the CIA) and took advantage of 'treason' inside.
In doing this, they rely on the 'triumphalists' in the United States claiming
that Gorbachev and part of the Soviet elites surrendered to the West and/or
converted to Western values. The criticism of elitist 'new thinking' that
resulted in the 'wrong' ending to the Cold War, became a popular theme
among Russian ex-liberals [derzhavniki].[16] Unfortunately, most of these
critics do not bother to support their arguments with documentary
evidence.[17]

The bitterness which followed the Soviet Union's collapse continues to
be the main obstacle to serious and sober discussion on the end of the Cold
War in Russia. Before the disintegration, Marshal Sergei Akhromeyev,
critical of 'new thinking', still could assess the international changes as a
generally positive development. In 1990–91 Akhromeyev wrote:

> All who knew the real situation in our state and economy in mid-
> 1980s understood that Soviet foreign policy had to be changed. The
> Soviet Union could no longer continue a policy of military confron-
> tation with the US and NATO after 1985. The economic possibilities
> for such a policy had been practically exhausted.

In his opinion, the economic crisis in the USSR was intensifying, and it
was mandatory for the Kremlin leadership to end the arms race.[18] After
1991, however, Akhromeyev's friend and co-author Georgi Kornienko
unequivocally criticized Gorbachev's and Shevardnadze's foreign policy
and claimed that the American goal was not to end the Cold War, but to
destroy the Soviet Union and now to weaken Russia. The thesis that the
Cold War 'is not over' is wide-spread today among Russian communists
and ultra-nationalists.[19]

The Gorbachev camp (his assistants Anatoly Chernyaev, Georgi Shakhnazarov, and Gorbachev himself) treats the end of the Cold War as a separate issue from the collapse of the great power, and their writings 'cross-breed' with the research of Matlock, Archie Brown, and most Western academic writers. To their credit, they are the only students of the subject in Russia who present impressive empirical evidence and analysis on the end of the era of confrontation. They continue to claim that 'new thinking', with its emphasis on 'common interests of humanity', provided the only possible alternative to the Cold War and the 'old thinking' that generated enmity, bipolarity, and the arms race. They claim that rejection by the Gorbachev leadership of the systemic confrontation with the West was organically linked to domestic reforms, de-Stalinization, and, most important, the need for the survival of mankind in the nuclear age.

There are attempts, largely by Western political scientists and theorists of international relations, to approach the topic in a systematic and synthesizing manner, checking against the evidence all existing approaches, such as structural 'Realism', the impact of domestic politics, the analysis of ideas, and the role of leaders.[20] A heated discussion took place during 1992–95 between the adherents of Realism and their critics, who claimed that under Gorbachev Russian foreign policy 'became increasingly inconsistent with power transition and other realists theories', and that the Soviet withdrawal from Eastern Europe was even more anomalous.[21] In general, these lines of debate – in several forms – will probably continue to define research priorities in the years to come.

The new evidence

The background to 'the turn' were years of extreme and increasingly dangerous US–Soviet confrontation, unprecedented in its acuteness since the Cuban Missile Crisis. We have learned recently that some in the Soviet military and security establishment were on the brink of a genuine war scare. This war scare, in one observation, was a reflection of the Kremlin's 'pessimistic assessment of the "correlation of forces" and the ever-widening gap in the USSR's technological lag behind the West'. Not only Soviet ideologists, but the military heard Reagan's 'evil empire' rhetoric with great apprehension.[22] By the early 1980s the Soviet rulers had already quietly buried the 'Brezhnev doctrine', no longer wanted to consolidate their regime with the help of external threats, and just wanted to normalize Soviet–American relations without losing the superpower's prestige. Some elements of the future 'new thinking' of Gorbachev had been around already in the early 1980s, for instance the assertion that nuclear danger made some old dictums of *realpolitik* obsolete.[23]

After 1984 both sides, including President Reagan, began to look for a way out of the dangerous deadlock, while tensions remained high. The turn away from crisis, however, did not end a Soviet–American confrontation that lasted for several more years. The reduction of this confrontation and, presumably, the end of the Cold War, happened in at least three distinct stages.

The first stage (1985–early 1987) was marked by an increasingly vigorous 'peace offensive' by the Soviet leadership. A young, energetic leader recognized that the old foreign policy that led the USSR into Afghanistan and 'gave a pretext' to the Reagan Administration 'to dismantle détente', was a losing proposition – a virtually unanimous consensus in Soviet elites.[24] Gorbachev set before the diplomatic establishment and the KGB the task to wind down the costly arms race and to reduce confrontation as a *sine qua non* for reforms of the country and economy.

Reagan's Strategic Defense Initiative (SDI) program became Gorbachev's nemesis, an embodiment of everything that he vowed to overcome with his new foreign policy. On the technological level, his task forces of scientists and military experts convinced him that the Soviet Union needed only '10% of the [US] expenses for a countersystem that would be sufficient'.[25] But this was too much for Gorbachev. The defeat of the SDI remained Gorbachev's priority at the Reykjavik Summit in October 1986 where his 'supertask' was 'to prevent the next round of the arms race'. He was afraid that the USSR

> will be pulled into an arms race that is beyond our capabilities, and we will lose it, because we are at the limit of our capabilities. Moreover, we can expect that Japan and the FRG could very soon join the American potential ... If a new round begins, the pressure on our economy will be unbelievable.[26]

The military and some defense scientists tried to use Gorbachev's concern to get more funds. The General Secretary continued to raise the issue of SDI until the spring of 1987, when it virtually disappeared from the Politburo agenda.[27]

In some ways, Gorbachev's 'peace offensive' was remarkably similar to that of Stalin's successors in 1953–55: in both cases the Soviet leadership faced an urgent need for economic recovery and change (*tak dalshe zhit nelzia*) and desperately sought to wind down an arms race with the technologically superior West that could cripple Soviet economy and society. At first Gorbachev opted for a propagandistically attractive plan of complete nuclear disarmament (the high military command strongly preferred it to any partial and more realistic initiatives on arms reductions).[28] Later, in a search for 'more butter than guns', he initiated the first radical change in Soviet military doctrine since Khrushchev's attempts in 1959–60. Also Gorbachev, using economic arguments, came with proposals to reduce strategic arsenals by half and decided to ignore the British and French, as well as 'forward-based' US nuclear forces in arms control calculations. The military intensely disliked both decisions, but they, as in Khrushchev's time, bowed to the political authority of Gorbachev.[29]

And there was always a possibility of a backlash against the West, similar to the one that had occurred in Soviet foreign policy after 1957. The Reagan administration, like the Eisenhower administration, ignored the Kremlin's good will and continued to harass the Soviets here, there, and everywhere.[30] Reagan wanted radical nuclear disarmament, but his administration continued to wage the Cold War against the Soviet Union in the worst possible ways, by supplying 'Stingers' to the fundamentalists in Afghanistan, by continuing the technological arms race and even flexing its military muscles against the weakest enemies, such as in Nicaragua. After the US air strike against Libya, Gorbachev fulminated at the Politburo: 'We cannot cook anything with this gang [of Reagan].' He threatened to freeze high-level dialogue with the administration.[31] But unlike the post-Stalin leadership in Korea, Gorbachev did not manage to end the Soviet Union's own foreign war in Afghanistan quickly; it became 'his war' as much as the Vietnam War became Nixon's war: he simply could not face a public fiasco there, for both international and domestic reasons.[32]

What made Gorbachev's 'peace campaign' distinct from Khrushchev's, beside the changed international circumstances, was 'new thinking'.[33] The trials and errors of his predecessors persuaded Gorbachev, Shevardnadze, and their advisers to reject the traditional bargaining methods in diplomacy; they began to look for a 'conceptual breakthrough' in relations with Reagan. The Soviet leader also began to view Reagan as a nuclear abolitionist and perhaps a partner, not an enemy.[34] The Gorbachev camp unanimously claim that the Gorbachev–Reagan talks at Geneva and then Reykjavik were crucial.[35] From Reykjavik on, Gorbachev sought to engage Reagan in a 'breakthrough' to end the Cold War. To achieve this, he was prepared to make 'concessions' to gain American trust. A most important 'concession' around the time of Rejkyavik and after was the release of Andrei Sakharov from exile and a quiet relaxation of the KGB's grip on the dissidents inside the USSR.[36] The Soviet leadership apparently still believed that the 'peace campaign' could work if it were coupled with liberalization inside the Soviet Union; the KGB and its propaganda apparatus carried out costly and highly sophisticated 'active measures' to propagandize 'new thinking' and to dismantle the 'enemy image' in American and West European public opinion.

In the second phase (1987–mid-1988) both the American and the Soviet leadership became, finally, engaged in a process of reduction of armaments and tension. In the Reagan administration, the most extreme cold-warriors in the NSC, the CIA, and the Pentagon – weakened by the Iran–Contra scandal – were on the way out, and the more pragmatic course of George Shultz, increasingly supported by the President himself, became an official policy of the administration. Still, the initiative for change stayed almost wholly on the Soviet side. The authoritarian character of the Gorbachev leadership was a factor that, ironically, facilitated the departure from old ways. Gorbachev inherited power from the Kremlin's 'old guard', but unlike them, he was not constrained by imperialist and conservative complexes. He surrounded himself with intellectual advisers, and learned very fast. Gorbachev was also learning from his interaction with foreign leaders (Reagan, Schultz, Margaret Thatcher, François Mitterand, later Helmut Kohl, Rajiv Gandhi, and European Social Democrats).[37]

Soviet elites had been exposed to transnational dialogue and communications for decades, but the effect of these external influences varied according to position and personal beliefs. Many Soviet diplomats and KGB officials, as a result of this exposure, lost any illusions about 'socialism' in their country, but this drove them not to liberal reformism, but to cynical careerism. They remained loyal apparatchiks even after many years of service abroad. In Gorbachev's case, however, intense exposure coincided with the trend of his own mind: foreign leaders became his alternative 'reference group' where he shaped his new initiatives and ideas and overcame the old ones. Later Gorbachev's lieutenants discovered, with joy or indignation, that the leader of the CPSU, unlike the other reformer Nikita Khrushchev, had no personal 'limits' in parting ways with Stalin's legacy internally and externally.[38]

The summit in Washington in December 1987 and the 'nuclear zero' agreement on the INF (Intermediate Range Nuclear Forces) was another milestone in Gorbachev's education. He returned to Moscow not only with the promising outlines of more disarmament agreements to come (preservation of ABM, number of warheads on strategic missiles, sea-based cruise missiles), but convinced that his direct contact with the American establishment and the logic of disarmament would eventually erode 'the myth about the "Soviet military threat"'. Reagan and American society ceased to be enemies for Gorbachev and his close advisers.[39]

But those changes in thinking had to reveal themselves in public intentions and policies; if not, the state of Soviet–American relations could have easily stopped at the level achieved during the détente of 1972–76. Like then, summits and chemistry between leaders were crucial, and arms control remained at the center. Although Reagan began to trust Gorbachev personally, he remained an intense foe of the Soviet communist system, and was buffeted by skeptical warnings about Soviet intentions from the CIA especially.[40]

The 'Nina Andreeva affair' in the spring of 1988 – the direct criticism of his policies in Soviet media – forced Gorbachev to choose between the control of the press and glasnost. His conscious choice of the latter made him begin to plan an all-out political reform to dismantle 'the system' of central party control over all aspects of economic and social life. He and his advisers also came to perceive that the renunciation of the set practices of communism was a cornerstone in their strategy to end Soviet–West confrontation: they believed that the United States, if denied the scarecrow of a 'Soviet threat', would no longer be able to continue the arms race and global anti-Soviet policies. Reagan's personal admission during the Moscow Summit (May 1988) that the Soviet Union was no longer 'a focus of all evil' signified to the Soviet reformers that the Soviet–American confrontation could be replaced by partnership.

On the eve of the emergency Nineteenth CPSU Party Conference, Gorbachev argued at the Politburo that the arms race and Cold War confrontation could be ended only through unilateral concessions from the Soviet Union, in violation of the old 'zero-sum game' approach that, as he argued, had brought 'us to the brink of war'.[41] Gorbachev and Shevardnadze told the party and foreign policy establishment that Soviet foreign policy and the concept of 'class struggle' had contributed to the Cold War. From now on there would be a new foreign policy based on the search for consensus and 'all-human values'. The idealistic thrust of this form of 'new thinking' (disarmament, complete national self-determination, etc.) was reminiscent more of Wilsonianism than Leninism.

These changes in political theory were decisive and even revolutionary, and determined the pace and scale of changes in Europe in the following three years. Dismantling the communist foundation of Soviet foreign policy overthrew the old 'legitimacy' of the Soviet empire without offering anything to replace it. At the same time, 'new thinking' dispensed not only with old ideological concepts, but with the boundaries of *realpolitik*; in the view of the reformers, 'realism' justified bipolarity and confrontation, hence it had to be discarded. For Gorbachev's opponents *realpolitik* was mother's milk; they would perhaps have agreed to get rid of the 'socialist' perspective and 'proletarian internationalism', but they cared about power and empire. But Gorbachev and his 'new thinkers' did not, and, in retrospect, they claim today that more 'realist' practices and bargaining would have never ended the Soviet–American confrontation.[42]

Here lies the divide between them and 'realists' both in Moscow and in Washington. From the latters' perspective, this revolutionary leap was highly risky, since the Soviet leadership unilaterally discarded the traditional Cold War system before agreeing with the West on the terms of an end of geopolitical confrontation and the arms race. While the Cold War was radically dismantled inside the Soviet establishment and Soviet society, arms control plodded slowly along at START and MBFR talks in Europe, and in Germany Warsaw Treaty and NATO forces still faced each other.

In 1988–89 the scene was set for the peaceful collapse of communist regimes in Eastern Europe. Under pressure from Gorbachev, the old Soviet military doctrine and the doctrine of the Warsaw Pact, with their emphasis on the geostrategic importance of Central Europe (to dissuade NATO from a first nuclear strike by threatening a conventional *blitzkrieg*) had been abolished, and replaced with 'sufficient defense'. The Politburo members frankly admitted among themselves that 'socialist integration' with Eastern Europe had failed and the USSR had become a net donor to the other WTO (World Trade Organization) countries, 'a provider of cheap resources'. The former jewels of Stalin's empire, Poland and East Germany, began to look like liabilities, politically and economically, for Gorbachev and the reformers.[43]

At the same time, nobody in Moscow, Eastern Europe, or even in the United States surmised that the collapse of the East European order was near. Soviet reformers believed that transformation would lead to 'national communist' regimes and would not endanger the Warsaw Pact. For Eastern European reformers the 'Brezhnev doctrine' was alive and well; they checked the Kremlin cautiously for limits to their autonomy, without getting any response. A CIA analyst recalls that back in 1988 he never asked himself what East Europeans would do, if they realized they were free to reform themselves. A revolution in international affairs was about to begin, and nobody foresaw it.

During the third phase (mid-1988 to end of 1989) the deep Soviet–American détente[44] continued, but the main stage was taken by the collapse of communism in Eastern Europe and inside the Soviet Union itself. Gorbachev began to lose control over politics in the Soviet Union, while in the United States Reagan's romantic enthusiasm with disarmament was replaced by the very unromantic, cautious conservatism of the Bush administration.[45]

There had been no consensus in Washington on Reagan's 'romance' with Gorbachev. Contrary to the Reagan 'outsiders', most of the new Bush Administration had been associated with the détente of the 1970s (most of them worked for the Ford Administration and later believed that public dissatisfaction with détente thwarted Ford's reelection in 1976); they feared that the Gorbachev–Reagan 'détente' might be again replaced by confrontation. Robert Gates, Bill Cheney, and Brent Scowcroft dismissed 'new thinking' as atmospherics at best and a deception campaign at worst, especially since Gorbachev posed as a neo-Leninist, and gave no inkling of abandoning the goals of communism. Soviet withdrawal from Afghanistan placated them only in part, because the Soviet client still ruled in Kabul with substantial Soviet assistance and the Soviets continued to support other regimes in the Third World.

At the same time, the professional Russia-watchers (the CIA's Bureau of Soviet Analysis, Ambassador Jack Matlock in Moscow) realized that after the Nineteenth Party Conference changes had become irreversible; they became convinced that the confrontation between communism and capitalism, the centerpiece of the Cold War, was over. But they could not, at least initially, win the new Bush administration over. During its first months in power it remained totally dominated by old concerns; only after six months, in June 1989, did Bush decide to move 'beyond containment' and toward engaging the Soviet Union in the process of peaceful changes in Europe and elsewhere.

In the Politburo the members had to face up to the uncertain future of Soviet allies in Eastern Europe. In January–February 1989, Aleksandr Yakovlev and Georgi Shakhazarov solicited a number of analytical papers from academic and state institutions, and most of them predicted an overall crisis of the alliance. There were frank conclusions that Soviet allies were already quietly rejecting 'socialism' and were 'in the powerful magnetic field' of the West. Looking at scenarios, one paper concluded that if the ruling parties did not make concessions to the opposition forces, there would be 'a political eruption'. Another predicted 'a most acute social-political conflict with an unfathomable outcome'.[46]

Gorbachev and his advisers assert in their memoirs and interviews that they rejected not only military involvement, but any interference in Eastern Europe. This is supported by documentary evidence: Gorbachev's assistant in charge of the 'socialist bloc', Georgi Shakhnazarov, wrote to Gorbachev in a memo in October 1988 that, 'In reality all of them need changes, although we do not tell them this publicly to avoid criticism for trying to impose our perestroika on our friends.'[47] One reason for the policy of non-interference was put best by Fedor Burlatsky: 'We have given our allies so much bad advice in the past that we now hesitate to give them good advice.'[48] The guilty conscience of 1956 and 1968 weighed on the Gorbachevites as part of their generational experience.

And there were other reasons. One of them Jacque Levesque describes as 'reformist illusions', the idea that reformed communists or social democrats might take over in Eastern Europe and that the GDR would remain a stalwart of the Soviet alliance. Another reason was the fear that Soviet military intervention would be an unmitigated disaster. A paper from the Bogomolov Institute warned that if the USSR tried to intervene on behalf of the conservative forces, it 'will most evidently signify the end of perestroika, the crumbling of trust of the world community in [our reforms], but will not prevent the disintegration of the ... systems in these countries'. The whole of Eastern Europe, the memo continued, might explode.[49]

Nobody in Moscow contemplated military intervention, because the Politburo did not contemplate it. But the absence of any policy with regard to Eastern Europe appears puzzling in retrospect. Remarkably, even in the spring–summer of 1989 there was no attempt to create a 'fire brigade' on Eastern Europe inside the leadership; experts on the region behaved as if struck with complete political impotence. In a sense, the external empire continued to exist after 1987 only because Eastern Europeans did not yet realize that they could just walk away from their shackles. When Eastern

Europe did explode and communist regimes there went down without a fight, the Kremlin did not just not intervene, it hardly noticed. In late 1989, Gorbachev and other Politburo members were truly overwhelmed by burning domestic issues. Already since May 1989 it was clear for some in the Soviet leadership that the USSR itself might be a casualty of the processes unleashed.[50] Besides the failing economy and the financial crisis, the domestic political crisis of the system became the main concern of the leadership.

With the joyful breach of the Berlin Wall and the beginning of the process of German reunification driven by West German Chancellor Helmut Kohl, the main obstacle for dismantling the Cold War structures in Europe disappeared. The road was open to 'one Europe' – from the viewpoint of Gorbachev and the 'new thinkers' this certainly meant the end of the Cold War. The Bush administration agreed at a summit in Malta in December 1989 that the confrontation was definitely over. In the eyes of Bush, as in Reagan's earlier, Gorbachev became 'a friend'. However, for many in Washington, as the Soviet Union 'lost' East Germany and was disintegrating as a superpower, Gorbachev was quickly becoming a lame duck; it was plausible to expect a coup against him by hard-liners and the military. Some even believed that some form of Soviet–American confrontation might return. This mood, supported by important interests and old habits, but also by the turmoil in the USSR, died hard in Washington. President Bush himself made a Freudian slip in his Christmas address of 1991, when he equated the end of the Soviet Union with the end of the Cold War.

A new history of the end of the Cold War?

The Soviet potential to wage the Cold War was always vastly inferior to that of the United States. This has long been known (but not always publicly admitted) in the West. The end of the Cold War revealed just how overextended the Soviet Union had become in the conflict with the West. The most important aspect of Gorbachev's 'learning process' and a most crucial one to explain the evolution of his foreign policy is his own growing realization of this fact – the biggest and most momentous of Soviet secrets.

When Gorbachev began his term, he, like Khrushchev, Kosygin, Brezhnev, and Andropov before him, expected to produce a quick economic revival ('acceleration'). His illusions were based on his poor knowledge of Soviet economy beyond the agricultural sector for which he had been responsible, and on his ideological belief in 'the great potential of socialism' (shared by the whole Politburo, from Yegor Ligachev and Nikolai Ryzhkov to Alexandr Yakovlev). However, in December 1988 Gorbachev admitted at the Politburo:

Today we cannot tell even the party [about the burden of defense/security expenditures]. If we today tell how much we extract from our national revenue for defense, this may negate [Gorbachev's disarmament] speech at the United Nations. In no other country is it so bad. Perhaps only in poor countries, where half of their budget goes for military spending.[51]

Only a future research project can determine what percentage of the Soviet GNP by the end of the 1980s was really spent on the Cold War – figures vary from 10 percent of direct costs to 70 percent of indirect costs related to military, defense, international assistance, and propaganda needs. All in the Soviet echelons of power (who later blamed Gorbachev for 'treason') agreed that the country could no longer bear the burden of the arms race, and that arms-limitation agreements with the United States must be reached.[52]

Of course, it could be said that Gorbachev was guilty of turning a creeping crisis into a galloping one. But throughout the Cold War the Soviet economy was a tale of two cities: on the one hand, the military–industrial complex (its secret core and supporting structure), on the other, the decaying remainder. The militarized part of economy was a new and much better economy, and for a while it was the engine of technological progress in the USSR. But everything not essential for defense continued to lag behind; in the 1980s Gorbachev directed the secret military economy to boost consumer industries, but it was too little and too late.

The apparently robust figures of Soviet growth in the 1950s and 1960s impressed many, and in the 1970s the ability of the Soviets to achieve a form of strategic parity led some Cold Warriors in the United States to panic. And this was not just in the Committee on the Present Danger; there was a widespread belief in Western quarters, even in the intelligence community, that the Soviet Union had become a true superpower. In fact, Khrushchev desperately searched for an equivalent of Eisenhower's 'New Look', to alleviate the burden of defense expenditures. He never succeeded, and in the late 1960s Khrushchev's successors reversed gears in the name of achieving a strategic parity, which led to enormous expenses covered only by the sale of oil and other resources. This new 'big leap', after so many others in the past, undermined the Soviet economy in ways from which it could never recover.[53]

The blatant inferiority in economic and financial resources, the global outreach of the Soviet empire, the fragility of its allies, and the costs to the quality of life inside the empire eventually led to the erosion of the will to wage the Cold War.[54] In the Soviet Union the reformist part of the elites had by the end of the 1980s decided 'to say farewell to arms'. However, what current critics of the Gorbachevites regard as a 'betrayal' was a natural reaction to the profound economic and financial crisis of the central planning system aggravated by awkward reforms. This crisis developed parallel to the process of ending the Cold War.[55] As Marx would have been glad to hear, in one sense 'material' economic factors determined the 'ideas' in the Soviet case.

Historical experiences and ideological blinkers explain why the Soviets had for so long been willing to sustain the uneven burden of world competition with the United States. Historians of Russia and the Soviet Union now give these factors as much prominence as geography and society.[56] During the Cold War these approaches succumbed to the tendency to dismiss Soviet propaganda, and broad trends in scholarship went against employing such nebulous factors as national experience and ideology. The end of the Cold War makes a case for their rehabilitation.[57]

The new evidence shows how important was the fading of the traumatic memories of June 1941 in the Soviet leadership during the 1980s. People from the generations who survived World War II tended to take all potential threats very seriously, and especially the threat of the American nuclear arsenal and American military bases. Once the dynamic of confrontation was set, it was not hard for Soviet propaganda to keep the generational fear of war simmering. Marshals, generals, and the architects of the military-industrial complex had the image of burning cities of 1941 in their minds when they argued that nothing should be spared in defense preparedness.[58] This factor, I would argue, was the main psychological block delaying the impact of the nuclear revolution in the Soviet Union until the 1980s.

It was the physical disappearance of the war-time age cohorts which made the generational shift of 1985 possible. The June 1941 experience was replaced with the experience of the decades of the Cold War. The economic problems posed by the Soviet system all of a sudden appeared not as a lesser evil, but as evil incarnate. The ethos and principles of the Soviet elites changed accordingly, and, in the end, some of them felt nothing but cynical pragmatism toward the empire they lived in and worked for.[59] This happened first at the leadership and elite level, but with glasnost it spread among the public at large.

The importance of the collapse of ideology in 1986–88 for the end of the Cold War has been amply confirmed by the Politburo minutes we now have. As I have stressed before, Soviet ideology, as far as foreign policy was concerned, was a combination of revolutionary myths and imperial *realpolitik* (the revolutionary-imperial paradigm).[60] When some of the central tenets of this ideology were removed from foreign policy in 1988, 'new thinkers' threw away *realpolitik* as well.[61] The most striking evidence of the difference that made was the reaction of Anatoly Chernyaev, one of Gorbachev's closest foreign-policy advisers, to the collapse of communism in Eastern Europe. On 5 October 1989 he wrote in his diary:

> In a word, the total dismantling of socialism as a world phenomenon has been proceeding ... Perhaps it is inevitable and good ... For this is a reunification of mankind on the basis of common sense. And an ordinary fellow from Stavropol [i.e., Gorbachev] set this process in motion.[62]

'New thinkers' did not fully anticipate the geopolitical consequences of this 'dismantling',[63] but, on the other hand, they were willing to take extraordinary risks with the Soviet international position in order to reach their aims. Gorbachev's advisers never regretted the Soviet withdrawal from Central Europe and the reunification of Germany. In their eyes, neither ideology nor the victory over Nazism could legitimize the existence of an empire in contemporary Europe. Their position can be understood only as an effect of both the rejection of ideology and the transcendence of historical experience, and first and foremost June 1941.

By contrast, American Cold War ideology proved to be resilient and strong, and its 'imperial' components survived the concussions of the 1960s; Wilsonianism and belief that the United States was the world-wide protector of 'liberty' outlasted Leninism. Ironically, as the 'new thinkers' began to emulate Western values, this reinforced, to the point of smugness, the tenets of American Cold War ideology.[64]

The Cold War experience produced breakdowns in the imperial will of both antagonists, but at different times. The first such breakdown occurred in the United States, and became the main reason for détente in the early 1970s. Undermined both by the Vietnam War and by domestic discontent, the American will to geopolitical confrontation was substantially weakened. Reflecting this, the Carter administration initially was ready for a far-reaching departure from the superpowers' antagonistic ways. However, the Soviet leadership, despite its growing economic problems, was completely unprepared for dialogue. It was ready, however, for agreements that reflected its understanding of the security interests of the USSR.[65]

In the United States the political backlash against détente and the determination to restore its hegemonic position in the world led to Ronald Reagan's victory and the restoration of a strong Cold War consensus. During the 1980s the US financial system was at the hub of the rapidly expanding world financial system of capitalism; the increase of military spending in a robust capitalist economy created a Keynesian 'multiplication' effect. The Reagan administration was determined to 'turn the tide' against the Soviet Union everywhere in the world, and some elements of the Administration even led a 'crusade' to 'win' the Cold War.

The breakdown in the Soviet imperial will occurred in the second half of the 1980s and underpinned Gorbachev's search for détente. For reasons that are beyond Cold War studies, primarily in the economic sphere, the Cold War consensus in the Soviet Union collapsed completely. Despite a 'local war' in Afghanistan, fear of war was largely non-existent among younger Soviets. Because of this, imperial pride was replaced by pacifism and radical anti-statism. The shocking revelations of glasnost about the Stalinist past paralyzed even those who still adhered to the traditional consensus. This paralysis of imperial will may explain why there was little opposition to Gorbachev among the military, the KGB, and party stalwarts until 1990. It seems that most of those who *post facto* criticized Gorbachev for 'betrayal' after 1990 had supported his foreign-policy innovations in 1986–89.

The new Cold War history shows that it was not only the resources, but the goals of the Soviet Union and the United States which were very different. Détente remained a consistent goal of Soviet foreign policy after Stalin, but it was not for most US administrations. From 1953 on there were intermittent 'peace offensives' from the Soviet side, and Khrushchev even expected to end the Cold War on acceptable terms, including the recognition of a 'Yalta system' in Europe. In 1967 Andrei Gromyko stated flatly in his secret memorandum to the Politburo that the main goals of Soviet foreign policy could be reached more easily in the atmosphere of détente.[66] The outcome of the détente of the 1970s favored the Soviets. In 1975 the Helsinki Agreements, despite its 'third basket', brought the Soviet rulers to fulfillment of their long-time program of European stability with acceptance of Soviet domination in Central Europe, recognition of post-war European borders, and the expansion of Soviet positions in the developing world. Inside the country, the Soviet repressive machine completely suppressed internal dissent, and most dissenters 'agreed' to emigrate. No wonder that in the late 1980s Gorbachev and his assistants tended to think in terms of this past experience and were convinced that past attempts to reach a 'truce' failed only because the Kremlin was guided by ideological impulses and allowed itself to be sucked into proxy wars in the Third World, such as in Afghanistan.

The political structure of the Soviet Union facilitated switches from periods of hostility and propaganda confrontation to peace campaigns and rapprochement with the enemy. Public opinion and adverse pressures, which are institutionalized in American society in the form of trade unions, ethnic lobbies, or Congressional opposition, had little role in the Soviet system. Meanwhile, the same generational memories that propelled the Soviets to combat readiness, also called for a peace-loving leader. Gorbachev's authoritarian, highly personal style of conducting foreign policy in partnership with Eduard Shevardnadze is reminiscent, in form, if not in substance, of the Nixon–Kissinger style in early 1970s.[67] And initially, Gorbachev, like Nixon, succeeded in becoming in the eyes of the vast majority of his countrymen the architect of peace.

The role of the leader was always crucial in explaining Soviet contributions to the turns in the Cold War. Above the importance of social movements, changing economic conditions, or generational shifts, the Soviet part in the starting and the ending of the Cold War, in its great crises and periods of détente, can be explained largely by the actions of Soviet leaders at the pinnacle of power. Most recent evidence suggests that without Stalin, his extraordinarily strong and evil character, his unbending suspicious will, and his uncanny ability to see the future through the lenses of 'worst case scenarios', the Soviet Union might not have dared to engage in geopolitical rivalry with the Anglo-American powers.[68]

In a similar way, the foundation for a new Soviet foreign policy had been set when Gorbachev came to power. Later, social and nationalist movements came to prominence, but this does not change a bit the immense importance of the Gorbachev factor in the end of the Cold War. This factor alone accounted for the lack of violence at the turn of the 1980s.[69] Gorbachev moved towards the end of the Cold War, violating every prescription of Realism in international relations.[70] His personal relationship with Ronald Reagan and George Bush was also very important – an emerging understanding, and then friendship, between the leaders facilitated a non-violent transition.

Stalin and Gorbachev were both General Secretaries of the CPSU, but the contrast between them could not have been greater. Stalin could be viewed, with a caveat, as an extreme, special case of 'realist' in international relations: he placed the main emphasis on geostrategic games, hard bargaining over territories, gambling over resources; he had no place for intentions – the reason he miscalculated Hitler in 1941. He had a strong ability to keep his eye on the ultimate goals, even under stress. Although he almost always failed to foresee a crisis, he reacted to it with ruthless determination. He cared for small details and held his foreign ministers on an extremely tight leash. Gorbachev, by contrast, never bothered to develop specific policies and tactics, he left everything for history, politicians, and ultimately people (of Eastern Europe, Germany, finally the Soviet Republics) to decide. He acted under the illusion that, in doing so, he could atone for the mistakes and crimes the USSR had committed against its allies in the past – at one point quoting the Russian poet and diplomat Feodor Tyutchev, implying that he wanted to remake the Union and its alliances not by 'iron and blood, but by love'.[71] And even today he does not admit a final judgment on the failure of his intentions.

In the end, it was not the bad guys who lost to the good guys in the Cold War. During the years of confrontation the United States was repeatedly tempted to use its vast superiority in power to end 'the communist threat' once and for all, including the devilish temptation to use nuclear power. It is a testimony to American common sense (and probably prudence, given the Soviet atomic arsenal) that the plans of forward pressure and 'roll-back of communism' were replaced by more patient approaches – including consistent attempts to influence Soviet elites and erode 'the enemy image' inside the Soviet Union by a combination of radio propaganda and cultural and other exchanges. While force had bred only resistance and counterforce, this gradualist and prudent approach gave history the much needed time to allow the communist experiment and the imperial drive in the Soviet Union to erode and wither away.

The pressure from the West in the early 1980s revived Cold War tensions, but it is hard to see it as a decisive factor in the end of the Cold War world order. The ending was, in a way, a 'victory' of the West, but the attempts of some US leaders to take credit for this victory cannot be corroborated by the new evidence from the Soviet side. The role of longer-term processes within the Soviet Union (the erosion of ideology, the pent-up desire for relaxation) played a much greater role than the short-term measures of the Reagan or Bush administrations.

On the other hand, the personal roles of Gorbachev and other 'new thinkers', decisive as they were in the turn from the Cold War, should not be over idealized. They let the war in Afghanistan continue, needlessly, for three more years under their leadership. In concrete terms, their new foreign policy gave them only limited achievements, with the INF treaty as its apogee. What finally ended the Cold War was the process of liberalization inside the Soviet Union that they unleashed and over which they later lost control. As a domestic reformer, Gorbachev failed terribly – which can be testified to by his treatment by the vast majority of his countrymen. The end of the Cold War was, in many ways, the byproduct of this failure. The new evidence demonstrates dramatically that it was not only Gorbachev's 'good will', but also the progressive paralysis of his 'revolution from above', the lack of guidelines and orientations, that made possible the collapse of communism in Eastern Europe.

For future generations, it may not be so important, after all, why and how the Cold War ended. It is over, and this is all that matters. In future annals of world history I think the name of Gorbachev may remain more prominent than the names of those who 'won' the Cold War, and perhaps rightly so. But then the Cold War was never a morality play and its end also precludes unambiguous moral interpretations.

NOTES

The materials used as background for this chapter include the documentation in the Archive of the Gorbachev Foundation, open to researchers since 1995. Also, this author was fortunate to be part of a series of projects aiming at explaining the end of the Cold War, including several 'critical oral history' conferences: at Princeton in 1993 and 1995 and at Musgrove, St Simon Islands (1–3 May 1998) and at Brown University (7–10 May 1998). For the last two conferences the author held numerous meetings with Soviet/Russian veterans and helped prepare voluminous briefing books of documents which include 'highlights' from the Archive of the Gorbachev Foundation and US official documents obtained through the Freedom of Information Act. The author thanks the organizations and individuals who helped him with this new evidence, particularly the National Security Archive, its director Thomas Blanton and research director Malcolm Byrne; the Cold War International History Project and its past directors James G. Hershberg, David Wolff, and its present head Christian Ostermann, the Archive of the Gorbachev Foundation, including Professor Vladlen Loginov and Dr Sergei Kuznetsov; and Gorbachev's assistants Anatoly Chernyaev and Georgy Shakhnazarov.

 1 John Lewis Gaddis, *The Long Peace: Inquiries into the History of the Cold War* (New York: Oxford University Press, 1987).
 2 A remarkable self-reassessment can be found in John Lewis Gaddis, *We Now Know: Rethinking Cold War History* (Oxford: Clarendon Press, 1997), esp. pp. 281–95.
 3 Among recent contributions are Michael H. Hunt, *Ideology and US Foreign Policy* (New Haven, CT: Yale University Press, 1987); Melvyn P. Leffler, *A Preponderance of Power: National Security, the Truman Administration, and the Cold War* (Stanford, CA: Stanford University Press, 1992); Geir Lundestad, *The American 'Empire' and Other Studies of US Foreign Policy in Contemporary Perspective* (New York: Oxford University Press, 1990); Susan Strange, 'The "Fall" of the United States: Peace, Stability, and Legitimacy', in Geir Lundestad (ed.), *The Fall of Great Powers: Peace, Stability, and Legitimacy* (Oslo: Scandinavian University Press, 1994), pp. 197–211.
 4 Alexander Shubin, *Istoki perestroiki 1978–1984* [The roots of perestroika, 1978–1984], vols I–II (Moscow: 1997); Dimitry Furman, 'Nasha strannaia revolutsiia' [Our strange revolution], *Svobodnaia mysl*, no. 1, 1993; Vladimir Sogrin, 1985–1995, Realnosti i utopii novoi Rossii [Realities and utopias of a new Russia], *Otechesvennaia istoriia*, 2 (March–April 1995): 3–16; Vladislav Zubok, 'The Collapse of the Soviet Union: Leadership, Elites, and Legitimacy', in Lundestad, ed., *The Fall of Great Powers* and its Russian version in *Polis*, 1, 1995.
 5 Robert M. Gates, *From the Shadows: The Ultimate Insider's Story of Five Presidents and How They Won the Cold War* (New York: Simon and Schuster, 1996), p. 575.
 6 Peter Schweizer, *Victory: The Reagan Administration's Secret Strategy That Hastened the Collapse of the Soviet Union* (New York: Atlantic Monthly Press, 1994).
 7 George P. Shultz, *Turmoil and Triumph: My Years as Secretary of State* (New York: Scribner's, 1993); Jack Matlock, *Autopsy on an Empire: An American Ambassador's Account of the Collapse of the Soviet Union* (New York: Random House, 1995); Remarks of Douglas MacEuchan, CIA Chief of Soviet Analysis in the 1980s, at the Brown University conference, 'Understanding the End of the Cold War: The Reagan–Gorbachev Years', 7–10 May 1998. The transcript of this conference is still not available and I will refer to my notes. Subsequently: 'notes at the Brown University conference'.
 8 Matlock, *Autopsy on an Empire*, pp. 84–5; also Matlock's comments on the paper of Thomas Bierstecker, Richard Ned Lebow, and Richard Herrmann, presented at a workshop of the Mershon Center, Ohio State University, September 1997.
 9 A remark of Robert McFarlane, notes at the Brown University conference.
10 Gates, *From the Shadows*, p. 566.
11 Matlock, *Autopsy on an Empire*, pp. 16–17.
12 Raymond Garthoff, *The Great Transition: American–Soviet Relations and the End of the Cold War* (Washington, DC: Brookings Institution, 1994).
13 Archie Brown, *The Gorbachev Factor* (New York: Oxford University Press, 1996), p. 237.

14 William Curti Wohlforth, *The Elusive Balance: Power and Perceptions during the Cold War* (Ithaca, NY: Cornell University Press, 1993), p. 290.

15 Jacques Levesque, *The Enigma of 1989: The USSR and the Liberation of Eastern Europe* (Berkeley, CA: University of California Press, 1997), p. 252.

16 Gleb Pavlovsky, 'How They Destroyed the USSR', *Nezavisimaia Gazeta*, 14 November 1996, p. 5; for criticism of this thesis for 'primitivism' see Georgi Mirsky, ibid., 22 November 1996.

17 See Valerii Boldin, *Krushenie p'edestala: shtrikhi k portretu M. S. Gorbacheva* [Collapse of the Pedestal: Details for M.S. Gorbachev's Portrait] (Moscow: Respublika, 1995) and its English-language version *Ten Years that Shook the World: The Gorbachev Era as Witnessed by His Chief of Staff* (New York: Basic Books, 1994); Vladimir Kriuchkov, *Lichnoe delo* [Personal files] (Moscow: Olimp, 1996); Leonid V. Shebarshin, *Ruka Moskvy: zapiski nachal'nika sovetskoi razvedki* [The Hand of Moscow: Reports from the head of Soviet intelligence] (Moscow: Tsentr–100, 1992) and *Iz zhizni nachal'nika razvedki* [From the life of a head of intelligence] (Moscow: Mezhdunarodnie otnosheniia, 1994); Nikolai S. Leonov, *Likholetie* (Moscow: Terra, 1997); Valentin Falin, *Die Politische Erinnerungen* (Munich: Droemer-Knaur, 1993) and his *Die Perestroika und der Zerfall der Sowjetunion*, Hamburgerbeiträge zur Friedensforschung und Sicherheitspolitik, Heft 77 (Hamburg: April 1993).

18 S. F. Akhromeev and G. M. Kornienko, *Glazami marshala i diplomata: kriticheskii vzgliad na vneshniuiu politiku SSSR do i posle 1985 goda* [With the Eyes of a Marshal and a Diplomat: A Critical View of Foreign policy of the USSR before and after 1985] (Moscow: Mezhdnarodniie otnosheniia, 1992), pp. 314–15; see also the criticism of Gorbachev and Shevardnadze's foreign policy in the last chapter of Anatoly Dobrynin, *In Confidence: Moscow's Ambassador to America's Six Cold War Presidents* (New York: Time Books, 1995) and Anatoly Gromyko, *Andrei Gromyko v labirintakh Kremlia* [Andrei Gromyko in the labyrinth of the Kremlin] (Moscow: IPO 'Avtor', 1997).

19 A particularly notorious example was a letter from Oleg Baklanov, Valentin Varennikov, Vladimir Kryuchkov, and Nikolai Leonov to Director of the Watson Institute of Brown University, Thomas Bierstecker, in April 1998, in which they declined to participate in a conference on the end of the Cold War, claiming that it still 'continues'.

20 This is the focus of the Mershon Center–Brown University's project on 'understanding the end of the Cold War'. For four explanations, see Thomas Bierstecker, Richard Herrmann, and Richard Ned Lebow, 'Understanding the End of the Cold War', draft paper presented at the conference at the Mershon Center, the Ohio State University, September 1997.

21 Quoted in Richard Ned Lebow, 'The Long Peace, the End of the Cold War, and the Failure of Realism', *International Organization*, vol. 48, no. 2 (Spring 1994); John Lewis Gaddis, 'International Relations Theory and the End of the Cold War', *International Security*, vol. 17, no. 3 (Winter 1992/93); William C. Wohlforth, 'Realism and the End of the Cold War', *International Security*, vol. 19, no. 3 (Winter 1994/95): 91–129; Ted Hopf, 'Getting the End of the Cold War Wrong', *International Security*, vol. 18, no 2 (Fall 1993): 202–8; Thomas Risse-Kappen, 'Did "Peace Through Strength" End the Cold War? Lessons from INF', *International Security*, vol. 16, no. 1 (Summer 1991): 162–88.

22 Ben B. Fischer, *A Cold War Conundrum: The 1983 Soviet War Scare* (Center for Study of Intelligence, September 1997); Lt-Gen. Vladimir I. Slipchenko at the Brown University conference said that Reagan's rhetoric in 1983 made the Soviet armed forces maintain 'maximum, highest-level combat readiness' for a long time

(author's notes).

23 Shubin, *Istoki perestroiki*, vol. I, ch. 2; Zubok, 'The Collapse of the Soviet Union', p. 165; Gromyko, *Andrei Gromyko*; also discussion on the quiet death of the 'Brezhnev doctrine' at the conference at Musgrove (author's notes).

24 On Soviet torments over the dismantling of détente, see Dobrynin, *In Confidence*.

25 Politburo Session, 24 March 1986, notes of Anatoly Chernyaev, the Archive of the Gorbachev Foundation, Fund 2, Opis 1.

26 Politburo Sessions 4 and 8 October 1986, notes of Anatoly Chernyaev, the Archive of the Gorbachev Foundation, Fund 2, Opis 1.

27 See, for instance, Politburo Session, 23 and 26 February 1987, notes of Anatoly Chernyaev, the Archive of the Gorbachev Foundation, Fund 2, Opis 1.

28 A lively and informative discussion took place at the Brown University conference regarding the origins of a January 1986 plan of a nuclear-free world by Gorbachev. Former head of Soviet delegation at MBFR negotiations at Vienna, Ambassador Oleg Grinevsky, claimed that Akhromeyev, Kornienko, and other 'traditionalists' did not, contrary to their claims, seek disarmament – on the contrary, they wanted to prevent it (author's notes at the conference).

29 Lt-Gen. Vladimir Slipchenko and Lt-Gen (ret.) Nikolai Detinov at the conference at Brown University (author's notes).

30 Chernyaev recalled his 'surprise' and Gorbachev's 'irritation' at this back in 1986 and even later; the conference at Brown University (author's notes).

31 Politburo Session, 15 April 1986, notes of Anatoly Chernyaev, the Archive of the Gorbachev Foundation, Fund 2, Opis 1.

32 Chernyaev makes this point in his *Shest let s Gorbachevim* [Six Years with Gorbachev] (Moscow: Progress-Kultura, 1993); Shevardnadze's foreign policy assistant Sergei P. Tarasenko confirmed this at the Brown University conference (author's notes).

33 On the 'new thinking', its origins and foreign policy implications, see Archie Brown, *The Gorbachev Factor*; see also Robert D. English, 'Sources, Methods, and Competing Perspectives on the End of the Cold War', *Diplomatic History*, vol. 21, no. 2 (Spring 1997): 283–94.

34 Anatoly Dobrynin, who was at this time still Gorbachev's chief adviser on American affairs, writes that 'the president [Reagan] proved to be a much deeper person than he first appeared ... Reagan was endowed with natural instinct, flair, and optimism', which allowed him to achieve what the best strategists thought to be unattainable, *In Confidence*, p. 609.

35 Conversations of M. S. Gorbachev with R. Reagan at Reykjavik, 11–12 October 1986, from Gorbachev's archive, *Mirovaia ekonomika i mezhdnarodniie otnoshenia*, Moscow, nos 4, 5, 7, 8, 1993; parts 2 and 3 are translated in FBIS-USR-93-087, 12 July 1993 and FBIS-USR-93-113, 30 August 1993.

36 Anatoly Chernyaev's impression is that Gorbachev stopped regarding the 'human rights' issue as a concession to foreign policy needs only when he decided to change the political system of the USSR in the spring of 1988 (conversation with the author, Providence, RI, 8 May 1998).

37 The minutes of most of these conversations between 1986 and 1990 are open at the Archive of the Gorbachev Foundation in Moscow. Some, as the Reykjavik summit, are published. See also Conversation of M. S. Gorbachev with G. Shultz, 23 October 1987, *Mirovaia ekonomika i mezhdunarodniie otnosheniia*, Moscow, nos 10–11, 1993. For the impact of Margaret Thatcher's visit on Gorbachev see Chernyaev's notes from the Politburo session, 2 April 1987, the Archive of the Gorbachev Foundation, Fund 2, Opis 1.

38 The absence of inner 'limitations' translated later in 1989 into the absence of 'limits'

for change in the Soviet empire – the discussion on the end of the Cold War in Europe, Musgrove (author's notes).

39 'Results of Visit to the US', a memo from A. Chernyaev to Gorbachev, 17 December 1987; Chernyaev's notes from the Politburo, 17 December 1987, the Archive of the Gorbachev Foundation, Fund 2, Opis 1 (translation by Svetlana Savranskaya).

40 The disagreements split the American intelligence community. Experts of SOVA (Bureau of Soviet Analysis in the CIA) who had begun to see Gorbachev's foreign policy as a serious departure from old ways created by the severe economic problems of the USSR remained in the minority in bureaucratic battles against the CIA, and particularly military colleagues. Douglas MacEuchen, head of SOVA, even contemplated resignation in 1987 (his remarks at the conference at Brown University, notes by the author).

41 Gorbachev said, according to Chernyaev's notes: 'There are stupid dialectics here: if they do it, we also will. There were opportunities – yes, but we got wound up. If you look closely – we were always catching up, and we did not use political methods to achieve our objectives in a proper manner ... We were not capable of using our peace-loving capabilities in a reasonable way.' At the same session, Andrei Gromyko, posing as a reformer as well, recalled that Khrushchev suggested that they stop building nuclear bombs and admitted that under Brezhnev 'we continued to stick to the principle: they are racing, and we are racing, like in sports' (translation of Svetlana Savranskaya), Chernyaev's notes of the Politburo meeting, 30 June 1988, The Archive of the Gorbachev Foundation, Fund 2, Opis 1.

42 Chernyaev, Shakhnazarov, and Tarasenko at the Brown University conference and the conference at Musgrove (author's notes).

43 Chernyaev's notes from the Politburo meeting, 10 March 1988, the Archive of the Gorbachev Foundation, Fund 2, Opis 1.

44 The term 'deep détente' to define Soviet–American relations after 1987 was used by Wohlforth, 'Realism and the End of the Cold War', p. 95. It agrees with the evidence.

45 Both Soviet reformers and their American sympathizers felt that, because of the change of administration the momentum of 1986–88 was halted. Chernyaev calls 1989 'the wasted year', and Matlock's title for the early Bush foreign policy is 'Washington fumbles' (the author thanks Thomas Blanton, who brought to his attention this similarity).

46 A memo of the International Department of the Central Committee, 'On the Strategy of Relations with European Socialist Countries', (?) February 1989 and a memo from the Institute of World Socialist System (Bogomolov), February 1989. Professor Jacques Levesque obtained both documents from private sources and donated them to the National Security Archive, Washington, DC. They were translated for the Musgrove conference. For the analysis of the Soviet discussion on the future of Eastern Europe, see Levesque, *The Enigma of 1989*, pp. 68–90.

47 He added in the same memo: 'We should clearly see ... that in the future any possibility to "put out" crisis situations by military means must be fully excluded. Even the old [pre-Gorbachev] leadership seems to have already realized it, at least with regard to Poland', 6 October 1988, *Tsena Svobodi*, pp. 368–9. The 'new thinkers' contend that Gorbachev's position on non-use of force not only flowed from the pragmatic experience of the past, but was deeply personal and moral, Chernyaev at the Musgrove conference.

48 Interview in *Die Presse*, April 1988, see explanations in Charles Gati, *The Bloc That Failed: Soviet–East European Relations in Transition* (Bloomington, IN: Indiana University Press, 1990), pp. 76–7 and Levesque, *The Enigma of 1989*, pp. 68–74.

49 'Changes in Eastern Europe and their impact on the USSR'.
50 See the Politburo meeting on 11 May 1989 on the situation in the Baltic Republics, A. B. Veber (chief ed.), *Soiuz mozhno bylo sokhranit: Belaia kniga: dokumenty i fakty o politike M.S. Gorbacheva po reformirovaniiu i sokhraneniiu mnogonatsional-nogo gosudarstva* [The Union could have been preserved: White Book: Documents and facts on M. S. Gorbachev's policy for reforming and preserving the multinational state] (Moscow: Aprel-85, 1995).
51 Record of the Politburo Meeting, 27–28 December 1988, *Istochnik*, 5–6, 1993; and the even more radical version in Chernyaev, *Shest let s Gorbachevim*, pp. 255–6.
52 See Akhromeyev's opinion cited above. Also Chairman of the Council of Ministers Nikolai Ryzhkov in interview with Michael McFaul in the summer of 1992, the Hoover Institution's oral history project, cited in Wolforth, 'Realism and the End of the Cold War', p. 113. The figure of 70 percent was mentioned by Chernyaev and Shakhnazarov without a source reference during the Brown University conference.
53 Nikolai Detinov at the conference at the Brown University (author's notes); also see Nikolai Simonov, *Voienno-promyshlenniii kompleks SSSR v 1920–1950-e gg.* [The USSR military-industrial complex from the 1920s to the 1950s] (Moscow: Rosspen, 1996).
54 For a comparative perspective on imperial overstretch and decline, see Stephen A. Schuker, *The End of French Predominance in Europe: The Financial Crisis of 1924 and the Adoption of the Dawes Plan* (Chapel Hill, NC: The University of North Carolina Press, 1976), Paul Kennedy, *The Rise and Fall of the Great Powers: Economic Change and Military Conflict from 1500 to 2000* (New York: Random House, 1987); Lundestad, ed., *The Fall of Great Powers*.
55 Marshall Goldman, *What Went Wrong with Perestroika?* (New York: Norton, 1991).
56 They are reflected also in the best studies of George F. Kennan, Adam Ulam, and a number of scholars and diplomats with 'classical' education.
57 John Gaddis in *We Now Know* (pp. 286–90) 'rehabilitates' the ideological factor in Cold War studies, but also talks about the historical experiences of the Soviets, about defeated Germans, raped German women, etc.
58 Detinov's remarks at the Brown conference reiterate what is known through anecdotes.
59 On the discussion about this transformation, including the feeling of inferiority or *Haßliebe* toward the West, see Vladislav Zubok, 'The Collapse of the Soviet Union', pp. 164–5.
60 See Zubok and Pleshakov, *Inside the Kremlin's Cold War: From Stalin to Khrushchev* (Cambridge, MA: Harvard University Press, 1996); also Martin Malia, *The Soviet Tragedy: A History of Socialism in Russia, 1917–1991* (New York: Free Press, 1994).
61 Robert English, 'Sources, Methods, and Competing Perspectives on the End of the Cold War'.
62 The Archive of the Gorbachev Foundation, Fund 2, Opis 2.
63 The best study on this is Levesque, *The Enigma of 1989*.
64 George Shultz wrote: 'The Soviets were picking up our ideas and playing them back to us as though they had just invented them. That was fine with me. The more Gorbachev wanted to play the role of "creative world statesman for peace", by coming to our agenda, the more we should stand back and applaud him in that performance.' Shultz, *Turmoil and Triumph*, p. 894; Wohlforth, 'Realism and the End of the Cold War', p. 121. Unlike Gaddis (*We Now Know*, p. 288) I do not set apart Wilsonianism and *realpolitik* in US foreign policy.
65 These conclusions are based on the results of the Carter–Brezhnev project of

Brown University, the Norwegian Nobel Institute, the Cold War International History Project, and the National Security Archive, in particularly several critical oral history conferences that took place during 1993–95.

66 The document is published in Dobrynin, *In Confidence.*

67 Shakhnazarov, Gorbachev's foreign-policy assistant, admitted that systemic, radical changes in foreign and domestic policies of the USSR could be carried out only 'by the czar'. It was necessary for Gorbachev to act like a tsar, in order to succeed as a reformer.

68 Vladimir O. Pechatnov, 'Notes on Stalin's correspondence with V. Molotov and the Politburo in the fall of 1945 (from the Archive of the President of the Russian Federation)', presented at the workshop 'Stalin as a Cold War statesman', Moscow, 20 March 1998.

69 In the enormous literature on Gorbachev, even in Archie Brown's significant study, this point gets short shrift. Many in the West obviously believe that the 'non-use' of force in 1989 was 'overdetermined' and therefore inevitable. I have been arguing since 1993 that 'Gorbachev's choice to remain "a good Tsar", to avoid force, proved to be decisive ...', in *The Fall of Great Powers*, p. 169. Explanations of this feature of Gorbachev's character and his leadership style are sought in Eric Shiryaev and Vladislav Zubok, 'Gorbachev and the end of the Cold War: A Historical-Psychological Approach', unpublished paper.

70 This point is absent in the otherwise excellent article of William Wolhforth, 'Realism and the End of the Cold War'.

71 In *Far Away, So Close*, a feature film by Wim Wenders.

Index

abolitionism, 92

Acheson, Dean, 52, 55, 81, 82–3, 93, 293

Adenauer, Konrad, 245, 246, 248–9, 251, 254, 333

Adomeit, Hannes, 187

Advanced Research Project Agency, 218

Afghanistan, 34; Soviet war against, 17, 157, 234, 238, 329, 348, 358; Soviet withdrawal, 352; US military aid, 349

Africa, 16, 31, 51, 57, 182, 190, 267, 272, 293, 295, 329, 332; see also names of countries

Aircraft Nuclear Propulsion program, 218

Akhromeyev, Sergei, 346

Albania, 326

Aliev, Geidar, 238

Allen, Woody, 304

Allied Control Commissions, 283

Allies, 242, 248, 289, 292

Almond, Gabriel, 165

American Association for the Advancement of Slavic Studies, 315

American Civil War, 83, 84, 87, 91, 92, 93

American Revolution, 86, 93

Amin, Hafizullah, 32

Anderson, Major Rudolf, 318

Andreeva, Nina, 350–1

Andropov, Yuri Vladimirovich, 116

Angola, 67, 330; civil war 1976, 332

anti-communist rhetoric, 4, 45, 65, 92, 294

anti-fascism, 94

Arbatov, Georgy, 235–6

Archilochus of Paros, 110

Argentina, 158

Aristotle, 89, 162

arms race, 13, 106, 156, 207–23, 310–11, 346, 348, 349, 351, 355

Aron, Raymond, 180

Asia, 51, 52, 53, 57, 112, 151, 182, 208, 245, 267, 272, 286, 293, 295; East, 2, 12, 17, 19, 31, 46, 234, 281; Eurasia,

44; Northeast, 48, 54; Southeast, 31, 54; Soviet Central, 173; see also names of countries

Attlee, Clement Richard, 111, 287

Augustus, Emperor, 240

Austria, 115

authoritarianism, 173

autocracy, 35

Backchannel, 328

Bagehot, Walter, 164

Bahr, Egon, 254

Balkans, 4

Baltic, 292

Basic Treaty 1972, 333

Bay of Pigs 1961, 109, 115, 117, 118, 316, 317

behaviourism, 165, 166, 167

Beijing, 34, 46, 53–6, 234, 237, 263–73, 303, 305–7, 315, 320

Belgium, 51, 294

belief systems, 3, 7, 108–10

Beria, Lavrentii, 135, 233, 244, 252, 309

Berlin, 56, 75, 109, 115–16, 140, 253, 254, 308, 317, 318, 320, 333; East, 309; West, 248, 254, 307, 309

Berlin blockade, 51, 243, 248

Berlin crisis, 106, 303, 307–11, 314, 315, 316

Berlin, Sir Isaiah, 110

Berlin Wall, 105, 254, 354

Berlin Wannsee 1947, 247

Bernstein, Barton, 66

Bessarabia, 292

Bevin, Ernest, 287, 288, 289, 291

Bidault, Georges, 290

Bierut, Boleslaw, 167

'biological reductionism', 164

bipolar systems, 7, 28–9, 111, 136, 159, 190, 304–7

Bismarck, Otto Eduard Leopold, Fürst von, 249

Bissell, Richard, 117

Printed in the United States
75110LV00001B/16-45

9 780714 681207